A HISTORY OF WOMEN'S EDUCATION IN THE UNITED STATES

Courtesy of Bigelow, Brown and Company, New York

PLATO

A HISTORY OF WOMEN'S EDUCATION IN THE UNITED STATES

By
THOMAS WOODY

VOLUME I

55996

1966
OCTAGON BOOKS, INC.
New York

Copyright 1929 by Science Press

Reprinted 1966
by special arrangement with Mrs. Thomas Woody

OCTAGON BOOKS, INC.
175 FIFTH AVENUE
NEW YORK, N.Y. 10010

LIBRARY OF CONGRESS CATALOG CARD NUMBER: 66-17495

Printed in U.S.A. by
NOBLE OFFSET PRINTERS, INC.
NEW YORK 3, N. Y.

LC
1752
.W6
1966

TO
FRANK PIERREPONT GRAVES
INSPIRING TEACHER, COLLEAGUE AND FRIEND

"Women from fourteen years of age are flattered with the title of mistresses by men. Therefore, perceiving that they are regarded only as qualified to please the men, they begin to adorn themselves; and in that to place all their hopes. It is worth while, therefore, to fix our attention on making them sensible, that they are esteemed for nothing else, but the appearance of a decent, and modest, and discreet behavior."—EPICTETUS.

PREFACE

About ten years ago I began assembling material for a History of Education in the United States. Little progress had been made when it became evident that there were numerous gaps in information on a vast number of subjects. Clearly these had to be dealt with before a complete, reliable, general history could be prepared. Particularly impressive was the comparative silence —in some educational histories, almost complete—on the subject of women's education; and equally striking, the scant attention given her emancipation and education in the general histories of the country. The latter, written in recent years, have indeed improved in respect to this question. But, a generation ago, Bush's remark, in his *History of Higher Education in Massachusetts,* might well have been made of the whole country: "While we have modern histories, political, philosophical and educational histories, we still lack one that duly takes into view the education of woman." These volumes are the outcome of an effort to satisfy myself as to the nature of the revolution that has been brought about in the position and education of women in the United States. It is hoped that they may, partially, yet admittedly imperfectly, bridge the gap in our information on this subject; and that they may lead to something better.

The principles underlying the assignment of material to volumes one and two have been primarily logical, and secondarily chronological. In the first volume there is, of course, a definite turning point in the chapter dealing with the New Concept of Woman's Education. Preceding the "New Concept," girls' education was determined chiefly by notions transplanted from abroad; plus, certainly, some unavoidable influences of a pioneer environment. Rush's new conception stressed the need of an education adapted to American women, even though many of his ideas harmonized with those abroad. From his day forward, the female seminary, the high school, common school, and normal school developed more or less rapidly and, to a great extent, interdependently. The discussion of this new concept and the institutions which helped realize it in practice, run naturally through the next century. It has seemed more appropriate to

honor the logical relation of these topics than to sacrifice them in
the interest of a formal delimitation of chronological periods.

As the transplanted ideals and practices, plus primitive environment, were fundamental determining factors in girls' education of the early days; and, as increasing wealth and stability
of settlements, relaxing of religious restraints, and growth of
culture in municipal centers, gave a new tone to their education
in the last half of the eighteenth and the early years of the nineteenth centuries; so the vastly changed economic place and function of women, the extension of suffrage, transcendentalism, the
movement for equal rights and many other reform movements
concerned with women, or with which women concerned themselves, furnish the basic reasons for, and condition the development of, new opportunities for woman's education with man
which has taken place in the past hundred years. These new
opportunities were either (1) new institutions created for the
purpose, (2) an extension of institutions begun in the preceding
transition period between Colonial beginnings and 1825, or (3)
modifications of men's institutions so as to provide for women as
well.

The appearance of these volumes marks approximately the
centennial of the agitation, and provision, for advanced education for women. They are not concerned exclusively, however,
with advanced education. The opening of the "golden paths"
of elementary and secondary schools was quite as significant, preparing for gradual equalization of participation in higher and
professional education.

"Woman" has been punctuated as a question from ancient
times; but during the past seventy-five years the mark has been
bigger and blacker than ever. Some phases of this question
about herself, she has answered in the past two generations.
This work contains a partial record of her answers. If we were
not such literalists it might be called a history of women's emancipation in the United States, though it makes no pretence of
dealing exhaustively with political emancipation. In the broader
sense it is, though comparatively little space is given to facts of
the more recent phases of her emancipation.

The aim has been to present a connected narrative, letting contemporary records and the literature of the day, so far as possible, tell the story of changes that have taken place in ideals,

practices, and institutions. No individual portraits have been attempted, nor connected histories of particular institutions. This leaves much to be desired; but while much detail of personal and institutional history might be added if space were unlimited, it is believed the general picture here presented would not be materially changed. A complete history of any of the women's colleges would require a volume at least. It is somewhat singular that although many colleges for men have prepared satisfactory histories, it is seldom true of those for women. Let me suggest to the many friends and officials of women's colleges, who have so cordially assisted me, the desirability of preparing as complete, documented histories as their archives will permit. I shall be especially pleased if such institutional histories bring to light more facts which will serve to correct any distorted picture or erroneous statements in this.

The bibliography contains a partial list of (I) catalogs, *MS.* minutes and records, laws, student papers, diplomas, court records, and similar materials; (II) newspapers, whose files shed light on current conceptions of women's position and education and furnish descriptions and advertisements of contemporary institutions; (III) books and pamphlets; and (IV) periodical publications, journals and proceedings which have been found useful, contributing definitely to the formation of my mental picture of the evolution of women's education, though not all are quoted or referred to directly in the text. In addition, acknowledgment should be made to some fifteen hundred authors whose books and articles, covering our general history, have contributed in a more general way to my views; but the general accounts are known to every one and, with the articles, would but extend the list, rather than contribute a different view of the subject. Many of the materials, under the first two heads, are inaccessible to most students; they have been examined by me personally. Their location is generally indicated in brackets. The books, periodicals, and proceedings, most of them at least, are available in the best libraries; but most of the local material has been found only at a distance and badly scattered.

My obligations are numerous. The following institutions, publishers, and authors have graciously given permission to quote or use illustrations from their publications, which are cited in footnotes and the bibliography: M. B. Fuller's *Wrongs of Indian*

Womanhood, published by Fleming H. Revell Company, New York; C. W. Sams's *Shall Women Vote?,* Neale Publishing Company, New York; W. D. Hyde's *The College Man and the College Woman,* Houghton Mifflin Company, Boston; Paul Monroe's *Sourcebook in the History of Education,* The Macmillan Company, New York; Alice D. Miller's *Are Women People?,* Doubleday, Doran and Company, Garden City, New York; the *Bay Psalm Book,* Dodd, Mead and Company, New York; Theodor Mommsen's *History of Rome,* Charles Scribner's Sons, New York; Belle Squire's *Woman Movement in America,* A. C. McClurg and Company, Chicago; H. M. Olin's *Women of a State University,* G. P. Putnam's Sons, New York; A. H. Wharton's *Colonial Days and Dames* and Mary N. Stanard's *Colonial Virginia, Its People and Customs,* J. B. Lippincott Company, Philadelphia; Hester Dorsey Richardson's *Sidelights on Maryland History;* the edition of Jowett's *Plato,* published by Bigelow, Brown and Company, New York; Arthur W. Calhoun's *Social History of the American Family* and the *Documentary History of American Industrial Society,* edited by J. R. Commons and others, The Arthur H. Clark Company, Cleveland, Ohio; Elizabeth Blackwell's *Pioneer Work for Women,* Aristotle's *Politics,* and Crèvecoeur's *Letters of an American Farmer,* J. M. Dent and Sons, London, and E. P. Dutton and Company, New York; W. H. Small's *Early New England Schools,* Ginn and Company, Boston; and Helene Lange's *Higher Education of Women,* published by D. Appleton and Company, New York; the Women's Bureau, United States Department of Labor, Washington; Rhode Island School of Design, Providence; Moravian Seminary and College, Bethelehem; Ursuline Sisters, New Orleans; Oberlin College, Oberlin; Columbia University; Vassar College, Poughkeepsie; Woman's Medical College of Pennsylvania, Philadelphia; Hobart College, Geneva, New York; Pennsylvania German Society, Philadelphia; Professor Arthur O. Norton and the Alumnae Association of the Framingham, Massachusetts, State Normal School; Professor Paul Monroe; Mr. Herbert Croly; Mr. Charles F. Heartman. To many others, my indebtedness is acknowledged in the appropriate pages and the bibliography.

It would be a pleasure to acknowledge my obligations specifically, by naming the hundreds of librarians, school and college officers, and other correspondents, who have so willingly and

effectively aided me by locating and loaning material, and especially those whom it has been my pleasure to meet personally.
To name all is impossible. However, I may mention The Library
of Congress, New York Public Library, the Library of the American Antiquarian Society, Worcester, Massachusetts, Boston
Public Library, The Athenaeum Library, Boston, the Public
Library and the library of the Historical Society of Pennsylvania, Philadelphia; the state libraries of Pennsylvania, New
York, New Jersey, Connecticut, Massachusetts, Maine, Ohio, Indiana, Illinois, Iowa, Wisconsin, Tennessee, Kentucky, Virginia,
North Carolina, South Carolina, Alabama, Mississippi, Louisiana
and Georgia; and the libraries of the University of Michigan,
University of North Carolina, Columbia University and the University of Pennsylvania; all of which have given indispensable
aid. Numerous smaller city, college, and state historical libraries,
several of which are designated in sections I and II of the bibliography, have been useful.

To Professors Paul Monroe, Willystine Goodsell and William
Heard Kilpatrick, for the inspiration of their work, teaching,
and appreciative, constructive criticism, the author recognizes a
greater obligation than he can hope to express adequately; and,
finally, to Matilda E. Shafer, Naomi Norsworthy, Frank Pierrepont Graves, Edward H. Reisner, Wilhelmine Lawton Woody,
John Harrison Minnick, Anna Slogoff, James A. Mulhern and
Lucy Gwynne Branham, for appreciative insight, encouragement
and assistance by word and deed, he acknowledges deep obligations and expresses such thanks as they alone can understand.

Notwithstanding these and other obligations he is, nevertheless,
solely responsible for what is done or left undone.

THOMAS WOODY.

FEBRUARY 8, 1929.

TABLE OF CONTENTS

VOLUME I

ILLUSTRATIONS

A HISTORY OF WOMEN'S EDUCATION IN THE UNITED STATES

CHAPTER I

CONCEPTION OF WOMEN'S POSITION AND EDUCATION IN OTHER LANDS

I. *Before the Renaissance*

The education of women on a grand scale, in the United States, is of recent date; their higher education is a development of the past seventy-five years. This would seem strange were it not that this fact offers little or no contrast to the annals of other lands. From the days of our primitive ancestors women have generally occupied a sheltered place and have not, therefore, received a higher cultural or professional training such as would enable them to deal with large affairs, remote from the fireside. Rare exceptions to this rule have indeed merited the approval of all mankind, as witness the wife of Rama, Lady Tsao, Sappho, Hypatia, Cornelia, Paula, Mary Wollstonecraft, Harriett Martineau, or Olive Schreiner.

Among nature peoples, "where girls received any training at all it usually took the forms of housewifery and agriculture, with drill to the point of drudgery." Thus Todd tersely describes the practical education of primitive girls.[1] This education in drudgery had its *raison d' être* in the fact that woman's labor was very important for the successful tribal life. Even "where little home training is bestowed upon the boys, their sisters early become miniature housewives. And where both sexes are formally taught, the girls usually come first."[2] The only division of labor that existed was along sex lines; the male was huntsman and warrior, while the female cared for shelter and prepared food and clothing.[3] As for puberty ceremonies, which had to be

[1] *Primitive Family*, 185.
[2] *Ibid.*, 165–6.
[3] See Thomas: *Sex and Society*, 55–172.

passed through before one became recognized as a mature member of the tribe, "boys, and even more frequently girls, are subjected to them."[4] These ceremonies were filled with instruction, drill and torture; ofttimes seclusion, fasting, and silence were imposed in order that moral stamina might be tested as well as physical ability and endurance. No more elaborate education was deemed necessary for women, and the products of her labor, when she was married, were the property of the male.[5] In this economically enforced union there was at first little of sentiment; only with the passage of time did the family relationship claim permanency, and the rights of husband inviolability; and the violation of these rights was often regarded more as an infringement upon property than otherwise. When a savage offered his wife to a guest, he merely did as he would with his own possessions.[6] But as "where the treasure is, there will the heart be also," so sentiment gradually grew into the relationship and the beautiful ideal of the family arose. When man came to cherish his wife and daughters as flowers, treasured for their beauty and sweetness, their acquisition of "accomplishments" began to seem desirable. Nevertheless, the limits to which "accomplishments" might extend have generally been rather definitely fixed by custom, in earliest as in most recent civilizations, and those who dared exceed them have run the risk of being thought "unwomanly," "insane," or both.

The earliest civilizations that have left literatures give evidence of the fact that love and reverence came to play a great rôle in the family. Thus Dauuf advised his son: "Give thy heart to learning and love her like a mother." Nevertheless women were subject to man's dominion and had little encouragement to intellectual endeavor beyond the rudiments. In short, one must be impressed by the fact that woman was regarded as a beautiful, lovely, delicate possession, to be loved and protected, not as an intellectual competitor of man; as Ptah-Hotep put it: "If thou art successful and lovest the wife of thy bosom, fill her stomach and clothe her back. Make glad her heart during the

[4] Todd: *Primitive Family*, 193.

[5] Compare with Westermarck: Position of Woman in Early Civilization [*Sociological Papers of the London Sociological Society*, I, 147–60.]

[6] *Ibid.*, 45, 47; consult also Tylor: *Primitive Culture*, 2 vols.; and Spencer and Gillen: *The Native Tribes of Central Australia*.

time thou hast." Likewise in the *Negative Confession* it is clear that purity of women has come to be a virtue, and the defilement of it a sin.[7] The Egyptians were generally monogamous, save the wealthiest and most powerful;[8] and this is a surer mark of their advancement than any intellectual opportunities that can be pointed out. Likewise, among the Chaldeans, if bride and bridegroom were of the same level, or equal in fortune, an oath could be exacted from the man that he would take no second mate during the lifetime of the first; and if the agreement were broken, the first wife should be free and receive alimony. The master's relation with female servants, however, was not affected by such agreement.[9]

Practical training was, of course, necessary in order that the labor of daily life might be properly performed. For while middle class, or well-to-do, families had slaves to look after cattle, cook, carry water, grind corn, weave, or watch the children, all such labor in poor families had to be done by the women.[10] Since these activities occupied so much of her time, it is only natural to find her education largely vocational.

In ancient China, great stress was laid on education of a formal type for men, and the rewards of honor, high political position, and social distinction were for those who proved their capacity by success in the system; but examinations leading to these preferments were only for men. Woman's sphere was the home, for as the book of *Li Ki* explains "men should not speak of what belongs to the inside of the house, nor the woman of what belongs to the outside;"[11] and her chief virtues were filial piety,[12] flexibility or adaptability,[13] humility, piety, fidelity, activity in the performance of the various housewifely duties, obedience, chastity, and reticence.

[7] "Hail, thou serpent Uamemti, who comest forth from the house of slaughter, I have not defiled the wife of a man."—*Literature of the Orient*, Fitzgerald edition, translations by various Oriental scholars, edited by E. Wilson, 104–6.

[8] Maspero: *Dawn of Civilization*, 267 *ff*.

[9] *Ibid.*, 735 *ff*.

[10] Maspero, in his *Dawn of Civilization in Egypt and Chaldea*, 317 *ff*., gives an interesting picture of the household, describing the women making bread and weaving linen on a horizontal loom.

[11] Part XII, Bk. 10, Sec. 1, trans. by Legge.

[12] Jen Hsiao: *Nei Hsun*, Ch. I (Headland, translator) quoted by Lewis.

[13] Lady Tsao: Nu Chih, Ch. III.

The following extract from Bk. X of *Li Ki*[14] shows clearly enough the trend of the girl's training: "(Sons') wives should serve their parents-in-law as they served their own. At the first crowing of the cock, they should wash their hands, and rinse their mouths; comb their hair, draw over it the covering of silk, fix this with the hairpin, and tie the hair at the roots with the fillet. They should then put on the jacket and over it the sash. . . . Thus dressed, they should go to their parents and parents-in-law. On getting to where they are, with bated breath and gentle voice, they should ask if their clothes are (too) warm or (too) cold, whether they are ill or pained, or uncomfortable in any part; and if they be so, they should proceed reverently to stroke and scratch the place . . . They will ask whether they want anything and then respectfully bring it . . ."

For three months prior to her marriage a Chinese girl was taught especially "the virtue, the speech, the carriage and the work of a wife."[15] With such rigid conformity to passive virtues it is not strange that even highest talents were often obscured and few celebrated women appeared in China, nor that since the Sung period there has been such a proverb as "A woman without ability is normal."[16] Whether it be for good or ill, few can break the restraints imposed by social custom. Some Chinese girls, fortunately situated, did, indeed, receive unusual advantages, because of their fathers' wealth and interest in their education. Lady Tsao says she was "ignorant" and "stupid" but "had the good fortune to receive the special favor of my father,"[17] while Jen Hsiao "studied poetry and classical books" at the same time that she learned carefully her duties as a woman. This education received by fortunate daughters, certainly by not more than one in three or four of all women of China, was one of "accomplishments," as described suggestively in the words of the *San Tze Ching*.[18] The unusual event of woman's cultural training also appears in the old quotation:

[14] Translation by Legge, in the *Sacred Books of the East*, ed. by Max Müller, Vol. XXVII.

[15] *Li Ki*, Bk. XLI, Ch. 10.

[16] Quoted by Lewis from Kiang: "Woman and Education in China" (unpublished).

[17] Quoted by Lewis: *The Education of Girls in China*.

[18] See Kuo: *The Chinese System of Pub. Ed.*, 53.

"Tsae Wan Ke could play upon stringed instruments;

"Seay Tao Wan likewise could sing and chant.

"These two though girls were intelligent and well in-
    formed;

"You then my lads should surely rouse to diligence."[19]

Not only were girls generally uneducated in the literary sense,
but their arrival among kinsmen was not greeted as joyously as
that of sons. Kwei Chunk Fu, dealing with infanticide, explains: "To destroy daughters is to make war upon Heaven's
harmony. The more daughters you drown the more daughters
you will have; and never was it known that the drowning of
daughters led to the birth of sons."

For hundreds of years the Chinese conception of woman's
place and education remained the same; but it changed rapidly
once foreign commerce of ideas and materials began. After the
opening of five Chinese ports in 1842, the first school for girls
was opened at Ningpo by Miss Aldersey in 1844. Numerous
institutions followed, established by various denominations; and
in 1897 was opened the first girls' school established and supported by the Chinese themselves, and managed by—women.
About fifteen years later, "the latest statistics available" showed
"a total of 270,692 girls in school."[20] As the total number of
girls in China at that date was probably over 28,000,000, a great
discrepancy appears between the girl population and the school
attendance. This discrepancy, however, is being rapidly reduced
by the efforts to extend the benefits of the public system to girls
and boys alike all over China.

The degraded position[21] woman occupied in India, and the
consequent lack of educational opportunities, is indicated in the
wisdom of the sages. Vishnu Sarma appears, at one time, to
recognize greatness in females when he says: "Every book of
knowledge which is known to Oosana or to Vreehas Patee is by
nature implanted in the Understanding of Women." But when
we understand that these are the deities of love and cunning, his
true meaning is undisguised. Elsewhere the seer states his low
opinion of the sex more directly: "Women, at all times, have

[19] Quoted by Lewis: *op cit.*, 12.

[20] *Ibid.*, 41.

[21] See the work of Dubois: *Hindu Manners, Customs, and Ceremonies,*
especially Chaps. 16–19.

been inconstant, even among the Celestials . . .; woman's virtue is founded upon a modest countenance, precise behavior, rectitude, and a deficiency of suitors'' and "infidelity, violence, deceit, envy, extreme avarice, a total want of good qualities, with impurity, are the innate faults of womankind.'' And, as for giving such a dangerous person any freedom, he advises: "In infancy, the father should guard her; in youth, her husband; in old age, her children: for at no time is a woman fit to be trusted with Liberty.''[22] It is her first duty to minister unto and worship her husband as a god. "Let a wife,'' says the *Skanda Purana,* "who wishes to perform sacred ablution, wash the feet of her lord, and drink the water: for the husband is to a wife greater than Shankar or Vishnu. The husband is her god, and priest, and religion: wherefore abandoning everything else, she ought chiefly to worship her husband.'' Her condition is that of continuous slavery (a rope and a rod are named as the supports of her husband's authority), and in this inferior position she has nothing to do with the *Vedas* or any road to wisdom.

The condition of Mohammedan women in India offers little or no variation from that of the Hindu. A traveller tells this significant story[23] which illustrates their life: "A woman was seen sitting half in the sun and half in the shade, while by her side were some broken bricks, a stick and a rope, and some hot and cold water in different vessels. Some one asked her why she was sitting half in the shade, and half in the sun. She answered that her husband was a grass cutter and she could not tell whether in cutting his grass he was at that time in the sun or in the shadow; but, whichever it was, she wanted to sympathize with him, and so felt both heat and cold at the same time. She added also, in explanation, that she did not know which he would prefer on his return, hot or cold water, so she had both ready. Also, if he were in a bad temper and wished to beat her, he would choose between the stick and the rope, or throw the pieces of brick at her. The prophet, hearing this, replied that she was truly a good woman, and deserved to go to heaven.''

The nineteenth and twentieth centuries have seen beginnings of amelioration of woman's hard lot. About 1820 the modern movement for her Christian education was begun in India, first

---

[22] *Manu,* V, 147–66.
[23] Related in Fuller: *Wrongs of Indian Womanhood,* 271–2.

by the Baptist Missionary Society, the missionaries of the Established Church, the Free Church of Scotland, the London Missionary Society, and later others.[24] But there are, even yet, many difficulties in the way of woman's education and in 1918, as a general rule, there was as yet "little provision . . . in the government schools of India, vernacular or Anglo-vernacular, for the education of girls." Their education was generally carried on in special private schools, save in the Central Provinces where the Government had taken control. The greatest difficulties to overcome are: securing women of proper character, education and caste to serve as teachers; interesting women of position in the work of school committees; and, more than anything else, the ancient antagonism to the idea of woman's education must be combatted. Nevertheless, in spite of difficulties, in 1916–17 about 1,300,000 native Indian girls were receiving instruction, this figure representing an increase of 29.2 per cent. for the preceding five years; and more significant than the figures themselves is the fact that the age-long antagonism begins to weaken. Some authorities say: "Indian public opinion has clearly changed from the former attitude of positive dislike to the education of girls and is now much more favorable as regards every community. . . ." Professional men now wish to marry their sons to educated girls who can be in a real sense companions and helpmeets; therefore education is beginning to be valued by parents as improving the marriage prospects of their daughters.[25]

Among Semitic peoples it appears there was a high regard for woman.[26] But here, also, it was her value as represented in her virtues of thrift, industry, foresight, business judgment, devotion to her family affairs, skill in the crafts, and goodness of heart that caused her praises to be sung, rather than any realization of mental excellence. It is clear that woman occupied a more

[24] For an interesting account see *History of Native Female Education in Calcutta* (anonymous), 1858.

[25] *Biennial Survey of Education*, 1916–18, II, 244.

[26] For good accounts see Simon: *L'éducation et l'instruction des enfants chez les anciens Juifs d'apres la Bible et le Talmud, Leipsic*, 1879; Strassburger: *Geschichte der Erziehung und des Unterrichts bei den Israeliten . . . bis auf die Gegenwart*, Breslau, 1885; Swift, in *Education in Ancient Israel* (Open Court, 1919), gives a brief account of woman's education.

strategic position in earliest times than she did later. Children[27] traced their descent from her, while Deborah,[28] Jael,[29] and others were wise in large affairs. Gradually, however, woman became more and more hemmed in by restrictions, devoting her energies to religion and household affairs, while man dominated the intellectual field. Always, of course, she occupied an important place in the education of her girls, but it is well known that daughters were less esteemed than sons,[30] and, certainly, their education usually stressed religion, dancing, manners, morals, music, and the domestic life. Though instructed in reading, the critical study of the law was not encouraged, and this field of intellectual endeavor was controlled by men. In the oft-quoted passage from the *Proverbs*,[31] which sets forth the ideal

27 Consult *Genesis*: XXXVI, where it appears that Esau's children traced their line from the female rather than the male.

28 *Judges*, IV and V.

29 *Judges*, IV, 18–24.

30 "Well to him whose children are boys; woe to him whose children are girls."—*Talmud*.

31 "A worthy woman who can find?

"For her price is far above rubies.

"The heart of her husband trusteth in her,

"And he shall have no lack of gain.

"She doth him good and not evil

"All the days of her life.

"She seeketh wool and flax

"And worketh willingly with her hands.

"She is like the merchant-ships;

"She bringeth food from afar.

"She riseth also while it is yet night,

"And giveth food to her household,

"And their task to her maidens.

"She considereth a field, and buyeth it:

"With the fruit of her hands she planteth a vineyard.

"She girdeth her loins with strength,

"And maketh strong her arms.

"She perceiveth that her merchandise is profitable;

"Her lamp goeth not out by night.

"She layeth her hands to the distaff,

"And her hands hold the spindle.

"She spreadeth out her hand to the poor;

"Yea, she reacheth forth her hands to the needy.

"She is not afraid of the snow for her household;

"For all her household are clothed with scarlet.

"She maketh for herself carpets of tapestry;

woman, it is interesting to note that, while she proves her goodness and worth in many ways, it is ''her husband [who] is known in the gates, when he sitteth among the elders of the land.'' From this picture of Hebrew life it is evident that the signs of dawn presaged largely the increase of woman's recognition as a home builder, and, in a fashion, presented her as a superior creature. However, her intellectual bent was as yet unguessed, untried.

Among the Persians, who, Herodotus says, had learned ''unnatural lust from the Greeks,'' it was common for a man to have several wives and more concubines. Nevertheless the ties of family were sacred, children were highly regarded, and the wife's duties were wholly of a domestic nature. Sons were in care of the women to five years of age, so as not to afflict their father if they died. ''Next to prowess in arms,'' says Herodotus, the greatest excellence was ''to be the father of many sons.''[32] Every year the king made rich gifts to the man who could show the greatest number. Nothing is said of excitement over the birth of a daughter. As learning was the possession of men, chiefly the *Magi*, as the greatest glory was to be strong in battle, and as so much emphasis was put on the rearing of children, one must conclude that Persian women were little if any better off than those of other Oriental countries.

To Hegel, Greece was ''a point of light'' in history; and, in the sphere of woman's education, it was given to a Greek philosopher to hold up a great light. However, the earliest practice of the Greeks was not far beyond that of other ancient peoples of their day, except notably Sparta, where women had great power and freedom, though not great intellectual attainments. The origin of this freedom, and the results, are accounted for

''Her clothing is fine linen and purple.
''Her husband is known in the gates,
''When he sitteth among the elders of the land.
''She maketh linen garments and selleth them;
''And delivereth girdles unto the merchant.
''Strength and dignity are her clothing;
''And she laugheth at the time to come.
''She openeth her mouth with wisdom;
''And the law of kindness is on her tongue.
''She looketh well to the ways of her household,
''And eateth not the bread of idleness.''—*Proverbs*, XXXI, 10–31.
[32] *History*, I, 136.

by Aristotle in the *Politics*.[33]   Their greatness, on this score, rests primarily on the advancement of a new theory of woman's capacities.   That the actual social and political position of woman was low indeed, is indicated by the fact of Solon's law against the sale of daughters or sisters into slavery by male relatives, which suggests that formerly they had been regarded as property.   Before his time the punishment for violation of a free woman was at the discretion of the magistrates.   Solon was the first who instituted a penalty of 100 drachmas for such an offense.[34]

In the home, woman found her sphere as wife and mother, whose chief tasks were concerned with the physical welfare of the family.   When a Greek wife crossed her husband's threshold, the axle of the nuptial chariot was broken.   A faithful conservative view of the domestic character and labors of woman is clearly set forth by Xenophon in the *Economics*, wherein he describes the education of the wife of Ischomachus: " 'But,' said I, 'Ischomachus, I would very gladly be permitted to ask you whether you instructed your wife yourself, so that she might be qualified as she ought to be, or whether, when you received her from her father and mother, she was possessed of sufficient knowledge to manage what belongs to her.'   'And how, my dear Socrates,' said he, 'could she have had sufficient knowledge when I took her, since she came to my house when she was not fifteen years old, and had spent the preceding part of her life under the strictest restraint, in order that she might see as little, hear as little, and ask as few questions as possible?   Does it not appear to you to be quite sufficient, if she did but know, when she came, how to take wool and make a garment, and had seen how to apportion the tasks of spinning among the maid-servants? for as to what concerns the appetite, Socrates,' added he, 'which seems to me a most important part of instruction both for a man and for a woman, she came to me extremely well instructed.' 'But as to other things, Ischomachus,' said I, 'did you yourself instruct your wife, so that she should be qualified to attend to the affairs belonging to her?'   'Not, indeed,' replied Ischomachus, 'until I had offered sacrifice, and prayed that it might be my fortune to teach, and hers to learn, what would be best

[33] Bk. II, Ch. IX.
[34] Compare Grote: *History of Greece*, I, 602.

for both of us.' 'Did your wife, then,' said I, 'join with you in offering sacrifice, and in praying for these blessings?' 'Certainly,' answered Ischomachus, 'and she made many vows to the gods that she would be such as she ought to be, and showed plainly that she was not like to disregard what was taught her.'"

Having explained to his wife how he chose her from among all the rest, and her parents chose him in like manner, he continued: "'To these remarks, Socrates, my wife, replied, 'In what respect could I cooperate with you? What power have I? Everything lies with you. My duty, my mother told me, was to conduct myself discreetly.' 'Yes, by Jupiter, my dear wife,' replied I, 'and my father told me the same. But it is the part of discreet people, as well husbands as wives, to act in such a manner that their property may be in the best possible condition, and that as large additions as possible may be made to it by honourable and just means.' 'And what do you see,' said my wife, 'that I can do to assist in increasing our property?' 'Endeavor by all means,' answered I, 'to do in the best possible manner those duties which the gods have qualified you to do, and which custom approves.' 'And what are they?' asked she. 'I consider,' replied I, 'that they are duties of no small importance, unless indeed the queen bee in a hive is appointed for purposes of small importance. For to me,' continued he, 'the gods, my dear wife,' said I, 'seem certainly to have united that pair of beings, which is called male and female, with the greatest judgment, that they may be in the highest degree serviceable to each other in their connection. In the first place, the pair are brought together to produce offspring, that the races of animals may not become extinct; and to human beings, at least, it is granted to have supporters for their old age from this union. For human beings, also, their mode of life is not, like that of cattle, in the open air; but they have need, we see, of houses. It is accordingly necessary for those who would have something to bring into their houses to have people to perform the requisite employments in the open air; for tilling, and sowing, and planting, and pasturage are all employments in the open air; and from these employments the necessaries of life are procured. But when these necessaries have been brought into the house, there is need of some one to take care of them, and do whatever duties require to be done under shelter. The rearing of young children also demands shelter, as well as the preparation of food from the fruits of the earth, and the making of clothes from wool. And as both these sorts of employments, alike those without doors, and those within, require labour and care, the gods, as it seems to me,' said I, 'have plainly adapted the nature of the woman for works and duties within doors, and that of the man for works and duties without doors. For the divinity has fitted the body and mind of the man to be better able to bear cold, and heat, and travelling, and military exercises, so that he has imposed upon him the work without doors; and by having formed the body of the woman to be less able to bear such exertions, he appears to me to have laid upon her,' said I, 'the duties within doors.' "[35]

The advantages of a literary education belonged to the *hetaerae,* and between them and the wife a great gulf was fixed.[36] Above, in the words of Ischomachus, we have a description of the ideal housewife and her virtues. If we turn to the comic poets and satirists we find the lowest estimate of women. According to Sularion, "Women are an evil, but . . . it is not possible to have a household without evil, for to marry is an evil, and not to marry is an evil." Another says: "A man has only two pleasant days with his wife, one when he marries her, the other when he buries her." Another says many things are evil, but none "such a terrible evil as woman. No painter can adequately represent her; no language describe her."

The early center of the woman's movement was Sappho, a poetess, whom Plato called the "Tenth Muse" and to whom Aristotle and Herodotus referred in terms of great respect. Her productions have by common judgment been ranked with those of the best male poets. Strabo says that in the whole period of time of which there is any record there does not appear a single woman that could rival her even in a slight degree.[37] Thus he bears witness to the unusual character of her accomplishments, and suggests, at the same time, the rarity of woman's intellectual development in contemporary Greece. Some authorities credit Sappho with establishing a school wherein her pupils were taught the art of poetry (the chief means of culture at the time) and

[35] Monroe: *Sourcebook,* 38–41.
[36] Grote: *History,* II, 509–10.
[37] Strabo: *Geography,* II, 391.

were urged to free themselves from the shackles of ignorance. To the ignorant she said, "Dying, thou shalt lie in the tomb, and there shall be no remembrance of thee afterwards, for thou partakest not of the roses of Pieria: yea, undistinguished shalt thou walk in the halls of Hades, fluttering about among the pithless dead." In *The Distaff*, Erinna, pupil of Sappho, depicts the sadness of the young woman forced to the toil of the loom whereas she preferred to cultivate the muses.

Likewise, around Aspasia, first mistress, and later wife, of Pericles, there developed a coterie who represented the movement towards woman's intellectual emancipation. Among this group of *hetaerae* there were doubtless women of every sort of character, and our opinions as to their morals have probably been shaped by knowledge of the worst, sometimes very scantily supported by data. Of the character of Aspasia, however, there is the judgment of careful scholars that she has been accused on "very doubtful evidence," and the evidence may have been created for political purposes; of her beauty, culture, conversation, ability, and the influence she exerted on men and women, there is no doubt. Nevertheless the popular distrust of, and contempt for, such intellectual women as Theodote and Aspasia points clearly to the fact that, in general, Athenian society regarded woman as properly employed in the household and did not favor her education for a place in public life.

Even the greatest philosopher-scientist, who, as a later satiric wit said, could tell what "the soul of an oyster is like," could explain "the sperm and conception and the shaping of the embryo," and "how far down the sunlight reaches into the sea,"[38] could not fathom the intellectual capacities of woman. Aristotle continued, in some respects, to follow the trend of Eastern thought, believing that woman was controlled by a "submitting principle" rather than a "governing one," and dominated by an irrational rather than a rational soul: for "it is evident then that both parties [men and women] ought to be virtuous; but there is a difference between them, as there is between those who by nature command and who by nature obey, and this originates in the soul; for in this nature has planted the governing and submitting principle, the virtues of which we say are different, as are those of a rational and irrational

[38] Lucian: *Philosophies for Sale.*

being. It is plain then that the same principle may be extended farther, and that there are in nature a variety of things which govern and are governed; . . . thus a slave can have no power of determination, a woman but a weak one, a child an imperfect one." Again, dealing with the virtue, courage, "The courage of the man consists in commanding, the woman's in obeying."[39] This nature of woman is that which determines the kind of education, for in a later passage we are assured that "it is necessary that both wives and children of the community should be instructed correspondent to the nature thereof, if it is of consequence to the virtue of the State, that the wives and children therein should be virtuous . . .;" and this is true, for women are one-half the free persons and the children the future citizens. As for the final limitation of woman's freedom in society, that is determined by the same principle that fixes her relation to her husband, for: "As to the indulging of women in any particular liberties, it is hurtful to the end of government and the prosperity of the city; for as a man and his wife are the two parts of a family, if we suppose a city to be divided into two parts, we must allow that the number of men and women will be equal."

The conservative nature of Aristotle's conception of women's capacity is doubtless due to his willingness to observe facts and be guided by them; and the facts, generally observable up to and including his day, led naturally to the conclusions that women were not rational contrivers, executives, and judges, but emotional creatures, possessed of a good physical being and irrational souls, who, however, lacked the supreme virtue and capacity for the highest happiness. His views are, certainly, the more unexpected since he was acquainted with those of his master, Plato; but the latter offered to the scientific, fact-searching mind no conclusive proofs to support his theory of like capacities in man and woman. And as his thesis was unconvincing to his pupil, so it was to untold numbers of men throughout succeeding generations and civilizations. But, even if unproved, the theory of Plato is interesting for its originality and remarkable for its prophetic character. The introduction of his argument for the education of women the same as men

[39] Taken by permission from the Everyman's Library edition of Aristotle's *POLITICS*, published by J. M. Dent & Sons, Ltd., London, and E. P. Dutton & Co. Inc., New York. Book I, Ch. XIII.

suggests the common current attitude towards them ("The part
of men has been played out, and now properly enough comes the
turn of the women"), but disillusionment follows i mmediately:

"What do you mean?

"What I mean may be put into the form of a question, I said:
Are dogs divided into hes and shes, or do they both share equally
in hunting and in keeping watch and in the other duties of
dogs? or do we entrust to the males the entire and exclusive care
of the flocks, while we leave the females at home, under the idea
that the bearing and suckling their puppies is labor enough
for them?

"No, he said, they share alike; the only difference between
them is that the males are stronger and the females weaker.

"But can you use different animals for the same purpose,
unless they are bred and fed in the same way?

"You can not.

"Then, if women are to have the same duties as men, they
must have the same nurture and education?

"Yes.

"The education which was assigned to the men was music
and gymnastic.

"Yes.

"Then women must be taught music and gymnastic and also
the art of war, which they must practise like the men?

"That is the inference, I suppose."[40]

It is observed, at once, that some of these proposals may appear ridiculous, such as women exercising in the palaestra;
but, says Plato, one of the best sayings is, and ever will be,
"that the useful is the noble and the hurtful is the base," and
that he who laughs at this novelty "is ignorant of what he is
laughing at or what he is about." Again the question is foreseen
that, since there are admitted differences in the sexes, ought
there not to be different tasks for different natures? Plato de-
livers himself from this difficulty by wittily arguing that, if it
is admitted that hairy men differ from bald men, and bald men
are to be cobblers, then hairy men should be forbidden to be
such, and continues:

"That would be a jest, he said.

"Yes, I said, a jest; and why? because we never meant when
we constructed the State, that the opposition of natures should

[40] *The Republic,* Bk. V.

extend to every difference, but only to those differences which affected the pursuit in which the individual is engaged; we should have argued, for example, that a physician and one who is in mind a physician may be said to have the same nature.

"True.

"Whereas the physician and the carpenter have different natures?

"Certainly.

"And if, I said, the male and female sex appear to differ in their fitness for any art of pursuit, we should say that such pursuit or art ought to be assigned to one or the other of them; but if the difference consists only in women bearing and men begetting children, this does not amount to a proof that a woman differs from a man in respect of the sort of education she should receive; and we shall therefore continue to maintain that our guardians and their wives ought to have the same pursuits.'"[41]

Thus the conclusion is finally agreed upon that some women, just as some men, will show an aptitude for healing, others not; some a capacity for music, others not; some a love for military exercises, others not; some will love true wisdom and have the virtues of the philosopher, while others are unconcerned. Such differences within the female sex shall determine occupations, just as in the male they mark him for an artisan, warrior or philosopher.[42]

As in the case of his educational scheme at large, so in regard to the education of women, Plato's theories had no immediate effects. But they have been suggestive to students of the question to this day. A revival of interest in the question in modern times, has, interestingly enough, stimulated more scientific investigations, partial results of which, at least, accord with the views of the visionary philosopher.[43]

We have allowed considerable space to the presentation of the Greek views, ranging from the conservative lines of Xenophon to the dream of Plato, and have permitted them to speak in their own words, not without purpose. For with but little, if any,

[41] *Ibid.*

[42] It should be noted that elsewhere, *Timaeus* for example, Plato set forth the well-known doctrines of woman's inferiority.—Jowett's translation, Bk. V, 461, 498, 513, etc.

[43] Compare data reported by Thorndike: *Ed. Psychology*, III, Ch. 9.

exaggeration, it may be said that in their works there are presented most of the arguments for and against the equality of men and women that have appeared until recent days. Musonius repeats the views of Plato; Luther's are similar to Xenophon's, which thus became widespread and influential among Christian people; Rousseau's Sophia is taught by her husband; while Defoe, Mill, Mary Wollstonecraft, Harriett Martineau, and their followers, again take up the claims of Plato. Psychologists now, borrowing a leaf from the statistician, gather much more objective data, but not always conclusive, substantiating or refuting the ancient theses.

During the early Roman period, education was of very limited character both for boys and girls, being a preparation, by way of apprenticeship to father and mother, for the everyday duties of life. But with the establishment of elementary schools, girls probably began to share with their brothers the advantages of the rudiments of reading, writing, and arithmetic. But here her scholastic training came to an end, while her brother continued in the schools of the *grammaticus* or *rhetor* to study grammar, history, geography, ethics, philosophy, and, to the Roman the consummation of all arts, oratory; and, if he were very fortunate, he studied at a university, perhaps at Athens. The daughter, however, was fully employed in mastering domestic affairs. An ancient epitaph describes her lot thus:

"Stranger, it is but little I would say;
"Pray tarry here to read it all. This is
"A lovely woman's most unlovely tomb.
"Claudia was the name her parents gave.
"She loved with all her heart the man she wed.
"Two sons she bore and one of these on earth
"She leaves, the other underneath it laid.
"Gracious her bearing, and her voice was sweet.
"She kept her house, spun wool. All's said. Depart.[44]

But if her school education was limited, her economic and social importance was recognized; she was no mere menial in the home. Mommsen depicts her situation clearly: "Woman did not indeed occupy a position inferior to man in the acquiring of property and money; on the contrary the daughter inherited

[44] Translation of Professor William C. Lawton.

an equal share with her brother, and the mother an equal share with her children. But woman always and necessarily belonged to the household, not to the community; and in the household itself she necessarily held a position of domestic subjection— the daughter to her father, the wife to her husband, the father-less unmarried woman to her nearest male relatives; it was by these, and not by the king, that in case of need woman was called to account. Within the house, however, woman was not servant but mistress. Exempted from the tasks of corn-grinding and cooking which according to Roman ideas belonged to the menials, the Roman housewife devoted herself in the main to the superintendence of her maid-servants, and to the accompanying labours of the distaff, which was to woman what the plough was to man. In like manner, the moral obligations of parents towards their children were fully and deeply felt by the Roman nation; and it was reckoned a heinous offence if a father neglected or corrupted his child, or if he even squandered his property to his child's disadvantage.''[45]

In the last two centuries of the pagan era, with Rome's ex-pansion, military successes, and increasing wealth, great changes began to appear, intimately affecting the status of women. The rigid regulations of the family became lax indeed. Grisettes and boy-favorites became common; and luxury in dress, orna-ments, and eating began to supplant old Roman simplicity. With it came a large degree of emancipation of women. Hideous crimes were committed by women against their husbands, for the sake of wealth or political ends. The old law that women were subject to their fathers, husbands, or nearest male relatives, was now evaded and they became mistresses of great wealth.[46] Strenuous measures to curtail this tendency availed nothing. With wealth, domestic labors became a less entrancing field of endeavor. ''Hitherto the women of the household had them-selves attended to the baking of bread and cooking; and it was only on the occasion of entertainments that a professional cook was hired. . . . Now, on the other hand, a scientific cookery began to prevail. In the better houses a special cook was kept.''[47] Bakers' shops sprang up in Rome about 171 B. C., and imported foods and wines vied with Roman products.

[45] *Ibid.*, V, 391 *ff.*, and III, 121.
[46] *Ibid.*, V, 391 *ff.*, and III, 121.
[47] *Ibid.*, V, 391 *ff.*, and III, 121.

With wealth and release from the humdrum duties of life came increasing leisure and opportunity for cultivation of intellectual interests. Plutarch says Pompey's second wife was instructed in letters, geometry, philosophical discussions, and in playing on the lyre; Calpurnia, the wife of Pliny the Younger, was educated and interested in literary affairs.[48] The path of learning, however, was pursued but irregularly, for the school training prepared boys and young men for public affairs and oratorical display—which women did not need in the decadent days in order to secure their ends. Though higher education of women does not appear to have become widespread in practice, there did appear a higher conception of woman's mental talents and a belief that she could be improved by studies as were men. Musonius, in the latter half of the first century A. D., wrote:

"If, then, the same virtues must pertain to men and women, it follows necessarily that the same training and education must be suitable for both. For in the case of all animals and plants, the application of the proper treatment ought to impart to each the excellence belonging to it. Or, if both men and women should have to possess equal skill in playing the flute, or in performing on the harp, and if this were necessary for their livelihood, we should impart to both equally the requisite instruction. But if both ought to excel in the virtue proper to mankind, and to be in an equal measure wise and temperate, and to partake in courage and righteousness the one no less than the other, shall we not educate them both in the same manner, and teach both equally the art by which a human being may become good? . . .

" . . . And when one asked him if women too should study philosophy, he began, somewhat in this way, to teach that they should. Women, he said, have received from the gods the same reason as men, the reason which we use in dealing with each other, and by which we discern, in regard to each act, whether it is good or bad, noble or base. So, too, the female has the same perceptions as the male—seeing, hearing, smelling, and so forth . . . So, too, not only men, but women also, have by nature the desire and the adaptation for virtue; for the latter, no less than the former, are so formed as to be pleased with noble and righteous actions and to disapprove the contraries of these. This

[48] Donaldson: *Women; Her Position and Influence in Ancient Greece and Rome*, 120.

being the case, why should it belong to men principally to inquire and consider how they shall live nobly—which is the province of philosophy—and not principally to women? Is it because it is fitting for men to be good, and not for women?

* * *

"For some will say that the women who visit philosophers must generally become bold and presuming when, leaving their household occupations, they live surrounded by men, and practice discussions, and argue subtly, and analyse syllogisms, while they ought to be sitting at home spinning. But I am so far from approving of women who are studying philosophy leaving their proper avocations and devoting themselves solely to discussions, that I should not even think it fit for men to do this. But I say that they ought to engage in all the reasonings with which they occupy themselves for the sake of their avocations. For as medical speculations are useless unless they conduce to the health of the human body, so if a philosopher holds or inculcates any doctrine, it is of no value unless it promote the virtue of the human soul. . . ."[49]

Into the Roman world of loose morals Christianity came. It might have been expected that this new faith would improve the situation of women; for had not Christ, during his ministry, appeared to women as well as to men? Had he not held lofty conversation with a woman who had had five husbands and was then living with one not her husband? Did he not, after his resurrection, appear first before Mary, out of whom he had cast seven devils? Surely this suggested an impartiality in the treatment of men and women. Nevertheless, though women occupied considerable space in the Gospels, there was no specific doctrine regarding women put forth—only suggestive incidents, and attitudes. But in the writings of Paul there appeared restrictions which seem to set women off as an inferior, dependent class. "I suffer not women to teach" and "if they have questions let them ask their husbands" indicate his spirit. This is in sharp contrast to the degree of freedom in social and political life which women had become heir to in the great days before the dawn of Christianity; and, however much the new religious enthusiasm affected moral conditions, it cannot be shown to have

[49] Quoted from Professor Muir's translation in Laurie's *Hist. Survey of Pre-Christian Education*, 428 *ff.*

promoted women's intellectual advancement to the degree claimed by enthusiastic writers,[50] but rather appears to have limited the sphere of their activities. Beyond religious instruction, early Christians apparently accepted the household education as the only necessity, unless, indeed, one would renounce the world completely and enter a nunnery. Education of the latter sort, the most intellectual in content allowed Christian daughters, is described by Jerome in his letter to Laeta. This was written at the beginning of the fifth century (403), and breathes the ascetic spirit which pervaded men's as well as women's education under the ecclesiastical regime. The principles of pedagogy and moral training are sound but the purpose and limits are narrow:

"Thus must a soul be educated which is to be a temple of God. It must learn to hear nothing and to say nothing but what belongs to the fear of God. It must have no understanding of unclean words, and no knowledge of the world's songs. Its tongue must be steeped while still tender in the sweetness of the Psalms.

* * *

"Get for her a set of letters made of boxwood or of ivory and called each by its proper name. Let her play with these, so that even her play may teach her something.

* * *

"Moreover, so soon as she begins to use the style upon the wax, and her hand is still faltering, either guide her soft fingers by laying your hand upon hers, or else have simple copies cut upon a tablet; so that her efforts confined within these limits may keep to the lines traced out for her and not stray outside of these.

* * *

"When Paula comes to be a little older and to increase like her Spouse in wisdom and stature and in favor with God and man, let her go with her parents to the temple of her true Father, but let her not come out of the temple with them. Let them seek her upon the world's highway amid the crowds and the throng of their kinsfolk, and let them find her nowhere but in the shrine of the Scriptures, questioning the prophets and

[50] Such advancement of position is depicted, for example, in the *Addresses* of Thomas Grimké, 107.

apostles on the meaning of that spiritual marriage to which she is vowed.

* * *

"And let it be her daily task to bring you the flowers which she has culled from Scripture. Let her learn by heart so many verses from the Greek, and let her be instructed in the Latin also.

* * *

"She ought to rise at night to recite prayers and psalms; to sing hymns in the morning; at the third, sixth, and ninth hours to take her place in the line to do battle for Christ; and, lastly, to kindle her lamp and to offer her evening sacrifice. In these occupations let her pass the day, and when night comes let it find her still engaged in them. Let reading follow prayer with her, and prayer again succeed to reading. Time will seem short when employed on tasks so many and so varied.

"Let her learn, too, how to spin wool, to hold the distaff, to put the basket in her lap, to turn the spinning wheel and to shape the yarn with her thumb. . . ."[51]

But if limits were narrow, within them a great deal of activity took place. Miss Eckenstein showed conclusively, in her study of *Woman Under Monasticism*, that particularly from the sixth to the eighth, and in the twelfth centuries, women shared the intellectual life of their day and some even achieved reputations as creators of poetry and art. Others were notably skilled in penmanship, acted as translators, transcribers, and illuminators. In the early Middle Ages some abbesses were prominent in political affairs. Hild of Whitby (b. 627) became a very prominent abbess, presiding over a monastery from which five men arose to the episcopacy.[52] That it was, nevertheless, a man's world may be suggested by the fact that the five *men* became bishops. All in all, however, woman's life of this period does not appear in as subdued a light as is usually assumed. The nun Hrotsvith (b. 932) produced metrical legends, seven dramas "in the style of Terence, and contemporary history in metrical form;[53] while of Herrad's *Hortus Deliciarum*—an encyclopedic work telling in pictured pages the wisdom of her age—it has been said that "few illuminated manuscripts . . . acquired a fame so well deserved.

51 St. Jerome's Letter to Laeta, 403 A. D. [*R. C. E.*, 1867-8, 371-6.]
52 Eckenstein: *Woman Under Monasticism*, 82 and 89 *ff*.
53 *Ibid.*, 160-1.

. . ."[54] St. Elizabeth of Thuringen († 1231), St. Hildegard of Bingen (1098–1178), and St. Elizabeth of Schönau (c. 1129–1165) were prominent in the more generally approved fields of philanthropy and prophecy. Of them it was written, in 1158, that "in these days God made manifest His power through the frail sex, in the two maidens Hildegard and Elizabeth, whom he filled with a prophetic spirit. . .";[55] and Bernard of Clairvaux wrote Hildegard: "They tell us that you understand the secrets of Heaven and grasp that which is above human ken. . . ." The Benedictine Convent of Helfta in Saxony, under the leadership of the Abbess Gertrud, was a center for literary activity, chiefly of mystic character.[56]

II. *Influence of the Revival in Italy and England*

The humanistic revival is generally credited with great influence in the intellectual emancipation of women; and, considering the extremely narrow spirit of the preceding age, some of the humanistic views are, by contrast, notable. The spirit of the time is different—worldly and human rather than ascetic, otherworldly, or superhuman. Dante is inspired by Beatrice; Petrarch by Laura. They are not ashamed. The spirit of the world of chivalry and joyous aestheticism begins to rise to its ascendancy over that of drab asceticism, which had renounced lovely things because they were sinful. This change in attitude naturally affected the conception of women's education. And while one effect of it was to defend her right to cultural education and free activity in the literary field, another was to emphasize again her place in the home—but a home enlightened by cultural interests, rather than within convent walls. True it is that prominent women of this period, such as Cecilia and Battista di Montefeltro, followed the habitual custom of religious retreat. But education was increasingly esteemed for cultural and social values in ordinary secular life. The transition was certainly gradual, and there was undoubtedly social disapproval of woman's education and emancipation from social conventions. Woodward[57] calls attention to the fact that Isotta was "under

[54] *Ibid.*, 238 *ff.*
[55] *Ibid.*, 257, quoted from *Annales Palidenses* in Pertz: *Mom. Germ. Script.*, XVI, 90.
[56] *Ibid.*, 328–53.
[57] *Vittorino da Feltre*, 249.

the ban of social opinion'' at Verona because of her correspondence with Guarino, her teacher. That was inevitable, but
women of the upper class continued for a time to be instructed
by the greatest schoolmasters, and their new rôle in general was
defended by the ablest scholars. Vittorino taught the ladies of
the House of Gonzaga; Guarino da Verona, Ginevra Nogarola;
and Ascham, of *Scholemaster* fame, Queen Elizabeth. Women
studied Greek and Latin grammar; literature; the Christian
fathers; works of moralists, poets, and orators; history; geometry, and arithmetic. As the good life was the goal, religion was
never to be omitted; and, as suggested, the new woman was to
continue to serve in a religious capacity, but in the home preferably.

The intelligent capacities, that some philosophers had denied
women, readily showed their presence in this hospitable environment. The names of Mildred Cooke, Margaret Roper, Katherine
Parr, Margaret Ascham, and Joanna Arundel come readily to
mind. Elizabeth, according to her enthusiastic master, ''atteyned
to soch a perfite vnderstanding in both the tonges, and to soch a
readie vtterance of the latin, and that with soch a judgement, as
they be fewe in nomber in both the vniversities, or els where in
England, that be, in both tonges, comparable with her Maies-
tie.''[58] Cecilia, Isotta, Ginevra Nogarola, Battista di Montefeltro, Paola, and Lady Jane Grey are likewise praised for their
learning. The latter was found by Ascham one day reading
Plato's *Phaedo*, while the rest of her family and friends were
hunting in the park. To his question she replied, ''I know all
their pleasure in the park is but a shadow to that pleasure that I
find in Plato: Alas, good folk, they never felt what true pleasure
meant.''[59] Erasmus puts into the mouth of the ignorant abbot
the age-old objections raised by common people to woman's education:[60] ''Ladies should have something to divert them''; ''women have nothing to do with wisdom''; ''a spinning wheel is a
woman's weapon''; ''it is not safe for a woman to know Latin'';
''books destroy women's brains, who have little enough of themselves''; and ''a wise woman is twice a fool.'' Magdada turns
on him with such keenness, defending her rights to joys of intel-

---

[58] *The Scholemaster*, Bk. II.
[59] *Ibid.*, 100–2.
[60] Bailey: *All the Familiar Coloquies of Erasmus*, 253 *ff.*

lectual cultivation, that finally the old monk asks in despair, "How came I to fall into this woman's company?"

But if such arguments of Antronius were often heard, it is equally true that from the Renaissance onward there appeared an increasing array of advocates of woman's education in England, France and Germany. These prophets were, indeed, without many practical followers.[61] Had it been otherwise with practice, there had been no need of prophets.

Ascham's *Scholemaster* appeared in 1571. Ten years later, Richard Mulcaster, a realist in educational philosophy, published his *Positions*,[62] wherein he defended the education of "young maidens." He is, however, no great insurgent reformer. His first reason is that the practice of the country allows it (England of the sixteenth century appears unusually hospitably inclined to women's education), and he but acquiesces in that practice. He says specifically, "I set not young maidens to public grammar schools, a thing not used in my country, I send them not to the Universities, having no precedent thereof. . . ." He refers with approval to the views of Plato that "all virtues be indifferent, nay all one in man and woman, saving they be more strong and durable in men, weaker and more variable in women. . . ." Since "their aptness calls for it," that is another argument for their receiving education; and, finally, the noble effects of education on the sex—where it has been granted—warrants the continuance of the practice.[63]

Society of England in the seventeenth and eighteenth centuries proved less favorable to women's education than in the sixteenth.[64] The earlier free spirit of humanism congealed into

[61] Compare Cannon: *Education of Women during the Renaissance.*

[62] See pp. 166–82.

[63] "Is Anacreon a good poet, what say you to Sappho? Is Bacis a good prophet, what say you to Sibill? Was Sesostris a famous Prince, what say you to Semiramis? Was Servius a noble King, what say you to Tanaquill? Was Brutus a stout man, what say you to Porcia? Thus reasoneth Plutarch . . ."—Quoted from Mulcaster's *Positions.*

[64] A book of great interest appeared in London in 1624, under the title of *The Mother's Legacie, To Her Unborn Child*, by Elizabeth Jocelin. It is pervaded by great piety and devotion, but much learning is deprecated as likely to lead to evil. "I desire, if the child be a daughter, her bringing up may be learning the Bible, as my sisters do, good housewifery, and good works; other learning a woman needs not: though I admire it in those whom God has blest with discretion, yet I desired not much in my own, having seen that sometimes women have greater proportion of learning than wisdom . . ."—*R. C. E.*, 1904, I, 666.

Ciceronianism in the schools; the days of the great Elizabeth
and her reputation for learning were over;[65] autocratic excellence
gave way before democratic mediocrity; Puritanism with its
return to simplicity in religion was inclined to adopt once more
for women the educational standards of primitive Christians.
Whereas, up to the time of Henry the Eighth, nunneries had
offered educational stimulus and opportunities to women, he
destroyed many of them, along with monasteries and chantry
schools.[66] The effect of this diminution of educational encouragement in time made itself evident in an indifference to, and
even a disbelief in the possibility of, their education. Paul's
advice to women—that they ask their husbands—was taken seriously by those in New England who had to deal with Anne
Hutchinson and her ilk. This decline accounts for the predominant note in literature advocating the education of women,
which came from the pens of Mrs. Makin (1673), Mary Astell
(1697), Daniel Defoe (1692), Pope (1729), Hannah More
(1799), Mary Wollstonecraft (1792), Darwin (1798), Sydney
Smith, and John Stuart Mill. The prevailing note that here
contrasts sharply with Ascham and Mulcaster is the demand for
educational facilities and reproof of that unjust social disapproval of woman's learning. Ascham and Mulcaster were happy
in promoting woman's education in a society that believed in it,
or at any rate tolerated it, for all "as their means would bear
it." The protagonists of the succeeding centuries sought to gain
that advantage for women generally, regardless of wealth, provided they were mentally capable of appreciating it. That is,
a distinct movement for women's intellectual emancipation appeared in the latter part of the seventeenth century, which slowly
achieved a small measure of success until women were admitted
to the universities in the nineteenth. This intellectual emancipation was accompanied by a similar movement in social, economic,
and political life.

Let us return to the period of the Restoration. In 1673, Mrs.
Makin issued *An Essay to Revive the Antient Education of Gentlewomen, in Religion, Manners, Arts and Tongues, with an
answer to the objections against this way of Education*, wherein,
although she understands that it is an age which counts learn-

[65] See Stephens: *Workfellows in Social Progression*, 105–9.
[66] See Leach: *English Schools of the Reformation*.

ing and virtue pedantic things, she, nevertheless, proceeds to sharply challenge such a customary view and to set forth her own. Education of women, she says, has been so long out of practice that people have generally come to believe the sex is not endowed with reason, and hence incapable of education. "A learned woman is thought to be a comet that bodes mischief, whenever it appears. To offer to the world the liberal education of women is to deface the image of God in man, it will make women so high, and men so low, like Fire in the housetops it will set the whole world in flame." She urges education, but advises women againt seeking preëminence. "I verily think, Women were formerly Educated in the knowledge of Arts and Tongues, and by their Education, many did rise to a great height in Learning. Were Women thus educated now, I am confident the advantage would be very great: the Women would have Honour and Pleasure, their Relations Profit, and the whole Nation Advantage. . . . Were a competent number of Schools erected to Educate Ladyes Ignorance, and how industrious the next Generation would be to wipe off their reproach. I expect to meet with many Scoffes and Taunts from inconsiderate and Illiterate Men, that prize their own Lusts and Pleasure more than your Profit and Content. I shall be the less concern'd at these, so long as I am in your favour; and this discourse may be a Weapon in your hands to defend yourselves, whilst you endeavour to polish your Souls, that you may glorify God, and answer the end of your Creation, to be meet helps to your Husbands. Let not your Ladiships be offended, that I do not (as some have wittily done) plead for Female Preeminence. To ask too much is the way to be denied all. God hath made Man the Head, if you be educated and instructed, as I propose, I am sure you will acknowledge it, and be satisfied that you are helps, that your Husbands do consult and advise with you (which if you be wise they will be glad of) and that your Husbands have the casting-Voice, in whose determinations you will acquiesce."[67]

Mrs. Makin also undertook to reply to the objections raised to women's education. To the objection, "If we bring up our daughters to learning no persons will adventure to marry them," she answers that learned men will seek learned wives and that

[67] Quoted from the excellent work by Reynolds: *Learned Lady in England, 1650–1760*, 280–1.

there is no danger of overstocking the market with educated women. She further explains that the ancient ideal set forth in Solomon's praise of the good housewife implied a good education, else she could not have done all she was reputed to have done. When it is maintained that "women are of ill natures" and will abuse their education, she retorts, "Men also abuse their Education." If women are of "low parts," so often are men; if women do not wish education, so also with many boys; if a learned woman appears ridiculous because it is not customary, she avers this is a bad custom; if women are soft, delicate, weak, then strengthen them by education.[68] These objections and answers are very similar to those that appeared in Barksdale's *Learned Maid*, in 1659, a translation of Anna Van Schurman's treatise on ladies' education. "The wits of women are too weak for the study of letters," it is said, but she replies: "Not all men have 'heroical wits' yet they are not excluded from studies . . ." and so forth. The conclusion is finally drawn: "Wherefore our thesis stands firm: A Christian maid, or woman may conveniently give herself to learning. . . ."[69]

Mary Astell (b. 1668), well educated because of her father's solicitous care, came to live at London when she was twenty years old. Six years later her *Serious Proposal to Ladies for the advancement of their true and greatest interests* appeared, in which she recommended a plan for a woman's college, or nunnery of the Established Church, wherein religion and education were to be cultivated at the same time. Bishop Burnet, referred to elsewhere for his backward views on the subject of woman's education, appears to have discouraged practical coöperation in the scheme, and it came to naught. It was, notwithstanding this failure, of great consequence in the history of women's education and in a few years was followed by a similar scheme proposed by Daniel Defoe. Astell's *Proposal* concerned itself with the erection of "a retreat from the world for those who desire that advantage, but likewise an institution and previous discipline to fit us to do the greatest good in it." Here was, indeed, a great forward-looking program, so much so that she realized the difficulty of its securing a hearing. "The men, by interest and inclination, are so generally engaged against us, that

68 *Ibid.*, 283–5.
69 *Ibid.*, 274–5.

it is not to be expected that any man of wit should arise so generous as to engage in our quarrel and to be the champion of our sex against the injuries and oppressions of his own. Those romantic days are over, and there is not so much as a Don Quixote of the quill left to succor distressed damsels.'' Not only did she despair of defenders; she denounced the unequal interest taken in boys' and men's education:

''In the first place, Boys have much Time and Pains, Care and Cost bestowed on their educations, Girls have little or none. The former are early initiated in the Sciences, are made acquainted with Antient and Modern Discoveries, they Study Books and Men, have all imaginable encouragement; not only Fame, a dry reward now-a-days, But also Title, Authority, Power, and Riches themselves which purchase all things, are the reward of their improvement. The latter are restricted, frown'd upon, beat, not *for* but *from* the Muses; Laughter and Ridicule that never-failing Scare-Crow is set up to drive them from the Tree of Knowledge. But if in spite of all difficulties Nature prevails, and they can't be kept so ignorant as their masters would have them, they are stared upon as Monsters, Censur'd Envy'd and every way discouraged, or at the best they have the Fate the Proverb assigns them: *Virtue is praised and starved.*''[70]

But the unexpected knight came riding. Almost coincident with her thought, in part, ran that of another—Defoe, a Quixote of parts, used to fighting for human emancipation, and not afraid of losing battles. His essay seems to have been written in 1692 but was not published until 1697, when it appeared as one of his *Essays on Projects*. His proposal varies from Astell's inasmuch as he breaks with the monastic ideal. He was a staunch and open fighter for religious and civil liberty. To seclude women for their education seems to be unnecessary. Yet he does not wish to ''exalt the female government in the least,'' and is convinced that women of sense and education will not seek to usurp the places of men. This education is to be of the completest sort—no trimming merely because they are women, no limitation save that of capacity: ''To such whose genius would lead them to it, I would deny no sort of learning. . . . The capacities of women are supposed to be greater, and their senses

---

[70] Quoted from the Preface to *Reflections on Marriage* (1706) by Reynolds: *Learned Lady in England,* 1650–1760, 300.

quicker than those of the men; and what they might be capable
of being bred to, is plain from some instances of female wit . . .
which upbraids us with injustice, and looks as if we denied women
the advantage of education, for fear they should vie with the
men in their improvements. . . .''[71]

It is, he thinks, ''one of the most barbarous customs in the
world, considering us as a civilized and a Christian Country, that
we deny the advantages of learning to women.'' We reproach
them with folly and impertinence, but ''one would wonder, indeed, how it should happen that women are conversible at all;
since they are only beholden to natural parts, for all their knowledge. Their youth is spent to teach them to stitch and sew, or
make baubles. They are taught to read, indeed, and perhaps to
write their names, or so; and that is the height of a woman's
education. And I would but ask any who slight the sex for their
understanding, what is a man (a gentleman, I mean) good for,
that is taught no more?

''The soul is placed in the body like a rough diamond; and
must be polished, or the lustre of it will never appear. And 'tis
manifest, that as the rational soul distinguishes us from brutes;
so education carries on the distinction, and makes some less
brutish than others. This is too evident to need any demonstration. But why then should women be denied the benefit of instruction? If knowledge and understanding had been useless
additions to the sex, GOD Almighty would never have given them
capacities; for he made nothing needless. Besides, I would ask
such, What they can see in ignorance, that they should think
it a necessary ornament to a woman? or how much worse is a
wise woman than a fool? or what has the woman done to forfeit
the privilege of being taught? Does she plague us with her
pride and impertinence? Why did we not let her learn, that
she might have had more wit? Shall we upbraid women with

[71] Defoe on The Education of Women [Aitken: *Later Stuart Tracts*, IV,
281–4.] This suggests the ideas of Johnson and the lines of Pope, written
about 1720:

''In beauty and wit
''No mortal as yet
''To question your empire has dared:
''But men of discerning
''Have thought that in learning
''To yield to a lady was hard.''

MARY WOLLSTONECRAFT

folly, when 'tis only the error of this inhuman custom, that hindered them from being made wiser?''

The essay must be read in its entirety to appreciate its spirit, the completeness of his attack on entrenched prejudice and practices. He becomes the most daring knight, espousing the cause of woman's emancipation from mere drudgery, when he says: ''. . . I take it upon me to make such a bold assertion, that all the world are mistaken in their practice about women. For I cannot think that God Almighty ever made them so delicate . . . glorious . . . agreeable . . . delightful . . . with souls capable of the same accomplishments with men . . .[72] to be only stewards of our houses, Cooks, and Slaves.''

In the next century two very prominent figures emerged who left an impression upon the literature of women's education.[73] Hannah More (1745) and Mary Wollstonecraft (1759) both became teachers for a time, and later achieved a reputation, the one for her *Strictures on the Modern System of Female Education* and *Coelebs Hunting a Wife,* and the other by her *Vindication of the Rights of Women.*

The *Strictures on Female Education* appeared in 1799. While it was a much read and influential book, it was not of the same

[72] This idea of equal mental powers is on the increase and appears often. It appears in Mary Astell's work, again and again in Defoe's, and later in that of Joseph Addison.—See the *Guardian,* Sept. 8, 1713. Pope, too suggests, in ''Sandy's Ghost'':

> ''Ye ladies, too, draw forth your pen
> ''I pray where can the hurt lie?
> ''Since you have brains as well as men,
> ''As witness Lady Wortley.''

[73] Reference should also be made to Burton's *Lectures on Female Education,* 1794, in which, for the most part, he took a decidedly liberal stand. Nevertheless, his work was not calculated to arrest the attention and stir up the minds of men as was Wollstonecraft's. He recalls with approval the learned women of England in the sixteenth century and points with pride also to Madame Dacier's translation of Homer, Mrs. Carter's version of Epictetus, and the accomplishments of Mrs. Trimmer, Miss Murry, and Mrs. Macauley. Woman's duty is in domestic economy, but though this is important, it ''is not sufficient that you are taught the Domestic Arts.'' He is nevertheless conservative: ''It is not necessary, neither is it expedient for the purpose of civil society, that girls should be educated in the same manner as boys; but were a similar plan to be adopted, the women, without doubt, would be as well informed in the system of human knowledge as the men.''

kind as that with which it has been bracketed. It was pervaded throughout by an emphasis on Christian training, the evils of dissipation and amusements, and the worldly spirit which was incompatible with Christian life. All education must lead to a religious life; history and geography are to be used for a moral purpose; still another chapter deals with "the use of definitions, and the moral benefit of accuracy in language." Godwin speaks of education as a means to lead from bondage to freedom; but with More, "their knowledge is not often like the learning of man, to be reproduced in some literary composition, nor ever in any learned profession. . . . A lady studies, not that she may qualify to become an orator or a pleader; not that she may learn to debate, but to act." Women are to read books, not so much to be able to talk about them as to secure improvement and the formation of habits. She does not so much hope to bring forth a new education that is to change woman's sphere, as to denounce and ridicule the vain formal education of "accomplishments" and the tendency to seek after amusements rather than serious, solid benefit. "Pursuit of knowledge," she explained, had not caused any considerable number of women to become "examples of the dereliction of family duties" (as many opponents of women's education claimed); and if there were cases, it was probably true that "Hoyle, and not Homer" had "robbed her children of her time and affections. For one family which has been neglected by the mother's passion for books, an hundred have been deserted through her passion for play."[74]

It might be concluded, from the religious and moral note repeatedly struck, that Hannah More merely denounced the baubles in "female" training of the day; but she did much besides that. The principle of selection, which she laid down, makes it clear that she hoped to see women educated as rational creatures, not as objects of flattery:

"To woman therefore, whatever be her rank, I would recommend a predominance of those more sober studies, which, not having display for their object, may make her wise without vanity, happy without witnesses, and content without panegyrists; the exercise of which will not bring celebrity, but improve usefulness. She should pursue every kind of study which will teach her to elicit truth; which will lead her to be intent

74 More: *Strictures*, II, 108–9.

upon realities; will give precision to her ideas; will make an exact mind; every study, which, instead of stimulating her sensibility, will chastise it; which will give her definite notions; will bring the imagination under dominion; will lead her to think, to compare, to combine, to methodise; which will confer such a power of discrimination that her judgment shall learn to reject what is dazzling if it be not solid; and to prefer, not what is striking, or bright, or new, but what is just. That kind of knowledge which is rather fitted for home consumption than foreign exportation, is peculiarly adapted to women.''[75]

Caroline Dall, in *College, Market and the Court*,[76] states that, in her study of English books upon the subject of woman's advancement, she was depressed by the great lack of literature up to about 1800, when a sudden flood of it seemed miraculously to appear. This literature, or a great part of it, is a monument to the influence of Mary Wollstonecraft. Yet her *Vindication*, which aroused so much criticism and denunciation, would scarcely be regarded as revolutionary today. It was, indeed, a scathing criticism of much already written on the subject by such authors as Rousseau, Fordyce, Gregory and de Stael; it pointed out as the chief reason of woman's inferior position in society, her improper education, or none. She wrote in her introduction: "... I have turned over various books written on the subject of education, and patiently observed the conduct of parents and the management of schools; but what has been the result? a profound conviction, that the neglected education of my fellow creatures is the grand source of the misery I deplore; and that women in particular, are rendered weak and wretched by a variety of concurring causes, originating from one hasty conclusion. The conduct and manners of women, in fact, evidently prove that their minds are not in a healthy state; for, like the flowers that are planted in too rich a soil, strength and usefulness are sacrificed to beauty; and the flaunting leaves, after having pleased a fastidious eye, fade, disregarded on the stalk, long before the season when they ought to have arrived at maturity. One cause of this barren blooming I attribute to a false system of education, gathered from the books written on this subject by men, who, considering females rather as women

[75] *Ibid.*, 6.
[76] Pp. 84–5.

than human creatures, have been more anxious to make them alluring mistresses than rational wives; and the understanding of the sex has been so bubbled by this specious homage, that the civilized women of the present century, with a few exceptions, are only anxious to inspire love, when they ought to cherish a nobler ambition, and by their abilities and virtues exact respect.'"[77]

Published in 1792, the *Vindication* furnished an antidote for Rousseau's conception of woman's education, which had appeared a generation before. Her criticism of the popularly accepted ideas at once secured the severest condemnation for herself and her views. Fordyce, whose *Sermons* she quotes in order to demolish, provokes her greatest disgust when he writes:

". . . I am astonished at the folly of many women, who are still reproaching their husbands for leaving them alone, for preferring this or that company to theirs, for treating with this and the other mark of disregard or indifference; when, to speak the truth, they have themselves in a great measure to blame. Not that I would justify the men in any thing wrong on their part. But had you behaved to them with more respectful observance, and a more equal tenderness; studying their humours, overlooking their mistakes, submitting to their opinions in matters indifferent, passing by little instances of unevenness, caprice, or passion, giving soft answers to hasty words, complaining as seldom as possible, and making it your daily care to relieve their anxieties, and prevent their wishes, to enliven the hour of dulness, and call up the ideas of felicity: had you pursued this conduct, I doubt not but you would have maintained and even increased their esteem, so far as to have secured every degree of influence that could conduce to their virtue, or your mutual satisfaction; and your house might at this day have been the abode of domestic bliss.''

"Is not [this] the . . . portrait of a house slave?" she cries. "Such a woman ought to be an angel—or she is an ass—for I discern not a trace of the human character, neither reason nor passion in this domestic drudge, whose being is absorbed in that of a tyrant's.'' "If women be ever allowed to walk without leading strings, why must they be cajoled into virtue? Speak to them the language of truth and soberness . . . and let them be

[77] *Vindication,* 6.

taught to respect themselves as rational creatures. . . . It moves my gall to hear a preacher descanting on dress and needlework; and still more to hear him address the British fair, the fairest of the fair, as if they had only feelings.'' It is her belief that all writers of this character "have contributed to render women more artificial, weaker characters, than they would otherwise have been; and, consequently, more useless members of society. . ."; for they "render women pleasing at the expense of every solid virtue.''[78] Mrs. Piozzi's advice, "Seek not for happiness in singularity; and dread a refinement of wisdom as a deviation into folly,''[79] and her opinion that "a woman will pardon an affront to her understanding much sooner than one to her person,'' are, to her, odious in the extreme; but not more so than de Stael's eulogium on Rousseau in which she praises him for having assisted women to descend from their usurped throne and seated them upon that "to which they were destined by nature.''[80]

In the same year appeared an interesting *Plan of Female Education* by Erasmus Darwin. Another edition was published, in Philadelphia, in 1798. It discussed the wide range of problems connected with the operation of a boarding school, but of greater significance was his advanced view in recommending many scientific studies for girls.[81] That this range of science which he recommends "may perhaps be thought to include more branches . . . than is necessary for female erudition,'' he recognizes; but "as in male education the tedious acquirement of ancient languages for the purpose of studying poetry and oratory is gradually giving way to the more useful cultivation of modern sciences, it may be of advantage to ladies of the rising generation to acquire an outline of similar knowledge. . . .'' The purpose of this accession of scientific knowledge, or of any education for that matter, was not, with him, as it was with Wollstonecraft, to emancipate women from a degraded bondage, but to enable them to be better companions. It is to improve their conversation by more up-to-date studies that he urges them to study the botany of Linnaeus, in translation, the textbook of Lee, and

[78] *Ibid.*, 22.
[79] *Ibid.*, 109.
[80] *Ibid.*, 110.
[81] *Plan of Female Education*, 54–60.

Curtis' botanical magazine; the elements of chemistry by Lavoissier, and the philosophy of chemistry by Fourcroy; mineralogy should precede chemistry, but he knows of no book to recommend that is made easy enough; while "astronomy, mechanics, hydrostatics and optics, with the curious addition of electricity and magnetism, may best be acquired by attending lectures in experimental philosophy, which are occasionally exhibited by itinerant philosophers."[82]

All this to improve their conversation; but even this purpose was much too advanced for people generally. It was against the ignorant view that educated women were pedantic, affected, and immodest, that Sydney Smith made his oft-quoted, characteristically witty, statement:

"It is said that the effect of knowledge is to make women pedantic and affected; and that nothing can be more offensive than to see a woman stepping out of the natural modesty of her sex, to make an ostentatious display of her literary attainments. This may be true enough; but the answer is so trite and obvious, that we are almost ashamed to make it. All affectation and display proceed from the supposition of possessing something better than the rest of the world possesses. Nobody is vain of possessing two legs and two arms—because that is the precise quantity of either sort of limb which everybody possesses. Who ever heard a lady boast that she understood French?—for no other reason, that we know of, but because everybody in these days does understand French; and though there may be some disgrace in being ignorant of that language, there is little or no merit in its acquisition. Diffuse knowledge generally among women, and you will at once cure the conceit which knowledge occasions while it is rare. Vanity and conceit we shall of course witness in men and women as long as the world endures; but by multiplying the attainments upon which these feelings are founded, you increase the difficulty of indulging them, and render them much more tolerable by making them the proofs of a much higher merit. When learning ceases to be uncommon among women, learned women will cease to be affected.

* * *

"To suppose that any mode of education can create a general jealousy and rivalry between the sexes, is so very ridiculous

[82] *Ibid.*

that it requires only to be stated in order to be refuted. The same desire of pleasing secures all that delicacy and reserve which are of such inestimable value to women. We are quite astonished, in hearing men converse on such subjects, to find them attributing such beautiful effects to ignorance. It would appear, from the tenor of such objections, that ignorance had been the great civilizer of the world. Women are delicate and refined, only because they are ignorant; they manage their household, only because they are ignorant; they attend to their children, only because they know no better. Now, we must really confess, we have all our lives been so ignorant as not to know the value of ignorance. We have always attributed the modesty and refined manners of women to their being well taught in moral and religious duty—to the hazardous situation in which they are placed—to that perpetual vigilance which it is their duty to exercise over thought, word, and action—and to that cultivation of the mild virtues, which those who cultivate the stern and magnanimous virtues expect at their hands.''[83]

In the succeeding century probably no single writer had as great an influence as John Stuart Mill, whose essay on the *Subjection of Women* was first published in 1869. Women's emancipation had indeed been agitating the minds of many, even in our own country, but it occupied little time in the minds of the most influential people. Here was a champion not to be ignored by any. Mill's *Political Economy* and his *Logic* were in the hands of students generally, and this support of an acknowledged logician and economist at once lent weight to the struggling cause. He attacked directly the principle of inequality, and maintained: ''That the principle which regulates the existing social relations between the two sexes—the legal subordination of one sex to the other—is wrong in itself, and now one of the chief hindrances to human improvement; and that it ought to be replaced by a principle of perfect equality, admitting no power or privilege on the one side, nor disability on the other.''[84] Moreover, the existing principle of inequality has no basis in experience to prove its superiority, no other having ever been tried; likewise, the theoretical advantages of inequality are not known for society adopted it without ''deliberation, or forethought, or any social ideas, or any notion whatever of what con-

[83] Quoted in *Godey's Lady's Book*, Nov. 1855, 401–2, 403.
[84] Mill: *Subjection of Women*, 208.

duced to the benefit of humanity or the good order of society.''
In his view, the prevailing inequality ''arose simply from the
fact that from the very earliest twilight of human society every
woman (owing to the value attached to her by men, combined
with her inferiority in muscular strength) was found in a state
of bondage to some man.''[85]

The result of this subjection has been to make what is called
woman's nature ''an eminently artificial thing—the result of
forced repression in some directions, unnatural stimulation in
others. . . . It may be asserted without scruple, that no other
class of dependents have had their character so entirely distorted
from its natural proportions by their relation with their masters;
for, if conquered and slave races have been, in some respects,
more forcibly repressed, whatever in them has not been crushed
down by an iron heel has been generally let alone, and if left
with any liberty of development, it has developed itself according to its own laws; but in the case of women, a hothouse and
stove cultivation has always been carried on of some of the
capabilities of their nature, for the benefit and pleasure of their
masters. Then, because certain products of the general vital
force sprout luxuriantly and reach a great development in this
heated atmosphere and under this active nurture and watering,
while other shoots from the same root, which are left outside
in the wintry air, with ice purposely heaped all round them,
have a stunted growth and some are burnt off with fire and disappear; men, with that inability to recognize their own work
which distinguishes the unanalytic mind, indolently believe that
the tree grows of itself in the way they have made it grow, and
that it would die if one half of it were not kept in a vapour
bath and the other half in the snow.''[86]

We have now passed in review the ideas of many of the most
prominent advocates of woman's education in England, but
many whose work is less well known were, nevertheless, remarkable for their liberal sentiments and would repay a more
complete survey than can be included here. Among these were
Lord Collingwood, whose letters, revealing a great interest in
the education of daughters, were often quoted in early American
pedagogical journals; and Samuel Wilderspin, who, in his *Sys-*

[85] *Ibid.*, 214.
[86] *Ibid.*, 244–5.

tem of Education for the Young, devoted several pages to the discussion of the weaknesses of female education and the ways whereby it should be improved. Harriett Martineau, a most brilliant woman, celebrated for many literary productions, among which were *Household Education, Society in America,* and *A Retrospect of Western Travel,* stoutly maintained "that the brain which will learn French will learn Greek; the brain which enjoys arithmetic is capable of mathematics." And if women are said to be "light-minded and superficial," the obvious answer is that their minds should be the more carefully sobered by grave studies and the acquisition of exact knowledge.[87]

The complete duality of character in men and women is held up to ridicule by Emily Davies in her *Higher Education of Women*: "The conception of character which rests on the broad basis of a common humanity falls into the background, and there is substituted for it a dual theory, with distinctly different forms of male and female excellence. Persons who take this view are naturally governed by it in their conceptions of what women ought to be. Having framed a more or less definite idea of the masculine character, in constructing the feminine helpmeet they look out, if not for the directly opposite, for what they would call the complimentary qualities, and the conclusion quickly follows, that whatever is manly must be unwomanly, and *vice versa*. The advocates of this view usually hold in connection with it certain doctrines, such as, that the man is intended for the world, woman for the home; man's strength is in the head, woman's in the heart; the man's function is to protect, woman's to soothe and comfort; men must work, and women must weep; everywhere we are to have a sharply marked division, often honestly mistaken for the highest and most real communion. Closely connected with these separatist doctrines is the double moral code, with its masculine and feminine virtues, and its separate law of duty and honour for either sex."[88]

Emily Shireff, in *Intellectual Education* (1858), sounded a note like that of Olive Schreiner, in *Woman and Labor,* by declaring that woman must secure her improvement "not by angry clamour or proud contention, but by proving [her] own capacity; by rendering [herself] fit for higher social and domestic influ-

[87] *Household Education,* 270–2.
[88] (1866) Pp. 16–18.

ence.''[89]   Since women had no professions, she held that it is all
the more necessary to educate them in order that they may experience ''from within what comes to the more active portion of
mankind from without.''   Education of women for the home is a
great good, but ''in educating a young girl we must feel that her
future is too uncertain, too much beyond her own control, to
venture to train her for a position that may never be hers.   The
only safe course is to hold up individual perfectness, as far as
such a term may be used . . . , as the aim of education; in other
words the harmonious development of all her powers, as her own
individual right and duty; to train her, in short, as God's
Creature, not as man's subordinate.''[90]

It is probably true, as Dr. Johnson observed, that ''man is, in
general, better pleased when he has a good dinner on his table,
than when his wife talks Greek''; and it is, indeed, a rare accomplishment to be able to translate Epictetus, embroider beautifully, and make a pudding!   The consummation of all these
things was devoutly to be wished for, but the rarity of the
performance no doubt caused many mere men to think the combination an impossibility.   Whether the seat of opposition to
woman's education truly lay in the stomach, the heart, or the
head, is a difficult riddle to unravel; but certain it is that there
was a voluminous literature published, though of a monotonous
sameness of character, to counteract, denounce and deride the
views of friends of woman's education, already touched upon.
Such conceptions as those found in the *Lady's New Year's Gift
or Advice to a Daughter* by the first Marquis of Halifax (1688),
the *Letters* of Lord Chesterfield, the *Autobiography* of Bishop
Burnet (about 1710), the *Sermons to Young Ladies* by James
Fordyce, and others of like character point as clearly to the
almost complete passing of the sixteenth century's tradition of
learned women as does the voice of protest which arose from
Astell, Defoe and Wollstonecraft.[91]   Chesterfield, who probably
typified best the prevailing attitude, and who especially attacked
the views of Mary Astell, gave it as his sentiment:

''I leave 'em a mighty empire, Love.   There they reign absolutely, and by unquestioned right, while beauty supports their

[89] *Op. cit.*, 276.
[90] *Ibid.*, 19–20.
[91] Stephens: *Workfellows in Social Progression*, 114–17.

throne. They have all the talents requisite for that soft empire,
and the ablest of our sex cannot contend with 'em in the profound knowledge and conduct of those arcana.'' If any ''are
deposed by years, or accidents'' (loss of beauty), and if any ''by
nature were never qualified to reign,'' they ''should content
themselves with the private care and economy of their families
and the diligent discharge of their domestic duties. . . .

''Women, then, are only children of a larger growth; they have
an interesting tattle, and sometimes wit; but for solid reasoning,
good sense, I never knew one in my life that had it; or who
reasoned or acted consequentially for four-and-twenty hours together. . . . Their beauty neglected or controverted, their age
increased, or their supposed understandings depreciated, in-
stantly kindles their little passions, and overturns any system
of consequential conduct, that in their most reasonable moments
they might have been capable of forming. A man of sense only
trifles with them, plays with them, humors and flatters them, as
he does with a sprightly, forward child; but he neither consults
them about, nor trusts them with serious matters; though he often
makes them believe that he does both; which is the thing in the
world that they are proud of; for they love mightily to be dab-
bling in business (which by the way they always spoil); and
being justly distrustful, that men in general look upon them in
a trifling light, they almost adore that man, who talks more
seriously to them, and who seems to consult them; I say, who
seems; for weak men really do, but wise men only seem to do it.
No flattery is either too high or too low for them. They will
greedily swallow the highest, and gratefully accept the lowest;
and you may safely flatter any woman, from her understanding
down to the exquisite taste of her fan. Women who are either
indisputably beautiful, or indisputably ugly, are best flattered
upon the score of their understandings: but those who are in a
state of mediocrity are best flattered upon their beauty, or at
least their graces; for every woman, who is not absolutely ugly,
thinks herself handsome; but not hearing often that she is so,
is the more grateful, and the more obligated to the few who tell
her so: whereas a decided and conscious beauty looks upon every
tribute paid to her beauty only as her due; but wants to shine,
and to be considered on the side of her understanding. . . . It
is, therefore, absolutely necessary to manage, please and flatter

them: and never to discover the least marks of contempt, which is what they never forgive."[92]

Because of the popularity of his *Letters*, Chesterfield's view was widely known and unquestionably furnished arguments to minds less brilliant against the proposed innovations against tradition, thus acting as a deterrent to the movement. In similar fashion Bishop Burnet, because of his position, was probably able to discourage wealthy patrons who would have furthered the practical realization of Mary Astell's scheme.

Fordyce, in the eighteenth century, found that woman's complaint that men sought to repress women by keeping them in a state of ignorance was "without any foundation adequate to the bitterness with which it has been made. Are you desirous of knowledge, and what hinders your attainment of it? Is there any law or statute by which you are prohibited . . . to read or think if you are so minded?" He implied later that her lack of mental culture depended upon her greater love of expensive gowns, plays and novels. ". . . It is both an idle and unthankful pretense to plead that they want either opportunity or leisure for any one study benefitting their sex."[93]

His views, elsewhere expressed, are very similar to those of Chesterfield and Rousseau. But in order to rule in the "empire which belongs to [women]" he advises that history, biography, memoirs, voyages and travels, geography and astronomy be read, and asks rhetorically: "Permit me to ask, whence it proceeds that studies like these are neglected by the generality of your sex? Is it because they are not calculated to inflame the fancy, and flatter the passion; or because to relish them to purpose, requires some degree of solidity and judgment? . . ."[94] As to the first, I scruple not to declare my opinion that Nature appears to have formed the faculties of your sex, for the most part, with less vigor than those of ours; observing the same distinction here, as in the more delicate frame of your bodies. . . . But you yourselves, I think, will allow that war, commerce, politics, exercises of strength and dexterity, abstract philosophy, and all the abstruser sciences, are most properly the province of men."

[92] *Ibid.*, 143–4, 145–8.
[93] Fordyce: *Sermons to Young Ladies*, 170–1.
[94] *Ibid.*, 160–5.

All of this, many of the feminist leaders would decidedly *not* "allow." It was the complete assurance, the assumption of all wisdom, and the patronizing attitude that roused the "gall" of Mary Wollstonecraft. "I am sure," said Fordyce, "those masculine women that would plead for your sharing any part of this province equally with us, do not understand your true interests. There is an influence, there is an empire which belongs to you, and which I wish you ever to possess: I mean that which has the heart for its object and is secured by meekness and modesty, by soft attraction, and virtuous love."[95]

There is a distressingly pathetic characteristic in human beings and the societies they create which must, if only for the moment, depress the student of the past: a tendency to boast of their straightforward progress and believe in it. But such as has been made has been decidedly slow, especially in fields where it has depended upon the acceptance of a new idea. We naturally expect that enlightened men of the nineteenth century would have been influenced by ideas of the seventeenth and eighteenth; and, indeed, many were. Yet it gives us pause to find that the phrases and ideas from Aristotle to Halifax, Chesterfield, and Fordyce provide the mental furnishing of many of the "best" minds of the nineteenth century. It is encouraging to remember, however, that we are apt, in our search for signs of progress, to stress the long line of traditional thought that occupied the minds of the great personages in conservative groups from generation to generation, and forget, momentarily, that progress has been made by those who have risen unknown from inconspicuous places, bearing the divine fire.

On account of the sameness of the view of woman's capacity which appears in so many works, it would not be a profitable expenditure of time and space to present them at length. Let it suffice to name some of them and to hear those who are most qualified to be spokesmen of their time. Chirol, in the *Best System of Female Education* (1809) ;[96] Ruskin, in his *Letters and Advice to Young Girls and Ladies* (1879) ;[97] "A friend of the sex," in *Sketches of the History, Genius and Disposition . . . of the Fair Sex* (1812) ;[98] Gisbourne, in *Duties of Women*

[95] *Ibid.*
[96] Pp. 4–10.
[97] Pp. 33–4.
[98] Pp. 118–21, 141–2, and 143–5.

(1820) ;[99] Abbott, in *The School Girl* (1840) ; Arthur, in *Advice to Young Ladies* (1866) ;[100] Dana, in *Woman's Possibilities and Limitations* (1899) ;[101] and others, interspersed between and extending beyond these dates, continued to hold to the idea that woman's intellectual capacity was as different from man's as her physical.   None, to be sure, would have her ignorant, but all would have her know her place—the home; they are, likewise, in general agreement as to what constitutes her best preparation for the home.   Ruskin, describing her nature and sphere, says:

"We are foolish, and without excuse foolish, in speaking of the 'superiority' of one sex to the other, as if they could be compared in similar things.   Each has what the other has not: each completes the other, and is completed by the other: they are in nothing alike, and the happiness and perfection of both depends on each asking and receiving from the other what the other only can give.

"Now their separate characters are briefly these.   The Man's power is active, progressive, defensive.   He is eminently the doer, the creator, the discoverer, the defender.   His intellect is for speculation and invention; his energy for adventure, for war and for conquest, wherever war is just, wherever conquest necessary.   But the woman's power is for rule, not for battle,—and her intellect is not for invention or creation, but for sweet ordering, arrangement, and decision.   She sees the qualities of things, their claims and their places.   Her great function is Praise: she enters into no contest, but infallibly judges the crown of contest."[102]   He continues:

[99] Pp. 14–18.

[100] Pp. 57–8.

[101] Pp. 11–19.

[102] Ruskin: *op. cit.* Compare Gisbourne: *op. cit.*, 16–18; also the statement of Arthur: "By keeping this division in the mind, the difference between the sexes, when stated, will be clearly apparent.   A man has will and understanding, and a cerebellum and cerebrum by which they act; and so has a woman.   In this they are alike.   But in man the understanding predominates, and in woman the will; and here they are different.   If this be so, we may, of course, expect to find a larger development of the cerebrum, or upper brain, in man, and a larger development of the cerebellum, or lower brain, in woman; and this is so.   A man's head is higher, and fuller in front, than a woman's while a woman's head is broader and larger behind than a man's."—*Op. cit.*, 152–3.   A like view is found in Dana: *op. cit.*, 11.

"And wherever a true wife comes, this home is always round her. The stars only may be over her head; the glowworm in the night-cold grass may be the only fire at her feet: but home is yet wherever she is; and for a noble woman it stretches far round her, better than ceiled with cedar, or painted with vermilion, shedding its quiet light far, for those who else were homeless.

"This, then, I believe to be,—will you not admit it to be,—the woman's true place and power? But do not you see that to fulfill this, she must—as far as one can use such terms of a human creature—be incapable of error? So far as she rules, all must be right, or nothing is.[103]

Arthur was greatly disturbed because "we have in this day a class of intellectual ladies who boldly contend for the absolute equality of the sexes, and who write books for the purpose of proving this doctrine, and spreading it through society. . . . Some of the books written . . . contain views of the most pernicious character, striking still more deeply at the very foundations of social well being.[104] As might be supposed, few of these writers understand or teach what is true in regard to marriage. And this is no matter of wonder; for how can any one, who is not able to see the true difference between the sexes, teach what is true in regard to their union?"[105] Abbott denounced the movement in more vehement language, illustrating amply the fashionable contempt felt in the middle of the century for women who were too forward in leaving their wonted sphere:

"Now and then you see an Amazon, a female monster, who, like Mary Wollstonecraft, lays aside all delicacy and loveliness of her sex, and, with brazen faced effrontery, wishes to destroy all distinction between male and female, and to mingle with men in the most masculine and indelicate of employments. She will unblushingly harangue popular assemblies. She will go without protection, by day or by night, into the most excited crowds.

[103] Ruskin: *op. cit.*, 33–4; see also Hardy: *The Five Talents of Woman*, 15–16 and 18–19.

[104] Compare, for example, with the views of Frances P. Cobbe, who deplored the fact that public spirit in women was not encouraged; that women were expected to pay taxes but possessed no corresponding rights.—*The Duties of Women*, 174–5.

[105] Arthur: *op. cit.*, 148–50.

How revolting and unnatural is such a spectacle of female character.''[106]

There are, then, many false notions in the air about woman's place in society and the requisite education that will help her to find it. Conservatives recommend what might be called a ''guarded education'' to keep her and her interests centered in home life. One writer seems to feel that this careful education is most necessary, for, as he sees it, ''the consequences [of a lack herein] are far more fatal to the community than the neglect of that of man; since his vices and crimes more frequently proceed from the passions with which woman inspires him, than from the defects of his education.''[107] Because of the grave tendency to take part in affairs outside, to favor education to that end, and the grave consequences to society, he therefore advised a ''domestic education'' relating to the ''Health of the Body; the Cultivation of the Mind; and the improvement of the Heart;'' for ''the best boarding school is, at least, good for nothing; or what amounts to the same thing . . . is not adapted either to the constitution or to the destination of woman.''[108]

Having examined the prosaic utterances of those ranged on both sides of the controversy, we may recall their essential arguments in the words of the poet. Tennyson, in *The Princess*, suggests the accepted views of people generally, the prophetic outlook of those who would found a college, and also the results that some foresaw. The beginning of the evil lay in theories:

''. . . There were widows here,
''Two widows, Lady Psyche, Lady Blanche;
''They fed her theories, in and out of place
''Maintaining that with equal husbandry
''The woman were an equal to the man.
''They harp'd on this; with this our banquets rang;
''Our dances broke and buzz'd in knots of talk;

106 *Op. cit.;* compare also with Lord Lyttleton's lines of *Advice to a Lady*:
''Seek to be good, but aim not to be great,
''A woman's noblest station is retreat;
''Her fairest virtues fly from public sight,
''Domestic worth, that shuns too strong a light.''
107 Chirol: *op. cit.;* the author apparently is somewhat inclined to agree with Pope: ''Men some to pleasure, some to business take; but every woman is at heart—a rake.''
108 *Op. cit.*

"Nothing but this; my very ears were hot
"To hear them: knowledge, so my daughter held,
"Was all in all: they had but been, she thought
"As children; they must lose the child, assume
"The woman: then, Sir, awful odes she wrote,
"Too awful, sure, for what they treated of,
"But all she is and does is awful; odes
"About this losing of the child; and rhymes
"And dismal lyrics, prophesying change
"Beyond all reason. . . ."

This assumption of the woman ran counter to the old belief which held:

"Man for the field and woman for the hearth:
"Man for the sword and for the needle she:
"Man with the head and woman with the heart:
"Man to command and woman to obey;
"All else confusion. . . ."

But these old beliefs are precisely the most objectionable to the new women, for they know that convention beats them down. To overcome their inferiority, which is but bringing up, Lelia would build—

"Far off from men a college like a man's,
"And . . . teach them all that men are taught."

Out of this opportunity for equal culture of the mind the new sphere of woman is to emerge. Henceforth she is to be an equal, helper and companion:

". . . Everywhere
"Two heads in council, two beside the hearth,
"Two in the tangled business of the world,
"Two in the liberal offices of life. . . ."

The crude ways, barbarous laws, and subjection to man are all of the past:

"Henceforth thou hast a helper, me, that know
"The woman's cause is man's: they rise or sink
"Together, dwarf'd or godlike, bond or free:"[109]

The actual practice in English education of women, while these two extremes were being urged, appears to have strongly favored an education of "accomplishments." As Smith said, no doubt with some exaggeration, "Everybody speaks French and for that reason no one is apt to boast of the attainment." De Wahl, in

[109] *The Princess* [*Works of Tennyson*, III (Macmillan, 1903)].

Hints on Training of Girls at School (1847), asked: "What is the common acceptation, with reference to girls, of this word education? Is it not this, that if a girl has been taught two or three foreign languages, if dates and facts of history have been forced upon her memory; if she have worked through the first few rules of arithmetic; if her fingers can execute mechanical difficulties in music, and if she can copy a drawing, she is said to be educated?" As would be expected, this training, so far as it contained advanced academic subjects, was justified on the basis of the prevailing formal discipline. The "accomplishments" were, no matter if superficial, real assets as a step towards marriage in approved circles, for without them one must be a *sitzengebliebene Ball-Mutter*. Darwin, as stated, deplored the slavish adherence to an education based solely on languages and literature and recommended sciences; but conservative practice was afraid of such an innovation, for "books of chemistry or electricity and all that might lead them prematurely to making philosophical experiment we would still keep from them."[110] This was undoubtedly true of English boarding schools, as it was also the general truth regarding many "female" academies and seminaries of the United States which began to offer girls their first opportunity for study.

The dreary drudgery of the routine is described by De Wahl: ". . . Dates—isolated facts; mere memory-work; mnemonical chronologies, in which the pupil has the double task of learning some meaningless symbol or verse by which the date is to be remembered, when the date itself, if the simple act of remembering it be an acquaintance with history, would surely be sufficient. *Poetical* chronologies! alas for poor Poetry. Such jumbles of sense and sound; such pitiable doggerel rhyming to accomplish, what? a mere mechanical memory of dates and facts. Can any one call this History; and does any one *retain* this mere word knowledge? Moreover, would it be worth having even if it could be retained? Let the girl leaving school, her education finished, speak for herself. She can tell you where every English reign commenced and ended; she has possibly attained to the same knowledge of the royal succession in France; she can repeat the names of the Roman emperors without misplacing them, and

[110] *Guardian of Education* (London, 1803), 2: 408—quoted by Kilpatrick: *Sourcebook in the Philosophy of Education.*

she will not make any serious mistake about the divisions among the Greeks, the rise of Macedonian power, and its fall before that of the Romans. But ask her about the general progress of civilization; refer to the *causes* which have produced the great changes among dynasties and powers; speak of History as a picture of man in his gradual advancement from the mere fighting, murdering animal of olden times, to the intelligence and intellectual cultivation of the present day; ask her whether she has thought of the difference in the glory pertaining to an Alexander and a Julius Caesar, or to such men as Penn, Jenner, Watts, and Cooke, with his magnificent application of the powers of Galvanism. She will probably look at you with astonishment, and tell you that her lessons contained nothing of the kind.'"[111]

One of the greatest faults in English, as in American, schools was a lack of regard to health or attention to physical education. De Wahl devoted twenty-eight pages of her text to this question, calling for reform by stressing play, physical examination, and hygienic conditions in schools, for both work and play. Stodart, also, bewailed the lack of attention to health. Girls have, in general, for too little exercise and are shut up for too many hours engaged in sedentary employments.[112] She quotes *The Castle of Indolence* and declares it describes the situation of women of England in her day (1844), as well as a century before. The reason is to be found in a wrong system of female education. The lines follow:

"Here languid beauty kept her pale-faced court,
  "Bevies of dainty dames of high degree
"From every quarter hither made resort,
  "Where from gross mortal care and business free,
"They lay, poured out in ease and luxury:
"Or should they a vain show of work assume,
  "Alas! and well-a-day! what can it be?
"To knot, to twist, to range the vernal bloom,
  "But far is cast the distaff, spinning wheel, and loom."

Stodart's approval of the last lines suggests a high regard for domestic skills of her grandmother. This is also to be seen in her approving comment on Madame Campan, who advised Napoleon that the way to benefit the coming generation most was to educate a race of mothers.[113]

[111] *Op. cit.*, 92-4.
[112] *Principles of Education*, 24 and 247-8.
[113] *Ibid.*, 267.

A much more cheerful view of the subject of girls' education was taken by Thomas Gisbourne, who held that in the cultivation of the female understanding essential improvements had been made. It is recalled, however, that his conception of woman's place in the world was narrow; hence the improvement he speaks of has rather to do with method and content of school work, and not with acceptance of a higher plane on which the whole question of her training must rest.

"In the cultivation of the female understanding essential improvements have taken place in the present age. Both in schools and in private families there prevails a desire to call forth the reasoning powers of girls into action, and to enrich the mind with useful and interesting knowledge suitable to their sex. The foundation is laid by communicating to the scholar a rational insight into the formation and idioms of her native tongue. The grammatical blunders, which used to disgrace the conversation even of women in the upper and middle ranks of life, and in conjunction with erroneous orthography to deform their epistolary correspondence, are already so much diminished, that in some years hence it may perhaps no longer be easy to find a young lady, who professes to be mistress of the French language, and is at the same time grossly ignorant of her own. Geography, select parts of natural history, and of the history of different nations, antient or modern, popular and amusing facts in astronomy and in other sciences, are often familiar to the daughter in a degree which, at the very moment that it delights the parent, reminds her how small a portion of such information was in her youth imparted to herself. Of the books, also, which have been published within the last twenty years for the purpose of conveying instruction to girls, though some of them approach too nearly to the style and sentiments of romances, a considerable number possesses great merit; and most of them are abundantly more adapted to interest the young reader, and thus to make a lively and permanent impression on her understanding, than those were to which they have succeeded. Some improvement, too, though certainly not so much as is desirable, appears to have taken place in the choice of French books used at schools and in domestic education. And learners of that language are perhaps called upon less frequently than was heretofore the case, to convert the exercises of religion into French lessons."[114]

[114] Gisbourne: *op. cit.*, 42–4.

A Mother, in *Thoughts on Domestic Education* (1829), suggested that every well-educated young woman ought to set up for herself the following standards to be reached through her studies. This may, without doubt, be accepted as a faithful epitome of the objectives generally aimed at in English girls' schools, and also striven for, partially at least, even by those who could not attend schools. The end of studies is:

"To read well, and write a good hand; to have a thorough knowledge of all needleworks, of arithmetic, of geography, of the French language; to possess considerable acquaintance with general history, a closer intimacy with that of her own, and to be familiar with the best poetry, travels, essays, &c.; to acquire an improved skill in any one branch of painting or drawing; as excellence in 'painting flowers,' or 'drawing landscapes,' or 'sketching heads'; to attain a moderate execution of music, with correct time and pure taste, so as to please others and amuse herself; also some insight into the Italian language, botany, natural history, and all the branches of natural and experimental philosophy, as astronomy, &c.; [and] perhaps a peep into mathematics and the Latin language."[115]

In discussing the views of Ascham on girls' education, it was noted that he did not "set" them "to public grammar schools" nor did he send them to the universities.[116] The usage in his day favored education at home with a tutor. Public schools for girls are of recent development, whether in England, Germany, France, or the United States. The sixteenth century and the seventeenth, unless we include monastic institutions on account of their educational services, knew almost nothing of them, the eighteenth but little more, while upon the nineteenth fell the burden of their development and full acceptance as quite as essential to social welfare as those for boys. But their growth in

[115] *Op. cit.*, 24–5; criticism of the prevailing worship of 'accomplishments' for women may be found in Bennett: *Letters to a Young Lady*, 3–5, and *Strictures on Female Education*, 1–2, 23–4, 25, and 27–8. The spirit of the criticism is very similar to that of Hannah More: "Music, Drawing, accomplishments, dissipation and intrigue—everything but solid knowledge—everything but humility—everything but piety—everything but virtue!"

[116] Bremner points out that he may have meant only his part of the country, though this is by no means certain; and that girls were not excluded expressly from the endowments of many schools, but that "boys simply took possession of what was meant for both sexes."—*Education of Girls and Women in Great Britain*, 70 *ff*.

point of numbers, as well as the expansion of the course of study, has been phenomenal in the latter half of the nineteenth and first quarter of the twentieth centuries.

Myra Reynolds, in her *Learned Lady in England,* calls attention to the beginning of domestic science in the "Pastry Schools" at the time of Queen Anne. Her statements rest upon the quotation from Ashton's *Social Life in the Reign of Queen Anne* wherein he says, "All young ladies at Edw. Kidder's Pastry School in little Lincoln's Inn Fields are taught all sorts of Pastry and Cookery, Dutch hollow works and butter works. . . ."[117] He appears to have had four schools, at any rate, at this time. But probably the first encouragement ever written for such schools was by Sir William Petty, who in 1647 was author of *The Advice of W. P. to Mr. Samuel Hartlib for the Advancement of Some Particular Parts of Learning.* Herein he said that "for the Females, they will be making Pyes with Clay, making their Babies Clothes, and dressing them therewith, they will spit leaves on Sticks, as they were roasting meate, they will imitate all the talke and Actions which they observe in their Mother and her Gossips. . . . By all which it is most evident that Children do most naturally delight in things and are most capable of learning them."[118]

At the middle of the eighteenth century, boarding schools for ladies, the fount of polite accomplishments, appear to have increased in number, at any rate in and near the large cities. James Malcom[119] says that near London "two or three houses might be seen in almost every village, with the inscription, 'Young Ladies boarded and educated,' to which all kinds of tradesmen sent their children to be taught." Here young ladies, received by governesses, were turned over to French and dancing masters who prepared them soon to be contemptuous of their parents' deficiencies; here they were allowed to continue the vulgarisms of their native tongue while they acquired a foreign tongue—Boarding School French—a tongue little understood in France! The *Idler* of 1750, if we may rely upon its evidence (doubtless exaggerated), would lead to the conclusion that this was a Golden Age of female learning: "Scarcely a

[117] Ashton: *op. cit.,* 19.

[118] Quoted from Stephens:*Workfellows in Social Progression,* 113.

[119] *Anecdotes of the Manners and Customs of London in the 18th Century,* I, 328.

wench was to be got for all work, since education had made such numbers of fine ladies that nobody would now accept a lower title than that of waiting maid, or something that might qualify her to wear laced shoes and long ruffles and to sit at work in the parlor window."[120]

But if there is some truth in the foregoing statement, it is more true that the difficulty of getting laboring girls was due rather to economic factors than the great access of education. Even a century later (1864), when a Royal Commission was named to investigate the condition of boys' secondary schools, and the memorial to include an examination of girls' institutions was also granted, a most deplorable condition was revealed. Notwithstanding the fact that probably the best schools were visited in the selected districts, it was found that they were generally in the hands of persons who had not even an elementary idea of the task they had undertaken. The report of the Commission, published in 1867, disclosed that "want of thoroughness and foundation; want of system; slovenliness and showy superficiality; inattention to rudiments, undue time given to accomplishments and those not taught intelligently or in any scientific manner;" and "want of organization" characterized the ladies' schools.[121]

One of the first results of the investigation was the formation, in 1871, of the "National Union for improving the education of women of all classes" by women of prominence such as Lady Stanley of Alderley, Miss Gurney, and Mrs. Grey. Its purposes were, especially:

"1. To promote the establishment of good and cheap day schools for all classes above those attending the elementary schools, with boarding houses in connection with them, when necessary, for pupils from a distance.

"2. To raise the social status of female teachers by encouraging women to make teaching a profession, and to qualify themselves for it by a sound and liberal education, and by thorough training in the art of teaching, and to secure a test of the efficiency of the teachers by examinations of recognized authority,

[120] Quoted from Reynolds: op. cit., 267–8.
[121] Quoted by Roberts: Education in the 19th Century, Ch. V; also Bremner: Education of Girls and Women in Great Britain (1897), 74–7. See, too, The Woman's Library (ed. by McKenna), I, 5–6.

and subsequent registration.''[122]   It began at once the formation
of the Girls' Public Day School Company (1872), patronized by
Princess Louise, Lady Stanley, Mrs. Grey, and others, the purpose of which was to secure funds to establish schools that were
equipped to give to girls the very best possible education, or, at
any rate, to measure up to that given boys in the Great Public
Schools. The first school of the Company was opened at Chelsea,
in 1873. In 1900, it had 33 schools and over 7,000 pupils. The
changes of larger significance in English life that had come
about in the generation before 1900, and in which women had
come to play a large part, were described enthusiastically by
Miss Gadesden:

''When the first High Schools were opened the women trained
to work and capable of working on special lines were few and far
between.

''The want was recognized and deplored by all who needed
their assistance. Miss Beale, Miss Buss, Mrs. Grey put in the
front of their programme the training and teaching of women
and the testing of their powers and capacity. Thirty years ago
the notion that a well-born woman should belong voluntarily to
a profession was repugnant to parents and relations. That a
woman should teach, or be obliged to earn her living, meant that
she became an object of commiseration to all who knew of her
misfortune.

''Well might the 'National Union' speak of 'raising the social
status of female teachers.' Women there were then who by force
of character and nobility of aim rose above all prejudices and
carried on bravely and successfully the work which they were
inspired to do. Even for them the difficulties were great; for
the mass idleness was the only genteel occupation. The new
schools have changed all that. The need for teachers created
and encouraged the supply, and the modern spirit is all in favour
of women undertaking not only teaching but any occupation, and
adopting any profession for which by nature, capacity and training they are best fitted. Honour to work and to workers is the
rule, and it is beginning to be fully realized that through her
work, and because of her work, the modern woman claims and
holds a position among those who are honoured in the land.

''The High Schools and Colleges are sending out their pupils

[122] Quoted from Roberts: *op. cit.*

to be trained as Doctors and Nurses, Factory Inspectors, Poor Law Guardians, Sanitary Officers, Teachers, Lecturers, Examiners. In business and in professions and in the performance of their home duties, where these call them, they are justifying the confidence of those who have so nobly and strenuously advocated the right of every woman to receive the education best suited to her power and capacities, and who have borne the heat and burden of the day in putting this within her grasp.

"Not the least of the peaceful revolutions of the 19th Century is that which has made English Schools places of real education and training, which has raised the ideal of woman's vocation, and which has brought home to thousands the conception of what is due from them to their homes and to their country and placed it within their power to realize their ideal."[123]

Not only has the secondary education of girls made rapid progress in England since 1860, but that of collegiate grade also. The reform movement of the first half of the century stirred a desire for higher learning in many circles that had been closed to thoughts of woman's capacity for such activities. It began to appear as though—

"Lilia . . . would build
"Far off from men a college like a man's
"And . . . teach them all that men are taught."

About 1852 Miss Murray, one of the Maids of Honor to the Queen, began to raise money for the purpose, in which work she was assisted by professors of Kings College. A house was secured where courses were to be offered "in all branches of female learning," and this became the basis of Queens College, chartered in 1853. At first lectures were introduced apologetically by professors who seemed ill at ease in their new rôle as promoters of female college education. Professor Maurice is credited with having made an interesting, if awkward, observation on the ability of women to learn mathematics:

"We are aware that our pupils are not likely to advance far in mathematics, but we believe that if they learn really what they do learn they will not have got what is dangerous but what is safe. I cannot conceive that a young lady can feel her mind in a more dangerous state than it was, because she has gained a

[123] *Ibid.*, 103–4. Consult also Burstall and Douglas: *Public Schools for Girls*, which gives rather full treatment of the subject in England.

truer glimpse into the conditions under which the world in which it has pleased God to place her, actually exists."[124]

Adams[125] wrote in 1880 that woman's education had in the past few years attained the position of a public question. The Cambridge examinations for girls had been established in 1864; five years later Girton was opened; and Newnham was begun in 1871 but had no regular hall till 1875. Nevertheless, while great progress had been made, she pointed out that old views were slow to give way and that woman was not yet free to be educated for herself: "Yet it would be folly to suppose that the battle is won, that the old prejudices have been absolutely conquered, the old traditions finally extirpated; that society, as a whole, has been taught to recognize the claims of woman in their entirety, or is prepared to allow her that full intellectual and moral freedom which it allows to man. No very great progress has been achieved towards equality of treatment; for example, our daughters are still, to a great extent, denied participation in the funds and other benefits that the endowed schools of the country offer to our sons; and equality of treatment cannot be hoped for until men are brought to understand their own vital concern in the freest possible development of the education of women.

"We are met at the outset by the consideration, for what object is woman to be educated? Is she to be trained exclusively to play her part as wife and mother, or to do her duty in whatever station in life events may place her? That is, is her education, so far as man can influence it, to be controlled by a selfish or a generous aim? Is the cultivation of her faculties to be limited to a particular sphere, or so broadened as to enable her in after-life to choose a field for herself? . . ."[126]

Much of her statement was still true at the close of the century. While there were nearly three hundred women students in Girton and Newnham, and though there were many more who were reading for degree examinations throughout the country, they were, nevertheless, still on unequal footing. In 1897, there was a grave controversy over degrees for women at Cambridge, and, even as late as 1920, women were still seeking admission to

124 Roberts: *op. cit.*, 86–7.
125 *Woman's Work and Worth*, 368–9.
126 *Ibid.*

"full membership" in that University.[127]   But it has now been long admitted that university education is desirable—for at least a great number.   That education will unfit woman to be wife or mother, that the physical strain will be too great, or that she is intellectually incapable of mastering higher branches of knowledge, were serious arguments a generation or two ago, and unquestionably acted as deterrents, but are now only slumbering memories in the social mind of a busy world and come to the surface only in some sequestered nooks, still undisturbed by events of fourscore years.

[127] Consult *London Times Educational Supplement*, Oct. 15, 1920.

CHAPTER II

CONCEPTION OF WOMEN'S POSITION AND EDUCA-
TION IN OTHER LANDS (*Continued*)

I. In France

Influences from France and Germany, as well as from England, came to bear upon the education of women in the United States, some causing a negative, others a positive acceleration. Particularly the writings of their leading exponents of woman's training were widely quoted. Fénelon, Rousseau, Necker, Aimé-Martin, and Jean Paul Richter, as well as numerous writers of less significance, are often spoken of, approvingly or disapprovingly, during the formation of American ideas on the subject, in the nineteenth century. It is therefore of consequence to note the views held by representative men, and the practical realizations by way of institutions for woman's education.

For our present purpose we need not retrace the earlier centuries of French history, for, so far as the education of women is concerned, France, England and Germany have much the same general tradition of at least some "learned ladies" during the mediaeval period; ideals of the seventeenth century spring from similar traditional soil. Indeed, the Palace School of Charlemagne, with its studious queen, has reflected glory upon both France and Germany, according to desire. And well it might. Lange's statement[1] that the "difficult art of reading and writing," as also a "knowledge of the Psalter," were the possession of all women is unquestionably as true of the territory of France as of Germany. The great Charles commanded the clergy, in numerous edicts, to teach their parishioners—men, women and children—at least the Creed and the Lord's Prayer. If the learners proved recalcitrant they were to be flogged and forced to fast; and if still rebellious, to be brought before the king himself.[2] Wherever education of women appears at all, before the secularization of French schools in the latter part of the nineteenth cen-

[1] *Entwickelung und Stand des höheren Mädchen-schulwesens in Deutschland*, 1.

[2] Paulsen: *German Education*, 13–14.

tury, it is permeated by religious influence. Not only is its
character uniformly religious, but the quantity is uniformly limited. Madame Campan declared, in the nineteenth century, that
only within the past fifty years had attention been paid to the
education of women.[3]

Among the notable institutions for girls' education, which began to break the tradition of monastic ecclesiastical influence and
substitute for it that of the state, were St. Cyr, founded by Louis
XIV (1686), and given into the care of Madame de Maintenon,
for the education of daughters of noblemen; Écouen, by Napoleon
in 1807, for daughters and sisters of the Legion of Honor; and
St. Denis (1809), for daughters of officers of higher rank. In
these schools, national purpose eclipsed religious or ecclesiastical
ends. The purpose "is to educate mothers," said Campan to
Napoleon, when asked what was "wanting in order to train up
young people properly in France." "Right," Napoleon replied,
"for therein lies a complete system of education and it must be
your endeavor, Madame, to form mothers who know how to educate their children." Religion, instead of being the end, became
the means of education, thus serving the state. Napoleon
wanted "women who believe, and not women who reason. . . .
Religion is an important matter in a public institution of girls.
It is, whatever one may say about it, the surest guarantee for the
mothers and for the husbands. . . . The weakness of women's
minds, the fickleness of their ideas, their destination in the social
order, the necessity for a constant and perpetual resignation and
for a sort of indulgent and ready charitableness, all this can be
obtained only through religion, through a charitable and gentle
religion."[4] These schools were naturally quite apart from the
ordinary primary schools, and since they catered only to a small
group, Duruy, in 1867, might well hold that nothing had been
done by the State for secondary education of girls.[5]

Convents played a leading rôle in the education of girls,[6] notwithstanding the anti-clerical tendency of the Revolution. Num-

[3] Campan: *De l'education*, I, 225.

[4] *Correspondance de Napoleon*, I, No. 12, 585, quoted by Kilpatrick:
Sourcebook in the Philosophy of Education, 10.

[5] *Instructions aux recteurs*, quoted by Farrington: *French Sec. Schs.*,
314.

[6] Reich: *Woman Through the Ages*, II, 112, makes some interesting comments on convent education of girls in France.

erous private schools, as well, had of course sprung into existence, especially in or near large cities. These were often merely "venture" schools, similar to the "boarding" institutions that sprang up in England and America also, and about the same period. Jules Simon, in 1867, declared them "futile and incomplete"—a judgment similar to those passed at various times on the same type of schools in England and the United States. An increased interest in the education of girls was apparent in the creation of a commission of three women (1844) to investigate these private schools, both lay and ecclesiastical. The effect of this commission's work was salutary, and for a time it was generally understood that a system of girls' *collèges*, similar to those for boys, would be established by the government. Definite reaction set in, however, in 1850, with the passage of the Falloux law; and it appeared to be long before the prophetic claim of Olympia de Gonges, of Revolutionary days, could come true: "Woman has the right to mount the scaffold; she must also have a similar right to mount the platform of the orator."

However, improvement of facilities was not far distant. Following a suggestion of Duruy, the Association for Girls' Secondary Education was created and secondary courses for girls came into being, 69 of them by 1887. On this as a basis, the lycée or the collège could, and some did, build. In 1880 the law providing secondary schools for girls, after vigorous opposition by ecclesiastics, was finally passed. The first lycée under the new law was opened at Montpelier in 1881; others followed soon after, and by 1907 there were 47 lycées, 61 collèges, and 63 secondary courses, in all of which combined there were 33,843 pupils.[7] The creation of secondary schools for girls was followed by the establishment of a higher normal school at Sèvres (1882) where teachers (a few at any rate) might be prepared to occupy the positions created by the new secondary system. It was planned at the same time (1880) to create a women's university, but this failed of support. Since then, however, women have been admitted generally to French universities. In the earlier period, keeping in mind Renan's criticism of the French universities (1864) that they were shamefully inferior to the German, and in all of them there was not "any movement productive of research," one may well believe that women did not lose much by

[7] Farrington: *French Secondary Schools*, 318.

their absence. In respect to the admission of women, French universities were far ahead of the German. In 1896, however, fifteen universities were recognized by law, and since that time have increased in importance. None of these institutions are closed to women.

An American woman was first to apply for entrance to a French university in 1868, and this was followed by those of other nations soon after. The Collège of Sèvigné was established for women in 1880, at Paris, by the Society for the Propagation of Instruction Among Women. Foreign women have, generally, patronized the French universities more than the French women. A Roumanian, Mlle. Belsesco, and a Frenchwoman, Mlle. Chauvin, were the first to receive the Doctor's degree. The Bachelor's and Master's degrees had, of course, been attainable for some time. The present century has seen a great increase in the number of women at French schools. In 1910 there were 3,830 women, 2,033 native and 1,797 foreign, in French universities. By 1925, the number of women in French universities had risen to 7,706; there were 37,834 men.[8]

The facts in the practical development of facilities for the education of women in France are important as a background and as a measure with which we can compare American movement in the same direction; but these facts were not influential in forming our opinions or our practice. Indeed they are seldom mentioned in the literature dealing with the rise of women's education here. On the other hand, our views followed very closely those expressed by numerous French authors. Fénelon and Rousseau have, no doubt, been most often quoted and most influential.

Nettement[9] declared that Fénelon and Madame de Maintenon gave voice, in the seventeenth century, to the idea that Christianity should be the foundation of all education for women. This, of course, was no innovation but merely the pursuit of the Christian tradition—that of the Apostles, the church fathers and Christ himself. The truth of this statement is apparent; but, whether it was an innovation or not, Fénelon's forceful message called attention to the fact that in the seventeenth century too little was thought about any education for women. He says:

[8] *Educational Yearbook*, 1925, 166.
[9] *De la séconde Éducation des Filles*, 386–7.

"Nothing is more neglected than the education of girls. Custom and maternal caprice often decide the matter entirely, and it is taken for granted that little instruction should be given to their sex. The education of boys is regarded as a most important affair with reference to the public welfare; and although almost as many mistakes are made in it as in the education of girls, at least the world is convinced that, there, much wisdom is unnecessary to success. On that subject, the most competent persons have undertaken to lay down rules. How many teachers and colleges for boys do we see! What vast expenditures in their behalf for editions of books, for scientific researches, for methods of teaching the languages, and for the choice of professors! All these great preparations are often more pretentious than effective, but at least they mark the lofty conception that the world has of the education of boys. As for girls, it is said, they should not be learned; inquisitiveness makes them vain and affected: it is enough for them to know how some day to manage their households and to obey their husbands without argument. Men do not fail to make use of the fact that they have known many women whom learning has made ridiculous, after which they think themselves justified in blindly abandoning their daughters to the guidance of ignorant and indiscreet mothers."

His conservatism is readily seen in his acceptance of the current view that women could not do many of the tasks usually undertaken by men; and he would not have them attempt such a thing. Women must not be made "ridiculous blue stockings"; they must not engage "in studies that may turn their heads; they are not destined to govern the state, to make war, or to minister in holy things; so they may pass by certain extended fields of knowledge that belong to politics, the art of war, jurisprudence, philosophy and theology. Most of the mechanic arts, even, are not suited to women, who are fashioned for moderate exertions only. Their bodies as well as their minds are less strong and robust than those of men. As a compensation, nature has given them for their portion neatness, industry, and thrift, in order to keep them quietly occupied in their homes."

"Women are weaker than men, but what follows from this natural weakness of women? The weaker they are, the more important it is to strengthen them. Have they not duties to fulfil, and duties, too, that lie at the foundation of all human life? Is it not the women, who ruin or uphold families, who regulate every detail of domestic life, and who consequently decide what touches the whole human race most nearly? In this way they exert a controlling influence on the good or bad morals of nearly all the world. A discreet, diligent, pious woman is the soul of an entire large household; she provides in it alike for temporal and spiritual welfare. Even men, who have exclusive authority in public, cannot, by their decisions, establish a real prosperity unless women aid them in its achievement.''[10]

The specific recommendations are of such interest, and his practical recommendations impressed American readers so favorably (note the similarity of the views of Benjamin Rush), that we quote them at length. They are self-explanatory.

''Teach a girl to read and to write correctly. It is shameful, but very common, to see women, who have intellect and politeness, know not how to pronounce well what they read. They either hesitate, or they sing out in reading; instead of which, they ought to pronounce in a simple and natural tone, but firm and united. They fail still more grossly in the orthography, or in the manner of forming or connecting their letters in writing. . . . It is also necessary that a girl should understand the grammar of her own language. It is not necessary that she should learn it by rules, as scholars learn Latin in classes. Accustom them only, without affectation, not to take one tense for another; to make use of proper terms to explain their thoughts with order and clearness, and in a short and concise manner. You will by this means enable them, one day or other, to teach their children to speak well without any study. . . .

''They ought also to know the first four rules of arithmetic. They would become useful to yourself, by often making them keep your accounts. It is an occupation very distasteful for many people; but habit acquired in infancy, joined to the facility of doing quickly by the help of rules, all sorts of accounts the most embroiled, diminishes greatly this distaste. We well know, that exactness in accounts often makes the good order of a house.

''It would be well also that they should know something of the principal rules of justice. For example, the difference that there is between a legacy and a donation; what is a contract; a substitution; a division of co-heirs; the principal rules of the

---

[10] Fénelon: *Education of Girls*, 11–13.

rights and of the customs of the country in which we live, to render these acts valid; that which is meant by common property; what is meant by goods movable, and immovable. If they marry, all their principal affairs will turn on this.'' Nevertheless, he points out "how incapable they are of going far into the difficulties of rights. . . .

"All this seems to me important, as it may be a means of preventing women from feeling too much impassioned on these affairs, and from giving themselves up blindly to certain advisers, enemies of peace, when they are widows, or mistresses of their fortune, in any other state. They ought to listen to their people of business, but not to be wholly guided by them.

"It is right that they should mistrust themselves in the processes which they are persuaded to undertake. Let them consult persons of a more enlarged knowledge, and more attentive to the advantages of an accommodation; and finally, let them be persuaded that the principal cleverness in law suits, is to foresee the inconveniences of them, and to know how to avoid them.''

Girls of breeding ought to be instructed so as to look after their property interests and be encouraged to think of establishing charity schools for the poor; and also of setting up "traffic in certain foreign countries'' which may relieve their misery. From this point, Fénelon proceeds to describe girls' literary education:

"After this instruction, which ought to hold the first place, I believe that it is not useless to suffer their capacity, to read profane history; it is even a means of giving them a disgust to comedies and romances. Give them, then, the Grecian and Roman histories; they will there see prodigies of courage and disinterestedness: do not let them be ignorant of the history of France, which has its beauties; mix those of the neighboring countries, and the relations of distant countries which are judiciously written. All this serves grand sentiments, provided we avoid vanity and affectation.

"It is generally thought, that a girl of quality, who is well brought up, should learn Italian and Spanish, but I see nothing less useful than this study, unless she be attached to the person of some Spanish or Italian princess, like our queens of Austria and Medicis; otherwise, these two languages serve for little but to enable them to read dangerous works, calculated to augment their defects. There is much more to be lost than to be gained by this study. That of the Latin would be much more rational, for it is the language of the church; a fruit would arise from it, and an inestimable consolation from understanding the sense of the words of the divine office at which they so often assist. Those even who seek for beauty in language, would find it much more perfect and more solid in Latin, than in the Italian or Spanish, where there remains a *jeu desprit,* and a vivacity of imagination without rule. But I would only have those girls learn Latin, who have a firm judgment and a modest conduct; who would know how to study it for what it is worth; who could renounce vain curiosity, and who would hide what they would have learned, and who would seek it only for their edification."

Poetry and eloquence are to be permitted if the young lady's judgment is "sufficiently solid" to withstand the "embroiling of the imagination" that may result from such study. Music and painting must be taught in the same cautious way, for they are of the "same genius and taste." Besides, he recalls that the ancient philosopher believed it necessary to banish "effeminate melody" from his ideal republic; and that Spartan magistrates broke up musical instruments "whose harmony was too delicious." This censorship is not to go so far as to exclude music that tends to a right end, such as the poetical works which the Hebrews have sung. Indeed, he believes that "sacred music and poetry would be the best of all means to give a disgust to profane pleasures. . . ." Therefore, he concludes, somewhat after the manner of Aristotle, that "it is better to give a regulated course to the torrent than to try to stop it."

Painting, Fénelon believed, could be more "easily turned to good" in the education of girls, and without it their works are apt "not to be well conducted." Particularly, it is asserted that "almost all that we now see in stuffs, laces, and in embroidery, are in bad taste . . . confusion, without design, without proportion." This state of affairs would be improved and women would "undeceive themselves if they were to consult the painters." They would learn to give more thought to harmony and "noble variety" and less to the "irregular caprice of fashion."

Finally, education must be adapted to probable conditions of life:

"We ought to consider in the education of a girl, her condition, the situation where she will probably pass her life, and the profession which she may be likely to embrace. Let us be careful that she conceive no hopes above her condition. There are not a few persons whom it has cost dear to have raised their hopes too high; that which would otherwise have rendered them happy, becomes disgusting from the moment that they have conceived the hope of a state above them. If a girl be destined to live in the country, turn her mind early to the occupations which will engage her there, and suffer her not to taste the diversions of the town; show her the advantages of a simple and active life: if she be of a moderate condition in the town, do not let her mix with those of the court; this commerce would only serve to make her acquire an air unsuited and ridiculous. Shut her up within the bounds of her condition, and give her for a model those who the best succeed in it; form her mind by those things which will occupy her during her life; teach her the economy of a commoner's house, the care which it is necessary to take of the receipts of rents both for the town and country, that which regards the education of children, and, in short, the detail of other occupations in affairs of commerce, in which you foresee that she may have to enter, when she will be married."[11]

In the education of women, says Fénelon, we must consider besides the good that they do if properly brought up, the evil they may cause in the world when they lack a training that inspires virtue. For a bad education produces more harm in women than in men, and the excesses of the latter proceed from the bad influence of their mothers and "passions awakened at a later age by other women."[12] Moreover, their education is of first import on another ground; namely, that "notwithstanding the authority of men in public affairs, it is evident that they cannot effect any lasting good, without the intervention and support of women."

In the next century, Rousseau put many of the same ideas into circulation. In his statements can be recognized the play of a brilliant yet erratic mind, dressing up ideas long accepted and marshalling them in mimic battle up and down the page—mimic battles, for there were few opponents to contend against his dog-

[11] *Ibid.*, 95–104.
[12] This argument was also made by Chirol, see p. 46.

matic views. Some of his statements may indicate either a lack of observation of the subjects discussed or else failure to distinguish between effect and cause. But if inaccurate, paradoxical, and irrational, the popular statement Rousseau gave to the world on women's education was destined to become widely influential. It was generally read, and quoted; many copied his views in their writing, apparently, who did not maintain any acquaintance with his *Émile*.

Rousseau began by insisting on the fundamental differences commonly accepted between men and women, and argued for a different education. Men and women ought to act in concert, but not do the same things; their duties have a common end but are themselves different. Since he accepts these differences as fundamental, and the duties as different, he begins at once to describe the relation that must exist between the two and to what end the education of girls must be shaped:

"On the good constitution of mothers depends, in the first place, that of children; on the care of women depends the early education of men; and on women, again, depend their manners, their passions, their tastes, their pleasures, and even their happiness. Thus the whole education of women ought to be relative to men. To please them, to be useful to them, to make themselves loved and honored by them, to educate them when young, to care for them when grown, to counsel them, to console them, and to make life agreeable and sweet to them—these are the duties of women at all times, and what should be taught them from their infancy."[13]

Women are then the servants of men and, as he says elsewhere, "dependence being a state natural to women, girls feel that they are made to obey."[14] Obedience is the controlling principle which operates in religious as well as domestic life. He contends that: "Every daughter should have the religion of her mother, and every wife that of her husband. Even were this religion false, the docility which makes the mother and the daughter submit to the order of nature expunges in the sight of God the sin of error. As they are not in a condition to judge for themselves, women should receive the decision of fathers and husbands as they would the decision of the Church."[15]

[13] Payne's translation, 263.
[14] *Ibid.*, 269.
[15] *Ibid.*, 275–6.

In her domestic subjection she may be yoked with an authority as unjust, false, or vicious as the religious doctrine she is forced to accept merely because it is authoritative, but she must "preserve the tone" of her sex, whose virtue is docility. More at length it is argued that:

"There results from this habitual restraint a docility which women need during their whole life, since they never cease to be subject either to a man or to the judgments of men, and they are never allowed to place themselves above these judgments. The first and most important quality of a woman is gentleness. Made to obey a being as imperfect as man, often so full of vices, and always so full of faults, she ought early to learn to suffer even injustice, and to endure the wrongs of a husband without complaint; and it is not for him, but for herself that she ought to be gentle. The harshness and obstinacy of women serve only to increase the wrongs and the bad conduct of husbands; they feel that it is not with these arms that their wives should conquer them. Heaven has not made them insinuating and persuasive in order to become waspish; has not made them weak in order to be imperious; has not given them so gentle a voice in order to use harsh language; and has not made their features so delicate in order to disfigure them by anger. When they become angry they forget themselves; they often have reason to complain, but they are always wrong in scolding. Each one ought to preserve the tone of his sex. The husband who is too mild may make a woman impertinent; but, unless a man is a brute, the gentleness of a wife reforms him, and triumphs over him sooner or later."[16]

The chief goodness allotted to women is that of heart; even though her temper may "degenerate into unruliness" and she may "forget herself," her docile submissive nature triumphs at last and her eagerness to make amends almost transforms her fault into a virtue. Rousseau finds that "the reason which leads man to a knowledge of his duties is not very complex" and that which leads woman to a knowledge of hers is still more simple.[17] This he accepts as true, and hence it becomes a natural basis for opposition to woman's higher education; for he lays down the principle that as their duties are different so must be their education, the other justification being that woman's capacity is not

16 *Ibid.*, 270.
17 *Ibid.*, 279–80.

equal to higher learning. He closes the passage, in which he declares that "works of genius are out of her reach," by condemning her to read the book of the world (for "woman observes while man reasons"), and then adds that she must be more like a nun in the cloister than a woman of the world:

"The search for abstract and speculative truths, principles, and scientific axioms, whatever tends to generalize ideas, does not fall within the compass of women; all their studies ought to have reference to the practical; it is for them to make the application of the principles which man has discovered, and to make the observations which lead man to the establishment of principles. All the reflections of women which are not immediately connected with their duties ought to be directed to the study of men and to that pleasure-giving knowledge which has only taste for its object; for as to works of genius, they are out of their reach, nor have they sufficient accuracy and attention to succeed in the exact sciences, and as to the physical sciences, they fall to that one of the two which is the most active, the most stirring, which sees the most objects, which has the most strength, and which exercises it most in judging of the relations of sensible beings and of the laws of nature. Woman, who is weak, and who sees nothing external, appreciates and judges the motive powers which she can set to work to offset her weakness, and these motive powers are the passions of men. Whatever her sex cannot do for itself, and which is necessary or agreeable to her, she must have the art of making us desire. She must therefore make a profound study of the mind of man, not the mind of man in general, through abstraction, but the mind of the men who surround her, the mind of the men to whom she is subject, either by law or by opinion. She must learn to penetrate their feelings through their conversation, their actions, their looks, and their gestures. Through her conversations, her actions, her looks, and her gestures she must know how to give them the feelings which are pleasing to her, without even seeming to think of them. They will philosophize better than she can on the human heart, but she will read better than they can in the hearts of men. It is for woman to discover, so to speak, an experimental ethics, and for us to reduce it to a system. Woman has more spirit and man more genius; woman observes and man reasons. From this concurrence there result the clearest light and the most complete science which the human mind can acquire of itself—the surest knowledge, in a word, of one's self and others which is within the scope of our species. And this is the way in which art may incessantly tend to perfect the instrument given by nature.

"The world is woman's book; when she reads it wrong, it is her fault or some passion blinds her. However, the real mother, far from being a woman of the world, is hardly less a recluse in her house than a nun in her cloister."[18]

By a rough classification the arguments about woman's position and education may all be grouped under three heads: first, the most conservative, which utterly restrict her, making her at best a tolerably intelligent, obedient, slave; second, those that give her a measure of freedom by taking a half-step forward towards her higher education, arguing that by this pure intelligent mother-influence the life of society may be improved at the fountain head; and third, the most radical, that propose equality of opportunity in education, in political, social and economic life, maintaining that woman need not, unless she desires, pay her obligation to society, biologically, any more than men, but should be equally free to choose a literary, scientific, or industrial career. It is difficult to classify men and women; but arguments lend themselves more readily to such treatment. Arguments of one or another of the three groups are found to be predominating in their general acceptance at one period or another. The middle of the eighteenth century witnessed the gradual rise into ascendancy of the views of the second class; and insofar as Rousseau expressed the slavish conception of woman, he must be regarded as the most influential exponent of it, though his views have had many imitators and followers.[19]

In France, the beginning of the new conception is visible, however, in the work of Madame Necker de Saussure, *Progressive*

18 *Ibid.*, 281–2.

19 Nettement, in *De la séconde Éducation des Filles*, 388–9, gives an interesting summary of the service of Rousseau in particular, and eighteenth century philosophy in general. Rationalism, which would free humanity from the yoke of the church, subjected it to another intolerable yoke. Rousseau would have women grow old in a perpetual infancy, always believing what their husbands told them to believe. Under Napoleon a reaction took place. Madame Campan, advising Napoleon as to the proper education of girls, returned to the seventeenth century principle of Fénelon, that religion ought to be the foundation of all education of girls.

Education, 1828–1838, in which her chief interest is the life, nature, and education of women. Her views resemble those of Hannah More in some respects, particularly in that she desires a substantial education of the intellect, not the trappings and accomplishments usually thought so essential in both England and France. Following Rousseau, as she did, her work offers an interesting contrast to his, and her ideas find warm acceptance on the part of those who were at once disgusted by Rousseau's low estimate of women and, at the same time, not ready to go to the length of advocating their complete emancipation. She does, however, advocate the opening of some professions, such as teaching. These beginnings of vocational opportunity logically prepared the way for the greater extension of activities of productive nature; and with her greater rôle in everyday life partially accepted and becoming daily more so, political freedom came as a logical step.

Madame Necker's break with the views of Rousseau as to the inequalities in the nature of man and woman is much more gradual than with his views of woman's possible capacities and the range of her future activities. She admits that "their nature [men's] is superior to ours,"[20] but maintains that "the inequality is not so great as now appears." Yet "they have, we think, an internal power, an intensity of will, stronger than ours. Theirs is that instinct of dominion, theirs that firm and haughty nature, which raised the Romans over nations more civilized and polished than themselves. Ours are the gifts of the conquered nations which in their very inferiority, have a character of dignity and beauty."[21] She understands, it appears, that man's supremacy is largely due to his arrogant will and "instinct of dominion," for elsewhere she says, "They are neither more religious, less selfish, nor more virtuous, nor, perhaps, more intelligent than us. . . ." She would not have been surprised at Dr. Angell's declaration recently "that for brilliancy his women students had been found to be equal to, and even better than the men."[22] Having these capacities woman's lack of distinctive accomplishments in fields of literature or science has then been due to the fact that "these faculties have been always

[20] *Progressive Education*, 48–9.
[21] *Ibid.*
[22] As quoted by the *Phila. Inquirer*, October 19, 1925.

kept in the rear, or surpassed by those of men, and have followed at a humble distance the line of development pursued by the stronger sex."[23] Her weaker nature has been absorbed in the stronger nature of man. In this fact she finds "the real design of our Maker"; in this position woman has the opportunity for an immortal influence, for it extends to future generations. "If woman responds to the call of God, the improvement of the human race will be her aim."

Similar views as to woman's function as formative agent in her household are stressed by Aimé-Martin in the *Education of Mothers*.[24] He is not, however, in agreement with Madame Necker as to the broader, more substantial education which is to prepare her for this service. According to Necker, woman's life is not to be limited to the household, as she explicitly declares later: "We say private life, as distinguished from political life for we do not mean . . . that the action of women should be restricted to the interior of their homes."[25] But if she is not to lead a life entirely private, her purpose is, nevertheless, chiefly to improve it, "to animate, embellish, sanctify it"; and this, she avers, is a noble career. She stabilizes the family, which, she thinks, is a most important service; for, "Whatever in political organization is not founded on the true interests of families, soon disappears or produces only evil. . . ." By her service to families, woman helps to pour "by a thousand channels a purer element into society."

That she may perform this larger service to society chiefly through her family, it is necessary that she be more broadly educated than if she is to be only cook and general servant. Moreover, the status of her future spouse is as yet unknown and, indeed, may vary from time to time. To meet this unknown or changing situation requires a broad, sound education. She continues: "With the sort of capacity that I would desire her to possess, a woman might be, in turn, a manager of real estate, keeper of books, a compiler of facts and results for statements or memorials; an enlightened critic, to select in various works passages that suit the purposes of those she loves. Finally, in

---

23 *Progressive Education*, 32–3.
24 Pp. 40–1, 52–3, and 93–4.
25 *Progressive Education*, 34–5.

the absence of other assistance, she might carry on, or direct the education of her children, with the aid of good books.''[26]

One of the chief difficulties in the way of realizing this broad education is the fact that future wifehood is always kept in view; and with a single narrow objective it is difficult, if not impossible, to arouse interest in broad training, since the ''evident utility'' decreases in proportion as the future objectives are limited.[27] ''Is it not evident that such views tend to giving the whole attention to the exterior?'' It is thought that figure and talents of a superficial sort are exhibited in public society and cannot be hid—therefore these must be improved. But ''who will ever interrogate the young girl on her principles, her knowledge, her gentleness in private? All this, it is hoped will be taken for granted, and the more or the less will not be remarked. Thus the great objects of intellectual education, the harmonious development of faculties, . . . [are] overlooked by mothers.''[28] The possibility of developing an ''enlightened mind'' is exchanged for a few ''small accomplishments'' with such regularity that it has become a system, and a firm belief prevails that deeper knowledge is of no use to a woman. Under such a system, ''how can we wonder at the narrow views of women?''

Recommending that a general preparation for life be attained, Madame Necker fell into the generally accepted belief in a formal discipline of the mind: ''Consequently, your lessons will continue to consist in strengthening exercises, more than in instructions . . . , that all your faculties . . . be exercised.'' Logically she believes in the all powerful formative influence of education, and warns young ladies: ''If you do not early get the habit of studying vigorously, indolence, so contagious in your sex, will gain upon you; you will then remain always inferior, and your salutary influence will be a nullity.''[29] Algebra, geometry, natural history, natural philosophy, and chemistry are stressed for training the reasoning power;[30] while Latin, German, history, geography, and poetry are to cultivate the memory and imagination. Fine arts, such as music and drawing, needlework, and domestic

26 *Ibid.*, 90.
27 *Ibid.*, 64–5.
28 *Ibid.*, 53–5.
29 *Ibid.*, 91–2.
30 *Ibid.*, Ch. IV.

duties receive a great deal of attention, because of direct importance in the home.

Physical education is emphasized because of the great lack of attention to it formerly, and the consequent lack of health among women. The latter has become so customary that nothing else is expected. The influence of Madame Necker's views on Mrs. Phelps, Catherine E. Beecher, Mrs. Willard, and other prominent women who stimulated a movement for physical training for girls in America,[31] makes it necessary to consider her statement of the needs more fully. Her description follows:

"We are now so accustomed to see debilitated women, that for want of good models, the ideal of the female form is impaired in many imaginations. What style of beauty is most commended in the novels of the day? Is it a brilliant complexion, the graceful elasticity and vivacity of youth? No, it is a slender aerial form, a sylphlike shape, an interesting paleness, occasionally relieved by a delicate rosy hue; it is an expressive look slightly tinged with melancholy;—but most of these indications are precisely those of weak health: the extreme delicacy of form, the colour which comes and goes, the languishing look, announce nothing favorable to the future mother, to the wife who will, perhaps, be called to aid her husband in adversity. And, in the meantime, these descriptions fascinate the imagination of a young girl, and even of her mother, and make them fear to destroy charms so attractive. One young girl is afraid to eat lest she should become too fat, another fears to walk lest her feet should grow too large—what misery!

"We do not desire to form Clorindas or proud Amazons; no, indeed, but the opposite extreme into which the feminine race has fallen in our day, proves that it has degenerated. This is complained of everywhere, in England, in Switzerland, and in America, perhaps most of all. The victims of maternity are multiplied; widowers still young often sadden our view; physicians advise mothers not to nurse their children, lest both should remain weak. The number of orthopedic institutions, sad and uncertain correctives of defective education, bear witness to its fatal consequences. How does it happen that in an age where medical science has made astonishing progress, the science of health should be so far in the rear with respect to women, to that

[31] See Beecher's *Physiology and Calisthenics* (1856).

half of the human family on which chiefly depends that of the whole race? To them will be due the existence of a generation healthy, active, vigorous; or soft, feeble, enervated, and subject to a too excitable nervous system, as women so often are.

"In towns especially, physical inactivity has very deplorable effects. It is thought enough to lead out young girls to walk a little when the weather is fine; but what elasticity can they gain from a measured pace where they are required to hold themselves straight, to guard their looks, their clothes, and to speak very low? Hardly is their circulation accelerated sufficiently to give their limbs a little warmth. The muscles of the arm, the shoulders, the back, remain inactive; those muscles, so necessary, which unite the bones and prevent them from giving way, which keep the spine in its proper place, those muscles gain no strength. The spine, soft and flexible, yields under the weight of the head and arms, and soon curves in the feeblest place."[32]

To correct these evils a system of calisthenics is heartily approved:

"In this age, so favourable to establishments for education, might not in most of the towns places be obtained where young girls might have strengthening exercises, without being exposed to view? Under the inspection of persons respectable enough to make the parents easy, they might take great pleasure in these free exercises, where buoyancy of spirits and the motion of the blood would combine their salutary effects. There also might be prepared all the apparatus of female gymnastics, and proper mistresses to superintend and teach.

"This has been the object of particular solicitude in the United States. It appears, that at least around New York, physical education is very bad; since, in a journal to which I am indebted for some of my preceding remarks, a physician has published, that he does not know eight or ten girls in a hundred who enjoy perfect health. He assigns the evil to three principal causes; one is the abuse of warm drinks, especially tea; and then the compression of the stomach and sides in corsets habitually too tight; and thirdly, the want of sufficient exercise. To these causes he adds some moral ones; contrarities, the irritation they produce, and, in short, whatever impedes the course of the spirits and impairs the natural gaiety. Attention once directed to this

[32] Necker: *op. cit.*, 123–4.

subject, it was inquired, what corporeal exercises would best suit young girls? Thence has arisen a new art, to which is given the name of calisthenic; a word which signifies beauty and strength. This art, already practised in the schools, produces, they say, effects very superior to the common gymnastics, and to dancing. Books with engravings describe the various movements proper to obtain the double object in view. . . ."[33]

Recognizing that "customs are become much less inconvenient to women" now than formerly, "that women are already in France legally relieved of every yoke but marriage," and that they have been entering rapidly into many cooperative philanthropic activities for the past century, she finds that there is every reason for the improvement of their preparation so that they may make use of these new fields of endeavor. Their activities have, indeed, already suggested to some that women wish to leave their sphere, but this view is "unjust to them." "It must, however, be remarked, that all this movement is not agreeable to men: obliged to approve its results as philanthropists, they take no pleasure in it as individuals. It is, to their eyes, a step towards independence; and whether from the weakness of self-love, jealousy of authority, or of opinion, or vague fears of the extravagances not uncommon among women, they have too much antipathy for these associations not sometimes to treat them with ridicule and contempt."[34]

That the advantages of a more liberal education may raise some other questions in turn does not disturb the author. The objection of some, that if girls master music rather than merely get a smattering of it, we may be faced with the possibility of female Mozarts, does not possess much reality for her. It will at least be long before such fame is achieved and the early sound education of the reason will "enable her, either to accept without too much danger the lot of celebrity, or to cast it from her."[35] But since such an event need not be expected more than once in a century, it demands little attention. There is greater likelihood that the new education will open up to her the vocation of teacher; in fact, "were mothers to offer as a motive to their daughters the hope of one day instructing other young females, they would move a powerful lever which otherwise they could

[33] *Ibid.*, 125–6; also consult Chapter III, Vol. II, of this text.
[34] *Ibid.*, 64–5.
[35] *Ibid.*, 106.

not reach. The business of teaching is adapted to women. . . ."
American writers took this cue and urged women to become
teachers that they might have a useful employment in society.
It was here that women found their first important public
rôle.[36] The great immediate advantages to the home are seen by
Necker, as also their possible service to the children of the poor;
but even greater remote consequences may appear. They may
come to find a delight in the search of truth for its own sake, the
advancement of science, as great as that which men have felt;
"they would come to feel the great difference between the pre-
tended resources to which they resort merely to pass the time,
and those in which they advance towards an important object.
Women need not limit their hopes of success to the arts and to
light literature; and experience would soon convince them that
studies more serious and calm would produce more durable and
less dangerous pleasure."[37]

II. In Germany

As intimated in previous pages, the position and education of
women in German lands during the Middle Ages were much the
same as elsewhere in Christendom. After the Reformation, as
in other countries, the ideal for woman was wifehood and motherhood. The institutions that had provided women an opportunity
to share the general education of former days were destroyed.
Luther gave it as his judgment[38] that men were "to pilot the
State and people safely, and to good issues; women to train up
well and to conform in good courses both children and servants."
Secondary and higher schools were organized to prepare for the
more important professions and, since these were not open to
women, there was no ready argument for their admission to
higher education. Luther entertained the idea that women, too,
might become teachers, and declared that the most promising
children, whether male or female, "we should leave . . . longer
at schools, or, perhaps, keep them there altogether. . . ." This
idea, however, gained little headway in early German practice.[39]

[36] See Chapter X.

[37] *Ibid.*, 66–8.

[38] In the *Address to the Councilmen of all the Towns of Germany*, 1524.

[39] In 1887 Prussia had 10.6% women teachers to compare with 32% in
Switzerland, 53% in Italy, 54% in France, 69% in England, and 90% in
the *cities* of the United States—*R. C. E.*, 1887–88, 75 and 360.

There is an old German saying to the effect that *Kinder, Küche* and *Kirche* represent the sphere of women; and this has been generally true until the time of the modern movement for women's emancipation, which has had a stimulating effect upon the growth of facilities for her education. Paulsen, in his *German Education*,[40] maintains that the lack of facilities for woman's education accounts for the fact that German society was a male society "until well into the 18th century"; that the French *Salon* was not an accepted idea, and, indeed, was little affected until the latter part of the century. This homely conception of woman is reflected in oft-quoted passages of her greatest poets, Goethe and Schiller. The former's lines, " *Die Hand, die Samstags ihren Besen führt, wird Sonntags dich am besten caressiren,*" suggest the woman, busy in housewifely art, as the most desirable for man; while Schiller's *Würde der Frauen* lauds women for their virtue and loving service but pictures them as "weaving heavenly roses into this mundane life" while man eternally roams.[41]

Jean Paul Richter (1763–1825), often called by Germans *Der Einzige,* takes a very human and sympathetic view of woman's position but pokes fun at her weaknesses and urges her to attend to her first work, the bringing up of her children.[42] Whimsically he satirizes the custom of putting children out in the care of

---

[40] P. 233.

[41] "*Ehret die Frauen! sie flechten und weben*
"*Himmlische Rosen ins irdische Leben*
"*Flechten der Liebe beglückendes Band,*
"*Und in der Grazie züchtigem Schleier*
"*Nähren sie wachsam das ewige Feuer*
"*Schöner Gefühle mit heiliger Hand.*

"*Ewig aus der Wahrheit Schranken*
"*Schweift des Mannes wilde Kraft;*
"*Unstet treiben die Gedanken*
"*Auf dem Meer der Leidenschaft;*
"*Gierig greift er in die Ferne*
"*Nimmer wird sein Herz gestillt;*
"*Rastlos durch entlegne Sterne*
"*Jagt er seines Traumes Bild.*"

[42] "*Allein, bevor und nachdem man Mutter ist, ist man ein Mensch; die mütterliche Bestimmung aber, oder gar die eheliche, kann nicht die menschliche überwiegen oder ersetzen, sondern sie muss das Mittel, nicht der Zweck derselben sein.*"—Richter: *Levana,* 89.

nursemaids. Jacquelina confesses that "all last year did I not
see my two youngest children, Josephine and Peter, only once a
day, at breakfast, and that merely because I wanted to finish a
novel and a piece of worsted-work; and, also, because my noble
friend, the princess, for whom I was working it, had taken up
her residence here. Only this consideration can tranquillise my
conscience, that I took the greatest trouble to procure a trust-
worthy nurse for my little ones, who promised me to treat them
as a real mother; and may Heaven punish her if she was ever
inattentive to so dear a trust, or ever let my precious lambs go
out of her sight for a moment, or ever left them in the hands of
strangers! Ah, God! when I think of the possibility of such a
thing! But, alas! what do such creatures know of the anxieties
of a tender mother's heart?"[43]

The tendency to a showy education for women is deplored by
Richter, but in this he observes, though his observation is open
to question, a basic reason in female desire. ". . . If there
were a Miss Robinson Crusoe on a desolate island, with no one
to please but her own reflection in the water, she would yet every
day make and wear the newest fashions. . . ." Education is
often for show, much as dress is, he said, long before Spencer
published *Education*. Especially he notes it in female bringing
up and condemns it. But, in place of the "accomplishments,"
he does not recommend a broader, deeper training, but rather an
education useful for the home life which she is to provide:

"Sin not against your daughters, nor blasphemously offend
the spirit of God, by showing and recommending, even indirectly,
any excellence they may possess, be it art, science, or the sanc-
tuary of the heart, as a lure to men, or bait for catching a
husband: to do so is truly to shoot wild fowl with diamonds, or
to knock down fruit with a sceptre. Instead of making heaven
a means and handle for this earth, we should, in the highest
possible degree, elevate this as a means of attaining that. Only
an understanding of the general regulation of a house,—order,
knowledge of house-keeping and similar matters, should be
spoken of as valuable for the future groundwork of the marriage tie. The so called lady-like accomplishments are, at most,
but garlands of flowers by which Cupid may be bound; but
Hymen, who breaks through these, and garlands of fruit too, is

[43] *Ibid.*, 218; also 224–5.

best guided and held by the golden official chain of domestic capability.''[44]

Since he does not approve of formal accomplishments, it is quite natural that he finds objections to the system of boarding schools for girls, where they lose sight of and sympathy for the home life which is to be their greatest province. Girls' day schools are better.[45] A most difficult rôle is assigned to woman, one which depends much more upon temperament than upon institutional training. Still, cheerfulness and gaiety can be cultivated:

''Laughing cheerfulness throws sunlight on all the paths of life. Peevishness covers with its dark fog even the most distant horizon. Sorrow causes more absence of mind and confusion than so-called levity. If a woman can perform this comedy impromptu in married life, and occasionally enliven the serious epic of the husband, or hero, by her amusing heroic ballads, or get up, as the Romans did, a merry farce against misfortunes, she will have bribed and won joy, and her husband, and her children.

''Wherefore, ye mothers, do not merely suffer but assist your daughters to become externally French girls, internally German, and to convert life into a comic poem which surrounds its deep meaning with merry forms. . . . Then let the dear merry children laugh to their hearts' content among one another and especially at any grave pompous man who comes among them, even were he the author of this ninety-seventh paragraph.''[46]

Karl von Raumer, in his *Education of Girls*[47] presents a more orderly treatment of the subject, but fundamentally conservative. Similar in many respects to Richter, he condemns vigorously the nursemaid education which compels children to adopt the standards of thought and action of servants, whereas they should have only the best examples.[48] For intellectual cultivation he recommends that girls study reading, writing, French, English, arithmetic, singing, piano, drawing, botany, history (but not so

[44] *Ibid.*, 240.

[45] *Ibid.*, 243, 244–5.

[46] *Ibid.*, 266–7.

[47] Republished from Barnard's *American Journal of Education* for March and June, 1861.

[48] *Op. cit.*, 297.

thoroughly as in the case of men); and for domestic success they should achieve dexterity with needle and thread, knitting, and other housewifely employments. The practice of limiting girls' education to nothing but the latter—domestic training—is bad, for " . . . in default of an appropriate higher culture, the minds of girls will become interested in a very useless and indeed dangerous way, in things of the idlest and foolishest kind."[49] Other evils are either sternly condemned or ridiculed, such as: the rather universal practice of educating girls "in such a way that they will soon get married, no matter to whom, provided he only has a good income;[50] the slavish pursuit of "singing and playing which girls learn for exhibition in society . . ."; the custom of learning "empty stuff, nonsensical conversational phrases" from French governesses, themselves often uneducated, who merely drill children to speak as "starlings and parrots" but do not instruct them, for they cannot; and the pernicious system of boarding school education which takes girls "from the domestic circle where God meant them to live."[51]

Throughout, a substantial education is preferred. This is seen clearly in his recommendations concerning the literature to be placed in the hands of girls. He realizes that fashions prevail in literature as elsewhere. "Romances of Chivalry," "family romances, bandit, and ghostly romances, as also mystery tales of one kind or another, all come and go, are the rage and then forgotten." He trusts they may remain forgotten and that girls may "read over and over again the best standard works." Girls should not be permitted to choose for themselves from a whole collection, and "still less . . . from a circulating library."[52]

Quite evidently, Von Raumer examined woman's education primarily from the standpoint of social needs rather than individual desire. He began and ended with the family and her place in it. The improvement of society, so ardently sought after by many through reforms of state or church, he held, could only be achieved by putting at its basis the healthy family life: "But my own belief, on the contrary, is, that it is from the

[49] Ibid., 332.
[50] Ibid., 297–8.
[51] Ibid., 364.
[52] Ibid., 338.

smallest of all these spheres, the family, that new life, blessing and health, must come, to church and state; that both state and church, no matter how perfect the forms of their organization, must be mere forms, quite empty, or at most imperfectly filled out, as long as the families which constitute them remain corrupt. Nor can such families themselves, such unhealthy and corrupt members of state and church, reach a condition of real prosperity, until they rid themselves of the same corruption; and least of all, can good results be hoped for, if that corruption still remains, from the education of girls, which is a matter so entirely included in and depending upon the family.''[53]

As previously stated, modern elementary education for girls in Germany began with the Reformation. In Luther's instructions it was stated, '' . . . Your little girls too may easily find time enough to go to school for an hour a day, and yet do all their household duties; for they now devote more than that to overmuch play, dancing and sleep.'' The possibility of higher education for a limited number, superior in intelligence, is also asserted.[54] The practical realization of this plan for elementary education is indicated in the many *Schul- und Kirchenordnungen*. Bugenhagen provided in the Brunswick *Kirchenordnung* (1528) that four schools for girls be established at four places so that they might not have to go far from home; in 1534 an *Ordnung* extended these schools to all towns and lengthened the school day to four hours. Elementary subjects—reading, writing, singing, Bible and Catechism—were taught.[55] At Hamburg, the regulation concerning women teachers was incorporated in the local *Kirchenordnung* (1526) which specified that, when possible, girls' schools were to be provided under the care of ''mature, pious women, who shall instruct the girls'' in reading, religion, and spinning, admonishing them to be punctual and diligent that they might become ''capable housewives.''[56] Similar instructions appeared in Pomerania, Brandenburg, Saxony, and elsewhere throughout Protestant Germany in the sixteenth

[53] *Ibid.*, 366–7; also numerous German views on ''Female Education,'' *R. C. E.*, 1867–68, 377–84.

[54] *Address to the Councilmen* . . . 1524; see also p. 180.

[55] Barnard: *German Teachers and Educators*, 160.

[56] Lange: *Entwickelung und Stand des höheren Mädchen-schulwesens* (1893), 4.

century. No doubt some orders were no more than that; but certainly others resulted in opening special girls' schools. In the Catholic sections the Ursuline sisters, established in 1535, and also the Hieronymians, offered facilities for girls' education. But, for the most part, this schooling was dominated by religion and was largely elementary as in Protestant institutions. Some instances of "learned" women in the sixteenth century are recorded by Cannon,[57] such as Margaret von Staffel, poetess, and the Countess Matilda, who was also interested in poetry and influential in bringing about the creation of the University of Freiburg, by her husband, and that of Tübingen by one of her sons.

In the next century, with the destructive effects of the Thirty Years' War to contend against, there came a decline of girls' schools; girls were again often received into the inferior *Winkelschulen* and Hedge Row schools. The outstanding events of the century, relating to this subject, were the work of Comenius, who asserted that "boys and girls, both noble and ignoble, rich and poor, in all cities and towns, villages and hamlets, should be sent to school";[58] and the interest fostered by his follower Ratke who secured, through the Duchess Dorothea von Weimar, a temporary school in which 231 boys and 202 girls were enrolled. This proved a failure, as most things to which Ratke put his hand; but it was probably influential in shaping the policy of the Weimar school system, wherein provision was made for girls and boys to attend to the twelfth year. Ernest the Pious, Duke of Gotha, established a system, 1642, whereby children of both sexes were to attend school until they were "well versed in religion and the rudiments";[59] and a school for girls, of various classes, was established by Francke at Halle in the last decade of the century. In the latter, Francke was much under the influence of the ideas of Fénelon. The chief purposes being the good life and domesticity, he emphasized Christianity and household management. Accomplishments such as French and handiwork were not omitted since they helped adorn the housewife. Greek and Latin were included since they were necessary for thorough study of religious sources.[60]

[57] *The Education of Women During the Renaissance,* 154 *ff.*
[58] *The Great Didactic,* 66.
[59] Nohle, 43.
[60] Barnard: *German Teachers,* 407 *ff.;* also consult Lange: *op. cit.,* 6.

The reawakening interest in girls' education at the end of the seventeenth century became much more noticeable about the middle of the eighteenth, following in general the trends already indicated in England and France, though scarcely as vehemently championed by its advocates as was the case sometimes in the former. Lange[61] records the fact of increasing literature about the latter half of the eighteenth century;[62] but, as noted elsewhere, practical achievements were slow to follow. The *Herzogliche Töchterschule* (1786) at Dessau, a monument to the experimental work of Basedow, but established by the munificence of Prince Leopold Franz, may be mentioned as an important practical result; but here the purpose was to give "useful and needful instruction" to girls of the middle class, for the improvement of "home life." Other prominent schools founded by societies or by royal favor were the Elizabeth School at Berlin (1748), one similar to it at Frankfort-am-Main (1749), and *St. Maria Magdalena Töchterschule* at Breslau, in 1767.

The reform literature of the preceding century was appreciably augmented in the early nineteenth by Gleim's *Erziehung und Unterricht des Weiblichen Geschlechts* (1810) and Rudolphi's *Gemälden Weiblicher Erziehung* (1807);[63] and reform in practice was brought more and more unavoidably to the attention of the state by the rapid rise of private schools for girls in all the greater cities. These schools, however, generally continued in practice the accepted views of girls' training—*i.e.*, directing them towards home life as the consummation of all things. School life terminated early, usually at fourteen or sixteen years of age. The private schools continued to be of great importance, serving as a stimulus to the state to provide more schools and also as an encouragement to women, offering the tools, as it were, wherewith they might work, and enabling them more intelligently to seek for their emancipation. In 1887, the secondary schools of Prussia had 70.5% boys and 29.5% girls; of these

---

61 *Op. cit.*, 7.

62 E.g., *Von der Notwendigkeit des Studierens, insonderheit der Frauenzimmer*, Leipzig, 1753; *Über Frauenzimmerschulen*, Zurich, 1770; *Über die Notwendigkeit der Anlegung öffentlicher Töchterschulen für alle Stände*, Wolfenbüttel, 1786; *System der Weiblichen Erziehung, besonders für den mittleren und höheren Stand*, 1787.

63 Lange: *op. cit.*, 8.

girls, approximately a half were in private schools. At that date there were no women in the German universities.

A change in regard to public secondary education of girls was foreshadowed in the convocation of teachers of girls' schools (1872), which prepared a memorial on the subject of state assistance, and the establishment of the General German Association for the Higher Education of Girls, at Hanover, in the same year. A year later the Minister of Education in Prussia (Falk) convened the heads of girls' schools to consider the problem.[64] Governmental action, however, did not come till 1893.

Other events, assisting in the furtherance of women's demands, but which can only be named here, were the establishment of the *Lette-Verein*, in the sixties; the *Allgemeiner Deutscher Frauenverein*, organized (1865) at Leipzig; the *Frauen Bildung-Reform-Verein* at Wiemar, in 1888; and similar groups. These had varied activities, but most prominent among their interests was the improvement of facilities for higher education. The latter two, especially, agitated for such recognized secondary schools as would prepare girls to enter the universities.[65]

Recognition came, at last, to the efforts of these organizations, in an official rescript (May, 1894) which provided a fixed curriculum for the *höhere Mädchenschulen*. Women were to be permitted to teach in the upper grades, and if a man were head, then a woman was to be the associate. They were, however, only nine years in length, whereas the boys' were ten; and another reason for disappointment lay in the fact that though they were under provincial authorities, yet they were not recognized as secondary schools. By 1897, only 39 girls' schools (Prussian) had been ranked as equal with boys.[66] In Germany, as elsewhere, it is to be noted that advancement came through individual and private enterprises. In 1893, Miss Lange opened a school in Berlin to give graduates of the *höhere Mädchenschulen* sufficient preparation to take the leaving examination (*Abiturienten*) which had to be passed in order to qualify for the university; but the university was not yet open to them. In the same year, a similar school at Carlsruhe was begun by the *Frauen Bildung-Reform-Verein* and, in 1894, another in Leipzig. Preparation for the

[64] *Ibid.*, 15.
[65] *Ibid.*
[66] Russell: *German Higher Schools*, 130 *ff.*

Abiturienten might at this time be obtained at the Victoria Lyceum (Berlin), the Humboldt Academy, and in the *Realkurse*
for women controlled by the *Wissenschaftlicher Zentralverein* of
Berlin.[67]

Thus the close of the nineteenth century saw German women
prepared—a few at least—for university educational opportunities. But this boon was only occasionally, and reluctantly,
granted.[68] Heidelberg and Göttingen were among the first to
admit women, but the courses were mostly attended by foreigners. Freqnently they were allowed only as *Hospitaninnen* and
Zuhörerinnen (auditors), not being a part of the university nor
able to take a degree. The attitude of German universities was
apparently less liberal than the French.[69] At Berlin and Jena
the opposition was greatest, though the accounts given of professors' actions in some cases seem to have been overdrawn. Following an exaggerated report, in a Berlin journal in November,
1895, that Erich Schmidt, the historian, and Treitschke had
expelled ladies from classes with violence and used harsh language, a journalist undertook to find out what professors'
opinions really were about the presence of women at the universities. The replies indicated only a few who categorically
declined all compromise. On the other hand, there were
extremely few who revealed a sympathetic attitude. Some
believed that women would have a wholesome effect on the
intellectual life, while others thought they would prove a great
distraction. Most uncompromising in his objections was Wusten-
feld, octogenarian professor of philology at the University of
Göttingen, who declared: ". . . I am absolutely opposed to the
admission of women to academic studies or to any profession
whatever which demands a learned education."[70] Professor
Gierke, of the law faculty at Berlin, attempted to be more
rational in his position, but his reason most feminists, doubtless,
held to be nothing but an excuse. In part, he said: "We live
in serious times. The German people have something better to
do than to make rash experiments in female education. The one
thing that concerns us is that our men should be men. It is al-

[67] Lange: *op. cit.*, 35.
[68] Russell: *op. cit.*, 416 *ff.*
[69] See an article in *Littel's Living Age*, CCXIV (1897), 83–5.
[70] *Ibid.*

ways a sign of decadence when we are reduced to demanding of the women a virility in which the men are lacking.'' This represents one view of the opponents. Even ardent friends of woman's education subscribed to the view that the state should not experiment with costly higher education for women, but that private wealth should be devoted to its encouragement, and cited the examples of foreign countries to prove their point. But the excuse that the state was too poor to offer the highest education to women did not much affect the suffragists, who pointed out that many women (about half of the upper classes) would probably not marry; that they would not become dependent; and that they must therefore be equipped to take a real place, professionally, in an active world. The number of women increased in the universities during the early years of the twentieth century. Just before the war there were 56,691 men, 4,057 women and 8,000 auditors. In 1923 these figures had increased to 76,608 men, 8,761 women, and 17,500 auditors.[71]

Under the present constitution, women have a new place in German life. Men and women over twenty years of age have received the ballot, while rights and duties are, theoretically at least, equal.[72] In 1923–24, 37 women deputies were seated in the *Reichstag* and 117 were scattered throughout the several legislatures of the states of the Republic.

[71] *Educational Yearbook* of the International Institute of Teachers College, 1924, 319–20.

[72] Constitution, articles 22, 109 and 128 particularly, given in Brunet: *The New German Constitution*, 303, 323 and 326.

CHAPTER III

CHANGING CONCEPT OF WOMEN'S ABILITY, POSITION AND EDUCATION IN THE UNITED STATES

I. Mental Inequality Versus Equality

In the realm of affairs of the mind, it is difficult, even now, to prove or disprove a theory; before the advent of an experimental psychology, it was necessarily more so. The Colonial inhabitants of the Atlantic coast continued, in their wilderness homes, to be satisfied with the notions that had served their fathers; and it was long before any new conclusion was reached regarding the mentality of women. Allusion has been made to views which were common in England, France, and Germany. It is needless to say that in America these ideas persisted as a dominant force until very recent years and, even now, are often found in sequestered minds, here as elsewhere.

In the nineteenth century, articles copied from English periodicals appeared often on this subject. In 1860, *Littell's Living Age*[1] quoted an article from *The Saturday Review,* wherein the question of equality of intellect was summarily disposed of. The author admitted that all men are interested in the education whereby women are formed, and "perhaps the view that a natural equality of intellect exists in women, and demands a similar education with that bestowed on men, may, in courtesy, be called plausible"; but, he said, "The great argument against the existence of this equality of intellect in women is, that it does not exist. If that proof does not satisfy a female philosopher, we have no better to give. . . ." The same belief in widely differentiated capacities of male and female mind is found also in the utterances of President Eliot and others of his generation. Replying to Colonel Higginson, a staunch advocate of women's education, he said: "When Col. Higginson asks if the male and female mind are not the same, we would answer no, very distinctly. The male and female minds are not alike. Sex penetrates the mind and the affections, and penetrates deeply and

[1] LXIV, 184.

powerfully. . . . Now, women differ from men more than men differ from each other; that is to say, there is a fundamental pervading difference between all men and all women which extends to their minds quite as much as to their bodies. . . ."[2] Those who championed the opposite view were few, but they did arise in every century.

In the eighteenth century, William Alexander, in his *History of Women*,[3] held that women were more inferior to men in highly developed civilizations; there, women, for lack of proper occupations, certainly became inferior physically; and "such is the influence of body upon mind, that to this laxity of body we may fairly trace many, if not all, of the weaknesses of the mind, which we are apt to reckon blemishes in the female character. . . . But there is a further reason for the greater difference between the sexes in civil, than in savage life, which is the difference of education; while the intellectual powers of the males are gradually opened and expanded by culture in a variety of forms: those of females are commonly either left to nature, or, which is worse, warped and biased by frippery and folly, under the name of education."[4] Not only has man, in his opinion, cherished this idea of differentiation on this earth; he has also, ofttimes, denied to her the immortality he himself prizes.

Branagan, in his treatise on the *Excellency of the Female Character*,[5] took the same view, imputing the degraded idea of women's ability "to error in education, a wrong association of ideas in youth, which is handed down from one generation to another . . . till that hypothesis, which is, in fact, an insult to common sense, daily experience, and the nature of things, is, by custom, reduced to a natural supposition, a received opinion." The current education suffices to make women "the most vain, capricious, versatile, gaudy, and affected mortals in the creation"; but so far as their capacity to be anything more is concerned, he maintains it is equal, if not superior, to that of man; moreover, he confesses he is astonished that such a brilliant man as Lavater could have believed in such inequality of gifts to the sexes. "Had he listened to the captivating brilliancy of the

---

[2] Quoted from Orton: *Liberal Education of Women* (1873), 321.
[3] Phila., 1795, II, 46–7.
[4] *Ibid.*
[5] (1808) Pp. 81, 82–3, 101, and 118–19.

elocution of Aspasia, and ascertained the depth of her philosophy
. . . ; had he recognized the sublime Corinna, contending with and
winning the prize from Pindar . . .; had he investigated with
candor the ingenious, though abstruse writings of Wollstonecraft; had he been present in the councils in which Queen Elizabeth presided . . . he would, undoubtedly, have been of a different opinion. Indeed, I cannot help believing, that the contempt for the mental capacity of the sex, expressed by many
learned authors, proceeds more from envy than ignorance. . . .''[6]

During the nineteenth century there appeared many men—
and women, too, for that matter—who had a profound respect
for the intelligence of ''females,'' though not necessarily accepting the idea of equality. Carter, Gallaudet, Mann, and Barnard come readily to mind as men who attributed great intelligence to women and offered them new opportunities to prove
their possession. The new profession of teaching, as also the
foundation of women's colleges, offered laboratories in which the
test was to be made. Little can be said of this test at the moment,
save that women began to distinguish themselves in these and
also in other competitive enterprises. Maria Mitchell, who some
may say was too enthusiastic about her young women and hence
not to be trusted, made the following comment on her charges
at Vassar: ''I have a class of seventeen pupils, between the ages
of sixteen and twenty-two. . . . I allow them great freedom in
questioning, and I am puzzled by them daily. They show more
mathematical ability and more originality, than I had expected.
I doubt whether young men would show as deep an interest. Are
there seventeen students in Harvard College who take mathematical astronomy, do you think?''[7] If Miss Mitchell's estimate
stood alone, it would count for little; presidents of institutions
admitting women with men have frequently commented on the
equal, or superior, excellence of the work of the former.[8] Since
the sixties, and especially in the generation since 1890, there has
been accumulated a great fund of data concerning physical and
mental traits of men and women. Thorndike stated, after reviewing these data: ''On the whole the differences, reported in the

6 *Ibid.*, 118–19.

7 Quoted from Dall: *College, Market and the Court,* 44; compare also
Sch. and Soc., Oct. 9, 1926, 458.

8 See Chapter V, Vol. II, for many varieties of opinions on this subject.

case of the less easily measurable features of intellect, character and behavior, are of the same magnitude as those found in objective tests. They do not require any amendment of the general rule that sex is the cause of only a small fraction of the differences between individuals. The differences of men from men and women from women are nearly as great as the differences between men and women."[9]

It was an ancient belief, expressed frequently, that women were weaker and more variable than men. In more recent times, the latter half of the statement was often minimized, if not even reversed, and greater variability attributed to men than to women.[10] This view, it appears, has been based more on opinion than adequate objective measurement of traits. Dr. Leta Hollingworth has summarized the findings, to date, as follows: "(1) The greater variability of males in anatomical traits is not established, but debated by authorities of perhaps equal competence. (2) But, even if it were established, it would only suggest, not prove, that men are more variable in mental traits also. The empirical data at present available on this point are inadequate and contradictory, and, if they point either way, actually indicate greater female variability. . . ."[11]

In connection with these recent differences of opinion among psychologists as to the precise differences between men and women, as also in regard to the variability of their capacities, it is interesting to recall the statement of President Angell as to the performance of women in his classes: "I think I may fairly speak, from my years of experience, during which I have taught many thousands of women, . . . I may say that there is little difference between my students, except that I generally had to attract the males a little more violently to have them attain the requirements. But I think I may say for sheer brilliancy many of the women under my charge have proved themselves superior to many of the men I have ever met and certainly have taught.

[9] *Educational Psychology*, III, 205.

[10] Compare Jastrow: *Psychology of Conviction*, 296–7.

[11] Quoted by Parsons: Sex and Genius [*Yale Review*, July, 1925, 745–6]. Compare also with Thorndike: *op. cit.*, III, 193–6; Hollingworth's article in *Am. Jour. Soc.* (Jan., 1914), XIX, 528–9; Thompson: *The Mental Traits of Sex*, 169 *ff.*; and Bernard Hollander, as reported in an address before the Ethnological Society in London.—*Phila. Inquirer*, Jan. 20, 1927.

Whatever the fundamental differences may be that mark those of us who are male and those who are female . . . [they do not] cut very deeply into the procedure of collegiate education. They are of an order we can disregard for that purpose.''[12] This statement is similar to many made by professors in colleges during the past generation. The verdict has been, in general, that woman's ability to do high grade academic work at any rate equals, and certainly often excels, that of man, if we judge by the work actually done. The work done does not of itself imply there are no differences, but rather that they are not consequential. But, if it is true that they are not consequential, why have few women made their mark? Castle found but 891 women of note (and 237 of them biblical characters) mentioned in three of six standard works of reference. ''It is a sad commentary on the sex that from the dawn of history to the present day less than one thousand women have accomplished anything . . . recorded as worth while. [But] one cannot evade the question,—is woman innately so inferior to man, or has the attitude of civilization been to close the avenues of eminence against her?''[13]

II. The Sphere of Woman

In Colonial days, just as there existed no real question as to the intelligence of women, it being generally accepted that they were inferior, so likewise there had arisen no doubt as to the sphere of woman. The Margaret Winthrops, Mercy Warrens and Phillis Wheatleys were too scarce, during this period of transplanting, to allow any disturbing sense of woman's greater sphere which might be opened up by means of education. Even though a woman gave the first ground on which a free school was erected in the Bay Colony, her sex was zealously excluded from the benefits of schooling; and many of the New England towns appear, at first, to have considered the admission of girls to their schools as ''inconsistent with the design'' thereof. These views were somewhat modified about the Revolutionary period, when, for example, Norwich, Connecticut, gave girls permission to attend early in the morning before the boys arrived and after they had gone home in the evening.[14]

[12] Address reported in the *Phila. Inquirer*, Oct. 19, 1925.

[13] Castle: *Statistical Study of Eminent Women*, 90.

[14] See Dexter: *History of Education in the United States*, 427; and Chapter IV of this work.

Woman's preparation for her allotted sphere—the home—was obtained through apprenticeship to her mother, in the home; and it precluded any attention to a more formal schooling, costly in time and money, which led away from the hearth. A certain reliance and independence was, doubtless, cultivated in our Colonial mothers; but it was, as a general rule, a self-reliance in practical duties of the home, rather than in the affairs of the wide world. Mrs. Adams, even as late as her day, regretted, in comparing France and America, that the latter gave little encouragement to the cultivation of the female mind. In fact, she says it was the custom to "ridicule female learning," and in the best families of New England, education extended to nothing more than reading, writing, and arithmetic. Her own education along broader lines she attributed to John.[15] The colleges of the day were given over to the training of ministers, and since women could not enter that profession, there was not the slightest reason for their contemplating such a step. Moreover, the idea prevailed that an educated wife was, after a fashion, an infringement upon the domain of man; that the wife of Winthrop lost her mind because she left her proper domestic duties and indulged herself in literary pursuits; and that, at any rate, to seek culture of the mind was to transgress the law of God, who had given her the home and fixed her in it. Wharton, in a delightful book, *Colonial Days and Dames,* quotes significant lines which she attributes to "some crabbed bachelor" who, "heavily fined for remaining in the single state from which no fair lady would help him to escape . . . ," must have written them as a model to be copied on a little girl's sampler:

"One did commend to me a wife both fair and young
"That had French, Spanish, and Italian tongue.
"I thanked him kindly and told him I loved none such,
"For I thought one tongue for a wife too much,
"What! love ye not the learned?
"Yes, as my life,
"A learned scholar, but not a learned wife."[16]

The Dutch and the Germans were noted for their thrift and, whether in the settlements of New Netherlands or those of Pennsylvania, we find the ideal wife was economical and industrious.

15 See Ch. IV.
16 Wharton: *op. cit.,* 195–6.

We recall the homelike picture drawn in *The Letters of An American Farmer* by Hector St. John, a Frenchman, who described the existence of the pioneers in Pennsylvania about the time of the Revolution. This is a lifelike picture of a Colonial home; in it there was little demand for a woman of cultured mind but the greatest need for a cheerful and efficient domestic worker. The independence acquired by the women of Cape Cod, during the absence of their husbands, is likewise described by him as a natural development. Rush, in his *Account of the German Inhabitants of Pennsylvania,* declared that "to fear God and to love work, are the first lessons they teach their children. They prefer industrious habits to money itself; hence, when a young man asks the consent of his father to marry the girl of his choice, he does not inquire so much whether she be rich or poor, or whether she possess any personal or mental accomplishments—as whether she be industrious, and acquainted with the duties of a good housewife." For, as an old German adage has it, *"Eine fleissige Hausfrau ist die beste Sparbuechse."*[17] It was Rush's view that the many newspapers printed in the German language[18] had diffused knowledge widely among them and that there were but few of either sex that could not read; but, he says, "many of the wives and daughters of the German farmers cannot write."[19]

In the English Quaker settlements, whether in Pennsylvania, New York, New Jersey, Delaware, Virginia, the Carolinas, or New England, there was a liberal attitude towards the elementary education of girls. The sphere of Quaker women was, as in the case of the others, the home; and it was there that her influence counted for most. But the Quaker meeting had been, from the beginning, the public forum for women. Fox's doctrine did not deny the leading of the *inner light* to women. Thus their ministry was recognized and they too, with men, went forth among the nations "preaching the word." The Quaker leader insisted on a return to primitive Christianity, and did not recognize as authoritative the injunction of St. Paul. It was by reason of this encouragement to women that Mary Dyer fell

[17] Rush: *op. cit.,* 68 and 69–70.

[18] For a special study of this question see Knauss: *Social Conditions Among Pennsylvania Germans.*

[19] Rush: *op. cit.,* 105.

afoul of the laws of the theocratic state in New England, about 1659.[20] It also paved the way for the free entrance of women of the Society into various reform movements, such as the abolition of slavery,[21] temperance, and the emancipation of women. The elementary schools were, from the first, open to girls as well as boys. Fox, 1667, set up a special school for girls at Shacklewell, in England, and in his letters urged the attention of parents and meetings to the question; while in America the colonists followed the example of the London Yearly Meeting in establishing schools. The name of a woman teacher in the Friends' schools of Philadelphia appeared in 1702.[22]

But, as said, this greater freedom to enter into public questions did not seek to impair the home influence of woman. That was her greatest duty. But in the home she was an equal. A simple declaration, in the presence of witnesses, with invocation for divine aid to maintain faith, was the only thing needed to legalize marriage. As Lucretia Mott put it, there was neither "assumed authority nor admitted inferiority; no *promise of obedience.*"[23]

In the Colonial South, the sphere of women was in the home, just as it was in New England or the central colonies. Everywhere the marriageable age was earlier than now. Calhoun states that "in Seventeenth Century Virginia if the father made a gift to his daughter it was customary to insert a proviso in case she married before sixteen."[24] One clandestine marriage was found in which "the wife was not past her twelfth year." Marriages at thirteen, fourteen, and fifteen years of age were common; while, according to one contemporary, a girl who was unmarried at twenty was "reckoned a stale maid. . . ." After twenty-five the situation was considered hopeless.[25] Marriage

20 Consult Hallowell: *Quaker Invasion of Massachusetts,* 56 *ff.;* and Ellis: *The Puritan Age and Rule,* 434 *ff.*

21 Women delegates from the Society of Friends in America attended the World's Anti-Slavery Convention in London, 1840, but were ruled out by the English abolitionists.

22 Woody: *Early Quaker Education in Pennsylvania,* 22, 53, and 208.

23 Quoted from Butler: *Woman's Work and Culture,* XLV–XLVII.

24 Reprinted by permission of the publishers, The Arthur H. Clark Company, from Calhoun's *Social History of the American Family,* I, 245.

25 *Ibid;* consult on marriage also Bruce: *Soc. Life of Va.,* Ch. XVII; and Weeden: *Economic and Social History of New England,* I, 217–19, 293–5, 412, etc.

was not only at an age of immaturity, both of mind and body, but was arranged for a price. Women sold themselves for their passage to America, wives were sold into Virginia to meet the demand of the lonely settlers, and even in later times, and in the wealthier classes, marriage settlements were quite businesslike.[26] Considering these facts, it is not surprising that women were generally considered the playthings of men; and women like Margaret Brent, of Maryland, only serve to bring out in sharp relief the position accorded to the majority, whose duties were to spin, sew, and do general housework. Their education seldom went beyond the merest rudiments, and many missed these. Only in the case of the wealthier families, where the system of tutorial education prevailed, were daughters sometimes instructed more liberally in the free time not used for the instruction of sons. This mode of education became more common in the latter half of the eighteenth century, when, as one writer says, ''The gentlemen of Virginia, taught by the experience of many years, . . . '' began to appreciate and reverence ''the nobleness, the purity, the gentleness of woman'' and accorded her '' . . . the unstinted and sincere homage . . .'' she deserved.[27]

This statement, with some variation, could be applied to most of the earlier settlements. As their safety and permanence became more certain, as economic conditions improved, more and more culture and freedom became a possibility for men. In turn, there was a gradual amelioration of woman's lot, but her function as home-maker continued to be the most highly regarded. Her education, the quantity of which was gradually increased in the boarding schools of the latter part of the eighteenth century and the early nineteenth, dwelt chiefly upon the acquisition of accomplishments, that she might embellish the home and society of her husband. This conception of her education was destined to continue until new fields of activity, outside the home, began to open before her. To make her service in these new fields effective, a more substantial education was then urged, and gradually obtained.

To quiet the unrest that began to be apparent in the early nineteenth century; to silence the slender arguments that were

[26] Calhoun: *op. cit.*, I, 253–4.

[27] Reprinted by permission of the publishers, The Arthur H. Clark Company, from Calhoun's *Social History of the American Family*, I, 275.

put forth in favor of woman's larger sphere, there descended a
deluge of opinions from persons of high and low estate, expressed
privately in letters and publicly in speeches, sermons, and
periodicals, to show that woman's true sphere must not be for-
saken, but that she must be better educated to fill it adequately.
Numerous articles appeared in such educational magazines as
the *Common School Journal, Connecticut Common School Journal, American Journal of Education, Annals of Education,* and
others, stressing the "task assigned to women," "the maternal
relation," the "sphere of female influence," "the moral agency,"
"mother's counsel," "mother's care," "mother's touch," and
so on *ad infinitum.* Articles of this character predominate from
the beginning of educational periodicals, about 1819 and 1826,
until the middle of the century. A sample of this voluminous
literature is given below. It is a "letter from a father to his
daughter," quoted from the *Charleston Observer.*

"She is to occupy the place, and exert the influence of a
mother. I speak now of the race. Here, under divine appointment, she applies the plastic hand to a moral and intellectual
existence, at its starting point for eternity. None will deny that
the children of every family take their character principally
from the mother of that family. Through life, they yield fruit
according to the seed sown—the character imprinted in the nursery and in the parlor. Through eternity they retain this character. What kind of education can qualify her to discharge the
arduous and responsible duties of such a situation? If the
physical nature of that child is disordered, the learned and skilful physician is called in to prescribe. To administer spiritual
instruction and relief, requires the learning of a divine; and the
masters in intellectual philosophy alone, are competent to its
intellectual training. Here we must see what sort of education
that mother needs. She must know, and know intimately too,
the physical, intellectual, and moral nature of the being she
educates, and be able to apply the principles of true philosophy
in the training of it.

"The influence of a mother's counsel and a mother's care
might be referred to, if additional support were needed to affirm
this position. The mother's hand laid upon the feverish temple,
that kind hand is forever remembered. That touch is felt as if

there were an abiding impression made by it, perhaps through life. The moral instruction she then whispered in the ear, remains bright and impressive in memory's storehouse. The look of love or gentle reproof, of approbation or censure, exist like durable forms in the mind. The mother is ever before the mind, and when the pride of intellect has transported the man in maturity beyond the influence of even sound argument and rational conviction, he remembers the lessons of that mother and feels their truth. By a law of his nature, he is held by that mother's influence, and whenever he feels it, he becomes docile. I may here illustrate my remark by a reference to the testimony of the celebrated, witty, eccentric, and eminent John Randolph. Through a life uncommonly various in public incident and honors, he said to a friend, 'I should have been an infidel, had it not been for the influence exerted on me by my mother, as she taught me to kneel at her side, and fold my little hands, and say, 'Our Father who art in Heaven, &c.'

"Similar results will be found, if we consider the power of female influence in all the other relations of life, as a wife, a daughter, a sister, or a friend. She always exerts a great, often a controlling influence.

"Look into families.—Who regulates the terms of social intercourse? What gives character to the conversation, and who prescribes laws there? It is the mother, daughter, sister, the female members of the family. The husband, father, brother, the young men of every community, are influenced in every department of labor and of duty by a constant reference to the opinions, the approbation of those whom they may meet in the hallowed society of home. Here is the centre of influence. The man is brutal, who can see unmoved a tear on the cheek of an affectionate wife; who can willingly excite a blush for a father's wrong on a daughter's face; or wound a sister's confiding feelings; or trifle with a lady's frown. Men are accustomed to speak and act as they think will meet the approbation of female society. This fact shows at once the importance that the sentiments of female society should be such as to form a correct standard of public opinion, and her conversation embrace a range of subjects worthy of the attention of men; of immortal men; subjects suited to the great duties of life, the interests of an eternal life.

HOME, THE CENTER OF MATERNAL INFLUENCE IN SOCIETY

"The place which the female occupies in society, and the influence she exerts, requires the most complete moral and intellectual education, to prepare her for her duties. She may not only 'learn to read, and write, and cypher,' but she ought to have her mind and character formed by whatever can adorn or give strength to the intellect. And why should she not? She has a whole life to live—why not spend it rationally? She must be always doing something. The mind must think. Why may she not as well be wise as frivolous? Why may she not as well be devoted to literature as to fashion? Why may not the conversation of mixed companies, which occupies so large a share of our time and attention, be rational, literary and improving, instead of being, as it too often is, vain, unprofitable and dissipating?

"Every view we can take of the bearing of female influence on the character and destiny of our race, enforces the importance that female education should be of the most substantial kind. I think but little of a young lady's ability to pencil a rose, or polish a wax flower. I would rather see you able to analyze the flower itself, plucked in its season fragrant with its native sweets, glowing with its native, inimitable colors, and enamel. I prize at a low rate the graces, which consist in exact and measured genuflections, curved lines or angles. I would have you cultivate a sound understanding, and quick sense of propriety in all your intercourse with society, in all your intercourse with yourselves. The character which will be thus formed under the influence of a meek and quiet spirit, will recommend you to approbation, when every design of art will fail.

"I would not have a lady inattentive to her person; much less, contemptuous of the ordinary forms of social intercourse; but I give it to you as the deliberate result of my observations on society, that true grace of personal manner, so far as that is a subject of education, depends far more on a correct sense of propriety, and on intellectual education, than on any physical training of the dancing master, or rules of art. A ride on horse back, or a botanical ramble, or a walk in the fresh air of the early morning, or even the necessary effort to put your own room in order before you leave it, furnish a more uniform and safer exercise, uniting the pleasant and profitable, than all the physical discipline which can result from mere pleasure or constraint. I should rather see you able to cook well a penny loaf or lead a charity enterprise, than to cut the 'pigeon wing,' in 'measured motion,' or to dance a cotillion.

"A reference to the condition of females in society, and the general principles on which their education would be conducted, is necessary to justify the manner in which I have directed your education.

"Whatever may contribute to elevate the standard of female education, and to promote a proper female influence, adds weight to a lever of tremendous power, and lengthens its shaft."[28]

A second characteristic view, which was shortly to vie with the first for emphasis, was that women should be educated sufficiently to enable them to extend their forming influence to children in the public schools. This appeared but logical. If the school was to usurp the work formerly done by the home, the mother's influence ought to follow into the school. Otherwise society would suffer the consequence, it was argued.[29]

The great bulk of Americans, however, did not think highly of this newly proposed freedom for women. Mann, Gallaudet, Carter and others were considered a little visionary. The popular feeling of horror for the dissolution of the home, which even then was foreseen, as also reverence for that bulwark of the nation, are seen in the following quotation from the monumental *Godey's Lady's Book:*

"OUR homes—what is their corner-stone but the virtue of a woman, and on what does social well-being rest but in our homes? Must we not trace all other blessings of civilized life to the doors of our private dwellings? Are not our hearth-stones guarded by holy forms, conjugal, filial, and parental love, the corner-stone of church and state, more sacred than either, more necessary than both? Let our temples crumble, and capitals of state be levelled with the dust, but spare our homes! Man did not invent, and he cannot improve or abrogate them. A private shelter to cover . . . two hearts dearer to each other than all in the world; high walls to exclude the profane eyes of every human being; seclusion enough for children to feel that mother is a holy and peculiar name—this is home: and here is the birthplace of every secret thought. Here the church and state must come for their origin and support. Oh! spare our homes. . ."[30]

[28] Reprinted in the *American Annals*, VI, 503–5.

[29] Numerous essays in the journals mentioned bear out this statement.

[30] *Godey's Lady's Book*, September, 1856, 213.

The importance of preserving the home for its social service, and the duty of women as educators of their children, were sternly urged by Coxe in *Claims of the Country on American Females;*[31] Todd, in *The Daughter at School* (1854) ; Butler, in *The American Lady* (1851) ; Webster, in a statement quoted by *Godey's Lady's Book* (January, 1852) ; Starrett, in *Letters to a Daughter* (1892) ; and Hyde, in *College Man and College Woman* (1906). Some variations occur through the years, but the sentiment of the first is much like the last on this point.

Butler found the duties of women, in 1851, to be: ''First; In contributing daily and hourly to the comfort of husbands, of parents, of brothers and sisters, and of other relations, connexions, and friends, in the intercourse of domestic life, under every vicissitude of sickness and health, of joy and affliction. Secondly; In forming and improving the general manners, disposition, and conduct of the other sex, by society and example. Thirdly; In modelling the human mind, during the early stages of its growth, and fixing, while it is yet ductile, its growing principles of action. Children of each sex are, in general, under maternal tuition during their childhood, and girls until they become women.''[32]

Hyde, in 1906, under the influence doubtless of economics, gave a tang of the new science to his utterance: ''In a broad way, subject to exceptions and qualifications . . . the manly economic ideal is the effective direction of production; the womanly ideal is the beneficient ordering of consumption.''[33] ''Goods are not immediately useful when produced in large quantities. Food must be prepared and served. The house must be furnished and kept in order. Cloth must be fitted to the person who is to wear it, and kept cleanly and presentable. Children must be separately reared and individually trained. Hospitality must be extended. The sick must be nursed and the aged must be cared for.

''The right rendering and ordering of these and kindred services is woman's distinctive economic function. Happy is the woman who as daughter, sister, wife, mother, finds herself excused from the task of direct economic production by the gen-

31 2 volumes (1842).
32 *Op. cit.,* 14–15.
33 *Op. cit.,* 195–6.

erous devotion of father, brother, husband, or son, and can find the economic justification of her life in this ministry and superintendence of the common household consumption. For it is a function just as necessary, just as useful, just as honorable as law, or banking, or commerce, or agriculture, or manufacture, or transportation. It is a function for which women are by nature and taste eminently fitted, and for which most manly men are conspicuously unfit. It is a wise distribution of economic functions which assigns in this broad way the direction of economic production to men, and the ordering of economic consumption to women.''

For women of the class who will not marry and who must therefore ''earn the whole or a portion of their living,'' he provides that they may enter fields of ''production for immediate consumption,'' such as ''nursing, domestic service, teaching, typewriting, retailing in small communities, work for wages or salaries in factories or offices, practice medicine, acting, music, the management of such local industries as serve patrons personally known to the manager. . .'' And he thinks they may have a certain advantage in these over men. But women are ''doomed to financial failure'' if they enter the arena of ''production on the large scale, production for the speculative market . . ., production in competition and collision with the vast shifting, hostile, stubborn facts and forces of the world.''[34] He shudders, apparently, at the risks involved in entering ''these exclusively masculine vocations, such as mining, manufacturing, transportation, law, banking, commerce, wholesale trade, [which] involve a degree of strain, a kind of contact, a sort of emotional and mental attitude which not one woman in a million can stand without either disaster or deterioration. For the producer of a general commodity comes into intense competition with everybody in his line of business. He is exposed to severe strain, enormous risk, frequent quarrels, perpetual antagonism. He must be constantly alert to adapt methods and processes to changing conditions and varying demands. He must make important decisions instantaneously; take risks by telegraph which hang in the balance between profit and loss for weeks and months; strike hard blows swiftly; deal resolutely with dishonest contractors, insolvent debtors, striking workmen, incompetent agents, un-

[34] *Ibid.*, 195–200.

scrupulous competitors, corrupt politicians, fickle customers, treacherous friends, and secret enemies almost every day of his active business life. In this strife of contending interests, where good and bad meet on equal terms, asking no favor and giving no quarter, in the face of enmity and calumny, fraud and deception, men manage to turn out their product, and make their enterprises a success, without a very large proportion of physical breakdowns, and without the destruction of their personal character. Under these conditions the normal woman could not succeed in more than one case in ten thousand; and even then she would be almost sure to perish on one of the two rocks that guard the narrow passage—nervous prostration or hardening of heart. No law today forbids a woman from entering these competitive careers. The womanly ideal forbids it; and it does so on the ground that the womanly ideal is of such supreme worth, to herself and to her children, to her family and to the world, that she ought not to run the risk of losing it for the sake of the largest rewards these competitive careers hold out to the winners.''[35]

From the foregoing it is clear that the ideal place for woman is in the home; that only when a home is out of the question may woman acceptably enter other activities; and that, even when forced to earn all or part of her living, she must be banished from the world of large affairs, for they are ''exclusively masculine occupations'' and to enter them would be to transgress against ''the womanly ideal.''

R. J. Condon, in The Girl in the Home,[36] stressed making ''home life . . . the center of their thoughts and interests . . .'' for the girls of Helena, Montana. This was to be accomplished by teaching ''what a girl needs to know, in relation to herself . . . in relation to the family . . . in relation to her friends . . . home decorations . . . and occupations.'' Under the latter caption were mentioned possible ways of earning money while at home, industry, and economy of expenditures. No occupation seems to have been considered except home-making. The character of instruction may be judged by reference to the list of books recommended for the use of girls.[37]

[35] *Ibid.*

[36] See *The Intelligence*, Jan. 15, 1904, 69–70.

[37] ''*Making Home Happy*, Avery-Stuttle . . .; *Sunshine at Home* . . .; *The Art of Good Manners*, Dare . . .; *What a Young Girl Ought to Know*,

Ex-president Eliot recently expressed a similar view regarding education for home-making. But the number who will not marry and who must earn a living in the world of business has greatly increased. "The secondary and higher education of women has been greatly improved during the past forty years; but it has not been sufficiently affected by the considerations that all women should be prepared in youth for maternity. . . . ." This end he holds to be the one for the loss of which there can be no adequate compensation. "Woman is freer in American Society today than . . ." ever before, and has gained many advantages, but also has faced disadvantages, the greatest being the loss of "the happiest, most informing, and most serviceable occupation of the female sex—the bearing and bringing up of children. . . .

"No accessibility for women to the callings or professions which until recently have been open only to men can compensate women for the loss or stunting of their opportunity for rendering loving and devoted service. No economic gains for women, no better access to the social excitements and so-called pleasures which city life affords, can possibly compensate young women for any impairment of their chances to win the natural joys of normal family life. No social or political service can bring women opportunity to contribute to the real progress and development of mankind comparable with that of the healthy wife and mother who bears and brings up from four to eight children."[38]

Thus it appears, from the foregoing pages, that the maternal, housewifely ideal for women is very persistent. Voluminous quotations might be found to show its prevalence today. Still others might be given to show the new ideal of woman's sphere; for, in spite of protests, she has, willingly or not, been taken from the home, to a very remarkable extent. The family has greatly declined in importance, and the husband in authority. No longer can it be said with truth, as it was in the "Fabulous Forties:"

Wood-Allen . . .;*Nineteen Beautiful Years*, Willard . . .;*Winsome Womanhood*, Sangster . . .; *Our Business Boys and Girls: Art of Good Manners*, Clark-White; *Helps for Ambitious Girls*, Drysdale; *Go right on Girls*, Ryder; *The Five Talents of Women*, Hardy; [and] *"Chats with Girls on Self-Culture*, Chester."—*Ibid.*

[38] Eliot: *A Late Harvest*, 67–8, and 71.

"The father gives his kind command
"The mother joins, approves;
"The children all attentive stand
"And each, obedient, moves."[39]

The schools have attempted to fill the office of foster mother, insofar as instruction is concerned; the nineteenth century has seen the removal of industry from household to factory; and into the school and factory women have gone seeking employment. In the period from the forties to the present, numerous vocations between the two extremes, not so maternal as the office of the school ma'am, not so rigorous as that of factory laborer, have been opened to woman. To this entrance of women into men's domain the Civil War, doubtless, gave considerable impetus. As the ancient jingle put it: "Just take your gun and go; for Ruth can drive the oxen, John, and I can wield the hoe." Into these occupations women have come on an equal competitive basis with men, 'accepting no favor and giving no quarter.' Capital has been no more chivalrous in its treatment of women than it has been humanitarian in its treatment of male workers. They have likewise become highly respected members of the professions. In 1836, there were, according to Miss Martineau, seven occupations open to women; these were teaching, needlework, keeping of boarders, labor in cotton mills, bookbinding, typesetting, and domestic service. But Calhoun points out that this is an error and maintains that there were over a hundred occupations open to women in 1837.[40] Since then they have increased many fold. In 1845, there were 55,828 men and 75,710 women in textile manufactures of the United States. This greater proportion of women as employees appeared in figures for other types of manufacturing as well. But as employers women lagged far behind, only 7,000 being listed.

Dall, in *College, Market and the Court*,[41] mentioned women as employers in the manufacture of gloves, glue, gold and silver leaf work, caps, hose, India rubber, lamps, pickles, preserves, saddles and harness, shoes, snuff, cigars, stocks and suspenders, trusses,

[39] Quoted from J. N. Danforth: *The Token of Friendship, or Home the Center of the Affections*, Boston, 1844, by Minnigerode: *Fabulous Forties*, 74–5.

[40] Calhoun: *Soc. Hist. Am. Family*, II, 182.

[41] Pp. 202–7.

umbrellas, cards, watch crystals; they were also hair weavers, laundresses, leechers, milliners, morocco workers, nurses, paper-hangers, physicians, soda-room keepers, typers and stereotypers, upholsterers, photographers, phonographers, house and sign painters, button makers, fruit hawkers, tobacco packers, box makers, embroiderers, fur sewers; and in the West, reapers and hay-makers.   This was in 1845.

Today, women are to be found in almost every occupation, be it as paid laborer, employer, or professional expert.   They have become politicians, lawyers, consular agents, magistrates, physi-cians, managers of big business, heads of educational institutions, scientists; they even play the dangerous, nerve-racking game of commercial gambling in the stock and grain markets, not to men-tion hazardous bootlegging, in which one woman has achieved the title of "Queen."   Even as men: they have been successes and failures; they have been sympathetic and heartless; wise and in-telligent, as well as ignorant, foolish; corrupt politicians and honest public servants; criminals and law-abiding citizens.   In the varied rôles women have found a place, to an extent that fades the wildest fancies of their grandmothers, and even those of some who advocated woman's freedom to labor.   In 1880, 14.7% of the population ten years of age or over, or 2,647,157, were "gainfully employed" females; in 1900, 18.8% or 5,319,-397, and in 1920, 21.1% or 8,549,511, ten years of age and over, were thus employed.[42]   These figures, certainly, include neither male nor female bootleggers!   Meantime the marriage percent-age for females of all classes in the United States has risen from 56.8% in 1890 to 57% in 1900, 58.9% in 1910, and 60.6% in 1920.   The percentage of married males has risen in the same period from 53.9% to 54.5%, 55.8% and 59.2%.   But, in spite of this increased percentage of unions for all classes, it is true that the home does not function today as a center of interests of children, mothers and fathers, as it did fifty years ago.

III. The Limits of Women's Education

During the first century and a half of our existence on the American continent, little attention was given to the education of women, either in theory or in practice.   The literary and in-

[42] *Abstract of the Fourteenth Census*, 1920, 481.

tellectual interests of Anne Hutchinson, Anne Bradstreet, Mercy
Warren, Elizabeth Ferguson, Deborah Logan, Sussanna Wright,
Hannah Griffitts, and Mrs. Stockton were exceptions to the
rule.[43] The prevailing conception of their intelligence, and the
belief that women were destined for the hearth, effectually
quenched any latent ambition for higher education. Such education as was afforded, if it had any definite goal in this life,
looked towards a satisfactory marriage. The practice herein
reminds one of the experience of the woman missionary who was
teaching a class of Indian girls the parable of the ten virgins:
noticing an amused smile on one burnished face, she learned that
in translation into the Indian tongue the text read that "ten
maids lighted their lanterns and went out to look for a husband."
This was the purpose of woman's education in early days.[44] She
was to be capable in the household; if so, she was acceptable to
man. If, in addition, a woman had attainments of an intellectual sort she might find a husband; but the "learned wife" was
not sought after. Her elementary education in reading, which
was more often provided than any other, was considered desirable for religious purposes.   In 1812 "a friend of the sex" urged
that being "born for a life of uniformity and dependence, what
they have occasion for is reason, sweetness, and sensibility, resources against idleness and languor, moderate desires and no
passions. Were it in your power to give them genius, it would
be almost always a useless and very often a dangerous present.
It would, in general, make them regret the station which Providence has assigned them, or have recourse to unjustifiable ways
to get from it.   The best taste for science only contributes to
make them particular. It takes them away from the simplicity
of their domestic duties, and from general society, of which they
are the loveliest ornament.

"Intended to be at the head of a house, to bring up children
to depend on a master, who will occasionally want their obedience
and their advice, their chief qualifications are to be the love of
order, patience, prudence and rightmindedness."[45] The author
recognizes that "the more agreeable talents" they could add to

[43] Wharton: *Colonial Days and Dames.*

[44] Compare Draper: *American Education*, 258-9.

[45] *Sketches of the History, Genius and Disposition of the Fair Sex*
(anonymous), 262.

these virtues, the better and happier they would be; but he mentions specifically that they are only to taste "elements of parts of learning." So much, apparently, is considered safe and will not make them 'particular.'

It would be a mistake to assume, however, that there were no friends who advocated the higher education of women. Benjamin Rush, DeWitt Clinton, Charles Burroughs, and Thomas Gallaudet, in the latter part of the eighteenth and the early nineteenth centuries, respectively, were firm advocates of the idea. Rush, in his essay, "Thoughts upon Female Education . . ." (1787), declared he considered it proper for them to study English language and grammar, writing, bookkeeping, geography, history, biography, travels, astronomy, natural philosophy and chemistry, in addition to vocal music, religion, dancing, as also, and of first importance, the duties of the house. Yet he says, "I am not enthusiastical upon the subject of education." For he has noticed that a formal education of many superficial accomplishments has in the past been a concomitant, if not indeed a sign of decay, and he prays that one spot of earth may be preserved as a monument to the effects of a good education.[46]

The practical facilities for improving girls' education began to develop about the second quarter of the eighteenth century. The Ursuline Convent for girls was established in New Orleans in 1727 and continues its work to this day. The Bethlehem Female Seminary was established in 1742 in Pennsylvania, and to this, after 1785, came girls from widely separated districts. Other female seminaries and academies sprang up in the latter part of the century and a profusion of them in the first half of the nineteenth.[47] In these day and boarding schools, a formal education of polite accomplishments began to prevail. Certain prominent institutions, such as those at Bethlehem, Philadelphia, Salem, Troy, and Ellicotts Mills, undoubtedly sought to steer clear of too much frippery and urged a more "solid" and "disciplinary" education. The female academy and seminary may be said to have been the prevailing type of institution for girls' education from 1750 to 1865. Large numbers of them secured official recognition from the state; others, quite as important, were not recognized by state charters of incorporation. During

46 *Essays, Moral, Literary and Philosophical*, 89.
47 See Chapters VIII and IX.

the last forty-five years of the period the high school and the normal school, as also many colleges, real and nominal, began to compete for patronage.

The normal school became an important agency[48] because of its specified vocational aim and the need of the public schools for cheap teachers in every state as soon as they were established; whereas the high school, or the seminary, usually intended to give a good English education, with the addition, in some instances, of a year's normal training. Catherine E. Beecher[49] urged that every seminary of the higher sort should have a normal department "in which every young lady may have an opportunity of adding to the advantages of the ordinary course of education, all those peculiar advantages which distinguish a normal school from other institutions. Every woman ought to be trained to act as an educator; and not only so, no woman ever ought to be considered as qualified to become the head of a family till she has been practically exercised in this her highest professional duty." Gallaudet, in the *Connecticut Common School Journal*,[50] declared, "We must, I am persuaded, look more to the other sex for aid in this emergency, and do all in our power to bring forward young women of the necessary qualifications to be engaged in the business of common school instruction."

But while normal schools, and the normal departments of the high schools and seminaries, were devoting their energies towards procuring a solid and useful education, the ordinary course of the seminaries, leading to the M. P. L., M. F. A., and the M. P. A. degrees, was tending more and more to formal accomplishments. Criticism of this tendency became common in North and South. Margaret Fuller fitly described the education of her sex: "Women are now [1839] taught, at school, all that men are. They run over, specifically, even *more* studies, without being really taught anything. . . . Women learn without any attempt to reproduce [their learning in active life as men do]. Their only reproduction is for purpose of display."[51]

Hundley, in his *Social Relations in our Southern States* (1860),[52] stated that "the daughters are often quite uneducated

48 See Chapter X.
49 See the *True Remedy for the Wrongs of Women*, 56–8.
50 I, 10.
51 Howe: *Margaret Fuller*, 83.
52 Pp. 72 and 100.

in the current literature of the times, and in all things else evince a simplicity of mind and character altogether refreshing. Sometimes, 'tis true, they are sent to Boarding Schools (which are becoming more common in the South of late years), are there exposed to a false and shallow system of hot-bed culture for a few sessions; and emerging therefrom in due time make their debut in life, possessed of fully as much pride and affectation, as well as conceit and vanity, as of artificial graces of person and manner; and boasting a superficial knowledge of twenty different branches of learning, but in reality having a perfect mastery and comprehension of none.''

Beecher declared[53] that women were not trained for their professions—*i.e.*, to be housekeepers, wives, mothers, nurses of young children, seamstresses, and domestics—but rather showered with tinsel that distracted their attention from their proper work. Samuel Lewis, speaking for Ohio, expressed the same sentiment: We do not ''furnish instruction for females, at all adapted to their sphere in life, or such as will be likely to elevate their views, refine their taste and cultivate that delicacy of sentiment and propriety of conduct which the good of the country, no less than their own happiness, requires. It should be kept in mind that the females in our schools will be the mothers of the next generation, and what shall be the character of that generation depends on what education we furnish to the present.''[54]   A satirical thrust at the formal ''finishing school'' education, made to appeal to a more popular audience, appeared in *Harper's New Monthly Magazine* in 1858:[55]

''With a spick and span new, superfine education,
''Befitting a maid of such fortunate station,
''Miss Mary Degai had just made her debut,
    ''From the very select,
        ''Genteel, circumspect,
''Establishment kept by—it can not be wrong
''Just to mention the name—by one Madame Cancan.
''This Madame Cancan was a perfect Parisian,
''Her morals infernal, her manners elysian.

''She was slender and graceful and rouged with much art,
''A mistress of dumb show, from ogle to start.

[53] *Harper's New Monthly Magazine*, XXIX (1864), 766.
[54] *Com. Sch. Jour.*, I, 69.
[55] P. 434.

"Her voice was delightful, her teeth not her own—
"And, a cane-bottomed chair when she sat seemed a throne.
"In short, this dear, elegant Madame Cancan
"Was like a French dinner at some restaurant—
"That is, she completely was made a la carte,
"And I think she'd a truffle instead of a heart!
"But then what good rearing she gave to her pupils!
"They dressed like those elegant ladies at Goupil's
"One sees in the prints just imported from France;
"With what marvelous grace did they join in the dance!
"No Puritan modesty marred their tournure—
"Being modest is nearly as bad as being poor—
"No shudder attacked them when man laid his hand on
"Their waists in the Redowa's graceful abandon,
"As they swung in that waltz to voluptuous music;
          "Ah! did we but see
          "Our sisters so free,
"I warrant the sight would make both me and you sick!
"Thus no trouble was spared through these young misses' lives
"To make them good partners, and—very bad wives."

The above criticisms were aimed at formal accomplishments
which occupied so much time in schools. Yet Mrs. Phelps (1833),
and others, urged that daughters should be sent to schools
rather than taught in the home: "We see, then, that however
beautiful in theory it may be to educate girls at home, it is not
easy in practice. The mother herself who sets out with the resolution to persevere in teaching her child, or in superintending
her education, will at length feel that there are difficulties and
evils growing out of her excessive anxiety. . . ."[56] Brackett also
held that there was something of a discipline and social responsibility given in the school which could never be obtained at home,
and that the schools that advertised themselves as "like homes"
simply did not know what either the home or the school should
be.[57]
Many who were interested in girls' education at boarding
schools sought to reform their showy proclivities by urging an
attention to the discipline of the mind. Mrs. Phelps[58] regarded
the mind as a garden, wherein are planted the seeds of various
faculties which are to be improved by cultivation. Thus she ex-

[56] Phelps: *Lectures to Young Ladies*, 35–6.
[57] *Woman and the Higher Education* (1892), 164–5.
[58] *Op. cit.*, 69–70.

plained in *Hours with My Pupils*:[59] "We would not be instrumental in educating masculine women, but we seek to enlighten, refine and elevate the female mind and character." Butler found "the great uses of study to a woman are to enable her to regulate her own mind . . .";[60] and Todd believed the discipline of such faculties as memory, attention, and reason to be the most important end of a girl's training.[61]   Brackett also, in 1892, found the purpose, in the last analysis, was to make the girl "level-headed."[62]

As the belief in the discipline of 'solid' studies rose to its height—and this received a great impetus with the establishment of the first genuine colleges, for the most part after the war—the zeal for the lighter accomplishments subsided to a considerable degree. For the decline of interest in embroidery, fine stitching, and other arts which had occupied our grandmothers, Woolson assigned the economic reason, the cheapness and rapidity of manufacture of substitutes by machine production: "Machinery now produces finer stuffs than any we could fabricate at home with shuttle and thread; and it supplies, also, the greater part of the ornaments to be added, in the form of braids, gimps, cords and ribbons. The sewing of silk into traceries of flowers, leaves, and other designs, is too wearisome for these busy days; and though fashion endeavors now and then to revive it, it is fast becoming an obsolete art, except as a matter of purchased labor. A simple process of braiding is the most we now attempt: and even that is put on by household sewing-machines, over a pattern stamped by an invented process. The delicate arabesques in tambour cotton on muslin and cambric, over which our mothers spent so many precious hours of their youth, no longer flourish, when French products of this kind are so beautiful, and those of Hamburg machines so cheap; and the picturing of bouquets in silk floss, once so popular, meets with the same neglect. Indelible ink has made the old-fashioned samplers superfluous, since there is now no need to stitch through the alphabet, preparatory to the marking of clothes. Embroidery, then, properly so called, may be reckoned as a lost accomplishment.

[59] (1841), pp. 31-2.
[60] *The American Lady* (1851), 156-7.
[61] *The Daughter at School* (1854), 11–17, 37–9, 39–41, 44–6.
[62] *Woman and the Higher Education*, 177–8.

"Worsted work has taken its place; but it is an unworthy successor; for while the embroideries of early times require some originality of design and artistic skill, this, whether it be canvaswork or crocheting, aims at nothing better than the servile copying of a purchased pattern. And when manufacturers have gone so far as to supply the market with figures already complete, leaving nothing to be done but the filling in of a uniform background, we may consider it as the amusement of children. Any woman possessing the ordinary modicum of brains should seek a higher employment for elegant leisure; for this not only stupefies thought, but impairs the eyesight and injures health. And to a cultivated taste, the product of such toil can never be half as beautiful as a square of silk damask or brocade."[63]

To provide a cure for the "want of reasoning capability, impetuosity in forming judgments," and the "irresolute pertinacity" of the female sex, E. L. S. argued, in *The Nation,* that the step then in progress seemed most practicable; that is, to "give our daughters the mental discipline and the breadth of outlook which young men get in a good college. . . ."[64] Beecher, in her *True Remedy* (1851),[65] had urged the necessity of "permanent female institutions on the college system." This step had been taken some time previously, technically at least. Oberlin (Ohio), for nearly fifty years, and Macon (Georgia), Perkiomen Bridge (Pennsylvania) and Poughkeepsie (New York), for shorter periods, had been seats of a women's education which aimed to be, though it was not, the equivalent of that in men's colleges. In 1852, the American Women's Educational Association had been formed, having as its purposes the uniting of "American women of all sects and parties in an effort to secure to their sex a liberal education, honorable position, and remunerative employment in the appropriate profession of woman, this profession being considered as embracing the training of the human mind, the care of the human body in infancy and sickness, and the conservation and domestic economy of the family state"; this they held could be accomplished best by "endowed institutions for women in which the college plan of organization shall be adopted. . . ." *Godey's Lady's Book*

[63] *Woman in Am. Soc.* (1873), 57-9.
[64] XXIX (1879), 365.
[65] Pp. 52-5.

remarked, reassuringly, that "it will be seen that the purpose of the association is by no means to transplant women from the position which Divine Providence has assigned them."[66]

But if domestic ends were prominent in the statement of the Association, it must be recalled that the women's colleges which were actually created attempted to imitate, as nearly as possible, the formal curriculum of the men's college—so much so, that it has led to arguments as to priority of establishment. It has been urged that certain women's colleges were not truly colleges because they did not have the standard men's college curriculum.[67] There was some reason for such a standard, of course, for did not the woman's college aim at the degree; and must not the degree represent a standard value or accomplishment? Why should a woman not receive the degree, if she did the same work? This question, in doggerel, appeared in *Littell's Living Age*.[68]

> "Ye fusty old fogies, Professors by name,
> "A deed you've been doing, of sorrow and shame:
> "Though placed in your chairs to spread knowledge abroad,
> "Against half of mankind you would shut up the road.
> "The fair sex from science you seek to withdraw
> "By enforcing against them a strict Salic law:
> "Is it fear? is it envy? or what can it be?
> "And why should a woman not get a degree?"

Significant, indeed, is the change of attitude on the part of those promoting the idea of women's education from the early part of the century to the end of it. The establishment of the "female college" encouraged a greater independence on the part of women. In 1819, when Mrs. Willard put her "plan for improving female education" before the legislature of New York, she appealed to the "enlightened politicians"; whereas Maria Mitchell, about sixty years later, declared that all women desired was the enlightenment of their present rulers.

Some proponents of woman's collegiate education[69] urged that the higher mental culture would not only *not* take women away from the home, but would make them better companions. "How often you find wives complaining that their husbands are taken

---

[66] September, 1855, 276–7.
[67] See *Before Vassar Opened*, 1–80.
[68] (1869) C, 578—copied from *Blackwood's Magazine*.
[69] See, for example, *The Nation*, XLIII (1886), 96.

up with their books, and have not a word for them.   This is because the wives don't care for what the books contain; they have no liking nor knowledge of these things, and their husbands find nothing to say to them." But if specific objectives of the above sort made an appeal to some, the great purpose of a college education was held by most to be the discipline of powers of observation, reflection, perception, attention, memory, and reason. "We do not aim to train a woman for a sphere, profession or calling"[70] represents the view of many college presidents of the past century and the present. "When men complete the college curriculum they rarely have definite ideas of what course they will pursue. Why should women be expected to have definite plans? All must await developments, and whatever those developments may be, the college bred woman is better equipped to meet them."[71] This was written in 1893. The tendency of the newer college education was doubtless the target of the satirical sonnet:

"I idolize the *Ladies*! They are fairies,
"That spiritualize this world of ours;
"From heavenly hot-beds most delightful flowers,
"Or choice cream-cheeses from celestial dairies,
"But learning, in its barbarous seminaries,
"Gives the dear creatures many wretched hours,
"And on their gossamer intellect sternly showers
"SCIENCE, with all its horrid accessaries.
"Now, seriously, the only things, I think
"In which young ladies should instructed be,
"Are—stocking-mending, love, and cookery!—
"Accomplishments that very soon will sink,
"Since Fluxions now, and Sanscrit conversation,
"Always form part of female education!"[72]

The criticism of this exclusive attention to a formal cultivation of the faculties appears often, especially in later years. In 1874, Beecher[73] quoted the following criticism of women's education by Greeley:

"I go into one of our public schools, and before me are boys who are to work in shops or mills or till the soil all their lives,

[70] McCabe: *American Girl at College*, 4–5, and 14.
[71] *Ibid.*
[72] Quoted by Hamilton in *A New Atmosphere*, 48–51.
[73] *Educational Reminiscences*, 178–9.

and there are girls who are to be wives and mothers of farmers and mechanics; to cook, sew, darn, wash, starch, and make butter and cheese; and when I see them studying Algebra and Trigonometry and Logarithms, and making astronomical calculations, I ask, not whether such studies are not useful for some purposes and persons, but whether this does not preclude or take the place of what would be more useful, what they will urgently need to know, and what would perhaps equally tend to mental discipline and growth. If they were studying Sanscrit or Russian I should not say such knowledge is not desirable, but I should say they gain this by neglecting what would be far more useful in after life.

"Let me illustrate: There are thousands in this city of virtuous amiable women who can earn only a pauper's livelihood by long protracted labor, and often in unhealthful circumstances. Some of them have invalid parents or sisters or little children to support, or wish to educate a dependent young brother or sister. But they have been *trained* to no particular business, while every place that pays will find enough who are trained. I profoundly pity the noble and helpless thousands whose life is without joy and whose future is without hope, and I protest against the false training all over our land that is rearing thousands more to push them into untimely graves. But how is this to be remedied? I reply, by so transforming our current education that every woman shall be *trained to do well one or more useful things* which will be always in demand, and also by striving to educate the popular mind to consider *all useful work honorable*.

"This very day there are thousands of refined and expensively educated women vainly seeking employment. Yet every one of them could find employment and high wages had she been trained to be a skillful and scientific cook. Our cooking now is done chiefly by the ignorant, and the results are simply abominable. Our city spends yearly fifty million for food, and at least ten million is squandered in bad and wasteful cooking, beside the waste of health and comfort."

In 1900, Edward Bok declared:

"There is no doubt that the average girls' college would be more useful to girls themselves, and to American domestic life in general, if the practical components of a woman's life entered a

little more into its curriculum. Girls are turned out by our colleges with diplomas telling us how efficient they were in the
physiology class, and yet they have absolutely no practical knowledge of their own healthful dressing or hygienic eating. I must
confess that in my editorial experience I have come across more
atrocious chirography in letters from college girls than I would
have believed possible. Some day our girls' colleges will wake
up to the fact that for a girl to be able to write an intelligent
letter, properly punctuated, and in a handwriting which does
not drive a man clear to profanity, is likely to be of more value
to her than the gift to glibly decline a Latin verb. It is a better
mixture of the practical with the less useful that is needed in the
management of girls' colleges. As it is now, the college gives a
girl only mental resources. It should go further, and give her
also a fund of practical knowledge from which to draw when she
becomes a wife, a mother, and a homekeeper. That is the field
for the women's colleges—not, by any means, becoming mere
practical outfitters, but adding the practical to the mental.' "[74]

These criticisms have been popular. In fact, any criticism of
the college is popular today. In spite of them, colleges continue
to study many subjects that seem useless to some people. This
practice of college faculties probably will continue. It is, nevertheless, true that many practical subjects have crept into college
curricula and are credited towards the coveted degree. The
effect of this wide extension of the elective principle, combined
with the increasing wealth of America, is largely responsible for
the fact that the matriculates at our higher institutions have increased phenomenally, whereas the students have not.

IV. Political Freedom

In a fourth field, that of political affairs, a change has occurred
in the past seventy-five years, equal at least to the transformation
of views as to woman's intelligence, her household sphere, and
her education. Not only do women now vote, but they are police
magistrates, mayors, representatives in legislative halls, and governors of states. To obtain this measure of equal participation
in the government they were taxed to support required a long
struggle, more severe than that to acquire an education or a place

[74] *Jour. of Education* (1900), LII, 85.

in commerce and industry. Woman's admission to the educated world was, no doubt, one of the most significant steps, for from this position of vantage she could more intelligently work for her political freedom. Edward Everett viewed her opportunity for education as extremely important, declaring that, "with the acknowledged equality of women in general intellectual endowments . . . with her admitted superiority to man in tact, sensibility, physical and moral endurance, quickness of perception, and power of accommodation to circumstances, give her for two or three generations equal advantages of mental culture, and the lords of creation will have to carry more guns than they do at present, to keep her out of the enjoyment of anything which sound reasoning and fair experiment shall show to be of her rights."[75]

So much for a prophecy. The real problem of women was to gain a new freedom—freedom to be themselves. It was generally urged by anti-suffragists that those who would vote were only cheap imitators of men. There is little to support such a contention save the obvious fact that some women affected a superficial imitation of men's clothing.

To support the opposite view there is the ringing note that is found in suffragist speeches, pamphlets, and books, in favor of woman's freedom to find herself. This spirit is perhaps best typified in the declaration of independence adopted by the Woman's Rights Convention at Seneca Falls in 1848. Herein it was declared that "in view of this entire disfranchisement of one half of the people of this country, their social and religious degradation, in view of the unjust laws above mentioned, and because women do feel themselves aggrieved, oppressed, and fraudulently deprived of their most sacred rights, therefore they do insist upon an immediate admission into all the rights and privileges which belong to them as citizens of these United States. . . ." A more humorous view of the movement for woman's freedom was presented in "The Times That Try Men's Souls," written by Maria W. Chapman and read at the convention.[76]

The desire for individual freedom as a woman, not merely as a citizen, was voiced in the work of Dora Marsden, who at the

[75] Quoted in R. C. E. (1867-8), 384.

[76] For an interesting account of the convention, giving text of resolutions, etc., consult Littell's Living Age (1848), XVIII, 423-4.

same time called attention to the reason behind the conservative attitude towards such freedom. She declared the difference between bond women and free women to be that the former "are not spiritual entities . . . are not individuals." They complement and "round off the personality of some other individual." "Women as a whole have shown nothing save 'servant' attributes." Now they demand to be free, to be individuals, to be themselves rather than complements to someone else; and it is this that conservative men fear. Their fear is that which "an engineer would have in guaranteeing an arch equal to a strain above its strength."[77]

Anne B. Hamman declared that "no one who understands the feminist movement, or who knows the soul of a real new woman would make the mistake of supposing that the modern woman is fighting for the vote, for education, and for economic freedom, because she wants to be a man. That idea is the invention of masculine intelligence. Woman is fighting today, as she has all the way up through the ages, for freedom to be a woman."[78] She acknowledges the importance of woman in the home, but maintains that, at present, women have to win battles for their homes in the fields of business and politics:

"Women's sphere is the home. Granted, gladly. But that no longer means that woman's sphere lies within the four walls of her own house. There is not a phase of home-making in our complex modern life that does not bring a woman into contact with the business of the outside world. It is her duty to see that her household has wholesome food. This means dealing with the beef trust, the ice trust, the milk trust, the health board, the makers of the pure food laws. It is her duty to educate her little children. She is then concerned with educational boards and commissions, with the sanitation of schoolhouses, with the laws regulating immigration, and the treatment of contagious diseases. In a word, her feminine duties bring her into direct contact with 'big business' and politics. The problems of the home can not be settled by the individual woman, working for her own husband, her own home, her own children. They can only be solved

[77] Quoted in Dell: *Women as World Builders*, 93-6, and 103-4; similar views were also expressed by Emma Goldman.

[78] From her answer to an article by Prof. Beyer—See the *Educational Review* (1914), XLVII, 296-7.

by all women—and men—working together for all homes and all children. This means not less motherhood, but broader motherhood, for women. Thousands of women who have no children are doing mother-work in the world for everybody's children. No mother heart will be afraid of the ballot if with it she can bring about better conditions for the coming generations.

"Woman is demanding that she be free to marry the man of her choice, free to rear beautiful, healthy children in happy homes. A woman is not free to choose her mate so long as she must choose someone. So long as home-making in the narrow sense is the only occupation open to her, she is forced to marry. Therefore she must have the possibility of useful labor and self-support until she meets the man she wishes to marry."[79]   Only by means of such independence can she be free to avoid such a marriage as that referred to in "The World Is All Awry," used some forty or fifty years ago when suffragists were far from their goal:

> "Rare women who would stir the world
> "If they only had a chance,
> "Are busy sewing patches
> "On a worthless husband's pants;
> "For it so frequently occurs
> "That the gods will strangely plan
> "To wed an all-gold woman
> "To a hollow pewter man."[80]

One of the most favored means of attack upon the position of the conservative anti-suffragists was ridicule. This was used freely by both sides, but the position of the latter appears to have been most open to such attacks. Alice Miller's *Are Women People?* Stetson's *In This Our World,* and Higginson's article, "Ought Women to Learn the Alphabet?" which was published in the *Atlantic Monthly,*[81] may have carried as much convincement as the staider arguments by Lucretia Mott, E. C. Stanton, and others.

Higginson summarized Sylvain Marechal's "Plan for a Law Prohibiting the Alphabet to Women"—which had, in 1801, been suggested to Napoleon when he was about to remodel religion, government, and education—and then asked ironically whether

[79] *Ibid.*
[80] Quoted in the [Philadelphia] *Evening Public Ledger.*
[81] (1859) III, 137 *ff.*

the recent events in our several states—the concession by most states of the right of married women to hold property; the granting of control over their earnings in Maine, Massachusetts, Connecticut, and Pennsylvania; and the extension of suffrage in some questions, especially educational, in some—did not warrant the belief that these evils were the fruits of learning. "Surely," he said, "here and now, might poor Mr. Marechal exclaim, the bitter fruits of the original seed appear, and the sad question recurs, whether women ought ever to have tasted of the alphabet. . . ."[82] Stetson gave pointed expression to a thought as old as Plato, and seriously proposed by Olive Schreiner; namely, that women should, like other female creatures, be accepted as co-workers, rather than forced to be parasites:

> "The female fox she is a fox;
> "The female whale a whale;
> "The female eagle holds her place
> "As representative of the race
> "As truly as the male.

> "The mother hen doth scratch for her chicks,
> "And scratch for herself beside;
> "The mother cow doth nurse her calf,
> "Yet fares as well as her other half
> "In the pasture free and wide.

> "The female bird doth soar in air;
> "The female fish doth swim;
> "The fleet-foot mare upon the course
> "Doth hold her own with the flying horse—
> "Yea, and she beateth him!

> "One female in the world we find
> "Telling a different tale.
> "It is the female of our race,
> "Who holds a parasitic place
> "Dependent on the male."[83]

Mrs. Gilman also satirized the dominion of the male, and the submissive docility of the female:

> " 'O come and be my mate!' said the Eagle to the Hen;
> " 'I love to soar, but then
> " 'I want my mate to rest
> " 'Forever in the nest!'

[82] *Ibid.*

[83] From the poem "Females" in Stetson: *In This Our World,* 169-71.

YORK COLLEGE PENNSYLVANIA LIBRARY

55996

"Said the Hen, 'I cannot fly
" 'I have no wish to try,
" 'But I joy to see my mate careering through the sky!'
"They wed, and cried, 'Ah, this is love, my own!'
"And the Hen sat, and the Eagle soared, alone."

Alice Miller, in "A Consistent Anti to Her Son," ridiculed the idea that women could not, because of their refined nature, run the risk of the moral and physical dangers that would beset them at the polls.[84]   The view was suggested, to name one instance, by Crothers: "Lost, somewhere on the road to the polls, by twentieth-century women, the chivalrous deference that once was theirs.   This heirloom of mediaeval workmanship was highly valued for its associations."[85]

Against the arguments for freedom, only suggested in the preceding pages, there was the universal practice of limiting woman to her "proper" sphere, denying her political privileges.   There were almost none in the eighteenth century to sustain the views of Mrs. Adams that American independence should have won and secured the privilege of freedom for American women, as well as for men.   The early nineteenth century, while marked by the appearance of many able advocates for woman's education, cannot boast the names of many political emancipators.   Rush, Burroughs, Carter, Mann, Gallaudet, and Catherine Beecher were content, for the most part, to take the one step to a better education.   Coxe, in her *Claims of Our Country on American Females* (1842), had little sympathy for political emancipation. The ultra reformers who had "raised their banners, ostensibly in the cause of injured woman," she thought, had argued so ingeniously and plausibly "that many ambitious and unprincipled, as well as injudicious minds . . . " had been allured to their standards.   It is not woman's duty to rail at the position to which she has been assigned, but rather to prepare herself for it.[86]   Forty years later Eliot, in *The North American Review*, appeared gravely concerned over the fact that "girls are being prepared daily, by 'superior education,' to engage, not in child bearing and house work, but in clerkships, telegraphy, newspaper writing, school teaching, etc.   And many are learning to believe

[84] Miller: *Are Women People?* 11–12.
[85] Crothers: *Meditations on Votes for Women* (1914), 62.
[86] *Op. cit.*, 15–16, and 34.

that, if they can but have their 'rights,' they will be enabled to compete with men at the bar, in the pulpit, the Senate, the bench."[87]   Dana, in *Woman's Possibilities and Limitations* (1899.), was inclined to the opinion that woman has been a most potent influence for good in the past and that "she can do vastly more; and that, too, without interfering with home, and without detracting from the charm of her womanly personality." "Why should it be thought necessary for her to step into man's place in order that she may discharge her duties to the State?"[88]

The loss of "womanly charm" has apparently been most feared by the opponents of woman's taking part in politics and most carefully guarded against by the advocates of the same. At the present moment, when some of the ends which they sought have been won, when women convene upon every conceivable pretext in all parts of the world, it is urged that the retention of womanly character is essential, and possible, in the bustling world of business and politics. Jane Addams is reported recently to have said: "Imitating men is only a little worse than being suppressed by them. . . . Women must not lose the essentially feminine qualities. Masculine women are not emancipated, as they seem to think. The important thing for women to learn is to express themselves."[89]

[87] August, 1882.

[88] *Op. cit.*, 88–90.

[89] As reported in the [Philadelphia] *Evening Public Ledger*, March 27, 1924.

CHAPTER IV

EARLY EDUCATION OF GIRLS IN NEW ENGLAND

I. Religious Influence

The New England girl of the Colonial period was born into a deeply religious atmosphere, charged with a goodly measure of harsh theology that swiftly disposed of childhood. Fear of the Lord seems, by these old ancestors of ours, to have been held to be the "beginning of wisdom"—if not indeed both the beginning and the end. The drab character of such literature as came from women's pens, as well as men's, is accounted for by the dreary theological conceptions as well as by the hardness of their life in an almost unbroken wilderness. Even the sunny soul of little Phillis Wheatley was unable to break away from the sinister motif of her Puritan religion:

> "Then begging for the spirit of our God
> "And panting eager for the same abode
> "Come, let us all with the same vigour rise
> "And take a prospect of the blissful skies."[1]

This was written at the period of the Revolution, when education for girls was becoming much more common and religious conceptions were much less harsh than a century before. The fears that crowded the timid little souls are suggested in the words of Judge Sewall, wherein he described the anxieties of Betty, his daughter. She had first been touched by reading a sermon entitled, "Ye shall seek me and shall not find me," and also by the sentiment expressed therein that "Ye shall seek me and die in your sins." Mather's question, "Why hath Satan filled thy heart?" also perturbed her. Asked whether she prayed, she said she did but was afraid her prayers were unanswered. Later, Sewall says, she told him she "was afraid she should go to Hell" and asked him to pray to God to "pardon her Sin and give her a new heart"; and he adds, "I answerd her

[1] From "On the Death of Rev. Dr. Sewall" (1769), in the *Poems and Letters of Phillis Wheatley*, 35.

Fears as well as I could, and prayd with many Tears on either part; hope God heard us."[2]

Calhoun quotes the words of Cotton Mather, who wrote thus of his little girl: "I took my little daughter Katy (aged four) into my study and there told my child that I am to die shortly and she must, when I am dead, remember everything I now said unto her. I set before her the sinful condition of her nature and charged her to pray in secret places every day. That God for the sake of Jesus Christ would give her a new heart. . . . I gave her to understand that when I am taken from her she must look to meet with more humbling afflictions than she does now she has a tender father to provide for her."[3]

The sermons of great length which were heard on Sunday frequently constituted, in published form, their only diversion in literature, and one cannot wonder at the fact that children were wrought up to a fearful pitch. There were then no amusing tales of the doings of *Three Little Pigs, Town Mouse and Country Mouse,* or *How Little Topknot Lost Her Topknot.* These would have been considered, if not bad, at any rate useless, because they lacked the moral teachings so much desired. Mather's work, called *Some examples of Children in whom the fear of God was remarkably Budding before they died; in Several Parts of New England,* or Wigglesworth's *Day of Doom* were much preferred. There were others called *The Prodigal daughter or the disobedient Lady Reclaimed* and *Examples of Youthful Piety.* The *Day of Doom,* no doubt, expressed the conception of infant damnation adequately:

> "Then to the Bar all they drew near
> "who died in infancy,
> "And never had or good or bad
> "effected pers'nally;
> "But from the womb unto the tomb
> "were straightway carried,
> "(Or at the least ere they transgress'd)
> "who thus began to plead:
>
> " 'If for our own transgression,
> " 'or disobedience,
> " 'We here did stand at thy left hand,

[2] Van Doren: *Sewall's Diary,* 130, 132.

[3] Reprinted by permission of the publishers, The Arthur H. Clark Company, from Calhoun's *Social History of the American Family,* I, 108-9.

" ' just were the Recompense;
" ' But Adam's guilt our souls hath spilt,
" ' his fault is charg'd upon us;
" ' And that alone hath overthrown
" ' and utterly undone us.

" ' Not we, but he ate of the Tree,
" ' whose fruit was interdicted;
" ' Yet on us all of his sad Fall
" ' the punishment's inflicted.
" ' How could we sin that had not been,
" ' or how is his sin our,
" ' Without consent, which to prevent
" ' we never had the pow'r?' "

But the only answer of the stern judge to their plea is:

" ' A crime it is, therefore in bliss
" ' You may not hope to dwell;
" ' But unto you I shall allow
" ' The easiest room in hell'

* * *

" Yea now it would be good they could
" themselves annihilate,
" And cease to be, themselves to free
" from such a fearful state.
" O happy Dogs, and Swine, and Frogs,
" yea, Serpent's generation!
" Who do not fear this doom to hear,
" and sentence of Damnation!"[4]

Perhaps the Puritan maiden also dipped into the *Spiritual
Milk for Babes.* Then there was the old *Bay Psalm Book* (1640)
whose "groanings" must have filled her heart:

" All my desires before thee, Lord;
" Nor is my groaning hid from thee.
" My heart doth pant, my strength me fails
" And mine eye sight is gone from mee."

Again the lament:

" My heart is smote, & dyde like grasse,
" that I to eate my bread forget:
" By reason of my groanings voyce
" my bones into my skin are set.
" Like Pelican in wildernes,

[4] Wigglesworth: *The Day of Doom*, 68–73.

> "like Owle in desart so am I:
> "I watch, & like a sparrow am
> "on house top solitarily."[5]

In the eighteenth century there was a gradual introduction of some Mother Goose rhymes. A family collection belonging to Mrs. James A. Holmes, Long-meadow, contains a number of titles in lighter vein, such as *A Pretty Plaything* (1794), and *Tom Thumb Folio, or a New Plaything for Little Giants.* In this family of the late eighteenth century, little Jemima possessed for heavier reading a 1799 edition of the Bible, an *American Spelling Book,* 15th edition, and a copy of *Rural Felicity or the History of Tommy and Sally.* For the doleful pages of the old *Bay Psalm Book* there had been substituted the more cheerful hymns of Isaac Watts, *Divine Songs attempted in Easy Language for the Use of Children* (1790).[6] But if there is a more cheerful note in the books for children, it is quite true that moral and religious sentiments still occupy a great place. These lines illustrate the character of the contents:

> "I must pray
> "Both night and day
> "Before I eat
> "I must entreat
> "That God would bless
> "To me my meat.

> * * *

> "It is a sin
> "To steal a pin
> "Much more to steal
> "A greater thing
> "I'll beg my bread
> "from Door to door
> "Rather than steal
> "My neighbor's store."[7]

In the period of the Revolution we still find a rather terrifying note in sermons to children. A Boston schoolgirl, of 1771, reports to her family, as nearly as she can remember, the gist of

[5] Facsimile ed. of the *Bay Psalm Book.* Dodd & Mead: New York, 1903.
[6] See a list of books mentioned in the (Sunday) *Springfield Republican,* May 11, 1924.
[7] *Ibid.*

the preacher's (Mr. Beacon's) message: "He said he would lastly address himself to the young people; My dear young friends you are pleased with beauty, and like to be thought beautiful but let me tell ye—you'll never be truly beautiful till you are like the King's daughter, all glorious within. All the ornaments you can put on while your souls are unholy make you the more like whited sepulchres garnished without, but full of deformity within. You think me very impolite to address you in this manner but I must go a little further and tell you, how coarse soever it may sound to your delicacy, that while you are without holiness your beauty is deformity—you are all over black and defiled, ugly and loathsome to all holy beings, the wrath of the great God lies upon you and if you die in this condition you will be turned into hell with ugly devils, to eternity.

"My aunt says a miss . . . can't possibly do justice to the subject in Divinity and therefore had better not attempt a repetition of particulars that she finds lie (as may easily be concluded) somewhat confusedly in my young mind."[8]

Etiquette for children is indicated in a suggestive little book, quoted by Calhoun in his *Social History of the American Family*: "Never sit down at the table till asked, and after the blessing. Ask for nothing; tarry till it be offered thee. Speak not. Bite not thy bread but break it. Take salt only with a clean knife. Dip not the meat in the same. Hold not thy knife upright but sloping, and lay it down at right hand of plate with blade on plate. Look not earnestly at any other that is eating. When moderately satisfied leave the table. Sing not, hum not, wriggle not. Spit nowhere in the room but in the corner. . . . When any speak to thee, stand up. Say not I have heard it before. Never endeavor to help him out if he tell it not right. Snigger not; never question the truth of it."[9]

II. *Attitude Towards Learning*

The attitude of Puritan New England towards intellectual improvement on the part of woman was decidedly unfavorable. It has given rise to the statement that the hardest lot of New

[8] *Atlantic Monthly*, August, 1893, 220.
[9] Reprinted by permission of the publishers, The Arthur H. Clark Company, from Calhoun's *Social History of the American Family*, I, 112–13.

England mothers was that they had to live with the Puritan fathers! The daily attentive study of the Holy Scriptures, which were held to be the true source of all wisdom and discretion, was certainly a general practice, but mental improvement went little beyond this limit. Even in this field of devout learning woman was forbidden to wander far, for she had to accept views upon authority. Contrary views were apt to get her into trouble. The injunction of St. Paul, "I permit not a woman to teach," was enforced in the case of Anne Hutchinson. It was the sober judgment of the best minds "that though women might meet (some few together) to pray and edify one another; yet such a set assembly, (as was then in practice at Boston,) where sixty or more did meet every week, and one woman (in a prophetical way, by resolving questions of doctrine, and expounding scripture) took upon her the whole exercise, was agreed to be disorderly, and without rule."[10]

It is possible that this historic incident was not without influence in shaping the attitude of the colonists towards women's education. Perhaps it would be better to say it confirmed a belief, long impressed by practice, that women's minds were not strong enough for learning:[11] that they easily became unbalanced in the pursuit of abstract ideas. It was, at least, upon the assumption that learning for women was unnecessary that the colonists acted; and even as late as the Revolutionary period, Mrs. Adams could not but lament that it was fashionable to ridicule "female learning." Indeed, most young ladies who possessed intellectual charms must have been able to summarize their attainments with the familiar couplet, as did she:

"The little learning I have gained
"Is all from simple nature drained."

A dialogue of 1744, which "may serve for any part of New England," suggests the stiff-necked character of the opponents of education for girls and portrays the longing of some mothers for accomplishments for their daughters. The wife insists:

[10] Winthrop: *Hist. of New England*, I, 240.

[11] Eliza Southgate, as late as 1804, commented on the still prevailing view: "Sprightliness is in favor of females and profundity of males. . . . I found the mind of a female, if such a thing existed, was thought not worth cultivating."—Cook: *A Girl's Life Eighty Years Ago*, 56–9.

"My dear, you'll breed this girl a very fool,
"Why don't you put her to the dancing-school?
"See how she holds her head and treads her toes,
"Like a meer Bumpkin, when she stands or goes
"Is so shame-fac'd, tho' enter'd in her teens
"That she looks downward, like a sow in beans
"Prithee, my dear, consider and bestow
"Good breeding on her for a year or two."

But the husband declares he likes—

"... to see
"Young maidens full of bashful modesty
"If that's her only fault, 'e faith, my pence
"Shall never fly to teach her confidence
"'Tis hard to find a girl but learns that faster
"Than it is fit she should without a master"

Rather than send her to a dancing school,

"Prithee, good madam, let her first be able
"To read a chapter truly in the Bible,
"That she may'nt mispronounce God's people, popel,
"Nor read Cunstable for Constantinople;
"Make her expert and ready at her prayers
"That God may keep her from the devil's snares;
"Teach her what's useful, how to shun deluding
"To roast, to toast, to boil and mix a pudding
"To knit, to spin, to sew, to make or mend,
"To scrub, to rub, to earn and not to spend,
"I tell thee wife, once more, I'll have her bred
"To book'ry, cook'ry, thimble, needle, thread
"First teach her these, and then the pritty fool,
"Shall jig her crupper at the dancing school."

Now the wife uses the deadly argument that their inferior neighbors are educating *their* daughters; and history witnesses that, eventually, she won the debate.

"You see my neighbor Grub, that sorry fool
"Can keep his daughter at a boarding-school;
"Nay Smug the Smith gives all his children breeding
"And sends them out to writing and to reading;
"I'm sure we live as well, and save as much,
"Why should you then so small a matter grudge?
"Prithee consent, you'l ne'er the sooner break
"'Tis hard we cannot scrape for one poor chick
"An only daughter, and a hopeful girl,
"Who if she'd breeding might deserve an Earl.''[12]

[12] *Boston Ev. Post*, Dec. 10, 1744.

In this early period any education higher than that secured in the dame school must have come through individual effort, writing and reading in private. Abigail Smith's lack of schooling was due not only to lack of facilities near at hand, but also to ill health. She occupied her time in reading and, on one occasion, wrote: "I have taken a great fancy for reading Rollin's Ancient History . . . and find great pleasure and entertainment from it. . . ."[13] Again, she gave a critical judgment of the type of histories that were being published on the American Revolution, remarking on the unfairness of the treatment given France and Holland.[14] Mercy Warren, too, was a brilliant student—in Alice Brown's opinion, the equal of her brother, with whom she was taught by the Rev. Jonathan Russell.[15] She read Raleigh's *History of the World*, which was loaned her by the tutor, and became a lifelong enthusiastic student of history and politics.[16] Mrs. John Quincy Adams was an interested reader of French and English literature and an entertaining letter writer. But she was apparently filled with the ancient idea of female mental inferiority that had not yet been conquered, for she wrote, though conceivably in gentle irony, ". . . Was my mind sufficiently strong or capacious to understand, or even to comprehend the study of ancient and modern philosophy, I am certain I should derive very great advantage from [it] ; but you certainly forgot when you recommended it, that you were addressing the weaker sex. . . ." Of ancient philosophy she says it was quite out of her reach, except the dialogues of Plato, which she read but did not thoroughly understand. Moderns such as Locke, Berkeley, Reid, Hume, and Tucker puzzled, amused, astonished, disgusted, and diverted or put her to sleep, each in his turn.[17]

Another conspicuous instance of learning, in early Colonial days, was Anne Bradstreet, the daughter of Governor Dudley, whose poetic lines breathe something of the bitterness she felt because of the social disapproval of "female wits":

[13] Quotations are made from her *Letters*, published by Little and Brown (1840).

[14] *Ibid.*, 14 and 343–4.

[15] Brown: *Mercy Warren*, 25–6.

[16] *Ibid.*, 23–4.

[17] Holloway: *Ladies of the White House*, 265–7; see also 282.

"I am obnoxious to each carping tongue
"Who says my hand a needle better fits,
"A Poets pen all scorn I should thus wrong,
"For such despite they cast on female wits:
"If what I do prove well, it won't advance,
"They'l say it's stoln, or else it was by chance."

Phillis Wheatley, a little Negro girl who was purchased by a gentleman of Boston in 1761, is another rare example of learning in spite of obstacles. In less than sixteen months she learned English and was able "to read the most difficult parts of the Sacred Writings"; and to this she added such a knowledge of Latin literature and mythology as to embellish her poetry with references to them and astonish the native Bostonians, who marvelled that a mere child, and a slave at that, could be "inspired by the Muses." Her lot being fortunately cast in a well-to-do family, where private studies were encouraged, she might well celebrate "Being Brought from Africa to America":

"'Twas mercy brought me from my Pagan land,
"Taught my benighted soul to understand
"That there's a God, that there's a Saviour too;
"Once I redemption neither sought nor knew,
"Some view our sable race with scornful eye,
" 'Their color is a diabolic die.'
"Remember, Christians, Negroes, black as Cain,
"May be refined, and join th' angelic train."[18]

So much for exceptions to the generalization that 'female learning was ridiculed'—and it may be recalled that Thomas Jefferson ridiculed the productions of Miss Wheatley; they help, merely by their scarcity, to prove the rule that schools were few and suggest, certainly, that many people must have believed, as did Mrs. Means, in the nineteenth century, that "book larnin' don't do no good to a woman." The effects of this disparagement of woman's powers, and of the lack of incentives to learning, are mentioned by Eliza Southgate:

"Necessity is the nurse of all the great qualities of the mind; it explores all the hidden treasures and by its stimulating power they are 'polished into brightness.' Women who have no such incentives to action suffer all the strong energetic qualities of the mind to sleep in obscurity; sometimes a ray of genius gleams

18 *Poems and Letters of Phillis Wheatley*, 92.

PHYLLIS WHEATLEY

through the thick clouds with which it is enveloped, and irradi-
ates for a moment the darkness of mental night; yet, like a comet
that shoots wildly from its sphere, it excites our wonder, and we
place it among the phenomenons of nature, without searching
for a natural cause. Thus it is the qualities with which nature
has endowed us, as a support amid the misfortunes of life and
a shield from the allurements of vice, are left to moulder in
ruin. In this dormant state they became enervated and impaired,
and at last die for want of exercise. The little airy qualities
which produce sprightliness are left to flutter about like feathers in the wind, sport of every breeze.''[19]

If we turn but a moment to the letters of Mrs. Adams, it is
possible to learn what was the accepted education for women in
Puritan New England about the period of the Revolution. For
though she was much better educated than most, and lamented
that facilities were limited, it appears that she loyally held to
many of the established ideas of proper training.

Her own broader education she owed, in part, to the liberal
views of her husband; and it must be understood that much of
the treasure of cultivated minds was obtained by conversation
and correspondence with cultured people. Certainly it could
not come from the schools where the three R's were the usual
limit. To these were added, in rare instances, music and dancing. Mrs. Adams stressed the importance of early attention to
religion and a useful education for domestic life.

''True, genuine religion is calm in its inquiries, deliberate in
its resolves, and steady in its conduct; is open to light and conviction, and labors for improvement. It studies to promote love
and union in civil and religious society. It approves virtue, and
the truths which promote it, and, as the Scripture expresses it,
'is peaceable, gentle, easy to be entreated.' It is the author of
our hope, the ornament of youth, the comfort of age; our support in affliction and adversity, and the solace of that solemn
hour, which we must all experience. Train up my dear daughter,
your children, to a sober and serious sense of the duty which
they owe to the Supreme Being. Impress their infant minds
with a respect for the Sabbath. This is too much neglected by
the rising generation. Accustom them to a constant attendance
upon public worship, and enforce it by your own precept and

[19] Cook: *Girl's Life Eighty Years Ago*, 58-9.

example, as often as with any convenience you can attend. It is a duty, for which we are accountable to the Supreme Being."[20]

Regarding a useful education, she wrote:

"It behooves us who are parents or grandparents, to give our daughters and granddaughters, when their education devolves upon us, such an education as shall qualify them for the useful and domestic qualities of life, that they should learn the use and proper improvement of time, since 'time was given for use, not waste.' The finer accomplishments, such as music, dancing, painting, serve to set off and embellish the picture; but the ground work must be formed of more durable colors.

"I consider it an indispensible requisite, that every American wife should know herself how to order and regulate her family; how to govern her domestics and train up her children. For this purpose, the all-wise Creator made woman a help-meet for man, and she who fails in these duties does not answer the end of her creation."[21]

The deep impression of her own New England training is revealed in her shocked utterances upon being thrown into French society, which contrasted so sharply with her own. She wrote: "As to the ladies of this country, their manners appear to be totally depraved. . . . I have never seen a female model here of such unaffected, modest, and sweetly amiable manners as Mrs. Guild, Mrs. Russell, and many other American females exhibit."[22] Yet at another time she admitted: "I have received every mark of politeness and civility. The ladies here are well-educated, well-bred, and well dressed."[23] Of one of the friends of Dr. Franklin she wrote with charming frankness:

"I should have been greatly astonished at this conduct, if the good Doctor had not told me that in this lady I should see a genuine Frenchwoman, wholly free from affectation or stiffness of behaviour, and one of the best women in the world. For this I must take the Doctor's word; but I should have set her down for a very bad one, although sixty years old and a widow. I own I was highly disgusted, and never wish for an acquaintance with any ladies of this cast. After dinner she threw herself upon a

20 *Letters*, 427.
21 *Ibid.*, 440.
22 *Ibid.*, 388.
23 *Ibid.*, 420.

settee, where she showed more than her feet. She had a little lap-dog, who was, next to the Doctor, her favorite, and whom she kissed. This is one of the Doctor's most intimate friends, with whom he dines once every week, and she with him.''[24]

Likewise, Mercy Warren, who managed to secure a considerable education in the midst of the inhospitable environment, revealed in her satirical advice to a young lady what the usual attitude was regarding women's learning:

''If you have a Taste for the Study of History let me Urge you not to Indulge it, lest the Picture of human Nature in All Ages of the World should give your Features too serious a Cast or by becoming acquainted with the rude State of Nature in the Earlier Ages—the Origin of Society, the Foundations of Government & the Rise and Fall of Empires, you should Inadvertently glide into that unpardonable Absurdity & sometimes Venture to speak when Politicks happen to be the Subject.—In short, Science of any Kind beyond the Toilet, the Tea, or the Card Table, is as Unnecessary to a Lady's figuring in the Drawing Room as Virtue unsully'd by Caprice is to the Character of the finished Gentleman.—She may be the admiration of the *Ton* without the One & He the Idol of popular Fame without the Other.''[25]

That the acquisition of an elaborate education required an unusual degree of effort may be judged from another case of phenomenal intellectual achievement. We are told that Mary Moody Emerson, who was born about 1774, was accustomed to the reading of such authors as Milton, Young, Akenside, Clark, Jonathan Edwards, and the Bible. A picture of her constant endeavor to learn while, at the same time, she carried on the work of the household, may be gained from a page of her diary: ''Rose before light every morn; visited from necessity once, and again for books; read Butler's Analogy; commented on the Scripture; read in a little book, Cicero's Letters—a few; touched Shakespeare; washed, carded, cleaned house, and baked. Today cannot recall an error, nor scarcely a sacrifice, but more fullness of content in the labors of a day never was felt. There is a secret pleasure in bending to circumstances while superior to them.'' With this devotion to learning she coupled an economy in household and personal expenditures which is now-a-days

[24] *Ibid.*, 252–3.
[25] Brown: *Mercy Warren*, 23–4.

almost incomprehensible: "I had ten dollars a year for clothes and charity, and I never remember to have been needy, though I never had but two or three aids in those six years of earning my home."[26]

The books read, in case one read at all, possessed a solidity that would oppress a modern "maid of learning." Histories, natural and political, and the philosophers just mentioned were no doubt to be found in a number of libraries, or borrowed from friends.[27] "Milton, Watt's *Lyric Poems*, Young's *Night Thoughts*, Hervey's *Meditations*, the *Tatler*, and Addison's *Spectator* were not scarce, though not generally diffused. *Pamela, Clarissa Harlow*, and an abridgement of Grandison were in a few hands and eagerly read; and the *Adventures of Robinson Crusoe* was the chief work . . . for the young." Such, one writer considers, was the literary pabulum on which they were fed in the late eighteenth century.[28] The books had to be of substantial character to keep their place alongside the Bible. Puritan women mastered the economics of the *Proverbs* wherein the "worthy woman" is described. Most cloth was home-made and clothing was manufactured from it by the daughters and wives. If occasionally a gown was purchased, very probably home-made cloth was bartered for it.

It is evident, from many and varied sources, that a broader, richer culture, determined to a great extent by native factors, was developing in the Colonies from the early years of the eighteenth century. This culture, and the increased economic stability back of it, underlies many of the changes appearing here and there in reference to girls' education.[29] Near the last quarter of the century sentiment changed rather decidedly, and this is reflected in the gradual opening of town schools and the creation of private institutions to provide for girls the special education it was felt they should have.[30] Dilworth, in his

26 Weeden: *Economic Hist. New England*, II, 861–2; *Lectures and Biographical Sketches*, by Emerson, X, 402.

27 For refeerence to early New England libraries see Wertenbaker: *The First Americans*, 241 *f*.

28 *Am. Annals of Education*, I, 522–3.

29 For a good general account see Adams: *Provincial Society*, especially Chaps. IX and XI.

30 *Am. Annals of Education*, I, 522–6; see also Jameson's treatment of changing "Thought and Feeling" in his *American Revolution Considered as a Social Movement*, 115–57.

Schoolmaster's Assistant, at the middle of the century, recommended that girls be allowed to go to school as early and as long as boys did; but this certainly was not general practice.

'Senex,' writing in the *American Annals of Education,* tells of the enthusiasm for 'female' education that began to appear late in the eighteenth century and, in particular, of his own interest in, and experiment upon, the subject: "In an oration which I was called upon to deliver as a collegiate exercise, I warmly advocated the importance of 'Improvement in the education of females.' I contended that science would never reach its acme, while the influential half of our race, to whom the training of the rising generation is committed, were left in ignorance of it.

"In pursuance of the purpose I had formed, of acting as well as speaking, on this subject, an evening school, of 5 evenings in a week, was opened, for 12 weeks. About 20 young ladies attended. Lowth's Grammar, and Guthrie's Geography, were studied well and reviewed. At the end of the term, in the presence of the faculty of ————— College, the parents, and others, they passed an examination that did them honor, and delivered addresses of their own composition. Each brought her essay or letter, neatly copied, for the perusal of the spectators. This was the first female school, it is believed, that ever was attempted in New England, above the common district schools.

"When, at length, academies were opened for female improvement in the higher branches, a general excitement appeared in parents, and an emulation in daughters to attend them. Many attended such a school one or two quarters, others a year, some few longer. From these periods of attendance for instruction in elementary branches, arose higher improvements. The love of reading and habits of application became fashionable; and fashion we know is the mistress of the world."[31]

III. *Educational Opportunities*
a. *The Dame School*

The dame schools appeared early in New England's history, and to these girls and little boys might go. In the seventeenth and eighteenth centuries they filled the place later taken by the

[31] *Am. Annals,* I, 522–6.

infant schools and kindergartens at the beginning and end of the
nineteenth century, respectively. This was an English institution of long standing, of which Crabbe had written his classic
lines:

> "When a deaf poor patient widow sits
> "And awes some twenty infants as she knits—
> "Infants of humble, busy wives who pay
> "Some trifling price for freedom through the day,
> "At this good matron's hut the children meet
> "Who thus becomes the mother of the street:
> "Her room is small, they cannot widely stray
> "Her threshold high, they cannot run away:
> "With bands of yarn she keeps offenders in,
> "And to her gown the sturdiest can pin."

The reference to Mrs. Jupe—teacher of the Ipswich School in
1639—is doubtless to a dame school.[32] New Haven recorded a
school of Goodwife Wickham in 1651. Sudbury had "two dame
schools, one on each side of the river," in 1680.[33]

While the dame school was open to girls, its most important
function was to give little boys the rudiments of English that
they might enter the town schools. Many of them were entirely
private, being held in the home of the dame; but public interest
in them was evinced in the case of some towns at an early date.
As early as 1682, Springfield agreed with "Goodwife Mirick to
encourage her in the good work of training up children, and
teaching children to read, and that she should have three pence
a week for every child that she takes to perform this good work
for."[34] At Woburn and Winchenden public encouragement was
also given. Weymouth, 1700, Waterbury, Connecticut, in 1702,
Haverhill, 1707, Lexington, 1717, Wenham in 1746, and Gilsum,
New Hampshire, as well as other towns, show by their records
that the dame school was at any rate quasi-public.[35] That the
dame school continued to play a rôle of such importance as to
claim the attention of the town school committees is shown in
the case of Medford in 1819, when it was reported "that the
town contains 158 girls over the age of seven years. . . . That
the town contains 117 children of both sexes over four years of

---

[32] Bartholomew: *Record of the Bartholomew Family*, 32.
[33] Small: *Early New England Schools*, 164.
[34] Dexter: *Hist. of Educ. in the U. S.*, 425.
[35] Small: *op. cit.*, 164 *ff.*; and Dexter: *op. cit.*, 425.

A DAME SCHOOL

age and under seven years of age, that require to be taught in the summer season by women teachers. . . . That the committee be authorized to employ three women teachers for six months beginning about the first of May, who are to teach the girls of all ages from four years old and upwards, and the boys from four years old to seven, unless they are sufficiently qualified to go to the master's school.'' This was accordingly done.[36] Medford had made partial provision for girls to go to the master's school in 1766.

Of the interior of the dame school little need be said. Simplicity and crudeness marked it. The homely utensils of the kitchen were scarcely out of sight. The curriculum was decidedly limited, but many of the dames certainly could not have been called "mistresses" of it. The alphabet, some spelling, writing, reading, and numbers, according to the ability of the dame, constituted the more ambitious studies; and to these were added knitting and sewing for girls, which, no doubt, the dame taught more successfully than the rest.

The capacity of the dames for teaching must have varied greatly. One of the most ignorant is doubtless described by a resident of Industry, Maine:

"An old maiden lady was employed occasionally a short time to teach children their letters and to spell out words. Her school was kept one month in my barn. She did what she could to teach the young ideas how to shoot, but was quite incompetent. I visited her school on one occasion and she had a small class advanced to words of three syllables in the spelling book, and when they came to the word 'anecdote,' she called it 'a-neck-dote' and defined it to be 'a food eaten between meals.''[37]

The very opposite extreme is described in the epitaph of Miriam Wood of Dorchester, who died in 1706:

"A woman well beloved of all her neighbors
"For her care of small folks education, their number being great,
"That when she died she scarcely left her mate
"So wise, discreet was her behavior
"That she was well esteemed by neighbors
"She lived in love with all to dye
"So let her rest to Eternity."

36 Small: *op. cit.*, 171–2.
37 *Ibid.*, 169.

A HORNBOOK OF THE EIGHTEENTH CENTURY

Somewhere between these two examples of ignorance and cultivation were the great majority whose chief task was to "keep offenders in." As with their intellectual qualifications, so also their moral fitness for teaching varied greatly. The townsmen found Mrs. Kimball to be of "sober conversation." But in New Haven a little girl who was brought into court in 1651 for "prophane swearing," having used such expressions as "by my soul" and "as I am a Christian," rested her only defense on the fact that she learned bad language from the dame whose school she attended.[38]   Others, it seems, managed to get through their tasks only by resorting to a doze now and then, or, perhaps, a little "nip" of New England or Santa Cruz rum.   Perhaps the dame made the way of learning attractive, as Prior suggests:

> "To Master John the English maid
> "A Horn book gives of gingerbread;
> "And that the child may learn the better,
> "As he can name, he eats the letter."

b. The Town School

The place of girls in New England town schools has been a rather obscure subject.   On this question individual cases can be cited from the town records to show that they were admitted and again that they were not.   The practical results following the towns' votes are more difficult to ascertain.   Small, after a search of the records on this particular point, says that "here are seven direct votes making 'females' eligible for the public schools, and five cases of implied permission.   They are all the gleanings from the records of nearly two hundred towns."[39]   Martin came to a similar conclusion.[40]   The status in the various towns whose records take cognizance of girls' education may be briefly reviewed, as it is revealed in fragmentary statements.

On July 22, 1639, "Mr. Bartholomew offered to entertain Mrs. Jupe (teacher of the Ipswich School) freely for a year without charge, if she have health, but if she prove sick, the charge to be borne by the publicke."[41]   If the primary authority for this statement is unquestioned it shows, however, nothing beyond the fact that a woman was employed in teaching—probably a dame school.   Martin declares, "No girls went to a master's school until 1769 in Ipswich."[42]   Sewall, in his diary, says little Hannah Sewall, eight years old, was run over by a horse while going

[38] *Ibid.*, 164.
[39] *Education* (1902), XXII, 534.
[40] *Ibid.* (1900), XX, 323–6.
[41] Bartholomew: *Record of the Bartholomew Family* (1885), 32, quoting Ipswich Records.
[42] *Education* (1900), XX, 323 *ff.*

to school in Schoolhouse Lane. Here again the probability is that there was a dame school in the lane.

In 1639, after the establishment of the town school at Dorchester, it was left to "the elders and the seven men for the time being (selectmen) whether maids should be taught with the boys or not," and the action does not appear to have been favorable to the "maids."[43] In 1649, Hampton, New Hampshire, agreed with John Legat to teach the children of the town "both male and female, which are capable of learning, to write and read and cast accounts." The later records, however, do not show that this direction was carried out in practice.[44] Dedham, in 1652, raised the question "whether the town require that girls be taught in the school or not," but no answer is found in the records concerning their decision. Rehoboth (1699) employed Robert Dickson for six months "to do his utmost to endeavor to teach *both sexes* of boys and girls to read English and write and cast accounts." Other towns, such as Northampton, Hatfield, and Wheatley, are reported to have had girls in attendance for a short time at least; and in the case of the last, it is said "no one remembers the time when girls did not commonly attend school and pursue the same studies as boys."[45] The situation in general, however, seems to be more nearly represented by the case of Farmington, Connecticut, where, in 1687, money was voted "for the maintenance of a school for the year ensuing, for the instruction of all such children as shall be sent to it to learn to read and write the English tongue." Objections are recorded a year later regarding this inclusion of the females in the educational provision: "Whereas the town at a meeting held Dec., 1687, agreed to give £20 as is there expressed, to teach all such as shall be sent, the town declare that by *all such* is to be understood only *male* children that are through their hornbook." Hopkins Grammar School, in 1680,[46] excluded all girls "as improper and inconsistent with such a grammar school as the law enjoins and is the design of this settlement." Wallingford is said to have provided for both boys and girls at a meeting held November 27, 1678, when it was ordered that three pence per

[43] *Ibid.*; see also Small: *Early New England Schools*, 275.
[44] Small, 276.
[45] *Ibid.*, 277.
[46] *Barnard's Journal*, IV, 710, gives the date as 1684.

week be paid "by all scholars, both male and female," towards the support of the schoolmaster.[47]   Rehoboth also voted, in 1699, for a master to teach "both sexes" to read, write, and cast accounts.   In Hatfield it has been said that girls attended from the first.[48]   Small points out, however, that from 1695 to 1699 none were on the school lists; that in 1700 there were but 4 girls and 42 boys; while in 1709 there were "16 girls in a class of 64."[49]

David McClure, a teacher in Portsmouth, New Hampshire, 1773[50] said: "Opened school, consisting the first day of about 30 Misses.   Afterward they increased to 70 or 80; so that I was obliged to divide the day between them and one half came in the forenoon and the other in the afternoon.   They were from 7 to 20 years of age. . . . I attended to them in reading, writing and arithmetic and geography principally.   This is, I believe, the only female school (supported by the town) in New England, and is a wise and useful institution."

A court decision of Hartford, 1655, ordered administrators of an estate to "educate the children, learning the sons to read and write, and the daughters to read and sew well."   Another decision, a year later, set forth that "the sons shall have learning to write plainly and read distinctly in the Bible, and the daughters to read and sew sufficiently for the making of their ordinary linen."[51]

It appears that not until the latter half of the eighteenth century was the admission of girls to the town schools more generally practised,[52] and the change of attitude throughout the last half of the century was slow.   Equal provision was sometimes not made until well into the nineteenth century.   In 1766,[53] the town of Medford gave its committee "power to agree with their schoolmaster to instruct girls two hours in a day after the boys are dismissed," while in 1787 it was arranged that girls attend "one hour in the forenoon and one in the afternoon for

[47] *Hist. of Wallingford*, quoted by Stewart in his *Hist. of Religious Education in Conn.*, 90–1.

[48] Martin: Early Education of Girls in Mass. [*Education*, XX, 323–6].

[49] Small: Girls in Colonial Schools [*Education* (1902), XXII, 533].

[50] Dexter: *Hist. of Ed. in the U. S.*, 427.

[51] Small: *Early New England Schools*, 278.

[52] *Am. Annals of Education*, I, 522–6.

[53] According to Martin: *op. cit.*, 1776.

four months." Three years later we learn "that girls have liberty to attend the master's school the three summer months." In 1794 they stipulated that the two sexes should attend school at different hours, and that girls should attend from May first to the first of October. The school day was to be eight hours long and equally divided between boys and girls. Nevertheless, not before 1834 did the town vote "that the school committee be directed so to arrange the town schools that the girls may enjoy equal privileges therein with the boys *throughout the year.*"[54]

The custom of having girls attend at hours when boys were not present appeared in a number of towns. Nathan Hale, New London, 1774,[55] said: "I have kept during the summer, a morning school between the hours of five and seven, of about twenty young ladies: for which I have received twenty shillings a scholar by the quarter." At Newburyport, in 1792, girls were admitted to the master's school, "in summer when boys were few," for an hour and a half after school. In 1804, the town created four girls' schools which were open for six months "from six to eight in the morning, and on Thursday afternoon," which was a holiday for the boys. At Essex, a local historian says a few girls attended the town school (about 1782) but they were "only those who thought a good deal of themselves."[56] Haverhill, in 1790, provided a school for girls an hour in the morning and afternoon, between May and September. The Salem school committee was authorized, in 1793, to provide for education of girls in reading, writing, and ciphering; but nothing was done before 1812 more than to permit them to attend an hour at noon and another in the afternoon.[57] The Reverend Eli Forbes, in 1790, urged the town of Gloucester to provide for the education of girls—"a tender and interesting branch of the community that have been neglected in the public schools of this town."[58]

Concerning the status of 'female' education in Boston a few years earlier (1782), John Eliot wrote to Jeremy Balknap: "We don't pretend to teach ye female part of ye town anything

[54] Small: *op. cit.*, 281. Italics mine.
[55] Dexter: *History of Educ. in the U. S.*, 427.
[56] Martin: Early Ed. of Girls in Mass. [*Education*, XX, 323–6].
[57] *Ibid.*
[58] *Ibid.*

more than dancing, or a little music perhaps, (and these accomplishm^t must necessarily be confined to a very few,) except ye private schools for writing, which enables them to write a copy, sign their name, &c., which they might not be able to do without such a privilege, & with it I will venture to say that a lady is a rarity among us who can write a page of commonplace sentiment, the words being well spelt, & ye style & language kept up with purity & elegance.''[59]

In 1789, Boston took a step towards the education of girls in public schools by ordering: ''That there shall be one writing school at the south part of the town, one at the center, and one at the north part, that in these schools the children of both sexes shall be taught writing and also arithmetic in the various branches of it usually taught in the town schools, including vulgar and decimal fractions.

''That there be one reading school in the south part of the town, one at the center, and one at the north part; that in these schools the children of both sexes be taught to spell, accent, and read both prose and verse, and also be instructed in English grammar and composition.''

Girls were admitted only one-half of the year, however—the summer—and not until 1828 did they attend the year round. It also seems that they attended (at any rate, in 1794) at hours when boys were not in the school. In 1790 there were 539 girls in all the schools, their number being slightly less than that of boys.[60]

Benjamin Mudge, in an oft-quoted statement, says, regarding Lynn, ''In all my school days, which ended in 1801, I never saw but three females in public schools, and they were there only in the afternoon to learn to write.''[61]

From the data concerning the individual towns it appears that the school laws of the early seventeenth century had no significance so far as the rapid advancement of education for girls was concerned. These town schools were animated by Calvinism and the English spirit in education and existed for

[59] Quoted in Kittredge: *The Old Farmer and His Almanack*, 229–30. He refers doubtless to the general usage, but not particularly to the public schools.

[60] Small: *op. cit.*, 279.

[61] *Ibid.*, 279.

the education of men to the service of state and church. This wider service was not open to women and hence there was little argument in favor of their education as a public concern. Martin summarized the situation in regard to girls' education most adequately as follows: "First, during the first one hundred and fifty years of colonial history girls did not attend the public schools, except in some of the smaller towns, and there only for a short time; second, about the time of the Revolution, when public thought was quickened, the subject of the education of girls was widely agitated; third, against much opposition the experiment was tried of sending girls to the master's school for a few hours in a day during a part of the year, but never in the same rooms or at the same time with the boys; fourth, this provision extended only to the English schools, no instruction being provided in Latin or even in the higher English branches; fifth, it was not until the present century was far advanced that girls and boys shared alike the advantages of the higher public schools."[62]

The above statement was made concerning Massachusetts. In 1770, one writer states that "common schools were opened to every child, and the expense of instruction paid by the public, partly by the school fund which was then small, and partly by town taxes."[63] These schools were kept open for six, four, three, or two months, depending upon the size and wealth of the district. Spelling,[64] reading, writing, and sometimes the first rules of arithmetic, were taught. "The assembly's Catechism was repeated at the close of every Saturday forenoon school." Girls were never taught arithmetic, says this author, but boys were known who mastered the first four rules of it. There were no separate classes for the girls, though they generally sat on separate benches.

Dwight, in the early nineteenth century,[65] completed his observations of education in New England by saying:

"I have now given you a summary view of the schools in Connecticut. With little variation of figure, light, or shade, it will serve as a portrait, sufficiently exact in this respect, of New

[62] *Op. cit.*
[63] *American Journal of Education*, V, 421–3.
[64] *Ibid.*; Dilworth's book was used.
[65] *Travels in N. E. and N. Y.*, IV, 287–8.

England at large, the state of Rhode Island excepted. In Massachusetts, New Hampshire, and Vermont, schools are everywhere established. They are often styled parochial schools. You will not suppose that each parish has a school, distinguished by this title; but that each parish has a sufficient number of schools to admit all the children which it contains. To these little seminaries the children of New England are universally sent, from two, three, four, and five years of age, to the period in which they have learned to read, write and keep accounts. In many of them, other instructions are added, according to the skill and disposition of the instructors, and the wishes of the parents. At the earliest periods, children of both sexes are placed under the direction of female teachers, and, at more advanced stages of their education, under that of men. I speak of the common schools only. It ought to be observed, that throughout a considerable part of the country, the female pupils, whether placed under the instruction of men or women, are sent to separate schools.''

Thus it appears that also in Connecticut the public schools had been gradually opened to girls. Dwight estimated between 40 and 78 thousand children in school in Connecticut about 1800. Girls, he said, usually left school at 12 or 14 years of age.[66] This fact lies back of the admonition that was given by Thomas in the *Farmer's Calendar* for December, 1808: ''Now let your boys and girls attend school. Send them to the Common School, rather than to an academy. Fun, frolick and filigree are too much practised at the academies. . . . Let them have a solid and useful education.''[67]

A slight glimpse of the interior of this 'Common School' at a little later date may be obtained from Burton's *District School As It Was*.[68] For a disciplinary measure the ''boys were made to sit in the girls' seats, amusing the school with their grinning awkwardness, and the girls were obliged to sit on the masculine side of the aisle with crimsoned necks and faces buried in their aprons.''[69]

66 *Ibid.*, I, 148.
67 Quoted in Kittredge: *Old Farmer and His Almanack*, 228 *ff*.
68 Published in 1833.
69 *Op. cit.* (Ed. of 1852), 56.

The education of the academies was more elaborate, of course, than that attempted by any of the town schools, aiming at a secondary grade of schooling. But in spite of Mr. Thomas and his fears on account of the frivolous education of the academies, or new private schools, their vogue continued to increase. In time they were to become a most effective agency in opening up educational opportunities generally for girls.[70] The academies were preceded by an extremely versatile and variable institution—the adventure school, whose proprietor-master or mistress was willing, for a price, to teaching anything desired.

In many of the larger cities of eighteenth century New England, adventure masters offered opportunities for girls which were not accessible to them in the town schools. Instruction in social accomplishments, such as music and dancing, and fancy needlework, were very generally afforded after the middle of the century. Mr. Peter Pelham (1743) announced in the *Boston Evening Post*[71] that he had been for nine years ''under the Tuition of an accomplished Professor of the Art of Musick'' and was now ready to serve ladies and gentlemen as a tutor in music and dancing, either at his father's house or his school in Leveret's Lane. Other dancing, or dancing and music, masters were B. Glaan, M. Boullay, Mr. Nugent and Mr. Carter.[72]

In 1763, the *Providence Gazette* advised readers that ''very good encouragement'' would be given ''any person who understands Fencing, Dancing and the Violin,'' who would ''set up a school in the Town of Providence.''[73] Dancing was somewhat of a novelty at that date, and the notice was a signal to call forth a lengthy discussion.[74] In 1768, J. Baptist Tioli, who had ''had the honor of teaching the principal nobility in England and Ireland, and some very respectable personages in America, offered to teach the minuet, double minuet, quadruple minuet, paspie, gavotta, alouber, hornpipe [and] country dances,'' pro-

[70] See Chapters VIII and IX for more complete treatment of the rise of the academy.

[71] June 20, 1743, 2, col. 2.

[72] *Boston Ev. Post*, Apr. 10, 1794, 2, col. 2; *Mass. Spy or Worcester Gaz.*, July 12, 1797, 4, col. 4; Sept. 6, 1797, 3, col. 4; and *Independent Chronicle* [Boston], Oct. 21, 1802, 4, col. 4.

[73] *Providence Gaz. and Country Journal*, Jan. 15, 1763, 3, col. 3.

[74] A defense of dancing appeared in the *Prov. Gaz.*, Feb. 5, 1763, 3, cols. 2 and 3.

vided enough attended.[75]   Instruction for boys and girls was to
be separate until after a month, when they were to attend together, "at which time their respective parents, inclined to
speculation will have free access." Tioli taught violin also. In
1774, William Billings taught the "art of Psalmody in all its
branches" to such as were "desirous of being instructed."[76]

Similar music and dancing schools were established in Newport, Rhode Island, by William Pope, dancing and fencing
master, and a master of psalmody who performed at Mr. Bradford's school house.[77] Mary Cowley announced her dancing
school in 1764, stating several interesting rules to secure the
"decency, agreeable to that most approved accomplishment":
"I expect every lady that attends for the pleasure and improvement of their dancing, will be punctual at sunset, as no lady
shall be admitted an hour after, except a stranger. No lady
shall engage, either in school or out, to dance with any gentleman without my approbation. No lady shall refuse being taken
out by any gentleman that's admitted by a ticket, without giving
a sufficient reason, on pain of being publickly reprimanded, and
immediately dismissed. No gentleman nor lady shall come in an
undress. No gentleman shall be admitted without a ticket.
None to be admitted that don't dance. The number of gentlemen not to exceed sixteen. The hours from five to nine."[78]

The private teachers of ornamental and plain needlework were
numerous in Boston and other towns of New England. At their
schools young ladies were assured of being taught plain and
ornamental needlework, tapestry, embroidery, marking, pattern
drawing, wax work, transparent "filagree," painting upon glass,
Japanning, quill work, featherwork, gold and silver embroidery,
imitation of Brussell's lace, shell work, flowers for the head,
"shaded work in colors," Dresden work, flowering on muslin,
making "furbelow'd scarfs," quilting, flourishing, turkey work,
and spinning. Among those advertising these 'mysteries' were
Margaret Laitaill, Mrs. Condy, Mrs. Hiller, Elinore and Mary
Purcell, Elizabeth Murray, and Jane Day.[79] An unusual type

75 *Ibid.*, July 9, 1768, 3, col. 3.
76 *Ibid.*, May 28, 1774, 3, col. 3.
77 *Newport Mercury*, June 20, 1768, 3, col. 3; and Jan. 8, 1770, 4, col. 2.
78 *Ibid.*, Oct. 15, 1764, 3, col. 3.
79 *Boston Ev. Post*, Apr. 30, 1739, 4, col. 2; Mch. 15, 1742, 2, col. 2; Feb.
8, 1748, 3; Apr. 22, 1751, 2, col. 1; Apr. 1, 1751, 2, col. 2; Apr. 30, 1759, 3,

of school was proposed, in 1768, by a woman in Newport, who would teach "young misses . . . to spin, in the best manner, either flax, wool or cotton." It was hoped she would receive encouragement as she was "thoroughly acquainted with the business" and it seemed such a school was "much wanted."[80] It should be noted, too, that the 'mystery' of cooking was not entirely neglected, though references to it are comparatively rare. Margaret Mackellwen had a "pastry school" in Boston in 1736, but may have given as much or more of her time to painting on glass, plain work, flowering, marking, and embroidery;[81] and Mrs. Mary Campbell, of Newport, in 1759, proposed to teach young ladies "pastry and many other parts of cookery."[82]

Another prevalent type of private school for girls combined instruction in some accomplishments with reading, writing, and ciphering. Mary Turfrey offered "education" to young gentlewomen of Boston in 1706, but did not specify constituent elements;[83] at George Brownell's House, writing, ciphering, dancing, treble violin, flute, spinet, English and French quilting, embroidery, flourishing, and marking were offered as attractions in 1712;[84] similar schools were announced at the house of James Ivers, in 1714,[85] and by the Misses Southerlands in 1784.[86] Possibly Mrs. Day's school, in 1762, was of the same sort.[87] At Newport, Sarah Osborn and Elizabeth Allen combined reading and writing with plain and ornamental work and knitting.[88] Adventure schools which taught 'substantial subjects' and ignored the accomplishments were frequently opened to girls after 1750.

---

col. 3; Apr. 20, 1767, 4, col. 2; *Boston News Letter*, Aug. 20–27, 1716; *Newport Mercury*, May 8, 1759, 3, col. 2.

[80] *Newport Mercury*, Apr. 25, [?] 1768; this may have been the same as advertised later by Sarah Geers, at "John Fryer's House on the Point."— May 16, 1768, 3, col. 3.

[81] *Boston Ev. Post*, Nov. 29, 1736, 2, col. 2.

[82] *Newport Mercury*, Aug. 14, 1759, 4, col. 1.

[83] *Boston News Letter*, Sept. 9, 1706.

[84] *Ibid.*, Feb. 22–Mch. 2, 1712, 2, col. 2.

[85] *Ibid.*, Apr. 12–19, 1714, 2, col. 2.

[86] *Independent Chronicle and Universal Advt.* [Boston], Sept. 23, 1784, 4, col. 4.

[87] *Boston Evening Post*, June 21, 1762, 4.

[88] *Newport Mercury*, Dec. 19, 1758, 4, col. 1; July 4, 1768, 3, col. 3.

It is possible that Pelham's "writing and arithmetick school," "from candle light till nine . . . for the benefit of those employed in business all the day," was open to women as well as men.[89] William Elphinstone advertised his writing school for both sexes from twelve years of age to fifty, in 1755;[90] and Joseph Ward, in 1769, offered reading, spelling, writing, arithmetick, English grammar—"the misses" to be taught "at such hours as it will suit them best to attend."[91] In 1774, William Payne made a strong plea for the study of English grammar, as "well worthy the attention of youth" who "are designed to act any considerable part in life," and added that "writing and arithmetic will be taught to such as desire it, and letter writing in form." As for the "ladies who chuse to be instructed at home [they] may be waited on with the utmost complaisance and strictest attention, as . . . the business requires, and . . . as shall be most convenient."[92]

At Newport, Rhode Island, Thomas Green had a school for girls only, in 1767;[93] and Ebenezer Bradford, in 1770, opened a "morning school for young misses" in which he taught "writing, arithmetic, and the English language grammatically."[94] At Providence, Benjamin Stelle proposed (1767), if "twenty scholars" appeared, to continue a school for girls in "writing and arithmetic, which hath been much neglected in this town." The hours were to be from six to half after seven in the morning and in the afternoon from half past four till half past six.[95]

Theodore Foster went Stelle one better, proposing to hold a school for girls, in the present Latin School room, from half past five in the morning till a quarter of eight. His conception of his school, which was to run for three months, suggests the early female seminary: "Those young Ladies, who have an inclination thereto, shall have an opportunity of learning English Grammar, by Rule, which is to be the first exercise in the morning. Then each successively, and in order, shall read a Portion

89 *Boston Ev. Post*, Sept. 19, 1748.
90 *Ibid.*, July 14, 1755, 2, col. 1.
91 *Ibid.*, May 1, 1769, 3, col. 2.
92 *Ibid.*, Nov. 28, 1774, 4, col. 2.
93 *Newport Mercury*, Apr. 20–27, 1767, 3, col. 3.
94 *Ibid.*, May 21, 1770, 4, col. 3.
95 *Prov. Gaz.*, May 30, 1767, 3, col. 3.

of Fordyce's Sermons to young Women, which is to be succeeded by the exercise of Writing and Arithmetic.—Every Saturday he proposes, shall be dedicated to Reading, and studying the Grammar of the English Language, when some strictures and Observations will be made upon writing and composing of letters.''[96]

French was becoming a very popular study for girls in the New England cities by 1770, though fewer masters are noted there than in New York, Philadelphia, and the cities of the South, such as Baltimore and Charleston. William Lyons offered to teach French at Boston in 1719, but did not mention ladies.[97] Lewis Delile, in 1772, informed the public he would teach French "in its native purity," and that when his school was not open he would wait on ladies and gentlemen at their homes.[98] In 1775, at Providence, a young gentleman from Boston announced he would teach "young gentlemen and ladies," either in classes or at their homes, "any Branch of common Education, in the most concise and accurate method, . . . arts of Elocution, and epistolary writing . . . also the Latin and French languages grammatically, if required.''[99]

Schools of the adventure type formed a worth while addition to the slender facilities for girls' education afforded by the towns. They were important in themselves, but more important as the predecessors of the more elaborate academy or seminary which, in time, was put upon a firm basis, and in many cases chartered by the states. They appeared first in the larger towns before the Revolution, and in smaller places after that date. The opening of town schools to girls in some instances—Boston, for example—was probably, in part, a result of their influence. A few more of these prominent private schools may be noticed.

A writer in the *American Journal of Education*[100] says he personally knew of private girls' schools at Boston, Hartford, and another place which he does not call by name, before 1776. Soon after 1776, he himself taught two young ladies who had been instructed by a clergyman. In these cases the girls were to learn marking, needlework, dancing, reading, and to improve their

[96] *Ibid.*, May 25, 1771, 3, col. 3.
[97] *Boston News Letter*, Oct. 26–Nov. 2, 1719.
[98] *Boston Ev. Post*, Mch., 16, 1772, 4.
[99] *Ibid.*, June 17, 1775, 4, col. 2.
[100] V, 421–3.

manners.   In 1779, during the vacation, two students of Yale College kept a school for young ladies at New Haven, teaching arithmetic, geography and composition.   One of them, in his senior year, held a school there during the winter of 1779–80; there were twenty-five students who studied grammar, rhetoric, composition and geography.   The success of these efforts led to a similar school soon after in the town of Newburyport.[101]   Bingham opened his private school for girls in 1784,[102] in which he taught them writing, arithmetic, reading, spelling, and English grammar.   There can be no question but that the success of the small private schools, and the more ambitious undertaking of Bingham, was influential in shaping the town's action (1789) in making some formal provision for admission of girls.   This influence of private initiative upon public action is seen in a great number of cases.

In the same year the town of New Haven was favored in the establishment of an institution of similar character by Jedediah Morse.   About 1785, Dwight opened a school for young ladies at Greenfield Hill, Connecticut,—an academy—where he taught the "higher branches of education";[103] and in 1789, a Female Academy was opened at Medford, which was attended by students from many states.   "The place was delightful and airy, containing ample and commodious buildings, and fruit gardens of about five acres."   It continued about seven years and was influential in pointing out the practicability of the scheme of "female education."[104]   In 1790, Woodbridge, "the Columbus of Female Education," as he called himself, created another school for girls at New Haven.   These represent the beginning of the academy movement in New England, as far as girls are concerned.

It was probably in the school at Medford, or its successor, that Eliza Southgate was "finished."   Mrs. Rowson's school occu-

101 *Ibid.*
102 Though this was a private school, it was approved by the Selectmen of Boston.   Two years later, Matthew Simpson was allowed to keep a school for both sexes, teaching "writing, arithmetic and mathematics."   See Small: *Early New England Schools,* 279.
103 Dwight: Women at Yale Graduate School [*The Forum* (1892), XIII, 457 *ff.*].
104 *Am. Jour. Education,* V, 421–3.

TITLE PAGE OF BINGHAM'S *Young Lady's Accidence*

pied the estate of Timothy Bigelow, Medford, from about 1797 to 1803, when it was removed to Newton.   Eliza's letters when she was fourteen years old mention that she studied arithmetic, writing, reading, French, geometry, geography, dancing, embroidery and music;[105] but it must be remembered that she had

[105] In connection with music as a school study it is interesting to recall Brissot de Warville's comments in his *New Travels*, 95–6; ''Music, which

already been at school—probably the town school—at Scarborough, Maine. She wrote for special permission to study music and French—the latter because she was advised it would not take much time, as the lessons were only two hours long and came twice weekly. Arithmetic and geometry, however, were her greatest concern, and she early promised to send a copy of her "Arithmetic" to her mother. "Cyphering" had to be finished before geometry was taken up, and the latter had to precede geography. Her teacher thought that nine months for arithmetic would do, if she were diligent, but he did not want to give her a superficial knowledge only. She wrote she would be "very happy and very grateful if you thought proper to let me tarry that time. I have cyphered now farther than Isabella did, for I have been through practise, the Rule of Three and Interest and two or three rules that I never did before." What an anxiety is contained in that simple request that they may think it proper for her to 'tarry' for nine months! Later she wrote of happy completion of the work. "I have been busy in my arithmetic, but I finished it yesterday, and expect now to begin my large manuscript Arithmetic . . . [later] I have finished my large manuscript Arithmetic and want to get it bound, and then I shall send it to you. I have done a small Geometry book and shall begin a large one tomorrow, such a one as you saw at Mr. Wyman's, if you remember."[106]

Here was a remarkable little girl. We are not surprised at some of her advanced views[107] when we remember her ambition and her implied valuation of an education: "I have a great desire to see my family, but I have a still greater desire to finish my education."[108] It recalls another estimate made in the back of a little school book by one to whom the golden paths of learning had just been opened:

their teachers formerly proscribed as a diabolic art, begins to make part of their education. In some houses you hear the forte-piano. This art, it is true, is still in its infancy; but the young novices who exercise it, are so gentle, so complaisant, and so modest, that the proud perfection of art gives no pleasure equal to what they afford. God grant that the Bostonian women may never, like those of France, acquire the malady of perfection in this art! It is never attained, but at the expense of the domestic virtues."

106 Cook: *A Girl's Life Eighty Years Ago*, 8, 11, and 15.

107 See page 175.

108 Cook: *op. cit.*, IV–V.

MANUSCRIPT ARITHMETIC OF LUCRETIA KIMBALL, BRADFORD ACADEMY (1811)

"Next unto God, dear Parents, I address
"Myself to you in humble thankfulness
"For all your care and pains on me bestowed
"And means of learning unto me allowed
"Go on I pray and let me still pursue
"These golden paths the vulgar never knew."

The condition of the schools, wherein the "golden" opportunity was offered, was not always inviting. Eliza Southgate wrote of the first school she attended at Medford: "We get up early in the morning and make our beds and sweep the chamber, it is a chamber about as large as our kitchen chamber, and a little better finished. There's four beds in the chamber, and two persons in each bed, we have chocolate for breakfast and supper."[109] Dr. Southgate removed her to the school of Mrs. Rowson. Of her she wrote that she was "so mild, so good, no one can help loving her; she treats all her scholars with such a

[109] *Ibid.*, 4-5.

tenderness as would win the affection of the most savage brute. . . ."[110] To Octavia, who went to boarding school after Eliza had returned "to begin life itself," she sent the almost maternal admonition: "I think, my dear sister, you ought to improve every moment of your time, which is short, very short to complete your education. In November terminates the period of your instruction. The last you will receive perhaps ever, only what you may gain by observation. You will never cease to learn I hope; the world is a volume of instruction, which will afford you continual employment—peruse it with attention and candor and you will never think the time thus employed misspent. I think, Octavia, I would not leave my school again until you finally leave it. You may—you will think this is harsh; you will not always think so; remember those that wish it must know better what is proper than you possibly can. Horatio will come on for you as soon as your quarter is out. We anticipate the time with pleasure; employ your time in such a manner as to make your improvements conspicuous. A boarding-school, I know, my dear Sister, is not like home, but reflect a moment, is it not necessary, absolutely necessary to be more strict in the government of 20 or 30 young ladies, nearly of an age and different dispositions, than a private family? Your good sense will easily tell you it is. No task can be greater than the care of so many girls, it is impossible not to be partial, but we may conceal our partiality. I should have a poor opinion of any person that did not feel a love for merit, superior to what they can for the world in general. I should never approve of such general love. I say this not because I think you are discontented, far from it—your letters tell us quite the reverse and I believe it. Surely, Octavia, you must allow that no woman was ever better calculated to govern a school than Mrs. Rowson. She governs by the love with which she always inspires her scholars. You have been indulged, Octavia, so we have all. I was discontented when I first went from home. I dare say you have had some disagreeable sensations, yet your reason will convince you, you ought not to have had. You had no idea when you left home of any difference in your manner of living. I knew you would easily be reconciled to it and therefore said but little to you about it."[111]

110 *Ibid.*, 17.
111 *Ibid.*, 29–31.

That education to the point of literacy became the rule for a considerable number of girls, at least by the close of the Colonial period, is suggested by the fact that many women, particularly in populous centers, were engaged in business involving the necessity of writing, reading, and the use of accounts.[112]

The status of Colonial men and women, so far as literacy is concerned, has, however, never been adequately studied. The facts found, though incomplete, may be set down for what they are worth. At any rate, they are suggestive. At the invasion of New Haven in 1779, ten women made depositions concerning outrages committed by soldiers. Of these, seven signed their names and three made their marks. Fewer men made depositions in this case, but all signed their names.[113] These cases are too few to warrant much attention. Kilpatrick reported that 11 per cent of 179 men in Suffolk County, Massachusetts, made marks in signing deeds, 1653 to 1656; and 11 per cent of 199 men, between 1686 and 1697. Fifty-eight per cent of 48 women made marks in the first period named; and 38 per cent of 130 women made marks in the second period. In New Netherlands, a study of 154 names of women showed 60 per cent illiterate. Of 274 men at Flatbush, 19 per cent made marks; while at Albany 21 per cent were illiterate.[114] Weber reported 23.9 per cent illiteracy among German men.[115] In Virginia, Bruce found 40 to 46 per cent of illiteracy among men; among women who signed deeds and depositions in Virginia, he found that 75 per cent were unable to sign their names.[116]

Whatever may have been the exact state of things as to writing in the several colonies, it is perfectly certain that there was a much greater percentage of illiteracy among women than men; it is likewise certain that both men and women spelled abominably—but the women probably more erratically.[117] This was a universal weakness. The great Webster was not yet. When one compares the spelling of the generation preceding him and that of the one which followed him, one is compelled to agree

[112] See pp. 162 ff.; also consult Dexter: *Colonial Women of Affairs.*
[113] *Records of Conn.,* 1778–1780, II, 544–61.
[114] *Dutch Schools of New Netherlands,* 228 ff.
[115] *Charity School Movement,* 14.
[116] *Institutional History of Va.,* I, Ch. XVIII.
[117] E.g., a letter from Elizabeth Belknap to Hezekiah Wyllys [*Coll. Conn. Hist. Soc.,* XXI, 402].

with his own estimate of his influence, 'that it was truly remarkable.'[118]

IV. Economic, Social and Political Condition

As women did more housework than anything else, it is interesting to note what duties were usually performed by the housewife herself or by servants, if the position of the family made possible the employment of assistance. Herein, the rules laid down in English guides to housewifery, such as Tusser's *Five Hundred Points of Good Husbandry*, his *Book of Housewifery*, and *Derictions for ye Maides in ye House*, are suggestive, though they do not exactly fit the situation of early Colonial settlers, far removed from the convenience of their old English homes. Certainly the duties prescribed for special maids were often of necessity performed by the wife alone.[119] Later there were plenty of servants for those who could afford the luxury.[120] Besides these, the New England housewife was sometimes assisted by poor girls who were apprenticed to learn an occupation, and in the meantime, perhaps, taught to read.[121] Tusser named "Brewing, Baking, Cookery, Dairy, Scouring, Washing, Dinner matters, Afternoon Works, Evening Works, Supper matters, [and] After supper matters" as the groups into which woman's duties fell. Brewing was important not only to prepare drink for the household and laborers but also to feed swine.

> "Brew somewhat for thine
> "Else bring up no swine."[122]

The following duties, in *Derictions for ye Maides*, from the papers of Captain Stewart, were not necessarily performed by maids in New England, but they show what the English wife must have felt called upon to do in order to have a well-regulated household. Possibly in this orderly arrangement of duties lay

[118] Webster's answer to Cobb: *To the Friends of American Literature*, an eight-page pamphlet, 1829.

[119] Compare Salmon: *Domestic Service*, Chaps. III and IV.

[120] Typical advertisements of white servants—*Boston News Letter*, Oct. 5–12, 1713; *Boston Ev. Post*, Dec. 14, 1741 and May 24, 1742.

[121] *Col. Rec. R. I.*, V, 40; *Early Records of Town of Providence*, XII, 85.

[122] Quoted by Earle: *Margaret Winthrop*, 58–60.

the foundation of that reputation which the wives of New England have borne to the present day.

"Mondays. Look out the foule clothes, and cale the maids and sit or stay by them till they be all mended.

"Tuisdays. Clene the Romes and Shers from ye great Rome to the nersery, and ye beads on ye Tope and botom, and dust ye feathers.

"Wednesdays. Clene all the Romes Chers and beads onder and Tope with ye feathers from the nersery to ye Eyll Chamber.

"Thursdays. Clene ye Hall and Parlors windows tables chears and Pictors below stairs.

"Fridays. Scoure all the grats, tongs, and Hand-Irons.

"Saturdays. Clene the Store house, Shelfs and Dressers.

"Every-day. Once for one houre in ye fore-noone goe throught all ye Romes and see it doith not Raine into them, and dust them all downe, and swipe them.

"Dery-maid. Wash yor dery every day, and for yor milke and butter doe as you will be dericted. Churne Tuisdays and Fridays. Sarve ye Swine and Pouletrey night and morning; and for the Hogesmeat any of the Servent-mens shall carry that out for you. Observe well the time for seting all sorts of yor Pouletrey; Once every weeke make your House breed, an the same shall helpe you need it.

"Cooke-maid. Washe yor Chitchen every night, and the Larders every other day, Shelfes and dressers; and scour the puter we use every friday night, and all ye Rest of ye Puter once every month. Kepe your chitchen exthrodinary clene. To helpe upon washing dayes ye reste of ye maides wash. And make all ye Maides bring downe their candell-stickes ye first thing in ye morning to be made clene."[123]

A year before the Declaration of Independence, Abigail Foote wrote in her diary the duties which occupied her time. From it, one may judge that few changes had been made in domestic tasks throughout the Colonial existence—though to card "two pounds of whole wool" did make her feel "Nationly."

"Fix'd gown for Prude—Mend Mother's Riding-hood—Spun short thread—Fix'd two gowns for Welsh's girls—Carded tow —Spun linen—Worked on Cheese basket, Hatchel'd flax with Hannah, we did 51 lbs. a-piece—Pleated and ironed—Read a

[123] *Ibid.*, 55–6.

sermon of Doddridge's—Spooled a piece—Milked the cows—
Spun linen, did 50 knots—Made a Broom of Guinea-wheat straw
—Spun thread to whiten—Set a Red dye—Had two scholars
from Mrs. Taylor's—I carded two pounds of whole wool and
felt Nationly—Spun harness twine, scoured the pewter."[124]

Although the New England colonist was greatly impressed
with the idea that woman's sphere was in the home, the number
of occupations entered outside the home was greater than has
generally been believed. A study of newspaper advertisements
of the eighteenth century shows that, particularly in the larger
cities, women entered numerous fields in the industrial and commercial world. This is especially true of women in Boston,
New York and Philadelphia. Dexter, in her study of *Colonial
Women of Affairs*, concluded, after counting the advertisements
of the first half of 1773, that probably 9 per cent of the merchants were women. The businesses in which they engaged
were various, the list embracing the selling of dishes, hardware,
cutlery, dry goods, books, drugs, tobacco, wines, diamonds—a
variety of jewelry in fact—and groceries. Besides shopkeeping,
Colonial women often kept taverns and sometimes were interested in privateers. In industrial life they were found as
seamstresses, repairers of umbrellas, wigs and fans, and manufacturers of soap, candles, and many kinds of baked and preserved foods. The range of occupations included smithing,
management of land, and smuggling. These findings vary considerably from those reported by Dwight, in the early nineteenth century, who says, "The employments of women of New
England are wholly domestic. The business which is abroad, is
all performed by men, even in the humblest spheres of life."[125]
It must be recalled, however, that he is here contrasting the
foreign custom of having women work in the fields with the prevailing custom in America.[126]

A few specific cases of occupations other than housekeeping
may be noted. Numerous items in the early records of Provi-

124 From Abigail Foote's diary, quoted in Talbot's *Education of
Women*, 7–8.
125 *Travels in New England*, IV, 459–63. Compare Weeden, I, 366, 398 and
436; II, 731–2, and 885; and Calhoun: *Soc. Hist. Am. Fam.*, I, 101.
126 For a study of women in various occupations, consult Dexter: *Colonial
Women of Affairs*.

dence show that women were licensed to keep public houses and were frequently licensed to "retale strong drinke," the period of time usually being one year.[127] Susanna Warner was apprenticed, in 1713, to learn the "art and mystery of a tailor," and to "learne to Read." To secure these gifts and also "two new sutes of apparill" at the end of six years, she promised "true and faithfull service," not to "frequent Taverns nor ale houses," not to "absent herself neither by night nor by day," not to "comitt Fornication," nor to "Contract Matrimony with any Person."[128] Another cut "gentle-women's hair in the newest fashion."[129] Joanna Perry operated a bookshop in Boston in 1717; while Mrs. Nutmaker, 1742, sold everything that women and children could conceivably put on.[130] A lady staymaker advertised in Boston in 1717; and Mary Crebb, in 1739, did "all kinds of fancy work for the public."[131] Hannah Chapman (1748) made and sold a "mixture that will cure the itch, or any other breaking out, by the smell of it"; but she seems to have overestimated the efficacy of her medicine, or advertising was ineffectual, as Marryat and others noted the prevalence of that complaint nearly a century later.[132] The woman shoplifter was not unknown.[133]

In all the colonies women were recognized as competent midwives.[134] Among those famous in New England were Mrs. Wiat, Mrs. Whitmore, Mrs. Fuller, Elizabeth Phillips, and Anne Hutchinson. The midwife was regarded as an important public servant. The *Newport Mercury*, in 1760, took note of the death of Mrs. Mary Turner, aged eighty-seven, "an experienced midwife, and otherwise useful in the community, by assisting those who labored under the Disorders incident to the Human body, with her advice and remedies." Notwithstanding she had thirteen children living and ninety-eight grandchildren, "she retained her reason and memory to the last; [and] employed

---

[127] E.g., *Early Records, Providence*, VI, 44 and X, 112, wherein Mary Prey and Anne Tirpin were so licensed.

[128] *Ibid.*, IX, 5–6.

[129] *Boston News Letter*, Aug. 20–27, 1716.

[130] *Ibid.*, June 17, 1717; *Boston Ev. Post*, Apr. 12, 1742, 2, col. 1.

[131] *News Letter*, Sept. 30, 1717; *Post*, Feb. 12, 1739, 2, col. 2.

[132] *Boston Ev. Post*, Mch. 21, 1748, 4.

[133] *Boston News Letter*, Dec. 22, 1712.

[134] See "Entrance of Women into Medical Schools," Ch. VII, Vol. II.

all her leisure hours in reading.''[135] Some made more or less
definite preparation for their profession; such was Mary Bass,
who had ''studied under the Direction of some of the most
eminent Professors in New England'' and said she could show
certificates ''signed by gentlemen of the faculty, whose Veracity
will not be questioned.''[136]

Teaching, on a very limited scale it is true, was among the positions first opened to women. A Mrs. Jupe is named as teacher
of the Ipswich School—a dame school presumably—in 1639;[137]
these dame schools, either as private ventures or encouraged by
the towns, were quite common. At Wenham, 1746, Mrs. Kimball
was ''approved of and approbated to keep school in our town to
teach children and youth to read and write, she having behaved
in sober conversation.'' Official recognition by the town also appeared in Gilsum, New Hampshire, where Rachel Bill was
approved of for teaching: ''These may certify whom it may concern, that having examined Miss Rachel Bill concerning her
qualifications for a school dame, cannot but judge her a person
qualified for that business, and as such do hereby recommend
her wherever a door shall be opened for her improvement,
Clement Sumner.''[138]

But if she was free to earn a wage in the dame school, it did
not follow that the wage was always hers. There are many instances in which the dames' salaries were paid to husbands. A
townsman in 1765 entered this minute: ''Gave an order in
favor of Mr. Andrew Tucksbury for the sum of £2–6 lawful
money for his wife's schooling twelve scholars, each 17 weeks
and three days, at three shillings and two pence one farthing
per week.''[139] Small also mentions the case of a schoolmistress,
as late as 1817, in Medford, who had been ''employed for this
work at twenty-five dollars a month and board'' and whose husband ''for about a year and a half [drew] with great regularity
both his own salary and his wife's.''[140]

The records of Connecticut show that a woman on one occasion
bound books, and in another instance was given permission to

135 Feb. 26, 1760, 4, col. 1.
136 *Providence Gazette*, Aug. 3, 1776, 4, col. 1.
137 See p. 138.
138 Small: *Early New England Schools*, 178.
139 *Ibid.*, 173.
140 *Ibid.*, 170.

operate a ferry. Mrs. Elizabeth Short received £50 from the public treasury, in 1714, for binding two thousand copies of the Confession of Faith.[141] Mary Dudley, of Saybrook, was recognized by the Colonial government as a partner of Stephen Wittlesey in the building and operation of a ferry.[142] Records of this sort are not numerous; and certainly these occupations were not usual for women, though printing and publishing of newspapers was frequently taken over by widows at the death of their husbands.

Hector St. John, in *Letters of an American Farmer,* gives the women of Nantucket a very independent character, which, he says, is derived from their being obliged to transact business while their husbands are away on long "sea excursions." "This ripens their judgment and justly entitles them to a rank superior to that of other wives. . . . The men, at their return, weary with the fatigues of the sea . . . cheerfully give their consent to every transaction that has happened during their absence. . . . 'Wife, thee has done well' is the general approbation they receive. . . . What would they do without the agency of these faithful mates?"[143] Ability in commercial affairs, which appeared so often in the larger cities, likewise attracted his notice in one particular instance:

"The richest person now in the island owes all his present prosperity and success to the ingenuity of his wife: this is a known fact which is well recorded; for while he was performing his first cruises, she traded with pins and needles, and kept a school. Afterward she purchased more considerable articles, which she sold with so much judgment, that she laid the foundation of a system of business, that she has ever since prosecuted with equal dexterity and success. She wrote to London, formed connections, and in short, became the only ostensible instrument of that house, both at home and abroad. Who is he in this country, and who is a citizen of Nantucket or Boston who does not know Aunt Kesiah? I must tell you that she is the wife of Mr. C——n, a very respectable man, who, well pleased with all her

[141] *Col. Rec. of Conn.,* V, 1706–1716, 423.

[142] *Ibid.,* VI, 212, 284 and 323.

[143] Taken by permission from the Everyman's Library edition of Crèvecoeur's *Letters of an American Farmer,* published by J. M. Dent & Sons, Ltd., London, and E. P. Dutton & Co., Inc., New York. Pp. 146–7.

schemes, trusts to her judgment, and relies on her sagacity, with so entire a confidence, as to be altogether passive to the concerns of the family. They have the best country seat on the island, at Quayes, where they live with hospitality, and in perfect union. He seems to be altogether the contemplative man.

"To this dexterity in managing the husband's business whilst he is absent, the Nantucket wives unite a great deal of industry. They spin, or cause to be spun in their houses, abundance of wool and flax; and would be forever disgraced and looked upon as idlers if all the family were not clad in good, neat, and sufficient homespun cloth. First Days are the only seasons when it is lawful for both sexes to exhibit some garments of English manufacture; even these are of the most moderate price, and of the gravest colors: there is no kind of difference in their dress, they are all clad alike, and resemble in that respect the members of one family."[144]

Marriage was the most common state for women of early New England, as it generally is in newly forming societies. Girls frequently married under sixteen years of age and men under twenty. Some towns assigned lots to men after their marriage, while others—Hartford for example—laid a fine of 20 shillings on those who did not marry. The Plymouth Court enforced the old ordinance that a single man could not live alone.[145] To be reckoned an "ancient maide" was then, and has generally been, till recently, a reproach. Of not many could it be said, as it was of a woman of Plymouth, that they were godly old maids, never married.[146] Naturally, early marriage meant the shortening of the school period and reduced learning to little beyond the apprenticeship training at the mother's hands and a smattering of rudiments, possibly obtained at the dame school.

If marriage was early, courtship was hasty. Men were busy, and there were few social affairs, in the earlier years, for the entertainment of the young, however common they became in the latter part of the eighteenth century. Calhoun, after a careful study of this aspect of woman's life, says: "In more than one instance a lonely Puritan came to the door of a maiden he had never seen, presented credentials, told his need of a

144 *Ibid.*, 148–50.
145 Weeden: *Econ. and Soc. Hist. New England*, I, 293 *ff.*
146 Calhoun: *Soc. Hist. Am. Family*, I, 69.

housekeeper, proposed marriage, obtained hasty consent, and notified the town clerk, all in one day. On one occasion a bold fellow removed a rival's name from the posted marriage notice, inserted his own, and carried off the bride. After his death she married the first lover. Another Lochinvar kidnapped a bride-to-be on the eve of marriage.''[147]

But it sometimes happened that neither the Captain nor John Alden 'asked,' but were 'asked' by the Puritan maiden. The sad predicament of Cotton Mather is related in his diary:

''There is a young gentlewoman of incomparable accomplishments. No gentlewoman in the English Americas has had a more polite education. She is one of rare wit and sense and of a comely aspect; and . . . she has a mother of an extraordinary character for her piety. This young gentlewoman first addresses me with diverse letters, and then makes me a visit at my house; wherein she gives me to understand, that she has long had more than an ordinary value for my ministry; and that since my present condition has given her more of liberty to think of me, she must confess herself charmed with my person to such a degree, that she could not but break in upon me, with her most importunate requests, that I should make her mine, and that the highest consideration she had in it was her eternal salvation, for if she were mine, she could not but hope the effect of it would be that she should also be Christ's. I endeavored faithfully to set before her all the discouraging circumstances attending me, that I could think of. She told me that she had weighed all those discouragements but was fortified and with a strong faith in the mighty God for to encounter them all. . . . I was in a great strait how to treat so polite a gentlewoman. . . . I plainly told her that I feared, whether her proposal would not meet with unsurmountable opposition, from those who had a great interest in disposing of me. However I desired that there might be time taken to see what would be the wisest and fittest Resolution. . . . In the meantime, if I could not make her my own, I should be glad of being any way instrumental, to make her the Lord's. . . . She is not much more than twenty years old. I know she has been a very aiery person. Her reputation has been under some disadvantage. What snares may be laying for me I know not.''

[147] Reprinted by permission of the publishers, The Arthur H. Clark Company, from Calhoun's *Social History of the American Family*, I, 52.

Later he wrote: ''All the friends I have in the world . . . persuade me, that I shall have no way to get from under these confusions but by proceeding unto another marriage. Lord help me, what shall I do? I am a miserable man.''[148]

There was likewise a certain Mrs. Hicks who, although the records do not tell that she proposed outright, must have used subtle arguments. ''She came over in a vessel from England, unattended apparently, and at once brought to her feet and to the altar a merchant of Salem, reputed to be worth £30,000.''[149]

In the married state, women, as a rule, had little legal independence. St. John gave special reasons to show why those of Nantucket became independent in business. We have already pointed out that women teachers frequently received their wages *through* their husbands—if at all. To give deed to a property, it appears they generally made memorials to the court to grant them permission.[150]

The inheritance of married women in Connecticut was regulated, as follows, in 1696; some such provision was made in other colonies. ''Ordered by this Court that when any man dieth intestate leaving an estate, his widow if any be (shall have besides the third part of his reall estate during her life) a part also of his personall estate equall to his eldest child, provided it exceed not a third part of ye s^d personall estate, which said part of her husbands personall estate shall be her own forever.''[151]

Considering the disability with which the law invested woman and the complete powers which were lodged in the hands of her husband—he might beat her, provided he did it for her own good—it is not strange that domestic happiness was frequently broken, or that the wife ran away. The following are representative of complaints made by wives.

[148] Mather's *Diary* [Mass. Hist. Soc. *Collections*, Seventh Ser., Vol. VII, Part I, 457–8, 477].

[149] Weeden: *Econ. and Soc. Hist. of New England*, I, 299–300.

[150] For a single example: ''Upon the memorial of Mrs. Abigail Lord of Hartford, liberty and full power is granted to her by this Court, to give a deed to Joseph Petty of Coventry for a parcel of land lying within the township of Coventry, which her late husband, Mr. Richard Lord of Hartford, in his life time sold to said Petty and did not give a deed for. Also she is impowred, upon the receipt of money due upon any mortgage of lands made to her deceased husband, to release and quit claim unto the respective mortgagers, their heirs, &c.''—*Col. Rec. Conn.*, V, 314.

[151] *Col. Rec. Conn.*, IV, 1689–1706, 167.

In 1691, the fathers of Providence noted:

"Whereas their is a Complaynt made by Hannah Pierce unto ye towne that her husband hath locked her out of doers & hath sold his farme shee desiring the townes Assistant. The towne doe refer the matter to ye next quarter day & for Ephraim Pierce, then by warning to appeare before the towne to Answere the Complaynt of his sd wife his sd wife also there to appeare."[152]

A notice, in the *Boston Evening Post*[153] informed the public: "William McAlpine has no servants that have deserted their business or run him in debt. But his wife, whom he has repeatedly beat and abused, and finally kick'd out of doors, has (to shun his further abuses) removed from him. She has not run him in debt or taken anything out of his house, but her own property, which no man of humanity could refuse."

Generally the husband opened hostilities, in a public way, by advertising the wife's misdemeanors. Nearly always he said she had "eloped" his "bed and board," or had run him into debt.[154] Alexander Mason asserted that his wife had "failed in her attempt upon his life" but continued to "ruine his Estate."[155] Honour Rook, it was declared, had by "divers notorious actions greatly injured" the business and interests of her husband;[156] and Bridget Southworth had "hearkened to the Counsel of some of her wicked neighbors," absented herself, and continued to live abroad, in "breach of the marriage covenant."[157]

Early laws were aimed at the reduction of frivolity, petty vices, personal extravagance, and the prohibition of satisfaction of cravings for this world's vanities. Law concerned itself with the most trifling details of private life of the home. Single women, or wives, if their husbands were absent, could not take in lodgers because of the "appearance of sin," and married folks were on occasion reproved for their "uncivil carriage."[158] The *Newport Mercury*[159] published a satire on the "Boston Sabbath" as it was controlled by law:

152 *Early Records, Providence*, VIII, 179.
153 Nov. 7, 1763, 3, col. 2.
154 E.g., *Newport Mercury*, Feb. 26, 1760, 4, col. 1; June 16, 1766, 4, col. 2.
155 *Boston News Letter*, May 16–23, 1715.
156 *Boston Ev. Post*, May 14, 1744, 4, col. 2.
157 *Ibid.*, Aug. 31, 1741, 2, col. 2.
158 Weeden: *op. cit.*, 293–4.
159 May 19, 1761, 3, cols. 2–3.

"In ancient days, 'twas God's most sacred will,
"T' expound his law on Sinai's lofty hill;
"Whose top terrific, issu'd clouds of smoke,
"And thus amidst the flames, the Great Eternal spoke;
"Six days, said he (and loud the same expressed)
"Shall men still labor, on the seventh rest;
"But here alas in this great pious town
"The' annul his law and thus prefer their own,
"And let it be enacted, further still,
"That all our people strict observe our will:
"Five days and half, shall men and women too,
"Attend their business, and their mirth pursue:
"But after that, no man without a fine,
"Shall walk the streets, or at a tavern dine,
"One day and half, 'tis requisite to rest,
"From toilsome labor, and a luscious feast
"Henceforth, let none, on peril of their lives
"Attempt a journey, or embrace their wives;
"No barber, foreign or domestic, bred,
"Shall once presume to dress a ladies head
"No shops shall spare, on the preceding day,
"A yard of ribbon or an ounce of tea.
"Five days and half, the inhabitants may ride
"All round the town, and villages beside!
"But if by chance they lose their destin'd road,
"'Tis our command, they lodge that night abroad.
"From hence 'tis plainly seen, how chang'd indeed
"That sacred law, which God himself decreed!
"In this one act they think to merit Heav'n,
"By taking half a day from six, and adding it to seven."

Notwithstanding the slur at Boston, the General Assembly of
Rhode Island, in 1762, passed an act "to prevent stage plays,
and other theatrical entertainments . . ." which "occasion great
and unnecessary expenses, and discourage industry and frugality
[and] likewise tend generally to increase immorality, impiety
and contempt of religion."[160] Any one letting a house to be
used for such purposes was to be fined £50 for each time so used.

Families who spent their time in idleness were to be "presented." It is related that while the Pilgrims were in Holland
Parson Johnson married a stylish widow, much to the chagrin
of his congregation; and that for her "garrish" and proud
apparel she was condemned and ordered to "discontinue ye
whalebones and starcht Ruffs, ye Muske, and ye Ringes"; and

[160] *Col. Rec. R. I.*, VI, 324 ff.

to substitute for her "Schowish Hatt" a modest "Taffety or Felt"; and whatever she wears not to "sett it so Toppishly." In 1673, thirty women and maids together, from the towns of Springfield, Northampton, Hadley, Hatfield and Westfield, were presented because they were "persons of small estate" and "wore silk contrary to law." Three years following, 38 women and 30 men were presented, "some for wearing silk, some for long hair, and other extravagancies."[161] This was after a half century of Colonial existence; within less than another ten years the situation appears to have changed remarkably and we find the selectmen of the five towns arraigned before the court for non-enforcement of the law.

Any reference to a preference for silks and long hair cannot but recall *The Simple Cobbler of Agawam,* who, though he remained in America but a short time, returning to England before 1647, undoubtedly expressed the contempt of true Puritans everywhere for the vanities of the world. He condemns, "with all the indignation" possible, the "nugiperous Gentledame," who inquires what dress the Queen is in this week or "what the nudiustertian fashion of the Court; with egge to be in it in all haste, what ever it be; I look at her as the very gizzard of a trifle, the product of a quarter of a cypher, the epitome of Nothing, fitter to be Kickt, if she were of a kickable substance, than either honour'd or humour'd. . . .

"I point my Pen only against the light-heel'd beagles that lead the chase so fast, that they run all civility out of breath, against these Ape-headed Pullets, which invent Antique foolfangles, merely for fashion and novelty sake. . . .

"It is beyond all account, how many Gentlemens and Citizens Estates are deplumed by their feather-headed Wives, what useful supplies the pannage of England would afford other Countries, what rich returns to itself, if it were not slic'd out into Male and Female fripperies. . . ."[162]

The prevalence of belief in witchcraft in New England made life very hazardous for women. Frequently they were compelled to appear before the court even though the accusations were

[161] Weeden: *op. cit.,* 289.
[162] *The Simple Cobbler of Agawam,* 19–20, and 22–3.

slight.[163]   Women who were merely "Common Scoulds" were to be "punished with the Ducking Stools."[164]

Throughout the eighteenth century the old Puritan vigilance was gradually more and more relaxed, so that by the Revolution there was in Boston, and in other ambitious places, a great amount of fancy dress and fashionable society.   The hair was often dressed over a roll, such as that described by Anne Green Winslow, a little school girl, in 1771: "I had my heddus roll on; Aunt Storer said it ought to be made less, Aunt Deming said it ought not to be made at all."[165]   Women of style wore high bonnets of silk or satin, high-heeled shoes, silk stockings, and huge gowns of silk or brocade distended over hoops.   The fashion of hoop-skirts was fully established by 1727.   Weeden says: "Such a breezy revolution in the volume of petticoats did not come in without profound ethical disturbance and physical portents, according to the magnitude of the change.   The good women had hardly adjusted their trains to the enlarging demand of fickle Fashion, when Nature, by an unusual disturbance, frightened the poor dames into narrower draperies.   An earthquake occurred, and the people of a considerable town in Massachusetts were 'so awakened by this awful Providence that the women generally laid aside their Hoop Petticoats.' "[166]   A string of gold beads, thirty-nine in number, frequently adorned the neck.   One proverb had it that a woman was "so poor she hadn't a bead to her neck."[167]   A Young Man's Journal (1783–1874) gives a lively impression of the gay society that had become common.   He mentions many assemblies which are attended by the ladies, and is thoroughly convinced of the supremacy of the ladies of New England over those of New York.   At Litchfield he is "favored with the presence of the most angelic form in a female"

163 Will and Doom, or the Miseries of Connecticut [Coll. Conn. Hist. Soc., III, 233 ff.].

164 Col. Rec. R. I., I, 185; but that New England was much like the rest of the United States is shown by the fact that, as late as 1829, Mrs. Anne Royall was tried as a common scold in Washington, D. C., and the Navy racked its brains to devise a ducking stool for her.—Porter: Life and Times of Anne Royall, 134 ff.

165 Atlantic Mo., August, 1893, 219.

166 Op. cit., II, 537–8.

167 Ibid., II, 859–60.

that he ever saw, whose skin is "like paper" but "animated with a little of the vermillion. . . ."

That stylish dress was a point of pride in the cities is suggested by the fact that a little school miss at Boston, in 1771, was greatly disturbed because of her outfit: "I hope Aunt won't let me wear that black hat with the Red Dominie for the people will ask me . . . what I have got to sell as I go along the street . . . or how the folks at New Guinea do? Dear Mamma you don't know the fashions here. . . . I beg to look like other folks. . . ." But when she was provided with yellow coat, black bib, apron, "pompedore," shoes, cap, locket, pin, gloves, new cloak and bonnet, she said, "They all liked my dress very much."[168] The cloak and bonnet cost "an amazing sight of money" and she was inclined to think "Aunt Deming would be frightened out of her wits at . . . it. . . ." These fashion notes of pre-Revolutionary Boston are mixed with a description of the girl's studies, an attempt to describe a sermon, a bit old-fashioned —which retained many of the terrors held forth to earlier generations—the ministers' gowns, and an assembly where she had the honor to "open the diversion of the evening in a minuet with Miss Soley." But, if we are inclined to think her more interested in the fashions and assembly than in the lessons and sermon, she proves by her own statement to have retained a good degree of industry:

"I have finished my shift, I began it 12 o'clock last Monday; have read my Bible every day this week, and wrote every day save one. . . . I have spun 30 knots of lining yarn and partly new footed a pair of stockings for Lucinda, read a part of the Pilgrims Progress, copied a part of my text journal, . . . played some, tucked a great deal, laughed enough and I tell Aunt it is all human nature if not human reason. . . .[169]

"Aunt says I have been a very good girl today about my work, however I think this day's work may be called a piece meal; for in the first place I sewed on the bosom of uncles shirt, mended two pairs of gloves, mended for the wash two handkerchiefs (one cambric), sewed on half a border of a lawn apron of Aunt's, read a part of the xxi Chapter of Exodus and a story in the Mothers Gift."[170]

[168] *Atlantic Mo.*, August, 1893.
[169] *Ibid.*
[170] *Ibid.*

On the whole, life at the Revolutionary period seems to have been very pleasant. St. John, in describing the customs of Nantucket, comments on the "custom of incessant visiting" which "has infected every one, and even those whose husbands do not go abroad. . . . When the good man of the house returns from his labor, he peaceably goes after his wife and brings her home . . . meanwhile the young fellows, equally vigilant, easily find out which is the most convenient house, and there they assemble with the girls of the neighborhood."[171] They marry early and settle down, as "the title of master of a family necessarily requires more solid behavior and deportment. . . ." Brissot de Warville says: "The young women here enjoy the liberty they do in England, that they did in Geneva when morals were there . . . and they do not abuse it. Their frank and tender hearts have nothing to fear from the perfidy of men. Examples of this perfidy are rare; the vows of love are believed; and love always respects them, or shame follows the guilty."[172] Of Bostonian mothers, he says "they are reserved," "somewhat frank, good and communicative" and "entirely devoted to their families. They are occupied in rendering their husbands happy, and in training their children to virtue."[173] Apparently the new society could not quite sweep away the customs of olden time when, as the chronicler put it, "the Hyacinth follows not the sun more willingly than she her husband's pleasure."[174]

At Salem, Massachusetts, de Warville writes: "It was cold, and we had a fire in a Franklin stove. These are common here, and those chimneys that have them not, are built as described by M. de Crèvecoeur: they rarely smoke. The mistress of the tavern . . . was taking tea with her daughters; they invited us to partake of it with them.—I repeat it, we have nothing like this in France. It is a general remark through all the United States: a tavern-keeper must be a respectable man, his daughters are well dressed, and have an air of decency and civility."[175]

[171] Taken by permission from the Everyman's Library edition of Crèvecoeur's *Letters of an American Farmer*, published by J. M. Dent & Sons, Ltd., London, and E. P. Dutton & Co., Inc., New York. P. 147.
[172] Brissot de Warville: *New Travels*, 95–6.
[173] *Ibid.*
[174] Weeden: *Econ. and Soc. Hist. of New England*, I, 301.
[175] *Ibid.*, 448.

Early in the nineteenth century, Josiah P. Quincy depicted the accelerated gaities of life at the chief city: "In the regions of fashion dancing still continues the rage. Private balls are numerous, and little cotillion parties occur every week. The dancing disease having gradually ascended till it reached the middle-aged, now begins to descend on the other side of the hill and attacks the old. . . . The public balls were quite neglected except the last, which, being the first of January, was crowded and brilliant—though not, say the fashionables, very genteel.

"The night before last, as my cold was better," continues a society girl of the period, "I ventured to Mrs. James Perkin's, who gave a ball to more than two hundred people in town, with their children and in some cases grandchildren. It was very pleasant, well-conducted and perfectly satisfactory to all tastes. They had dancing for the young, cards and conversation for the old and for those who love eating an excellent collation of solid good things in the side-board style."[176]

With a very few exceptions, women of Colonial New England appear to have thought very little about their equality or inequality with men. Barnes says that in "our colonial period women had a large influence in determining community questions, and, in Massachusetts, under the old Providence Charter, they voted for all elective officers for nearly a hundred years."[177] But by the time of our independence women were not voting, and the privilege of determining who should vote was left by the constitution to the states; the decision for male suffrage was unanimous. Abigail Adams and Mercy Otis Warren are exceptions to the general rule that no voice was raised to demand that independence be secured for women as it was for men. Mrs. Adams wrote to her spouse: "Do not put such unlimited power in the hands of the husbands. . . . Remember the ladies, and be more generous and favorable to them than your ancestors."[178]

Eliza Southgate, about 1800, expressed her views rather independently on the subject of marriage and education, but denied that she was a disciple of Mary Wollstonecraft, though she al-

[176] See the *Memorial History*, IV, quoted by Crawford: *Old Boston Days and Ways*, 402–3.

[177] Barnes: *Women in Modern Society*, 174; compare Porter: *Suffrage in the United States*.

[178] Robinson: *Mass. in the Women Suffrage Movement*, 8–9.

lowed her "to have said many things which I cannot but approve." Women and men should have separate spheres of action and women should be "under the same degree of subordination that they now are"; but "to cultivate the qualities with which we are endowed can never be called infringing the prerogatives of man. Why . . . were we furnished with such powers unless the improvement of them would conduce to the happiness of society? Do you suppose the mind of woman the only work of God that was made in vain? The cultivation of the powers we possess, I have ever thought a privilege (or I may say duty) that belonged to the human species, and not man's exclusive prerogative."[179]

She not only defended woman's right to an education but her right not to marry. "I do not esteem marriage absolutely essential to happiness, and that it does not always bring happiness we must every day witness in our acquaintance. A single life is considered too generally as a reproach; but let me ask you which is the most despicable—she who marries a man she scarcely thinks well of—to avoid the reputation of an old maid—or she, who with more delicacy, than marry one she could not highly esteem, preferred to live single all her life, and had wisdom enough to despise so mean a sacrifice, to the opinion of the rabble, as the woman who marries a man she has not much love for—must make. I wish not to alter the laws of nature—neither will I quarrel with the rules which custom has established and rendered indispensably necessary to the harmony of society. But every being who has contemplated human nature on a large scale will certainly justify me when I declare that the inequality of privilege between the sexes is very sensibly felt by us females, and in no instance is it greater than in the liberty of refusing those we don't like, but not of selecting those we do."[180]

[179] Cook: *Girl's Life Eighty Years Ago*, 60–1.
[180] *Ibid.*, 36–9.

CHAPTER V

EARLY EDUCATION OF GIRLS IN NEW YORK, PENN-SYLVANIA, DELAWARE, AND NEW JERSEY

I. *Religious, Social, and Economic Condition*

Everywhere religion has played an important rôle in education. This has been most conspicuous in early stages of civilization; the American colonies were no exception to this general rule. We have already noted that religion occupied an important place in the life of children as well as adults of New England. In the central colonies it was no less true. Nevertheless, we have to deal here with a different religious bias. In New England, the combined influence of Calvinism and the traditional English conception of education resulted in no provision for girls, in the earlier years, beyond the rudiments gained somewhat irregularly in the dame schools. The elementary town schools did not open to them as a general rule until the latter part of the eighteenth century, and then but a few hours, at the most inconvenient time, when boys did not occupy the master's attention.

In some of the central colonies we find a more equitable treatment granted to girls, and this is in part traceable to different religious conceptions. The Friends accepted, in a most complete sense, the idea of equality of all men, inasmuch as they held that in all there dwelt a measure of the divine. All possessed the *inner light*, whether male or female. And since men became ministers of the 'word' without the classical education obtained in the ecclesiastical colleges of the day, so also did women. There was no denial of their privilege of speaking. The inefficacy of higher learning to form true ministers was set forth by numerous Quaker leaders.[1] The belief was persistent. Of Rebecca Hubbs, a woman preacher, it was said: "Her schooling was much neglected and her literary acquirements were very slender. But the seasoning virtue of Divine Grace and an humble obedi-

[1] Woody: *Early Quaker Education in Pa.*, 4, 11, 31.

177

ence to its teachings were eminently instrumental in raising her up out of her low estate. . . . With this meagre equipment of secular learning she travelled to all the yearly meetings from New England to North Carolina and into the then Western communities.''[2]

But if the higher learning of the ecclesiastical college was not encouraged, and if male and female ministers were sometimes not well instructed, there was a general insistence on the necessity of establishing elementary schools—for boys and girls— apprenticeship training in some craft or business, and strict moral and religious training for both sexes. The elementary school, equally open to the sexes, is, however, the chief distinguishing feature.[3] Equality prevailed in family life; in marriage there was no promise of obedience.[4]

Wherever the Germans settled they generally established elementary schools in connection with their churches; and in these elementary institutions, controlled by the church, the congregation and ministers sought to bring practice into accord with Luther's pious wish: "Would to God that each town had a girls' school in which girls might be taught the Gospel for an hour daily, either in German or Latin. . . ."[5] Promising talent, both in boys and girls, was to be cultivated far more extensively and for a longer time, in order to prepare them to be teachers. These were more than pious wishes to the earnest German and, in both his homeland and America, elementary schools were created. But that the establishment was slow in the rigorous environment of the wilderness is not to be doubted; and statements of Rush, for example, show that elementary education did not obtain everywhere.[6] It should also be pointed out that, although education in the rudiments and religion was allowed to girls, there was no doctrine of equality sufficient to open up the ministry to women. Since the ministry in those days was the great arena of public influence, the German women·continued to concern themselves with *Kinder, Küche*, and *Kirche;* and in

2 *A Memoir of Rebecca Hubbs,* 12–13.

3 For the beginning of schools see p. 197.

4 See *Rules of Discipline* (1828), 43–51; and marriage form, 1719, in Christian and Brotherly Advices (*MS.*), 398.

5 Painter: *Luther on Education,* 147; see also Ch. II, 82 *ff.*

6 Rush: *Account of the German Inhabitants of Pa.,* 105; see also *Hallische Nachrichten,* I, 144 *f.*

the latter they listened always to men. The minor German communities, whether Mennonite or Dunker, contributed no novelty in the education of girls. They had little place for any education, and so far as the position of women was concerned they followed the usual German practice.

The Moravians' view demands our attention not so much because of difference from that of Luther, but because they were energetic in the practical realization of school facilities. In their educational activities they were guided by the fundamental views spread abroad by their powerful leader, Comenius. As for women, he held they were fully as capable as men; and further asserted, "The more we occupy their thoughts, the less will there be place for the rashness which springs from empty minds."[7] Moreover, in the *School of Infancy, or The Mother School,* he provided that for six years the instruction of the young was to be by the mother who, by directing the observation, was to teach the beginning of meta-physics, physics, optics, astronomy, geography, chronology, arithmetic, history, geometry, statics, mechanics, dialectic, grammar, rhetoric, economics, polity, morality, piety, and religion. Naturally, the content of the foregoing subjects was not to be gained from books, but from his surroundings; the aim was to sharpen the interest in, and the observation of, the objective world, as a basis for further learning.

In New Netherlands the prevailing influence was that of the Dutch Reformed Church, combined with the secular power. While women of New Netherlands did not have such freedom under their religious system as did those professing the Quaker faith, insofar as elementary education was concerned they shared equally.[8] The Dutch Reformed Church, being Calvinist, held to the supremacy of the male as indicated in the form for the confirmation of marriage: "You, who are the bridegroom, must know, that God hath set you to be the head of your wife . . . instructing, comforting, protecting her as the head rules the body . . . [and to the wife] you are to love your lawful husband, to honor and fear him, as also to be obedient unto him. . . . You shall not exercise any dominion over your husband, but

[7] See *The Great Didactic,* 67–8.
[8] See p. 195.

be silent. . . ."⁹   As for entering the ministry, that was un-
thought of.   The Calvinist influence was not limited to Pennsylvania and New York, but was prominent in New Jersey where
colleges for the training of the ministry were established in the
eighteenth century.   In Delaware, too, in the Dutch and English
settlements, Calvinistic thought appeared, but was weakened
there as in New Jersey by the presence of many different religious persuasions.

But if the way was left open for the elementary education of
girls in the central colonies, it is true that their everyday duties
were very similar to those of New England.   In New Netherlands the care of the house and the dairy, spinning, baking, brewing, knitting, raising poultry, and many other domestic employments kept them busy.   Indeed, if anything, the Dutch women
seem to have been more preoccupied with these affairs than the
English.   Kalm wrote of the economy and industry of the
women of Albany:

"The inhabitants of Albany are much more sparing than the
English.   The meat which is served up is often insufficient to
satisfy the stomach, and the bowl does not circulate so freely as
amongst the English.   The women are perfectly well acquainted
with economy; they rise early, go to sleep very late, and are
almost over nice and cleanly, in regard to the floor, which is frequently scoured several times in the week.   The servants in the
town are chiefly negroes.   Some of the inhabitants wear their
own hair, but it is very short, without a bag or queue, which are
looked upon as the characteristics of Frenchmen; and as I wore
my hair in a bag the first day I came here from Canada, I was
surrounded with children, who called me Frenchman, and some
of the boldest offered to pull at my French dress."¹⁰

In spite of educational handicaps the English "were inveterate
letter-writers and diarists," whereas the Dutch were "neither
penwomen nor talkers."¹¹   Travellers were frequently impressed
with the idea that the society of the Dutch was very dull.   Even
the celebrated Catherine Schuyler was "very frugal, industrious

⁹ The Constitution of the Reformed Dutch Church of N. A. (1840 edition),
124–8.
¹⁰ Kalm: *Travels into N. A.*, II, 266–7.
¹¹ Humphreys: *Catherine Schuyler*, 8, 9–11.

and methodical.''[12] Rochefoucauld-Liancourt declared: ''The few I got acquainted with looked extremely dull and melancholy. They live retired in their homes with their wives, who are sometimes pretty but rather awkward in their manners, and with whom they scarcely exchange thirty words a day, although they always address them as 'my love.' ''[13] In a *Young Man's Journal a Hundred Years Ago,* the young tutor-to-be of Yale College found Dutch society equally dull, in 1783–84. He was chiefly disgusted with their custom of drinking at funerals, and the attempts of some of those he met to appear learned. He commented particularly on the fact that ''not a single lady'' was present, though it was a female corpse; again, he said, ''No ladies were present,'' and concluded it must be due to the vile habit of having ''wine, pipes, and tobacco'' rather than ''prayer'' and ''human condolence'' at these affairs.[14] Ladies are mentioned at a few dances, but the proud son of New England was not impressed with Dutch beauty. Others were not so harsh in their judgment. Humphreys[15] quoted the ''unfriendly testimony of a Tory historian'' to the effect that Catherine van Rensselaer, at least, was ''a lady of great beauty, shape and gentility.'' This Lossing confirmed: ''Delicate but perfect in form and feature; of medium height, extremely graceful in her movements and winning in her deportment. . . .''

Dutch matrons, notwithstanding their natural tendency to plumpness, appear to have accepted the dictates of fashion of the eighteenth century when the hoop skirt made its appearance. The latest fashions of Europe were often made known by sending dolls dressed *à la mode,* rather than fashion plates. Humphreys quotes one correspondent who refers to the hoop skirt vogue as follows: ''The petticoats which began to heave and swell before you left, are now blown up into an enormous concave, and rise more and more every day.''[16]

In order that some girls might have the advantage of a larger society, it was customary for those who lived at a distance to send their daughters for a visit to relatives in New York. This was

[12] *Ibid.,* 22.
[13] *Ibid.*
[14] Baldwin: *Young Man's Journal,* 193–208.
[15] *Op. cit.,* 22.
[16] *Ibid.,* 23.

182 WOMEN'S EDUCATION IN THE UNITED STATES

customary, of course, only in well-to-do families which by intermarriage had many worthwhile "connections."

The Germans of all times, from the days of Tacitus to the present, have been credited with great energy and industry. In their
removal to American soil these traits were not lost; instead, the
building of a new society challenged them and stimulated an increased activity. They showed a grave concern for economic
prosperity, though extremely poor to begin with, Pastorius asserting that in the early days Germantown might well have been
called "Armentown"—city of the poor. Its prosperity, he says,
came from flax spinning and weaving, to which the inhabitants
devoted themselves assiduously. A paper mill also was early
established. They were diligent farmers. As early as 1751,
86,000 bushels of wheat, 120,000 barrels of flour, and 90,743 bushels of maize were exported, which came very largely from the
German farms. It is maintained that Christopher Ludwig, who
provided the Continental Army with bread, drew supplies chiefly
from the German farmer. Stiegel laid out Mannheim in 1758,
establishing an iron foundry and smelting plant. A wagon factory, glass works and smith shop, too, arose. Stiegel's stoves and
Sauer's printing establishment were monuments to German
achievement, just as was Franklin's to the English.

Franklin said of the Germans' industry that "when any of
them, the English, happen to come here, where labor is much
better paid than in England, their industry seems to diminish in
equal proportion. But it is not so with German laborers; they
retain their habitual industry and frugality they bring with
them, and, receiving higher wages, an accumulation arises that
makes them all rich."[17]

Rush declared the Germans were successful because the first
thing they did was to build a good barn for cattle; good dwellings came in the second generation. They selected good farming
land, showing judgment, grubbed out stumps and built fences to
keep their cattle from straying. Sutcliff observed, somewhat
later, that the "German residents in this country have a character for greater industry and stability than those of any other
nation."[18] Children were taught to love work and to fear God.

17 A Letter to Peter Collinson [*Vide* Sparks: *Works of Benjamin Franklin*, VII, 66].

18 *Travels* (1805), 34.

About 1764, Christopher Dock, schoolmaster at Skippack and Germantown, wrote *One Hundred Necessary Rules for the Conduct of Children,* published by Christopher Sauer.[19] Naturally, in the primitive homes at first set up, the German housewife had a heavy burden in tending the garden, milking cows, making butter and cheese, and preparing meals in crude fireplaces. In harvest time the women frequently left the spinning wheel for a time and helped the men to cut, collect, and draw into the barns the produce of the land.[20] "Even sixty years ago there could be seen the *Baurbursch,* the youthful peasant, at the side of him, the *Baurmädchen,* the peasant girl, the classic *puella rustica,* wielding the sickle. . . ."[21]

The foregoing suggests, at any rate, the truth of the German maxims: "An industrious house-wife is the best money-safe" and

"He that earns and saves will be
"Rich for certain, you shall see."[22]

The German was always more concerned with his future daughter-in-law's industrious habits and domestic duties than with her personal beauty or mental accomplishments.[23]

The Swedish settlers were likewise noted for their high appraisal of industry and thrift, and their women occupied a place of significance comparable with the Dutch, but their independence appears to have been greater than that of German women. Certainly the data is insufficient for a conclusive statement, but a Swedish pastor has been credited with the statement that: "I found it best to avail myself of some Sunday . . . [when women were present], who in many houses rule more than the men, [and who] might have opportunity to hear what was presented, and thereafter, for their part both agree and direct for the best."[24]

[19] Brumbaugh: *Works of Christopher Dock,* 167 *ff.*
[20] Rush: *Account of the German Inhabitants of Pa.,* 66–7.
[21] *Ibid.*—a note added to Rush's account by I. D. Rupp.
[22] *Ibid.,* 69–70.
[23] Concerning the change in the economic situation about the time of the Revolution, see Knauss: *Social Conditions Among the Pennsylvania Germans,* 119 *ff.*
[24] Reprinted by permission of the publishers, The Arthur H. Clark Company, from Calhoun's *Social History of the American Family,* I, 192.

De Crèvecoeur, in *Letters of an American Farmer,* drew an attractive picture of domestic life as he found it in Pennsylvania:

"When I contemplate my wife, by my fire-side, while she either spins, knits, darns, or suckles our child, I cannot describe the various emotions of love, of gratitude, of conscious pride, which thrill in my heart and often overflow in involuntary tears. I feel the necessity, the sweet pleasure of acting my part, the part of an husband and father, with an attention and propriety which may entitle me to my good fortune. It is true these pleasing images vanish with the smoke of my pipe, but though they disappear from my mind, the impression they have made on my heart is indelible."[25]

The English communities in the central colonies are in many ways more comparable to those of New England than the German of their own locality. English Quaker women were industrious about household affairs, although, by means of the Quaker meeting, the way was open for them to share in a public capacity the life of the colony. At all times the practical side of education was stressed for girls as well as boys. Fox urged the apprenticeship of youth to all manner of customary trades for the sake of economic independence;[26] and a girls' school was early set up in England to teach them all things "civil and useful." Even as late as the War of Independence, Sally Wister wrote in her journal that she put "a stocking on the needles and intends to be mightily industrious." One morning she arose "at half-past four" and ironed "industriously till one o'clock."[27] Like all other maids of the day, she was skilled with the needle and no doubt worked many "curious" samplers. But she was also interested in the society of her "merry companions"; she had a good education in literature for that day, in addition to the "accomplishments" that were coming to be popular, particularly in the greater cities. Many of her leisure moments were passed in "reading and chatting." One day she "read and worked by turns."[28]

[25] Taken by permission from the Everyman's Library edition of Crèvecoeur's *Letters of an American Farmer,* published by J. M. Dent & Sons, Ltd., London, and E. P. Dutton & Co., Inc., New York. P. 24.

[26] Woody: *Early Quaker Education in Pa.,* 10.

[27] Myers: *Journal of Sally Wister,* 13–16, 17.

[28] *Ibid.*

But Quaker discipline did not encourage gay society or fancy dress; and though, in time, it became more tolerant of both, in the actual practice of members, there was a continual emphasis on plain living and simplicity of dress. In 1726, the yearly meeting of Burlington was "willing in the pure love of Truth . . . to caution and advise our Friends against those things we think inconsistent with our ancient Christian Testimony of Plainness in Apparel, some of which we think proper to particularize,—As first that immodest fashion of hooped Petticoats or the imitation of them, either something put into their petticoats to make them sit full or wearing more than is necessary or any other imitation whatsoever which we take to be but a Branch springing from the same corrupt root of Pride. And also that none of our Friends accustom themselves to wear their Gowns with superfluous folds behind but plain and decent, nor to go without Aprons nor to wear superfluous Gathers or Pleats in their Caps or Pinners. Nor to wear their Heads dressed high behind, neither to cut or lay their hair on their Foreheads or Temples. And that Friends are careful to avoid wearing striped shoes."[29]

And well might the Friends feel a "concern" on the subject of dress: for a grave temptation was being devised by the clever shopkeepers even at that early day. In 1731, all who read the Philadelphia papers were advised to ". . . inquire of Peter Lloyd in Second Street, Philadelphia, who has a choice parcel of strip'd and plain mantua-silks, lustrings, mohairs, satins, burdets, sattinets, persians, crapes, poplins, Berylians, Camblets, Callimancoes, yard-wide stuffs; and sundry other goods just imported, to be sold at reasonable rates."[30] Throughout the advertisements of the Colonial papers of New York and Philadelphia there is the ever-present idea of fixing women up so as to be attractive to men. This is the characteristic view of the time, whether it be in the decoration of her mind—for which she studied grammar, French, writing, and so on, at an adventure school, and later at academies—or the perfection of her personal appearance, for which advertisements offered the most attractive articles of silk and satin, latest high-heeled shoes, rings, necklaces, pendants, and "stays made to such perfection as to con-

[29] *Min. Burlington Yr. Mtg.*, 1726.
[30] *American Weekly Mercury*, Apr. 22–29, 1731.

tribute the greatest elegance to a genteel shape, and cause those who are not, to appear so. . . ."[31] It was against a fashion-ridden world that the Quaker and Puritan took their stand in favor of simplicity.[32]

The great sphere of Quaker women was the home; and the primary object of the young woman was matrimony. But, as an intelligent member of the household, she needed an education. Mrs. Knowles, a Quaker woman, depicted the happy effect of education on the housewife who, when the pudding bag bursts, "calms her maids by learned disquisitions and proceeds to make a fresh pudding, out of the mixture; whereas the ignorant housewife thinks a hobgoblin is in the pot, and gets into a perfect state of flurry."[33] Nevertheless, the fear was as common in the central colonies as in all others, that man loved "a learned scholar but not a learned wife." An adventure master advertised, in 1765, that young ladies should not be "discouraged on account of age through fear of not obtaining a spouse" as he had already given "the finishing stroke in education to several of the reputed fine accomplished ladies in New York, some of which were married within two, three, or four years afterward."[34]

In Pennsylvania, intermarriage played an important rôle in the final assimilation of the varied stocks that went to make up the American. "Melting-pot" has become a byword. In Crèvecoeur's *Letters* one sees the 'melting' process going on, the part played in it by women and men of various religious persuasions, as also of many national stocks: ". . . What then is the American, this new man? He is either an European, or the descendant of an European, hence that strange mixture of blood, which you will find in no other country. I could point out to you a family whose grandfather was an Englishman, whose wife was Dutch, whose son married a French woman, and whose present four sons have now four wives of different nations. He is an American, who, leaving behind him all his ancient prejudices and manners, receives new ones from the new mode of life he has embraced, the new government he obeys, and the new rank he holds. He becomes an American by being received in the broad lap of our Great Alma Mater. Here individuals

31 *N. Y. Gaz. and Wkly. Mer.*, May 4, 1772.
32 For example, compare *The Simple Cobbler of Agawam*, p. 171.
33 Quoted by Wharton: *Col. Days and Dames*, 125–6.
34 *Ibid.*

of all nations are melted into a new race of men, whose labours and posterity will one day cause great changes in the world. Americans are the western pilgrims, who are carrying along with them that great mass of arts, sciences, vigour, and industry which began long since in the east; they will finish the great circle. The Americans were once scattered all over Europe; here they are incorporated into one of the finest systems of population which has ever appeared, and which will hereafter become distinct by the power of the different climates they inhabit. The American ought therefore to love this country much better than that wherein either he or his forefathers were born. Here the rewards of his industry follow with equal steps the progress of his labour; his labour is founded on the basis of nature, self-interest; can it want a stronger allurement? Wives and children, who before in vain demanded of him a morsel of bread, now, fat and frolicsome, gladly help their father to clear those fields whence exuberant crops are to arise to feed and to clothe them all; without any part being claimed, either by a despotic prince, a rich abbot, or a mighty lord. Here religion demands but little of him; a small voluntary salary to the minister, and gratitude to God; can he refuse these? The American is a new man, who acts upon new principles; he must therefore entertain new ideas, and form new opinions. From involuntary idleness, servile dependence, penury, and useless labour, he has passed to toils of a very different nature, rewarded by ample subsistence.—This is an American.''[35]

But if most accounts of Colonial life depict a happy domestic circle with women in the center, one must not conclude that this is the whole truth. Our forefathers knew broken homes, elopement, divorce, and separation, though they did not treat them statistically. Not all homes were happy, and the results were runaway wives and infidelity on the part of the husbands. From an examination of the newspapers of Philadelphia and New York, which were a veritable ''school for scandal,'' sufficient cases appear to illustrate this point.[36]

[35] Taken by permission from the Everyman's Library edition of Crèvecoeur's *Letters of an American Farmer*, published by J. M. Dent & Sons, Ltd., London, and E. P. Dutton & Co., Inc., New York. Pp. 43–4.

[36] Satisfactory statistical treatment of this data is at least difficult, perhaps impossible, but a complete study of this question would repay the investigator of Colonial social conditions.

Wives of Colonial New York and Philadelphia are charged with "elopment," "extravagant conduct," "drinking strong drink,"[37] leaving "her sucking babe," "continually running [the husband] in debt," "some misdemeanors," "leading a dissolute life," behaving "in a vile manner to her husband," and using the husband "very ill." For these wrongs, which he published, the husband revenged himself by refusing to pay bills incurred by the wife. Some not only refused to pay bills incurred, but warned others that they took her in at their peril, or offered to prosecute "to the utmost extent of the law" people who should "entertain" the eloped wife.[38] A typical notice may be given from about the middle of the period. "Whereas Alice, the Wife of Wm. H———, of Phila., Marriner, has behaved herself in a vile Manner to her said Husband, and is endeavoring to run him in Debt; this is to forewarn all Persons from trusting or

New-York, August 24, 1758.

ALL Persons are forbid to truft *Mary* Smith, the Wife of *Patrick Smith*, of the City of *New-York*, Mariner ; for he will pay no Debts of her contracting from the Date hereof.   311¶   PATRICK SMITH.

ADVERTISEMENT OF REFUSAL TO PAY BILLS INCURRED BY THE WIFE, NEW YORK GAZETTE, SEPT. 18, 1758

giving the said Alice any credit on his account; for he will pay no Debts she shall contract from the Date hereof. . . . N. B. Said Alice is now in N. Y."[39]

When wives were independent enough and able to answer these complaints, the columns of the paper were utilized by them as by the men; but few cases were noted in which reply was made. One husband appears to have been forced to rectify an error made in his advertisement. He admitted later that he had "inadvertently" advertised his wife as "eloped" whereas he merely "intended" to say "absenting."[40]   Lydia A———

37 The following, however, became no cause for divorce: "Sunday last one Rachel Twells of this city died suddenly and the Coroner's Inquest having sat on the body brought in their verdict, that by drinking too plentifully of rum and other strong liquors she came by her death. 'Tis said she had drank 16 drams of rum and 2 mugs of strong beer that day."—*Pa. Gaz.,* June 19, 1735.

38 *Am. Wkly. Mer.,* Aug. 19–26, 1736.

39 *N. Y. Gaz.,* revived in the *Weekly Post Boy,* Feb. 20, 1748-9.

40 *Pa. Gaz.,* July 21, 1748.

answered her husband's notice of their agreed separation by a full statement "to let the public know the reason, . . . that in about three years he spent near three hundred pounds of my estate and was never sober one week in the whole time. . . ."[41] Some cases, but not as many, appeared in which the wife rebelled against her husband's ways, although he had not advertised her for any reason (it seems he had none). Let the following example suffice:

"I, Sarah S———, Schoolmistress, the wife of William S———, take this method to inform the public not to trust or credit the said S——— on my account, for I shall never pay any more of his contractions; my living shall go no more after that date as it did last March to uphold his whores, he abused me, and turned me out of doors; his credit and his living came by me, but he forgot that and lives in adultery; now to get more, I will if I can, but I will not trust it to that false man; I nine years have been his wife, though he for a widower doth pass, when he meets a suitable lass; for his wicked doings I never more can him abide, nor he never more shall lie by my side. SARAH S———."[42]

In a study of the advertisements it should be remembered that the worst facts were doubtless presented; that many cases of separation and elopement were not advertised; and that, as a general rule, the woman's side of the question did not appear in print. That there were some suspicious characters abroad, posing as school mistresses, is pointed out by several public notices, of which the following is typical:

"Notice is hereby given to all good people not to take precents which come of a strolling woman who goes under the name of Elizabeth Castle, alias Morrey. She pretends to be a schoolmistress, tayloress and staymaker, embroiderer and doctoress. She is of middle stature, high schouldered, grey eyed, and very well qualified in lying, cheating, defrauding, cursing, swearing, drunkenness, talebearing, backbiting, mischief making among neighbors and is reported to be a thief. She carries with her a quantity of pieces that shine like gold by which means she hath deceived several women and children, to their great prejudice. She squeaks when she speaks and hath done damage in New-

41 *Ibid.,* Nov. 17, 1763.
42 *Ibid.,* Dec. 27, 1775.

town, Chester County. This is but little of what might be said in the bonds of truth. Thomas Thomas.''[43]

We have spoken thus far only of women occupied in the home circle. A glimpse of another group, the servants, white and black, who were sold, sometimes to pay their passage to this country, may be gained from the newspapers.[44] These servant women were quite numerous, if we may judge from the number of notices of sale and the items regarding runaways. Judging, so far as possible, from the inadequate evidence of the notices, most of them were probably uneducated, but some laid a claim to learning and passed as schoolmistresses. They were generally listed as Irish, Scotch, English, Dutch, Welsh, and Negro. With the exception of Negroes, the Irish and Scotch predominated. The indentures were generally for a period of five or seven years, and it was indicated how long the indenture had to run. The servants were recommended by their masters or mistresses as able to do a great variety of things: general ''housework,'' ''Country work,'' ''nursing,'' ''sewing at extraordinary or plain work,'' baking, brewing, cooking, washing, spinning, work in the field, dairy work, quilting, etc. In these occupations, they are generally described as 'likely girls,' 'capable,' 'very handy,' 'choice,' 'well-recommended,' 'very good,' etc. Occasionally more specific virtues are named, and the fact that mention is made of them may suggest their absence in others.

Typical notices are given, the last one only being in any way exceptional: ''A likely young Dutch servant woman's time for three years to be disposed of, she is a very good seamstress at Extraordinary or plain work, and pretty handy at housework; those inclined to purchase her time may agree with Anthony Furnas, in Philadelphia.''[45]

''To be sold a Dutch Servant Woman, who has two years to serve, she understands Country or Town Business, and is a very good spinner. Enquire of the printer hereof.''[46]

''To be sold An Irish Servant girl's time, being 4 years and 3 months; she is fit for either town or country and is a very good spinster. Enquire of the printer hereof.''[47]

[43] *Ibid.*, Mar. 1745.
[44] Chiefly the *New York Gazette*, the *Weekly Post Boy, Pennsylvania Gazette*, and the *American Weekly Mercury.*
[45] *Am. Wkly. Mer.*, June 3–10, 1731.
[46] *Ibid.*, Apr. 20, 1738.
[47] *N. Y. Wkly. Post Boy*, Mar. 7, 1747–8.

"Just imported . . . a parcel of likely English and Irish Servants, men and women; and are to be disposed of, by William Hartly, Thomas Robinson or Lawrence Anderson, on board the said Snow now lying off opposite to Market Street Wharff."[48]

To be sold, "A Young Wench about 29 Years old, that drinks no strong Drink, and gets no children; a very good drudge. Enquire of the printer hereof."[49]

That the indentured woman had no easy life, and sought to better it, is suggested by the number of runaways advertised every week. These notices offer little information beyond that recorded above, unless it be in the way of fashion notes for servants. They seem to have been as much overburdened with apparel as their mistresses. One had on "two suits of apparel, the one a blue stuff jacket and petticoat, the other a brown shalloon gown, and light colored petticoat, oznaburgh shift, blue stockings and old shoes."[50] Two examples of this class are given: the first one is typical; the second more unusual and interesting because of the woman's "pretention" to being a school mistress.

" . . . The other woman named Eleanor Traynor, black hair, fresh coloured, a very lusty woman, and has on a stuff gown mixed with red and white, but appears to be mostly Red, and a petticoat of stamped calico with a dark stamp; one other gown of striped stuff lined with striped stuff of a contrary stripe, a petticoat of second Mourning Crape, a pair of blue worsted stockings and wooden heel'd shoes. Ozenbrig shirt and some other old working clothes. I hear they pass for man and wife, and that he calls himself John Williams, and she Modesty."[51]

"Run away, about the first of June last, from the plantation of Mr. William Alexander, near the head of Elk River in Cecil County, a servant woman named Mary Dawson alias Murphy, aged about 40 years, born in Ireland, professes herself a Roman Catholic, takes a great deal of snuff and is much given to liquor, she is of small stature and thin of body, pretends to be a school mistress and writes a good hand. She wears a cloath colored Callimanco gown. Whoever secures her and gives notice to the

[48] *Pa. Gaz.*, July 6–13, 1738.
[49] *N. Y. Gazette,* revived in the *Wkly. Post Boy,* Feb. 20, 1748–9.
[50] *Pa. Gaz.*, Dec. 16–23, 1729.
[51] *Am. Wkly. Mer.*, May 11, 1721.

printer hereof or to the subscribed at the above Plantation, so that she be had again, shall have Forty shillings as a reward and reasonable charges.'"[52]

A pathetic glimpse at the life of the indentured girl is revealed in an advertisement of Elizabeth Everton who, in 1740, had been indentured by her mother to Edward Thompson at Fairfax, Virginia. The term of her service having expired, she returned to Pennsylvania and was in the household of Thomas Downing of East Caln, whence she "made considerable enquiry and took great pains" to ascertain whether her mother were still living.[53]

It has been pointed out that the primary economic function of women was to take care of the household and, among the Germans, at times, to labor in the fields. But the generally accepted view has been that this was her *sole* function. From an examination of contemporary businesses, however, it appears at once that a considerable number of women engaged in them. In the newspapers of New York and Philadelphia, the following occupations are mentioned which indicate that women did many things besides managing homes for husbands: needlework (*i.e.*, making objects to sell), store keeping, teaching, sewing; doing general housework, wet-nursing, spinning, footing old stockings, making gloves, acting as midwives; manufacturing "ointment for the itch" and "hair cloth and hair lines of all sorts"; "weaving sives," keeping taverns and coffee houses; making candy, dressing buckskin, making powder and wigs; quilting, boarding school children, manufacturing and selling "tar-water"; professional cake baking, cleaning, dyeing, turning; keeping delicatessen and millinery shops, making preserves, pickles, pickled fish, and ointment for curing bald heads; curing sturgeon, running laundries, acting, brewing, tailoring; and serving as matrons in hospitals, governesses of children, and nursemaids.[54] Besides, they appear as manufacturers of treacle, merchants of all manner of wares, executrices of estates, managers of printing and publishing establishments (usually after the death of their husbands), and in numerous other affairs.

[52] *Ibid.*, August 22, 1734.
[53] *Pa. Gaz.*, Mar. 30, 1758.
[54] Based on items mainly from the *Pennsylvania Gazette*, *American Weekly Mercury*, *New York Gazette*, *New York Mercury*, and the *Weekly Post Boy*.

Philadelphia had no reason to suffer a shortage of treacle, as competition was lively. On March 23, 1721, this notice appeared:

"Mary Banister's Sovereign Spirit of Venice Treacle sold for her by David Brientnall and Francis Knowles, is now, she being dead, rightly prepared by her Daughter, who employs the same persons to sell it, and no other in this City of Philadelphia."[55] This was followed by another advertisement of the "only genuine article": "Elizabeth Warnaby's Right and Genuine Spirit of Venice Treacle, truly and only prepared by her in Philadelphia, who was the original and First Promoter of it in this City, is still sold by her at her shop in High Street near the Market: As also the Spirit of Scurvy-Grass."[56]

Lack of space forbids a long array of these interesting announcements. The following, however, are fairly typical of those inserted by women who were engaged otherwise than in housekeeping. The first three depict the woman producer, the next two the woman merchant, and the last two those who were "content to teach":[57]

"Sarah Lancaster, Sive-weaver, that did live in Market street, is removed into Arch Street, a little up from Second street, on the right hand; where she follows the said business; and buys good horse hair, in the usual manner."[58]

* * *

"Notice is hereby given that Ann Page, widow of John Page, of second street, Philadelphia, turner, deceased, intends to continue the turner's business in its various branches, viz., for carpenters, joiners, chairmakers, etc., lignum vitae mortars and pesils, molds for wagon, cart and cheese-boxes, bench screws. Also iron turning for the West Indies, and mill spindles. N. B. Spinning wheels are also made, mended, and sold at reasonable rates. The continued favours of her late husband's customers will be duly acknowledged by Ann Page."[59]

[55] *Am. Wkly. Mer.*

[56] *Ibid.*, March 30, 1721.

[57] For a more complete survey of the activities of Colonial women, the reader is referred to Dexter: *Colonial Women of Affairs*.

[58] *Pa. Gaz.*, May 3–10, 1739.

[59] *Ibid.*, Sept. 30, 1756.

"Jane Moorland from London living at the back of Mrs. Thornhill's house, in Laetitia Court, Philadelphia, begs leave to inform the public that she prepares and sells sausages, black and white puddings, Tripes and cow-heels. Likewise pickled sheeps tongues; which she sells ready boiled, or green, out of the pickle. Whoever is pleased to favor her with their custom, may depend on all the above articles being done from the best receipts, and in the nicest manner. N. B. Said Jane Moorland keeps stall on market days, the second below the court house, in the Jersey market."[60]

* * *

"To be sold by Ann Alsop, in the House Capt. Joseph Wilson, removed out of last year: Very good Muscovada Sugar, Raisins, Oatmeal, Pepper, Chocolate, Coffee and loaf sugar, fine writing Paper and Sealing Wax."[61]

* * *

"Just imported in the Snow Two Brothers, Capt. Marsden, from London, and to be sold by Hannah Brientnall at the sign of the spectacles, in second street, near black horse alley, a variety of the finest crystal spectacles, set in temple, steel, leather or other frames. Likewise true Venetian green spectacles for weak or watery eyes, of various sorts. Also concave spectacles for short sighted persons, magnifying and reading glasses, telescopes, perspectives, with multiplying glasses; and glasses for Davis's quadrants, etc."[62]

* * *

"Wants Employment, A single woman who can be well recommended for her honesty and fidelity, is well qualified to instruct children of both sexes in all that is necessary for their years and would go in a gentleman's family, in Town or Country, on reasonable Terms. . ."[63]

* * *

"A young woman of a creditable family, about 15 years old, who has been regularly taught the three r's, needlework and French is willing to live in a good family by the year, in the quality of a seamstress. . ."[64]

[60] *Ibid.*, Dec. 31, 1761.
[61] *N. Y. Gaz.*; revived in the *Wkly. Post-Boy*, Nov. 16, 1747.
[62] *Pa. Gaz.*, Mar. 30, 1758.
[63] *N. Y. Gaz.*, Dec. 16, 1762.
[64] *N. Y. Gaz. and Wkly. Mer.*, Apr. 29, 1771.

II. Elementary Education of Girls

That elementary education was frequently provided for girls on the same basis as for boys, in the central colonies, seems now to be little open to question. The influence of the churches, combined, in the case of New Netherlands, with the civil authority, definitely favored it. This has been shown conclusively in the studies of Kilpatrick, Woody, Weber, and Rohrbach, covering the Dutch, English Quaker, and German communities, respectively.[65]

Kilpatrick, going back to the Zeeland regulations of 1538, found that provision was made therein for "separate schools . . . for boys and girls when this is feasible. Where this is not feasible the said boys and daughters shall be separated as much as possible from each other. . ."[66] He goes on to quote the work of Douma, who said of the latter part of the century, that "the pupils, girls and boys separated from one another, sit on low benches without backs. The girls sit in a corner all by themselves."[67] The regulations of the seventeenth century carried the same provisions. It would be expected that the custom of the old country continued to be the practice of the new, and such is the final conclusion. But Kilpatrick found no "explicit statement, prior to 1733, that girls did attend the Dutch schools of America."[68] Then it was stated that "the school children, both boys and girls, should recite. . ." Hamilton's statement, in 1744, also is quoted, showing there were "about 200 scholars, boys and girls," at school in Albany, which was a typically Dutch town. Nevertheless, lacking the explicit reference to girls at school in the earliest years, Kilpatrick showed conclusively, by reference to wills and marriage contracts, that girls' schooling was taken as a matter of fact. In 1632 a contract was made, insuring the sending of Jan and Rasel, "minor children," to school and "teaching them a trade." Others name specifically

[65] Kilpatrick: *Dutch Schools of New Netherlands;* Woody: *Early Quaker Education in Pennsylvania* and *Quaker Education in the Colony and State of New Jersey;* Weber: *Charity School Movement among the Germans;* Rohrbach: *Lutheran Education in the Ministerium of Pennsylvania (MS.);* also Wickersham: *History of Education in Pennsylvania,* for a more general account.

[66] *Op. cit.,* 30.

[67] *Ibid.*

[68] *Ibid.,* 217.

reading, writing and a trade, as the things to be taught;[69] sewing is also named. Wills, of a slightly later date than the marriage contracts, also specified reading, writing, and learning a trade. Any possibility of English influence, at the end of the century, may be safely discounted inasmuch as the Dutch were not inclined to follow English leadership; and, had they been so, English practice would have led in the direction of discrimination against girls.[70] Therefore the author convincingly concludes that "all these [facts] seem to put it beyond a reasonable doubt that in the ordinary Dutch Parochial school, girls as well as boys attended, at least until they learned to read."[71] Recently, this conclusion has been confirmed by a schoolmaster's tuition bill which has come to light, showing that girls attended with boys at Albany.[72]

In the Dutch town and village schools the master was generally the servant of the church as well as the school. He taught the three R's and religion by means of prayers and the Catechism of the Dutch Reformed Church. School opened at eight in the morning and, except from eleven to two, continued till four in the afternoon. The school rules left by Valckoogh seem to have been devised for boys chiefly, but this does not indicate that girls did not attend; laws are made to control the worst elements of society, and do not imply the absence of the best:

"Those who do not take off their caps before a man of honor,
"Who run and scream and swear,
"Who race wildly or improperly through the streets,
"Who play for money or books, or who tell lies,
"Who chase or throw at peoples' ducks or animals,

* * *

"Who play with knives or run their hands thru their hairs,
"Who run into the fields, or jump into the hay with sticks,
"Who stay at home without the teacher's or parent's leave,
"Who make noise in church or who buy candy,
"Who do not say prayer at table, before lessons,
"In the morning or in the evening,

69 *Ibid.*, 218.

70 Consult Ch. IV for discrimination against girls in New England town schools.

71 Kilpatrick: *op. cit.*, 219.

72 By letter, dated Dec. 27, 1927, Kilpatrick refers to *Flatbush Town Records*, Papers Nos. 6897 and 6904, Hall of Records, Kings Co., Brooklyn, N. Y.

"Who tear their hair, or spoil their paper,
"Who call one another names here,
"Who throw their bread to dogs or cats,
"Who wish to keep what they find in school,
"Who spit in the drink of another, or step on his dinner,
"Who run away from school and do not tell it,

* * *

"Who do not go nicely to church and home again,
"And who read these rules and do not mind them,
"Shall receive two paddlings (placken) or be whipped."[73]

Kilpatrick lists, from various sources, a number of school-books, with some of which the Dutch maidens were doubtless compelled to become acquainted. Prominent among these, besides the A B C books, were titles indicating religious and moral instruction, such as Catechisms, Bibles—large and small—, "Steps of Youth," "Exquisite Proofs of Man's Misery," "Last Wills," and "Hours of Death."[74]

In common with the rest of the world of that time, the Dutch did not offer girls a secondary education. But in the learning of hymns, psalms, prayers, and catechisms the little girls appear to have done well. At a contest, about 1698, "the girls, although fewer in number, had learned and recited more, in proportion, than the boys." But as there were fewer girls—about half as many, in this instance—it is possible that the proportion of girls to boys in the school was about the same. The figures on illiteracy show a much greater part of illiterates were women—which would be expected, if it were true, as Kilpatrick thinks probable, that girls often left school before learning to write.[75]

As already stated,[76] the founder of Quakerism in England laid emphasis on the proper education of both boys and girls. Schools were established at Waltham and Schacklewell for boys and girls respectively.[77] Meetings were set up for both men and women,

[73] Kilpatrick: *op. cit.*, 31-2.

[74] *Ibid.*, 223-5. Titles mentioned were: written and printed Histories of Tobias; Histories of David; Last Wills; Hours of Death; Exquisite Proofs of Man's Misery; General Epistles; Catechisms; A B C books; Arts of Letters; Succinct Ideas; Steps of Youth; Books of the Gospels and Epistles; Short Way, by Megapolensis; Bijbels; Psalm boecken; Vraegboechjens van Aldegonde; books of Evangelists; historical schoolbooks; books of Cortimus; song books; books of Golden Trumpets.

[75] *Ibid.*, 149, 227, 229; see p. 159.

[76] P. 178.

[77] Woody: *op. cit.*, 10.

insuring the latter a proper share in the work of the Society.[78] The Yearly Meeting of London, established in 1672, began early to concern itself with education in keeping with Fox's advice. In 1690, the "advices" of this meeting mentioned specifically the provision of "school masters and school mistresses who are faithful Friends, to teach and instruct their children."[79]   A year later they were "glad to hear" care was being taken "in some places . . . providing schoolmasters and school mistresses. . . ."[80] The continual references to schoolmistresses seem to indicate no discrimination against girls.   A practical education was desired. Penn wanted his children to be "husbandmen and housewives." Budd, in 1685, recommended a system of education which, though not put into operation, may be considered a faithful description of Quaker views, so far as provisions for girls are concerned:

"That schools be provided in all towns and cities, and persons of known honesty, skill and understanding be yearly chosen by the Governor and General Assembly, to teach and instruct boys and girls in all the most useful arts and sciences that they in their youthful capacities may be capable to understand, as the learning to read and write true English and Latin, and other useful speeches and languages, and fair writing, arithmetic and bookkeeping; the boys to be taught and instructed in some mystery or trade, as the making of mathematical instruments, joinery, turnery, the making of clocks and watches, weaving, shoemaking or any other useful trade or mystery that the school is capable of teaching; and the girls to be taught and instructed in spinning of flax and wool, and knitting of gloves and stockings, sewing, and making of all sorts of useful needlework, and the making of straw work, as hats, baskets, etc., or other useful art or mystery that the school is capable of teaching."[81]

The instruments of government drawn up 1682, 1683, and 1696, and also the laws of the Quaker assembly, in 1683, all refer to the "good education of youth," which the Quakers interpreted to mean male and female youth; and the first school, 1683, was actually called into being by the Provincial Council, in keeping

78 *Ibid.*, 16.
79 *Ibid.*, 20.
80 *Ibid.*, 21.
81 *Ibid.*, 36–7.

with Penn's provisions.[82]   Enock Flower was employed to "learn to read English," write and cast accounts;[83] there is no documentary proof that he taught girls, but the Quaker practice would make it appear reasonable that he may have done so.   In 1696, Thomas Holme, judge of the Philadelphia County Court, described educational facilities of the town, which included those for girls:

> "Here are schools of divers sorts,
> "To which our youth daily resorts.
> "Good women, who do very well,
> "Bring little ones to read and spell,
> "Which fits them for writing; and then
> "Here's men to bring them to their pen,
> "And to instruct and make them quick
> "In all sorts of Arithmetick."[84]

In 1702, the minutes of Philadelphia Monthly Meeting mentioned Olive Songhurst, schoolmistress, whose salary they raised from five to ten pounds.[85]   She was the first woman named as schoolmistress in the minutes of Philadelphia, but many more appear throughout the century.   That it was customary to send girls to the town, where they could be better instructed, is suggested by the following letter (1702) concerning the progress of "prisila":

"The few liens comes to salute thee and fore prisila which I hope are in helth as blessed be the God of all our mersies I am at this writing.   I long to hear from you both and how prisila likes being at scool and how the like her and whether she thinks that shee will lern anything worth her while to be kept at cool here.   I have sent her some thred to knit me too pares of golves and herself on if there be anough for to mak so much if not one for me and one for her.   bid her be a good gerl and larn well and then I shall love her. . . . thy most affectionate sister Abigail . . ."[86]

[82] The law of 10/I/1683 declared: "All persons in this Province and territories thereof, having children, and all the guardians and trustees of orphans, shall cause such to be instructed in reading and writing; so that they may be able to read the scriptures; and to write by that time they attain to twelve years of age."—Linn: *Laws of Pa.*, 142.

[83] Woody: *op. cit.*, 42.

[84] Quoted by Wickersham: *Education in Pennsylvania*, 277.

[85] *Min. Phila. Mo. Mtg.*, 27/I/1702.

[86] Woody: *op. cit.*, 182.

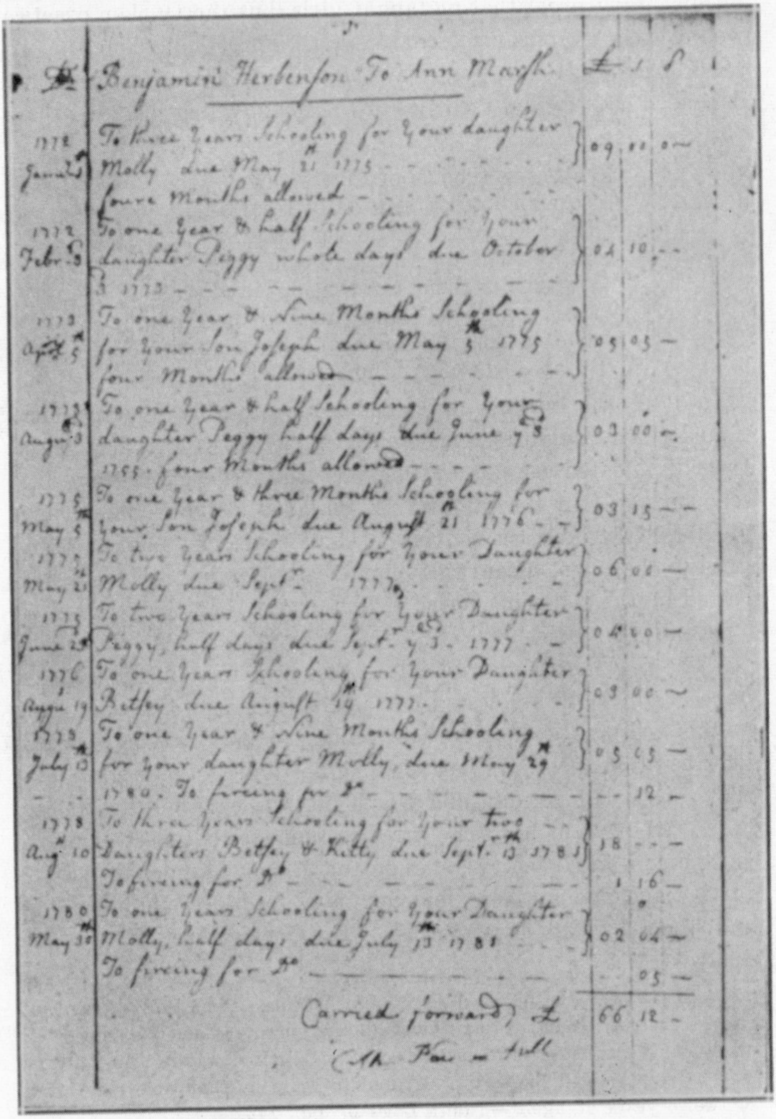

Dr.	Benjamin Herbenson To Ann Marsh	£	s	d
1772 Janu 20	To three Years Schooling for Your daughter Molly due May 21 1775 – – – – – fourе Months allowed – – – –	09	00	0 –
1772 Febr 3	To one Year & half Schooling for Your daughter Peggy whole days due October 3 1773 – – – – – – – – –	04	10	– –
1773 April 5	To one Year & Nine Months Schooling for Your Son Joseph due May 5 1775 four Months allowed – – – – –	05	05	–
1773 Augt 3	To one Year & half Schooling for Your daughter Peggy half days due June 3 1775 · four Months allowed – – – –	03	00	–
1775 May 5	To one Year & three Months Schooling for Your Son Joseph due August 21 1776 – –	03	15	– –
1775 May 21	To two Years Schooling for Your Daughter Molly due Septr 1777 – – – –	06	00	–
1775 June 23	To two Years Schooling for Your Daughter Peggy, half days due Septr 23 1777 – –	04	10	–
1776 Augt 19	To one Years Schooling for Your Daughter Betsey due August 19 1777 – – –	03	00	~
1778 July 13	To one Year & Nine Months Schooling for your daughter Molly, due May 29 1780. To fireing for Do – – – – – –	05	05	–
– –		– –	12	–
1778 Aug 10	To three Years Schooling for Your two Daughters Betsey & Kitty due Septr 13 1781	18	– –	–
	To fireing for Do – – – – – – – –	1	16	–
1780 May 30	To one Years Schooling for Your Daughter Molly, half days due July 13 1781 – –	02	04	–
	To fireing for Do – – – – – – – –	– –	05	–
	Carried forward £	66	12	–

Accot Pass – [illegible]

Account Book of Ann Marsh, Philadelphia (1772–1780)

A number of schools were established from time to time under the control of the Board of Overseers of the Public School, and in these women were very generally employed. Rebecca Burchall taught for many years, at times girls only, and again both boys and girls. Other teachers were 'Widdow' Mellor, Ann Thornton, Deborah Godfrey, Mary Gosnold, Mary Jones, Mary Wiley, Rebecca Jones, Ann Redman, Ann Pattison, Jane Loftus, Susannah Brittain, and many others, too numerous and monotonous to catalog.[87] A report, in 1784, listed ten schools. That of William Brown had twenty-nine girls; the one under Mrs. Clarke, fifteen boys and girls; and Ann Marsh's had about fifty boys and girls. The schools taught by Sarah Lancaster, Mary Harry, Joseph Clarke, and Mary McDonnell probably had girls, alone or with boys, but it is not specifically stated.[88]

There is nothing to indicate that girls ever attended the Latin school, though no evidence appears to show that higher learning was considered unnecessary for, or harmful to, women. In fact, Budd seems to have had in mind that girls might be taught Latin.[89] But the most advanced school, specifically for girls, reported by the minutes of the Trustees of Penn Charter School or the Monthly Meeting, was that of Anthony Benezet, 1754, in which he was to teach "Reading, Writing, Arithmetic and English Grammar."[90] Thus, if Sally Wister "received some instruction in the higher classics and literary studies," or gained "some knowledge of Latin and French," as her Journal suggests, Benezet must have taught more than he was required to do;[91] or she may have acquired such knowledge at adventure schools which existed in the city. This school, taught by Benezet, was in the same building as the Latin School, but specific plans were made "to keep the girls separate from the boys." This would suggest the great improbability of their ever being taught in the Latin School itself. In 1799, Friends opened the Westtown Boarding School for boys and girls. This project had been contemplated since 1765.[92]

[87] A list has been compiled from the *Penn Charter School Minutes*, in custody of The Provident Life and Trust Company, Philadelphia.
[88] *Min. Phila. Mo. Mtg.*, 30/I/1784, 123 *ff.*
[89] Woody: *op. cit.*, 36–7.
[90] *P. C. S. M.*, 25/IV/1754.
[91] See Myers: *Journal of Sally Wister*, 13–16.
[92] Woody: *op. cit.*, 60, 73, 89, 145, and 151.

In educational work the Friends have always been philanthropists. Schools were opened freely to outsiders, and those too poor to pay were taught without charge. In this elementary charity education, women teachers played a prominent part. Many were employed by the Overseers to teach girls and boys at low cost, or at no cost, according to circumstances.

At the close of the century (1796), Anne Parrish, a Quakeress dedicated to works of benevolence, opened a school for poor girls in Pewter Platter Alley, Philadelphia. A few years later she was joined by other Friends (women) who formed a "Society for the Free Instruction of Female Children." In 1797 there were fifty pupils, to whom were taught "Spelling, Reading, Writing, Arithmetic, and Sewing." Grammar was mentioned as a sub-

ANNE PARRISH (1760–1800) FOUNDRESS OF THE AIMWELL SCHOOL

ject of instruction in the rules of 1805. In 1807, it was first appropriately called the Aimwell School. From 1821 to 1823, school was held in the well-known Carpenter's Hall. It is significant that for some years the ladies of the Association taught the school themselves, taking turn about. Later, regular teachers were employed. The Association and its school are a unique monument to women as managers. The school flourished until 1923, and since then its funds have been employed in educating poor girls at other schools. The complete financial transactions, over 129 years, are still preserved. It is interesting to note their attention to the pedagogics of teaching and of discipline. Limited space will not permit insertion of all the regulations, but the following set, drawn up in 1803, are suggestive of the practices. These are considerably more elaborate than those of 1798.

"Regulations

"Adopted by the Society for the free Instruction of Female Children.

"The School to be held from Nine O'Clock in the morning, until Twelve; and from half-past Two, until Five in the afternoon.

"All those scholars who write, are to be restricted to One Copy, when they first enter School in the morning and afternoon; except those who come in after Ten and Three O'Clock.

"First Class

"When they have finished one Copy, are to Cypher on second, fourth, and sixth day mornings; and on second, third, fourth, and sixth day afternoons, until it is time to get spelling; also on third day mornings, until a quarter past Eleven; when they are to commit to memory, some suitable pieces, selected from the Old or New Testaments, or other profitable books, which are to be said to the Teacher, in the afternoon; they are to stand in Classes, and the same propriety of pronunciation and voice to be required as in reading.

"To read in the New Testament, on second day morning; on other days of the week, other suitable books; reading to begin at Ten O'Clock.

"To read separately, on fifth-day morning before meeting; fifth-day afternoon they are to have their slates, and the Teacher is to give them verbally some lines, which the Scholars are to write on their slates, in the best manner they are capable; the Teacher is to examine such exercises carefully, and point out the errors to the Children, who are to write them in a column, and opposite to each word, put down what part of speech it is.

"On this afternoon, the arithmetical Tables are to be repeated, by all those who cypher, and cyphering omitted.

"To spell out of book every afternoon and on sixth-day afternoon in Classes; the word to be given but once;—portions of Grammar to be given on sixth-day afternoon, to be repeated to the Teacher, on second-day morning in a Class, after the second Class has read.

"Second Class

"Are to cypher on second, fourth, and sixth-day mornings, until a quarter past Eleven.

"Every afternoon, when they have written a copy, they are to be furnished with sewing.

"To read as mentioned for the first Class, and in every respect the same exercises for them, as for the First Class, except they are not permitted to cypher in the afternoons.

"Third and Fourth Classes

"When they have finished their Copies, are to be furnished with sewing.—To read in the New Testament on second day afternoon. Other afternoons, such books as are suited to their capacities.—reading to commence at Three O'Clock.

"To spell out of book, mornings, and afternoons, and on sixth-day afternoon in Classes, the words but once given out.

"Those Scholars, who have been accustomed to read in a Class, and say one lesson, are to omit reading in a Class, until afternoon. The small Children are to say One lesson in the morning, and One in the afternoon.

"Believing the Children lose some of the advantages of writing for want of method, and being brought forward too soon; it is agreed, to make it a practice, of keeping them in Strokes, until they can make a good bold Stroke; then to bring them on gradually, to the easiest letters;—after this, one copy of the same letters, beginning and going through the Alphabet again, with the addition of the letter M. to every letter;—by which means, they will learn to make good strokes, and round, and turn them properly. The Children are then to write One Copy of each letter in the Alphabet in capitals;—when they have made this progress in writing, it is thought, they may be put in joining-hand;— Figures are to be suitably interspersed.

"When the girls begin to cypher, they are to go through the small Assistant; and instead of copying their sums in a book, to use nothing but Slates; by this method, they will learn to make figures, and when they are capable of using the large Assistant, they are to set down, the rules and sums, in their cyphering books.

"It will probably be a means of exciting the Scholars to greater attention to their books when reading, if the Teacher sometimes stopt abruptly, the girl who was reading, and bid another take up the subject, where her Classmate left it, and if she could not perform such directions, she is to miss her turn, and the next in the Class to proceed.

"As the School is at present, in a state of great disorder; and as it must appear obvious to those, under whose care it is, that a very desirable point would be gained, could the Scholars, by unwearied efforts, be brought into due regularity, the labour of the Teachers would be less arduous, and the Children have greater opportunities of improvement in the different branches of education.

"It is concluded, that the Girls who read in Classes, stand with their faces towards the Teacher's desk, in a straight line, the Teacher to insist on their placing themselves in an erect posture, without inclining towards each other; the reading not to commence until each in the Class disposes themselves agreeable to direction.—Should any of the Scholars prove disobedient, after repeated persuasion, to do right; they are to be desired to go to their seats, and not permitted to read that morning: the same order to be observed by those who spell in Classes; and those Girls, who refuse to comply with the established rule, are to lose the advantage of spelling at that time.

"No Conversation, Whispering, or other Association, to be allowed the Scholars, during School-hours; and as the greatest exertions, will belong to the Teachers, in this part of the duty; it is requested, particular attention will be paid, and they not wearied in a portion of the work so necessary, but that they blend, repeated persuasion with due authority, until order and quiet reign in the School.

"The Scholars of every description, are to sit straight on the benches, and this rule not to be departed from, except the time employed in writing and cyphering. No work to be pinned on the lap, nor placing the feet on the benches in front.—no Scholar to be permitted to change her seat at pleasure; to walk about the School, or go to the closet, unless sent by one of the Teachers, on a necessary errand.—no more than two of the Scholars, are to stand at a time by Sarah Roche, or at the Teachers' desk.— those who are waiting for instruction, must quietly wait, until those who are standing have taken their seats.

"In the morning and afternoon, when business is finished, the work, books, etc., are to be put away, and the names of the Children to be called over; silence is then to be observed, and insisted on, by remonstrance and example, on the part of the Teachers: after a suitable pause has ensued, the Scholars are to be dismissed, in such a number, as will make the least confusion or noise.

"On second-day morning, and fourth-day afternoon, during the silence, a portion of the sacred writings is to be read aloud by one of the Teachers, selected from those parts, best suited to the capacities of children, and most likely to make an impression on their minds.

"As the best and most salutary Rules and Laws, are of little benefit, unless faithfully executed; it will be incumbent on every member of the Society, who is rightly interested in the important concern, strictly to adhere to those regulations, without partiality or wavering."[93]

An insight into some of the affairs of the school, such as provision of material, building, and caretakers, is gained from the account book of 1797, of which specimen pages are given below.

Besides instruction, a library was established, presumably filled with "solid" books, such as circulated in Friends' meetings; and

" 1797		SCHOOL	Dr.	L	S	d
3rd Month	2d	To Sundries from William Willson		3	16	10
		Cash expended for Books, etc.			18	9
		A Quarter of wood Hauling and Sawing			18	½
		Cleaning the House and lime			12	7½
		Removing			2	
4th Month	1st	Cash expended for books			13	6
		Do for worsteds			3	9
	10th	Sundries purchased by H. Hopkins		1	11	2
	19 ..	Cash for A Stone pitcher and pint mug			1	11½
		Half Dozen Thimbles 5½d)			1	4½
		A knife 11d)				
	29 ..	Boxes			13	2½
5th Month	9 ..	Benches & desks from F. Nesbitt		1	2	6
		A Dozen Juvenile Miscellanies		1	2	6
		For Half pound pins 2/9)				
		Half Hundred Needles 1/10½)			4	7½
7th Month	18 ..	A Collection of Tables in Arithmetic				
		half dozen 1/10½) .			3	4½
		sundries 1/6)				
		Peary King for 1 Quarters Rent		5		

L17 6 2½"

<hr />

[93] Regulations for the instruction of female children, 1803, among the Aimwell School Manuscripts; kindly loaned by Mrs. Howard E. Yarnall, 4727 Springfield Avenue, Phila., Pa.

1797		SCHOOL Dr.	L	S	d
11th mo:		To Cash paid for a stove pipe	1	4	4½
		12 Copy Books		6	
		Hauling a Box of drawers		1	4½
12th mo:	20th	A Quarter of Wood, 9/4½ hauling ½			
		Sawing and carrying it up 4/3½ 1d		15	1¼
		1 doz Spelling Books	1	2	6
		3 oz of Thread		3	7½
		2 doz Thimbles		1	4½
1st mo:	19th	Minute Book			11
1798		A Quarter of Wood sawing hauling		18	½
		1 doz Copy Books		5	
	25th	1 doz Thimbles			8
	28th	Quils			9
2d mo:	18th	1 oz of thread No. 22		1	5
	19th	Quarter of Hundred of needles			8
	21st	1 doz Copy Books		5	
3d mo:	5th	Cash laid out in tillets for work bags		14	9
		Tape thread		4	11½
	14th	Thimbles 1/ Thread & Needles		2	1
	20th	2 Hundred of Needles		4	1½
		2 papers of Pins 1/11 1 doz of Thimbles 8d		2	7
		1 Hundred slate pencils		1	10½
		Thread No. 26 1/6 No. 18 1/		2	6
		2 doz Copy books		10	

7   9   4½''⁹⁴

7   9   4½''[94]

the girls who, in the opinion of both teachers, had ''conducted well through the week . . .'' were allowed to take a book home from Saturday till Monday. Those who abused a book were not given one the next week-end. Those who finished their education at the school acceptably were to have the privilege of taking books from the library for a week at a time.[95]

Some space has been devoted to Quaker education of girls in Philadelphia. The same practices prevailed, though on a less elaborate scale, certainly, throughout the limits of the Philadelphia Yearly Meeting, which included much of New Jersey, Delaware, and Pennsylvania. The same is true for New York Yearly Meeting, New England, and North Carolina.[96]

[94] *Aimwell Sch. Acct Bk.*, 1797, 1 and 3.
[95] *Aimwell School Regulations*, 1802–1809.
[96] See Klain: *Quaker Contributions to Education in North Carolina*, 284–96, and his *Educational Activities of New England Quakers* (1928); Woody: *Quaker Education in the Colony and State of New Jersey;* also Wright: *Quaker Education in New York* (Master's dissertation at Columbia University, 1913).

Rules, for the observation of the scholars
in Friends Female School Woodbury.

1 The School is to commence the three months of
spring and Autumn, at half past eight in the morning and half past one in the afternoon closing at
twelve and half past four. — In summer at
eight and two, closing at five — In Winter at —
nine and one, closing at twelve and four.

2. Each scholar capable of reading in the Scriptures, should commit a small portion thereof to
memory every week, to be recited at such seasons, as the Teacher may —

3 The children are to avoid ___ any other noise;
when learning their lessons; and no conversation to be allowed, nor any child suffered to leave
her seat without permission from the Teacher

4 The scholars are required ___ ___ their Teacher
always treating her with ___ due to her station. — If however any should ___ obedience the circumstance should be represented to the visiting committee for their decision thereon

5 The Parents and Guardians are expected when they
enter a pupil, to pay for their time whether present
or not, unless kept at home by serious indisposition
in which case they are at liberty to send another child in her place

6 The children are affectionately desired to endeavour at all times to live ___ and harmony with
each other remembering ___ injunction of our
Holy Redeemer, to do unto ___ as we would
wish them to do unto us

RULES FOR WOODBURY FRIENDS' FEMALE SCHOOL

In communities where Lutheran, Moravian and Reformed elements were in control, efforts at education were at once made. The first Lutherans to arrive in the central territory were Swedes who landed at Cape Henlopen in 1638; and among these earliest scattered people—first Swedes, then Dutch and English, fighting for an existence in the wilderness—one scarcely expects to find schools. But there was an educational tradition in the homeland of the Swedes which they naturally hoped to carry on here; and, as in all religious communities, dependence for instruction was upon the ministers. The actual performance, however, does not appear to have been good. Acrelius, in 1759, said: "Forty years back, our people scarcely knew what a school was."[97] The first settlers were poor and ignorant and brought their children up in the same ignorance, "which is the reason why the natives of the country can neither write nor cypher. . . ." Yet something was done. In 1693 the Swedes requested by letter that "three books of sermons, twelve Bibles, forty-two psalm books, one hundred tracts, with two hundred catechisms and as many primers" be sent over, promising payment for them at once.[98] This letter makes the purpose of elementary education clear, as the catechisms and primers must have been designed for schools. The King donated, in response to the request, 400 primers and 500 catechisms, and many other books besides.[99] As for women at this time, the letter stated, "Our wives and daughters employ themselves in spinning wool and flax and many of them in weaving."[100] Torkillus, the first minister, in 1639, and Campanius, after 1643, must have performed what teaching was done; but that it was extremely difficult to keep regular schools, or build schoolhouses, can scarcely be questioned. The latter mentions that he preached on certain days and gave "daily instruction"; but what this was, is unknown. Torkillus is also mentioned as "teacher of the youth," Domine Lars, Sven Colsberg, Hans Stolt, Arvid Hernbom, John Göding, and Christopher Springer are similarly named as teachers; and, considering their later request

[97] *Hist. of New Sweden,* 351.
[98] Rohrbach: *Lutheran Education in the Ministerium of Pennsylvania* (*MS.*), 14; Clay: *Annals,* 43.
[99] Clay: *op. cit.,* 49.
[100] *Ibid.,* 43.

for the primers and catechisms, one would surmise that religion and reading were their first concerns in instruction.

The Dutch, at New Castle on the Delaware, were to provide a "house for a school" and a "school master," according to the constitution offered by the City of Amsterdam to its colonists at that place, in 1656. Evart Pietersen is the only master who kept school there, so far as known. He wrote, under date of August 10th, 1657, "I already begin to keep school, and have twenty-five children. . . ."[101]

From the above, it seems certain that the Swedes and Dutch had made arrangement for some schools between 1638 and 1682, when Penn's colony was established. The court records of Upland, March 12, 1678–9, also suggest that private teachers were employed by some.[102] Judging the Dutch schools to have been conducted much the same as those in New Netherlands, the presumption is that girls were here also taught reading, religion, and possibly writing, along with the boys. The Swedish Lutherans too, in all probability, taught the girls the primer and the catechism, at least—and possibly to write, as was the custom of Lutherans in Germany and Sweden. But of this there is no documentary proof.

The earliest educational work of the Germans in Pennsylvania was performed by the pietistic brotherhood, under the leadership of Kelpius, on the banks of the Wissahickon. Daniel Falckner wrote of this, in 1694: "We are now beginning to build a house here. . . . For we are resolved, besides giving public instruction to the little children of this country, to take many of them to ourselves and have them night and day with us; so as to lay in them the foundations of a stable permanent character."[103] Before the arrival of Kelpius, in 1683, the Mennonites had settled at Germantown. Here, in 1706, a meeting house was built which Wickersham says was also used as a school. In 1702, they established themselves at Skippack and, in 1725, erected a house for worship wherein a school also was kept. Here Christopher Dock, the pious Mennonite schoolmaster, taught for some time—according to some, as early as 1714, and certainly after 1718.[104] In

101 Quoted in Wickersham: *Education in Pa.*, 12.

102 *Ibid.*, 17.

103 Rohrbach: *op. cit.*, 18.

106 See recommendations of Smith: *A Brief Statement of the Province of Dock*, 12.

1750, he wrote the *Schulordnung*, usually considered the first book on school management in the United States. Wherever they settled, elementary schools went with their meeting-houses; for it was only the higher schools, which they associated with ecclesiastical tyranny, that they abhorred.

An interesting development of the work of early pietists is found in the community established at Ephrata by Conrad Beissel, into whom, the *Chronicon Ephratense* says, the spirit of Kelpius had entered. For a time he remained with the Dunkers but, differing on the question of the day of worship, disappeared, in 1732, and founded the community on the banks of the Cocalico Creek. The community was small, but active. In the Sisters' House, the work of their hands is preserved to this day. The rules of the Order of the Rose of Sharon, as they were called, required a certain number of hours to be spent in prayers, manual work such as spinning and weaving, and instruction and writing. Samples of their beautifully adorned script are exhibited now at the Sisters' House; but aside from assistance in preparing school books—*A B C Büchlein, Namen Büchlein,* and the *Rechnen Büchlein,* which were written by Master Hoecker— it does not appear that their painfully attained skill bore much fruit. About 1740, Hoecker and Sister Petronella began to teach the poor children of the community on Sabbath afternoons, both secular and religious instruction being given.[105]

From the days of Kelpius the number of Germans increased rapidly so that, by 1727, an act was passed by the assembly requiring all male ship passengers above sixteen years to take the oath of allegiance. Men of such sound judgment as Franklin and Logan became apprehensive for the stability of the English government in the Colony; and between 1750 and 1763 a great effort was put forth, by means of charity schools, to set up a safeguard by teaching Germans English.[106] These charity schools, Weber found, were for boys, their education being more important than the girls. There was, however, one exception: the school at New Providence, where girls were taught reading

---

[105] For an excellent account of the work of German sectarians consult Sachse: *German Pietists in Pa.*, three volumes; also a brief account in Wickersham's *Hist. of Education in Pa.*

[106] See recommendations of Smith: *A Brief State of the Province of Pa.*, 34 *ff.*

and sewing.[107]   Only twelve schools of any kind were actually
established, though twenty-five were at first planned.   The following extract shows that some supporters of the movement were
desirous of having the girls included in the program of the
society:

"... Secondly, as it may be of great service to religion and
industry, to have schools for girls also, we shall use our endeavors
with the honorable Society to have some few schoolmistresses
encouraged to teach reading and the use of the needle.   And tho
this was no part of the original design, yet as the Society have
nothing but the general good of all at heart, we doubt not they
will extend their benefaction for this charitable purpose also."[108]

William Smith estimated the German inhabitants, in 1759, as
"over 100,000."   Though this was too large, they were, no doubt,
numerous.   In their communities schools were created from the
start, but the greatest progress was made after 1750.   At the middle of the century there were probably as many as twenty schools
among Lutherans; in 1802, specific records show 62, but this number is incomplete.[109]

Before schools were established, children were sometimes instructed in private homes.[110]   And, no doubt, this occurred after
some schools were created, for as some observers wrote: "With
schools in the country it is very inconvenient with such bad roads
and rough weather for the poor children who have to go two,
three or four English miles.   The parents are for the most part
unable to provide as many shoes and necessary clothes as the
children wear out."[111]   Even as late as 1747, Weissinger
lamented in a letter to Ziegenhagen that "a large number of the
rising generation . . . know not their right hand from their
left. . . ."   Nevertheless, it is certain that as soon as the community could support a teacher, a pastor, or both, a school was
established.   Rohrbach, in a careful study of the church records,
found a school at Falckner's Swamp in 1704; and thereafter
they were established in various places, there being sixty-two on
record in 1802.[112]   In 1742, the Tulpehocken records mention "a

107 Weber: *The Charity School Movement in Col. Pa.*, 45.
108 *N. Y. Gaz.*, Mar. 17, 1755.
109 Rohrbach: *op. cit.*, 47–8.
110 Tyson: *Lutheran Ed. in Pa.*, 42.
111 *Hallische Nachrichten*, I, 178.
112 *Op. cit.*, 31–48.

schoolmaster . . . together with his wife . . ." who are "to teach the boys' as well as the girls' school."[113] Most of the records do not name boys or girls specifically. Some, such as the above, and also that for Philadelphia, in 1795,[114] specify both boys' and girls' schools. This was in accord with the general custom in Germany of having separate schools in large centers, whereas in poorer rural districts all attended the same school. Dock, in his *Schulordnung*, clearly indicated he had girls at his school. Referring to his method of receiving a pupil, he said: "If it is a girl, I ask the girls, who among them will take care of this new child and teach it."[115] Again he said, "The boys and girls occupy separate benches."[116] The wives of masters are referred to occasionally. For example, in 1750, the code of Augustus school (at Trappe) declared: "Not the slightest oath, or any idle talk, shall be heard in or out of school, on the part of the schoolmaster, his wife or his children."

The basis of all instruction was the A B C Book and the next step, learning the catechism, prayers, and psalms. Writing was probably not at first taught girls, such an acquirement being considered necessary only for boys. To arithmetic, girls did not aspire; and even for boys to be able to "figure Pike" was proof of great scholarship.[117]

The Reformed congregations do not figure prominently until after 1720. The earlier churches at Neshaminy, Bensalem, and Skippack were largely made up of Dutch. But in 1725, John Philip Boehm took charge of these three and also one at the Swamp. The earliest specific reference to teaching that must have included girls—though it is probable they were taught reading at least, by Boehm—is quoted by Wickersham, who says that the wife of Jacob Dubbs "was accustomed to gather the children of her neighbors into her kitchen in the afternoon and

[113] *Ibid.*

[114] *Ibid.*, 45.

[115] Brumbaugh: *Life and Works of Christopher Dock*, 104.

[116] *Ibid.*, 105.

[117] Rohrbach, *op. cit.*, 60, listed the following books used in schools of the eighteenth century: *Das A B C Buch und Namen Büchlein, Der Psalter, Das Glaubens Lied*, Stark's *Gebet Buch, Das Neue Testament, Deutsche und Englische Grammatik*, by Sauer, Luther's *Kleiner Catechismus, Anfang der Englischen Sprache*, Workmann's *Elementen der Geographie, Synopsis Mathematica Universalis, Der Geschwinde Rechner*, and Pike's *Arithmetic*.

teach them to read and write."[118] In 1746, Michael Schlatter
came to Pennsylvania and undertook the task of organizing the
scattered Reformed Churches. In 1747 the Coetus was established and, from 1753 onward, distributed money to masters,
sometimes assisting as many as ten schools in a year.[119] Schlatter
found a grave shortage of schoolmasters: ". . . Most of them
are not even provided with a good schoolmaster . . ." because of
poverty. As a remedy Schlatter raised money in Europe and,
in 1759, definite sums, ranging from £1½ to £8, were paid from
this fund to schoolmasters at Lancaster, Tulpehocken and elsewhere. In these schools and also at Conewago, Kreutz Creek,
Readingtown, Goshenhoppen and Falkner's Swamp, the typical
education, based on the Heidelberg Catechism and the Bible,
doubtless prevailed. The first was a guide to the second. On
the title page of an early edition this admonition was written:
"*Nach dieser Regel suchet in der Schrift.*"[120] The teacher
bound himself to "serve as chorister [and to read the sermon
when there was no pastor] to hold catechetical instruction with
the young, as becomes a faithful teacher and also to lead them
in singing."[121]

A glimpse of the school may be gained from the regulations
drawn up in 1760 for the school which had been established in
1753 at Philadelphia:

"When well organized Christian Congregations, for their
upbuilding, establish schools, it is very important to have competent God-fearing men for teachers, that becoming order and
propriety may be observed. On this account, the Elders and
Deacons of the Reformed Church in Philadelphia unanimously
agree to do all in their power for the welfare of such a well-
regulated school, and for the upbuilding of our congregation,
that all things may be done decently and in order. The following article is made, respecting the duty of the teacher, and the
amount of the salary he is to receive. He must be possessed of
the following accomplishments:

118 *Education in Pa.*, 128–9.
119 *Minutes and Letters of the Coetus of the German Reformed Congregation in Pennsylvania*, 89 *ff*.
120 Dubbs: *Hist. of the Reformed Church in Pa.*, 37.
121 Wickersham: *op. cit.*, 140.

"*First*, He must be qualified in reading, writing, arithmetic and singing—he must undergo an examination in these branches and be approved.

"*Second*, He must be one that takes a lively interest in, and helps to build up the Christian church; and must be also a God-fearing, virtuous man, and lead an exemplary life and must himself be a lover of the Word of God, and be diligent in its use as much as possible, among the children in school; and he must set a good example, especially before the young children, and avoid exhibitions of anger.

"*Third*, He shall willingly and heartily seek to fulfil the duties obligatory upon him, with love to God and to the Children; to the performance of which the Lord their Maker, and Jesus their Redeemer, have so strongly bound him.

"The following are the *Duties* incumbent upon the school-master.

"*First*, He is not to show partiality among the children, and he must receive them lovingly and without distinction.

"*Second*, He must teach six hours per day—three in the forenoon and three in the afternoon—unless, the number of scholars increases, when he must give them more time.

"*Third*, He must be judicious, and adapt himself to the various dispositions, and gifts of the children; and exercise patience, love and gentleness, as much as possible, in his teaching, that he may win their hearts and work with blessing among them.

"*Fourth*, He shall have power to correct and punish the children, though with moderation and forbearance, without animosity, or passion or anger; and in particular he shall not treat them in a spiteful manner, but shall rather consider the weakness of the children; and more particularly still he must refrain from all vexatious, abusive and disgraceful language.

"*Fifth*, He shall at all times open and close his school with a hearty prayer to God for his grace and blessing.

"*Sixth*, Besides teaching the children to read and write, he shall also train them to pray, and exhort them to continue the practice. And besides teaching them the Lord's Prayer (Our Father, etc.), he shall also teach them the articles of our Christian faith, the Ten Commandments, and several short, edifying, penitent prayers, as well as scriptural passages—which he must repeat to them and impress upon their attention. They must also be taught to live a Godly life; to remember their Saviour, and to be obedient to their parents, and to conduct themselves in a becoming manner, especially in receiving proper admonition.

"*Seventh,* If it is possible, and time will permit, he should sing several verses with the larger children, of pieces with which they are acquainted, and continue the practice from time to time, in order to instruct them in the art of singing.

"*Eighth,* All those children who are able to read shall diligently learn the Catechism by heart, and this shall be strictly followed up until they are able to recite all the questions and answers."[122]

At no time was a complete record of schools presented to the Coetus. In 1766, there were at least 28 congregations in the Coetus. These had 13 schools, with 432 children attending. This is inexact, since "the schools in the country begin with the winter and stop with the summer, and no certain account can be given." In 1776, 22 schools with 595 pupils, and, in 1783, 36 schools with 1,030 pupils were reported. In neither case was the report complete.

Although no specific mention of girls has been found in connection with the schools named, there is a probability that they were taught at least to read, and occasionally perhaps to write, this judgment resting on the practice of the Reformed congregation elsewhere (*e.g.,* in New Netherlands) and the custom of Germans at home ever since the days of Luther.

More significant than the foregoing was the work begun at Germantown, Bethlehem and Lititz, where the Moravians, acting for a time as a community in which each member lived as one of a family, founded schools for girls. The first school was begun at Germantown, in 1742, at the house of Zinsendorf; and, by 1747, there were fifty boys and girls, some of them coming from Philadelphia, Lancaster and New York. A similar school was opened at Nazareth in 1745, where twenty-eight boys and girls attended. In 1749, a Boarding School was opened, for Moravian girls only, but it was later (1785) thrown open to other denominations, as the Moravian Female Seminary. Other schools at Lancaster, York, Lebanon, Milton Grove, Emaus, and Oley should perhaps be named also, as it is probable that girls were educated there, as in Bethlehem, except that in small places

[122] Van Horne: *History of the Reformed Church in Philadelphia,* 32.

the boys and girls were taught together. In 1794, Linden Hall, a seminary for girls, was opened at Lititz; for a time it occupied the Sisters' House, but in 1804 a special building was erected.

III. Adventure Schools

Throughout the half century before the War of Independence, a new situation developed in the education of women and girls, due to the work of "adventure" masters. Their schools appear in considerable numbers in such cities of the central colonies as New York and Philadelphia.[123] They are conspicuous for several reasons: first, their number; second, the announced versatility of the masters and mistresses; third, their evident desire to teach what somebody wanted to learn,—a sensitiveness to social and economic needs; and fourth, for the fact that, so far as the writer has been able to ascertain, they taught such subjects as later appeared in academies and high schools. In other words, while the schools organized by Quakers, Dutch, and the various German congregations were satisfied with offering reading, writing, and religion to girls, these private masters and mistresses gave a taste of higher branches and languages—a part of secondary education. The experiments of Mrs. Rhodes, who taught French in 1723; John Guerbois (in New York), teaching Latin, French and arithmetic in 1752; Lucy Brown and Ann Ball, who advertised to teach French in 1771; and also numerous others, were possibly instructive to men like Benjamin Rush and DeWitt Clinton. Just after the Revolution we find Rush associated with a group in the establishment of a Female Academy of Philadelphia, the first in the city. This new institution, while it did not include all that private masters taught, went far beyond the usual elementary education. It had to compete with private masters, and the result was the elevation and extension of its course. Whether there be sufficient documentary proof of such influence or not, these private adventures were significant for their own sake.

The advertisements of private masters and mistresses, drawn chiefly from the *American Weekly Mercury, Pennsylvania*

[123] Extremely few, at least, were established outside the cities between 1720 and 1776. Although numerous advertisements of boys' schools, in nearby towns, appear towards the latter half of the period, such was seldom the case for girls.

Gazette, New York Gazette, and *The Weekly Post Boy,*[124] between 1720 and 1776, fall into five classes: first, those that specialized in a polite accomplishment, such as dancing; second, those teaching some accomplishments and domestic art; third, those teaching accomplishments and also one or all of the three rudiments; fourth, those that limited themselves to the rudiments, with, perhaps, a specialty of writing; and, fifth, those that made provision for some higher studies. While there is no strict adherence to chronology, we may say that the first class appeared prominently early in the period and continued throughout, while the fifth group was little mentioned at first but became prominent between 1750 and 1776. Advertisements of each group are quoted, either in full or in part.

Typical of dancing masters is the advertisement of Theobold Hacket:

"This is to give notice that Theobold Hacket dancing master (lately come from England and Ireland) has opened a dancing school in this city at the house where Mr. Brownell lived in Second Street, where he will give due attendance and teach all sorts of fashionable English and French dances after the newest and politest manner practised in London, Dublin and Paris, and will give all ladies, gentlemen and children (that please to learn of him) the most graceful carriage in dancing and genteel behavior in company on all occasions, that can possibly be given by any dancing master whatsoever. He will teach by the month or by the quarter as reasonable as any good master. N. B. If any be inclined to agree by the Great, or learn privately he will attend them duly either at their own houses or in his room (out of school hours), and that with the utmost discretion."[125]

The earliest newspaper reference found relating to the education of the female sex was in 1722, when notice was given in the *American Weekly Mercury*[126] that a person had arrived in Philadelphia who offered to give his services to educate the poor Negroes, men and women, without expense to their masters and mistresses, whether they were "Roman Catholics, Episcopalians, Presbyterians, Independents, Water-Baptists, or the people called Quakers."

---

[124] Some others were read; mostly duplicate advertisements were found.

[125] *Am. Wkly. Mer.* (Philadelphia), September, 1738.

[126] Feb. 19, 1722.

In 1731, 1750, and 1768 the following offers of instruction were published:

"Martha Gazley, late from Great Britain, now in the City of New York, makes and teaches the following curious works, viz. Artificial fruits and flowers, and other wax work, Nuns-work, Philligree and pencil work upon muslin, all sorts of needle work, and raising of Paste, as also to paint upon glass, and transparent for sconces with other works. If any young gentlewomen, or others, are inclined to learn any or all the above-mentioned curious works, they may be carefully taught and instructed in the same by said Martha Gazley, at present at Widdow Butler's near the Queen's Head Tavern in William Street, not far from Capt. Anthony Rutgers."[127]

"Anne Stockton, who lately advertised to keep an Ordinary, has declined, and is advised to teach young ladies to sew and embroider, and millenary. Any gentlemen or ladies that have any misses to send to her, may depend that due care will be taken in teaching: She likewise takes in plain work and dresses head clothes after the newest fashion; and young ladies boarded by ANNE STOCKTON."[128]

"Isabel Hewet, in Macclenahan's Alley, the corner house, next to St. Paul's Church, Begs leave to inform the public that she intends to open a school for the instruction of young girls in sewing sundry kinds of needle work, such as white and colored seam, drawing and flowering, Embroidery and dresden work. Those who are pleased to intrust the above Isabel Hewet with their children, may depend on being carefully attended. Also all kinds of needlework, done at the said place, after the best and neatest manner, and at the most reasonable prices."[129]

Numerous others taught sewing, darning, and "other needle work" to those who had practical domestic tastes; while plain work, samplars, quilting, knotting for bed quilts, Dresden work, 'enameling,' and 'japanning' had great vogue, apparently. Frequently the husband taught higher studies and announced his wife would teach certain accomplishments.[130] Thomas Carroll gave notice in the *New York Mercury* that he would teach—a

[127] *N. Y. Gazette*, Dec. 21, 1731.
[128] *N. Y. Wkly. Post Boy*, Jan. 28, 1750–1.
[129] *Pa. Gaz.*, Sept. 29, 1768.
[130] For example, see *N. Y. Gaz.*, April 1, 1751.

half column of subjects, naming everything conceivable—but explained that "he was not under the necessity of coming here to teach, he had views of living more happy, but some unforeseen and unexpected events have happened since his arrival here..." So he was driven to teach. To the list of diverse subjects which he would teach men, he added a *Nota Bene* (so far had fortune declined, that both had to teach!) that "Mrs. Carrol proposes teaching Young Ladies Plain Work, Samplars, French Quilting, Knoting for Bed Quilts, or Toilets, Dresden, Flowering on Cat Gut, Shading (with Silk or Worsted on Cambrick, Lawn, or Holland)."[131]

SCHOOL OF JAMES AND ELIZABETH WRAGG, ADVERTISED IN THE *New York Gazette or Weekly Post Boy*, APRIL 5, 1756

As stated, other schools combined accomplishments of sorts with the rudiments, and in a few instances "higher branches of Literature" were thus combined. Such a combination, for example, was offered "at the back of Mr. Benson's Brew-House" in New York, 1747;[132] "at James Bell's in second street," Philadelphia;[133] "at the house of Mr. Wiley in Broad street," New York;[134] and by Mary Robert, in Church Alley, Philadelphia, in

[131] *N. Y. Mer.*, May 6, 1765.
[132] *N. Y. Gaz.*, revived in *Wkly. Post Boy*, July 13, 1747.
[133] *Pa. Gaz.*, Oct. 12, 1752.
[134] *N. Y. Mercury*, May 16, 1763.

1766.[135] Reading, writing, and "spelling the English tongue" were the subjects combined, in the above cases, with plain and fancy work with the needle. Other schools of this kind were kept for many years by James and Elizabeth Wragg and Robert Savage in New York.

The fourth class of schools concentrated on such subjects as reading, writing—some engaging to teach all the hands—, arithmetic, vulgar and decimal, merchants' accounts, "the whole English grammar," and geography. These notices are found in great numbers after 1750. Some masters and mistresses taught

SCHOOL OF ROBERT SAVAGE, ADVERTISED IN THE *New York Mercury*, MAY 12, 1760

girls only; others both boys and girls. Mother MaGuire, who had for some time taught both, opened school especially for girls in 1770, because she had "frequently" been "solicited" to do so "by several respectable families."[136] The specialists were confident of overcoming every obstacle. A teacher of arithmetic explained that "the rules of . . . [it] will be peculiarly adapted to the sex, so as to render them concise and familiar."[137] But writing specialists were much more common, and they must have

[135] *Pa. Gaz.*, Sept. 11, 1766.
[136] *Ibid.*, Oct. 25, 1770.
[137] *Ibid.*, Apr. 17, 1766.

had a thriving business in those days when beautiful writing was still a highly valued art. William Elphinstone was a writing master for many years, at one time in New York and again in Philadelphia. Though he taught other subjects in his school, as shown in the facsimile, he appears to have been proudest of his skill as writing master. In earlier advertisements,[138] he offered to teach "persons of both sexes from twelve years of age to fifty, who never wrote before . . . to write a good legible hand in five weeks, at an hour per day . . . and such as write but indifferently may have their hands considerably improved . . ." When

SCHOOL OF WILLIAM ELPHINSTONE, ADVERTISED IN THE *New York Gazette*, SEPT. 18, 1758

he was in Philadelphia, in 1758, he had with him samples of pupils' achievements, with which to convince skeptical prospectives.[139] In September, 1758, he advertised his school in New York, where he taught much besides writing.

Another master of the pen who placed a high estimate on his profession was John Wingfield. According to his statement he had taught twelve or fourteen years and had obtained such a "compleat and approved Method" in teaching writing that he could do it in three months, for five dollars. His advertisements

138 See, for example, the *New York Gazette* for 1753.
139 *Pa. Gaz.*, Apr. 27, 1758.

are of especial interest here, as he was always careful to point out the utility of his art in case of the adversities of "the melancholy State of Widowhood."

Adventure schools which offered studies of more advanced character appeared, for the most part, after the middle of the century. Some, however, may be noted much earlier. Mrs.

SCHOOL OF JOHN WINGFIELD, ADVERTISED IN THE *New York Gazette*, JAN. 8, 1759

Rodes, for example, arrived in Philadelphia about 1723 and set out to "teach young ladies or gentlewomen to read and write French to perfection." With this she included "flourishing on muslin after the most expeditious way," lace work, embroidering of petticoats, and selling "very good Orange oyl" and "sweet-meats."[140] The teaching of French, English, and writing

[140] *Am. Wkly. Mer.*, May 16–23, 1723.

was also combined with needle- and shell-work by Mary Mc-
Allester.[141]

The great majority of these schools were taught by men and
attempted nothing but academic subjects. The wife is sometimes
mentioned, however, as willing "to teach some pieces of Ingenuity," if ladies require it. Instruction in the following subjects
was offered: reading, writing, arithmetic, Low Dutch, English,
French, Latin, Greek, merchants' accounts, algebra, logarithmical
and instrumental arithmetic, geometry and trigonometry, plain
and spherical, surveying, gauging, dialling, mensuration of

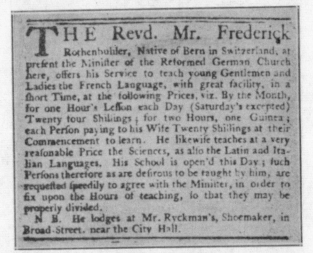

SCHOOL OF REVD. MR. FREDERICK ROTHENBUHLER, ADVERTISED IN THE
New York Mercury, JUNE 8, 1761

superficies and solids, astronomy, the calculation and projection
of the eclipses of the luminaries, planets, places, the projection
of the sphere upon the plan of any circle, navigation, uses of
charts and globes, geography, anatomy, and midwifery.

How many girls applied for instruction at these schools, and
whether they elected few or many advanced studies, is unknown.
But the opportunities were offered freely. Some masters advertised a great array of subjects, possibly to attract attention to
their versatility; but others were satisfied with one subject and
sought to show they were extremely well qualified in it. Such

[141] *N. Y. Mercury*, June 16, 1760.

was William Clajon, who had his ability to teach French certified
by the College in New York. Other masters desired to establish
a more definite school organization. Some referred to their
schools as academies and planned to take in boys; others would
take girls and boys, as was true of Jackson, in New York, 1765.
This was the first notice found advertising the "academy" for

SCHOOL OF ROBERT LEETH, ADVERTISED IN THE *New York Gazette-Weekly
Post Boy*, JUNE 17, 1751

boys and girls in New York and Philadelphia newspapers. The
name, however, was the only thing that distinguished his school
from many earlier ones. A little later, Poor's Academy for girls
was established in Philadelphia.[142] The Moravian School for
girls, established 1749, at Bethlehem, became a "Female Seminary" in 1785. Poor's "Female Academy" was similarly preceded, throughout a generation at least, by schools of like character, though not called by that name.

Besides the opening of the "golden paths" of learning in these

[142] Woodbridge says the school existed as early as 1780; references to
commencement, in 1787, have been found.

schools, there were numerous lectures on philosophical subjects. About 1750 and after, lecture courses were given in Philadelphia and New York on "Electrical Fire," and many other topics named under the head of Natural Philosophy. The lectures of Kinnersley and Evans attracted great attention, and were open

SCHOOL ADVERTISEMENT OF WILLIAM CLAJON, IN THE *New York Mercury,* JAN. 19, 1761

to ladies as well as men. Special encouragement was given to ladies' attendance by presenting a free ticket for them to each male subscriber.[143] A circulating library was started by Garrot Noel, for the winter, to promote useful knowledge.[144]

[143] See the *New York Gazette and Weekly Post Boy* and the *Pennsylvania Gazette,* in which similar advertisements appear.

[144] *N. Y. Gaz.,* Sept. 10, 1768.

Dr. Shippen was probably the first physician in Philadelphia (1765) who publicly offered women the opportunity to study midwifery. His announcement follows:

"Doctor Shippen, Junior, Having been lately called to the assistance of a number of women in the country, in difficult labours, most of which were made so by the unskilful old women

"An Academy" Proposed by Mr. Jackson, in the *New York Mercury,* April 22, 1765

about them; the poor women have suffered extremely, and their innocent little ones were entirely destroyed, whose lives might have been easily saved by proper management; And being informed of several desperate cases in the different neighborhoods which have proved fatal to the mothers as well as to their infants, and were attended with the most painful circumstances, too dismal to be related, he thought it his duty immediately to begin his intended course of lectures on midwifery and has prepared a proper apparatus for that purpose, in order to instruct women who have had virtue enough to own their ignorance, and apply for instruction, as well as all those young gentlemen now engaged in the study of that useful and necessary branch of surgery who are taking pains to qualify themselves to practice in different parts of the country, with safety and advantage to their fellow creatures.

"The doctor proposes to begin his first course as soon as a number of pupils sufficient to defray the necessary expense shall apply. A course will consist of about 20 lectures, in which he will treat of that part of anatomy which is necessary to that branch, explain all cases in midwifery, natural, difficult, and preternatural, and give directions how to treat them with safety to mother and child; describe the diseases incident to women and children in the month, and direct to proper remedies, will take occasion, during the course, to explain and apply those curious anatomical plates and casts of the gravid uterus at the hospital, and conclude the whole with necessary cautions against the dangerous and cruel use of instruments.

"In order to make the course more perfect, a convenient lodging is provided for the accommodation of a few poor women, who otherwise might suffer for the want of the common necessaries on those occasions, to be under the care of a sober, honest matron, well acquainted with lying in women, employed by the doctor for that purpose.

"Each pupil to attend two courses at least, for which he is to pay five guineas. Perpetual pupils to pay ten guineas.

"The female pupils to be taught privately, and assisted at any of their private labours when necessary.

"The doctor may be spoke with at his house, in Front street, every morning, between the hours of six and nine or at his office, in Letitia Court every evening."[145]

The chemists did not long lag behind the physicians. In 1798, Thomas Smith, in a lecture before the Chemical Society of Philadelphia, said:

[145] *Pa. Gaz.*, Jan. 31, 1765.

"I shall now present you with the last and most pleasing revolution that has occurred in chemistry. Hitherto we have beheld this science entirely in the hands of men; we are now about to behold *women* assert their just, though too long neglected claims, of being participators in the pleasures arising from a knowledge of chemistry. . . . What may we not expect from such an accession of talents? How swiftly will the horizon of knowledge recede before our united labours! And what unbounded pleasure may we not anticipate in treading the paths of science with such companions?"[146]

Throughout the period under discussion, numerous instances appeared in which women advertised, or were advertised for, to teach reading and writing and who could likewise "flourish," do

ADVERTISEMENT FOR A TEACHER FOR NEGRO CHILDREN, *New York Mercury*, AUG. 4, 1760

"plain work," "mark very well," and be "handy with children," if required.[147] St. Andrew's Society of New York, on Sept. 28, 1761, advertised, in the *New York Mercury*, "to employ such poor women as are capable of working, and for want of employ become the objects of the Society's Charity." A year before, a similar opportunity had been offered to a "sober

146 See Smith: *Chemistry in America*, 35 and 41.

147 For example, see *Am. Wkly. Mer.*, Oct. 2–9, 1729; *Pa. Gaz.*, Apr. 19, 1739; May 1, 1760, etc.; *N. Y. Mer.*, Mar. 16, 1761, etc. In Philadelphia alone, Wickersham stated there were, according to White's *Directory* of 1785, at least a hundred teachers of private schools, most of them women. J. Burnette Hallowell examined the *Directory* very carefully, however, in 1923, and found only 35 teachers named, of whom 17 were women.

woman'' to do a charitable work for Negroes, and at the same
time to find employment for herself.

From the study of newspapers we may draw certain conclusions concerning the educational facilities for girls in the two
cities. First, it is clear that a much greater number of private
schools offered instruction to boys than to girls; second, that
those for girls, as well as those for boys, increased notably after
1750; third, the disproportionate advantage of boys was fairly
constant throughout the period; and, fourth, that private facilities for girls and boys apparently suffered a great decline at the
War. The cuts, below, show the situation as accurately as it
can be described from the data collected. It must be kept in
mind, however, that, considering the nature of the sources, abso-

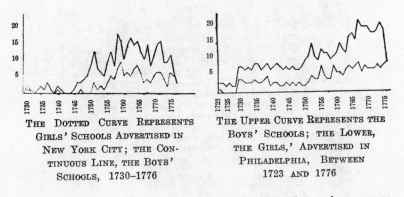

THE DOTTED CURVE REPRESENTS
GIRLS' SCHOOLS ADVERTISED IN
NEW YORK CITY; THE CON-
TINUOUS LINE, THE BOYS'
SCHOOLS, 1730–1776

THE UPPER CURVE REPRESENTS THE
BOYS' SCHOOLS; THE LOWER,
THE GIRLS,' ADVERTISED IN
PHILADELPHIA, BETWEEN
1723 AND 1776

lute statistical accuracy is impossible. Therefore, the curves
drawn suggest the tendency, rather than the exact number of
schools for either sex at any date. Some masters may never have
advertised, depending on reputation and interested pupils to tell
of their facilities. Quaker masters and mistresses did not use the
newspaper columns as much as others—at least in Philadelphia.
Others advertised irregularly, perhaps one year and not the next.
This may account for the sharp fluctuations of the curves.
Again, in turning over thousands of pages, some advertisements
have doubtless been overlooked.

From the newspapers of this same period may also be gained
some idea of the literature generally handled for the custom of
women. Among those noted, though no effort was made to make
an extensive or all-inclusive canvass, were *The Country House-*

wife and Lady's Monthly Director, Parts I and II,[148] the
Friendly Instructor or A Companion for Young Ladies and

This Day is published, and to be sold by

H·U·G H GAINE,

Bookseller, Printer and Stationer, at his Book-Store and
Printing-Office, at the Bible and Crown, in Hanover-
Square;

THE
DIRECTOR:
OR,
Young WOMAN'S best Companion.
BEING
The plainest and cheapest of the Kind ever published.
THE Whole makes a Complete Family Cook and
Physician. Containing above Three Hundred
easy Receipts in Cookery, Pastry, Preserving, Candy-
ing, Pickling, Collaring, Physick, and Surgery. To
which are added, plain and easy Instructions for cho-
sing Beef, Mutton, Veal, Fish, Fowl, and other Eata-
bles. Directions for Carving, and to make Wines.
Likewise Bills of Fare for every Month in the Year,
with a complete INDEX to the Whole. A Book
necessary for all Families. By Sarah Jackson. Collected for the Use of her own Family, and printed at
the Request of her Friends. The Third Edition. Corrected and greatly improv'd by the Author: Particularly
with an Addition of several new Cuts, which at one
View shew regular and easy Forms of placing the different Sorts of Dishes from two to nine in a Course, either in the middling or genteelest Manner. With a
Cut of 13 Dishes, shewing how to set off a long Table
in a common Way, or after the modern Taste: Not in
any other Book extant. Also several Cuts representing
the trussing of Fowls, &c. Dr. Mead's Account of a
Person bit by a mad Dog, and his infalliable Cure. The
Negro Cæsar's Cure for Poison, and likewise for the
Bite of a Rattle-Snake.

ADVERTISEMENT OF *The Director*, PUBLISHED IN THE *New York Mercury*,
OCT. 19, 1761

Young Gentlemen . . . ,[149] *Meditations on Divine Subjects*,[150]
The Lady's Preceptor,[151] *The Poor Planter's Physician, The*

148 *Am. Wkly. Mer.*, Sept. 25, 1740.
149 *Pa. Gaz.*, Dec. 17, 1745.
150 *N. Y. Gaz. and Wkly. Post-Boy*, March 26, 1750.
151 *Ibid.*, July 2, 1759.

FACSIMILE OF AN ADVERTISEMENT OF *The Lady's Preceptor, New York Gazette*, JULY 2, 1759

Matrimonial Preceptor,[152] *The Young Misses Magazine*,[153] *The Compleat House Wife or Accomplish'd Gentlewoman*,[154] *The British Housewife or the Cook, Housekeeper's and Gardener's*

152 *Ibid.*, Oct. 9, 1760.
153 *N. Y. Mercury*, Apr. 20, 1761.
154 *Ibid.*, Oct. 19, 1761.

Companion,[155] and *The Director or Young Woman's Best Companion.*[156] Another, "just published," was ". . . *The Ladies Friend,* being a treatise on the virtues and qualifications which are the brightest ornaments of the fair sex, and render them most agreeable to the sensible part of mankind. . . . To which is annexed, Real Beauty; or the Art of Charming, By an ingenious poet."[157]

Some books offered for sale at the bookstore of Garrot Noel, of New York, in 1762, suggest the character of girls' education. These books are suggested as proper gifts for "the entertainment

For the Use of MARRIED and UNMARRIED LADIES!
This Day is published, neatly printed in a Pocket Volume,
[Price SEVEN SHILLINGS.]
THE
MATRIMONIAL PRECEPTOR,
A COLLECTION
OF MOST EXCELLENT EXAMPLES
RELATING TO THE
MARRIED STATE,
In which every young LADY is directed in the Choice of
A HUSBAND;
In her Conduct to him. | The Duties of a good Wife.
The Folly of precipitate Matches | The Brutality of Husbands.
And a Thousand other Points essential to HUSBANDS, as well
as WIVES, are most incomparably treated upon.
By Mr. RICHARDSON, the Author of CLARISSA.
Mr. FIELDING, the Author of TOM JONES.
And several other elegant AUTHORS.
SOLD by JAMES RIVINGTON, at his Store in Hanover-Square,
over against Mr. M'EVERS's.

NOTICE OF THE PUBLICATION OF *The Matrimonial Preceptor,* IN THE *New York Gazette,* OCTOBER 9, 1760

and improvement of youth, in reading, writing, cyphering, drawing," and are especially "proper presents" at Christmas and New Year: *Lilleputian Magazine, or the Young Gentleman and Ladies Golden Library; Newtonian Philosophy, adapted to the capacity of young gentlemen and ladies; Polite Academy or Instruction for a genteel behavior and polite address in Masters and Misses; A Museum for Gentlemen and Ladies;* and many others. In 1759, Parker, publisher of the *New York Gazette,* began to

155 *Ibid.*
156 *Ibid.*
157 *Pa. Gaz.,* Mar. 14, 1771.

advertise a translation of *The Lady's Preceptor or letter to a lady of distinction on politeness*—taken from the French of Abbé D'Ancourt, "and adapted to the religion, customs and manners of the English Nation."

According to the description of these books, it appears they gave complete instruction on everything girls ought to know, from "their duty to God and their parents," and how to make "the choice of a Husband," to making the pastry, confectionery, preserves, pickles, cakes, creams, jellies, wines and cordials by means of which he might be fed and kept. For there is an old adage, no doubt containing some truth, that the way to a man's heart is through his stomach. *The Matrimonial Preceptor* gave advice to married and unmarried ladies, and threw in "a thousand other points, essential to husbands."

IV. Girls' Schools Worthy of Special Notice

In the foregoing, we have noted the rise of "adventure schools" which offered opportunities for girls' education, ranging from 'accomplishments' and the rudiments to grammar, French, Latin, Greek and many other studies. Specific mention should be made of other special schools, of more permanent character, that attracted pupils from a distance and were the forerunners of the network of academies and seminaries that, in the last quarter of the eighteenth century and first half of the nineteenth, spread over the whole of the states dealt with in this chapter, and constituted the chief source of training for girls. No substitute for them was found before the second quarter of the nineteenth century, when the high school began to offer competition; and not until after the Civil War were they really supplanted by the new institution.

Very early there existed a well-recognized school for girls at the little seaboard town of Lewes, Delaware, to which Deputy Governor Lloyd of Pennsylvania sent his daughters.[158] But though it was widely patronized its history is obscure and its work may not have been very advanced.

A school of conspicuous merit, established by the Moravians, first at Germantown in 1742, later at Bethlehem in 1749, catered to the needs of the Society until 1785, and was then opened to

[158] Wharton: *Col. Days and Dames*, 47.

other denominations. During the first century of its existence on the latter basis, more than seven thousand young women were instructed.[159] Some girls came from Nova Scotia, and many from Maine and other states of New England, as well as from central and Southern localities, to participate in its benefits.[160]

A third school, more permanent because officially under the Board of Overseers which controlled the Penn Charter School, was begun at the instance of Anthony Benezet, as described in the following minute: "Anthony Benezet informing the Board that as He is much solicited to keep a Morning Session for teaching Girls Reading, Writing, Arithmetick and English Grammar, after some Conversation agreed that if he will decline engaging in any Business which the Board may judge like to take his attention off the School, He shall be allowed a Salary of Eighty pounds for the Ensuing Year, and that He is not to take more than 30 Scholars for which he is to demand 40 shillings each the Amount of whose Schooling He is to account for with the Board in part for his Salary. And as some alterations are necessary in order to keep the Girls separate from the Boys in going to and from the School &c the Committee appointed are desired to get an Alley open'd from Chestnut St. to the School-house on the East side of the Lott and a Stair case made outside of the House leading immediately to the East Chamber."[161] This school was advanced, according to the prevailing standards. Possibly Benezet taught some French to those who desired it, though it was not specified in the minute. It was attended by girls from the 'best' families[162] though, knowing Benezet's philanthropic bent, it is probable he taught poor girls free. He resigned in 1755 and was replaced by Ann Thornton until 1757, when he returned and occupied the position until 1766, and occasionally thereafter. The school in 1767 was designated as "a morning school for poor girls," and so it seems to have continued until 1777. Reference is also made to William Brown, who took up the work of a girls' school until about 1784.[163]

[159] Wickersham: *Education in Pa.*, 158.

[160] See Chapter VIII, on "Seminaries," for further reference to Moravian Seminary.

[161] *P. C. S. M.*, 25/IV/1754.

[162] A list of the girls who attended, in 1757, is given in the *P. C. S. M.*, 21/II/1757.

[163] See the *Penn Charter School Minutes* for these dates.

Reference has already been made to the academy for both sexes proposed by Jackson of New York, in 1765. This was to have been a partnership between Wilson and Jackson. Mary McAllester opened a boarding school for girls in Philadelphia, in 1767;[164] and a more elaborate "academy" for females arose in Philadelphia about 1780. A writer in the *American Journal of Education*[165] said, "In 1780, in Philadelphia, for the first time in my life I heard a class of young ladies parse English." This was probably the predecessor of Poor's school.[166] The writer attributed the creation of this academy to the influence that the Moravian school for girls had had upon such men as Dr. Morgan and Dr. Rush.[167] The pamphlet published on the "Young Ladies Academy" stated, however, that "Mr. John Poor . . . opened an academy in the city of Philadelphia, June 4th, 1787, for the instruction of Young Ladies in Reading, Writing, Arithmetic, English, Grammar, Composition, Rhetoric and Geography. . . ." Certain prominent citizens—such as Benjamin West, Pelatiah Webster, Benjamin Say, and fourteen others—consented to act as visitors. From this date the institution was highly praised by the citizens, and in 1792 received a charter from the state. A regular course was offered, premiums were awarded for merit, diplomas were granted at the end of the course, and commencements filled with oratory marked the victory of the young ladies over ignorance. The following lines were written by a gentleman who attended the commencement of June 20, 1792:

> "On the soft accents of the female tongue,
> "To rapt attention every nerve was strung:
> "While decent confidence, and modest grace,
> "Diffus'd a lustre o'er each charming face!
> "Delightful task, t' expand the human mind,
> "With virtue, knowledge, sentiment, refin'd—
> "To teach th' aspiring faculties to soar,
> "And the bright realms of science to explore;
> "To form the maiden for th' accomplish'd wife,
> "And fix the basis of a happy life!"[168]

[164] Barnard's *Journal*, XXXII, 171.

[165] V, 421–3.

[166] Possibly the school of Andrew Brown—See *Pa. Gaz.*, Aug. 25, 1784, 3, col. 3, and Oct. 17, 1787.

[167] Wickersham: *Education in Pa.*, 279.

[168] From a pamphlet on the "Young Ladies Academy," in the State Library at Harrisburg, Pa.

The prominent place which the new institution held in the minds of its sponsors was indicated in the introduction to the pamphlet mentioned, which declared it was the first "in the United States, and perhaps in the world. . . ."[169]

Just at the end of the century (1799), Friends' Philadelphia Yearly Meeting opened a Boarding School at Westtown for boys and girls. This school was similar to other private and state-chartered institutions of secondary grade, often called male and female academies or seminaries. During its first seventy-five years of existence, the girls exceeded the boys by more than a thousand.[170]

[169] See p. 336.
[170] For an historical sketch see Dewees: *Hist. Westtown Boarding School.*

CHAPTER VI

EDUCATION OF GIRLS IN THE SOUTH TO ABOUT 1800

I. Views of Education in the South

Until recently, poor estimates have been held of education in the Colonial South. Historians have been wont to point proudly to the laws of 1642 and 1647 and the town schools set up in New England, and have drawn an unfavorable contrast between education in the North and South. Such interpretations are well known. McMaster declared that, "In the southern states, education was almost wholly neglected, but nowhere to such an extent as in South Carolina." The schools of New England were admitted to be "rude" but "incomparably better than could be found in any other section of the country."[1] McCrady undertook to correct this exaggerated view in a paper read before the Historical Society of South Carolina,[2] in 1883. He sustained his contention that McMaster was quite wrong as to the educational facilities available for boys, and as to the cultural level of the North and South, as represented by the newspapers supported; but as for the education of girls, he failed to present the case fully. Women, he stated, quoting Foote's *Sketches of North Carolina*, "prized beyond all price" an education for their husbands, brothers and sons; they "gloried in the enterprise and religion and knowledge . . . of their husbands and children, and would forego comforts and endure toil that their sons might be well instructed, enterprising men."[3] More than this he did not then show, though later, in his *History of South Carolina*,[4] some attention was given to the existence of schools for girls.

Other similar disparaging and misleading remarks have been made regarding the position and education of woman in the South. In 1894, Mary V. Woodward wrote: "The Southerner's

[1] *Hist. of the People of the U. S.*, I, 26, 27.
[2] *Colonial Education in South Carolina* [U. S. Bureau of Education, Circular of Information No. 3, 1888].
[3] *Ibid.*, 217; Foote: *op. cit.*, 512.
[4] Vol. II, 490–2.

standard of best womanhood has never been an intellectual one; it has been rather a standard of social and domestic graces and virtues . . .; in the minds of many Southerners, woman's intellectual enfranchisement is indissolubly connected with her political enfranchisement . . .; still another class think so meanly as to consider worse than superfluous any advantages of training not sanctioned by dateless and niggardly custom; . . . Southern ideals of womanliness contribute to the same result; [and] they make marriage the one objective of woman's life, home her only sphere."[5] These statements characterize the conceptions of woman's sphere and education in the North quite as much as in the South, as noted elsewhere in this work. When used to bring out a contrast between North and South they are, at least, misleading. It is the purpose of this chapter to record representative facts relative to the position of women and their education, to about 1800.

II. Conception of Woman's Sphere and Education

In the Southern colonies it frequently happened that first settlements were made by explorers and adventurers, not by whole congregations and families as in Northern and central colonies. As a result, encouragements were offered to induce women to come over as wives. Thus, Mrs. Forest and Anne Burras were the first two women to come to Jamestown in 1608; in 1609, the "Blessing" brought twenty women and children; and, in 1619, ninety women "of good character for wives" were sent out from England.[6] The recognized need of women is made clear in a record of the House of Burgesses of the same year, which provided "shares for their wives as for themselves, because that in a new plantation it is not knowen whether man or woman be the most necessary."[7] Again, it was regretted that "by the want" of women "there have sprange the greatest hinderances of the encrease of the Plantacon, in that most of them esteeminge Virginia not as a place of Habitacon but only of a short soiourninge . . . and to prevent so great an inconvenience hereafter whereby the planters minds may be the faster tyed to Virginia by the bonds of Wyves and Children, care hath been taken

[5] *Educational Review*, May, 1894 (VII), 468.
[6] Early: *Byways of Virginia History*, 152–3.
[7] *Journal* (1619–59), July 31, 1619, 6–7.

to prouide them younge handsome and honestly educated mayds. . . ."[8]

Another record recounts the shipment of "one widow and eleven maids," and sets forth how they were to be disposed of: "There hath not one of them been received but upon good commendations. . . . In case they cannot be presently married, we desire that they may be put with several householders, that have wives, until they can be provided with husbands. There are nearly fifty more that are shortly to come, and are sent by our honorable lord and treasurer, the Earl of Southampton, and certain worthy gentlemen, who taking into consideration that the plantation can never flourish till families be planted, and the respect of wives and children for their people on the soil, therefore having given this fair beginning, reimbursing of whose charges it is ordered that every man that marries them give 120 pounds of best leaf tobacco for each of them, we desire that the marriage be free, according to nature, and we would not have those maids deceived and married to servants, but only to such freemen or tenants as have means to maintain them. We pray you, therefore, to be fathers of them in this business, not enforcing them to marry against their wills."[9]

The settlement of Louisiana, in the early eighteenth century, repeated to a considerable extent the experience of Virginia. "With wives," said Iberville, "I will anchor the roving *Coureurs de bois* into sturdy Colonists."[10] In 1703, 1706, 1713, 1721, 1728 and 1751, girls were sent over, some of them possessed of character and industry; others with neither; some were declared too homely to get husbands, while others did not wish them, being disinclined to marriage, domesticity and living on corn bread. One, said Bienville, refused marriage, "though many good *partis* had been offered to her."[11]

Considering the pioneer conditions, the difficulty of making a living, the need of protection, the generally prevailing idea that woman's place was only in the home, and the undoubted fact, so often urged by the Virginia Company, that without families the "encrease" and stability of the Colony could not be secured, it

---

8 Kingsbury: *Records of the Virginia Company*, I, 566.
9 Early: *op. cit.*, 152–3.
10 King: *New Orleans*, 52; and Cable: *The Creoles of Louisiana*, 25, 38.
11 Hamilton: *Colonial Mobile*, 66; King: *New Orleans*, 54.

is but to be expected that Colonial women of the South found their life and work chiefly at the hearth side. This was no more true in the South than in the North; it has scarcely been more tenacious there than elsewhere. A contributor to the *Virginia Gazette,* in 1773, set forth that the true title to the designation of *lady,* indicated by the derivation of the name from *Leff-Day,* was truly earned by being a giver of bread.[12] Ladies were intended to be givers of bread; marriage brought them to their mansions or hovels, whence they distributed it to their households and to those in want.

That marriage, late in the eighteenth century, was still thought to be the only suitable culmination of a girl's life is attested by numerous epitaphs, letters, articles and poems published in the Colonial papers. To the question: "My dear! pray tell me what you were brought into the world for?" the young miss, if she answered to the point, replied: "A husband."[13] The "sovereign remedy for the ladies" was, in every case, a husband:

> "When first the nymph within her breast
> "Perceives the subtle flame,
> "She feels a something break her rest,
> "Yet knows not whence it came,
> "A husband 'tis she wants."[14]

In "A receipt to soften the hardest female heart" the belief was expressed that ". . . the flint in her heart will soon melt away" whenever young maid meets genteel youth—granted he be not too sincere, is ready with flattery, sighs, smiles and "a sprinkling of folly."[15] In early days most women were ready to marry and only the ugliest failed to find a spouse. Calhoun thus stated the case of the French girls sent over to Louisiana. One might say 'it was the custom of girls to marry early and die young.' Only a few exceptions to early marriage are recorded. A few unusual and talented women never married, possibly because of disappointment in love, or the death of a loved one, as in the case of Margaret Brent; but the situation of most unmarried women was probably similar to that of Mary Morgan, of

[12] March 4, 1773, 2, col. 2.
[13] *Ibid.,* Oct. 22, 1767, 1, col. 2.
[14] *North Carolina Journal,* Dec. 2, 1805, 4 col. 1.
[15] *Edenton* [N. C.] *Intelligencer,* June 4, 1788, 4 col. 1.

whom the *Virginia Gazette*[16] said that, though "fifty-five" and "unmarried," she merited "no Blame on account of her Virginity, for she certainly would have entered into the marriage State if any Man had thought proper to make his addresses to her. Nature has bestowed on her no Beauty and not much Sweetness of Temper. . . ."[17] The published notice of The Society for the Regulation of Good Manners, that "such as are very ugly" might be allowed to wear veils, conveys the same idea of contempt for the ill-featured woman.[18] The idea that woman's proper sphere was in the home continued to prevail in the nineteenth century, in the South as in the North. Even to go out "to teach school" was to risk one's social standing.[19] Whenever she places the "boundaries of her position at defiance," says one essayist, and makes "innovations upon the grounds of lordly man's estate," she loses the "halo of female beauty and confiding love that is the natural accompaniment to her proper sphere . . ."[20]

The Virginian women, in the eighteenth century, were noted for activity and frugality in the management of their households and for personal loveliness as well. They spun at the wheel, wove on the loom and cultivated their gardens. James Franklin said of the post-Revolutionary women of Virginia that, apart from amusements, chiefly dancing, they spent "their time in sewing and taking care of their families; for they seldom read, or endeavor to improve their minds. However, they are in general good housewives; and though they have not, perhaps, so much tenderness and sensibility as the English ladies, yet they make as good wives, and as good mothers, as any in the world."[21] Another writer credited them with reading the Bible and other books of moral and religious worth. The situation of women varied with the degree of wealth; and, while some were doubtless industrious and frugal, as described, others, who were better off and occupied large holdings, acted the rôle of fine ladies and depended on servants and slaves to do all things for them.

16 Nov. 19, 1772, 2, col. 1.

17 For same view at later date, see Calhoun: *op. cit.*, II, 218.

18 *South Carolina Gazette*, Nov. 5, 1753, 1, col. 2.

19 Fuller: *Pratt Portraits*, 175 *ff.*

20 *North Carolina University Magazine* (1859), IX, 100.

21 *The Philosophical and Political History of the Thirteen United States*, 91–2.

As for the Creole ladies of New Orleans, Mrs. Houstoun thought them quite indolent, only slightly educated and not possessed of many ideas beyond the subject of dress.[22] This estimate, however, is too severe according to some authors.

Of the girls in North Carolina, somewhat differently situated, Brickell said: they "are not only bred to the needle and spinning, but to the dairy and domestick affairs, which many of them manage with a great deal of prudence and conduct, though they are very young. . . . The women are the most industrious in these parts, and many of them by their good housewifery make a great deal of cloath of their own cotton, wool and flax, and some of them weave their own cloath with which they decently apparel their whole family though large. Others are so ingenious that they make up all the wearing apparel both for husband, sons and daughters. Others are very ready to help and assist their husbands in any servile work, as planting when the season of the year requires expedition. . . ."[23]

In aristocratic South Carolina there was great fondness for the traditions of English society, its manners, and its fashions.[24] The colonists imported furniture, horses, carriages, clothing, wigs, and the bricks for their houses. "Households were organized on the English model" and the presence of numerous servants, including butler, coachman, patroon, man-servant, maid-servant, tutor, nursemaid and seamstress, made work (apart from general oversight) on the part of the mistress of the household unnecessary. A description of the place of women in these wealthy households of the Carolinas, Virginia and Maryland is similar to that depicted at a later date when some of the best stock had migrated into the Blue Grass Country of Kentucky.[25] At least a part of the old traditions were carried westward into the wilderness.

Outside of the wealthiest circles, however, we see the women of the early Colonial period as energetic housewives, rather than as "fine ladies"; and even the aristocratic Miss Lucas, when she married Pinckney, recognized her obligations to domestic econ-

[22] Calhoun: *Soc. Hist. Am. Fam.*, II, 322; I, 231.

[23] *Natural Hist. of N. C.*, 32.

[24] McCrady: *Hist. of S. C.*, II, 513 *ff.*

[25] Clugston: The Collapse of Kentucky [*American Mercury*, VI, 267]; Semple: An Old Kentucky Home [*Atlantic Mo.*, LX, 40].

omy and the deference due to a husband. Before marriage she had done much practical work in the development of the culture of indigo and the manufacture of dyes.

With increasing wealth, consequent leisure, and the greater stability of society, gained through the years of Colonial life, a more general acceptance of the feudal conception of women came to prevail; gentlemen came to regard women as playthings rather than helpmeets—believed they should be educated for show rather than trained in domestic duties. In every city of the South, by the middle of the eighteenth century, schools of dancing and music masters began to be very popular;[26] and on the plantations Virginian gentlemen employed tutors capable of teaching their daughters accomplishments, while the boys were usually taught more substantial subjects. Wertenbaker, after surveying the situation in seventeenth century Virginia, concluded: "There is no proof that the colonists . . . regarded womanhood in any other than a commonplace light. They assigned to their wives and daughters the same domestic lives that the women of the middle classes of England led at that time."[27] By the time of the Revolution, however, it was clear that a great change was taking place. "The Virginia gentleman, taught by the experience of many years, was beginning to understand aright the reverence due the nobleness, the purity, the gentleness of woman."[28]

Considering that matrimony was the usual end of woman, what was the ideal character sought in a wife? Numerous references to the ideal spouse, some flippant, to be sure, but nevertheless indicative of prevailing thought, have been preserved. Epitaphs and notices, published in the newspapers after death, cannot be taken at face value so far as the individual is concerned; but they, and similar insertions, show the traits that were highly prized. We may note that the traits usually mentioned are "wit," "grace," "virtuous life," "kind," "obeying," "Beauteous form," "patience," "humility," "religious," "loyal," "not talkative," and "useful." When too many of these are combined in eulogy, one may well keep in mind the limitations of the epitaph.

26 See pages 281 ff.; Wertenbaker: *Patrician and Plebian in Va.*, 126.
27 *Op. cit.*, 82.
28 *Ibid.*, 87–8.

The wife of Thomas Williams (1746), the annalist declares, was

> "Sweet natured kind, giving to all their due
> "Supremely good and to her consort true
> "She'd differ not, but to his will agree
> "With condescending, sweet humility.
> "Tender and loving to her children dear
> "And to her servants not at all severe."[29]

The oldest legible tomb inscription in Virginia describes the wife of George Jordan (1650) thus:

> "Reader, her dust is here inclosed
> "Who was of witt and grace composed
> "Her life was virtuous during breath
> "But highly glorious in her death."[30]

Probably the epitaph of Mrs. Hannah Ludwell (who lived to the age of 52), buried at old Jamestown (1731), aptly summarizes the life of many an eighteenth century Virginian wife: ". . . She has left one son and two daughters. After a most exemplary life, spent in cheerful innocence, and the constant exercise of Piety, Charity and Hospitality, she patiently submitted to Death. . . ."[31] A veritable paragon of virtue was one who lived but half as long: "From a child she knew the Scriptures which made her wise unto Salvation: From her Infancy she learned to walk in the Paths of Virtue: She was beautiful but not vain: Witty but not Talkative; Her Religion was Pure Fervent Cheerful and of the Church of England: Her Virtue Steadfast Easey Natural: Her mind had that mixture of Nobleness and Gentleness as Made Her Lovely in the Eyes of all People. . . . [She was] the best of Wives [and] Made him the Happiest of Husbands. . . . Soon did she Compleat her Perfection, Soon Did She finish her Course of Life. Early was She Exempted from the Miseries of Human Life by God's particular Grace. Thus Doth He Deal With His Perticuler Favorites."[32]

The poetic soul who advertised his matrimonial ambitions in the *North Carolina Gazette*[33], near the end of the eighteenth

[29] Quoted by Stanard: *Colonial Virginia*, 349–50.
[30] *Ibid.*, 347.
[31] Copied from the tombstone, June 11, 1927.
[32] Stanard: *op. cit.*, 350.
[33] Sept. 3, 1796, 4, col. 1.

century, desired a beautiful queen, "cheerful cherub," and accomplished domestic economist, not under sixteen and not over twenty-two:

> "Wanted, for many a useful end,
> "By me a lovely Female friend,
> "To smooth the tedious path of life,
> "Namely a kind obliging wife. . . ."

In "Hints for young married women," the *Wilmington* [N. C.] *Centinel and General Advertiser*[34] depicted some of the pitfalls in the married state and the virtue needed to avoid them. "She has her husband's temper to study, his family to please, household cares to attend, and what is worse than all, she must cease to command, and learn to obey. She must learn to submit without repining, where she has been used to have even her looks studied." Who could accomplish it, save "a maiden virtuous without reservedness, wise without affectation, beautiful without knowing it?" Such a one was the wife described by the *North Carolina Journal:*[35] "The model of every virtue—the tender mother and loving wife. . . ."

Seldom or never does education appear to have been a highly prized possession of the deceased wife, but Evelyn Byrd, daughter of William Byrd, was celebrated for—

> "The various and excellent endowments
> "Of Nature Improved and perfected
> "by an accomplished Education
> "[which] Formed her
> "For the Happiness of her Friends:
> "For an Ornament of her Country. . . ."[36]

From sundry sources it appears that as a rule the "learned maid" was scarcely more desired in the South than in the North and a talkative, scolding one, never. One epitaph sarcastically records:

> "Beneath this stone, a lump of clay,
> "Lies Arabella Young,
> "Who, on the 24th of May
> "Began to hold her Tongue."

[34] June 18, 1788, 1, cols. 2–3.
[35] Aug. 24, 1795, 3, col. 3.
[36] Stanard: *op. cit.*, 351–2.

Still more pointedly the "Bachelor's Address or Proposal to the Maidens" makes clear the general skepticism as to a learned wife. His bride must be:

> "Not a mere wit, or perfect beauty,
> "Or who knows all things but her duty,
> "Who never learnt the art of schooling,
> "Untainted with the itch of ruling
> "Who not abroad, nor yet in his Dome
> "Will deign to teach her Husband wisdom. . . ."[37]

It was a common belief that women were to be won by cajolery, blandishments, and a flattering appeal to their vanity rather than to their reason:

> "Would you . . .
> "Endeavor what you can to please the Fair
> "Then you must flatter—you must learn to coax
> "Say witty things, some serious, mostly jokes
> "Praise all the pretty follis Cloe doth
> "Admire her witt, her air, her talk, her clothes,
> "Tell her, her eyes are soft, and often swear
> "You see ten thousand cupids dancing there. . . ."[38]

Such was the advice given to swains of Charleston, in 1735. Colonel Byrd's references to supping and prattling with the ladies, whose conversation was like "whip-sillabub," very pretty but nothing to it, give substantially the same impression as to the general attitude of men towards the intellectual endowments and accomplishments of women.[39] Woman's emptiness was set forth in a Carolina newspaper as follows:

> "Woman's a book of tiny size
> "Suited to catch the coxcomb's eyes;
> "In silks and muslins neatly bound,
> "And sometimes richly gilt around.
> "But what is strange in readers sight
> "This book oft' stands unletter'd quite!
> "The *frontispiece* is gayly drest.
> "*Blank paper* fills up all the rest ! ! !"[40]

The other extreme, a picture of independent young women, thinking for themselves and demanding sense in men's con-

[37] *Md. Gaz.*, Jan. 4, 1759, 2.
[38] *S. C. Gaz.*, July 5–12, 1735, 2, col. 2.
[39] Bassett: *Writings of Colonel William Byrd*, 361.
[40] *N. C. Journal*, Sept. 4, 1797, 4, col. 1.

versation, is found in the description of Maryland girls about 1660: "They are extreme bashful at the first view, but after a continuance of time hath brought them acquainted, then they become discreetly familiar and are much more talkative than men. All complimental courtships, drest up in critical rarities, are mere strangers to them, plain wit comes nearest their Genius; so that he who intends to court a Maryland girle, must have something more than the tautologies of a long-winded speech to carry on his design, or else he may (for aught I know) fall under the contempt of her own frown and his own windy oration."[41]

Marriages were made at early ages in all the Colonial settlements, North and South. Land was cheap, families large, and a new home could be established with relative ease. Women were not so numerous as men. Some girls married at thirteen, but fifteen and sixteen was a more usual age.[42] Brickell, of Edenton, North Carolina, said, "They marry generally very young . . . and she that continues unmarried, until twenty, is reckoned a stale maid."[43] Beyond twenty-five the case was hopeless. Marriage settlements appear generally to have been arranged carefully beforehand. A curious, and pathetic, instance of early marriage was that of Mrs. Lucy Drew, aged seventeen, "the amiable consort of Mr. John Drew," who "lived dearly beloved and died deeply lamented." But in her early marriage and death she appears to have measured up to the accepted standard of those days, for of her it was said:

"She's not well marry'd that lives married long;
"But she's best married, that dies marry'd young."[44]

From the general tenor of the foregoing, it might appear that women were quite unesteemed for their intelligence. But the habit of making wives the executrices of husbands' estates would seem to indicate that they possessed native shrewdness and business sense, even if not highly educated. In every Colonial newspaper file examined, the wife was named frequently as executrix,

---

[41] Richardson: *Sidelights on Maryland History*, I, 149.
[42] Raper: *Soc. Life in Colonial N. C.*, 12.
[43] Brickell: *op. cit.*, 31.
[44] *N. C. Journal*, Mch. 11, 1805, 3, col. 4.

and in many instances took over the business of her husband.[45] In Maryland, women appeared in the courts with power of attorney to settle estates, but were not, as some have believed, practicing attorneys, admitted to the bar.[46] Sometimes women were named on juries. When Judith Catchpoll was accused of infanticide, ten women were named to render the verdict.[47] When Luke Hill, in 1705, caused Grace Sherwood to be brought to court "in *suspection* of witchcraft," a jury of women was named to examine and determine whether she be "not like them."[48]

Several women might be named who were conspicuous for their intellectual interests and abilities, but it must be admitted that they stand out because they were uncommon. Mrs. An Cotton, of Q. Creeke, in 1676, published "an account of our late troubles in Virginia," wherein she set forth the difficulties with the Indians; and Margaret Brent, in 1647, became executrix of the estate of Leonard Calvert, and, later, as his attorney, demanded the right of voice and vote in the assembly—which was, however, refused.[49] Hannah Williams (1704) exhibited a remarkable interest in, and knowledge of, "Vipers and several sorts of Snakes, Scorpions and Lizzards . . . Insex . . . plants . . . [and] different Shells . . ." of South Carolina, some of which she sent, with "A Nest that is made by a wild bee," "ye Westo King's Tobacco pipe," and a "Queens Petticoat made of moss" to a friend in England. A promise was added to send "mocking birds and Red birds" the next Spring.[50] Dinah Nuthead and Elizabeth Timothy were publishers in Maryland and South Carolina, respectively;[51] and Mrs. David Hillhouse edited a paper in Georgia about 1800, while Clementine Rind was approved as state printer in Virginia in 1774.[52] Eliza Lucas of

---

[45] See newspapers listed in the bibliography; see pages 162 *ff.*, 192 *ff.*, and 257 *ff.* for women in business.

[46] Richardson: *Sidelights on Md. Hist.*, I, 149.

[47] General Provincial Court at Patuxent, Sept. 22, 1656, mentioned by Richardson: *op. cit., loc. cit.*

[48] Record of Princess Anne Co. Court, Jan. 3, 1705–6 [*Va. Hist. Soc. Collections* (1833), I, 73 *ff.*].

[49] *Md. Archives*, I, 215; see also *Harper's N. Mo. Mag.*, XCVII (1898), 229–30.

[50] Letter, Feb. 6, 1704–5, Charlestown, S. C. [*S. C. Hist. and Genealogical Mag.*, XXI, 5.]

[51] See pp. 261, 262.

[52] *Journal, House of Burgesses*, 1773–1776, 77 and 124–5.

South Carolina studied law and was interested in the cultivation of figs and the development of indigo culture as early as 1742.[53]

If the gentlemen were correct in their judgment that the best way "to win the fair" was to 'praise their witt and admire their clothes,' the ladies, by the middle of the eighteenth century, had ample opportunity to dress to be admired. In aristocratic and wealthy centers, fashionable attire was common much earlier; but the advertisements of gay attire were more frequent after 1750, and reached a peak about the Revolution. Elizabeth Cooper, of Charleston, offered to make "manteelets, riding habits, new fashion silk hats, velvet caps" and to 'dress heads' "after the newest and best fashion," in 1737.[54] Benjamin wished to provide ladies "with all sorts of Locks, and Tates de Moutons" and to cut "their hair in the most fashionable manner," in 1745.[55] Maria Hume, of Maryland, offered to sell "all sorts of millinery work, ladies head dresses, . . . hats, bonnets, cloaks, . . . slips, and Frocks, for young ladies, made in the newest manner," in 1768.[56] She was also willing to wash "laces, Blond Lace and Gauzes, to look equal to new" and also "silk stockings." The most elaborate arrays were offered, however, by a lady "just arrived from Paris," who, in 1794, dazzled "the ladies of Charleston" with an "assortment of goods" including gloves, dresses, ribbons, artificial feathers and flowers, gauze handkerchiefs, and silk purses.[57] Stay-makers flourished in the cities of every colony. One who made "stays, jumps and Sulteen Stays after the neatest best and newest fashion" assured the ladies he was not "exceeded by any master stay-maker now in being."[58]

In Virginia, just before the Revolution, Mary Dickinson and Mary Hill sold "best white lustrings, plain and flowered white and black satins, white Sarcenet, alamode, white and black persians, superfine white and black plain and flowered satin cloaks, Sarcenet and Persian shades Terefras, satin bonnets, black and white silk gloves and mits, red do., plain and netted gauze, Book muslin, stomachers and sleeve knots, laced and plain caps, . . .

53 McCrady: *Hist. of S. C.*, II, 267 *ff.*

54 *S. C. Gaz.*, Mch. 12–19, 1737, 3, col. 1.

55 *Va. Gaz.*, Oct. 24–31, 1745, 3, col. 1.

56 *Md. Gaz.*, Dec. 1, 1768, 3, col. 3.

57 *State Gaz. of S. C.*, Jan. 6, 1794, Supplement, 2, col. 4.

58 *Md. Gaz.*, June 21, 1759.

feathers . . . hats, best black and white satin shoes, calamancoes, . . . Breast flowers, Plumes, black and white Blond Lace, best handkerchiefs, common do., a variety of ribands, Fans, sewing silk, Silk Laces, Tape, Bobbin, Jacob's Ladder, Footing, Pins, needles, . . . skeleton ware, best French wax, necklaces, common do., silver watches, Paste shoe, knee, Hat and Shirt Buckles, Silver Thimbles, . . . best French earrings, common do., a variety of Paste Hair Sprigs and Pins, Marcasite do., Paste Combs, plain Tortoise shell and horn do., Bristol Sleeve Buttons and Studs, . . . Country made Gold and Silver work, . . . Jewels and Millinery Goods . . .[59] Tafetas, Chintzes, . . . Lockets, . . . Crosses, Garnet and Marcasite Hoops, Detto Tortoise shell lined with Gold, many little curious Watch trinkets, . . . Gold Bands, Buttons and Loops, Sword Knots, fine China Hose, Ladies Riding Hats, . . . blue and white satin pumps, white and blue satin Quilts, . . . missionet Laces, . . . Italian and silver stomachers, true Italian Fancy caps, nosegays, and Breast Flowers, Egrets and Plumes, fine striped bordered muslin, and lawn (laced and flounced) handkerchiefs, . . . Ladies silk, Kid, and Lamb gloves, Wool packs with Drop curls, netted Hoods, Gauze and laced caps, and many other articles too tedious to mention.''[60]

To the wealthier class in the South, life offered many diversions which were tabooed by the colonists of the Northern and central regions. But the differences have been exaggerated.[61] Some of the sports were only attended by ladies, but in many they took an active part. Brickell named horse racing, gaming (especially at cards and dice), cockfighting, wrestling, and leaping. Many went from North Carolina to Virginia to attend the horse races.[62] As for gambling, Smith says of North Carolina, "The ladies have never been known to play for money." Cock fights were frequently advertised in Southern Colonial newspapers.[63]

[59] *Va. Gaz.*, Jan. 24, 1771, 3, col. 1.

[60] *Ibid.*, Apr. 30, 1772, 3, col. 1; these are selected from among a great number.

[61] See Wertenbaker: *The First Americans,* Ch. XI.

[62] Brickell: *Natural Hist. of N. C.,* 39 *ff.*; according to Smith: *Hist. Ed. in N. C.,* 51, card playing and gambling had declined considerably by the early nineteenth century.

[63] E. g.: "At the House of Mrs. Eldridge [a tavern] on the Green, there will be a match of cock fighting, Five pairs of Cocks to fight five battles for 20 l. each, and 50 l. the odd battle.''

Music, dances, and dinners were probably the most favored diversions of ladies.[64] Balls and music and dancing school advertisements appeared far more often in the South than in the North at the same period. Some unusual attractions were frequently offered. Ladies and gentlemen were notified by the press that there would be a ball on Wednesday, April 26, and an assembly on Friday, the 28th, at Mrs. Degraffenreidt's, where "a likely young Virginia Negro Woman, fit for House Business, and her child" were "to be raffled for."[65] On the same date it was announced that there "will be a Public and Assembly at the Capitol" on Thursday the 27th, where "several Grotesque Dances, never yet performed in Virginia" will be demonstrated. Here also "valuable goods" and "a likely young Negro Fellow" were "to be raffled for."[66] Very often the dancing masters—for example, Mr. Valois, who taught both dancing and French—gave balls at their schools, where, as an attraction, they opened the dance with a performance by one of their students.[67]

Circulating libraries, some of short duration, were started in many of the cities; and generally the ladies were appealed to, as well as gentlemen, for subscriptions. Thus William Rind implored "such gentlemen and ladies who have any intention of subscribing to the circulating library . . . to give in their Names immediately, that the library may be opened, and such other books ordered by the return of the fleet as may be agreeable to the majority of the subscribers."[68] It should also be mentioned that South Carolina had a library after 1698, which, in 1700, was established by act as "the Provincial Library at Charles Town." Commissioners and trustees were named for its care.[69] There were some excellent private libraries.[70] It is difficult, however, to form a judgment as to the bearing of these libraries on women's learning. Burnaby characterized, perhaps too harshly, the activities of Virginian ladies as follows:

[64] Smith: *Hist. Ed. in N. C.*, 51; Franklin: *The Philosophical and Political History of the Thirteen United States*, 91; see also Calhoun's *Soc. Hist. Am. Fam.*, I, 311, for a description of the plantation family at dinner.

[65] *Va. Gaz.*, Apr. 7–14, 1738, 4, col. 2.

[66] *Ibid.*

[67] *S. C. Gaz.*, Feb. 7–14, 1761, 2, col. 2.

[68] *Md. Gaz.*, Sept. 9, 1762, 2, col. 1.

[69] *Statutes of S. C.*, II, 374.

[70] Wertenbaker: *The First Americans*, 257.

" . . . The Virginian ladies, excepting these amusements, and now and then going upon a party of pleasure into the woods to partake of a barbecue, chiefly spend their time in sewing and taking care of their families: they seldom read, or endeavour to improve their minds; however, they are in general good housewives. . . . "[71]

Before the law women occupied about the same position in the South and North, such laws as were passed in Virginia being similar to those of her neighbors.   In 1664, an act was passed "for explanation" of the manner of "assigning the thirds" of estates of persons intestate "to their widdows."[72]   Again, in 1673, another act was passed for the further "cleareing" of the question, about which there appears to have been "many doubts." By this it was explicitly stated that the husband might, by will, "devise more to his wife . . . but not lesse" than the third.[73] In Georgia it was agreed that widows should get their thirds as in old England.[74]   Special provisions were made whereby married women might acknowledge deeds for their property. Though Virginia permitted women to hold property, by law of 1699 she provided against "undue election of Burgesses" by the voice or vote of "women sole or covert," "infants" under twenty-one, or recusant convicts.[76]   An act of 1748, dealing with the punishment of felons, declared that, if a woman, "she shall suffer the same punishment as a man should suffer. . . . "[77]   Husbands were protected against their "Brabbling women," who "often slander and scandalize their neighbors," by an act of 1662, which provided that "after judgment passed for the damages the women shall be punished by ducking;" and if damages were assessed at more than 500 pounds of tobacco, the woman was to "suffer a ducking" for each 500.[78]

[71] Burnaby: *Travels*, 58.
[72] Hening: *Statutes of Va.*, II, 212.
[73] *Ibid.*, II. 303.
[74] Calhoun: *op. cit.*, I, 238.
[75] Hening: *op. cit.*, V, 410–11.
[76] *Ibid.*, III, 172; also Act of 1705, III, 238, and that of 1762, VII, 519–20.
[77] *Ibid.*, V, 546.
[78] *Ibid.*, II, 166–7.

There were many who rebelled against the limitations of woman's sphere. Thus one lamented the fate of "woman born to be controlled":

> "In youth a Fathers stern command,
> "And jealous Eyes control her will;
> "A lordly Brother watchful Stands,
> "To keep her closer captive still."

> "The Tyrant Husband next appears,
> "With awful and contracted Brow
> "No more a Lover's Form he wears,
> "Her Slave's become her Sovereign now."[79]

Another deplored the partiality of custom which gives men freedom and denies it to women:

> "Then Equal Laws let Custom find,
> "And neither sex oppress;
> "More freedom give to Womankind,
> "Or give to mankind less."[80]

Chafing under the restraints of man's tyranny, it is not strange to find instances of quarreling, conniving and runaway wives in Colonial homes, though moralists today would have us believe that the problems of domestic unrest and broken homes are only of recent origin. The character of runaway wives was generally described in the husbands' advertisements in which they declared the wives' infamies and that they would no longer be responsible for debts contracted by them. These, certainly, are not always to be trusted. The most frequent assertion was that the wife had contracted more debts than she should, had declared her intention of 'ruining her husband,' or had simply 'absented herself from his embraces.' Some were declared to have made threats against the husband's life; others were thought to have lost their senses. One was declared to have been "a naughty furious housewife for some years past and hath invented and reported certain slanders." Several were accused of living "in a criminal state" with other men. Generally, it appears, the husband felt the wife had eloped his bed and board "without the least provocation whatsoever!"[81]

[79] *S. C. Gaz.*, Nov. 21, 1743, 2, col. 2.

[80] *Va. Gaz.*, Oct. 15–22, 1736, 3, col. 2.

[81] *Md. Gaz.*, Dec. 23, 1762, 2, col. 3; Oct. 16, 1760, 3, col. 1; June 5, 1760, 3, col. 2; *Md. Jour. and Balt. Advt.*, Jan. 20, 1774, 3, col. 1; *Cape Fear*

Some husbands were more specific in their complaints. Nancy, it was said, had "wilfully neglected to perform any of the duties of a virtuous wife, and uniformly displayed an unparalleled and insatiable spirit of lasciviousness and disaffection," causing her spouse "all the horrors of a dreadful purgatory" for "ten years." By his version, the husband must have been most long-suffering, for he took no action until she ran away.[82] Ruth was advertised for bearing "into my family an adulterous child";[83] Polly had "meanly taken up with one Thomas Bennet, mate of a vessel";[84] Amy "made way with some of my effects";[85] Anne took "diverse sorts of household goods, very valuable" and secreted the same;[86] Martha took the liberty of "having some of my tobacco booked in her name";[87] and Elizabeth made an effort to sell some of her husband's estate.[88] Some notices claimed that women enticed youths to go away with them.[89]

Only occasionally did wives make any public reply. John Carr, having denied his wife, stirred her to energetic public notice that she could prove "by the Registry Book of St. Anne's Parish and sundry living evidences" that though he is not "worthy the name of husband, yet he certainly is mine."[90] A few wives took the initiative in advertising their husbands. Basheba Taylor described the dishonorable character of her husband's doings, which had culminated in his taking himself off "with a certain Patsey Norton, who is of a light complexion, black under the eyes, and extremely homely."[91]

Mercury (N. C.), Dec. 29, 1773, 2, col. 1; Fayetteville [N. C.] Gaz., Dec. 11, 1792, 3, col. 4; Va. Gaz., Aug. 24, 1751, 3, col. 2; Jan. 21, 1775, 3, col. 1; N. C. Gaz., Oct. 29, 1796, 3, col. 3; April 6 (?), 1796, 3, col. 3; S. C. Gaz., Oct. 14–21, 1732, 3, col. 1; and State Gaz. of S. C., Sept. 15, 1791, 3, col. 4.

[82] The Minerva (N. C.), Dec. 1, 1808, 3, col. 4.

[83] Md. Gaz., Mch. 29, 1759, 3, col. 3.

[84] N. C. Gaz., Mch. 18, 1797, 3, col. 2.

[85] Md. Gaz., Apr. 3, 3, col. 3.

[86] Ibid., June 9, 1747, 3.

[87] Va. Gaz., Feb. 1, 1787, 4, col. 3.

[88] Ibid., Mch. 20–27, 1746, 4, col. 2.

[89] Ibid., July 24–31, 1746, 6, col. 1.

[90] Md. Gaz., July 13, 1748, 4; many other instances were noted in which men denied that certain women were their wives and desired that no one should trust them—Md. Gaz., May 3, 1764, 2, col. 3.

[91] N. C. Journal, Aug. 18, 1806, 3, col. 4.

Domestic life must have had little glamour for the luckless Filmer Moore who said that his mother would rather live in a hollow tree than with his wife. In public notices, both wife and husband declared the other had eloped. The wife's father published a notice in her defense.[92] An interesting marriage agreement was made in Virginia (1714) whereby the property of husband and wife was secured against the anticipated predatory habits of both.[93]

From the plenitude of such cases of domestic infelicity, it appears that the Colonial home was probably not much freer from disturbance than that of today. A difference lay in this, however, that the grievances they paid to publish are now aired gratuitously. If there be a moiety of truth in the numerous published complaints, the reader is, in a measure, prepared for this sarcastic soliloquy ''On a Deceased Wife'':

> ''And is she gone? ah! gone, my luckless wife?
> ''Oh had she died but twenty years ago!
> ''It would have given comfort to my life,
> ''And saved my troubled house a deal of woe.
>
> * * *
>
> ''But now she's dead what lucky days for me,
> ''If she will never from the grave arise;
> ''How happy and contented shall I be
> ''While in the dust her lolling clapper lies.''[94]

Prepared, too, for the whimsical parody—

> ''To wed or not to wed—that is the question—
> ''Whether tis better still to rove at large
> ''From fair to fair, amid the wilds of passion
> ''Or plunge at once into a *sea* of marriage
> '' . . . to marry, take a wife
> '' . . . tis a consolation
> ''*Devoutly* to be wished—marry a wife—
> ''A wife—perchance a d-v-l—Aye there's the rub!
> ''For 'mongst that angelic sex, what d-v-ls are found
> ''When they have shuffled off the virgin mask
> ''Must give us pause—there's the respect
> ''That keeps a *prudent* man so long a *bachelor*!''[95]

[92] *Va. Gaz.*, May 9, 1771, 3, col. 2.
[93] *Va. Mag. of Hist. and Biog.* (1896–7), IV, 64–6.
[94] *N. C. Journal*, Oct. 30, 1797, 4, col. 1.
[95] *Ibid.*, Oct. 10, 1792, 4, col. 1.

As above noted,[96] Colonial women of the South were generally active in many ways; those who lived in idle luxury, sometimes pictured as an essential feature of the plantation in contrast to the North, were exceptions to the general rule in the early days. When the men had to be absent on business—and travel was slow in those days—a great deal of responsibility rested upon the mistress of the household.[97]   In North Carolina, it has been said that much of the outdoor work was performed by women.[98]   In the poorer sections this was no doubt true; and the same is true today in some Southern states.[99]   Always, inside the house, there was a vast amount of "spinning, warping,· weaving and quilting," clothing to make for the family and slaves, as well as the preparation of food and the care of the house to be attended to.[100] This work fell to the lot of the housewife and her children, save in wealthy homes where her task was oversight and direction rather than actual performance of labor with her hands.

Many women were owners or managers of estates.   The habit of naming the wife as executrix, on the death of the husband, has been mentioned.[101]   This was common in all colonies.   Only one case was noted in which the woman refused to serve.   She declared she would not "be any Ways concerned with [her] . . . husband's estate" and that "any one of his creditors may administer upon it."[102]   As for ownership and disposition of land, reference may be made to a few cases.   Mrs. Anne Partridge (1739) advertised she would sell a plantation of eighty-one acres;[103] Elizabeth Elbank (1794) offered "three hundred and sixty acres of uncleared, very good wheat and tobacco land, lying twelve miles from Halifax";[104] Rebecca Chamberlayne, of Virginia, advertised about 1,200 acres for sale in 1774;[105] and Margaret Haslen, of North Carolina (1797), offered to sell a half of

96 P. 242.

97 Calhoun: *op. cit.*, I, 278–9.

98 Brickell: *op. cit.*, 32.

99 Personal observations on two automobile journeys through the South, 1926 and 1927.

100 Ashe: *Hist. of N. C.*, II, 167–8.

101 *N. C. Journal*, July 27, 1795; see also p. 248.

102 *S. C. Gaz.*, Dec. 16–23, 1732, 3, col. 2.

103 *Ibid.*, Sept. 15–Oct. 13, 1739, 4.

104 *N. C. Journal*, Sept. 10, 1794, 4, col. 1.

105 *Va. Gaz.*, June 16, 1774, 3, col. 2.

a tract of 25,000 acres.[106]   Elizabeth Peay forbade anyone to buy
a certain tract from Charles Nodden, which she apparently had
leased for her lifetime.[107]   Wives and daughters were given
slaves, by last testament, not only as personal servants but also
to work in the fields.   Probably the best known, of those who
engaged in agriculture, was Eliza Lucas.   Her fame, however,
came from her experimental efforts in the cultivation of indigo,
which came to be, for a time, a source of great wealth to the
South Carolina planters.   Following her experiments, 1742–
1744, there was enough produced, in 1747, to warrant exportation
to England; and by·the time of the Revolution, the annual export
had reached 1,107,660 pounds.[108]

Single women, and widows, frequently sought places as housekeepers, in which capacity they performed a wide range of duties,
including attendance on young children and those approaching
senility, sewing, ironing, spinning, weaving, management of servants, slaves and poultry.   Others advertised as wet and dry
nurses.   These frequently stated they had had previous experience in families of their own.[109]

Closely allied to her usual occupation as housewife was that of
keeping taverns or ordinaries, wherein the good dame dispensed
meat and drink to all comers.   The widow of Jacob Colcock supported herself by "taking a few children to board."[110]   Occasionally, owners of taverns advertised for women "of good credit
and reputation" to manage public houses of entertainment.[111]
These tavern keepers were sometimes well enough known to occasion some mention in the press at death.[112]   A typical advertisement of the female tavern keeper follows:

[106] N. C. Journal, Jan. 21, 1797.

[107] Va. Gaz., Feb. 12, 1762, 3, col. 2.

[108] Ravenel: Eliza Pinckney, 102 ff.; McCrady: Hist. S. C., II, 267 ff.

[109] For instances see: Md. Gaz., Sept. 12, 1776; Sept. 13, 1753, 3, col. 1;
Apr. 16, 1767; Wilmington Chronicle and North Carolina Wkly. Advt., July
31, 1795, 3, col. 4; State Gaz. of S. C., Sept. 28, 1793, 3, col. 2; Sept. 6, 1790,
3, col. 4; [Charleston, S. C.] Columbian Herald, Nov. 14, 1793, 3, col. 4; Va.
Gaz., Mch. 4, 1773, 4, col. 1; Apr. 28, 1768, 2, col. 2; May 14, 1772, 2, col.
1; and Feb. 20, 1772, 3, col. 2.

[110] State Gaz. of S. C., Nov. 7, 1793, 1, col. 1.

[111] Md. Gaz., Apr. 2, 1761, 4, col. 2.

[112] E. g., Mrs. Warburton, N. C. Gaz., Jan. 30, 1778, 3, col. 2.

"I beg leave to acquaint my former customers and the Public in General, that I have just opened Tavern opposite to the Raleigh, at the Sign of the King's Arms, being the House lately occupied by Mr. John Carter, and shall be much obliged to the Gentlemen who favour me with their Company.—Jane Vobe. I am in want of a good Cook, and would be glad to hire or purchase one."[113]

The vocations of seamstress and milliner were highly favored. Some women, desiring such work, announced they would go to live in the homes of employers; frequently the planter advertised for "a compleat seamstress." Mrs. Alamode, itinerant milliner, announced she had combined that vocation with that of barber to the ladies.[114] Other specialists with the needle devoted themselves to the making of hoop-petticoats,[115] ran general tailoring shops,[116] did all manner of quilting—petticoats, coverlets, and so on.[117] One was noted who made "umbrelloes of all sorts of stuff at a reasonable rate."[118]

The foregoing performed in a public way the duties usually done at home; but many women engaged in affairs of the commercial, professional and industrial world, with which men were usually associated. Of this class, by far the greater proportion operated general stores; but some specialized. Maria Hume, Elizabeth Cooper, Mary Hill, and Mary Dickinson have been mentioned as dealers in fashionable wear for women.[119] Among the articles handled in the general stores were "Hartshorn," "Calves-feet and fruit jellies," "mackaroons," "Savoy Biscakes," "Barbadoes sweet meats" and "all sorts of confection-

[113] *Va. Gaz.*, Feb. 6, 1772, 3, col. 2. See also Oct. 3, 1771, 3, col. 1; Oct. 15, 1767, 2, col. 1; Aug. 5, 1775, 4, col. 2; June 6, 1751, 3; *Md. Gaz.*, May 27, 1756, 3; Mch. 18, 1762; May 12, 1747; Sept. 30, 1747; Dec. 23, 1747; Feb. 3, 1748; July 15, 1756; July 27, 1748; Aug. 30, 1759; and *S. C. Gaz.*, Jan. 7, 1764, 1, col. 1.

[114] *S. C. Gaz.*, Jan. 8–15, 1737; *N. C. Journal*, Extra, June 4, 1798, 1 col. 1; *Va. Gaz.*, July 4, 1771, 4; *S. C. State Gazette*, Jan. 9, 1794, 3, col. 4; and *Md. Gaz.*, Nov. 24, 1768.

[115] *Md. Gaz.*, July 9, 1752; June 6, 1754.

[116] *Ibid.*, Sept. 27, 1759.

[117] *S. C. Gaz.*, May 24–31, 1735, 3, col. 2; *Md. Gaz.*, Nov. 18, 1748, 4.

[118] *S. C. Gaz.*, May 24–31, 1735.

[119] *Va. Gaz.*, Apr. 30, 1772, 3, col. 1; Jan. 24, 1771, 3, col. 1; *Md. Gaz.*, Dec. 1, 1768, 3, col. 3; *S. C. Gaz.*, Mch. 12–19, 1737, 3, col. 1; see also the *State Gaz. of S. C.*, Jan. 6, 1794, Supplement 2, col. 4.

ery,"[120] pickled pork, hams, bacon and lard, toys, Strassburg
Rapee, Weston's and Scotch Snuff, hats, bonnets, cloaks, cardi-
nals, fans, and many other things.[121] The itinerant merchant
woman appeared in Mrs. Judith Miller who (1740) advised she
was going to the Ashley Ferry Fair and would carry a "variety
of goods to be raffled for."[122] Anne Catherine Greene advertised
a grocery,[123] and another acted as agent for a whip merchant at
Annapolis in 1747.[124]

A number of Colonial women of the South kept ferries, some
operating taverns in connection with them. Mrs. Sarah Flynn,
at Broad Creek Ferry(1764), had "good boats and skillful
hands" to carry people to and from Annapolis and announced
"good stables and provender for horses," as well as a "well furnished" tavern, as added inducements to patrons.[125] Mary Ann
Noble kept a ferry "over to Virginia to John Shurden's Landing" and also across the mouth of Piscataway Creek to William
Digges Landing.[126] Flora Dorsey was perhaps the best known
woman in this business in Maryland, having operated the Patapsco Ferry for many years. In 1759, she undertook to correct
the report of "a certain person in Baltimore Town" that her
attendance at the ferry was "very irregular and uncertain; . . .
due attendance is always given . . . [and] gentlemen and others
may be sure of a ready passage. . . ."[127] In Virginia, Janet
Mitchell and Mary Gibbons kept a ferry at Yorktown;[128] and
Jemimah Cannon ferried travellers over the Chowan River, in
North Carolina, "about 15 miles from Edenton."[129]

A manufacturer of clothing advertised in the *Maryland
Gazette* (1747) for women and children who could assist "in the

[120] Mrs. Stagg—*Va. Gaz.*, Oct. 31, 1738, 4, col. 2.

[121] [Charleston, S. C.] *Columbian Herald or the Southern Star*, Aug. 3,
1793, 4, col. 4; *Va. Gaz.*, May 9, 1771, 3, col. 3; *S. C. Gaz.*, May 8–15, 1736,
2, col. 2.

[122] *S. C. Gaz.*, Apr. 26–May 3, 1740, 4, col. 2.

[123] *Md. Gaz.*, Sept. 23, 1746.

[124] *Ibid.*, June 30, 1747.

[125] [Annapolis] *Md. Gaz.*, Mch. 22, 1764, 2, col. 2.

[126] *Ibid.*, Sept. 6, 1764, 3, col. 2.

[127] *Md. Gaz.*, July 18, 1759, 4.

[128] *Va. Gaz.*, Apr. 7, 1774, 3, col. 1.

[129] *State Gaz. of N. C.*, July 23, 1795, 3, col. 3; another by Ann Connor,
Pig-Point on Patuxent River—*Md. Gaz.*, Mch. 11, 1762; and by Elizabeth
Leidler, "Patomack"—*Md. Gaz.*, Dec. 16, 1773.

business of making duck and osnabrigs''; spinners were especially wanted.[130] Mary Stevenson, widow of John, announced, after his death, that she would carry on his business of glazier and painter.[131] Another widow who intrepidly entered upon the business her husband had founded was Mary Butler, who announced she had ''several good block makers'' and would supply customers ''with all sorts of blocks for ships, or other vessels, made in the best and cheapest manner, and with the greatest expedition. She likewise makes and mends pumps for ships and wells.''[132]

The vocations of teacher, printer, doctor, and midwife offered attractions to many women, though in the Colonial South they are not mentioned as frequently in the latter calling as in the North. Following is a typical advertisement of a woman who wished to go into a family as tutor, but was ready to accept other employment. The *Maryland Gazette* announced,[133] ''A young woman of unblemished character and liberal education, would be glad to undertake the instruction of young ladies in a gentleman's family, or the employment of a housekeeper. . . .''

In the field of printing, editing, and publishing there were several notable characters. Dinah Nuthead, of Maryland, after the death of her husband (1694), removed from St. Mary's to Anne Arundel County, the seat of the government, taking her husband's printing press with her. Though without education and little money, she petitioned, in 1696, for a license to print.[134] The license was granted; and, within ten days after making the petition, Dinah Nuthead with Robert Carvile and William Taylor gave bond for one hundred pounds ''lawful money'' for her good behavior in conducting the printing business. Dinah signed the document with her mark.[135] How long she continued to operate the press is not known; no imprints bearing her name have been found.[136]

130 Mch. 10, 1747, 3.
131 *S. C. Gaz.*, Oct. 11–18, 1735, 3, col. 2.
132 *Md. Gaz.*, May 27, 1756, 3.
133 June 14, 1764, 3, col. 1.
134 *Md. Archives*, XIX, 306.
135 *Ibid.*, XIX, 370; and XX, 449.
136 Wroth: *A Hist. of Printing in Col. Md.*, 13–14; compare Richardson: *Sidelights on Md. Hist.*, I, 147.

In 1732, Thomas Whitmarsh founded the *South Carolina Gazette,* which was, after his death a year later, taken over by Lewis Timothy. When the latter was accidentally killed (1738), his widow, Elizabeth, conducted the paper for about six years, her son being the printer. So far as known she was the first woman in America, possibly in the world, to conduct a newspaper.[137] When Peter Timothy, the son, died, about fifty years later, his wife followed the example set by Elizabeth and revived the *Gazette* July 16, 1783, serving also as state printer.[138]

A third interesting case is that of Clementina Rind who, on May 7, 1774, petitioned the Virginian Burgesses to "be appointed Printer to the Public in the room of her Husband . . . deceased. . . ." On the same date Alexander Purdie and John Dixon petitioned for the same privilege.[139] On the 24th of May, the petitions of all being read, and ballots taken, Mrs. Rind was declared elected by 60 votes to 27. Due to her death she occupied the position but a short time.[140]

Among others deserving mention are Anne Catharine Green, Sarah Updike, Mary Goddard, and Mrs. Hillhouse.[141] The first continued the press of Jonas Green, her husband, after his death in 1767.[142] The name of Sarah Updike (Goddard), mother of William Goddard, appeared for a time in the imprimatur of "S. and W. Goddard," publishers of the *Providence Gazette,* and later as "Sarah Goddard and Company."[143] Mary Goddard, William's sister, who learned practical typography and journalism from her mother, took charge of a newspaper in 1774 and carried it successfully through the war period. She was for fourteen years postmistress at Baltimore, leaving that position in 1789. Unlike several other women publishers, Wroth says of her: "She must be thought of . . . not simply as a business ex-

137 Salley: *A Century of the Courier* [*News and Courier* (Charleston, S. C.), Centennial Ed., 1803–1903, 3.]

138 *Ibid.,* 4; also Salley: First Presses of South Carolina [*Bibliographical Soc. Am.* (1907–8), II, 32, *ff.*]

139 *Journals, House of Burgesses, Va.* (1773–76), 77.

140 *Ibid.,* 124–5, and 264.

141 Georgia's first woman editor, who in 1804, when her husband died, took over the *Washington Gazette* and the management of the printing office—Knight: *Georgia's Landmarks,* I, 1047.

142 Wroth: *op. cit.,* 84 *f.*

143 *Ibid.,* 121.

ecutive whose part was to direct the labor of others, but as a craftsman whose manual labor was a considerable element in determining the success of her establishment."[144]

About the middle of the nineteenth century, when women tried to enter the medical profession, they had a sorry time of it. Even midwifery had fallen into the hands of men to a large extent.[145] But in Colonial days, in North and South, women advertised themselves freely as proficient in that profession.[146] Mary Rose, of Virginia, who had studied "under the direction and with the approbation of Doctors Pasteur and Galt," announced her practice of midwifery (1771) and assured ladies nothing would be spared to complete her in the "Knowledge of an art so eminently necessary to the Good of Mankind. . . ."[147] Mrs. Brown, of South Carolina, who "had a regular education in that line" and "received a diploma from the University of Edinburgh," with a "particular recommendation from Dr. Hamilton," arrived in Charleston in 1791 "with an intention of practicing" midwifery.[148] Mrs. Munro, likewise of Charleston, says she had "for these six years last past made it [midwifery] her sole study" and had also received "a diploma from Professor Hamilton" and "letters of recommendation to several of the most eminent Physicians in Charleston."[149] Mrs. Hughes had practiced midwifery in the West Indies "a number of years" when she came to Virginia in 1773. She announced her ability to cure "ringworms, scald heads, sore eyes, the piles, worms in children and several other disorders"; and she added, *"No cure no pay."*[150]

The midwife was not always such a specialist as to have devoted six years to study. With some, midwifery was a side line; with others, at best, it was only a major interest. Mrs. Hughes, while apparently no amateur, carried on a merchant business, dealing in ladies' socks, gowns, Brunswick dresses, cloaks, cardi-

---

[144] *Ibid.*, 144 *ff.*
[145] Gregory: *Man-Midwifery Exposed and Corrected.*
[146] "Man-midwifery" was, however, not unknown—*N. C. Journal*, Dec. 8, 1794, 4, col. 2.
[147] *Va. Gaz.*, Nov. 28, 1771, 2, col. 3.
[148] *State Gazette* (S. C.), Mch. 21, 1791, 1, col. 3.
[149] *Columbian Herald* (Charleston, S. C.), Aug. 31, 1796, 3, col. 4.
[150] *Va. Gaz.*, Dec. 16, 1773, 2, col. 3.

nals, bonnets, and calashes.[151]   Mary Kelsey dealt primarily in
"different sorts of spirituous Liquors, with a variety of dry
goods" which she sold "at the lowest rates"; but, at the same
time, she was "ready to attend all such as shall be pleased to
employ her as a midwife, having had many years experience
therein."[152]

Besides free white women there were many white indentured
women servants in the South as in the North who, by years of
service, paid the cost of their passage.   It has been said that
many of these indentured women were criminals.   The Massachusetts agent asserted that criminals were accepted as servants
in the Virginia, Barbadoes, Maryland and Carolina colonies.[153]
Doubtless there were some criminals among those who came;
but the sentiment of the Virginia Company, it appears, was
decidedly against bringing to the infant settlement the "weeds
of their native country"; and the popular belief that Virginia
was primarily an asylum for the idle, wretched, criminal, and
dissolute[154] has been dispelled by the facts set forth by Bruce
in his scholarly *Economic History of Virginia*.[155]   In 1624–5,
there were about four hundred and sixty-five servants, many
of whom had "barely reached maturity," and "it is hardly
probable that there could have been many representatives of the
purely criminal classes of England."   During the years following the Restoration, perhaps a larger proportion of men and
women of "loose and disorderly habit of life" were introduced
into the colony.[156]

Certainly it appears that there was an increased influx of un-
desirables after 1650.   Sollers cites certain orders of the Council
of State, 1654 and 1656, as well as reports, letters, and orders
of later date, encouraging the sending of convicts to English
plantations in America.[157]   The Barbadoes agent, contrary to the
assertion of the Massachusetts agent, declared convict women
would not be welcomed in the Barbadoes—where English women

[151] *Ibid.*

[152] *S. C. Gaz.*, Jan. 24, 1774, 4, col. 2.

[153] Sollers: Convict Laborers in Maryland during the Colonial Period
[*Md. Hist. Soc.* II, 24]; Calhoun: *op. cit.*, I, 250–1.

[154] Brown: *Genesis of the U. S.*, 456.

[155] I, Ch. 9.

[156] *Ibid.*, I, 601, 604–5.

[157] Convict Labor in Maryland [*Md. Hist. Mag.* (1907), II, 20 *ff.*]

were not put to labor in the fields—but that they would be accepted in Virginia and the Carolinas "where white women work in the fields."[158] It appears that no colonies were willing to receive convicts: Massachusetts desired to be excused from so doing, and Jamaica and New York likewise; Virginia and Maryland[159] passed laws against the importation of them. The fifty convict women, whose disposition had been the occasion for general protest against the reception of convicts, were finally sent to the Leeward Islands.[160] But if the colonies objected, the interest of "contractors" was so large and the influence of the crown so strong that convicts continued to be sent in. Scharf estimated the number of convicts brought to Maryland, before the Revolution, at "at least twenty thousand." Sollers cited numerous other studies, and made it clear that these were "criminals under the laws of England" and that "in Maryland and the other colonies they were looked upon as criminals and dangerous persons, and by experience they were found to be such ...''; that they are not to be confounded with political prisoners who were sometimes transported as servants to the colonies.[161]

Carolina encouraged the emigration of marriageable girls (1666), painting an attractive picture of their prospects: "If any maid or single woman have a desire to go over, they will think themselves in the golden age, when men paid a dowry for their wives; for if they be but civil, and under fifty years of age, some honest man or other will purchase them for their wives." And thirty years later (1697), when Massachusetts, Virginia and Maryland sought to be excused, the Carolina agent replied as follows to the letters of the Council of Trade and Plantations, requesting information as to the probability of receiving certain convict women: "You may be assured that the Proprietors will acquiesce in the Lords Justices' pleasure, if they transport them to Carolina. What reception they will find there I cannot say, though it will be better than elsewhere, for the most of the West Indian settlements (if not all, to my certain knowl-

---

[158] *Ibid.*, 24.

[159] The Maryland law of 1676 required the master of every vessel to take an oath "whether any servants on board his shipp be felons convict."— *Md. Archives*, II, 540.

[160] Sollers: *op. cit.*, 26.

[161] *Ibid.*, 46.

edge) will not receive woman convicts. If you resolve to send them to Carolina, I have a ship bound thither that will carry them at the usual rate, &c."[162]

White women who came over, whether of one sort of offender or another, were generally indentured for a period of years to pay for passage. As a rule they were house servants, though as to this authorities differ. One, quoted above, declared that white women worked in the fields in Virginia and Carolina;[163] but the author of *Leah and Rachel* (1656) stated, "The women are not (as is reported) put into the ground to work but occupy such domestic employments and housewifery as in England. . . ." But in a second breath he admits that "some wenches that are nasty, beastly and not fit to be so imployed are put into the ground. . . ."[164] That some labored "in the ground" would seem to be implied in the *Sot Weed Factor*, wherein one "Froe" berates another while they play at "Lanctre-Looe":

> "*D—n* you, says one,
> "Tho' now so brave
> "I knew you late a Four Years' Slave,
> "What if for Planter's Wife you go
> "Nature designed you for the Hoe."

Another laments:

> "But things are changed; now at the Hoe,
> "I daily work, and Barefoot go,
> "In weeding Corn and feeding Swine,
> "I spend my melancholy time."[165]

Moreover, the advertisements setting forth the qualifications of the servants to be disposed of not infrequently assert that they are "fit for Country or house Business."[166] Ballagh says, of those in Virginia, that they "were commonly employed as domestics."[167] And, while this in general was true, among some planters there was enough of a tendency to put them to work in the ground, "that thereby they may avoyd the payment of

---

162 *Ibid.*, 23–4.

163 P. 265.

164 Hammond: *op. cit.*, in Hall: *Narratives of Early Maryland*, 290–1.

165 Cook: *The Sot Weed Factor*, 26, 15.

166 E.g., "a swiss servant maid" advertised in the *S. C. Gaz.*, Jan. 17–24, 1735–6, 4, col. 1.

167 *White Servitude in the Colony of Virginia*, 69.

levies," that an act was passed, in 1662, whereby such women "working in the ground" were "to be accompted tythable, and levies paid for them accordingly."[168]

Certain it is that domestic work was the most common. Some of the women were accomplished and, besides doing housework, were able to handle the instruction of children. Thus "an English servant maid's time, . . . 3 years and 9 months," was advertised for sale; and it was specially noted that besides washing and ironing she could speak "very good French."[169] The servant women who were gifted with more than one tongue were, however, fewer than men and they were not so often disposed of as teachers as were the latter.

As a rule the white servant women were a greater source of trouble than Negro slaves, being much more inclined to run away. Acts for "the better governing and regulating white servants" were passed for the protection of the masters from loss of their mobile property. But Bruce asserts that a disposition to run away "was often accepted not as an indication of an incorrigible nature but of hard usage."[170] In Virginia, in 1671, the white servants were far more numerous than slaves, there being 6,000 of the former and but 2,000 of the latter.[171] Servants coming to the colony without formal agreement were usually sold for a period of years, depending upon their age: five years, if more than sixteen years of age; and, if under sixteen, until their twenty-fourth year. This was the law of 1661–2. At first they had been bound for four years if over twenty-one; five, if under twenty; and seven years if under twelve.[172] The servant's time might be sold and resold. Thus a "likely servant woman" with "six and a half years to serve," and whose "principal failing is drunkenness," was advertised in 1745;[173] another with "about four years to serve" who had "behaved herself peaceably, hon-

[168] Hening: *Statutes of Va.*, II, 170; another problem, growing out of the abuse of servant women by their masters who "got them with child," was met by requiring the woman to be sold for an additional two years' service, the income from which was to go to the vestry for use of the parish. —Act of 1662, Hening's *Statutes*, II, 167.

[169] *S. C. Gaz.*, Mch. 6–13, 1735–6, 3, col. 2.

[170] Bruce: *Economic Hist. of Va.*, II, 11.

[171] *Ibid.*, I, 572

[172] *Ibid.*, II, 3, 4.

[173] *Md. Gaz.*, June 21, 1745, 4.

estly and soberly'' and was ''not sold for any fault'' was offered in 1752;[174] another ''wench,'' with a husband, was to be sold because she ''is a very great scold.''[175]

Frequently the white servant women were given bad reputations in the advertisements relative to runaways. Margery Bailey, Elizabeth Piercy, Elizabeth Hawkins, and Mary Barrington were described as ''convict'' women.[176] Others seem to have been respectable, and even well educated;[177] but many, certainly, were not averse to carrying away as much clothing as they could lay hands upon.[178] In some cases, neighbors seem to have been suspected of abetting servants in their flight.

III. Education Afforded Girls in the South

The conditions of life in Southern settlements were so different from those of the North that to judge one section by the performances of the other is manifestly misleading. The town school of New England, with her concentrated and homogeneous communities, was clearly out of the question on Southern plantations. Families were scattered over such wide territories that the most natural solution of the educational problem, for girls as well as boys, among well-to-do planters, was found in following the practice of tutorial tuition as in England;[179] and, as in England, the education of the poor fell upon the church, philanthropists, and the apprenticeship system.

Aside from the encouragement of a college and the founding of certain free schools, educational legislation of Virginia followed that of England relative to the poor, orphans, and apprentices. As early as 1642–3, a general law enjoined guardians to educate orphans in the ''Christian Religion and the rudiments of learning.''[180] An act of 1672 recited the beneficial effects of

174 Ibid., Nov. 16, 1752, 2, col. 3.

175 Ibid., Jan. 25, 1776.

176 Md. Gaz., June 4, 1761, 3, col. 2; July 26, 1753, 3, col. 1; Aug. 30, 1745, 4; July 26–Aug. 2, 1734, 4.

177 Ibid., Jan. 22, 1756, 3.

178 N. C. Gaz., Apr. 15, 1757, 4, col. 2; Md. Gaz., Oct. 25, 1745, 4.

179 Benedict: Higher Ed. of Women in the Southern States [The South in the Building of the Nation, X, 259]; also Ramage: Local Government and Free Schools in S. C., 29 ff.

180 Hening: Statutes of Va., I, 260 f.; see also Maddox: Free School Idea in Va., 9.

English laws and required that Justices of the Peace in every county should enforce the laws of England against the "vagrant, idle and dissolute"; and that "county courts shall . . . place out all children whose parents are not able to bring them up apprentices to tradesmen, the males till one and twenty . . . and the females to other necessary employments, till eighteene years of age. . . ."[181] "The general supervision of such matters . . . belonged to the county courts" but it was "one of the duties of the Vestry . . . to take care of the poor of the parish." Records of their actions are, in some cases, still preserved. "In such cases a provision for instruction in reading and writing was generally inserted without regard to race or sex."[182] In case the vestries were negligent, "the county bench did not hesitate to act in their place." Thus in 1698, "Ann Chandler, orphan of Daniel Chandler," was "bound apprentice to Phyllemon Miller till 18 or day of marriage" and was to "be taught to read a chapter in the Bible, ye Lord's prayer, and ten commandments, and sempstress work." Rebeccah ffrancis (1690) was apprenticed till twenty-one years of age and was to receive "apparell, Linnen and Wollen . . . one able younge breeding cow . . . a compleat yeares schooling" and be "virtuously brought up" and "educated in reading ye vulgar tongue." Sarah Allen (1701) was to "be learnt to reade perfectly" and Grace Griswood was to be taught "to read, sew, spinn and knitt."[183] In case parents did not bring up their children "to an honest way of living as well as in ye Fear of God," they were to show cause why the children should not be bound out according to law.[184]

In North Carolina, where Quaker settlements were numerous, elementary education of girls was afforded on the same basis as that of boys.[185] As for legal provision, North Carolina passed a law in 1760, similar to those of Virginia, requiring orphans to be bound out by direction of the court, "every male to some tradesman, merchant, mariner or other person approved by the Court" to the age of twenty-one, and females to the age of eighteen; and

[181] Hening: *op. cit.*, II, 298.

[182] Tyler: Ed. in Colonial Va. [*William and Mary Quarterly*, V, 219].

[183] *Ibid.*, 222; see also Bruce: *Institutional Hist. of Va.*, I, 309 *ff.*

[184] Case of children of Mary Evans and Richard Bragby—Tyler: *op. cit.*, 223.

[185] Klain: *Quaker Contributions to Education in N. C.*, 284 *ff.*

the masters and mistresses were, besides providing food, clothing and shelter, to "teach or cause him or her to be taught to read and write"; and if it appear "that any such apprentice is ill used or not taught the trade, profession or employment . . ." then he or she may be bound to another.[186] In 1716, on petition of John Swain that his sister Elizabeth, bound out as apprentice, "be taught to read by her said master," it was "ordered that she be taught to read."[187]

Ramage divided the history of educational legislation in South Carolina into four periods, pointing out that in the Colonial years it was chiefly concerned with the education of the masses, and that only in the city was it possible to view education as a group problem.[188] It was in the city that the Society for the Propagation of the Gospel in Foreign Parts chiefly operated; and, according to their directions, it would appear that girls must have been admitted as well as boys, for they advise that, in "setting up of schools for the teaching of children, . . . widows of such clergymen as shall die in those countries" shall be encouraged "if they be found capable of that employment."[189] Numerous "free schools" were set up[190] but it is impossible to say to what extent they were open to girls. Of the South Carolina Society, formed about 1737,[191] it is known, however, that it paid the salary of "masters and mistresses for the education of both sexes." Girls were instructed till the age of twelve only; boys until fourteen. As none were admitted under eight years of age, girls could enter during a four-year period.[192] Possibly other philanthropic societies educated girls in a similar manner. Whether they were or were not provided for in the elementary work of the free school set up in Charleston by law, in 1710, is not made clear, but the presumption is that they were not.[193]

[186] *Laws of N. C.*, 1760, Ch. XIII [*State Records of N. C.*, XXV, 419–20].

[187] Court of Oyer and Terminer, Chowan Precinct (N. C.), Nov. 1, 1716, [*Col. Rec. N. C.*, II, 266].

[188] Ramage: *op. cit.*, 32–3.

[189] Dalcho: *Episcopal Church in S. C.*, 47.

[190] Ramsay: *Hist. of S. C.*, II, 352 *ff.*

[191] *Ibid.*, 362.

[192] McCrady: *Hist. of C.*, I, 489–90; also Ramsey: *op. cit.*, II, 362 *ff.*; the latter does not state definitely that girls were educated at the very beginning, but that such was the case at the time of his writing (1808).

[193] *Statutes of S. C.*, II, 342 *ff.*

Among those families of the Colonial South which were competent to provide for it, the education of daughters was given attention. Contrary to the practice of the Quaker and Puritan, the Southern gentlemen laid emphasis on social accomplishments which were not stressed, and scarcely tolerated, in the North until the rise of seminaries—for the most part, after the Revolutionary War. The chief elements of this social education were music and dancing. Jefferson required his daughter Martha to dance "three days in the week from eleven to one." The rudiments of reading and writing were generally included and attention was given to arithmetic in some cases. After 1750, French, painting, fancy needlework, and other subjects were frequently offered to young ladies in the schools of venture masters.[194] The reading recommended for young ladies was usually of a solid character but lighter literature was read, perhaps clandestinely. Naturally, there was considerable variation in different families. A descendant of Jefferson said, "Very little from books was thought necessary for a girl. She was trained to domestic matters . . . the accomplishments of the day . . . to play upon the harpsicord or spinet, and to work impossible dragons and roses on canvas."[195] In the case of Dolly Madison, "gentle arts of housewifery," "reading, writing and an uncertain quantity of arithmetic" made up her education. The writing was well taught, but her spelling was always erratic. Due to her Quaker family, the accomplishments had but little place in her education,[196] and she was "taught to ignore all those graceful accomplishments deemed so necessary in the formation of a woman's education." Of Martha Washington it was said, "She was in no wise a student, hardly a regular reader, nor gifted with literary ability . . .; such knowledge as she possessed of the world was gleaned from the few books she read, and the society of her father's friends, for she had never been farther from her home than Williamsburg."[197] John Baptista Ashe, in 1731, directed that his daughter, Mary, "be taught to write and read and some feminine accomplishments which may render her

194 See pp. 281 *ff.*

195 Wharton: *op. cit.*, 93 *ff.*

196 Goodwin: *Dolly Madison*, 1-2, 2-3, and 9-11; also Holloway: *Ladies of the White House*, 181-2.

197 Holloway: *op. cit.*, 15-16, and 23-4.

agreeable; and that she be not kept ignorant of what appertains to a good housewife in the management of household affairs."[198] Cullen Pollock, likewise of North Carolina (1749), desired that his "daughters have as good education as can be had in this Province."[199]

An interesting contrast between the education of daughters and sons is to be seen in these wills, and they are fairly representative, in that the sons of Ashe were to have "as liberal an education" as possible, studying reading, writing, "practical part of arithmetick," Latin, Greek, French, and, when they arrive at the "years of discretion," mathematics. Facilities for these studies were apparently thought better in Virginia, and thither they were to be sent. At manhood he hoped they would enter a profession or business, "the one to ye Law, the other to Merchandise," but in this they were to "follow their own inclinations." Pollock would have his sons get "what learning they can have in this Province" and then be sent "to Boston for farther Education."[200]

Thomas Parnell, of Virginia (1687), wished his sons to be brought up "in the fear of the Lord and to learn to write and reade."[201] John Savage directed his executors to put out three servants to provide education for his daughters;[202] Nicholas Granger (about 1640) secured the same end by setting aside "a definite number of cattle";[203] Clement Thresh, in 1657, provided, apparently, for the education of his daughter to the age of sixteen years.[204] Robert Gascoigne's daughter was to learn to read and sew; while the girls of William Rookings were to have "what education may be fitting for them." Still other cases of provision by will for the education of daughters have been cited by Bruce.[205] The daughter of Richard Burkland, however, was fortunate, for in 1663 he engaged a teacher "to give his daughter lessons in reading, and writing and casting accounts."[206] Just

198 Grimes: *North Carolina Wills*, 11–12.
199 Grimes: *Wills and Inventories*, 339.
200 *Op. cit., loc. cit.*
201 Stanard: *op. cit.,* 275–6.
202 Bruce: *Institutional Hist. of Va.*, I, 320.
203 Bruce: *Inst. Hist. of Va.*, I, 297.
204 *Ibid.*, 299.
205 *Ibid.*, 302, 304–5, 307.
206 Stanard: *Colonial Va.*, 280.

how how much was attempted in the "one year's schooling" offered to the daughter of Francis Browne is not known, but it may have included "accounts."

An interesting and instructive glimpse of a Virginian girl's education (1732) is gained from the letter of Bessy Pratt to her brother who was studying in England: "I find you have got the start of me in learning very much, for you write better already than I expect to do as long as I live; and you are got as far as the rule of three in Arithmetick, but I can't cast up a sum in addition cleverly but I am striving to do better every day. I can perform a great many dances and am learning the Sibell, but I cannot speak a Word of French."[207] Reading and writing were the most common accomplishments at first. Martha Laurens, of Charleston, it is said, could read by her third year.[208] Many references occur to "accompts" but this study did not go far in those days, even for many boys. After the middle of the eighteenth century, when settlements were firmly established and prosperous, musical instruments were "generally found in the home of the planter, who had his girls taught to play. . . . ." This accomplishment was not limited to the ladies, however. Special tutors were employed for instrumental music in the Carter family. Some of the gentlemen of the family were good musicians.[209]

The foregoing, with slight modification, may be considered the standard for a girl's education in the Southern colonies to the end of the eighteenth century. Ramsay says of women in South Carolina that they "are generally well educated. Several of them have highly cultivated minds and refined manners."[210] It is clear, however, that their education was generally with reference to men and their own future sphere as home-makers. Beyond the merest rudiments, the ornamental subjects were clearly emphasized, inasmuch as these made them agreeable embellishments of society and attractive ornaments of the home. The Carter household, as Fithian pictured it, was a very cheerful place because of the gaiety inspired by music and dancing. "A

[207] *Ibid.*, 112–13; also 272–3.
[208] Calhoun: *op. cit.*, I, 293.
[209] Fithian's *Diary*, 58 *f.*
[210] *History of S. C.*, 411.

young gentleman of Virginia'' elsewhere depicted its effect.
And still another broke forth in rhyme:

> "When Sukey to her harpsicord repairs
> "And, smiling, bids me give attentive ears,
> "With bliss supreme the lovely maid I view.''[211]

Whatever else may be said of ladies' education in the eighteenth century, either in the South or North, it must be admitted that it was designed to satisfy—the gentlemen, with few exceptions. Music and dancing by the ladies made the greatest appeal, naturally, but fine needlework was not without its admirers, as witness the following lines by "a gentleman of Virginia'' to "a Lady on a Screen of Her Working:''

> "A New Creation charms the ravish'd Sight;
> "Delightful Harmony of Shade and Light!
> "Art vies with Nature in a doubtful Strife,
> "The finish'd Copy, which and which the Life.
> "The Blooming Flow'rs the painted Bow excel;
> "The gay Delusion courts, and cheats the Smell.
> "What Beauty does Anemone disclose!
> "What flushing Glories the Carnation shews!
> "The Tulip here displays her motley Pride;
> "The Piony there in richest Crimson dy'd.
> "The Hyacinth, tho' rais'd by Phoebus' Pow'r,
> "Derives from Female Skill a fairer Flow'r.
>
> . . .
>
> "Here Silver Blooms of Golden Orange blow;
> "Stock-Gilly-Flowers there, and Jonquils glow,
> "And Leaves of chearful Green the Ground bestrew;
> "Refreshing Green, from Age preserve those Eyes,
> "By which you flourish in immortal Dies.''[212]

It was of education in the latter part of the eighteenth century, and early nineteenth, that Jefferson wrote that "a great obstacle to good education is the inordinate passion prevalent for novels, and the time lost in that reading which should be instructively employed . . . [contributes to] a bloated imagination, sickly judgment, and disgust towards all the real business of life.'' "Marmontel's new moral tales'' he considered good for girls, "but not his old ones.'' In this criticism Jefferson, writing in 1818,

[211] Quoted by Stanard: op. cit., 309 f., from the Va. Gaz., 1769.
[212] Va. Gaz., Dec. 3–10, 1736, 2, col. 2.

described the education given his own daughters as "a solid" one which would "enable them when become mothers, to educate their own daughters and even to direct the course for their sons" if fathers were lost, incapable or inattentive thereto. He especially recommended the reading of "Pope, Molière, Racine, the Corneilles" for "pleasure and improvement." French "is an indispensable part of education for both sexes." With the help of his daughter he prepared a list of books for girls' education, though he protested that this was a subject on which he had not thought much.[213] That he had really thought enough about it to make his judgments of value is suggested by the fact that, as early as 1779, he had introduced a bill in the General Assembly for the foundation of schools "for the training of all free children, male and female, for three years, in reading, writing and arithmetic."[214] This was ten years before girls were admitted to the schools of Boston, though, as noted before, a change was

[213] Letter from Thomas Jefferson to Nathaniel Burwell, Mch. 14, 1818 [*Missouri Hist. Soc. Collections*, IV, No. 4, 475 *ff.*]. See also Holloway: *Ladies of the White House*, 116–17, 141–2. The books named are: Les voyages d'Anacharis; Gillies' history of Greece; Gillies' history of the World; Livy in English; Sallust, English by Gordon; Gibbon's Decline of Rome; Tacitus, English by Murphy; Suetonius, English by Thompson; Plutarch's Lives; Lemprière's universal biography; Histoire ancienne de Milot; Histoire de France de Milot; Russell's Modern Europe; Robertson's Charles V.; Memoires de Sully; Vie de Henri IV par Perifixe; Louis XIV et XV de Voltaire; Historie generale de Voltaire; Baxter's History of England; Robertson's History of Scotland; Robertson's History of America; Botta's history of American Independence; Burke's & Girardin's history of Virginia; Joyce's Scientific dialogues; Histoire Natural de Buffon; Tully—Offices, English; Seneque par Lagrange; Morale et bonheur; Stanhope's Charron on Wisdom; Economy of human life; Sterne's Sherlock & Allison's sermons; Sermons de Masillon et Bourdaloue; The Spectator, Tatler, Guardian; Pike's Arithmetic; Pinkerton's Geography; Whateley on pleasure gardening; Pope's Illiad & Odyssey; Dryden's Virgil; Milton's Paradise Lost; Telemaque; Shakespeare's plays; Dryden's tragedies; Molière, Racine, Corneille; Don Quichotte, French; Gil Blas; Contes Nouveaus de Marmontel; Voyages de Campe; The Pleasing preceptor from the German of Vieth; Pope's works; Thomson's seasons; Lowth's English grammar; Walker's pronouncing dictionary; Dufief, French & English dictionary; Dufief, Nature displayed; *Novels:* Evenings at home by Mrs. Barbould; Miss Edgeworth's works; Lettres sur l'education; Vaillees du Chateau, Theatre d'education, and Theatre de societé by Mme. Genlis; Godwin's Caleb Williams.

[214] *The South in the Building of the Nation*, X, 294.

taking place in many New England towns. What the effect on girls' education in the South would have been, had Virginia followed the leadership of Jefferson on this occasion, can be surmised.

There are references which show that some girls of the socially competent class attended schools. About 1736, Mary Mason attended school for three years, paying two hundred pounds of tobacco a year for schooling and a thousand for board; Colonel Gordon reported in his diary, "Sent Molly and her maid Judith, to school to Mr. Criswell"; William Byrd sent his daughters, Susan and Ursula, to a school in England; and John Baylor, also of Virginia, sent four daughters to boarding school at Croyden, in England.[215] To these, various instances could be added. For many planters, however, a tutor in the household was the only solution for the educational problem. Such a tutor, if the children were numerous, ministered to them alone. Sometimes neighbors' children came in to be taught; again, children came to the house for a time "as boarders." Such arrangements seem to have been made in the cases of Richard Kellam's daughter and Martha Willett. Elizabeth Charlton was at Captain Jones', where "she was in care for her education," when she was persuaded to elope with John Severne.[216]

The best evidences of the prevalence of tutorial instruction, for girls as well as boys, are to be found in letters, wills, diaries, and newspaper advertisements, wherein planters sought qualified men and women for instructors or the latter sought employment, as the case might be. Maria Carter wrote her "dear Cousin" of being so confined "at school or with my grandma" as not to know "how the world goes on." She deplores being "awakened out of a sound sleep" by "some croaking voice" announcing that "Mr. Price"—the tutor—"is down stairs"; and that her life is so monotonous that "the History of one day" duly repeated "carries me through the three hundred and sixty five days, which you know compleats the year." When, finally, "Grandma uses her Voice, . . . I get up, huddle on my cloaths & down to Book, then to Breakfast, then to school again, & maybe I have an hour to myself before Dinner, then the same story over again

215 Stanard: *op. cit.*, 272–3, 287, and 289–90.
216 Bruce: *Institutional Hist. of Va.*, I, 323–5.

till twilight, & then a small portion of time before I go to rest.
. . .''²¹⁷

Another picture, replete with details of the tutor's life and
instructive as to what the daughters studied, has been left in the
Journal and Letters of Philip Vickers Fithian, who in 1773-1774
was a tutor in the household of Mr. Carter, of Virginia. Having
come from the North, and from a theological school—Princeton—
he was ill-fitted to enjoy to the fullest extent the social life of
his temporary home. Again and again he regretted that it has
not been "a part of my education to learn [dancing] what I
think is an innocent and an ornamental and most certainly, in
this province . . . a necessary qualification for a person to appear even decent in Company."²¹⁸

When school began, on November first, 1773, he had for pupils
two sons, a nephew, and five daughters. The eldest daughter
was "reading the Spectator, writing and beginning to cypher";
the second, reading the "Spelling Book and beginning to write";
the third was reading the Spelling Book; the fourth was "spelling in the beginning of the Spelling Book"; and the fifth, "beginning her letters." The two eldest daughters attended "Dancing School" and the eldest, Priscilla, aged about 16, was learning
to play the forte piano. Nancy was beginning "on the guitar."
Miss Prissy was "going to embroider" some flowers on linen for
a counterpane. Even the youngest daughter had "learned many
tunes and [could] strike any note or succession of notes perfectly
with the flute or harpsicord," being "never wearied with the
sound of music either vocal or instrumental." Vocal music was
indulged in by all, but a special tutor was not mentioned—as in
the case of instrumental music and dancing. Fithian mentions
having some of the younger children, girls and boys, "repeat
their Catechism."²¹⁹ Three months after his arrival, Prissy "began multiplication." Whether this advanced study was entered
upon solely out of deference to the fact that he found her
"steady, studious, docile, quick of apprehension," able to make
"good progress in what she undertakes" and to comprehend anything "I propose so soon as I communicate it to her"; or whether

²¹⁷ Stanard: *op. cit.,* 281.
²¹⁸ *Op. cit.,* 62, 75 and 76.
²¹⁹ *Ibid.,* 50, 75, 85-6, 122.

it was in the scheme of education designed for all the girls of the family, as they increased in years, is not made clear.

An interesting portrait of each daughter is given. Priscilla was eminently intelligent and teachable; Nancy, filled with curiosity, eagerness, friendliness, and words; Fanny, sedate and simple, strongly resembled her mother, "an elegant, beautiful woman"; Betsy was quiet and obedient; while Harriot was "bold, fearless, noisy and lawless, with a great fondness for music."

Society in Virginia, the young tutor found, was very hospitable and polite, the gentlemen not so much given to gaming as he had previously thought, but "some swear bitterly." Perhaps this habit was to be found among the ladies as well, for he makes particular note of the fact that Priscilla had "a sweet obliging temper" and "never swears, which is here a distinguishing virtue."[220]   Mr. Carter had a deep interest in music, good instruments—harpsicord, forte piano, organ, harmonica, German flutes and guitar—and was "indefatigable in the practice." Mrs. Carter took an interest in domestic affairs generally—the fowls, mutton, groves, fields, meadows, cattle and horses—was most solicitous for the welfare of those around her, "prudent, always cheerful, never without something pleasant, a remarkable economist, perfectly acquainted," he thought, "with the good management of children, entirely free from all foolish and unnecessary fondness," and also "well acquainted . . . with the formality and ceremony" commonly found in "high life."

The studies mentioned for the girls, while liberal compared with prevailing custom elsewhere in America, form quite a contrast with those of the boys of the family, who were instructed in Sallust (The Cataline Conspiracy), grammatical exercises, Latin grammar, English grammar and reading, writing and "Ciphering in Reduction," and subtraction. Judging from Mr. Carter's proficiency, the sons must have had opportunity to study music as much as desired; dancing was as necessary a part of a man's education as woman's; while horsemanship was undoubtedly an essential.

The tutor's day began when he was roused by a boy who came to light the fire at seven or a little after. By the time he was

[220] *Ibid.*, 82 *f.*

dressed the children were in the room below—the regular school-room—where they were heard "round one lesson" before the bell rang at eight o'clock. The children went out and at eight-thirty breakfast was served. At half-past nine, when breakfast was over, they all repaired to the schoolroom "till twelve," when the children were free. Dinner was usually at half-past two or three. From three-thirty till five they were in school again. Instruction seems to have gone on each day from Monday till Friday; but two of the daughters were excused from Fithian's instruction on Tuesdays and Thursdays, in order to practice music. Music and dancing frequently interrupted the regular routine. After school the tutor was free to "continue in the school room," sit in his own room, or sit "over at the Great House with Mr. and Mrs. Carter." Supper was usually begun at half-past eight or nine.[221]

Tutors frequently advertised for positions, but a majority of advertisements were inserted by families desiring teachers. In 1773, "a young gentleman . . . [with] Batchelor's Degree at Nassau Hall College in New Jersey" sought a place as "private or Publick Tutor" in Virginia.[222] Another, "properly quali-fied" and of "unexceptionable character," desired to instruct children in Latin, English, writing, and arithmetic, in 1776.[223] Still another, who had "received a collegiate education," wished to be tutor in a respectable family where he would give "liberal information" to "three or more sons"; and "any young ladies in the family might have an opportunity of acquiring the French language."[224]

Tutors were secured from many sources. As noted, some came from Northern colleges, others from England; still others were prepared in the institutions of Virginia. "Not infrequently, the tutor in a large family was a person under indenture. . . . Even among the convicts, there were found some who had received an excellent education in the most respectable English schools, and who were, therefore, fully competent, from the point of view of knowledge at least, to instruct the young."[225]

221 *Ibid.*, 60–1.
222 *Va. Gaz.*, Nov. 18, 1773, 2, col. 2.
223 *Ibid.*, Jan. 19, 1776, 3, col. 3.
224 *Ibid.*, Nov. 8, 1787, 3, col. 2.
225 Bruce: *Institutional Hist. of Va.*, I, 324, 328.

Relations between the planter and tutor were not always as agreeable as those described by Fithian. Bruce relates the dispute between John Matts and Charles Leatherbury. But good teachers were in demand; once secured and tested, the planter liked to keep them. John Brickell, in 1767, advertised that "if William Jones, teacher of Latin, . . . tutor to my children last summer," is unengaged and "will return to me, he shall meet with encouragement.[226]

The subjects with which the tutor had to be familiar were frequently specified. One must be "qualified" in "Latin, Writing and Arithmetick";[227] another must, "among other things," thoroughly understand "the mathematics";[228] another must be a "single man," "master of the Languages," able to "teach English and Arithmetic" and be of good "moral character";[229] another must be "capable of teaching the Classicks, Writing and Cyphering . . . [and] the French Language" and preferably "a middle aged person";[230] but, in many instances, only a knowledge of "reading, writing and arithmetic" was required.[231]

Women were frequently desired as tutors. Katharine Shrewsbury was employed by Richard Tompkins about 1693 for the education of his son.[232] Charles Fouchereaud wanted "a woman" to teach "reading and all Kinds of Needle-work"; none "under 20 or that has passed her grand climateric" were to be considered.[233] Another gentleman offered "good encouragement" to "a sober single woman" qualified to teach reading and "willing to live in a private family."[234] Sometimes the tutoress was to teach reading and sewing and also "undertake the management of a nursery of three or four children."[235] Generally, little was expected of the tutoress beyond the rudiments and an ability to handle children, but this was not universally the case. A

226 *Va. Gaz.*, Apr. 9, 1767, 3, col. 3.

227 *Ibid.*, Jan. 21, 1775.

228 *Ibid.*, Oct. 15, 1767, 2, col. 1.

229 *Ibid.*, July 18, 1771, 2, col. 1.

230 *Columbian Herald* (Charleston, S. C.), Mch. 31, 1794, 1, col. 1.

231 E.g., *S. C. Gaz.*, Aug. 7-14, 1755, 3, col. 1; *Va. Gaz.*, Feb. 12, 1762, 3, col. 2.

232 Bruce: *Institutional Hist. of Va.*, I, 327.

233 *S. C. Gaz.*, Sept. 11-19, 1755, 4, col. 3.

234 *Ibid.*, Feb. 25-Mch. 3. 1764, 6, col. 3.

235 *Va. Gaz.*, Sept. 24, 1767, 1, col. 3.

family, in 1793, desired "a female of good character" to undertake "tuition . . . in reading, writing and arithmetic"; but
specified that "if she understands French and Music," it will
be "the more agreeable."[236]

In the Southern colonies, schools of private masters and mistresses became prominent after 1750; before that time several of
them advertised, but were found chiefly in the greater cities.
These schools supplemented in an important way the work of
tutors in the household; indeed, the private master, in case his
specialty was dancing or music, frequently came to the house
to give lessons. They were important, however, not only as sup-
plements to other agencies of education, but as forerunners of
the first recognized institution for the higher education of girls—
the female academy or seminary. These schools appeared in
every colony of the South, as in the North. An examination of
advertisements from newspapers of North and South Carolina,
Virginia, and Maryland shows their chief characteristics.

Advertisements noted in papers published in these four Southern colonies fall naturally into the following classes: *first,* those
in which subjects are not specified; *second,* a group in which
sewing and reading received most emphasis, but others occasionally included; *third,* writing; *fourth,* vocal and instrumental
music; *fifth,* dancing; *sixth,* drawing, painting, riding, and so on;
seventh, French, with other studies sometimes included; *eighth,*
masters who offered a considerable number of studies such as
English, French, arithmetic, writing (similar to those called
academies); and, *ninth,* schools generally referred to as academies. Besides those falling under one of the above heads, a
single notice was found of "Peter Pekin, Pastry Cook from
Paris," who was "willing to teach, at Reasonable rates, all the
several Branches of his Business" while at the same time he
would gladly be "employed to make all sorts of Pyes, Tarts,
cakes" for gentlemen and ladies.[237]

The schools of the first class were numerous, judging from
their frequency in the papers examined; they were usually
taught by women and were for "children," "young children,"
or "children and servants," as a few advertisements stated.
While subjects were not named, they were, doubtless, quite ele-

[236] *State Gaz. of S. C.,* Sept. 21, 1793, 3, col. 3.
[237] *S. C. Gaz.,* Dec. 29, 1746, 3, col. 1.

mentary, similar to the dame schools of England and New England, which taught both sexes the rudiments of spelling, reading, writing, and numbers.   Jane Duthy announced her school (1759) and assured parents who would "favor her" of "utmost care and fidelity in teaching";[238] Sarah Norman, 'apprehending that there was no longer danger from the small-pox' returned to open her school in Charleston (1761) and announced she was "willing to take 3 or 4 boarders."[239]   A year later, Anne Hampton informed patrons that she was opening a school for "the care of their children or servants";[240] Mary Air notified the public in general and "her Friends in particular" that she had opened a school in 1773;[241] and similar examples are the schools of Tho. Crew and Elizabeth Dwight.[242]   Abigail Diamond (1750) intended to open a school "for young ladies to board or by the day" where all would "be properly instructed."[243]   Mary Stokes and Elizabeth Girardeau advertised similar day and boarding schools.[244]

The second type of school, also, was nearly always taught by women, but a few gentlemen attempted it.   The fact that it stressed an accomplishment—needlework—but also taught some rudiments, and even French, is probably sufficient to account for its greater frequence of recurrence than the first type.   This sort of school appeared in the earliest newspaper published in the South and increased in popularity after the middle of the century.   In 1734, Phillipene Henning advertised to teach "all sorts of needle work to perfection," make dresses, and teach "young ladies French and English";[245] M. Harward taught girls to "read embroider and flourish," "all sorts of needlework," and had "a person" who would teach them writing and cyphering;[246] and Jane Voyer offered to instruct "young ladies that have a mind to learn" in "Embroidery, Lace-work, Tapestry or other sort of needlework, Drawing and French," provided

238 *Ibid.*, May 12–19, 1759, 4, col. 1.
239 *Ibid.*, Jan. 17–24, 1761, 3, col. 1.
240 *Ibid.*, June 12–19, 1762, 1, col. 2.
241 *Ibid.*, July 19, 1773, 1, col. 2.
242 *N. C. Gaz.*, June 4, 1791; and *S. C. Gaz.*, May 23, 1771, 3.
243 *S. C. Gaz.*, Feb. 19–26, 1750, 3, col. 1.
244 *Ibid.*, Jan. 1, 1763, 1, col. 1; and Feb. 5, 1763, 4, col. 1.
245 *Ibid.*, Feb. 8–15, 1734–5, 3, col. 2.
246 *Ibid.*, Apr. 10–17, 1736, 4 col. 1.

they be not "under the age of 12."[247]   Numerous others advertised in Charleston papers to teach one or a combination of the
following subjects: "plain and sampler work," "embroidery,"
"plain needlework," "sewing and marking," "fine needlework,"
"Tent and Dresden work," and "Embroidery with silk, Cruels,
or silver and gold thread."   While some branch of needlework
formed the *pièce-de-resistance* in their offerings, the total of
their minor attractions makes a formidable array.   One, two, or
three of the following subjects were generally included: spelling,
reading, writing, music, dancing, drawing, arithmetic, French,
and reading "English in the most approved method."   Reading
occurred in almost every case, but dancing, French, drawing and
arithmetic very seldom.   Some of the women performed services
other than teaching.   Thus Elizabeth Ash would wash and iron
"Ladies Head-Cloaths in the best Manner"; Martha Logan
wished to lease "several lots" for a reasonable time to someone
who would build upon them; and Ann Imer would clean "all
Kinds of Laces, particularly Blown [?] Laces . . . as neat as in
London."   Generally, however, no other work or interest was
mentioned; and one announced specifically that she would "employ her whole time in this business" of teaching.[248]

The above are fairly representative.   A few others may be
noted.   Mary Salisbury, of Maryland, offered to teach young
ladies "all sorts of fine needlework, tapestry, embroidery, with
gold and silver, and every other curious work which can be performed with a needle, and all education fit for young ladies, except dancing."   Among things "fit" she included French,[249]
Mrs. Polk taught similar mysteries to young girls and, at the
same time, served ladies "in painting ribands, drawing all kinds

[247] *Ibid.*, Sept. 1–8, 1739, 3, col. 2.

[248] Ruth Lowndes—*S. C. Gaz.*, Aug. 22, 1743, 4, col. 2; Mrs. Hannah
Fidling, Jan. 24, 1743, 3, col. 2; Elizabeth Ash, Mch. 28–Apr. 4, 1748, 3,
col. 1; Martha Logan, Mch. 26–Apr. 2, 1750, 3, col. 2; Aug. 8–15, 1754, 3,
col. 3; Elizabeth Guy, Apr. 22–29, 1751, 3, col. 1; Anna Maria Hoyland,
Sept. 16–23, 1751, 2, col. 1; Jan. 13, 1757, 4, col. 1; Anne Hundley, Aug.
7–14, 1755, 4, col. 2; Eliz. Cossens, Dec. 4–11, 1755, 1, col. 3; Eliza White,
Jan. 13, 1757, 4, col. 1; Sarah Norman, Feb. 17–24, 1759, 2, col. 3; Elizabeth Screven, Dec. 22–29, 1759, 1, col. 2; Ann Imer, Jan. 12, 1767, 1, col.
2; Mary Corbett, Apr. 10–17, 1762, 4, col. 3; Mary Harriss, Mch. 6–13,
1762, 2, col. 2; Mrs. Wilkins, *State Gaz. of S. C.*, Jan. 23, 1794, 3, col. 4.

[249] *Md. Gaz.*, Feb. 28, 1754, 3, col. 2.

of patterns, particularly on silk and muslin . . . [and worked] gowns, shoes, ribands, men's waistcoats and ruffles in tambour, in the cheapest, neatest, and best manner.''[250] Maria Smith, perhaps a sister of Ann who was so influential in founding the Ann Smith Academy at Lexington, Virginia, opened a school in Winchester (1788) to teach ladies "reading, spelling, Tambour, Dresden Embroidery and all Kinds of plain and colored needlework. . . ." Writing and arithmetic also were to be taught at a special hour. She offered it as a testimonial that she had educated "some ladies of the first rank in these states. . . ." A later advertisement, of the same year, added geography, music, and dancing to the subjects to be taught.[251]

Like many arrivals in the colony who had to find something to support themselves, John Walker and his wife turned to teaching, offering classical instruction and improvement in morals to young gentlemen and "all kinds of needlework" to the ladies. These studies they conducted while the wife made all kinds of fancy work and helped to operate a store "at Mr. Cobb's new House," where they lived.[252] Similar "female accomplishments" were offered to society in Richmond by Mrs. Hodgson, who arrived from Norfolk where she had "had a very numerous school" "composed of the children of the most respectable families."[253] But "numerous" and "respectable" as it doubtless was, it could scarcely have competed with the establishment of "E. Armston, . . . better known by the name of Gardner" who continued a "school at Point Pleasant, Norfolk Borough, where is a large and convenient House proper to accommodate young Ladies as boarders; at which School is taught Petit Point in Flowers, Fruit, Landscapes, and Sculpture, Nuns Work, Embroidery in Silk, Gold, Silver, Pearls, or embossed, Shading of all Kinds, in the various Work in Vogue, Dresden Point Work, Lace ditto, Catgut in different Modes, flourishing Muslin, after the newest Taste, and most elegant Pattern, Waxwork in Figure, Fruit, or Flowers, Shell Ditto, or grotesque, Painting in Water Colours and Mezzotinto; also the Art of taking off Foliage, with

250 [Annapolis] *Md. Gaz.*, July 28, 1774, 2, col. 3.

251 *Va. Centinel or Winchester Mercury*, May 28, 1788, 3, col. 4; Oct. 21, 1788.

252 *Va. Gaz.*, Nov. 24, 1752.

253 *Ibid.*, Jan. 24, 1788, 3, col. 3.

several other Embellishments necessary for the Amusement of Persons of Fortune who have Taste. Specimens of the Subscriber's Work may be seen at her House, as also of her Scholars; having taught several Years in Norfolk, and elsewhere, to general Satisfaction. She flatters herself that those Gentlemen and Ladies who have hitherto employed her will grant her their farther Indulgence, as no Endeavours shall be wanting to complete what is above mentioned, with a strict Attention to the Behaviour of those Ladies intrusted to her Care.

"Reading will be her peculiar Care; Writing and Arithmetick will be taught by a Master properly qualified; and if desired, will engage Proficients in Musick and Dancing."[254]

Writing a beautiful hand is a rare accomplishment today— and almost as unnecessary as it is rare. But in Colonial days, when communication was chiefly by means of letters, writing was a necessary art. Masters specialized in the various hands, and were ready, with samples of writing, to convince prospective pupils that rapid progress was possible and a high degree of skill within reach. The writing master was frequently one who kept accounts for private business concerns, executed public and private documents, or perhaps a teacher of bookkeeping and kindred subjects. Men needed writing as a practical aid in business; and women did, too, no doubt, in many instances. But some women, as well as men, who were innocent of writing and other "book learning" conducted businesses. Though women engaged in many trades,[255] it must be assumed that their chief need of writing was for polite correspondence. To give them this elegant art, no master has been found in the Southern colonies equal to the celebrated William Elphinstone who for so many years taught writing in Philadelphia and New York. They may have existed, but were not so clever as he at writing glowing advertisements. Thomas Lyttleton, who had, for a time, been educating the youth of London in "writing, arithmetic (both vulgar and decimal), merchants accounts [and] geometry," advertised (1762) that "young Ladies are taught the Italian Hand."[256] "B. W., writing master" of South Carolina (1774) had "a few leisure hours every Day" which he was willing "to employ in waiting on

[254] *Va. Gaz.*, Feb. 27, 1772, 3, col. 3.
[255] See pp. 257 ff.
[256] *Md. Gaz.*, Jan. 21, 1762, 3, col. 1.

Ladies at their own houses, to teach them the Italian or any other hand''; more than that, he instructed them in ''that useful Part of Education, corresponding by Letter in a polite, familiar Style.''[257]   Again, Mr. Clifford, at ''terms very moderate,'' offered to teach ''writing, in all its different branches,'' to ladies and gentlemen. For this employment he felt himself ''perfectly adequate'' and offered to show ''specimens of his writing'' at the Coffee House, Harris's Hotel, and the ''different printing offices in the city.''[258]

Even ornamental needlework had its practical uses; reading, writing, arithmetic, and pastry wonders, too, had a utilitarian end; but private Colonial masters were not so stupid as to devote themselves wholly to such things! Passing by the rudiments and ornamental useful arts, we come to the most favored social accomplishments: music, dancing, drawing, painting, riding, and a knowledge of the French tongue. These subjects constituted a major part of the offerings of private masters. Music, French, and dancing masters were especially numerous, and presumably well patronized, in Charleston at an early date, and were always advertised after the founding of the first paper, 1732–3. Drawing and painting were close competitors, while opportunity was not lacking for instruction in languages such as Italian and Spanish. Other languages were offered, but probably few, if any, ladies studied them.[259]

Music masters of every description are represented. In 1739, ''a person lately arrived'' in Charleston offered to teach ''Young People in the art of Psalmody, according to the exact rule of the Gamut in all the various measures both of the old or new version''; another, with ''a collection of books for the purpose,'' wished (1753) to open an ''evening school for instructing Persons in plain Psalmody''; Elizabeth Smith, of Maryland, who had taught ''singing in sundry parts of this Province,'' proposed to open a school of Psalmody in Annapolis (1764); James Badger opened a school ''for the tuition of vocal music'' (1794); while ''vocal or instrumental music'' was offered by a teacher in North

[257] S. C. Gaz., Feb. 4, 1774, Supplement, 2, col. 2.
[258] S. C. State Gaz., Mch. 22, 1794, 4, col. 1.
[259] McCrady: Hist. of S. C., II, 490 ff.

Carolina, in 1795.[260] Some teachers simply taught music,[261] but most of them indicated their specialties: Mrs. Sully, the Forte-Piano;[262] Frederick Grundzweig, the Harpsichord, Viol, Guitar, and German Flute ("having a thorough Knowledge of those instruments");[263] Francis Russworm, the "Violin, German and Common Flutes";[264] Mr. Singleton, the Violin;[265] Thomas Woll, from the "Theater-Royal" in London, undertook to "teach Ladies and Gentlemen to play upon the Guittar";[266] and likewise "a young lady lately arrived in Williamsburg," in 1775.[267] Some music masters established schools; others would go into the houses of gentlemen as tutors; while still others would call at particular hours to give lessons. Some masters taught other subjects. Thus one offered to "teach arithmetic in all its Branches" and to show samples of his writing; another would show ladies how "to dance a minuet after the newest and most fashionable Method." As a rule, no number of pupils was specified as necessary to secure the teacher; but Mrs. Smith wanted a "sufficient number of scholars" for her vocal classes; and Singleton would "give attendance at York, Hampton and Norfolk," if there were "not less than six in any one place." Violin was to be taught "at a Pistole each per Month, and a Pistole Entrance. . . . " For "Guittar" at their houses the price was a guinea per month (12 lessons) or five guineas for six months.

The dancing master came more nearly to a complete concentration on his art than other masters. Only occasionally did he attempt to teach other subjects. One, however, was extremely versatile. In 1738, a school was advertised for teaching dancing, writing and cyphering, and a general store was run in connection with it;[268] Mr. Goodwin, formerly teacher and "principal Dancer at the Theater in Philadelphia" and now (1797) em-

260 *S. C. Gaz.*, Feb. 15, 1739, 2, col. 3; Nov. 16, 1753, 3, col. 1; [Annapolis] *Md. Gaz.*, Apr. 5, 1764, 2, col. 3; *S. C. State Gaz.*, Feb. 28, 1794, 1, col. 4; *N. C. Gaz.*, May 23, 1795, 4, col. 3.

261 *S. C. Gaz.*, June 2–9, 1753, 4, col. 1.

262 *S. C. State Gaz.*, Apr. 30, 1794, 4, col. 1.

263 *S. C. Gaz.*, Mch. 30–Apr. 6, 1747, 2, col. 2.

264 *Va. Gaz.*, May 16, 1771, 3, col. 1.

265 *Ibid.*, June 25, 1752, 3, col. 1.

266 *S. C. Gaz.*, Dec. 31, 1765, 2, col. 3.

267 Stanard: *op. cit.*, 313.

268 *S. C. Gaz.*, Aug. 31, 1738, 4, col. 2.

ployed at the Pittsborough (N. C.) Academy, offered instruction in dancing and playing the guitar;[269] James Cliquet taught dancing and "the Science of Defense";[270] and Thomas Pike introduced himself as "dancing, fencing and music master."[271]   A great number of schools—of the better sort, doubtless—advertised nothing but dancing instruction.   In the *South Carolina Gazette* (1732) there was a notice of the settlement of the estate of William Brawn, dancing master.   Though it is not stated that he had taught dancing in Charleston, it is probable he had done so.[272]   William Dering was teaching dancing, in 1749; Nicholas Scanlan, in 1750; the famous school of Andrew Rutledge was open "for the better education of young gentlemen and ladies, with the greatest dispatch and diligence," in 1761; and Francis Guy announced he had a "commodious room" and "commenced teaching dancing" in 1794.[273]

Anthony Smith opened his dancing school at Annapolis in 1759, and George Abington, in 1761.[274]   In Williamsburg the well-known actress, Sarah Hallam, after leaving the stage, opened a "Dancing School" where she hoped "Gentlemen and Ladies will be Kind enough in sending their daughters" and promised "entire satisfaction," for "no care or Pain on her part" would be wanting.[275]   Richard Coleman's School, at the Palace in Newbern, North Carolina, where he taught (1795) "from Candle light till nine-o'clock"; that of Mr. Loysel and Mr. Perrin (1796) in Newbern; Loysel's school in Wilmington (N. C.), to which he went from Newbern about 1798; and "a French Gentleman's school" (1798), established in North Carolina because he had ill health and wanted to leave Norfolk, Virginia, offered instruction in Terpsichorean art to the Tar Heel youth around the close of the eighteenth century.[276]

269 *N. C. Minerva and Fayetteville Advt.*, Nov. 4, 1797, 4, col. 3.

270 *S. C. Gaz.*, July 31–Aug. 7, 1749, 3, col. 1.

271 *Ibid.*, Oct. 22–29, 1764, 3, col. 2.

272 *Ibid.*, Aug. 5–12, 1732.

273 *Ibid.*, Dec. 4–11, 1749, 1; June 4–11, 1750, 1, col. 2; Jan. 31–Feb. 7, 1761, 2, col. 1; and *S. C. State Gaz.*, Mch. 4, 1794, 4, col. 4.

274 *Md. Gaz.*, Mch. 22, 1759, 3; Jan. 1, 1761, 3.

275 *Va. Gaz.*, Aug. 26, 1775, 3, col. 3; also Stanard: *op. cit.*, 250.

276 *N. C. Gaz.*, Nov. 7, 1795, 3, col. 3; Feb. 27, 1796, 3, col. 3; *Hall's Wilmington* [N. C] *Gaz.*, Mch. 29, 1798, 3, col. 1; *N. C. Journal*, Feb. 26, 1798, 3, col. 3.

To the very simple announcements of the foregoing dancing masters, that of Mr. Capus, lately arrived from the Royal Opera in Paris, formed quite a contrast. The former taught "dancing," but he, "the plain minuet, the minuet of the Graces, the Hunting, and the minuet de la Cour, with their respective Gavotes; the Allamande; with all the steps and figures for Cotillions, Country Dances and the Hornpipe." A "Private school" was provided for those who could not attend the "Public." In connection with dancing, scholars were taken in harpsichord, forte piano, violin, German flute, guitar, and violincello and the French language.[277] A year later Capus had joined with Moody "at the Mason's Hall" where they continued instruction in all the dances but ceased to advertise music and French.[278] Another specialist in dancing was Thomas Turner, who improved himself under "Monsieur Sicard (formerly pupil of Vestries) and Professor of Dancing in Philadelphia," and announced to Charleston and vicinity he would "introduce a variety of new steps and figures and minuet de la Cour."[279]

A few masters named the price for instruction: Anthony Smith, "a pistole a quarter, and half a pistole entrance"; Abington, a "Guinea entrance and a Guinea a quarter"; Sarah Hallam, "20 shillings Entrance and 4£ a year"; Capus, with an elaborate offering, was more expensive,—"one guinea entrance and 12 pounds per annum, payable every month in advance." Loysel, who appears to have encouraged dancing for its effect on the carriage of the body, assuring prospectives it would enable persons "to enter and leave a company in a polite manner," asked "six dollars a quarter" for day and "eight dollars per quarter" for night pupils, one half always to be paid on entering. Other masters were content to announce terms as "most moderate"; or as another one asserts, "his terms shall not exceed his deserts."

Drawing and painting were often taught in combination, sometimes by special teachers in connection with a dancing school— as in the case of Roberts, who taught the "art of Dancing" in Charleston in 1736;[280] or in a general boarding school, to those

277 *Va. Gaz.*, Jan. 11, 1787, 4, col. 3.
278 *Ibid.*, Feb. 28, 1788, 3, col. 2.
279 *State Gaz. of S. C.*, Sept. 13, 1790, 2, col. 2,
280 *S. C. Gaz.*, Mch. 27–Apr. 3, 1736, 2, col. 2.

who wished to pay for them as extra subjects.[281]   Again, drawing was taught as an adjunct to embroidery, that ladies might not need to depend on others to draw their designs for them.[282]   Mr. Rogers, who announced his school for both sexes in the Newbern (N. C.) paper, flattered himself that he should "meet with encouragement." "The ladies will find the utility of it in working needlework and drawing for their own amusement"; and "young gentlemen will likewise find it beneficial in . . . travelling . . . to sketch out the landscapes in any place or building."[283]   He painted portraits, "large and in miniature."   John Thomas, also, taught ladies to "shade with the Indian ink pencil," as "an amusement to their genius" and because it would be "serviceable to them in needlework."   This he did in addition to teaching "reading, writing, . . . merchant's accounts and navigation."[284]   Miniature painting, which became one of the favorite special studies in the academies of the early nineteenth century, was occasionally advertised in the latter part of the eighteenth.   Mr. Peter Henri announced a "school for miniature painting" in Charleston, in 1792.[285]

In the eighteenth century few people thought of physical exercises and recreation from the standpoint of its effect on health. Even dancing, which was so universally taught in the cities, was simply a diversion and social accomplishment to masters and pupils alike.   Almost a century elapsed before Dio Lewis began to popularize it as a physical health exercise.[286]   Riding as a sport and diversion was indulged in generally by gentlemen of the South, and occasionally by the ladies.   Thomas Griffith, just returned from Philadelphia (1775), announced he would break horses "for the road or menage" and teach "gentlemen and ladies to ride the same as is practised in the best schools in London."[287]

To the social graces of their children, derived from music, dancing, drawing, painting, and riding, Colonial fathers and

[281] E.g., Mrs. Lessley's school, where her husband taught "Drawing and Painting as usual."—*Ibid.*, Mch. 6, 1775, 4, col. 3.

[282] *Ibid.*, May 11–16, 1748, 4, col. 2.

[283] *State Gaz. of N. C.*, Oct. 4, 1787, 4, col. 2.

[284] *S. C. Gaz.*, Feb. 6–13, 1755, 4, col. 2.

[285] *State Gaz. of S. C.*, Mch. 22, 1792.

[286] See p. 103, Vol. II.

[287] *S. C. Gaz.*, Apr. 10, 1775, 3, col. 3.

mothers sought to add something a little more intellectual, but valued most, apparently, as an accomplishment—a knowledge of the French tongue.   To men of broad culture and deep knowledge, such as Jefferson, French was, certainly, not a mere decoration but as necessary a part of education as English—and for girls the same as boys.[288]   This view was, however, an exception to the general rule.   Moreover, it should be added that the smattering of French words obtained by a few months of instruction in the school of itinerant masters, here today and away tomorrow, cannot have been of much solid benefit to a majority of students.   That such schools were generally patronized in Southern colonies after 1750, and to some extent before, there is no doubt.   There were masters in all the better cities, and seldom did they lament a lack of patronage.   One, however, in North Carolina declared he had "not met with such encouragement as he deserves in teaching French" and promised "to continue but one month" if there was "no better encouragement"; he hoped some who wished to learn "that useful and genteel language" would not neglect the opportunity, as he was wanted where he might have "encouragement suitable to his merit."[289]

Numerous masters taught French and nothing else: among those in South Carolina were Francis Varambaut (1742); Mark Anthony Beselleu, who had a "French Evening School" (1747) and a "French and English Day School"; John Jasroffoy (1754); Lewis Lestarjette, "Master of Languages from Paris" (1773); and Mrs. Sody (1777), who hoped "her Pronunciation, Mode, and Assiduity" would, "upon Trial, merit Encouragement."[290]   Similar schools were announced, in North Carolina, by Gasper Beaufort (1778), who had just come from Philadelphia and was doomed to be disappointed at his reception; "Citizen" Gailliard who lived with "Citizen" Chaponell (1795) and desired to teach French "grammatically"; and Monsieur Reverchon (1796).   William Clajon, who had taught French in Northern cities, advertised a school for the "particular purpose" of teaching French, in Maryland, in 1756.[291]   Some gen-

[288] Page 275.

[289] *N. C. Gaz.*, Apr. 3, 1778, 4, col 1.

[290] *S. C. Gaz.*, May 22–29, 1742, 3, col. 2; July 13–20, 1747, 2, col. 2; Jan. 1, 1754, 3, col. 3; June 28, 1773, 1; Apr. 14, 1777, 4, col. 3.

[291] *N. C. Gaz.*, Mch. 6, 1778, and Apr. 3, 1778, 4, col. 1; June 20, 1795, 1, col. 3; Apr. 30, 1796, 3, col. 3; *Md. Gaz.*, Feb. 12, 1756, 3.

tlemen, such as the one who advertised in the *Maryland Gazette*
(1747),[292] David Delescure, "near the Quaker's Meeting in
Charleston" (1735–6),[293] and Benjamin Goy (1771)[294] were presumably far more accomplished and taught several languages, including Italian, English, and Portuguese, besides French. Bartholomew Le Petit, of Norfolk, Va., who offered to teach the
French tongue "in its greatest purity and elegance," having
made it "his favorite study for several years," likewise taught
writing and arithmetic, and carried on an evening school for
those "whose Business may prevent them from receiving Instructions in the Day."[295] Marquis de Clugney and his "family"
offered to teach French, vocal and instrumental music, dancing,
and drawing, in 1798.[296]

Far the greater proportion of French masters were natives of
France, born of French parents, and many were educated in
Paris—if all details of their announcements are to be trusted.
Two, Varambaut and Delescure, were readers of the French
church in Charleston; Clajon had been examined and certified at
the College in New York. A number of women, Widow Varnod,
Widow Bouchonneau, Mary Irwin (with Abraham Varnod) and
Mary Ann Valois, "just arrived in the Sally, from Paris," advertised as teachers of French in Charleston, and usually combined with it instruction in embroidery, other kinds of ornamental needle work, knitting, plain needlework, drawing, quilting—and reading and writing, in one instance.[297]

Beyond the schools of the rudiments and those of accomplishments there was a third type that taught a greater variety and
more advanced studies, usually to girls and boys. In this third

---

[292] June 16, 1747, 4.

[293] *S. C. Gaz.*, Jan. 17–24, 1735–6, 3, col. 2.

[294] *Ibid.*, Aug. 8, 1771, 1, col. 2.

[295] *Va. Gaz.*, Feb. 18, 1773, 2, col. 3.

[296] *State Gaz. of N. C.*, June 18, 1798, 4, col. 2.

[297] *S. C. Gaz.*, May 4–11, 1734, 3, col. 2; Jan. 1–8, 1750, 3, col. 2; Nov.
24–Dec. 1, 1759, 1, col. 3; other references to French and other language
schools may be mentioned: Mr. Sountaien's, Annapolis—[Annapolis] *Md.
Gaz.*, July 16, 1752; Alexander Rodahan, French, Latin and Italian—[An-
napolis] *Md. Gaz.*, Apr. 1, 1763; Mr. Curly, French and dancing, Baltimore—*Md. Jour. and Balt. Advt.*, Jan. 4, 1793; Gross and Bossier, French—
Md. Jour. and Balt. Advt., Feb. 12, 1793. By the end of the century they
were numerous.

group we see clearly the similarity to the academy and seminary course of study; but the school is still in the hands of a private master or mistress, is not subject to any trustees, and is not called "academy." A master for this more elaborate school was advertised for in 1775, in Virginia, when Port Royal desired a teacher "unexceptionable in point of character . . . to teach the English, Latin, and Greek languages in their purity and elegance, writing, arithmetic, accounts and the mathematics" in "a school for boys and girls."[298] Similarly, Bartholomew Le Petit advertised a school (1773) in Williamsburg, Virginia, where he would teach boys English, Latin, French, writing and arithmetic, and would wait upon ladies at their own houses.[299]

In South Carolina (1752), Henry Varnor announced he would teach reading, writing, arithmetic, merchants accounts, French, and needlework.[300] In 1768, it was announced, under the head of "Daniel's Island," that "young gentlemen and ladies may be taught English, Arithmetic, Latin, French and Spanish."[301] A year earlier, William Johnson, in an elaborate statement, called the attention of the public to his school where "children and youth of both sexes" were "instructed in Reading, Writing, Arithmetic, &c, agreeable to the following plan:

"I. In teaching the children to read, the strictest regard will be paid to an easy, graceful, yet manly pronunciation of the language; and in order to avoid those vicious habits of reading and pronouncing, which they so frequently acquire under persons not properly qualified for initiating them into the first principles of literature, he proposes to take children from their first setting out.

"II. Writing, he proposes to teach in that simple elegance which is its greatest ornament, avoiding all unnatural flourishing and useless decorations.

"III. As soon as they begin to write, he proposes to initiate them into the principles of the English Grammar, in a manner much more easy and familiar than that which is generally practised, and without much interfering with the ordinary business of the school.

298 Stanard: op. cit., 274.
299 Va. Gaz., June 3, 1773, 4, col. 1.
300 S. C. Gaz., Jan. 15, 1752, 2, col. 1.
301 Ibid., Jan. 11–18, 1768, 2, col. 4.

"It is a common, but too well grounded complaint, that a grammatical study of our own language seldom makes any part of the ordinary method of instructing youth in our English schools. To this neglect may justly be attributed the great incorrectness observable amongst almost all ranks of people in speaking and writing their native language: To remedy which, to teach the children to speak and write with propriety, is the point the proposer has in view; and experience has assured him that he has no reason to doubt of success.

"IV. Arithmetic he teaches in all its branches, both vulgar and decimal, together with Merchants Accompts, Trigonometry, and all the practical branches of the Mathematics, such as Gauging, Surveying and Navigation with the theory and practice of which he is well acquainted.

"V. At leisure hours, without much interfering with the business of the school, he proposes to teach the children of both sexes the Elements of Geography, by tracing out the boundaries, relative situations, latitude and longitude of all the kingdoms and countries of the world; giving, at the same time, a succinct account of their trade customs and manners. To which will be added all the principal problems in the Use of the Globe.

"VI. A course of experiments in Mechanics will likewise be exhibited, in which will be explained the construction, use and advantage, of the six mechanic powers, viz. the lever, the wheel and axle (commonly called the axis in peritrochio), the pully, the inclined plane, the wedge, and the screw, with their application to many important purposes in human life.

"VII. A course of lectures on select subjects in Natural Philosophy will also be exhibited, at proper seasons of vacation, as well for the instruction of the youth as of persons of riper years; to which his pupils will be admitted as a reward for their diligence and application to their studies, and to encourage them to proceed therein; but principally to cultivate in their tender minds a love of knowledge, and a taste for inquiring into the works of nature.

"As the above plan of English education is intended for general utility, the professor flatters himself with the hopes of meeting with encouragement, as he assures those parents and guardians who may be pleased to favor him with the care of instructing their children, that nothing shall be wanting on his part, that care and diligence, added to some considerable degree of experience, can supply, in order to bring the children forward in their learning, and to make their studies agreeable to them.''[302]

Similar schools, doubtless, but not as elaborately described, were those of Robert Gibson, William Nixon, McCormick and Edson, and Parker, near the close of the century.[303]

Of the broader type of school, for ''young ladies'' alone, may be named that of Mary Hext, who taught needlework and employed other masters for writing, arithmetick, dancing, and music in 1741;[304] that of Elizabeth and Rebecca Woodin (1764), teaching the ''most polite and useful branches of education . . . both French and English, writing, needlework, and dancing, &c,[305] to which were added, in 1767, reading, arithmetic, and music;[306] and that of Mrs. Alcock, in Maryland, offering English, French, geography, reading, writing, arithmetic, needlework, drawing and music.[307]

To a number of schools, offering a broader course of study, in the latter half of the eighteenth century, the appelation ''academy'' was applied. Walton announced such an ''academy'' in Charleston (1769), wherein the English language and the ''several other necessary and ornamental branches of Education'' were taught. History and geography were included, but whether as ''ornamental,'' ''necessary,'' or both is not known. The academy was open from nine to twelve and from three to six; and parents were to ''have free access to his Academy . . . to observe the mode of Education . . . and have a Perusal of any of his Lectures.'' The germ of the ''ladies' department,'' so common in the later academies, is seen in his announcement that ''a room . . . for young ladies, distinct from that'' of the gentlemen, is provided.[308] A later announcement named, specifically, ''moral philosophy'' and ''lectures upon oratory'' in addition to those above.[309]

[302] *Ibid.*, June 29–July 6, 1767, 3, col. 3.

[303] *S. C. Gaz.*, Feb. 31, 1791, 1, col. 2; May 2, 1794, 1, col. 4; *S. C. State Gaz.*, Oct. 29, 1796, 3, col. 1.

[304] *S. C. Gaz.*, July 30–Aug. 6, 1741, 3, col. 2.

[305] ''Little masters'' were taken, but only as day pupils—*Ibid.*, Oct. 15–22, 1764, 3, col. 1.

[306] *Ibid.*, June 22–29, 1767, 3, col. 1.

[307] *Md. Journal and Balt. Advt.*, Jan. 4, 1793, 4, col. 1.

[308] *S. C. Gaz.*, Dec. 7, 1769, 4, col. 3.

[309] *Ibid.*, Jan. 4, 1770, 2, col. 2.

In 1774, an academy for both sexes "under the patronage of several respectable gentlemen of this province" was announced in Queen-street, Charleston. This was in charge of a clergyman, once a teacher in Great Britain, and another who had "completed his studies at the University of Paris, where he rendered himself master of the French language." The subjects to be taught were "English Grammar, Latin, Greek, French, Writing, Arithmetic, Bookkeeping, Geography, Algebra, Geometry, &c. and different branches of Natural Philosophy." Apparatus was to be secured "as soon as possible" for "the experimental part

Mr. WALTON

Takes the Liberty of informing the Public,

THAT he has opened his ACADEMY for instructing YOUTH in the ENGLISH LANGUAGE, and initiating them in SEVERAL OTHER NECESSARY AND ORNAMENTAL BRANCHES OF EDUCATION, at Mr. Allwood's, in Queen-Street; where regular Attendance is given from Nine to Twelve in the Morning, and from Three to Six in the Afternoon.

Such Parents, who are pleased to favour him with the Care of their Children, may, whenever they chuse, have free Access to his Academy, in order to observe the Mode of Education and may likewise have a Perusal of any of his Lectures.

He purposes to attend young Ladies at their own Houses, as to instruct them in reading and speaking the English Language with Propriety, as well as to give them a Taste for Geography and History.

N. B. There is a Room at the Academy, for young Ladies distinct from that in which the young Gentlemen are to be.

WALTON'S ACADEMY, ADVERTISED IN *South Carolina Gazette*, DEC. 7, 1769

of Philosophy." "The frequent visits of parents and gentlemen of learning" were desired; and they were convinced "that the gentlemen of this Province who have distinguished themselves by their public spirited liberality to the northern academies," by sending children north to study, would be "still more ready to cherish any infant Seminary of Learning in their own Country."[310]

In 1790, "A lady, Capable of superintending the education of her sex" proposed to establish an "academy" "on an extensive

[310] *Ibid.*, Mch. 14, 1774, 3, col. 3.

plan . . . to introduce . . . pupils gradually to an acquaintance
with those arts and accomplishments . . . sought for as indispensable requisites by the more opulent classes of society.'' The
school was to open in the "large room in Beresford's Alley."
Visitors were to be chosen; pupils were to be divided into three
classes; premiums were to be awarded for merit in each class;
and promotions made at stated periods, after examinations "held
twice every year" under the inspection of the visitors. The
"plan" of organization, it seems, was more "extensive" and
more novel than the range of instruction, for the only studies
named were "grammatical knowledge of the English language,"
reading, writing, needlework (useful and ornamental), French,
geography, music, dancing and drawing.[311] To bring the "institution" before the public attention in a more effective way, the
"lady" who proposed to establish it "read a lecture on elocution," with tickets at five shillings each.[312]

A "French and English Academy," under Mrs. O'Connor, at
100 Tradd Street (1791), intended to teach young ladies French,
reading and English grammar. It was asserted that young
ladies of New York and Alexandria (Virginia, presumably) who
had been, "for several years, under the tuition of ignorant men
or more illiterate women" had acquired under Mrs. O'Connor
"the art of reading with observance of pause, emphasis, and
period, in the course of six or nine months."[313] In a later notice
of the "Academy," in addition to the above subjects, writing,
arithmetic, needlework, millinery, music, dancing, and drawing
were mentioned. Pupils were treated "with tenderness as well
as politeness"; and parents were to be consulted as to their
"regimen and diet." The young ladies' "own wishes" were to
be "reasonably indulged." To "excite emulation and animate
their diligence," parents and guardians were urged to attend
public exhibitions of reading "every day precisely at 12
o'clock."[314] Another "French and English Academy" was
operated at "No. 66 Meeting-Street" by a "governess" who
shunned "any parade which she probably might be entitled to"
(a thrust, probably, at the advertising methods of Mrs. O'Con-

[311] State Gaz. of S. C., Nov. 11, 1790, 4, col. 4.
[312] Ibid., Nov. 18, 1790, 3, col. 3.
[313] Ibid., Jan. 13, 1791, 2, col. 4; also Feb. 7, 1791, 1, col. 4.
[314] Ibid., Apr. 21, 1791, 1, col. 1.

PENSION FRANÇAISE.

*Conditions auxquelles Madame ̷ ARDI reçoit
en penſion des jeunes Demoiſelles & ſe
charge de leur Éducation.*

Pour Penſion, & leçons: de Grammaire Françaiſe, d'Écriture, d'Orthographe, d'Élocution,
d'Arithmétique, de Géographie, de Couture, &
divers Ouvrages à l'Aiguille; *par mois 14 piaſtres.*
L'Anglais, l'Italien, l'Hiſtoire, la Chronologie, le Deſſein, la Mythologie, & le Piano·Forte; *par mois 10 piaſtres.*
(On procurera auſſi des Maîtres pour la Danſe
& le Chant ſi les Parens le déſirent.)
Pour l'Entrée 10 piaſtres.
Blanchiſſage par mois 2 piaſtres. ̲
Les Penſionnaires auront ſoin de ſe pourvoir
des articles qu'il eſt d'uſage de porter avec ſoi
dans les maiſons de cette eſpece.
*Madame Rivardi croit ſuperflu d'aſſurer ici, qu'
elle veillera ſans relâche à la ſanté, & aux mœurs
de ſes Éleves.*

CONDITIONS POUR LES EXTERNES.

La Grammaire Françaiſe, l'Écriture, l'Orthographe, l'Élocution, l'Arithmétique, la Géographie, la Couture, & divers Ouvrages d'Aiguille;
par mois 4 piaſtres. d'Entrée 3 piaſtres.
La langue Anglaiſe; *p. m. 2 piaſ. d'E. 2 piaſ.*
La langue Italienne; *p. m. 2 p. & demie. d'E. 3 p.*
L'Hiſtoire, la Chronologie, la Mythologie;
par mois 2 piaſtres. d'Entrée 2 piaſtres.
Le Deſſein; *par m. 2 piaſt. d'Entrée 2 piaſtres.*
Le Piano-Forte; *par m. 5 piaſt. d'En. 2 piaſtr.*
Fleurs artificielles, Paniers dito; *par mois une
piaſtre & demie.*
Broderie·de toute eſpece; *par mois idem.*
Frankfort près de Philadelphie, 1802.
N·B. Madame Rivardi réſidera durant l'hyver
à Philadelphie.

SCHOOL ADVERTISEMENT OF MADAME RIVARDI, NEW ORLEANS *Moniteur de la
Louisiane*, AUG. 28, 1802

nor).[315] Mr. and Mrs. Paget, too, opened an academy for girls
at 6 Cumberland Street, where they taught reading, writing,
English grammar, arithmetic, practical branches of mathematics,

[315] *Ibid.*, Apr. 1, 1791, 2, col. 4.

geography, use of globes, needlework, and drawing.[316] Haller, a Swiss, opened an academy for girls at Richmond in 1798.[317] Many *pensions* for girls were advertised in the papers of New Orleans.

In the decade of the nineties the "academy" was frequently advertised in Maryland, Virginia, and Carolina papers. D. Searle, at Harvey's Neck, Perquimans County, North Carolina, advertised an academy for gentlemen and ladies, where were taught writing, arithmetic, English grammar, reading and speaking the English language, Latin, Greek, geography, navigation, surveying, bookkeeping, "and any other branches of learning usually taught in academies."[318] An announcement of an examination of the Pittsborough Academy in 1797 showed that ladies were in attendance.[319] According to the "Plan of Education" adopted by the trustees of Fayetteville Academy, it was to "be considered a school for the education of both sexes" and "a directress to superintend the female classes in education and manners" was to be engaged. English, Latin, Greek, history, geography, use of globes, *Belles Lettres,* mathematics, moral and natural philosophy, French, "other modern languages," music, drawing, and dancing were offered. The latter, however, must "not interfere with the usual exercises of the Academy."[320] Lumberton Academy, in 1798, was also designed for both sexes. David Kerr, "formerly . . . principal teacher and professor of languages in the University . . ." was secured as principal, and the "most zealous endeavors of the trustees and teachers" were put forth to make it "a seminary of good learning and good morals." The subjects of instruction were English composition, Latin, Greek, arithmetic, bookkeeping, geography, the use of globes, geometry, trigonometry, practical branches of navigation, surveying, elements of history, natural philosophy, moral philosophy, and needlework.[321]

In the foregoing, only those schools have been referred to which were open to girls, or for girls alone. There were, of course,

316 *Ibid.,* May 3, 1792, 1, col. 1.
317 Blandin: *Higher Ed. of Women in the South before 1860,* 311.
318 *State Gaz. of N. C.,* Jan. 22, 1789, 3, col. 3.
319 *N. C. Minerva and Fayetteville Advt.,* June 3, 1797, 3, col. 3.
320 *Ibid.,* June 30, 1798, 3, col. 3.
321 *Ibid.,* July 7, 1798, 3, col. 3.

many whose advertisements did not make clear whether they were for boys exclusively. Some of these, that may have admitted girls, were advertised between 1768 and 1778.[322]

[322] Rose, *Va. Gaz.*, Apr. 14, 1768, 3, col. 1; Burges, Oct. 24, 1771, 3, col. 3; Hoell, *N. C. Gaz.*, Sept. 2, 1774, 4, col. 2; one at Public School House, Newbern, June 30, 1775; George Harrison, July 31 and July 24, 1778, 4, col. 1.

CHAPTER VII

NEW CONCEPT OF WOMEN'S EDUCATION

In the past three chapters, reference has been made to the typical education of girls in New England, Central and Southern colonies. With few exceptions this education was of rudimentary character. But in the larger cities, private masters, free from the hampering restraint of the church, the town 'prudentials,' and the heavy hand of tradition, began to cater to young women by offering some higher studies. These new masters and their schools were the harbingers of a novel and more liberal conception of women's education.

To this new idea, contributions were made both by theory and practice, but probably the most numerous were made by the latter. Chief among the contributors to the thought of the movement were Benjamin Rush, DeWitt Clinton, Charles Burroughs, Emma Willard, Mrs. Phelps, Catherine E. Beecher, Thomas H. Gallaudet, William Russell and William Woodbridge. In practice, women's education gained much through the influence of the school of the Moravians at Bethlehem, Pennsylvania, 1749; John Poor in Philadelphia, about 1787; Caleb Bingham in Boston, 1784; George B. Emerson in Boston, 1823; Zilpah P. Grant at Derry, New Hampshire, 1824, and later at Ipswich, 1828; and Mary Lyon, first with Miss Grant at Ipswich and later at Mt. Holyoke, 1837. Emma Willard, Mrs. Phelps and Catherine Beecher are important for their practical work at Troy, New York, Ellicotts Mills, Maryland, and Hartford, Connecticut, respectively, as well as for their written and spoken encouragement of the movement. The new institutions which represented the actual effort toward woman's education were female academies and seminaries, the high schools, and the normal schools.[1]

We have already referred to the fact that the lack of educational facilities for girls came to be lamented by several people of intelligence near the close of the Colonial period. The last

[1] For the origin and development of these three institutions see Chapters VIII, IX, X, and XI.

quarter of that century, and the beginning of the next, saw a host of advocates of a higher education. As early as 1753, there appeared in the public press *An Essay on Woman,* wherein it was maintained that ''as to the capacity most women have for letters, it has been so conspicuous in all ages, that it can admit of no dispute; and did men, who have at present the power in their hands, think it safe to trust their natural ingenuity with the advantages of education they would soon find the difference betwixt the activity of their genius, and the Solidity, as they call it, of their own. . . .''[2] A score of years later, Neal wrote, with reference to the Female Academy of Philadelphia: ''To Vindicate the Rights of Woman, is a task as pleasing as it is uncommon. To show . . . the dignity, excellence and intrinsic worth of the Female Mind, is a generous, important and delightful exertion of genius. To direct the Fair Sex in the attainment of useful and ornamental acquirements . . . to caution against improper, nugatory and trivial pursuits, is an object of the greatest magnitude. . . .''[3]

In Benjamin Rush, 'female education' had a more able and influential advocate, even if the absolute originality[4] of his essay on the subject may be questioned. Though there is a distinct resemblance to the education of girls recommended by Fénelon, there can be no question of the effect of Rush's essay on opinion in this country. Not only was he influential in the establishment of the Academy of Philadelphia, but his writing was often quoted, and his example was proudly pointed to in the first half of the next century.[5]

Rush lays down the first principle that education of young ladies ''should be accommodated to the state of Society, manners and government of the country. . . .'' Therefore, ours must be different from that of France or Great Britain. The factors of American life which definitely influence female education are: first, early marriages, which leave little time for it, and that little time must be spent on ''the more useful branches of literature''; second, the ''state of property,'' which requires that every one in

[2] *N. Y. Gazette,* Mar. 5, 1753; see also an interesting ''. . . Essay by a young Lady, not sixteen'' [*N. Y. Gazette,* Apr. 16, 1767].

[3] Neal: *Essay on the Education and Genius of the Female Sex.*

[4] Good: *Benjamin Rush and his Services to American Education,* 226–34. Compare, too, pp. 62–66.

[5] See, for example, *Am. Annals of Ed.,* IV, 85–7.

BENJAMIN RUSH

America work to advance his fortune, makes it necessary that females be capable of assisting as "stewards and guardians of their husbands' property"; third, as the husband is taken from home on business, it follows that the wife must be prepared to intelligently educate her children; fourth, political freedom and men's possibility of taking part in the conduct of government requires that women "should be qualified to a certain degree by a peculiar and suitable education, to concur in instructing their sons in the principles of liberty and government"; and, fifth, the lack of a class of servants who know their duties, and do them, requires that female education be directed to domestic affairs— for, as he quotes an American woman, "They are good servants, who will do well with good looking after."[6]

His outspoken enthusiasm for an education differentiated from that of Great Britain, and his sharp criticism of our imitative tendency, may have given impetus to the rapid development of institutions which came about in the United States. "It should not surprise us," he says, "that British customs with respect to female education have been transplanted into our American schools and families. We see marks of the same incongruity, of time and place, in many other things. We behold our houses accommodated to the climate of Great Britain, by eastern and western directions. We behold our ladies panting in a heat of ninety degrees, under a hat and cushion, which were calculated for the temperature of a British summer. We behold our citizens condemned and punished by a criminal law, which was copied from a country where maturity in corruption renders public executions a part of the amusements of the nation. It is high time to awake from this servility—to study our own character— to examine the age of our country—and to adopt manners in every thing, that shall be accommodated to our state of society, and to the forms of our government. In particular it is incumbent upon us to make ornamental accomplishments yield to principles and knowledge, in the education of our women."[7]

The content of an American girl's education should consist of English language, so that she can read and spell correctly, writ-

---

[6] *Thoughts upon Female Education*—Commencement Address at the Young Ladies' Academy, Philadelphia, July 28, 1787; later published at the request of the visitors. In Rush: *Essays, Literary, Moral and Philosophical*, 75 *ff*.
[7] *Ibid*.

ing a "fair and legible hand," a knowledge of "figures and book-keeping," geography, chronology, biography, and travels, a general acquaintance with astronomy, natural philosophy and chemistry—of the latter, enough to be useful for domestic and culinary purposes—vocal music, dancing, poetry and moral essays. To these is added "regular instruction in the Christian religion" and an emphasis on the necessity of strict discipline, but not severity.

Instrumental music he would not encourage, not that he is insensible to the charms of it, but because it requires much time in practice and a great outlay of money for instruments and instructors, who charge "extravagant fees." The country is not yet ready for this. Likewise, the present "passion for reading novels" which "so generally prevails among the fair sex" is decried. They should read history, biography, and moral essays. Dancing, which he recommends, is to be a substitute for the "ignoble pleasures of drinking and gaming, in our assemblies of grown people"; but he looks hopefully to the time when developed conversational abilities will cause dancing to be "wholly confined to children." To Rousseau's principle of wasting children's time profitably he gives a qualified assent, for "we often impair their health, and weaken their capacities, by imposing studies upon them, which are not proportioned to their years."

Rush recognizes the experimental character of the academy and that the success of it can be determined only by "the future conduct and character of our pupils. To you, therefore, young ladies, an important problem is committed for solution; and that is, whether our present plan of education be a wise one, and whether it be calculated to prepare you for the duties of social and domestic life." In closing the address, he sets forth the excellent points of the academy organization: "By means of this plan, the power of teachers is regulated and restrained, and the objects of education are extended. By the separation of the sexes in the unformed state of their manners, female delicacy is cherished and preserved. Here the young ladies may enjoy all the literary advantages of a boarding-school, and at the same time live under the protection of their parents. Here emulation may be excited without jealousy,—ambition without envy,—and competition without strife. The attempt to establish this new mode of education for young ladies, was an experiment, and the

EMMA WILLARD

success of it hath answered our expectations. Too much praise cannot be given to our principal and his assistants, for the abilities and fidelity with which they have carried the plan into execution. The proficiency which the young ladies have discovered in reading—writing—spelling—arithmetic—grammar—geography—music—and their different catechisms, since the last examination, is a less equivocal mark of the merit of our teachers, than anything I am able to express in their favour."[8]

Early in the nineteenth century, DeWitt Clinton, prominent in the public affairs of New York, gave great encouragement to girls' education by word and deed. In 1819, he lamented the fact that "beyond initiatory instruction, the education of the female sex is utterly excluded from the contemplation of our laws."[9] A year later, he rejoiced over the success of the Waterford Academy and recommended its assistance by governmental subsidy: "As this is the first attempt ever made in this country to promote the education of the female sex by the patronage of government; as our first and best impressions are derived from maternal affection; and as the female character is inseparably connected with happiness at home and respectability abroad, I trust that you will not be deterred by common-place ridicule from extending your munificence to this meritorious institution."[10] In the years between 1819 and 1828 many female academies and seminaries were chartered by New York State; but from Clinton's death till 1835, legislative activity was very slight.[11] Clinton's efforts on behalf of high schools and his interest in the promotion of teacher-training, though not limited to girls, probably hastened the improvement of their opportunities in these fields.[12]

It may have been the suggestion of a woman that gave direction to Clinton's energetic action on behalf of girls' education. Emma Willard, born in 1787, educated first at a district school, and later at an academy presided over by Dr. Miner, in Berlin,

---

[8] *Ibid.*

[9] *Messages from the Governors*, II, 927; see also Fitzpatrick: *Educational Views of Clinton*, 52.

[10] *Ibid.*, II, 1018; the Female Academy, at Philadelphia, had been chartered January 9, 1792. See p. 337.

[11] Fitzpatrick: *op. cit.*, 121–4.

[12] *Ibid.*, 109 *ff.* and 118 *ff.*

Connecticut, had, at seventeen years of age, begun an educational career as teacher of a village school.[13] She came through this experience with credit, though it was embarrassing on account of the severe discipline required on the first day. In her own words, "Our school was soon the admiration of the neighborhood." After further study at the schools of Mrs. Royce and the Misses Patten of Hartford, she again taught in Berlin, Westfield and Middlebury. While at Middlebury (1814) she still had no idea of doing more than relieving her husband's financial embarrassment and teaching a better school than those around her. But within a year or two she formed "the design of effecting an important change in education by the introduction of a grade of schools for women, higher than any heretofore known." She began to write "an address to the ————— Legislature . . ." but for two years did not fill in the blank. Meantime she sought to avoid the objection that she was visionary, by improving her reputation as a teacher in her school at Middlebury. In 1818, she had five pupils from Waterford; and, regarding this as a favorable omen, she decided to present her "plan" to Governor Clinton of New York, to whom it went with this letter:

"SIR,—Mr. Southwick will present to you a manuscript, containing a plan for improving the education of females, by instituting public seminaries for their use. Its authoress has presumed to offer it to your Excellency, because she believed you would consider the subject as worthy of your attention, and because she wished to submit her scheme to those exalted characters, whose guide is reason, and whose objects are the happiness and improvement of mankind; and among these characters where can plans to promote those objects hope for countenance, if not from Mr. Clinton.

"The manuscript is addressed to a legislature, although not intended for present publication. The authoress believed she could communicate her ideas with less circumlocution in this than in any other manner; and besides, should the approbation of distinguished citizens, in any of the larger and wealthier states, give hopes that such an application would be attended with success, a publication might then be proper, and the manuscript would need less alteration.

[13] Barnard: *Memoirs of Teachers, Educators, and Promoters of Education,* 125–268.

"Possibly your Excellency may consider this plan as better deserving your attention, to know that its authoress is not a visionary enthusiast, who has speculated in solitude without practical knowledge of her subject. For ten years she has been intimately conversant with female schools, and nearly all of that time she has herself been a preceptress. Nor has she written for the sake of writing, but merely to communicate a plan of which she fully believes that it is practicable; that, if realized, it would form a new and happy era in the history of her sex, and if of her sex, why not of her country, and of mankind? Nor would she shrink from any trial of this faith; for such is her conviction of the utility of her scheme, that could its execution be forwarded, by any exertion or any sacrifice of her own, neither the love of domestic ease, or the dread of responsibility, would prevent her embarking her reputation on its success.

"If Mr. Clinton should not view this plan as its authoress hopes he may, but should think the time devoted to its perusal was sacrificed, let him not consider its presentation to him as the intrusion of an individual ignorant of the worth of his time, and the importance of his high avocations, but as the enthusiasm of a projector, misjudging of her project, and overrating its value. . . ."[14]

Clinton's favorable view of her proposal has already been referred to, in his message to the Legislature. The institution at Waterford was incorporated, and Mrs. Willard left Middlebury to take charge of it. Another law was passed which gave female academies a share in the literary fund. In 1820, Governor Clinton recommended further encouragement to the school at Waterford, and a bill appropriating $2,000 passed the Senate but was lost in the House. The Regents also decided that none of the literary fund could go to the school.[15] Other efforts to secure the Legislature's support, in 1821 and 1823, were in vain, and resulted in the disillusionment of Mrs. Willard.

The objections to a seminary for women, which had so many points in common with colleges for men, were anticipated. That some would find it absurd to think of "sending ladies to college," she was certain; and she hastened to "observe, that the seminary here recommended, will be as different from those appropriated

14 *Ibid.*, 136.
15 *Ibid.*, 144.

to the other sex, as the female character and duties are from the male.''[16] The social end of the system of education was clearly stated:

"As evidence that this statement does not exaggerate the female influence in society, our sex need but be considered in the single relation of mothers. In this character, we have the charge of the whole mass of individuals, who are to compose the succeeding generation; during that period of youth, when the pliant mind takes any direction, to which it is steadily guided by a forming hand. How important a power is given by this charge! yet, little do too many of my sex know how, either to appreciate or improve it. Unprovided with the means of acquiring that knowledge which flows liberally to the other sex,—having our time of education devoted to frivolous acquirements, how should we understand the nature of the mind, so as to be aware of the importance of those early impressions which we make upon the minds of our children? or how should we be able to form enlarged and correct views, either of the character to which we ought to mould them, or of the means most proper to form them aright?

"Considered in this point of view, were the interests of male education alone to be consulted, that of females becomes of sufficient importance to engage the public attention. Would we rear the human plant to its perfection, we must first fertilize the soil which produces it. If it acquire its first bent and texture upon a barren plain, it will avail comparatively little should it be afterwards transplanted to a garden.''[17]

Mrs. Willard not only proposed a new system, but urged its importance by pointing out faults in the existing mode of education:

"They are temporary institutions formed by individuals, whose object is present emolument; these individuals cannot afford suitable accommodations, nor sufficient apparatus and libraries; neither do they, or can they, provide a sufficiency of instructors either in number or capacity; in such schools a system of classification is not, and cannot be carried out; it is for the interest of such schools to teach showy accomplishments, instead of solid and useful learning; the teachers are accountable to no particular persons or board of trustees, and hence the pub-

16 *Ibid.*, 137–8.
17 *Ibid.*, 138.

lic are sometimes imposed upon by incompetent, unworthy or dishonest individuals; [and] in these schools, thus independent of supervision, absurd regulations, improper exactions, and unfaithful negligence, pass unquestioned.'"[18]

As to the principles upon which female education should rest, there are two: studies must be selected either because they "improve the faculties" or that they may be useful for future life. Thus she put women's education on an equal footing with men's. These principles, if recognized, would support a practice that would offset the usual tendency "to fit them for displaying to advantage the charms of youth and beauty," and "to prepare them to please the other [sex]." Nevertheless, she would not be "understood to insinuate that we are not in particular situations to yield obedience to the other sex" nor "that our sex should not seek to make themselves agreeable to the other."

The necessary features of the female seminary were to be:

"1. A building, with commodious rooms for lodging and recitation, apartments for the reception of apparatus, and for the accommodation of the domestic department.

"2. A library, containing books on the various subjects in which the pupils were to receive instruction, musical instruments, some good paintings to form the taste and serve as models for the execution of those who were to be instructed in that art, maps, globes, and a small collection of philosophical apparatus.

"3. A judicious board of trust.

"4. Suitable instruction; first, moral and religious; second, literary; third, domestic; and fourth, ornamental.

.   .   .

"5. There would be needed, for a female, as well as for a male seminary, a system of laws and regulations, so arranged, that both the instructors and pupils would know their duty; and thus, the whole business, move with regularity and uniformity.'"[19]

Emphasis is placed on "natural, mental and moral philosophy" in her discussion of the subjects of instruction. The "ornamental branches" are retained not because they are immediately useful, but because of their formal training value. She

18 *Ibid.*, 138–9.
19 *Ibid.*, 140, 141.

says of music: "The harmony of sound has a tendency to produce a correspondent harmony of soul. . . ." Regarding the systematic teaching of domestic science, she took advanced ground:

"It is believed that housewifery might be greatly improved by being taught, not only in practice, but in theory. Why may it not be reduced to a system as well as other arts! There are right ways of performing its various operations, and there are reasons why those ways are right; and why may not rules be formed, their reasons collected, and the whole be digested into a system to guide the learner's practice?

"It is obvious that theory alone can never make a good artist; and it is equally obvious that practice, unaided by theory, can never correct errors, but must establish them. If I should perform anything in a wrong manner all my life, and teach my children to perform it in the same manner, still, through my life and theirs, it would be wrong. Without alteration there can be no improvement; but how are we to alter so as to improve, if we are ignorant of the principles of our art, with which we should compare our practice, and by which we should regulate it?"[20]

In explaining the public influence of seminaries, Mrs. Willard took a position which was destined soon to be accepted by all who were connected with the rising systems of common schools. Seminaries were to provide better teachers for lower schools. And though Horace Mann declared, later, that seminaries and academies had for the past fifty years failed to provide teachers,[21] and therefore recommended the creation of normal schools, it must be recognized that the former prepared the way for an institution devoted entirely to training teachers. Nine years after Mrs. Willard's "plan" was presented to New York, James G. Carter presented a memorial to the Legislature of Massachusetts praying for the "establishment of a seminary for the education of teachers."[22] Her estimate of this significant function of the female seminary follows:

"Such seminaries would constitute a grade of public education, superior to any yet known in the history of our sex; and through them the lower grades of female instruction might be

20 *Ibid.*, 140.
21 *Ibid.*, 402
22 *Ibid.*, 190.

controlled. The influence of public seminaries, over these, would operate in two ways; first, by requiring certain qualifications for entrance; and secondly, by furnishing instructresses, initiated in their modes of teaching, and imbued with their maxims.

"Female seminaries might be expected to have important and happy effects, on common schools in general; and in the manner of operating on these, would probably place the business of teaching children, in hands now nearly useless to society; and take it from those, whose services the state wants in many other ways.

"That nature designed our sex for the care of children, she has made manifest, by mental as well as physical indications. She has given us, in a greater degree than men, the gentle arts of insinuation, to soften their minds, and fit them to receive impressions; a greater quickness of invention to vary modes of teaching to different dispositions; and more patience to make repeated efforts. There are many females of ability, to whom the business of instructing children is highly acceptable; and who would devote all their faculties to their occupation. They would have no higher pecuniary object to engage their attention, and their reputation as instructors they would consider as important; whereas, when able and enterprizing men, engage in this business, they too often consider it, merely as a temporary employment, to further some other object, to the attainment of which, their best thoughts and calculations are all directed. If then women were properly fitted by instruction, they would be likely to teach children better than the other sex; they could afford to do it cheaper; and those men who would otherwise be engaged in this employment, might be at liberty to add to the wealth of the nation, by any of those thousand occupations, from which women are necessarily debarred.

"Any one, who has turned his attention to this subject, must be aware, that there is great room for improvement in the common schools,—both as to the mode of teaching, and the things taught; and what method could be devised so likely to effect this improvement, as to prepare by instruction, a class of individuals, whose interest, leisure, and natural talents, would combine to make them pursue it with ardor."[23]

The work of Willard became widely known and her circle of influence expanded. In 1830, she went to Europe, visiting

[23] *Ibid.*, 141-2.

schools in England and France. Through an acquaintance her
"Plan" was introduced into South America, and a college was
later established at Santa Fè de Bogota.[24] Later she was instrumental in establishing a school for native teachers in Athens,
Greece. In 1838, she prepared a pamphlet, "Letter to the
Willard Association for the Mutual Improvement of Female
Teachers," and shortly thereafter left the seminary. After
1840, she became interested in the improvement of the common
schools of Connecticut, was elected Superintendent of the Common Schools of Kensington, and formed a Female Common
School Association. There she planned to institute the system
of assistant teachers previously used at the Troy Seminary, with
the threefold object of promoting their own education, making
them useful in the business of the school, and of training them
by actual service, as well as theoretical instruction, to become
teachers in full. Her criticism of the reading books used in the
Kensington schools is significant:

"I have collected and examined the school books used in the
Kensington schools. The amount of fiction put into the hands
of the children, in their daily lessons, strikes me with surprise
and regret. Truth is the mother of science, and the ancient ally
of virtue. Fiction may mislead, even when she intends to do
good—truth, never. The mind that feeds on fiction, becomes
bloated and unsound, and already inebriated, still thirsts for
more. And has not so much of the mental ailment of our times
been fiction, that this delirium of the mind has become an evil
so pervading that we ought resolutely to shun its source, and turn
now to the simple element of pure truth? Some of these books,
too, contain low and vulgar language. Who would send a child
among clowns to learn manners?"[25]

Through Barnard's report to the legislature and his *Common
School Journal,* her work became known in other states. Through
numerous books, both scientific and elementary treatises for the
introduction of students, she rendered a service to education in
general. Her service to female education, and especially to the
"great art of teaching," was celebrated in the following lines of
Christopher C. Cox:

24 *Ibid.,* 157.
25 *Ibid.,* 163.

"In the great art of Teaching we shall find
"Its best exponent is a female mind.
"In all that wins by manner or address,
"As in scholastic discipline no less;
"In varied knowledge, oratoric sway,
"The ready pen that knowledge to convey;
"The skill all sciences to understand,
"Grapple abstrusest problems, hand to hand;
"Our Trojan WILLARD stands aloft confest
"By all, the wisest, noblest, and the best!"[26]

To be recognized by her contemporaries as a great benefactor of female education was Emma Willard's fortune. All acclaimed her. Catherine Beecher, in her volume of *Reminiscences* (1874), declared she was "one of the earliest and most distinguished pioneers in the efforts to secure higher education for woman."[27] To that date 13,500 pupils had been instructed at the Seminary, a high proportion of whom had become influential teachers elsewhere.[28]

In the *American Journal of Education* (1828) there appeared an article based on an address of Charles Burroughs, delivered in Portsmouth, New Hampshire, which was highly applauded. It was published afterwards as a pamphlet of forty-four pages by Childs and March, Portsmouth. In this address he, too, attacked the education of "ornamental or superficial acquirements" and bespoke encouragement of "that high system of instruction, which calls into vigorous exercise all the faculties of the soul, strengthens it by culture, stores it with knowledge, plants every virtue in the heart; and exalts the character by intellectual and moral excellence. This should be the lofty aim of female education."[29] Education is important for the sake of woman's personal happiness, that of her family, and the best interests of society. These arguments, presented at considerable length, are quite similar to those of Rush and Willard, already quoted. Though not novel in its views, the influence of such an address,

[26] *Ibid.*, 155; read at the Commencement of Frederick [Md.] Female Seminary, July 8, 1858.

[27] P. 164 *f.*

[28] At Patapsco, Maryland; Philadelphia; Columbia and Charleston, South Carolina; Washington, Pennsylvania; Brooklyn and Montreal; see an account of the life of Emma Willard in *Godey's Lady's Book*, Sept. 1870, 276 *ff.*

[29] *Am. Jour. Educ.*, III, 53–8.

designed to catch popular attention, is not to be questioned. The
editors commented, with evident pleasure and approval, on the
eloquence of Mr. Burroughs' appeal. As it is typical of arguments for women's education, advanced during the twenties and
thirties, a part is quoted:

"Let me now close this address, my friends, by urging on your
attention and liberality the claims of female education. These
claims, you perceive, are of the highest possible character, connected with all that is lovely and beautiful in the condition of
man,—with the personal happiness of every individual, with all
the comforts of home, with the best interests of the community,
and even with the growth and prosperity of our country. They
are connected with the condition of the countless multitude of
unborn millions, that are yet to be wafted upon the current of
time to eternity. They are connected with our own momentous
destiny at the last dread tribunal of Jehovah. Learning pleads
for woman to bring her energies and her charms to its exalted
cause. Religion pleads for woman, that she may be guided by
its cheering light, and adorned with its precious ornaments; that
she may be admitted to the temple of its sublime doctrines and
holy truths, to its chambers, decked with curious and glorious
workmanship by the hand of God. Science pleads for woman,
to open before her susceptible mind the mysterious and splendid
exhibitions of omniscience and infinite benevolence in the works
of nature. Wisdom speaks, as from the throne of God, and
pleads with woman to take fast hold of instruction, saying, 'let
her not go; keep her, for she is the end of thy life.' Patriotism
pleads for woman, that she may dwell for ever in the land of
liberty and virtue; that she may lend her influence to advance
our national prosperity; and that, illumined by the purest principles and warmed by a holy zeal, she may inculcate such lessons,
as shall render her descendants the invincible defenders of freedom and the true faith. Where can genius so sublimely exert
herself, where can eloquence be so righteously employed, where
can governments so wisely legislate, where can wealth be so
profitably expended, as in aiding the cause of female education;
—a cause which, though accomplishing wonders in improving the
condition of the world, is yet far behind the spirit of the age,
and the demands of society? Let us now hope, that its claims
will be regarded; and that woman may soon realize all the bless-

ings that learning, refinement, genius, eloquence, the efforts of man and the power of the Gospel can possibly confer upon her; 'that our daughters may be as cornerstones, polished after the similitude of a palace.' . . . It is by providing High Schools of instruction for females, that you are to make them the best and most successful teachers in the land, to render them ministering angels to countless beings, and to multiply the joys of learning and virtue. Here then are we taught that the advancement of female education is one of the most efficacious means for promoting the public good. This will clothe society with new beauty and new blessings. On the exertions of the intelligent and pious of the present age rests the immense responsibleness of the future character of our country. It has become the imperious duty of every people, of every government, to make abundant provision for female education.''[30]

A few weeks after the address of Burroughs, Thomas H. Gallaudet delivered a stirring plea for woman's better education, at the opening of the building erected for the Hartford Female Seminary.[31] Gallaudet had already published an important pamphlet in favor of special institutions for training teachers,[32] and for that reason his message was the more readily received. Throughout the address there is found the wisdom of the practical schoolman, able to criticize the evils of the present system which he knows at first hand. Accepting the importance of training the faculties, a view common then, he declares that female education, even more than male, places a one-sided emphasis on the training of memory. This is so because parents ask for that which gives a good appearance; and a crammed memory makes more show than a sound understanding of fewer elements. "Of what do the recitations of the younger classes in schools consist? Of the mere repeating of what has been committed to memory." But there is another power of great importance,—that of drawing conclusions. This rational capacity, he maintains, can be developed, for example, by the inductive teach-

30 *Ibid.*

31 This address was published at the trustees' request by Huntingdon, at Hartford, 1820; and liberal attention was given it in a review in the March, 1828, issue of the *Am. Jour. of Educ.*, III, 178–87.

32 *Plan of a Seminary for the Education of Instructors of Youth*, Boston, 1825.

ing of reading and arithmetic rather than exclusive reliance on memorization of page after page.

Of the advantage of his new method, he says: "This mode of leading the youthful mind, in the exercise of its own powers, to arrive at general truths, not only produces a deeper interest, and a more fixed attention; but begets habits of independent and inventive thought, and trains the pupil to more extensive and vigorous efforts in all her future researches."

But there are difficulties in the way: "It requires, indeed, a considerable degree of labour, and withal not a little ingenuity on the part of the teacher. It seems, too, at first, to be but making rather slow progress. It does not give the young pupil quite so much the appearance of knowing a great deal on a variety of subjects, as the usual mode of taking every thing on trust, on the authority of the books, and of the teacher, and almost constantly doing little else than commit to memory;—but, if I mistake not, to whatever extent it is pursued, in the same degree, will be found an original, vigorous, active mind.

"I am aware, that the popular sentiment is, that in childhood, and during the earlier stages of education, it is the memory alone which can be cultivated to any considerable extent; and that, as the judgment has not acquired a sufficient degree of maturity, it is the better way for the young pupil to be laying up, as fast as possible, an abundant stock of knowledge for future use."[33]

Just as he would sacrifice showy accomplishments of the memory for the more substantial values of a rational education, so he condemns, somewhat like Milton, the lack of attention to "a correct knowledge of the mother tongue," which is sacrificed in practice, because to know some Virgil or Greek Testament, to read French or Italian, has been estimated of greater importance. He concludes: "In conducting the education of young ladies, therefore, whatever other languages, or branches of study they may have time to attend to, secure, at least, their correct knowledge of the English language; and if a sacrifice of any language must be made, let all others be sacrificed rather than this."

Third, he finds a "defect in the education of females . . . that they are not sufficiently taught the practical uses to be made of the knowledge they acquire; and not . . . qualified . . . for the actual business of life." This is a pertinent criticism, espe-

[33] *Am. Jour. of Ed.*, III, 178–87.

cially as the academy and seminary set out to do just that thing.
To remedy this defect, he makes an approach to the "project
method," in recommending the play store, merchant, and customers: "It would be no difficult thing for the teacher, and her
pupils to conceive, with the aid of a little imagination, transactions taking place in the school-room, which would furnish the
occasion for the pupils performing mentally precisely those calculations which they may afterwards make when these imaginary
transactions become real ones. Let the instructress be the merchant, and her pupils the customers. Let her sell her various
articles, at their various prices, and receive in payment different
kinds and sums, of money, for which often change is to be made.
—You can easily conceive what a multiplicity of questions in
mental arithmetic would grow out of these fictitious transactions."[34]

He closes by asserting that though "woman cannot plead at
the bar, or preach in the pulpit, or thunder in the Senate house,
. . . hers is no trifling eloquence," but one through which she
can exert a great influence by conduct and speech in her circle
of acquaintances and "in the retirement of her own family."

The services of Woodbridge (1794–1845) and Russell (1798–
1874) in the advancement of women's education are to be estimated highly, primarily for the fact that they provided an open
forum where advocates and critics might be heard. Russell, in
1826, founded the *American Journal of Education,* which became, in 1831, the *American Annals of Education,* the new name
given by the purchaser, William C. Woodbridge. Under both
managements, voluminous articles on the subject appeared, some
of them written by these men. Both had travelled abroad and
come back filled with enthusiasm for the Pestalozzian method,
common schools, normal schools,—and the education of women,
so closely connected with the last two.

Mrs. Phelps began her prominent educational work about 1830,
when she was acting principal at Troy during her sister's visit
in Europe. Later she was at the head of a girl's school at West
Chester, Pennsylvania. In 1831, with her husband, John Phelps,
she removed to Vermont where she prepared for publication her
*Female Student or Fireside Friend, Caroline Westerly, or the
Young Traveller,* her works on geology, botany, natural philoso-

[34] *Ibid.*

phy and chemistry. Later, 1841, she took up the direction of Patapsco Female Institute at Ellicotts Mills, Maryland.[35] This school came to have a reputation scarcely less than that of Troy itself. Upon her work there, and her books, the estimate of her services must rest. Certainly she was not an outstanding pioneer, as was her sister, for the principle that women's education must be provided for was now broadly accepted, though not universally.

In her books, too, she dealt capably with a vast array of topics and argued sanely for a thorough education of the rational individual, rather than the superficial polishing which generally prevailed. In her *Lectures to Young Ladies* (1833) she discussed the purposes of education, physical training, spelling, reading, grammar, ancient and modern tongues, geography, history, mythology, astronomy, chemistry, zoölogy, botany, mineralogy, geology, arithmetic, algebra, geometry, rhetoric, composition, intellectual philosophy, and accomplishments, such as music and dancing. The list is long, for her aim is comprehensive: "to prepare the young for the active duties of life and to enable them to fill with propriety those stations to which, by Providence, they may be called; . . . it consists in training the body to healthful exercises and elegant accomplishments, in cultivating and developing the mental powers, in regulating the passions, and above all in forming religious habits."[36] It is to attain 'development of the mental powers' that many sciences are introduced. But, as through all her discussion the religious purpose runs, so science is to be an important aid to religion. Her faith in the compatibility of science and Scripture is interestingly set forth in her recommendation of geology:

"To females, geology is chiefly important, by its effect in enlarging their sphere of thought, rendering them more interesting as companions to men of science,[37] and better capable of instructing the young. Especially does geology afford important aid to religion by confirming the truth of revelation. Infidels are confounded by the undeniable truth, that as the structure of the earth is investigated, and the secrets of its interior brought to light, the strictest coincidence is observed between them, and

[35] See *Hours with my Pupils* (1859), XIX–XXI.

[36] Phelps: *op. cit.*, 25 and 26.

[37] Compare Darwin's idea, p. 35.

the facts recorded in Scripture. 'I believe,' says Professor Silliman, 'the period is not far distant, when geology will be admitted
into the train of her elder sister, astronomy, and that both will
be eventually hailed as the friends and-allies of revealed religion.'

"The physical history of the Deluge is everywhere inscribed
upon the surface of the earth; upon its chasms and cliffs, its
valleys and mountains. For a knowledge of the moral cause of
these convulsions, we must look to the Scriptures; we there find
that 'God seeing the wickedness of man was great on the earth,
that every imagination of the thoughts of his heart was only evil
continually, and that the earth was filled with violence, resolved
to destroy man by a flood of waters.' We find that 'the waters
prevailed upon the earth an hundred and fifty days, and that all
the hills under the whole heaven were covered.'

"This one grand proof of the Scriptures, offered by geological
science, is enough to entitle it to the attention of the Christian,
for it furnishes sensible demonstration, broad and stable as the
earth, of the truth of that book. . . .'"[38]

From the standpoint of far-reaching activity, Catherine E.
Beecher was preëminent. Born in 1800, she devoted nearly fifty
years to educational projects; her seminary at Hartford was
opened in 1828, and her *Educational Reminiscences* appeared in
1874, four years before her death. Her labors were centered in
New England, at Hartford; Cincinnati, Ohio; Burlington, Iowa;
Quincy, Illinois, and Milwaukee, Wisconsin.

After an irregular education in the rudiments, but careful
instruction by precept and example in domestic economy, she
began at about the age of twenty to prepare to make herself independent by teaching. Having a practical goal in view, she
made rapid progress, first in music, and then in arithmetic,
studying Daboll's *Arithmetic* and Day's *Algebra,* and making
slight ventures into geometry, logic, chemistry and natural philosophy.[39] In arithmetic her independence of character began to
show itself in innumerable "whys"; and when she began to
teach it, she "taught as no book then did, and finally, made an

---

[38] Phelps: *Lectures,* 218–19; in addition to her books consult Barnard's
Am. Jour. of Educ., XVII, 611–17.

[39] *Reminiscences,* 29.

arithmetic . . .'' which was published, and received favorable comment from Professor Olmstead of Yale.

About 1823, she and her sister began the seven-pupil school in the upper room of a store, which soon grew in size to nearly 100 and (1828) became Hartford Female Seminary. Her experience upon presenting her plans for the new school to the town indicates the nature of the uphill fight for women's education: "This I submitted to some of the leading gentlemen of Hartford, and asked to have such a building erected by subscription. Many of them were surprised and almost dismayed at the 'visionary and impracticable' suggestion, and when it became current that I wanted a study hall to hold one hundred and fifty pupils, a lecture room, and six recitation rooms, the absurdity of it was apparent to most of the city fathers, and, with some, excited ridicule. But the more intelligent and influential women came to my aid, and soon all I sought was granted.''[40]

Her success soon conquered the skeptical and, a few years after inaugurating the school, she prepared for publication, at the request of the trustees, *Suggestions on Education,* describing her practice for the benefit of successors. In this book she first appeared distinctly as a reformer of woman's education—a rôle she continued to sustain. Her own comments show she was striving for an institution on the college plan, wishing to secure "as far as possible the division of labor and responsibility peculiar to our college system.'' To this theme she frequently reverted.[41] On the subjects of control and organization, improved methods of teaching, and the importance of introducing health exercises, she was always enthusiastic.[42] The latter interest led finally to the publication of *Physiology and Calisthenics,* in 1856. She tells of her conversion to the idea by "an English Lady'' who came to her Seminary: " . . . What interested us most was her assurance that, until maturity she had a curvature of the spine that was a sad deformity, being what was called a humpback, and yet there she was, a model of fine proportion and gracefulness.''[43]

[40] *Ibid.,* 33.
[41] *Ibid.,* 34. See also pp. 355, 368, 377, 388.
[42] See pp. 111 *ff.,* Vol. II.
[43] *Reminiscences,* 43; see also Ch. III, Vol. II.

CATHERINE E. BEECHER

But in the midst of such labors, and the additional excitement of a venture in public affairs, calisthenics were not enough to preserve her strength; and resultant ill-health caused her to urge all the more strenuously the need of organization on a college plan, so that responsibility might be shared.

Beecher's next work was the organization of the Western Female Institute at Cincinnati (1833), wherein she was assisted by Mrs. Stowe, Mary Dutton, and two other teachers taken from Hartford. Here, renewed efforts were made to create an endowment but, though the school was very successful, no one would take the responsibility in financial matters. The system of "co-equal" teachers was employed. Another project in her mind was to use the Institute as a distributing point, bringing qualified teachers from the East to meet the demand of the West. Eastern schools were now training more young women than could find satisfactory positions in the East, and the West was in need of such teachers. Travelling throughout New England, Beecher found numerous school heads who shared her views as to the importance of this supply of teachers; and numerous letters from the West showed that men of prominence knew of positions to be filled. The need of a placement service for women was indicated in a letter of Mary Lyon to Beecher, in which she replied to the latter's request for teachers:

"I have not forgotten you or your cause. I have received your circular, and now, with little time at command, I send in a few inquiries and suggestions.

"This object is a very great one and I hope it will accomplish for our country even more than any one could expect. Of the need of such an effort no one can doubt, and there are a *great many* women who have the heart to go and labor and suffer in the cause and receive but little earthly reward. But it is something to find them, and when found, still more to complete all needed negotiations.

"But my hope is not in women considerably advanced in age, who expect to remain unmarried; it is in young ladies scarcely out of their teens, whose souls are burning for some channel into which they can pour their benevolence, and who will teach two, three, or four years and then marry and become firm pillars to hold up their successors. If we could find teachers, who, unmarried, would devote twenty or thirty years to this work, we would not gain as much as by such a circulating system.

"As to the other sex, I regard them in a different light. They need not (like women teachers) leave their vocation when they marry in order to guide the house and nurture their children. And so God has given them *less versatility* and less power to enter successfully and *all at once* into what they undertake as their life work.

"In this view of the case there is a difficulty as to my immediate success in furnishing teachers for your enterprise. For young ladies must not only be willing to go, but must also gain the approbation of father, mother, or perhaps, brother or sister, or sister's husband.

"As the enterprise now is, it will be difficult to satisfy *very careful friends*. Just write to me of a particular place by name and that a teacher can have proper assurance of her paying expenses and a salary of say only $100, and I have little doubt that I can send you a good teacher with full consent of friends *as soon as I can find a safe escort*.

"But if I can only say I wish to send a teacher to Miss Beecher to spend a few weeks at Cincinnati in preparing for an unknown field with an unknown salary, and to be under obligation to an unknown donor, the case is different.

"You will not understand that I disapprove your mode of *commencing* your work. After your enterprise has made farther advance I hope to do more than I can do now. You will excuse me if my suggestions are borrowed from my own experience the last ten years. Having had many obstacles thrown in my own way, I anticipate them for others, and having been blessed with more success than I ever hoped, I am prepared to expect success for others as I do for you."[44]

But though all realized the need of the service, it proved difficult to find either the suitable man to handle such an undertaking, or the salary for him. To promote interest in the movement Beecher published anonymously *American Women, Will You Save Your Country?* and was also instrumental in the creation of the Boston Ladies Society for Promoting Education at the West, which actually sent many teachers. Through her volume, Governor Slade of Vermont became interested, first de-

[44] *Ibid.*, 97–9.

clined, and finally entered upon the work. Miss Beecher's letter to him set forth the many things the association might do:

". . . In its most comprehensive form this is an effort to place American Women in that true position designed by God, and relieve them from the miseries consequent on their present false position. Our Creator designed woman to be the chief educator of our race and the prime minister of our family state, and our aim is to train her to this holy calling and give her every possible advantage for the performance of its many and difficult duties.

"But, while this is our leading view, it includes several distinct departments, several of which are more readily comprehended than the more general object, and so we take one at a time, selecting such as the popular mind can most readily be led to appreciate. Our first measure presented to the public is the promotion of popular education as the only mode of saving our nation from ruin. This interests all patriots, and philanthropists of every class. To those who regard all enterprises in the religious aspect, it is offered as a missionary effort to save not only from temporal evils but from perils of the future life. To those who are laboring to secure woman's rights and remedy her wrongs, it is offered as the shortest, surest, and safest method.''[45]

After Slade's acceptance of the post, he severed his connection with Stowe's committee at Cincinnati, organized at Cleveland the Board of National Popular Education, and in many respects pursued a policy not entirely agreeable to Beecher who had been the inspiration of the movement. The essential ideas in her plan were: first, to have a paid agent in charge of teachers on their journey to the West, their location in schools, and their relief in case of necessity; second, to establish a few institutions for superior education of women in the West, with endowments and coequal teachers, which would continue to train future teachers, thus finally avoiding the difficult task of transferring them from New England. Slade believed voluntary committees in the West were sufficient to do all that was necessary, and Beecher yielded to his judgment.

Subsequent events seem to show a weakness in his plan, for, of the first class of teachers sent (thirty-three in number) and

[45] *Ibid.*, 106–7.

also the second (thirty-four in number), all of whom had had about a month's intensive training at Hartford before leaving, many were not given positions when they arrived in the West.[46] These wrote letters describing their unfortunate situation. Beecher later made a tour through Michigan, Indiana, Illinois, Missouri, Iowa, and Wisconsin to gather facts at first hand. She learned that schools were difficult to establish, chiefly by reason of: (1) the religious factions in the small communities (one village of four hundred inhabitants had twelve denominations); (2) political influences that entered into school affairs; and (3) prejudice, occasionally, against teachers from the East.[47] In one case she reported that, in the space of six months, "the divisions of society and the influx of poor teachers" had resulted in teachers being changed twenty times, "leaving the inhabitants utterly discouraged" with educational efforts. These observations led to a virtual break with Slade's work and her return to the original idea of establishing certain "model high schools,"[48] or seminaries on the college plan.

The essential features of her project, to which President Sturtevant of Illinois College gave his hearty approval, were: to establish high schools at central points on the college plan, with a faculty of co-equal teachers; to have trustees representing the chief religious denominations; to have teachers also of various denominations, so far as possible without sacrificing experience and culture to religious bias; to have a normal department in each, and a boarding house with it which could be a home for teachers in all emergencies; to have committees of ladies, representing the larger denominations, to select, train and otherwise care for teachers, either from abroad or from the home state; to locate these schools in larger towns only, whence students would be drawn, and so that those from a distance might be able to live in homes and thus avoid the necessary expensive buildings on the part of the school; and to employ women agents to raise endowments for such schools as they are raised for men's colleges.

The chief advantages of such schools in the West were believed to be: that they would be permanent centers of influence, training teachers for the surrounding communities; would raise the

[46] Ibid., 118.
[47] Ibid., 135.
[48] Ibid., 139.

standard of female education; stimulate other high schools to reach a higher standard; would be homes for the missionary teachers; communities would much prefer to secure a teacher from nearby than from a distance, inasmuch as a personal interview would be possible; the existence of such high grade schools at certain points would make it possible to secure the best teachers from the East who would not risk going West to an unknown school, which might or might not materialize; finally, they would train native daughters of the soil to become teachers.

An effort to put the above plan into operation was made at Burlington, Iowa, and Quincy, Illinois, where prosperous schools were maintained for a time; but no endowments were provided and the system of co-equal teachers was soon given up. Shortly thereafter, Beecher was invited to establish her plan in an institution in Milwaukee, with which a school formerly kept by Mrs. W. L. Parsons was to be merged. She offered to provide teachers, and also library and apparatus amounting to one thousand dollars, paid for out of her own funds and those supplied by ladies in the East, if the citizens formed a board of trustees from several denominations, provided temporary buildings, and guaranteed a certain sum in tuition fees. The school was opened and soon numbered more than one hundred students. Beecher drew a plan for the Milwaukee Normal Institute and High School, which later became Milwaukee Female College, and is now Milwaukee-Downer College. But money had to be raised to buy land and erect a building and no help was forthcoming from Slade's organization—the Board of National Popular Education—so a new organization, the American Woman's Education Association, was formed in New York City (1852) in which women were the controlling managers. This organization, with the aid of Mr. Parsons, soon raised funds which, together with those raised by Milwaukee, were sufficient to pay for the building, according to Beecher's plan.[49]

The organization of the American Women's Education Association marked the success of Beecher's efforts over nearly twenty-five years. It was an important agency till her death, in

[49] *Ibid.*, 154; see Wight: *Annals of Milwaukee College*, 1848–1891; a similar school was established at Dubuque, Iowa, under the charge of Mrs. Parsons.

1878. A circular, issued soon after its formation, shows clearly
the incorporation of her fundamental ideas:

"The education of woman, as conducted hitherto, has had very
little reference to her true vocation. Woman's profession, as the
educator of the human mind, the nurse of the sick, the guardian
of infancy, and the conservator of the domestic state, has in no
one of these departments been deemed worthy of *endowments*.
As the necessary result, everything in woman's education has
been more cared for than these. One of the most distressing results of this neglect has been the *appalling destruction of the
health of women*. The neglect of woman's profession has borne
no less severely on childhood than on woman, for the interests of
the two are inseparable. No proper provision having been made
to train woman for her profession or to provide her compensating
employ in it, the consequence is that there are now over *two million* children without teachers! To supply them properly *sixty
thousand* female teachers are needed at this moment, while every
year increases the demand. It was in view of these evils that
the American Women's Education Association was formed.
The leading measure to be pursued by this Association is the
establishment of permanent endowed institutions for women.
The mode of establishing such institutions shall be as follows:
An agent of this Association shall make this offer to some city or
large town in a section where teachers and schools are most
needed:

"First: That the citizens shall organize a Board of Trustees,
in which the various religious denominations of the place shall
be fairly represented; that these trustees shall provide temporary
accommodations and pupils enough to support four teachers;
that a primary and a high school department be organized, and
that the college plan of a faculty of teachers be adopted. These
teachers are to constitute a body of independent action and equal
power, matters of general interest to be submitted to a faculty
vote. On these conditions the Association shall furnish the institution with a library and apparatus, to the value of one thousand dollars. The first Board of Teachers shall be appointed by
the Association, with the advice and consent of the trustees, and
thereafter the faculty shall have the nominating, and the trustees the appointing, power.

"Second: As soon as the teachers have secured public confidence, and proved that they can work harmoniously together, the citizens shall erect a building at an expense of not less than ten thousand dollars, and engage to give gratuitous tuition to twenty normal pupils. In return, the Association shall provide an endowment of twenty thousand dollars, the interest of which shall furnish the salaries of three superior teachers, each having charge of one of the three departments set forth above, as constituting the profession of women. They also shall aid in the literary instruction. These three teachers, with the beneficiary normal pupils, and any others who may wish and be qualified to enter, shall constitute the normal department. The normal pupils shall act as assistants in the primary and high school departments, under the direction of the principal teachers."[50]

So great was her restless activity, in furthering the education of women, that her health was frequently endangered. From 1822, when the drowning of Alexander Fisher, off the coast of Ireland, blighted her love, she turned every energy to her adopted cause. She aimed, by curtailing attention to superficial accomplishments, to make woman's education practical, thus preparing her for a profession; she sought to make education secure by creating institutions with permanent endowments and the college plan of co-equal teachers; and, finally, by adequate attention to physical education and domestic science, she hoped to render women most useful and ornamental in the home, where, as mothers, they might improve individuals and benefit the nation.

Catherine Beecher wrote voluminously, the most important of her works being: *Suggestions on Education* (1829) wherein she described her method of education at Hartford for the preceding eight years; *The Moral Instructor* (1838); *True Remedy for the Wrongs of Women* (1851); *Letters to the People on Health and Happiness* (1855); *Physiology and Calisthenics* (1856); *Religious Training of Children* (1864); *Woman's Profession as Mother and Educator* (1871); and her *Educational Reminiscences* (1874). Besides these there were numerous letters, plans and proposals, from time to time, in connection with her favorite projects, or some reform which she deemed important. About 1845, she wrote *American Women, Will You Save Your Coun-*

[50] Wight: *op. cit.*, 8.

try? urging that only by providing literate and intelligent citizens, male and female, could disasters to society, such as revolution or social decay, be avoided. Very significant, too, was her *Domestic Economy,* the income from which provided much of the money wherewith she supported many an educational scheme.

Between 1750 and 1850 a great change in thought took place on the subject of woman's education. Rush pleaded primarily for a more substantial education for girls to offset the usual fripperies of education and to fit them for the home; Clinton, Gallaudet, Russell, Woodbridge, Burroughs, Emma Willard, and others stressed the social significance of woman as a teacher at home and in the schools; while Catherine Beecher crusaded for fifty years for permanently endowed institutions for women, without which their education could never be on an equal basis with men's. This change of ideal is shown even more clearly in the institutions themselves, some of which were fostered by those named above; others, however, founded by hands that rarely took up the pen, speak more eloquently than volumes concerning the change.

CHAPTER VIII

RISE OF FEMALE ACADEMIES AND SEMINARIES

I. Early Institutions

While men and women, from Benjamin Rush to Catherine Beecher, with skillful and breathless pens were actively publishing abroad a new ideal of woman's education, a vigorous, Herculean movement was gaining headway in the establishment of academies and seminaries.[1] The names "academy" and "seminary" are not very significant. The former seems to have been preferred, however, in the early part of the period, and the seminary more common in the later. There are "female" and also "male and female" seminaries and academies. The first institutions with which we are concerned were for girls alone and boys and girls together; but, in the nineteenth century, the coeducational institutions became much more common. Those that rose to prominence and exercised a large influence on women's education were designed and operated for, and frequently by, women.

Among the earliest schools for girls in the United States, though not at first strictly an academy, was the convent of the Ursuline Sisters, established in New Orleans, 1727. The Sisters came at the request of Governor Bienville, having assembled at Rouen, January 12, 1727. On February 22, they embarked on the *Gironde,* and after a perilous passage came to the city of New Orleans. They stopped frequently to visit inhabitants and on every hand were promised boarding pupils.[2] While the convent was being completed they occupied the country place of Bienville and, after August 7, 1727, began to teach both day and boarding pupils. Sister Madeleine Mahieu de St. Francis Xavier had charge of the former and Sister Marguerite Judde, the latter. That the service of the school was highly prized is witnessed

---

[1] The institutional development represented by normal schools and high schools is treated in Chaps. X and XI.

[2] Blandin: *Higher Education of Women in the South,* 22.

by the fact that a year later there were twenty boarders.[3] In 1734, they removed to their newly erected home, and in 1740 their share of the Colonial budget was 12,000 livres. It is said that "most of the ladies of the colony were educated at the Ursuline Convent," few going to Europe for that purpose. The earliest instruction does not appear to have extended beyond the rudiments, industrial training, and religion, but the school was without doubt the center of education for the girls of Louisiana and neighboring territory in the eighteenth century. In 1803, there were eleven sisters and 170 boarding pupils.

A prominent school for girls, tradition says, was early established at Lewes, Delaware, and to it deputy-Governor Lloyd of Pennsylvania sent his girls to complete their education.[4] But of its advanced character, too, there is no certainty.

In 1742, a boarding school was begun by the Countess Benigna Zinzendorf, at Germantown. After a continuous but checkered career it was finally located at Bethlehem, Pennsylvania, in 1749. Between 1742 and 1785, entrance was limited to the Brethren, there being but sixteen students in 1749; but, in March, 1785, "the subject of education being under consideration, it was concluded to formally open a boarding school for boys at Nazareth Hall and a similar institution for girls at Bethlehem, on Michaelmas next."[5] The first outside pupil, Elizabeth Bedell, arrived in 1786 and the following year three came from the West Indies and six from Baltimore. Four instructresses were employed by the end of the year; from this time the success of the school was assured. New York, Pennsylvania, Maryland, New Jersey, Rhode Island, Connecticut, South Carolina, Nova Scotia and the West Indies, at first, sent most of the pupils. During the first century the school ministered to more than seven thousand pupils. And from this beginning there has grown the present Moravian College for Women.

From the very beginning, simplicity and economy were emphasized, but to this school the most prominent families sent their children. Boarding and "common schooling" were obtainable, in 1790, for twenty pounds, Pennsylvania currency.[6] The

---

3 *Ursulines in Louisiana.* 12.

4 Powell: *Hist. Educ. in Delaware*, 61.

5 Reichel: *History of Bethlehem Female Seminary*, 29.

6 *Ibid.*, 83.

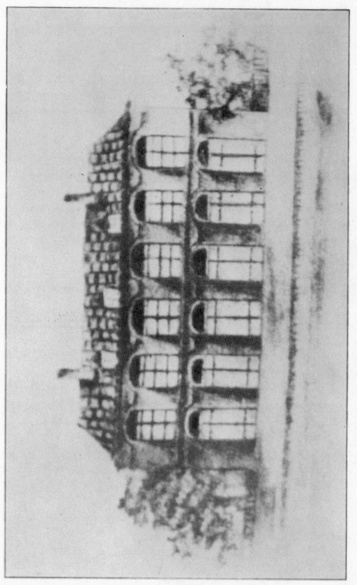

PROVISIONAL CONVENT OF THE URSULINES (1727–1734)

duties and the standard of deportment indicated in the regulations of 1788, long in use, give a faithful view of school activity and also reflect the general principles accepted by the Brethren as favorable to the proper education of girls:

"For the maintenance of order in schools conducted similarly to ours, it is indispensable to adopt definite rules and regulations, the observance of which conduces to the happiness and comfort of individuals and the community. If ever our school is to prove beneficial to its members, and through them to society, our daughters must endeavor to comply cheerfully and at all times with these few and wholesome requirements, as such compliance will lead to habits of order and general proper deportment.

"When the bell rings at half-past five in the morning, all are expected to rise immediately, and in silence await the word, from the tutoress who has them in charge for the day, to proceed to the dwelling-room, where sufficient time is allowed for making the necessary toilet.

"At six o'cock the bell rings for breakfast. Quiet and strict order should be observed in going to and returning from the dining-hall in company with the sister who is on duty. At table a hymn is sung, and the text for the day then read; and it is expected that you all join with cheerful hearts and voices, in thus praising your Lord, both before and after meals.

"As we have no servants to wait on our children, and we deem it well for young persons to learn to wait on themselves, one of our daughters from each room is appointed daily to sweep the room, dust the tables, and see to the proper disposition of the desks and chairs. After breakfast, each pupil attends in person to making her bed, and the different companies repair to their respective dormitories in company with their tutoresses.

"At eight o'clock the bell rings for school, and it is expected that the pupils have in readiness betimes what they need for recitation,—that they repair quietly to their classes, take their allotted seats, and, rather than indulge in noise and idle talk, silently implore God's blessing and aid, so that they may engage with pleasure and profit in the duties before them. A proper and erect posture, as highly conducive to health, should be carefully observed when seated at the desk or otherwise occupied.

"When the bell summons to children's meeting, our daughters should repair in silence to the chapel, two and two, in their respective divisions, attended by their tutoresses. No child is at liberty to excuse herself from attendance on this service. It would be a sad thing indeed if any of your number would not cheerfully devote a short half-hour to the praise and worship of her Redeemer. It is almost needless to add that boisterous deportment in returning from the house of God is also highly improper.

"In going to dinner, at a quarter of twelve, due order is likewise to be observed. At table, every thing should be done with decorum. If there is any thing needed, let one at a time make known her wants; otherwise, those of your number who serve at table will be needlessly disturbed. It is unbecoming in young misses at boarding-school to murmur at the food that is set before them, and to treat the gifts of God with disrespect. Whatever is not agreeable, let it remain untouched, without expression of dissatisfaction. Avoid all improper attitudes, such as leaning on your elbows, and the like; such deportment is indecorous, and inexcusable in well-bred children.

"The time after dinner till one o'clock is allotted you for amusement and recreation. Whatever is needed for the afternoon-classes should be got in readiness in this interval. Access is also allowed you to your trunks in the garret.

"The hours from one to four are for recitations and classes, which you are expected to attend punctually, confining yourselves as much as possible to your respective rooms, and avoiding needless walking and visiting to and fro in the house. After school, your tutoresses will always do you the pleasure of accompanying you to walk, on which occasion you should leave the premises quietly, and, while in the streets, manifest, by your whole deportment, respect for the quiet of the place, whereby you will win the esteem of the residents and do credit to those who are concerned in your training.

"And, finally, I hope all our daughters regularly engage in evening devotions before retiring for the day, and, after these, in composed and serious frame of mind, commit themselves to the safe-keeping of God.'"[7]

[7] *Ibid.,* 33 *ff.*

Bethlehem Female Seminary

Girls at the seminary, notwithstanding the careful regulations, seem to have had an enjoyable time. The journal, kept from day to day in the pupils' own hands, records many love feasts—customary among the Brethren—receptions, and farewell meetings. The great emphasis on music naturally made the school a cheerful place. On a spinning day they were awakened by a Sister's guitar: ''Awake, dear children, early rise, To pay your morning sacrifice, To God, the glorious King of kings. . .'' While they performed their tasks they recited appropriate couplets:

''I've spun seven cuts, dear companions allow
''That I am yet little, and know not right how;

''Mine twenty and four, which I finished with joy,
''And my hands and my feet did willing employ.''

For pastime, in the evening as well as on special ocasions, it was frequently the custom to have a play or dialogue which had been prepared by the girls. On Feb. 1, 1789, a play called ''Virtue,'' which some of the girls had composed, was performed at night. Another often performed, called ''Rural Life,'' was the production of Sister Langaard. Many others were written by Sister Kleist.

William Woodbridge credited the Moravian Seminary with influencing the creation of the Academy for Females at Philadelphia.[8] It is certainly true that many girls from Philadelphia were educated there; and Rush, Morgan, and others, were undoubtedly aware of the importance of the Bethlehem school, the special school that had been kept for years (since 1754) by Anthony Benezet,[9] and the private school kept by David James Dove, while he was a teacher at the Philadelphia Academy. However that may be, John Poor opened an academy, not later than 1787 (usually reputed to have been begun in 1780), ''for the instruction of young ladies in Reading, Writing, Arithmetic, English Grammar, Composition, Rhetoric, and Geography.''[10] Upon solicitation, seventeen gentlemen—including Benjamin West, Pelatiah Webster, Benjamin Say, and William Smith—agreed to serve as visitors. At the first examination, December

[8] *Am. Jour. Ed.*, V, 421–3.
[9] See p. 235.
[10] A pamphlet on the ''Young Ladies Academy.'' See p. 336.

3, 1787, six girls received premiums for excellence in reading, spelling, arithmetic, writing, English grammar, and geography, respectively.

The immediate popularity and success of the academy may be seen in the enrollment of one hundred pupils, reported in 1788, and also in the estimate of the order prevailing and the successful pursuit of studies: "The number of scholars was found to amount to one hundred. But, although no bodily correction, nor harsh treatment of any kind, be ever attempted in this seminary, yet so fully established, among the pupils, are the habits of good order and respect for their superiors, that in the whole course of the examination, which lasted two days, . . . the strictest order and decorum were preserved. And, indeed, with respect to the exhibition in general, it is no more than justice to say, that it is not easy to conceive how any thing of the kind could have been more perfect. In reading, in writing, in arithmetic, in geography, in English grammar, and in composition, such specimens were given of proficiency, not confined to a few individuals, but spreading itself on all sides through the classes in general, as even in this city would not a few years ago have been conceived practicable.[11]

Dr. Sproat, another visitor, likewise eulogized the institution in 1789: ". . . The instruction of female youth, till of late, has not been sufficiently attended to amongst us. Indeed it ought to be remembered, that a gentleman of a liberal education, and critical knowledge in Belles Lettres, has for some years past, been of eminent service in his instruction of young ladies in private families; but the Ladies' Academy, is a new institution in this city. And I cannot but hope, that the plan of female education, now adopted and prosecuted in this excellent seminary, will merit the approbation and patronage of all who wish well to the learning, virtue and piety of the rising fair of this metropolis. The proficiency these delicate pupils have made, in several branches of useful literature, not only displays the fertility of their blooming geniuses, but reflects honor on the abilities, and praise to the attention of their worthy Preceptor and his assistants in their instruction. Accuracy in orthography, a very necessary part of an early education . . . reading with propriety their native language . . . an acquaintance with En-

[11] *Ibid.*, 16–17.

glish grammar . . . writing a neat and beautiful character . . .
a knowledge of figures, with many of their valuable uses . . . a
general knowledge of the different parts of the terraqueous
globe . . . its divisions, inhabitants, and productions . . . such
knowledge of the planets that compose the solar system, and
their periodical motions . . . together with such a sketch of
history, as to remark the rise, progress, declension, and final
extinction of the most remarkable states, kingdoms and empires
. . . the virtues which contributed to their greatness, and the
vices which were productive of their ruin . . . these are such
valuable branches of literature, as are not only ornamental, but
in many respects exceedingly advantageous to the rising generation of the fair sex. Let it suffice to say, that such academical
improvements, tend to mollify the temper, refine the manners,
amuse the fancy, improve the understanding, and strengthen
virtue . . . to lay a foundation for a life of usefulness and
happiness here, and if rightly improved, for a blessed immortality
hereafter.''[12]

It is not the fortune of every master to hear his praises sung
during his lifetime, but such was the happy lot of John Poor.
The scarcity of educational institutions for girls made the
meanest facilities seem estimable. The following lines were
written by a young lady while a student at the Academy, about
1790:

> ''If modest merit is with honour crown'd
> ''Or happiness is by the worthy found,
> ''Her grateful wish will not be vain, who pays
> ''Not servile flattery, but deserved praise:
> ''Praise to the man who thus employs his care,
> ''On wisdom's plan to form the youthful fair:
> ''Oh! may thy cares their just reward obtain,
> ''Rich in each bliss, and only *Poor* in name.''[13]

In 1790, it was agreed that every pupil, upon conclusion of
her education in this seminary and passing a ''strict examination, shall be granted the following diploma, sealed by the
trustees:

''The Trustees of the Young Ladies' Academy of Philadelphia, having carefully examined Miss A————B————,

[12] *Ibid.*, 24–6.
[13] *Ibid.*, 37.

T HE novelty of a Female Academy established by a Charter of Incorporation, on account of its being the first in the United States, and perhaps in the world, has led many of its advocates in this city, and in several of the neighbouring states, to request a publication of this kind.

We have the pleasure to inform the public, that since the commencement of the Institution, we have been honoured with scholars from Cape-Florida, Georgia, Carolina, _____, Maryland, Delaware, New-Jersey, New-York, Connecticut, Rhode-Island, Maſſachuſetts-Bay, the Province of Main, Nova-Scotia, Canada, from several of the Weſt-India Iſlands, and from various parts of the state of Pennſylvania, but the greateſt number from this city.—In consequence of which we flatter ourſelves that the following sheets, by the candid, will meet with a kind reception.

FROM A DESCRIPTION OF THE FEMALE ACADEMY AT PHILADELPHIA (1792)

in spelling, reading, writing, English-grammar, arithmetic, geography, rhetoric and composition; do hereby make known, that she is well acquainted with those branches of literature; and at a public commencement hath been admitted to the highest honours of the institution. Desirous therefore of perpetuating the testimony of her merit; they have, in conformity to the charter and rules of the said academy, caused the seal of their corporation to be annexed to this Diploma, and the same to be witnessed by the names of the proper officers. Conferred this ————day of————in the year of our Lord, one thousand, seven hundred and ninety. . .''[14]

Two years later, the Academy was the first to be incorporated under the laws of Pennsylvania for the education of girls. It is the earliest, thus far found, in any part of the United States. Its charter, January 9, 1792, provided for not more than sixteen nor less than eight trustees, and fourteen were named at that time. Besides receiving the usual ''privileges, rights, powers, franchises,'' the trustees were to hold and sell real-estate, appoint officers, make by-laws, set examinations, hold commencements, and give premiums and diplomas. It was also provided that a new set of trustees could be elected upon a petition signed by any twelve subscribers; and that John Poor should be principal, and not removable, except for ''crime, misdemeanor, or disability either natural or civil.'' Following receipt of the charter, by-laws were at once drawn up relative to trustees' meetings, commencements, and the awarding of prizes.

Though the school was large, diplomas and premiums were not granted to many. At commencement, in the usual order of events, there came the procession of students, two by two, headed by the principal, and after them the trustees. Separating to right and left, they allowed the trustees to precede them into the church, where they were greeted by music. There followed a prayer, ''a salutatory oration'' and ''selected pieces well adapted to the female character'.' by several scholars, and more appropriate music. A valedictory was delivered ''with decency and propriety.'' Diplomas were then given to expectant hands and Mr. Poor gave his final charge to the graduates.

The addresses by young ladies at commencement are interesting for their defense of female education—possibly inspired by

14 *Ibid.*, 68.

Poor. Molly Wallace (1792) asserted, in defense of female orators: "We look not for a female Pitt, Cicero or Demosthenes," and then asked, "Why is a boy diligently and carefully taught the Latin, the Greek or the Hebrew Language, in which he will seldom have occasion to write or converse?" These are studied on account of the habits of study established, "so a young lady, from the exercise of speaking, . . . may acquire some valuable habits . . ." not otherwise obtainable. Another miss (1793) defended oratory for her sex with much more spirit, though the originality of her 'piece' may be doubted.

"Our right to instruct and persuade cannot be disputed, if it shall appear, that we possess the talents of the orator . . . and have opportunities for the exercise of those talents. Is a power of speech, and volubility of expression, one of the talents of the orator? Our sex possess it in an eminent degree.

"Do personal attractions give charms to eloquence, and force to the orator's arguments? There is some truth mixed with the flattery we receive on this head. Do tender passions enable the orator to speak in a moving and forcible manner? This talent of the orator is confessedly ours. In all these respects the female orator stands on equal,—nay, on superior ground.

"If therefore she should fail in the capacity for mathematical studies, or metaphysical profundities, she has, on the whole, equal pretensions to the palm of eloquence. Granted it is, that a perfect knowledge of the subject is essential to the accomplish'd orator. But seldom does it happen, that the abstruse sciences, become the subject of eloquence. And, as to that knowledge which is popular and practical,—that knowledge which alone is useful to the orator; who will say that the female mind is incapable?

"Our high and mighty Lords (thanks to their arbitrary constitutions) have denied us the means of knowledge, and then reproached us for the want of it. Being the stronger party they early seized the sceptre and the sword; with these they gave laws to society; they denied women the advantage of a liberal education; forbid them to exercise their talents on those great occasions, which would serve to improve them. They doom'd the sex to servile or frivolous employments, on purpose to degrade their minds, that they themselves might hold unrivall'd, the power and pre-eminence they had usurped. Happily, a more liberal way of thinking begins to prevail. The sources of knowledge are gradually opening to our sex. Some have already availed themselves of the privilege so far as to wipe off our reproach in some measure."[15]

In 1794, another school for girls, which was to become famous, was reorganized by the Moravians at Lititz, Pennsylvania. This institution, the present Linden Hall Seminary, had been a Moravian girls' school for forty-eight years, but began to receive others besides Moravians in 1794.[16] During the first century it was a close competitor of its sister institution at Bethlehem, so far as numbers of pupils may measure progress. Reference has already been made to a school for boys and girls established by the Friends at Westtown, in 1799.

It has already been shown[17] that some prominent private schools were created for girls in New England during the last quarter of the eighteenth century: the school of Jedediah Morse at New Haven, 1783;[18] Dwight's at Greenfield, about 1785; and a female academy at Medford, in 1789.[19] These, however, had no official recognition, such as a charter, nor was there any foundation or society to guarantee their continuance. The same must also be said of Bingham's school for girls, at Boston, in 1784. Its influence, however, on the opening of the town schools to girls (in 1789) enhances its significance; as also the fact that its head was author of three famous school

[15] *Ibid.*, 90–2.

[16] See Beck: Linden Hall, 1746–1921, in *A Century and Three Quarters of Life and Service.*

[17] Chapter IV.

[18] "A school for Young Misses—Gentlemen and Ladies are hereby informed that a school is opened in New Haven for the instruction of Young Misses in the following branches of Female education: Reading, Arithmetic, English Grammar, Geography, Composition, and the different branches of Needle Work. Said school will be taught by a gentleman and lady well qualified to instruct in the various branches above mentioned. Signed by Abel Morse. New Haven, Oct. 13, 1783." A later notice says, "The school lately opened in New Haven for the instruction of Young Misses, having succeeded beyond the most sanguine expectations of the subscriber, the customers of the said school and the public are hereby informed that he is encouraged to prosecute the plan he has adopted and proposes to furnish the school with a useful library and every other accommodation which may render it advantageous to its members."—This school was that of Jedediah Morse.—Atwater: *Hist. of New Haven*, Conn., 157 *ff.*

[19] Brooks and Usher: *Hist. of Medford, Mass.*, 298 *ff.*

books: *The Young Lady's Accidence, or a short and easy intro-duction to English Grammar, The American Precept*or (1794), and the *Columbian Orator* (1797),[20] Other schools, probably more nearly of secondary grade, were kept by two Yale men (1779–80), each a quarter of the year; one of them, William Woodbridge, had a school for girls at New Haven in 1780, where he imparted instruction in grammar, composition, rhetoric and geography.[21]

An academy that had a great career was established by Sarah Pierce, who began with one pupil at her home in Litchfield, 1792. She operated the school, incorporated as Litchfield Academy (1827), for forty years, during which time from 1500 to 2000 girls attended. Her brother, knowing she must help support the family, early conceived the idea of sending her to New York to be educated, and imparted this advice: "The short time you have and the many things you have to learn, occasions me to wish you would employ every moment for the purpose. I hope you will not miss a single dancing school, and that you will take lessons from Capt. Turner at other times, pray get him and Katy your friend, to instruct you in everything, in walking, standing and sitting, all the movements of which tho' they appear in a polite person natural, are the effects of art, which country girls never attend to and which you had best take the utmost pains, or you will never appear natural & easy in. I am somewhat fearful of that your old habits at your age can not be so thoroughly removed, as to give place to a natural careless genteel air, and which totally hides all the art of it. The Books I left with you I wish you not to read much in town, I want you to study the fashions, the art of pleasing to advantage and for this purpose to spare no neces-sary expense, and if you do not appear as genteel as any of the girls it will be your own fault, you must however pay a great regard to economy & always remember that every Dollar takes so much from my future prospects, on which you know that not only yours but mine and all our families happiness depends."[22]

[20] The *Independent Chronicle* [Boston], Apr. 1, 1802, 4, col. 1, carried an advertisement of "Elegant Pieces of Penmanship" to be sold by C. Bing-ham.

[21] Barnard: *Am. Jour. Ed.*, XXVII, 274.

[22] Vanderpoel: *Chronicle of a Pioneer School*, 6; and White: *Hist. of Litchfield*, 110 *ff*.

SALLY PIERCE

It should be mentioned, in passing, that while but few schools of a higher sort, especially designed for girls, appeared in the eighteenth century, there were others that were opened to boys and girls. In New England, the most prominent of these academies were Leicester, incorporated 1784, and the Westford Academy, incorporated 1793.[23] At Leicester, though girls and boys studied the subjects of the "English Department, it was many years before the former studied the languages and especially Latin." At Westford, the rules drawn up in 1792 specified that English, Latin, Greek, writing, arithmetic, speaking, geometry, logic, geography and music should be taught and that the school should be open to those of any nation, age, or sex who were "able to read in the Bible readily without spelling."[24]

II. Influential Academies and Seminaries of the Early Nineteenth Century.

In the nineteenth century there arose many prominent, influential schools that soon eclipsed the meagre record of the eighteenth. Bethlehem, Philadelphia, Lititz and Medford, although they had blazed a trail, and though the first and third continued to render important service to women's secondary education, yielded leadership to such influential centers as Troy, Hartford, and Ipswich. It is impossible to follow the dictates of interest and present the history of all the academies and seminaries fully enough to do them individual justice. Not even in one state can this be done. Brief reference is made to some of the earliest and most influential only, for through them and their imitators was practice in the education of women changed. Those that exerted the most profound influence on the whole seminary movement arose in the Northern states of the Eastern seaboard, their pupils ofttimes becoming the founders or principals of Western and Southern institutions. The honor of establishing the first exclusively female seminary in the nineteenth century, however, belongs to the South, where the Moravians opened their Female Academy at Salem, North Carolina, in 1802. With its influence few in the South can compare, though there were many and early imitators.

<hr>

[23] Washburn: *Hist. of Leicester Academy*, 27–8; Hodgman: *Hist. of Westford, Mass.*, 312 *ff.*
[24] Hodgman: *op. cit.*, 312 *ff.*

The earliest Northern academy[25] of the nineteenth century (Bradford, 1803), open to girls, was coeducational until 1836;[26] so, also, was the Friends' Academy (1812) at New Bedford.[27] The first incorporated for girls alone appear to have been at Pittsfield, in 1807,[28] and at Bath, 1808.[29] Those created for girls only, and exercising influence far and near, were the school of Catherine Fiske at Keene, New Hampshire (1814); Joseph Emerson's Ladies' Seminary at Byfield and Saugus, from 1818 to 1824, and later at Wethersfield (Connecticut); Troy Semi-

REWARD OF MERIT.

This certifies, that *Lavinia Bryant* by diligence and good behaviour, merits the approbation of *her* Friends and Instructer.

Sold by Cummings & Hilliard, at the Boston Bookstore, No. 1, Cornhill.

SUSANNA BRYANT'S CERTIFICATE OF MERIT, BRADFORD ACADEMY, 1818

nary (1821); the Adams Academy, Derry, New Hampshire, 1823, the first to be endowed exclusively for girls, in New England;

[25] *The Independent Chronicle* [Boston] advertised an academy for girls at Charlestown, Sept. 20, 1802, but it was of little consequence.

[26] Edward Kimball and 29 others bought shares to establish Bradford Academy. There were to be male and female departments, but Article 2 stated: "Instruction in the female apartment may be suspended whenever the proprietors judge necessary." Such a crisis never arose. As to teachers: "No young lady shall sustain the office of preceptress who is not a reputable person well versed in the science of Belles Lettres, embroidery and all kinds of fine needlework."—*MS. Minutes.*

[27] *Hist. Sketch of Friends' Academy*, 1876.

[28] *Laws of Mass.*, 1807, 56–7.

[29] *Ibid.*, 1808, 355–7.

George B. Emerson's private secondary school for girls at Boston, in 1823; Ipswich Female Seminary (1828); that at Hartford incorporated the same year, though in operation since 1823; the Abbot Female Academy at Andover, Massachusetts, in 1829; and Mount Holyoke Female Seminary, in 1837.

Catherine Fiske's school at Keene, New Hampshire, continued for twenty-three years, from 1814 to 1837, during which she taught some twenty-five hundred girls. In 1836, there were over a hundred pupils under the charge of the principal and six assistants. Miss Fiske's work was inspired by the maxim, generally accepted by enthusiasts for woman's education at that day, that it was "man's office to correct evil and woman's to prevent it."[30]

A similar school, in many respects, was kept by Joseph Emerson, first at Byfield, later at Saugus (1818–1824), and then transferred to Wethersfield, Connecticut.[31] Emerson had graduated from Harvard in 1789, where he was tutor for a while. The work of Emerson was highly complimented by the editor of the *American Journal of Education*,[32] especially on account of his "best manual hitherto published on the subject of practical education." Connected with the Seminary at Wethersfield, there was a preparatory school, open only before the regular seminary term, to fit girls to enter the former, and a collateral school, having a similar purpose, but which ran throughout the seminary term. The course was to embrace three seasons of twenty-eight weeks each, and "none but thorough scholars" were "ever to have standing in the Senior class." Some might have to take two years in passing from junior class to senior, but advancement would be immediate if ability were proved. Though his course was longer than those generally offered, he says "it is by no means as long as many ardent friends to female improvement may wish." But he is sure "the present state of our country seems not to justify the plan of so extended a course of female education, except, perhaps, for a small portion of our most opulent citizens." At any rate, "the humble plan of a course of eighty-four weeks, is the utmost which I now presume to adopt and . . . limited as it is, is something more than the plans

---

[30] *Am. Annals of Ed.*, VI, 235–6.
[31] Stiles: *Hist. of Wethersfield, Conn.*, I, 380 *ff*.
[32] I, 506–8.

which I have yet executed or . . . have been hitherto attempted. . . .''[33]

Emerson and his school have probably become well known because of his two prominent pupils who made history, one at Ipswich and the other at Mt. Holyoke. But it is clear, from a perusal of his numerous essays advocating female education, and especially that describing his scheme proposed for Wethersfield, that he was far above the average proprietor-principal of a girls' school.

His utterances were, in many ways, prophetic. He foresaw the day when higher institutions for the education of women would be regarded as necessary as colleges for men; but he added, when they ''shall be built, by whom . . . founded, and by whom taught, is yet for Providence to determine.'' 'Possibly, some of our children may enjoy their advantages.' The blood must have tingled in Mary Lyon's veins at such a vision.

Besides essays on the education of women, Emerson produced the *Evangelical Primer,* about 1812, and a *Poetical Reader,* in 1832.[34]

Troy Female Seminary, established by Emma Willard, has been said, with some exaggeration, to mark ''the beginning of higher education for women in the United States.'' Mrs. Willard began her career as a teacher by preparing herself first in a district school, which she did not rate highly, and by study directed by her father. Later she attended the 'academy' of Mr. Miner with her sister Lydia and, again at Hartford, studied Webster's *Grammar* and Morse's *Geography.* Beginning at the age of sixteen, she taught in Berlin and Westfield and, in 1807, began her school at Middlebury. In 1814, she opened a boarding school, which she left in 1818 to go to Waterford, New York, where she hoped for government support, having drawn up her *Plan,* approved by such men as Clinton, Jefferson, and John Adams, and presented it to the legislature.[35] Disappointed in the school at Waterford, and attracted by the offer of Troy to provide a building and grounds, she left in 1821. Concerning

[33] *Ibid.,* 539–44.

[34] See reference to Emerson's school in an account of the work of Z. P. Grant, Barnard's *Journal,* XXX, 615–16.

[35] See p. 307.

the failure of her *Plan* to gain support in the legislature she wrote bitterly:

"To have had it decently rejected, would have given me comparatively little pain, but its consideration was delayed and delayed, till finally the session passed away. The malice of open enemies, the advice of false friends and the neglect of others, placed me in a situation, mortifying in the extreme. I felt it almost to phrenzy,—and even now, though the dream is long past, I cannot recall it without agitation. Could I have died a martyr in the cause, and thus ensured its success, I could have blessed the faggot and hugged the stake. Once I had almost determined to seek permission to go in person before the legislature, and plead at their bar with the living voice, believing that I could throw forth my whole soul in the effort for my sex, and then sink down and die; and thus my death might effect what my life had failed to accomplish. Had the legislature been composed of such men as filled my fancy when I wrote my 'Plan,' I could have thus hoped in pleading publicly for women. Yet had such been its character, I should have had no necessity.

"It was by the loss of respect for others, that I gained tranquillity for myself. Once I was fond of speaking of the legislature as the 'fathers of the state.' Perhaps a vision of a Roman Senate played about my fancy, and mingled with the enthusiastic respect in which I held the institutions of my country. I knew nothing of the maneuvres of politicians. That winter served to disenchant me. My present impression is that my cause is better rested with the people than with their rulers. I do not regret bringing it before the legislature, because in no other way could it have come so fairly before the public. But when the people shall have become convinced of the justice and expediency of placing the sexes more nearly on an equality, with respect to privileges of education, then legislators will find it their interest to make the proper provision.'"[36]

Having obtained a building, Emma Willard began largely by her own efforts to train teachers, and in this she laid great emphasis on mathematics. The introduction of higher mathematics she was always prone to regard as epoch-making in the history of woman's education in this country.[37] It was her custom at

[36] Barnard: *Am. Teachers*, 145.
[37] *Ibid.*, 148.

Waterford and Troy to pursue some mathematical study, teach it herself, and finally turn the teaching of it over to one of her pupils, leaving herself free to develop another. Mathematics, chronology, and geography occupied most of her time. For her "time-maps," "Temple of Time," and *Chronographer of Ancient and English History* she received a medal at the World's Fair of London, in 1851.

When Dr. Willard died (1825), the Seminary lost the guardian of its health and suffered more severely the loss of service in money matters. She took up this task, however, and by systematic work and close devotion to business affairs, the readjustment was made. A great source of income was in the books of Mrs. Willard. By this time, too, the school was widely known, drawing students throughout the States, Canada, and the West Indies. This fame had come largely from the widely circulated *Plan*, the examinations of the school, private and public,[38] and the normal training of teachers whose services came to be demanded in all parts of the United States. This training of teachers, certainly, was not so much the product of an original purpose as the natural result of the method of teaching which had been constantly employed. Indeed, training of teachers was never an avowed purpose: Our "first object and mission has ever been to make it a model-school for teaching the broad sphere of woman's duties and accomplishments."[39]

Of the success of the Seminary, her biographer, Fowler, wrote: "Its success has been unexampled. For several years the attendance of pupils has numbered about four hundred, of whom more than one-third have been boarders. Teachers and officers number nearly thirty. It sends forth about twenty-five teachers each year. Since 1838, it has been under the charge of the only son of Mrs. Willard, John H. Willard, and his wife, Sarah L. Willard; the former having been for some years her business partner, and the latter having been connected with the institution for nineteen years previous to 1838, as pupil, teacher, and vice-principal. The same methods of instruction and discipline are

[38] It is said that some of the college professors who attended the Troy examinations were astonished at the success achieved; but although they approved, they did not invite her to attend their examinations.

[39] Barnard: *op. cit.*, 155.

continued, with such modifications as larger means and added experience naturally and happily induce.''[40]

Troy Seminary has been referred to as the ''Vassar College of New York a half century before the establishment of the institution at Poughkeepsie.'' The Seminary was, at any rate, a step toward collegiate education, and Emma Willard helped educate a generation to think favorably of permanent institutions for the education of women. After leaving the direct cares of the school behind, she was very active in the work of the common school revival and the Western Literary Institute. In 1846, she set out upon a tour of the South and West, covering some 8000 miles, visiting all the prominent cities. Everywhere she was received by girls' seminaries as a pioneer founder, and in many of them she was welcomed by her own pupils who had borne her message to remote, newly settled, regions of the country.[41]

Besides her celebrated ''Plan for improving Female Education,'' addressed to the New York Legislature in 1818, Emma Willard prepared numerous important textbooks which, judging from their excellent character and wide use, must have been influential factors in improving instruction in academies and seminaries throughout the Eastern half of the United States. These are listed below.[42]

The Adams Academy is peculiarly interesting because it appears to have been the first created by a bequest, from Jacob

[40] *Ibid.*, 156.

[41] Barnard: *Am. Teachers*, 125–68; Lord: *Life of Emma Willard;* Mayo: Common Schools of New York. . . . [*R. C. E.*, 1895–1896, I, 240–57]; *Educational Review*, XLIV (1912), 219–20.

[42] The Woodbridge and Willard Geographies and Atlases; School Geography and Atlas; Ancient Geography and Atlas; Geography for Beginners and Atlas (1822); History of the United States, or Republic of America, with an atlas (1828); Universal History in Perspective (1837); Abridgement of American History (1843); Temple of Time, or Chronographic Universal History (1844); A Chronographer of Ancient History (1845); A Chronographer of English History (1845); Historic Guide to accompany the Temple of Time, and other charts; A Treatise On the Motive Powers which Produce the Circulation of the Blood (1846); Respiration and its effects (1849); Last Leaves of American History (1849); Astronomy (1853); Morals of the Young (1857). In addition to these she published a Journal and Letters from Europe (1833), numerous magazine articles, and three addresses on women's education in Greece. [*Proc. of the 7th Convocation of the University of the State of N. Y.*, 81.]

Adams. When a principal was sought the trustees mentioned Miss Grant, then with Joseph Emerson. Though the latter was reluctant to lose her, he saw at Derry the possibility of realizing his hopes of a permanent institution for women and said to her: "If you can put into operation on right principles a permanent seminary for young ladies, you may well afford to lay down your life when you have done it."[43]

Thus, in 1824, Zilpah Grant took charge of the Adams Female Academy at Derry, New Hampshire, incorporated in 1823, and which, by her genius, was soon transformed into a first class school for girls. She was given the building without charge, but bore all other expenses herself, and had entire management of business and educational affairs. Mary Lyon worked with her during the summers, until 1828, when Miss Grant, due to some friction with the trustees, removed to Ipswich, taking Miss Lyon and many of her pupils with her.[44]

In 1823, George B. Emerson opened a private secondary school for girls, which was destined to be one of the most influential in Boston. Emerson had begun his teaching career while a student at Cambridge, teaching a district school at Kennebunk, Maine, during the long winter vacation, 1813–1814. In 1819, he became a tutor at Harvard, first in mathematics and then in Greek. Two years later he was chosen principal of the first high school in Boston, which post he occupied successfully for two years. At the end of that time he turned to his most important life work,— the education of girls. Largely because of his success in the English school, he was approached by William Sullivan, in a representative capacity, and urged to open a girls' school. It was argued that "the education of girls on such principles as [he] had adopted [was] of much more importance than that of boys, because mothers have almost the entire education of children. . . ." To this argument he yielded, being convinced he could do a larger service by properly educating the source of

[43] Quoted from Stow: *Hist. of Mt. Holyoke*, 29.

[44] Barnard: *American Journal of Education*, XXX, 616–7; it should be noted that Ipswich was not the first incorporated academy for girls in Massachusetts, as stated by Brown: *Making of Our Middle Schools*, 254; as early as 1807, Pittsfield Female Academy—see *Laws of Mass.*, 56–7—and 1808, Bath Female Academy—*Laws of Mass.*, 355–7—were incorporated by the state.

George B. Emerson

public virtue and domestic happiness.[45]   In this he followed the
advice of his friend Mrs. Eliot, and "always addressed his pupils
as immortal beings, preparing for life in this world, and a higher
life to come. . . ." He continued the school until 1855, when he
retired and travelled abroad. During this active service for
woman's higher education, he was also prominent in the work of
the Mechanic's Institution of Boston (1827), the American Institute of Instruction (1830)—before which he delivered an
impressive address on Female Education in 1831—and the Boston Society of Natural History (1830). He enthusiastically
supported another movement, very important for women—the
creation of normal schools. In 1836, he presented to the legislature a memorial in favor of raising the qualifications of teachers in the common schools. He was for many years a member
of the Board of Education of Massachusetts, and likewise prominent in the councils of the schools of Boston.[46]

Zilpah P. Grant, a pioneer in woman's education, scarcely second to Mary Lyon, Emma Willard, or Catherine Beecher, was
born in South Norfolk, Connecticut, 1794.[47] She received her
early education in the district school, where, according to her
biographer,

"Blackboard or crayon, globes or wall maps, there were none.
Nor any more were there school registers, or marks of any kind.
No one dreamed that intellectual excellence could be represented
by figures. It would as soon have been thought that faith and
love and every Christian grace could be registered by the Arabic
notation. Technical gradation was unknown. Scholars from
A B C to Algebra were gathered in the same room and attended
to by the same teacher. Reading and Spelling, Grammar and
Geography were conducted in classes. These were thoroughly
taught and apt to be thoroughly learned. Webster's was the im-
memorial and unquestioned speller. The New Testament was the
first Reader, and Caleb Bingham with his American Preceptor,
and Columbian Orator had no competitor. Booksellers' agents

[45] *Education* (1881), II, 178–82.
[46] Extracts from the *Reminiscences* in Barnard's *Journal*, XXVIII, 257–
74; also Vol. V, 417–26; Barnard: *Am. Teachers*, 333–43.
[47] Her biographer, J. P. Cowles, says she was second to none; indeed,
"before Miss Lyon and greater than Miss Lyon, was Miss Grant."—Barnard: *Am. Jour. Ed.*, XXX, 611 and 624.

were not, or had not discovered the field. Lindley Murray's Abridgment was the Grammar,—fastened and riveted with abundant and difficult parsing, and taught by those who understood it. In Arithmetic, Daboll's and Pike's were the text books, but every one worked his own way, and at his own rate. The lame only had help. The bright ones working independently, every step was solid progress. Many finished their Arithmetic without recitation, without assistance and without exhibition.''[48]

At fourteen, Miss Grant began to keep such a district school. She continued in active educational work until 1839 and was interested in it throughout her life. While teaching (1817) she began to study grammar, history, and English literature under Ralph Emerson, and became acquainted with Joseph Emerson[49] whose school, then at Saugus, offered superior advantages. The question of spending all her savings (fifty dollars) on further education then arose, and finally, despite protests of those who advised her "to marry and settle," she went to school. It was a great decision for her: the beginning of her educational adventure. At Saugus, she met Mary Lyon, who later assisted her at Derry; and, due to the help of Emerson, she secured a 'select' school for young ladies (1821) at Winsted, which she "kept" for two years and then removed to take charge of the Adams Academy, Derry, New Hampshire, 1824–1828.[50]

From 1828 to 1839, the history of Ipswich Seminary coincides with that of her life. A building had been erected by a joint stock company (1825) and a school opened for young ladies, first by Hervey Wilbur and then continued, till 1828, by James Ward. Between 1828 and 1835, Miss Grant and Miss Lyon coöperated to raise Ipswich to its greatest excellence. Miss Lyon's withdrawal (1835), to develop her cherished dream, left the entire burden on Miss Grant; on account of this and failing health she resigned the position in 1839. Since then there have been many principals. After 1844, it was for a number of years under the guidance of John P. Cowles.[51]

[48] *Ibid.*, XXX, 612–13.

[49] See p. 343.

[50] Hamilton: *An American Queen*, Ch. XXVI of Farmer's *National Exposition Souvenir*.

[51] *Am. Jour. Ed.*, XXX, 593–4.

IPSWICH FEMALE SEMINARY (CHARTERED, 1828)

The cherished vision of Miss Lyon seems to have been Miss Grant's also.   The failure of the trustees at Ipswich to respond with material aid was perhaps partially the cause of Miss Lyon's leaving in 1835, for she realized that her institution could never be created at Ipswich.   As early as 1834, Miss Grant had called a meeting of friends of the school and desired them to provide ample facilities, that the pupils and teachers might reside and teach under the same roof, rather than dwell in groups throughout the town and come to the Seminary building for instruction only.   They were favorably inclined to such views but did not take steps to realize such an institution, and Miss Grant, not having sufficient energy to do it all by herself, was forced to face inevitable failure and gradual decline of the institution.   It is worthy of notice that the new seminary, established by Mary Lyon, incorporated the facilities desired by her friend and, by virtue of them, laid the foundation for a permanent institution.[52]

As at Troy, the Ipswich school trained most of the assistant teachers.   This was necessary in the first generation of seminaries, for the teacher supply was not yet equal to the demand. At Ipswich, the number of pupils per teacher was at first twenty; but later, with the addition of teachers of vocal music, calisthenics, mezzotint and drawing, the number was reduced to fifteen.

Individual care of students was emphasized.   The school was divided into sections and each teacher assigned to one.   She was required to "acquaint herself with the health, habits, intellectual improvement, and moral and religious state of every young lady in her section; to attend to the investigation and recitation of a Bible lesson every week; to be the friend and adviser of each; to interest herself in everything that concerned their general improvement. . . . "[53]

Rule by sweet reasonableness was inaugurated, and no school regulation was introduced without some such preamble as: "When people come into society, each must give up somewhat of his natural rights.   A man living alone may eat, sleep, study, work, at his own hours.   When he comes into society there is a general good to be consulted; and when there is interference, that must set aside the individual preference."

[52] See p. 358.
[53] *Am. Jour. Ed.*, XXX, 620.

As in the better grade of female seminaries elsewhere, there was an effort to get rid of emulation as a means to encourage learning. No rewards were given, except a diploma or certificate to those who completed the three-year course—later reduced nominally to two. During her fifteen years' control of the school at Derry and Ipswich, only one hundred and fifty-six, of the sixteen hundred attending, received this certificate. But the formal mark of completion is not the criterion of usefulness, and there are few contemporary seminaries in New England that rendered greater service in building up the ideal of higher education for women. Also, a service was rendered to common school education in the West, many teachers being trained here before being sent to take charge of schools in Ohio, Indiana, Illinois, Iowa, and Wisconsin. As we are here concerned not only with the Seminary but quite as much with its foundress, it should be mentioned that she wrote several brief essays on the education of women, which appeared in the *Connecticut Common School Journal*.

Beecher says that her Hartford Female Seminary was begun in the spring of 1823 by two teachers. It was here, first of all, that she learned the lessons later published in her *Suggestions Respecting Improvements in Female Education* (1829).[54] In the beginning, these two young women proposed to do what all ladies' seminaries did—teach almost everything. She says:

"At that time, it was a general feeling in the community that the excellence of a school was indicated by the number of branches taught in it—so much so, that the common advertisements of the higher class of female schools set forth that one person proposed to be responsible for the instruction of pupils in from ten to twenty different pursuits, including often various languages and most of the branches pursued in colleges. In compliance with this custom, these ladies made similar proposals to the public. Gradually their school increased from fifteen to over seventy; and being accommodated with but one room, only these two teachers could be employed, while from ten to twelve branches were taught by them each day. Differences in the age or capacity of pupils necessarily multiplied the number of classes,

---

[54] The *Suggestions* were widely read and very influential. In 1840, the *Columbus* [Miss.] *Democrat* quoted them approvingly as "eloquent" and "striking." [Nov. 21, 1840, 1, col. 4.]

so that eight, ten, or in a few cases, fifteen minutes, were all that could be allowed for recitations, even to the most difficult and important branches.

"Thus, to the distracting duty of keeping in order and quietness so large a collection of youth, all full of life and animation, was added the labor of hearing a succession of classes at the average rate of one for every ten minutes. In attempting this no time could be allowed to explain or illustrate, and no apparatus was furnished for the purpose, not even so much as a blackboard. The teachers could only seek to discover as quickly as possible whether the pupils could repeat a form of words; and when that was attained, another class must come.

"The care of governing; the vexations from noise, irregularity, and mischief; the labor and distraction of mind incident to hearing such a number and variety of recitations; and the sickness of heart occasioned by feeling that nothing was done as it should be, exhausted all the animal strength and spirits ere each day was closed, so that nothing more could be attempted till the next day returned to witness the same unsatisfactory round of duties. All was perpetual haste, imperfection, irregularity, and the merely mechanical commitment of words to memory, without any chance for imparting clear and connected ideas in a single branch of knowledge. The review of those days is like the memory of a troubled and distracting dream; and nothing but a hope of remedy and relief, when time should have secured public confidence, sustained unremitting efforts to do all that could be done in such unfavorable circumstances."[55]

Finally the situation became unendurable, and when the pupils numbered about one hundred, the citizens formed the Hartford Female Seminary Association and provided for the erection of a building with suitable lecture and recitation rooms. A library was to be erected and "philosophical and chemical apparatus, together with globes, maps and charts, were to be provided." There were to be two terms per year of 22 weeks each, rather than the usual 'quarter' plan. Pupils were to be examined and classified at their entrance and set by their teachers to pursue the most useful branches first. Along with the regular studies there were special lectures held—at first chiefly by Miss Beecher—on moral, intellectual, and religious topics, the "formation of

[55] Beecher: *True Remedy*, 62 *ff.*

mental and social habits," the "evidences of Christianity," and the "best mode of studying the Scriptures."[56]

In the new building there was room for one hundred and fifty pupils. In order to improve instruction it was provided that: "Each teacher was responsible for the instruction of pupils only in two or three branches and received her classes at regular periods in her own recitation-room, while an hour was allowed for the most important recitations, and not less than half an hour to all. The teachers were allowed time to prepare themselves in their several branches, and, at the close of each term, conducted the public examination of all the classes committed to their care. One teacher was employed solely in enforcing the rules of neatness, order, and propriety, and in administering all the details of school government. She sat in the hall devoted to study, to preserve quiet; all permissions were to be sought from her; it was her business to send the classes to the recitation-rooms and to summon them back at the proper hour; and, in short, she relieved the other teachers of all care excepting that of instruction. At the same time, a regular course of study was instituted, and diplomas were awarded to all who completed this course."[57]

Miss Beecher was to have complete charge of the institution, and it was this provision, singularly enough, with the burdens that went with it, that was chiefly responsible for her later emphasis upon the necessity of a college system of co-equal teachers. The strain of the Hartford Seminary broke her health and she was compelled to leave to recuperate. Of this first experiment, however, she wrote: "The amount of intellectual activity and the delightful enthusiasm of interest that prevailed so universally, both among teachers and pupils, . . . exceeded anything of which I have ever known. . . ."[58]

Everywhere in educational circles the Hartford Seminary was regarded as unique. The editor of the *American Journal of Education* said, after describing the course at some length: "This undertaking we regard as one of peculiar interest. It is, so far as we know, one of the most liberal arrangements for the education of females . . . hitherto attempted in this country. . . ."[59]

[56] *Ibid.*, see also *American Journal of Educ.*, II, 252-3.
[57] Beecher: *True Remedy*, 62-7.
[58] *Ibid.*
[59] *Op. cit.*, II, 252-3.

Elsewhere it was pointed out that "it offers to young women a pretty fair opportunity of keeping pace, in some measure, with those of the other sex, who enjoy the advantages of a classical education."[60]

In 1833, Miss Beecher left the Hartford Seminary, removing to Cincinnati, and the school came under the care of a man who had a family and consequently could not devote his income to the support of the school as Miss Beecher had done. Later it was in charge of Miss Frances Strong who, with three of Miss Beecher's assistant principals, had operated the Huntsville Female Seminary in Alabama. Miss Beecher described it after leaving, and pointed out the reasons for failure.

"The decline of Hartford Seminary after I left was the necessary result of want of endowment. . . . Had [it] been endowed with only half the funds bestowed on our poorest colleges for young men, and the college plan of divided responsibilities thus been made permanent, most of my best teachers would have been retained, or, if removed at diverse intervals, their places would have been supplied by the highest class of teachers, as are college professorships."[61]

Surveying its whole history, she found therein the inherent weakness as contrasted with the men's colleges: "The preceding history of the Hartford Seminary shows a painful contrast to the advantages provided in colleges for young men. I began teaching and employing teachers without the previous preparation given to boys in preparatory schools, for no such had ever been offered to girls; and so I was obliged to train most of my teachers, as well as myself. Then no library or apparatus was provided, nor could the limited income from my tuition fees secure them. Then I was obliged to take the expenses and cares of housekeeping for several years, while all the instruction and government of the institution and finances rested on me alone. The selection and control of teachers and the course of study and the textbooks rested solely with me. Thus I had all the responsibilities which in colleges are divided among the faculty, treasurer and boarding housekeeper, and at the same time taught four and five hours a day."[62]

[60] *Ibid.*, III, 178–87.
[61] Barnard: *Am. Journal of Education*, XXVIII, 82.
[62] *Ibid.*, 81.

Few teachers have left as ungarnished a tale of their activities as did Gail Hamilton, who taught at Hartford High School. Her duties contrasted sharply with the laborious exertions of Miss Beecher in the private seminary:

"I am now comfortably settled in Hartford. Of course I do not feel at home as in Ipswich, but the change is very agreeable. I am boarding in a house with fifteen pupils and five teachers. The family is very pleasant. The school is about the same size as in Ipswich. I have five classes: three in Latin, one in Algebra, and one in Geometry. I have no care out of school. . . .

"I go down to school at half-past nine and stay till half-past twelve. There are four series of classes, but I am employed during only three of them. Consequently I have some three-quarters of an hour's rest after hearing my algebra, which comes first. Algebra is so familiar to me that I do not study it at all out of school. My next recitation is a class in Latin Reader. On this I spend, perhaps on an average, fifteen minutes out of school. Next comes a class in geometry. This I need to study, but do it when I am not employed, the hour after algebra. I go to school again at half-past two, hear a class in spelling for ten minutes, then have a class in Virgil. This I have taught so much that I study it but little myself, say from twenty minutes to half an hour. Then I have a class commencing Latin, which of course requires none of my time out of school. I reach home anywhere from four to half-past four. . . . My reading consists mostly of the *Tribune, Independent,* and the chance papers that come in my way. My literary efforts consist mostly in writing letters. I spend a good deal of time, in fact, on my pocket handkerchief, which really begins to look as though it might some day be finished."[63]

The Abbot Female Academy (Andover, Massachusetts) was incorporated and opened in 1829.[64] This school had no endowment, but depended at first on current income from students. Later it received benefactions from Sarah Abbot, of Andover, amounting to over ten thousand dollars, and other gifts from three citizens, George Davis, and John and Peter Smith, amount-

[63] Letters, I, 51–2, 53.

[64] Barnard's *Jour.,* XXX, 597. Note that the statement in Barnard's *Journal,* XXX, 597, is partially incorrect, since Pittsfield and Bath had incorporated academies or seminaries for females in 1807 and 1808, respectively.—See *Laws of Mass.,* 1807, 56–7; 1808, 355–7.

SARAH ABBOT

ing to fourteen thousand. The facilities were early improved by gifts of several cabinets of collections and pieces of 'philosophical' apparatus. The first catalog, 1832, listed eight trustees, five teachers, and seventy-four students.

Abbot Academy was unique in that it was presided over entirely by men in its early years. The course of study was not regularly pursued, nor were diplomas granted until after Miss Hasseltine took charge (1853). But a very liberal series of studies was offered, and the scholarship of Goddard, Schauffler, Lamson, Brown, and others, all college graduates, probably insured more excellent instruction than was available in most girls' academies of the thirties. In the first fifty years of its existence, about six thousand girls attended. "Particular attention" was to be "devoted to young ladies who may wish to qualify themselves to teach." It was designed "to afford every facility to young ladies for acquiring a thorough and extensive education." In the words of its constitution, "The primary objects to be aimed at in this school shall ever be, to regulate the tempers, to improve the taste, to discipline and enlarge the minds, and form the morals of the youth who may be members of it. To form the immortal mind to habits suited to an immortal being, and to instill principles of conduct and form the character for an immortal destiny, shall be subordinate to no other care. Solid and useful acquirements shall always have the precedence of those which are merely showy or ornamental."[65]

Mary Lyon, who, in her labor to establish Mount Holyoke Female Seminary, carried on the work begun by Joseph Emerson, her teacher, and Zilpah Grant, her co-worker, was born at Buckland, Massachusetts, 1797. First at a district school; then at Saunderson Academy in Ashfield, where she says she "was principally educated," and tradition says that she mastered Latin grammar in three days, to the complete marvel of the scholars and master, Elijah H. Burritt; again at Amherst Academy, where she studied chemistry under Eaton; and then, at twenty-four, under Emerson, at Byfield (1821), to whom she felt her debt was greater than to any other, she received the initial instruction and spiritual inspiration that were to sustain her labors for a quarter of a century in the interest of women's higher education.

[65] *Catalog*, 1832.

She began by teaching district school near her home, being paid the usual amount of $.75 a week and "board round"; and, after two terms with Emerson at Byfield, she became assistant teacher at Ashfield Academy, a place never before held by a woman. From 1824 to 1834, she coöperated with Zilpah Grant, whose acquaintance she had made at Byfield, at Adams Academy, and later at Ipswich Seminary, whence she withdrew to work out her own great experiment, which had been suggested by the words of her greatest teacher and cherished by Miss Grant as well. In this spiritual inheritance lay the secret of the religious emphasis at Mount Holyoke. Emerson had already published lectures on the millenium and regarded education of women as a necessary step towards it. He was deeply religious and converted Mary Lyon. She, in turn, converted more than a quarter of the Mount Holyoke students who attended during her lifetime.[66] The religious emphasis at Adams Academy resulted in friction with the trustees and the subsequent effort to found a permanent institution at Ipswich.

To promote the latter, Mary Lyon drew up a plan for The New England Seminary for Teachers (1832), but there was insufficient public enthusiasm at Ipswich to support it. A hopeful prospect in Amherst was also blighted about the same time. In 1834, Miss Lyon severed connection with the Ipswich Seminary, leaving to establish a school after her own heart,—she knew not exactly where, but at any rate in New England. Her ideas were clear. The institution was to be (1) for middle class girls, (2) much less expensive than most female seminaries, and (3) was to provide for domestic labor by students. Voluntary gifts were to erect the building. Low pay for teachers, combined with the foregoing features, was to reduce the cost of female education to at least the level of men's education.

A committee of men was named and funds sought, Miss Lyon herself collecting about $1,000 in two months in and around Ipswich. The early subscriptions varied from three of six cents each to those of a thousand dollars by Deacon Safford and Samuel Williston. Twenty-seven thousand dollars was raised by eighteen hundred subscribers in ninety localities, but Mary Lyon regarded the autograph guarantee of the ladies of Ipswich for

[66] Stow: *Mount Holyoke Seminary*, 22.

$1,000 as the true cornerstone of the new seminary.[67]   South
Hadley was selected as the location and on February 10, 1836, a
charter was granted to Mount Holyoke Female Seminary.
The school opened November 8, 1837, being the first established
by appeal to public philanthropy.   The gifts of money, made
upon the personal solicitation of Mary Lyon, were the best assurance that could be given that many of her neighbors believed in
her character, her power as a teacher and organizer, though
others doubted her vision.   Those best acquainted with female
education, Miss Grant and Miss Beecher, were both inclined to
think the new scheme wrong in adopting the idea of low pay for
teachers, for it would not draw the best talent.   To this argument
she replied with characteristic logic:

"While the public are so little prepared to contribute liberally
to an object like this, may it not be expedient that those who first
enter the field as laborers should receive as a reward so little of
'filthy lucre' that they may be able to commend themselves to
every man's conscience, even to those whose minds are narrow,
and whose hearts are not much enlarged by Christian philanthropy?   If such a course should be desirable at the commencement, how soon it would be no longer needful, time and experience alone can decide."[68]

The scheme according to which the Seminary was first conducted, was described in a circular, as follows:

"The teachers and pupils will constitute one family, and none
will be received to board elsewhere.   Except in extraordinary
cases none will be received under sixteen years of age.   If any
must be refused, preference will be given to those who have been
teaching.

"The school year will comprise four quarters of ten weeks
each.   The charge for board and tuition will be settled by experiment.   In the present fluctuating state of the market the
trustees will name a price for one quarter only at a time.   For
the first quarter they have decided to place board, exclusive of
fuel and lights, at thirteen dollars, and tuition at three dollars,
making the bill sixteen dollars for ten weeks, to be paid in advance.   As far as definite encouragement has been offered, it has
been that the regular bills for board and tuition would be from

[67] *Ibid.*, 59 *f.*

[68] *Ibid.*, 44.

one-third to one-half less than in existing seminaries.   It will be seen, on comparison, that the terms stated are not far from one-half charged elsewhere.   The expectations of the public will therefore be fully realized even if on experiment it be found that actual cost requires the charge to be somewhat higher hereafter. The domestic department will be in charge of a competent person.   All the members of the school will aid to some extent in the domestic labors of the family.   The time thus occupied will be so small that it will not retard progress in study, but rather facilitate it by the invigorating influence of a little daily exercise.

"The division of labor will be very systematic, giving to each young lady not much variety in a term, but enabling her to perform her part in a proper manner, without solicitude.   To each will be assigned that in which she has been well trained at home, and no one will receive instruction in anything with which she is entirely unacquainted.   It is no part of our design to teach young ladies domestic work.   This branch of education is important, but a literary institution is not the place to gain it. Home is the proper place for this instruction and the mother is the appropriate teacher.   Some may inquire, 'Why then this arrangement?'   We reply, that the family work must be performed—that it is difficult to find hired domestics, and to retain them when they are found—and that young ladies engaged in study suffer much in vigor of body and mind and in their future health, for the want of exercise.   The construction of the building and the family arrangements will render it convenient for the members of the school to take part in the domestic department, thus receiving and conferring benefit.   Daughters of well-bred families in New England have independence enough to do anything which will promote their best interests, and the best interests of those around them, and for such families this institution is designed.

"This feature of the institution will not relieve mothers from giving their daughters a thorough domestic education, but it will rather furnish additional motives to be faithful in this important duty.   Is it not a reflection on both mother and daughter, when the daughter cannot perform with skill and cheerfulness any domestic labor which is suitable for her mother?

"The plan for the domestic department is an experiment— but one respecting which there are sanguine hopes of success.

That the experiment may be a fair one, it is important that the plan should be executed on the principle of entire equality; that the labor should be performed as a gratuitous service; that all should participate; and that none should be received who are entirely unacquainted with domestic work, or who cannot cheerfully co-operate with others in carrying out these arrangements.

"In the formation of all the plans of this seminary it is kept in mind that the labors of any teacher are but temporary. Much care will be taken to adopt permanent principles and to mature a system which may outlive those who inaugurate it."[69]

From the above it is clear that Mount Holyoke never was an industrial or manual labor school in the proper sense. The labor was not performed primarily for an educational end, but for economy, as Miss Lyon said. The great benefit to those in poor or ordinary circumstances is evident in the fact that for sixteen years the annual charge per pupil was but sixty dollars.

At first they could receive but "about ninety" pupils, although there were requests for more than two hundred places. None under sixteen were to be admitted, and all were to remain at least a year.[70] After a short time, provision was made to accommodate the two hundred of the original plan and, during the life of Mary Lyon, about sixteen hundred girls attended the seminary. At the end of a half century, 12,500 students had been enrolled, nearly two thousand of whom had graduated. These students, during the first few years, came mostly from New England; later they were drawn from all sections of the United States, and many, too, from mission fields in foreign lands. They went out chiefly as teachers, home makers and missionaries. In 1877, the Memorandum Society had a record of 2,341—less than half of the total that had been connected with the seminary in the forty years. Stow[71] said that "Of these 2,341, 1,690 had taught since leaving the seminary; 77 of them twenty or more years; 260 between ten and twenty years; and 470 between five and ten years; making 807 that had taught five or more years. Twenty-one were physicians; 1,391 were married; 141, perhaps more, were or had been foreign missionaries. The number of city and home missionaries, known to be large, was not definitely ascertained."

[69] *Ibid.*, 72–3.

[70] An exception was made at the beginning of the first year.

[71] *Op. cit.*, 318.

Though religion played a prominent rôle in the life of most schools of the early part of the last century, and Christian character and usefulness were almost without exception reckoned as true objectives, especially appropriate for girls' schools, there is no exaggeration in saying that at Mount Holyoke there was probably more personal religious fervor than in any other single institution. Miss Lyon was prone to regard the success of her efforts to create the school as sealing a covenant with God for the advancement of His Kingdom. The journal of the seminary has many items of this or similar character: "At teachers' meeting Miss Lyon proposed that we mention the names of those here who are now missionaries either at home or abroad. . . . We then united in two prayers for them, Miss Lyon leading in one. . . . When Miss Lyon asked whom we wished to present for prayer, two, not Christians, were named. We knelt and prayed for them, then two more, and so on till twelve had been mentioned."[72]

At her death (1849) Miss Lyon had completed thirty-five years' service as a teacher and had ministered to more than three thousand pupils. Her whole life work was as fervid in spirit as her prayers. Nothing describes more fittingly her attitude towards her chosen endeavor than the lines cut upon the marble that marks her grave: "There is nothing in the universe that I fear but that I shall not know all my duty, or shall fail to do it."

After Mary Lyon's death, the Seminary passed first to the capable hands of Mary Chapin (1849–1867), Helen French (1867–1872), Julia E. Ward (1872–1883), and Elizabeth Blanchard (1883–1889). In 1888, the charter as seminary and college was received; five years later it became Mount Holyoke College.

Another famous institution was the Oread Collegiate Institute, established by Eli Thayer at Worcester, Massachusetts, in 1849. It was housed in a veritable castle, designed to accommodate six hundred girls. Its collegiate course was patterned after that of Brown University, and Thayer hoped to provide generous "mental culture, in no way inferior to that secured to the other sex by our colleges and universities." Furthermore, he planned to sell this education at cost.[73]

[72] *Ibid.*, 109.

[73] Wright: *Hist. of Oread Coll. Inst.*; Williams: *Hist. Worcester Co., Mass.*, I, 124 and 440.

MARY LYON

The states made out of the Northwest Territory became the missionary field for numerous advocates of higher education of women who had studied at schools in New England or the central states and had become teachers. Many felt, with Catherine Beecher, that the West had to be saved; and in her *True Remedy* and an essay entitled *American Women, Will You Save Your Country?* she made it clear that salvation was to come chiefly through education, and that woman's part in education was more important than man's.[74] The result was that the seminary movement arose and proceeded in the West after much the same manner as in New England, being determined both by a stock largely derived from thence and the missionaries sent out for the specific purpose of shaping educational affairs.

III. *Expansion of the Seminary Movement*

The academy and seminary movement grew at a phenomenal rate in the North, South, and West, though there were fluctuations in the individual states, according to the policy adopted regarding their encouragement. But throughout three quarters of the nineteenth century the seminary was the dominant agency of woman's advanced education. After 1850, the college—first only nominally, then actually—became a competitor. When secondary education became universally available in high school, academy, or seminary, the college was enabled to be more than a competitor of the latter, and offered collegiate instruction similar to, if not identical in all cases with, college education for men. To achieve this was difficult, as is suggested by the fact that so many colleges (real or nominal) were compelled by circumstances to run preparatory departments for their students. While it would be monotonous to catalog the numerous seminaries or academies of the several states, a few cases may be taken to illustrate the trend of the movement, the time of its rise, height, and gradual decline.

Massachusetts, in 1807 and 1808, incorporated the Pittsfield Female Academy and also one at Bath. The Bradford Academy and the Friends' Academy (New Bedford), coeducational, were begun in 1803 and 1812, the former becoming a girls' school exclusively in 1836, when "father Greenleaf" retired. As a gen-

[74] See her *Reminiscences;* and pp. 321 *ff.*

eral rule, however, Massachusetts' incorporated schools were for
boys or girls separately, those for the latter being created for
"the instruction of females in useful and elegant accomplishments." From an examination of the Laws of Massachusetts, it
appears that the female seminary movement was recognized as
important by the Massachusetts Legislature between 1830 and
1860, there being at least twenty-one individual acts passed for
their encouragement. With the Civil War, and thereafter, came
an almost complete cessation of incorporating acts, reliance being
placed upon the schools already established and the rapidly developing high schools. During the period of great legislative
encouragement (1830–1860) there were other specific acts in
favor of women's training and education besides those establishing seminaries. The Female Medical Education Society, Ladies
Physiological Institute (1850), and the New England School of
Design for Women (1853) are important instances.[75]

In Portland, Maine, Martin Ruter announced a school exclusively for girls, in 1812. Though not called "academy," instruction beyond the rudiments included English grammar and
geography, which had been among the distinguishing marks of
the new institution.[76] The same year Asa Lyman opened a
private academy for girls only, where he offered a practical education, "calculated to excite a fondness for mental investigation
and to promote intellectual and moral improvements."[77] Few
separate female academies, however, were established and fewer
were incorporated by Maine. Early academies, such as Hallowell, Berwick, Freyburg, Washington, and Portland, were, or
soon became, coeducational; at least they added female departments. For example, Hallowell, a strictly classical school, incorporated in 1791, established a female department in 1829;[78]
Maine Wesleyan Seminary, at Kent's Hill, admitted girls shortly
after its establishment, having seven girls and one hundred and
one boys in 1830;[79] and Waterville, Maine, Academy had two
girls and fifty-eight boys in 1831.[80] The female seminaries, as

[75] *Laws of Mass.*, 1850, 481; 1853, 681.
[76] *Eastern Argus* (Portland, Me.), Mch. 7, 1812, 4, col. 2.
[77] *Ibid.*, Oct. 8, 1812, 4, col. 3.
[78] Nason: *Old Hallowell on the Kennebec*, 55 and 212.
[79] *Catalog*, 1830.
[80] *Catalog*, 1831.

said, were few, and generally short-lived: thus Bath Female
Academy (1808) and Bangor Young Ladies' Academy (1818)
were extinct by 1851.   Oxford Female Academy (1827) was
never operated.   The Coney Female Academy became Coney
High School, and coeducational.[81]

In New York the earliest incorporated school for girls in the
nineteenth century was the Ursuline Convent (1814), which was
"to provide education for poor girls."[82]   The practice of incorporating separate schools for boys and girls was not so much
emphasized, though a considerable number of female seminaries
were created, especially from 1820 to 1840; and, again, from 1860
to 1870, several were incorporated.   From a comparison with
Massachusetts it is evident that New York was more favorably
inclined to the incorporation of the two-sex academy.   Prior to
1835, it was often specified that these seminaries or academies
should not receive a part of the literary fund; but, after 1835,
it was generally specified in the act that they should receive it.[83]
Some exceptions to this last, however, appeared.[84]   The rapid increase in special schools for girls, between 1819 and 1839, was
probably due more to the work of Mrs. Willard and the encouragement given by DeWitt Clinton than to any other two
promoters of the cause.

Although Pennsylvania had two special schools for girls—the
Moravian Seminary, opened to outsiders in 1785, and the Female
Academy in Philadelphia, 1784 (chartered in 1792)—and thus
led other states of the Union in officially recognizing the utility
of special agencies for girls' advanced education, it was not until
near the middle of the next century that vigorous, concerted
action in incorporating female seminaries occurred.   In 1838, a
general act was passed: "To encourage the arts and sciences, promote the teaching of useful knowledge, and support the Colleges,
Academies and Female Seminaries within this commonwealth,
there hereby is appropriated and shall annually be paid to the
said Colleges, Academies and Female Seminaries, in equal quar-

[81] *History of Education in Maine,* by the Superintendent of Public Schools,
84 *ff.*

[82] *Laws of N. Y.* (1814), 66; this probably gave only elementary instruction.

[83] *Laws of New York* for this period.

[84] For example, Female Academy of the Sacred Heart, *Laws of N. Y.,*
1851, 820.

terly payments, the sums following to wit: to each University and College now incorporated, or which may be incorporated by the legislature, and maintaining at least four professors, and instructing constantly at least one hundred students, one thousand dollars; to each Academy and Female Seminary, now incorporated, or which may be incorporated by the legislature, maintaining one or more teachers, capable of giving instruction in the Greek and Roman classics, mathematics and English, or English and German literature, and in which at least fifteen pupils shall constantly be taught in either or all of the branches aforesaid, three hundred dollars; to each of said Academies and Female Seminaries, where at least twenty-five pupils are taught as aforesaid, four hundred dollars; and each of said Academies and Female Seminaries, having at least two teachers, and in which forty or more pupils are constantly taught as aforesaid, five hundred dollars; but no Academy in any city or county of the state where a University or College is established, and receiving the appropriation made by this act, shall be entitled to receive the appropriation made by this act for the benefit of Academies; this section to continue in force for ten years and no longer."[85]

These seminaries were to be under an incorporated board of trustees (not over nine) empowered to (1) hold property having a yearly value of $3,000, (2) have a seal, (3) hold stated meetings, (4) employ and dismiss teachers, and (5) grant certificates to graduates. None were to be debarred from the position of trustee, teacher, principal or pupil "on account of his sentiments in matters of religion."[86]   Thirty-four such seminaries were incorporated in 1838 and 1839, after which the movement gradually declined.[87]   After 1850 several colleges were incorporated, most of which might, with greater propriety, have been included as seminaries.[88]

In Ohio, numerous female seminaries were incorporated in the period between 1830 and 1850.[89]   After 1852, due to a general

[85] *Laws of Pa.*, 1838, Sec. 4, 333–4.

[86] *Ibid.*, 1838, Sec. 7–13, 619–21.

[87] In 1840 it was stated that there were 33 female seminaries in operation and 57 academies, in which there were 1430 and 2465 students, respectively. —*Conn. Com. Sch. Jour.*, III, 161.

[88] See Vol. II, 146.

[89] Columbus Female Academy, 1831, 100; St. Mary's Female Literary Society, Marietta Collegiate Institute, and Western Teachers Seminary, 1832,

enactment providing for incorporation of educational institutions by any number of persons, not less than five, individual acts of incorporation ceased to appear in the laws.[90]   Barnard, in 1862, published data on 23 female seminaries and "colleges" of Ohio, including some of those given below.[91]   A rough comparison of the relative importance attached to the education of boys and girls may be gained from the fact that, up to 1851, Ohio had incorporated about one hundred and forty secondary schools and colleges for boys.   Girls probably attended some of these, though not mentioned in the incorporating acts.   Between 1831 and 1851, there were about thirty seminaries incorporated specifically for girls and at least one hundred and sixteen for boys, girls not being mentioned.   Thirteen, at least, were clearly for both boys and girls.[92]

Several of the seminaries were very ambitious.   As early as 1828, Steubenville Female Seminary had about a hundred pupils, a round dozen regular teachers, three assistant teachers, three assistant pupils and a matron.[93]   In 1830, Bethania Crocker, encouraged by the president and professors Scott and McGuffey of Miami University, founded Oxford Female Academy, which was incorporated in 1839, and later (1852) became "Oxford Female College."[94]   Granville Female Seminary was opened, in 1832, by Charles Sawyer.   It was little more than an elementary

---

4–5, 18; Chillicothe Female Seminary, 1833, 188; Granville, Western, and Circleville Female Seminaries, 1835, 87, 153, 321, respectively; St. Clairsville and Cleveland Collegiate Female Seminaries, 1837, 55 and 511; Norwalk Female Seminary, 1838, 210; New Hagerstown, Ravenna, and Worthington Female Seminaries and Oxford Female Academy, 1839, 344, 291, 141, and 80, respectively; Willoughby Female Academy, 1840, 155; Athens Female Academy, 1841, 65; Oakland Female Seminary, Methodist Female Collegiate Institute, and St. Mary's Female Educational Institute, 1843, 148, 146, and 46, respectively; Cooper Female Academy, 1845, 87; Felicity Female Seminary, 1848, 135; Springfield Female Seminary, Oxford Female Institute, and Mansfield Female Seminary, 1849, 263, 238, and 280, respectively; Defiance, Xenia, and Elliot Female Seminaries, and Soeurs de Notre Dame Institute at Chillicothe, 1850, 625, 637, 614, and 639, respectively; Cleveland, Sigourney, and Cody Female Seminaries, in 1851, 3, 12, 20, respectively.—*Laws of Ohio*, pages given after each date.

[90] *Laws of Ohio*, Apr. 9, 1852, 128 *ff*.

[91] *Am. Jour. Ed.*, XIII, 267–8.

[92] *Laws of Ohio* for the years concerned.

[93] *Am. Annals of Educ.*, IV, 577.

[94] *Laws of Ohio*, 1839, 80; and 1852.

school the first year but, in 1833, a full seminary course was offered. Later it became Shepardson College.[95] Another school at Granville was begun (1827) by Reverend Jacob Little and his wife, and taught first by Mary Ann Howe, one of his pupils. It was later incorporated; in 1867, the name was changed to "college" and English, classical and musical courses were offered.[96] The Western Female Seminary, incorporated at Oxford (1853), aimed higher than its name. Its directors insisted "the intellectual privileges of young ladies should be much greater than are commonly afforded them"; and aimed to provide discipline of the faculties "by drawing forth the mental energies" rather than by "ornamenting the surface." They sought a "permanent institution," erected a building 176 x 76 feet, costing $60,000, secured pledges for "a very respectable library" and set to work for an endowment of $125,000.[97] Though it was satisfied with the designation of "seminary," it required three years of Latin in the regular course (much more than many so-called "colleges") and its standards appear to have been above most seminaries.

The female seminary's rapid rise to popularity, in the thirties, may be seen in the city of Cincinnati. The city *Directory*,[98] in 1831, listed Dr. Locke's and Freusdell's female academies. In 1836, ten female academies were listed. One of these was the Western Female Institute, under the Misses Dutton and Tappan, which had been begun by Catherine Beecher and her sister when they removed to Cincinnati with their father, in 1833.[99]

Being solicited to establish a school "of a higher order than any then existing," Miss Beecher asked for $500 to buy equipment; and with the assistance of Mrs. Stowe, Miss Dutton, and two other assistant teachers whom she had trained at Hartford, the school was begun. Here the co-equal plan of teachers was tried. More scholars appeared than could be accommodated, and an effort was made to purchase a large building for housing a permanent school[100] and, likewise, to obtain an endowment from

95 *Old Northwest Genealogical Quarterly*, VIII, No. 4, Oct. 1905, 359–68.
96 *Ibid.*, VIII, No. 4, Oct. 1905, 317–58.
97 *First Circular, Western Female Seminary*, 1854.
98 P. 175.
99 *Cincinnati Directory*, 1829, 1831, 1834, and 1836–7.
100 Barnard: *Am. Jour. Ed.*, XXVIII, 82 *ff.*

the Hughes Fund. This was promised on condition that the former be done. Miss Beecher tried to raise the fund to buy the building, but her health failed in the task which became more difficult with the financial stress of 1837. Nevertheless, the school was continued by her teachers for five years, and failed only because of lack of a suitable building and the fact that the teachers found better positions elsewhere.[101]

How high an estimate was placed on these rising institutions of Ohio may be seen in the enthusiastic encomium expressed in the address of one of the visitors:

"One word only in regard to your institution. Everything indicates that you have been well and faithfully trained not only to perform regularly certain exercises, but to think and acquaint yourselves with history. You cannot but know, then, that in all ages and in all countries, up to a very recent period, your half (and the common parlance is equally complimentary and true) the better half of the species was viewed, as a race holding to man the relation of butterflies to eagles. Cast by the beneficence of Providence in a more delicate mould, you were considered in the light of statues, in which grace and beauty were the chief requisites, gaudy playthings in which mind was by no means necessary.

"All that has passed away, and, we hope, forever. A new era has dawned upon you, not the mental deliverance and independence of Miss Frances Wright, separating you from God and eternity, as it would emancipate you from this base thraldom of the past. But it has been proved, no longer to be contested, that you have minds capable of illimitable progress, differing, indeed, in some respects, from the male mind, but differing, perhaps, in your favor. It has been shown, in innumerable instances, that you are quite as susceptible of intellectual, and more docile to moral training than man; that thus you can become, what you were formed to be, an helpmate for him, his intellectual companion, his guide, philosopher, and friend, cheering existence with a mental radiance all your own, a mental radiance differing from that of man, only by that beautiful diversity, which marks all the works of God."[102]

[101] Beecher: *True Remedy*, 81–3.
[102] *Am. Jour. Ed.*, V, 230–1.

Numerous special schools for girls began to appear in Michigan in the twenties. Mrs. McKenney and Miss Sammons advertised schools in Detroit, in 1825 and 1826, but the exact nature of the studies was not stated.[103] Martha Baldwin's school offered many of the studies generally found in the seminaries.[104] The Detroit Female Seminary, under Miss Tappan and Miss Nichols, Resé's High School for Young Ladies, and St. Clare's Seminary for Ladies were advertised at Detroit, in 1833.[105] Miss Clark's school, at Ann Arbor, was announced the same year.[106]

In 1837, the legislature provided for establishing "branches of the University in the different parts of the state"; and section nineteen specified that "with every such branch . . . there shall be established an institution for the education of females in the higher branches of knowledge."[107] Several institutions were incorporated for girls only; among them, Marshall,[108] Utica,[109] Ann Arbor,[110] and Oakland female seminaries,[111] the Young Ladies' Seminary of Monroe City,[112] and the Michigan Female Seminary at Kalamazoo.

In Indiana, the act to incorporate "an University in the Indiana Territory" (1807) provided that the trustees, as soon as the funds would allow, should "establish an institution for the education of females" and make such by-laws for the same "as they may think proper."[113] In 1818, a "County Seminary Law" was passed, but the only state support was to come from fines for breaking the peace and from the "conscience money" of Quakers. These seminaries, therefore, though several were chartered, were never popular, especially in country districts; and, in 1852, the assembly ordered that county seminaries be sold, the proceeds, estimated at $100,000, to go to the common school fund.

[103] *Detroit Gazette*, Apr. 8, 1825, 2; Oct. 31, 1826, 3.
[104] *Ibid.*, June 6, 1826, 3.
[105] *Courier*, Aug. 14, 1833; *Detroit Jour. and Mich. Advt.*, May 1, 1833; and Sept. 25, 1833, respectively.
[106] *Detroit Jour. and Mich. Advt.*, Oct. 2, 1833.
[107] *Laws of Michigan*, March 18, 1837, 105.
[108] *Ibid.*, 1839, 88.
[109] *Ibid.*, 1844, 67.
[110] *Ibid.*, 1845, 109–11.
[111] *Ibid.*, 1849, 205–7.
[112] *Ibid.*, 1850, 23–6.
[113] *Laws of Indiana*, 1807, 436 and 444.

The constitutionality of the law for selling the seminaries was questioned, but the county seminaries were never revived.[114] The sale of seminaries was followed by a provision (1855) for the incorporation of high schools and academies.[115]

The general tendency was to favor coeducational institutions. A Female Seminary for Monroe County, at Bloomington, was incorporated, in 1833,[116] but schools with male and female departments were far more common. One of the most famous institutions, Washington County Seminary, under the leadership of John I. Morrison, laid great emphasis on the preparation of teachers. One of his pupils, Mrs. A. M. Coffin, says of his school:

"It was then not a common thing for girls to learn Latin and I well remember my surprise at Laura and Cornelia Leonard reading Horace to Mr. Morrison. The Seminary soon became famous. Pupils flocked not only from Washington County and from adjoining counties, from Louisville, New Albany, Jeffersonville, Charleston, Bedford, Paoli, Corydon, Indianapolis and other places. The house was too small to hold all the pupils. Many families of the town took boarders who attended the Seminary. . . .

"It was a mixed school, and all the better for that, as I take it. True the boys and girls occasionally fell in love with each other, but they will do that anyway and they will be less likely to make serious mistakes when they have studied and recited together and taken each other's mental caliber. There never were so many bright, pretty girls in any other school as that. Their presence made the boys behave better, and they were put on their mettle not to be excelled by them. I may mention Mary Bradley, who was among the foremost of the girls. Those who knew her then would testify as to her marked ability in all her studies."[117]

In Illinois, two academies, Madison and Washington, incorporated in 1819, and Monroe, in 1827, were permitted, as soon as funds would suffice, to establish institutions "for the education of females."[118] The practice of creating institutions with

114 Hendren: *Special Report On the Common School Fund of Indiana*, 12 *ff*.

115 *Laws of Indiana*, Feb. 28, 1855, 186–9.

116 *Ibid.*, 1833, 28 *ff*.

117 *Indiana Mag. of Hist.*, June 1926, XXII, 183 *ff*.

118 *Laws of Ill.*, 1819, 48 *ff*., 368 *ff*.; and 1827, 30–3.

permission to establish both male and female departments continued, about forty being so chartered between 1830 and 1860.[119] With the beginning of the fourth decade, however, the seminary for girls only became popular, as in other states, there being at least twenty-seven chartered between 1830 and 1860.[120]

A number of Illinois seminaries for women came to play a prominent rôle, having much more than local prominence and patronage. Such were the Jacksonville Female Academy, incorporated in 1835;[121] Monticello Female Seminary, opened in 1838 and chartered in 1840,[122] Illinois Conference Female Seminary and Rockford Female Seminary, both chartered in 1847.[123] The first of these had its origin in a meeting "of gentlemen favorable to the establishment of a Female Seminary" at Jacksonville, in 1830. The backing of such men as Samuel D. Lockwood, J. M. Sturtevant, John Ellis and ten others, who were named as a board of trust, was doubtless an important factor in securing its incorporation (the first in the state) at the hands of a reluctant legislature. The academy was formally opened in 1833, under Sarah C. Crocker, who had been recommended by Mary Lyon. Two years later, the first principal having married one of the trustees, a second, Emily P. Price, was secured upon the recommendation of Zilpah Grant of Ipswich. The new school was destined to be a center of great influence for the education of women, being created just as the public mind was beginning to be agitated on that subject. It was there that the Ladies' Educational Society was formed, having as its principal object the preparation of young women for teaching. The prevailing notions, against which the new experiment had to contend, are suggested in the views presented by a visiting delegation of ladies: "We hear you are about to form a class in Natural Philosophy?" Being informed such was the case, they opined it was not proper that "young ladies should study the sciences; if they can read and spell, write and count, it is all they need to know."[124]

[119] List made from *Laws of Illinois*, 1830–1860.
[120] *Ibid.*; a few were named college, high school, or institute, but their character was the same as the female seminary.
[121] *Laws of Ill.*, Jan. 27, 1835, 192–4.
[122] *Ibid.*, 1840.
[123] *Ibid.*, 1847, 52–4, and 124–6.
[124] *Semi-Centennial of Jacksonville Female Academy*, 1880, 8 ff.

Monticello Female Seminary, at Godfrey, was the result of the efforts of Benjamin Godfrey who, in 1834, confided to Theron Baldwin, who had been intimately connected with Mary Lyon's experiment at South Hadley, that he wished to spend his fortune philanthropically.[125] Baldwin was to take charge of the details. He travelled about five thousand miles, visiting and studying numerous Eastern schools. Mary Lyon was consulted. The building was ready by 1838, and Mary Cone, one of Miss Grant's teachers, was secured as the first principal.

In her *New England Girlhood*, Lucy Larcom described her indebtedness to this seminary which was at the time about twelve years old: "Its Principal—I wonder now that I could have lived so near her for a year without becoming acquainted with her,— but her high local reputation as an intellectual woman inspired me with awe, and I was foolishly diffident. One day, however, upon the persuasion of my friends at Vine Lodge, who knew my wishes for a higher education, I went with them to call upon her. We talked about the matter which had been in my thoughts so long, and she gave me not only a cordial but an urgent invitation to come and enroll myself as a student. There were arrangements for those who could not incur the current expenses, to meet them by doing part of the domestic work, and of these I gladly availed myself. The stately limestone edifice, standing in the midst of an original growth of forest-trees, two or three miles from the Mississippi River, became my home—my student-home— for three years. The benefits of those three years I have been reaping ever since, I trust not altogether selfishly. It was always my desire and my ambition as a teacher, to help my pupils as my teachers had helped me.

"The course of study at Monticello Seminary was the broadest, the most college-like, that I have ever known; and I have had ex-

---

[125] His total gifts amounted to $110,000. He said of the origin of his idea: "One morning in 1830, while lying in my bed recovering from a severe sickness, my wife came into the room and made some remarks as she left. Our little daughter who had just begun to lisp a few words, caught the remarks, and, while playing by herself on the floor, repeated them over and over for some time. This led me to reflect on the powerful influence of the mother on the minds, manners, habits and character of her children, and I resolved to devote a large part of my possessions to the intellectual and moral improvement of women."—Sketch of Monticello [*The Echo*, July, 1898, 4.]

perience since in several institutions of the kind.   The study of mediaeval and modern history, and of the history of modern philosophy, especially, opened new vistas to me.   In these our Principal was also our teacher, and her method was to show us the tendencies of thought, to put our minds into the great current of human affairs, leaving us to collect details as we could, then or afterward.   We came thus to feel that these were life-long studies, as indeed they are.

"The course was somewhat elective, but her advice to me was not to omit anything because I did not like it.   I had a natural distaste for mathematics, and my recollections of my struggles with trigonometry and conic sections are not altogether those of a conquering heroine.   But my teacher told me that my mind had need of just that exact sort of discipline, and I think she was right."[126]

Rockford Female Seminary was the outgrowth of a conference of churches of the Northwest, held in Cleveland, Ohio, June, 1844, at which it was decided there should be a college and a female seminary "of the highest order," one in Wisconsin and the other in Illinois.   Beloit was chosen as the college seat[127] and Rockford as the location for the female seminary, in 1845.   The same trustees served both institutions.   Subscriptions to a sum of $3,500 were sought for the girls' school and a charter secured February 25, 1847.   Many pledges failed and the opening was thus delayed.   Meantime, Anna P. Sill, from Phipps Union Seminary, Albion, New York, began a preparatory school (1849) called Rockford Female Seminary, wherein she was assisted by Hannah and Eliza Richards.[128]   The pupils numbered seventy the first term and were mostly under ten years of age.   It was not until September, 1850, that the contemplated Rockford Female Seminary, provided for by the charter, was assured.   In 1851, the trustees recognized Miss Sill's school as the preparatory department of Rockford Female Seminary.   In 1852, the seminary passed under the control of a separate board, though some members served also on the Board of Beloit College.[129]

126 *Op. cit.*, 265–7.

127 1844, and chartered Feb. 2, 1846.

128 Miss Sill had previously taught at Warsaw, Oakfield, and Cary Collegiate Institute, and came to Rockford at the solicitation of Rev. L. H. Loss.

129 Church: *Hist. of Rockford and Winnebago Counties*, 290 *ff*.

Miss Sill was made principal, in 1852, continued actively in that office till 1884, and as Principal Emerita till her death, in 1889.

Under her leadership, the seminary did high-grade work. In 1854, the collegiate department had four divisions: mental and moral philosophy; mathematics and natural science; history and English literature; and languages. The course at that time comprised four classes,—junior, middle, senior, and the course for resident graduates.[130] The work of each class was divided into three terms. By 1865, the collegiate course consisted of junior, junior middle, senior middle, and senior year; and the resident graduate year was still continued. In the first eight years, 1854–1861, eighty-two are said, by Church, to have completed the collegiate course.[131] Collegiate degrees have been conferred since 1887; on September 22, 1892, the name was changed to Rockford College.

A second effort to promote education of women in the West was made by Catherine E. Beecher, at Milwaukee. Before 1848, nothing of permanent character was done. In that year, Mrs. L. A. Parsons published a circular of the Milwaukee Female Seminary, which was "to take young misses from the primary schools and conduct them systematically onward to a thorough knowledge of the whole circle of sciences as taught in similar institutions."[132] The classes were preparatory, junior, middle, and senior. A boarding department was conducted.

At this time Mrs. Parsons became acquainted with the views of Catherine Beecher and, after correspondence, extended her an invitation to visit Milwaukee and make an appeal to the citizens on behalf of a permanent institution. This was accepted and an address was given September 11, 1850, at the school which had now become the Milwaukee Normal Institute and High School and, with the help of Miss Mortimer, was already operating on the coequal teacher plan. The address was warmly received, for, as one writer said: "Such a school as Miss B. proposes is exactly in keeping with the character and wants of this thriving City. . . ." The outcome was the surrender of the school by Mrs. Parsons and its incorporation, with a board of trustees,

130 *Catalog*, 1854–5, 17–18.
131 *Op. cit.*, 292.
132 Quoted by Wight: *Annals of Milwaukee College*, 2.

MILWAUKEE NORMAL INSTITUTE (DESIGNED BY C. E. BEECHER)

March 1, 1851.[133] From a circular issued that autumn, Miss Beecher's influence is clearly seen, for emphasis is placed on the fact that (1) it is non-sectarian, (2) it has an economical way of utilizing benefactions, (3) it operates on the college plan. (4) it aims to train women for their true profession, and (5) aims to assist them to find employment in their profession—teaching. Miss Beecher drew the plan for the new building and assisted in raising money, by a personal gift of $400, and through efforts of the Women's Education Association which employed Parsons to solicit funds. An endowment of $20,000 was proposed and for a time it seemed it would be realized, but such was not the case. Though, after ten years, with the need for more elaborate housing, there arose a misunderstanding between the trustees and Miss Beecher, which dragged on for six years and ended in the discontinuance of her active labor in its behalf, the institution still bore the impress of her genius. That this misunderstanding never destroyed the high regard of the community and trustees for Miss Beecher, is suggested by Wight's statement: "A character so majestic may well be the model, at this institution of her creation, for those pupils who, still unborn . . . were yet the objects of her vigilant and fostering care."[134]

By the charter of 1851, a perpetual board of trustees was created, with power to "direct and prescribe the course of study," procure necessary officers and teachers, grant "such literary honors and degrees as are usually granted by colleges and seminaries in the United States," give diplomas certifying the same, and also establish a normal department for the education of female teachers.[135] In 1853, the name was changed to Milwaukee Female College,[136] but the Bachelor's degree was not awarded until 1875. When Miss Mortimer resigned (1874), Professor Farrar, of Vassar, was named in her stead. Milwaukee College, as it was now called, began to imitate men's colleges in the course of study and greater emphasis was placed on Latin, Greek, and the sciences of chemistry and physics. In 1875, the diploma was issued in Latin rather than English, and conferred

[133] *Laws of Wisconsin*, 1851, Ch. 133.
[134] *Op. cit.*, 30.
[135] *Laws of Wisconsin*, 1851, Ch. 133.
[136] *Ibid.*, Ch. 257.

the rights and privileges pertaining to the degree of Bachelor of Arts.

Though the institution had been well patronized from the beginning, its number of graduates was small. In 1855, there were 252 in attendance; in 1875, 196; in 1880, 243; and in 1889, 160. The total number of graduates, to 1890, was 221, nearly half (101) of whom had received the Bachelor's degree.

A considerable number of institutions for the education of girls were chartered by Wisconsin;[137] in addition, numerous institutions, incorporated before 1860, were stated to be for both sexes, and provisions for girls were doubtless made in some institutions whose acts of incorporation do not specifically mention them.[138]

In 1853, Catherine Beecher visited Dubuque, Iowa, with the purpose of establishing a female seminary, to be fostered by the newly formed American Women's Education Association. A building was erected (1853) and instruction begun in 1854. An endowment of $20,000 was pledged on conditions similar to those in the case of Milwaukee, but was never fulfilled. Nevertheless, the school was very popular for a few years. In 1857–8, there were about eighty students, but lack of success in the scheme for endowment made it impossible to continue. One of the first three teachers was Mrs. L. A. Parsons, who had relinquished her school in Wisconsin, which later became Milwaukee Female College.[139]

Other promising but short-lived institutions were Mount Ida Female College (1855) at Davenport, Lyons [Iowa] Female College (1859), Mount Pleasant Female Seminary (1863), and St. Agatha's Seminary in Iowa City (1864).[140]

[137] Such as Sinsinawa Female Academy (1848); Columbia County (1850), Racine (1852), Kenosha (1855), Waukesha (1855), Mary Lyon (1856), Moundville (1856), Watertown (1856), and Judson (1855) female seminaries; Kenosha Female Institute (1852); Racine Female Collegiate Institute (1853); and Wisconsin Female College, in 1855.—Laws of Wisconsin, for the years named.

[138] List of incorporated institutions made from the Laws of Wisconsin to 1860.

[139] Wight: Annals of Milwaukee College, 8.

[140] Aurner: Hist. Educ. in Iowa, III, Ch. 4; other schools for girls might be named, such as the Ladies Seminary of Burlington, 1857, Mrs. O'Reilly's School for Young Ladies, Dubuque (1839), etc. They were short-lived, however, and some were rather elementary. Generally, the separate "female seminary" was not favored.—See Antrobus: Hist. Des Moines County, 163

From 1818 onward, Missouri encouraged the female seminary, though there were many institutions for both sexes as well as those for boys only.   Among the pioneer girls' schools were Madame Perdreville's (1818),[141] Mrs. Love's School for Young Ladies (1819),[142] the St. Louis Female Academy (1823)[143] the Washington School for Young Ladies at Franklin (1825),[144] Mrs. Peerce's School, Fayette (1826),[145] Bethlehem Monastery Female School, in Perry County (1826),[146] Paris Female Seminary,[147] and Miss Willard's Seminary for Young Ladies.[148]   The newspapers named below carried the advertisements of many others.   Some schools acquired more than a local reputation. Such was the Elizabeth Aull Female Seminary,[149] which continued till 1902.   The Lexington College for Women was incorporated in 1851.[150]

Incorporation of female seminaries in Missouri began early and continued at a rapid rate between 1830 and 1860, the number being about equal to those specifically incorporated for both sexes.   One of the latter sort was provided for in 1808, when St. Genevieve Academy was authorized to establish a female department as soon as possible.[151]   The rapid increase in popularity of separate girls' institutions, 1830–1860, is suggested by the fact that incorporations jumped from five, in the period 1830–40, to ten, 1840–50, and nearly forty between 1850 and 1860.[152]   In the same period, approximately eighty institutions were incorporated, no mention being made of provisions for girls.   Failure to mention them in the acts of incorporation need not imply, however, that girls were never taught in these schools, as female departments were sometimes attached without express authorization.

ff.; Goodspeed and Goodspeed: *Hist. Dubuque County*, 911 ff.   The *Laws of Iowa*, to 1860, reveal a strong preference for academies open to both sexes.

141 *Mo. Gaz.*, Sept. 11, 1818.

142 *Mo. Intelligencer*, Nov. 19, 1819.

143 *Mo. Republican*, Nov. 5, 1823. ·

144 *Mo. Intelligencer*, Oct. 14, 1825.

145 *Ibid.*, Feb. 8, 1826.

146 *Mo. Republican*, Nov. 23, 1826.

147 *Salt River Jour.*, Feb. 27, 1838.

148 *Mo. Republican*, Sept. 24, 1839.

149 *Laws of Mo.*, March 12, 1859.

150 Young: *Hist. of Lafayette County*, I, 211.

151 *Territorial Laws*, June 21, 1808, Pt. 1, 267.

152 From the *Laws of Missouri* for the period 1830–1860.

A study of the female seminaries in the South reveals but slight variation from the practices of the North. The movement arose about the same time.[153] As already noted, several schools for girls, in the latter part of the eighteenth century, had been opened in Charlestown, South Carolina, and elsewhere. These, though somewhat elementary as compared with later seminaries, were clearly the forerunners of the more advanced school.[154] The chief difference between North and South is that in the former the female seminaries declined earlier, due to a more rapid development of the public high school and a more favorable attitude towards coeducation.[155]

The first female academy of the nineteenth century was founded in 1802 by the Moravians at Salem, North Carolina. It carried on the same traditions as the Moravian school at Bethlehem, Pennsylvania. The first principal was named in 1802, and the first pupils came from a distance in 1804. Between 1804 and 1856, it was attended by 3,470 students who came from seventeen states. Though it became one of the most influential institutions of secondary grade in the South before the Civil War, it received no charter until 1866, and granted no diploma to graduates until 1877. Its influence was felt chiefly through the excellent teachers who received their training within its walls.[156] A eulogistic, but probably essentially fair, estimate of Salem Academy, written by J. H. Clewell, indicates the high regard in which it was held by the people of the South:

"No effort could accurately portray the permanent rôle which the Salem Academy for girls and women has played in the educational development, not only of North Carolina and the South, but of the whole country. Thousands of alumnae sent out since its inception, representing the ablest educators, the most refined and cultivated women—noble and grand in purpose—bless

---

[153] *Confederate Veteran*, Oct. 1907, 444.

[154] See pp. 295 *ff*.

[155] Alice Lloyd, in 1907, declared she would "welcome a successful refutation of the statement that south of Louisville there is not a public high school that fully meets modern standards of secondary education, and that south of Baltimore there is not a private secondary school for girls that ranks with the girls' Latin School of that city."—*Proc. of 10th Conference for Educ. in the South*, 1907, 220.

[156] Smith: *Education in N. C.*, 47, 118–20; also Blandin: *Hist. Higher Educ. of Women in the South*, 31–6.

SALEM FEMALE ACADEMY (1805)

nearly every community in America. The Salem Academy has ever stood paramount with the higher education of the country, and its aim has always been to afford a broad and liberal culture for women: to furnish to young woman an education in classics, mathematics, and sciences equal to that obtained in our best colleges for young men, and to add to these a special training in social culture, music, art, and conversation which shall better qualify her to enjoy and do well her life-work. The aim has been, not only to give the broadest and highest moral, intellectual, and physical culture, but also to preserve and perfect every characteristic of complete womanhood.''[157]

Though many academies were incorporated for boys after 1766, when New Bern Academy was established,[158] there were few especially for girls. Asheville, Louisburg, Milton, Shocco, Charlotte, Lincolnton, Hillsborough, Nashville, Greenville, Northampton, Hannah More, Salisbury, and Randolph female academies had been chartered by 1840, however, and up to 1860, at least twenty-two were added.[159] "Female departments," added to numerous academies, were by no means unimportant. Especially noteworthy were those of the Warrenton, Fayetteville, Hillsborough, Salisbury, and Raleigh Academies.[160]

One of the most prominent female academies of the South was that established by Elizabeth Roach, Washington, Mississippi,

[157] Blandin: *op. cit.*, 32–3; see also Reichel: *Moravians in N. C.*, Ch. XII.

[158] *Laws of N. C.*, Dec. 1, 1766.

[159] *Ibid.*, 1806, Ch. 79; 1814, Ch. 49; 1818, 90; 1820, Ch. 80; 1821, Chs. 50 and 72; 1824, Ch. 119; 1826, Ch. 58; 1830, Ch. 121; 1833, Ch. 46; 1839, Chs. 5 and 7, for those specified by name. For notices of Mrs. Gregory's Boarding School for Young Ladies (Hillsborough), Williamsborough Female Academy, Louisburg Female Academy, Warrenton Female Academy, Hillsborough Female Seminary, Milton Female Academy, and Shocco Female Academy, see *The Minerva*, Dec. 31, 1807, 3, col. 4; *The Raleigh Star*, Jan. 31, 1812, 1, col. 3; June 16, 1820, 3, col. 4; June 2, 1820, 3, col. 4; *Free Press* (Tarborough), Dec. 22, 1827, 1, col. 1; *Hillsborough Recorder*, July 13, 1825, 3, col. 5; Oct. 22, 1828, 3, col. 5; and *Free Press* (Tarborough), Jan. 8, 1830, 4, col. 4, respectively; see also Coon: *N. C. Schools and Academies*.

[160] Interesting accounts of these appeared in *The Raleigh Star*, Jan. 4, 1810, 1, cols. 2 and 3; Mch. 6, 1812, 1, col. 2; The [N. C.] *Minerva*, May 21, 1807, 3, col. 4; Dec. 24, 1807, 3, col. 4; Nov. 19, 1807, 4, cols. 2–3; Mch. 16, 1807, 3, col. 4; *Western Carolinian*, May 8, 1821, 3, col. 4; and Dec. 3, 1822, 1, col. 3.

and incorporated by the state,[161] to be under the superintendence of "members of the Methodist Conference." No religious test was, however, permitted. Land was given and work begun in 1818, but incorporation with a board of trustees, and the right to receive gifts, buy real estate, and confer degrees, was not

MANUSCRIPT CHARTER OF ELIZABETH FEMALE ACADEMY (1819)

accomplished before February 17, 1819. A lottery for the academy was announced in 1820.[162] As it was a Methodist institution, all places on the Board of Trustees were to be filled by members of the Mississippi Conference. The first president was Chillon F. Stiles, from whose care it passed in turn to Reverend

161 *Laws of Miss.*, 1819, 91.
162 *Miss. State Gaz.*, May 20, 1820, 2.

John Burruss, later to Reverend Drake and others, until it expired in 1843. This was the first institution, exclusively for girls, established by Mississippi after admission to the Union; and it rendered a very important service as a pioneer in the advancement of secondary education for girls in the Southwest. Claims that have been made relative to its collegiate standing cannot, however, be substantiated.[163]

The Academy was a flourishing institution in 1826, though it had just experienced a depression, when a complete report of its Governess, Mrs. C. M. Thayer, was reprinted in the *American Journal of Education*.[164] It had been in operation for eight years, but with its lack of orderly records she was not entirely in sympathy. She referred to the fact that her predecessor left no records, forcing her to rely upon her own initiative only. She introduced the methods of Lancaster and Pestalozzi, the utility of which she had already tested in St. Matthews Academy in New York. When she began (1825) there were but nine students, but before the end of the quarter (1826) there were forty-five, and at the end of the term, fifty-five. This period of great prosperity enjoyed by the Academy seems to have been largely due to the genius and popularity of Mrs. Thayer. Besides her great emphasis upon method, attention was given to classification of pupils and provision for their physical health. The classes were called minor, junior, senior, and honorary. Elizabeth Academy expired after a brief existence of about twenty-five years, similar schools having been established at Natchez, Port Gibson, Woodville, and elsewhere.[165] Many female seminaries were incorporated by Mississippi between 1830 and 1860.[166]

Other early notable female seminaries of the South, to which we may briefly refer, were: the Edgeworth Seminary, Greensboro, North Carolina (1840); in Kentucky, John Lyle's Female

[163] W. T. Harris said it was a college in everything but name—See Blandin: *op. cit.*, 43; C. B. Galloway's ''Elizabeth Female Academy—The Mother of Female Colleges'' [*Miss. Hist. Soc. Publications* (1899), II, 169–78] contains no justification to the rank of college. A degree, *Domina Scientiarum*, was given but the range of studies did not extend as far as many other academies.

[164] II, 633–7.

[165] Mayes: *History of Educ. in Miss.*, 46.

[166] A list of the academies, male and female, incorporated by Mississippi, published in Weathersby's *Hist. of Ed. Legislation in Miss.*, 66 *ff*.

Seminary (1806),[167] Nazareth Academy, Bardstown (1808), chartered in 1829,[168] Lafayette Seminary, Lexington (1821), Science Hill (1825), Georgetown Female Academy (1835),[169] and Georgetown Female Seminary, established in 1846 by Dr. J. E. Farnham;[170] in Tennessee, Moses Fisk's Female Academy at Hilham (1806),[171] Knoxville Female Academy (1811),[172] Maryville Female Academy (1813),[173] Nashville Female Academy (1817),[174] and Columbia Female Institute (1838) under Bishop James H. Otey;[175] and, in South Carolina, the celebrated Elias Marks Female Academy, at Barhamsville, near Columbia, Yorkville,[176] Barnwell,[177] and Pendleton[178] female academies and the Presbyterian Female Seminary, Anderson, in 1835.[179]

In Louisiana, not much was done for the education of girls beyond the labors of religious groups, the most conspicuous school being the Ursuline Convent (1727).[180] Numerous schools for

[167] Lyle was head of the Bourbon Academy, for both boys and girls, according to agreement Dec. 27, 1806. In 1810, he resigned and set up an independent girls' school.—MS. Record of Trustees of Bourbon Academy.

[168] Laws of Ky., 1829, 27 ff.; see the pamphlet, Nazareth: A Famous Convent School of the Southwest, n.d.

[169] Ibid., 1835, 77 ff.

[170] Gaines: Hist. of Scott Co., Ky., II, 295 f.; newspapers, such as the Western Citizen, from 1831 to 1865, and the Maysville [Ky.] Eagle, 1850 to 1860, carried voluminous advertisements, showing the keen interest in girls' education, especially from 1830 onward.

[171] Laws of Tenn., Sept. 11, 1806; Goodpasture: Life of J. D. Goodpasture, 21; and Goodspeed: Hist. of Tennessee.

[172] Laws of Tenn., Sept. 11, 1811, 116 f.

[173] Ibid., Oct. 18, 1813, 42 ff.

[174] Ibid., Oct. 3, 1817, 3–7; and Moore: Tennessee, The Volunteer State, I, 724.

[175] For others refer to Merriam: Higher Education in Tennessee.

[176] Acts of Assembly, Dec. 18, 1819, 51 and 54.

[177] Ibid., Dec. 21, 1822, 39–43.

[178] Ibid., Dec. 19, 1827, 50–2.

[179] MS. Minutes of the Trustees, 1835–1859; others, which aspired to the rank of colleges but offered courses more similar to the seminary and academy, were Johnson Female University, Columbia Female College, Marion Female College, Spartansburg Female College, Laurensville Female College, and Due West Female College.—See Acts of Assembly, Dec. 1852, 158; Dec. 1854, 331, 380 and 344; Dec. 1856, 523; and Dec. 1860, 907, respectively.

[180] Compare Fay: Hist. of Educ. in La., 123 ff.; King: New Orleans, 55 ff.; Cruzat: Ursulines of La. [La. Hist. Soc. Quart., Jan. 1919, 5–23]; Carroll: Papers on Colonial Education in La. [Am. Catholic Review, 1886–7]; and Rightor: Standard Hist. of La., 226 ff.

DIPLOMA ISSUED BY COLUMBIA (TENNESSEE) FEMALE INSTITUTE (1849)

girls, forerunners of the true academies, advertised in early nineteenth century papers of New Orleans.[181] The number advertised, however, is not as great as appeared in the papers of other cities at the same date.[182]

With the coming of Governor Claibourne, the legislative council of the Territory created the University of New Orleans.[183] One article of the incorporating act recited that:

"Whereas the prosperity of every state depends greatly on the education of the female sex, in so much that the dignity of their condition is the strongest characteristic which distinguishes civilized from savage society, be it further enacted that the said regents [of the University] shall establish such a number of academies in the territory as they may judge fit for the instruction of the youth of the female sex, in the English and French languages and in such branches of polite literature and such liberal arts and accomplishments as may be suitable to the age and sex of the pupils."[184]

Rightor says the academies herein proposed never actually materialized.[185] The preference of Louisianians was, however, for separate institutions for girls, and numerous schools were given official sanction by articles of incorporation, between 1830 and 1860.[186] That some, called colleges, were not really so, is indi-

[181] E.g., *Courrier de La Louisiane*, 8 Oct. and 22 Oct., 1808; 22 Oct., 1806; 2 Nov., 1808; and 26 Sept., 1807; see also Fortier's *Louisiana Studies*, 255 ff.

[182] Jackson and Natchez, Miss., Montgomery, Ala., Charleston, S. C., Richmond, or the larger cities of the North. The question naturally arises whether the relatively small number is due to the vogue of conventual education for girls, derived from the French and Spanish influences. Later in the century the number advertising in the *Daily Picayune*, for example, was much greater and more nearly comparable with those of other cities.

[183] *Acts of the Territory of Orleans*, Apr. 19, 1805, Ch. XXX.

[184] *Ibid.*, 314–15.

[185] *Op. cit.*, 232.

[186] The most important were: Clinton, 1830, 50; Covington and Ouachita, 1837, 113 and 140; Johnson and Greensburg, 1838, 51 and 52; Iberville, 1842, 304; New Orleans Female Collegiate Institute, Natchitoches Academy of the Sacred Heart, and Minden Female College, 1853, 204, 325 and 179; Avoyelles Academy of the Presentation, 1856, 38; Amité Female Collegiate Institute, Homer Female Collegiate Institute, Bastrop Female College, 1857, 267; St. Mary's Female Academy, 1858, 121; and St. Mary's Female Seminary, 1860, 116.

Marks Female Academy

cated by the fact that, though authorized to grant degrees, as was
the New Orleans Female Collegiate Institute (1853), the course
of study was to be English literature, French literature, history,
geography—ancient and modern—mental and natural philosophy, music, mathematics—including arithmetic, algebra and
geometry—chemistry and botany.[187]

Georgia incorporated the Harmony Grove, Culloden, Forsyth,
West Point, and Appling female academies in 1824,[188] 1834,[189]
1835,[190] 1837,[191] and 1839,[192] respectively. An interesting and
somewhat novel female seminary at Sparta was advertised and
described at some length, in 1829.[193] Others were situated at
Talbotton and Monroe.[194] Newton County Female Seminary was
incorporated in 1833, Lagrange Female Academy in 1833,
Lagrange Female Institute in 1847, and Lagrange Female College, 1849.[195] Clinton Female Institute was established in 1833
and merged (1839) with Georgia Female College.[196] The Monticello Female Academy and Gainesville Female High School were
advertised in 1836 and 1838, respectively.[197] Only a few "male
and female" academies were incorporated between 1820 and
1860. Among them were Union Hill, Medway, Cullodenville,[198]
Pataula,[199] and Iron Spring.[200] That joint male and female
academies were more common than would be suggested by the
acts of incorporation is shown in numerous advertisements, such
as the Macon,[201] Forsyth,[202] Hill,[203] and Hillsborough[204] acade-

---

[187] Act of incorporation, April 28, 1853.
[188] *Acts*, 1824, 19.
[189] *Ibid.*, 1834, 4.
[190] *Ibid.*, 1835, 5.
[191] *Ibid.*, 1837, 4.
[192] *Ibid.*, 1839, 11.
[193] *Sherwood's Gazeteer of Georgia* (Phila., 1829), 161-2.
[194] *Acts*, 1842, 4 and 11.
[195] *Acts*, 1833, 25-6; 1847, 120; White's *Historical Collections*, 651 *f.*
[196] See p. 161, Vol. II.
[197] [Macon] *Georgia Telegraph*, Feb. 11, 1836; Dec. 4, 1838.
[198] *Acts*, 1833, 22-5.
[199] *Ibid.*, 1837, 4.
[200] *Ibid.*, 1842, 3.
[201] [Macon] *Ga. Telegraph*, Apr. 2 and Aug. 20, 1835.
[202] *Ibid.*, Dec. 18, 1834, and Dec. 31, 1835.
[203] *Ibid.*, Nov. 20, 1834.
[204] *Ga. Messenger*, Dec. 24, 1823.

mies, all of which had both male and female departments. Certainly, it was a very general custom to open a "female department" if there was no separate school for girls in the vicinity.

About 1820, the Alabama Legislature began to evince an interest in seminary education for girls; and up to 1870, about seventy institutions had been specially incorporated for them.[205] The University of Alabama Code (1821) declared the trustees should select a site for a female institution, to be a branch of the University and governed by the same laws so far as possible. Section 17, of the Act of December 24, 1822, specified there "shall be established three branches of said University for Female Education." This provision, very similar to that of Louisiana (1805), authorized the legislature to locate the site and provided for twelve directors, for each seminary, to be elected by the University Board of Trustees. Not more than $100,000 was to be appropriated for the buildings of the three branches. The law seems to have been ineffectual, but the interest in female education, thus shown, is reflected in later individual acts incorporating female seminaries and colleges. The first of these were the Athens (1822), Tuscambria (1826), Sims (1830), and Tuscaloosa (1831) female academies.[206]

One of the most famous female schools was the Huntsville Female Seminary of Alabama, incorporated in 1831.[207] Near the end of Catherine Beecher's connection with Hartford Female Seminary she was asked by the Huntsville trustees to name a principal for them. She took this opportunity to propose a further experiment with her pet scheme of co-equal teachers. An endowment was to be secured. Her suggestion was accepted and four of her teachers, including Frances A. Strong as principal, went to Huntsville, while Miss Beecher and four other teachers went to Cincinnati. In her *Reminiscences,* the teachers at Huntsville were credited with six years of successful work;[208] but as they failed to secure a permanent endowment, three teachers left to secure better positions and the other because of ill

[205] List made from *Laws of Alabama,* 1818–1870; see also Weeks: *Education in Ala.,* Ch. II.

[206] *Laws,* 1822, 122; 1826, 63; 1830, 43; and 1831, 44.

[207] *Ibid.,* 1831, 46; by law of Jan. 21, 1831, Huntsville and all other incorporated academies of Alabama were exempted from taxation.

[208] In her *True Remedy,* 78, she said eight years.

Huntsville Female Seminary (1831)

A STUDENT'S REPORT OF 1835 (HUNTSVILLE FEMALE SEMINARY)

health.[209] The Seminary continued to play an important rôle in women's education; and prepared generation after generation of teachers in girls' private, and the public, schools of the state, and beyond its borders.

[209] *Reminiscences*, 80.

A few other institutions were conspicuously influenced by Northern teachers. Tuscaloosa Female Academy brought Mrs. Kinner and daughter from Hartford in 1831. An infant school was connected with it, in charge of Mrs. Reeder of Albany. With seven teachers, including those of the infant school and music department, "for whose competence the . . . trustees stand pledged," the latter urged that parents send their daughters with "full assurance that they will be ably instructed in the various branches, both useful and ornamental, of female education."[210]

Other early institutions of more than ordinary reputation were the Alabama Female Institute (1835) ;[211] Judson Female Institute, at Marion (1839) ;[212] Marion Female Academy and Seminary (1841) ;[213] and the Methodist Episcopal Female Institute, incorporated in 1843,[214] and, since 1889, called Athens College for Women. The Institute, in 1845, was said to offer the "most valuable facilities for acquiring . . . languages, mathematics and sciences . . . the frame work of education, as well as the light and more drapery accomplishments usually taught in female seminaries of the highest grade. Everything, indeed, . . . [for] a profound, brilliant and a pure education." At an examination the ornamental department exhibited wax work, embroidery, drawing, and painting.[215] Other later institutions have been mentioned by Blandin.[216]

Maryland incorporated the Baltimore Female Academy in 1809, authorizing a lottery for its support, this act being for the benefit of a girls' school already conducted by Sarah Browne and George Matchett.[217] The next to be incorporated was Cambridge Female Academy, in 1830; and others—Boonsborough Seminary, Patapsco Female Institute, Rockville Female Seminary, Hannah

210 *Spirit of the Age*, Dec. 7, 1831, 4, col. 3.

211 *Laws*, 1835, 98; and *Flag of the Union*, Aug. 1 and 8, 1835.

212 Blandin: *op. cit.*, 96.

213 *Laws*, 1841, 57.

214 *Ibid.*, 1843, 86.

215 [Athens] *Weekly Chronicle*, May 22, 1846, 2; and June 12, 1846.

216 *Op. cit.*, 56–125. References to Hanmer Hall—*Montgomery Daily Post*, July 14 and Oct. 2, 1860; Alabama Female Athenaeum—*Alabama Sentinel*, July 16, 1836; and Wesleyan Female Academy—*Flag of the Union*, Aug. 1, 1835.

217 *Laws of Md.*, Nov. 1809, Ch. 71.

Patapsco Female Institute

More Academy, Baltimore Academy of the Visitation, "for young females," St. Mary's County Female Seminary, and Frederick Female Seminary—followed in 1833, 1834, 1836, 1838, 1839, 1840 and 1842, respectively.[218] Of these the Patapsco Institute and the Frederick Seminary were the best known, the former being regarded as a finishing school for girls, many of whom had already attended other academies. More elaborate institutions were projected in the Baltimore Female College (1850), Baltimore Collegiate Institute (1853), and the Mount Washington Female College (1856).[219]

As mentioned, more or less pretentious academies for girls were advertised in Virginian papers in the latter part of the eighteenth century.[220] Early in the nineteenth, such institutions are found under the control of trustees, though frequently without being incorporated by the state. The earliest in Virginia was the Ann Smith Academy, of Lexington, said by the trustees to have been operated since "about 1807," when land was secured and subscriptions "amounting to several thousand dollars were raised." Plans were made to care for "about 100 pupils."[221] Its "very successful operation" was credited, by the trustees, to Ann Smith, who began teaching at Lexington in 1807.[222] Because of her devoted service, for which she would receive nothing more than payment of her expenses, they gave her name to the academy.[223] The school was well supported by students; and liberal gifts were made, about 1812, by fifty-two individuals, ranging from five to five hundred dollars.[224] Its first disaster occurred in the loss of Miss Smith, who left to teach in Fredericksburg, 1812. The trustees sought in vain for a successor of equal merit. Mr. Crusalles, from Richmond, Miss Hybert, from Fayetteville, North Carolina, Miss Benedict, from Danville, and Salina Nickolls from Winchester came for brief periods of ser-

[218] *Ibid.*, for the above dates, Chaps. 236, 86, 257, 189, 135, 190, and 256, respectively.

[219] *Ibid.*, for these dates, Chaps. 247, 69 and 241, respectively.

[220] See p. 281 *ff.*

[221] Trustees' *Memorial to Va. Legislature*, in 1821—*MS. Minutes*, in possession of Mr. Harrington Waddell, Lexington, Va.

[222] *Ibid.*, 23.

[223] It was thus advertised in the *Va. Gaz. and Gen. Advt.*, Nov. 3, 1809, 3, col. 5.

[224] *MS. Subscription List*, kindly loaned by Mr. Waddell.

vice, but the old popularity of the first few years was not easily reestablished. Other schools for girls, too, had been founded, which, it was admitted, "drained off pupils from this seminary." When it became involved in debt (1821) an appeal for aid was made to the legislature. The Virginian legislature, however, was as deaf as any other to appeals for aid which stressed the importance of "educated females' influence in society." This failing, all equipment was sold to pay the mason's bill but was restored through the munificence of John Robinson. Thus Ann Smith Academy was able to continue. In 1908, the property was conveyed to the town of Lexington for use of a high school; and, in 1910, the academy trustees gave $730 to the high school to create two "Ann Smith Academy Scholarships" for meritorious girls.[225]

This Virginian pioneer of the nineteenth century was soon followed by a host of female seminaries: Mrs. Byrd advertised Richmond Female Academy in 1808;[226] New Glasgow Female Academy was announced in 1818;[227] Miss A. Benedict opened a school at Danville in 1826, later the Danville Female Academy, incorporated in 1831;[228] and, in 1830, Mr. Sheffey began the Kalorama Seminary, in Staunton, which later became the Virginia Female Institute, chartered in 1844.[229] Clarkesville and Lynchburg incorporated female academies in 1836,[230] and many others followed in rapid succession. One of the most famous was Mary Baldwin Female Seminary, at Staunton, in operation since 1842, first called Augusta Female Seminary, and chartered under that name in 1845.[231]

Virginia is frequently designated as typical of educational life in the South. This general conception holds good, in the main, so far as the female seminary movement is concerned. The Southern states, as a general rule, continued chartering acade-

[225] *Ibid.*

[226] *Richmond Inquirer*, Jan. 7, 1808.

[227] *Ibid.*, May 29, 1818.

[228] *MS. Hist. of Danville, Va.*, by Geo. W. Dame; and *Laws of Va.*, 1831, 276.

[229] The *Staunton Spectator*; and *Laws of Va.*, 1844, 86.

[230] *Laws of Va.*, 1836, 241 and 245; advertisement of Clarkesville Female Seminary in *The Tobacco Plant*, Sept. 20, 1861.

[231] See Waddell: *Hist. of Mary Baldwin Seminary*, 7 *ff.*; and *Laws of Va.*, 1845, 105.

ANN SMITH ACADEMY (1808)

mies and seminaries longer than the Northern. In the North the seminary movement declined rapidly after 1860; in the South the decline is also marked, but many institutions of secondary grade continued to be chartered. Thus in Virginia, even as late as 1880–1890, there were at least ten special institutions chartered for girls. Others were incorporated since 1890, some of which have become well known: Belmont Seminary at Liberty (1890), Jeter Female Institute (1890), Ryland Institute (1892), Blackstone Female Institute (1892), Virginia Christian Female Seminary (1892), Wartbury Seminary (1894), Chatham Female Episcopal Institute (1894), Newport News Female Seminary (1896), Rawlings Institute (chartered 1900), Hollins Institute (1901), Sweet Briar Institute (1901), Bowling Green Female Seminary (1902), and several others.[232]

It should be observed that of more than thirty institutions incorporated between 1850 and 1859, ten were designated in the laws as "colleges" or "collegiate"; and from 1860 to 1869, fully half the institutions were thus indicated. After 1850, it was frequently specified that the institution could grant diplomas or degrees. This practice was general throughout the South.

Below there is shown the general tendency of growth of the female seminary in the South as represented by the combined efforts of Alabama, Kentucky, Maryland, Mississippi, and North Carolina. If all states were thrown together, the appearance of the graph would not be markedly different.[233] From 1820–1860, the activity of the combined states is similar, proportionally, to that of the single state of Virginia. Though the data have not been included after 1860, for the combined states, the laws show that the decline in other Southern states was similar to that of Virginia. It is made clear that the great day of the female seminary, so far as official encouragement by legislatures may be a satisfactory index, was from 1830 to 1860. When the female seminary idea was once established, it appears to have been preferred to the two-sex institution. Probably the economy of the latter was frequently a determining factor in causing its establishment, especially in small rural communities. Girls were, doubtless, sometimes provided for in those schools incorporated

[232] *Laws of Va.*, for the dates named.

[233] Lists from other states have been compiled and graphed, showing the same general tendency as above.

for boys.   The extent to which this is true can only be determined
by a study of each individual school's history.[234]   A comparative
view of the interest in secondary education for boys and that for
girls may be obtained from the fact that the ratio of incorporated

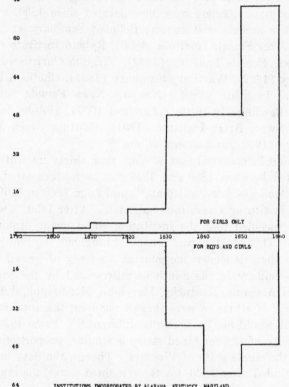

INSTITUTIONS INCORPORATED BY ALABAMA, KENTUCKY, MARYLAND,
MISSISSIPPI, AND NORTH CAROLINA, FOR GIRLS ONLY AND FOR BOYS
AND GIRLS, BETWEEN 1790 AND 1860.

boys' schools to incorporated girls' schools, leaving out of consideration the two-sex institutions, was generally, from 1820 to
1860, approximately 2.5 to 1.[235]   Before 1820, girls' schools were
scarce, while schools for boys flourished and were encouraged by
legislatures.[236]

[234] Weathersby mentioned a case or two wherein girls were admitted—
op. cit., 75; I have noted a few instances.

[235] Based on Laws of Louisiana, Kentucky, Maryland, North Carolina,
Mississippi, and Alabama.

[236] For example, see the Laws of North Carolina, 1766 to 1820: Tennessee,
1806–1820; etc.

From the foregoing it is evident that the incorporated female seminary in the United States rose to its height between 1830 and 1860, though variation is found in the several states. The number of incorporated schools is, of course, an incomplete measure of the educational facilities open to women, for numerous institutions were never thus officially stamped; but incorporation does represent crystallized public sentiment that approved of this mode of education for girls. Having secured this authorization for the female seminary, it was comparatively easy to take the next step: public recognition of the propriety of, and support for, higher—college or university—education of women, which became a *fait accompli* after the Civil War. Earlier colleges were often such in name only, and were experimental growths, in the soil and atmosphere best adapted to the seminary. The seminary movement, if we take the greatest institutions produced by it—for example, Troy, Salem, Elizabeth, Huntsville, Hartford, Mount Holyoke, Milwaukee—represents an experiment in curriculum, organization, and support, the successful outcome of which was the woman's college. In the meantime, there was developing a new type of secondary institution, the high school, which gradually took over such secondary school functions as had been performed by the academy or the seminary.

At the middle of the century, the female seminary, academy, or collegiate institute was to be found in almost every state of the Union; but a decline followed the war. In 1872, reports from twenty-nine states, to the Bureau of Education, showed 175 institutions called academies, institutes, seminaries, and, almost exactly a half of them, "colleges." Assuming that the reports were quite incomplete, and that many listed by the name of college were nothing but academies, we see that the seminary had, nevertheless, declined in importance. It is proof of its decline in popularity to find that communities preferred to create "colleges" instead of seminaries, even though they failed to reach the goal to which they aspired.[237] In the states which had been most active in the incorporation of seminaries, the decline is most evident. Pennsylvania, in a single biennium, had incorporated thirty-four; but, in 1872, only nine were reported; Virginia likewise had incorporated a great number, but only seven were reported; New York, Massachusetts, Ohio,

237 See *R. C. E.*, 1872, 792 *ff.*

Illinois, Alabama, and Mississippi reported eighteen, seven, six, five, three, and two, respectively. The reports to the Commissioner were doubtless very incomplete; but that many seminaries closed their doors or became something else is likewise true.

But the decline of the seminary did not leave women's education unprovided for. The incomplete reports for secondary education (1872) showed 43,794 female students, to compare with 37,957 males;[238] and the reports on "superior instruction of females," likewise incomplete, showed 11,288 students, distributed in colleges and seminaries throughout the United States. Of these, of course, the merest handful were doing genuine college work. But that much more remained to be done is suggested by the fact that the *Census* of 1870 showed 1,241,000 females, fifteen, sixteen and seventeen years of age.[239] The institutions which were reported and rated by the Commissioner as "superior" were distributed among the states as follows:

Alabama	8	Massachusetts	6	Oregon	1
California	3	Michigan	3	Pennsylvania	14
Connecticut	4	Minnesota	1	South Carolina	1
Delaware	1	Mississippi	5	Tennessee	8
Georgia	16	Missouri	5	Texas	3
Illinois	10	New Hampshire	3	Vermont	1
Indiana	3	New Jersey	3	Virginia	13
Kansas	1	New York	25	West Virginia	2
Kentucky	7	North Carolina	9	Wisconsin	3[240]
Maryland	3	Ohio	13		

238 *Ibid.*, XXXIV–XXXV.
239 *Ibid.*, XXXVII, 65.
240 *Ibid.*, XLVIII.

CHAPTER IX

THE FEMALE SEMINARY (*Continued*)

I. Purposes of Education in Female Seminaries

The aims of early seminaries were similar to those of the academy movement in general—to prepare for life, rather than exclusively for college, as the Latin Grammar School had done. From time to time, throughout the century and more (1750–1870) that the seminary offered the chief means of advanced education for women, various elements in this life preparation were stressed, such as: Christian religion and morals, domestic training, maternal influence and social usefulness, training for the teaching profession, accomplishments, physical health, intellectual enjoyment, and mental discipline.

Arising in the latter part of the eighteenth century, the female seminary naturally placed a great emphasis on religious and moral education; and, aiming at preparation for life, since woman's chief occupation was home-making, domestic training appeared as an ever-important purpose. These two, religious and domestic training, constituted the central objectives; the attainment of minor ones, stressed from time to time by various teachers of women's schools, contributed to the fuller realization of the religious and domestic purposes. Thus the appearance of "maternal influence and social usefulness" and the "profession of teaching" as objectives indicates merely the recognition of the facts (1) that maternal influence could be of social value to the group—if mothers were properly educated—by sending into it boys and girls who were well disciplined for life, and (2) that those who were not married could, nevertheless, exercise this maternal skill and benefit society by teaching school. Throughout the discussions it is evident that woman, by this social service, is merely to assist in the realization of God's plan in the world—to effect its salvation. Such specific *desiderata* as accomplishments, intellectual enjoyment, and physical health would at once contribute to her utility in, and adornment of, the home, while mental discipline would, it was believed, prepare her for anything. Belief in formal discipline of the mind is age-old, and appeared in the earliest seminaries, but it became a most prominent objective in the twenties, thirties, and later in the nineteenth century, with the increasing difficulty of prognosticating exactly what a girl would do when she was grown. After 1850, formal discipline as a purpose in education was stressed alike by female seminaries and women's colleges.[1]

The Ursuline Convent in Louisiana began its career in the education of girls, placing a strong emphasis on the religious purpose, including also preparation of an industrial character. In the Bethlehem Seminary religious instruction and forming correct habits were the first concern, though a sufficiently broad course of study was followed (after 1785) to justify somewhat the claim that the cultivation of the mental powers was also an objective.[2] Rush declared that the purpose of the Female Academy at Philadelphia, to whose graduates he was speaking, was to prepare for domestic, social, and religious life.[3] In each of these, but especially in the last two, there appears an emphasis upon the essentially equal necessity for religious and domestic training. And though, in practice, religious instruction in the seminary varied from a mere formal observance at some, to a fervid missionary activity, as at Mount Holyoke, and domestic training ranged all the way from practical work to mere shadows of domestic accomplishments, it is still true that seminaries everywhere paid homage to these objectives. To point out the prevalence of the first, it is sufficient to recall the religious zeal of such founders of schools as Joseph Emerson, Emma Willard, Zilpah Grant, Catherine Beecher, Mrs. Phelps, and Mary Lyon— all of whom, in a sense, dictated the purposes of other schools, established in the circle of their influence. Of George B. Emerson, who established a private school for girls in 1823, it was

---

[1] This change of purpose does not mean that the religious objective was entirely lost sight of but that it became less conspicuous. Some schools continued to name it as their chief end. Thus Bishop Lee Seminary, 1866, declared its purpose was to give ''to young ladies who may attend it, a thorough Christian education.''—See *Catalog*, 1866. Many others might be cited. The same is often true to-day. But back of this general, stated purpose there is a greatly changed course of study which indicates that the school has shifted emphasis.

[2] Reichel: *Bethlehem Souvenir*, 36.

[3] See pp. 302 *ff*.

said: "His constant aim was, first of all, to fill the hearts of the pupils with reverence for the laws of God, whether revealed in the Scriptures or discovered by reason; next to form habits of *self-control*, punctuality, and order, and to establish a profound sense of accountability to God for the proper use of all the talents with which He had been pleased to endow them."[4] Contributors to educational journals repeatedly stressed the all important religious basis of girls' education. The following will serve as an example:

"If the characters of young women were formed on the Christian model, if their minds were enlightened on the important subject of self-control, if their piety induced habits of self-examination, and religious principles imposed due restraints on the language and conduct;—in short, if they zealously and habitually sought to bring the temper and feelings into order and proper subjection, and tasked themselves to the daily and hourly duty of acting out the beauty and symmetry of the precepts of our Saviour; even though they might not extend their views so high or so wide in search of duty as to look forward to the maternal state, and consequently might continue ignorant and prejudiced on the subject of infant education; yet the evils caused by these deficiencies would be greatly mitigated, and counteracted, if not subdued."[5]

The fact that numerous early seminaries were created by religious organizations points also to the religious purpose. As late as 1872, of the 175 institutions for "superior instruction of females" reported to the Commissioner of Education, all but 67 were credited to religious denominations (and possibly some of these should have been).[6]

While domestic training constituted a purpose in both the theory and practice of the seminary from the very first of the period, the appeals for it became more vigorous in the nineteenth century. The Ursuline and Moravian schools practiced the teaching of household duties by doing them; later, with the evident tendency of the nineteenth century to pursue flashy accomplishments of little substantial value, there arose a vigorous demand that knowledge of domestic tasks should not be omitted. Further-

---

[4] Barnard: *Am. Teachers*, 338.

[5] *Am. Jour. Ed.*, IV, 127–32.

[6] *R. C. E.*, 1872, XLVIII.

more, at the same time, there arose a demand for a scientific domestic economy, voiced most authoritatively by Emma Willard and Catherine Beecher. This demand was variously expressed by others, less prominent: "When a-young married woman is first called to sustain the maternal relation, she is for the most part utterly ignorant of the whole field of operations into which she is so suddenly introduced";[7] "young women should endeavor to acquire a knowledge of family affairs. . . . Economy is so important a part of a woman's character . . . so essential to her performing properly the duties of a wife and mother, that it ought to have the precedence of all other accomplishments . . .";[8] and "we must begin with forming domestic habits, no quality is more essential to the dignity of the female character . . . the domestic disposition is best cultivated by giving domestic employments."[9]

The need for domestic science was clearly seen by Mrs. Willard, when she wrote that "housewifery might be greatly improved by being taught, not only in practice, but in theory. . . . It is obvious that theory alone can never make a good artist, and it is equally obvious that practice, unaided by theory, can never correct errors, but establish them."[10] Miss Beecher not only prepared her important book on *Domestic Economy*,[11] but declared domestic science as necessary for women as any professional instruction for men:

"And yet what trade or profession of men involves more difficult and complicated duties than that of a housekeeper? Where is skill and science more needed than in the selection, cooking, and economy of food? What wisdom and self-control are needed to perform all the duties of a wife! What can demand more practical science and skill than the care of infants and young children? What profession of man requires more knowledge and wisdom than the training of the human mind at its most impressible period? Where are science and skill more needed than in woman's post as nurse of the sick? And where

[7] *Am. Jour. Ed.*, IV, 36–9.
[8] *Ibid.*, III, 648–52.
[9] *Am. Annals of Ed.*, V, 360–3.
[10] Barnard: *Am. Teachers*, 140; see also p. 310.
[11] *Treatise on Domestic Economy for the Use of Young Ladies at Home and at School*, Boston, 1842.

is trained handicraft more important than in making, mending, and preserving the clothing of a family?

"And yet where is the endowment and where is the institution that has for its aim the *practical training* of woman for any one of these departments of her sacred profession?"[12]

The great revival of educational thought which carried successfully the movement to establish common schools also contributed to the extension of woman's influence and the enlargement of the purposes of her education: first, by declaring in oft-repeated speech and argument the far-reaching effect of the maternal influence in society; and, second, by offering woman the public profession of teacher.

In regard to the new social purpose, we find Horace Mann declaring that "without books, except in cases of extraordinary natural endowment, she will be doomed to relative ignorance and incapacity. Nor can her daughters, in their turn, escape the same fate; for their minds will be weakened by the threefold cause of transmission, inculcation, and example. Steady results follow from steady causes; under such influences, therefore, if not averted, the generations must deteriorate from the positive to the superlative, in mental feebleness and imbecility."[13] Another writer in the *American Journal of Education*[14] expressed a common belief in the social importance of woman's education when he said: "We are not willing to dismiss this subject without indulging a few thoughts on maternal influence. . . . The mental fountain is unsealed to the eye of a mother, ere it has chosen a channel or breathed a murmur. . . . She feels that she is required to educate not merely a virtuous member of society, but a Christian, an angel, a servant of the Most High. . . ."

But if many believed social reform would follow upon woman's education, and destruction and decay upon the lack of it, there were others (certainly many in the legislature that refused to support Willard's Seminary) who believed learning was of little use to women, would lead them from domestic duties and prove injurious to the best interests of society. Emma Willard made a plea for such a trial of the social utility of women's education

---

[12] *Harper's New Mo. Mag.* (1864), XXIX, 766; similar expressions may be found in most of Beecher's works.

[13] *Com. Sch. Jour.*, II, 144–5.

[14] I, 401–2.

as had never yet been attempted, and prophesied success for the nation that would break the new ground:

"Ages have rolled away; barbarians have trodden the weaker sex beneath their feet; tyrants have robbed us of the present light of Heaven, and fain would take its future. Nations, calling themselves polite, have made us the fancied idols of a ridiculous worship, and we have repaid them with ruin for their folly. But where is that wise and heroic country, which has considered that our rights are sacred, though we cannot defend them? that, though a weaker, we are an essential part of the body politic, whose corruption or improvement must affect the whole? and which, having thus considered, has sought to give us by education, that rank in the scale of being to which our importance entitles us. History shows not that country. It shows many, whose legislatures have sought to improve their various vegetable productions, and their breeds of useful brutes; but none, whose public councils have made it an object of their deliberations, to improve the character of their women. Yet though history lifts not her finger to such an one, anticipation does. She points to a nation, which, having thrown off the shackles of authority and precedent, shrinks not from schemes of improvement, because other nations have never attempted them; but which, in its pride of independence, would rather lead than follow, in the march of human improvement; a nation, wise and magnanimous to plan, enterprising to undertake, and rich in resources to execute."[15]

Numerous similar references might be made. Mary Lyon sought to reduce the cost of education and thus bring middle class girls to Mount Holyoke because through them a greater influence could be exerted than by educating a few from the "best families."[16] Catherine Beecher appealed to American women to save their country by educating themselves and devoting their lives to the education of others; and saw their greatest wrong in improper education, rather than in political dependence. A few items on the programs of the "College of Professional Teachers" suggest their recognition of the social argument for woman's education. The program of 1836 included an essay on Female Patriotism, by Mrs. Huntley Sigourney and

[15] Quoted by Phelps: *Lectures to Young Ladies*, 38–9.
[16] Stow: *Mount Holyoke Seminary*, 34.

that of 1837, a discussion on "The Inducements to Accept Teaching as a Life Profession," by Julia L. Dumont.   In 1838, Almira H. L. Phelps contributed a paper on "Female Education" and the next year, Anne W. Maylin read an essay on the "Pains and Pleasures of Teaching."[17]

Similar views as to social significance of female education were epigrammatically expressed, upon many occasions, by Charles McIver: "The cheapest, easiest, and surest road to universal education is to educate those who are to be mothers and teachers of future generations; . . . the proper training of women is the strategic point in the education of the race; . . . and educate a man and you have educated one person,—educate a mother and you have educated a whole family."[18]

RECOMMENDATION TO TEACH AN ENGLISH SCHOOL (1816)

With the establishment of public elementary schools the need for teachers became more acute, and recourse was had to otherwise unemployed women. Consequently there arose a demand that the seminary make one of its chief objectives the normal training of the teacher. Earlier seminaries trained teachers, but more or less unconsciously. The later ones, frequently established by an incorporating act of the state, made specific mention of the fact that this was a chief purpose. And though Mann at one time declared that for a half century academies and seminaries had failed to provide enough teachers for common schools,

[17] *R. C. E.* (1898–1899), I, 733–4.
[18] Quoted by Coon, *R. C. E.*, 1907, I, 336.

it is true that sending out teachers was among the greatest services performed by the schools at Troy, Hartford, Ipswich, Mount Holyoke, Patapsco, Cincinnati, Milwaukee, and others of less renown.   Thus Abbot Academy gave "particular attention" to ladies "who may wish to qualify themselves to teach";[19] and the institution at LeRoy, New York, had as "one principal object . . . to prepare young ladies to become teachers."[20]   At Salem, Indiana, Mr. Morrison's "leading object" was the same.[21] The incorporating acts of academies in Illinois frequently recited there should be "a department in which shall be taught branches . . . usually taught in common schools. . . ."[22]   And —to name no more—Pittston Seminary (Pennsylvania) aimed, among other things, at "the science and art of teaching."[23] Beecher emphasized the importance of this purpose in the seminaries by declaring (1851) that every seminary of the higher class shall have "a Normal Department in which every young lady may have an opportunity of adding to the advantages of the ordinary course of education, all those peculiar advantages which distinguish a normal school from other institutions. Every woman ought to be trained to act as an educator; and not only so, no woman ever ought to be considered as qualified to become the head of a family till she has been practically exercised in this her highest professional duty.

"The fourth point to be aimed at should be, to connect with every institution for training teachers, some organization to aid in providing employ for all who wish to act as teachers, and who need such assistance."[24]

With this new opportunity for social usefulness in a broader field, as teacher, there arose the new woman who, from her slight elevation on the rostrum of the school, gradually ascended to that of the public forum.   But many feared for her and still thought best not to give her much education.   The Western Literary Institute, for example, though for the most part progressive, resolved (1839) "that in the opinion of this college

[19] See p. 357; and *Catalog*, 1840, 12.
[20] *Am. Annals*, VII, 379.
[21] *Ibid.*, 332.
[22] E.g., *Laws of Ill.*, Mch. 2, 1839, 230–2.
[23] *Laws of Pa.*, 1866, 730.
[24] *True Remedy*, 56–8; see also chapter on Normal Schools.

the education of females, in order to be such as would at once attract the esteem and love of the other sex, and to elevate their own characters, should be based on the union of polite accomplishments with a thorough knowledge of housewifery.''[25] Miss Beecher suggested, however, in a later passage of her *True Remedy,* that there should be, besides positions in elementary schools, posts of greater importance in higher institutions, comparable with professorships in men's colleges. Shortly there were such, and many other opportunities began to open up such as medicine, law, and commercial and industrial pursuits.

Nevertheless, to enter upon strenuous studies similar to, if not identical with, those of men was, by many, considered hazardous; it would undo women's minds. At the same time, there was a widely credited rumor that the health of American women was declining—that they were rapidly becoming unfit to bear the succeeding generation. A safeguard against these dire results was found in the new fad of calisthenics; and, from the twenties on throughout the century, the preservation of health became a recognized purpose of the seminary, and later of the women's college.[26]

Concurrent with the entrance of women into fields of service outside the household, there was an increasing demand for her mental training. This was especially conspicuous from the first quarter to the end of the nineteenth century, and was but another way of expressing the purpose of the seminary to prepare for life; also, it signified the acceptance of the doctrine of formal discipline of the mind, generally held in men's colleges. At one time and another we find those prominent in the women's education movement of the period—and those who were not—giving their assent to this theory; and, as the theory was accepted, so, too, there came about a slavish imitation of the curriculum of the men's institutions.

Let us examine a few statements which defended this formal training value. Emma Willard urged attention to artistic subjects, such as music and painting, because of the harmonizing effect on the mind. Moreover, she believed the discipline of mathematics had, ''more than any one thing, been the cause of that stronger intellectual power by which the American women

25 *R. C. E.* (1898–99), I, 733–4.
26 For the development of physical education see Chapter III, Vol. II.

have now shown themselves capable of teaching, not only high subjects in the schools, but of investigating new ones, and of managing high schools as well as those for children."[27] A writer in the *American Journal of Education*, speaking of languages and mathematics, stated that "general mental improvement is the rational aim of such studies among females";[28] again, "the only question which should ever be put in regard to the education of females, is what . . . modern sciences will contribute most to the general improvement of the mind . . .";[29] and another suggested improvement of the faculty of imagination as the true purpose of education.[30]

Mrs. Phelps described this training of the mind as follows: "We may now consider the human mind as a garden laid out before us; he who created this garden, planted in it the seeds of various faculties; these do indeed spring up of themselves, but without education, they will be stinted in their growth, choked with weeds, and never attain that strength and elevation of which they are susceptible. In one part of our garden the germ of reason is seen to unfold itself, in another appears that of memory, in another that of judgment, until all the faculties of the intellect are in their full progress of development. The emotions and passions are mingled with powers of slower growth: while the intellectual gardener cultivates the latter with assiduous care, he knows that the passions need his most vigilant attention; that if they grow rank and unpruned, like the fatal Bohan Upas, they will poison and destroy the vital principle of virtue, and root out the moral harmony on which the beauty of the whole depends. Leaving the passions and emotions to be hereafter considered, our concern now is with those mental germs which belong to the intellectual department. The skilful gardener knows that his roses require one mode of culture, his tulips another, and his geraniums another; and that attention to one of these, will not bring forward the other. So ought the mental cultivator to understand that the germs of the various faculties should be simultaneously brought forward. This truth seems not to have been understood by those, who, bending all their

27 Barnard: *Am. Teachers,* 141 and 146; also p. 345 of this work.
28 II, 481-7.
29 *Ibid.,* 676-82.
30 *The Am. Ladies' Preceptor* (1821) 9th edition, 24-5.

efforts towards the cultivation of the memory, neglected the other powers of the mind.''[31]

Todd, in *The Daughter at School* (1854), set forth, at great length, the whole purpose of girls' education in terms of discipline. "The objects of study then are these:

"To give you power to command the attention. Till we have made many and long-continued efforts, this is no easy matter. You sometimes undertake to read a book, and while your eye runs over the pages or the lines of the page, the mind and the thoughts are off upon something else; and when you reach the bottom of the page, you know nothing of what you have been reading. When you are in conversation with another person, it often happens that you lose whole sentences, and have to assent to what he has said, though you know not what it is. Have you never found it so, my daughter? . . .

"A second object of study is to give you the power to hold the mind down to a subject or to a point, as long as is necessary. In doing a long sum in arithmetic, in demonstrating a difficult problem in Euclid, or in evolving a complicated question in algebra, you must hold the mind down to the point, and hold it there till you understand it and can explain it to others. When you write a letter, or a composition, you want the power to hold the mind or the thought till you know what to say [and] how to say it. How many people lose almost the whole of a lecture, or a sermon, or a public speech, because they cannot hold their minds fast till it is through! Perhaps two thirds of every sermon, and of every lecture and every valuable public effort of mind, are lost for the want of this power. It is the want of it that makes it so difficult for the school-girl to master her lesson. And it is to be acquired only by severe and continued application of the mind.

"The third object of study is to strengthen the memory. You know that some men are rich in conversation, welcomed everywhere, and their society eagerly sought, because they have at their command history, books, beautiful thoughts and great thoughts, all held fast by the memory, and all ready to be used at any time; while other men, who have read quite as much, are dry and barren of thought, and almost dull; they cannot recall any thing, they are sure of no fact, they are afraid to be ques-

[31] Phelps: *Lectures to Young Ladies* (1833), 69–70.

tioned about any date. Such a mind is a sliding plane, down which every thing hurries, and with no power to draw it up. . . .

"The fourth object of study is to strengthen the judgment. In all the departments of life, we need a balanced judgment. For the want of it, households are most wretched, homes are made unpleasant, property is squandered, character is never obtained, and life is almost lost. No lady can make a custard or a cooky, a jelly or a garment, spread a table or a cradle, without it, nor can a man well provide for his family, accomplish much in business, or gain in property or influence. It is an everyday commodity, and no day can be a happy one without its abundant exercise. . . .

"The fifth object of study is to cultivate the taste. People naturally differ much as to the possession of this power or faculty. One individual has a certain taste which makes her ladylike in her dress and address, while another is so deficient that she can in no possible circumstance deserve the title of lady. . . .

"The sixth object of study is to store the mind with knowledge, or to teach it where to find what it wants. In the course of the time necessary to discipline the mind so as to call it educated, you will have a vast amount of knowledge poured into the mind. Some of it will stay, but the greater part will run directly through and be lost. Still, the waters leave a tinge in the channel, and the banks through which they passed are richer than before. But at the completion of the course of study, you have new and enlarged and corrected views. You stand on a higher point of ground, and can see farther in every direction. You have also saved a great many things that are valuable. They are in the mind, not like drift-wood upon the shore, strewed anywhere; but they are stored away in the mind, in their appropriate places, labelled, numbered, and ready for use whenever wanted.

"One more object to be mentioned is to create habits of patient toil. If a man has a field of grass to mow, or a wheel to build, or if a lady has an article to sew, or a nice cake to make, each one can see, at every step, there is progress made. Each feels that it is but a short job, and then it will be done. But in study, the results of a day's labor are seen to be so small, if seen at all, that there is nothing to cheer. . . . How much patience is needed to get one lesson in Latin, or to make a single good recitation in algebra! Now you must multiply this toil as many times over as you have lessons. In the course of a week, and a year, how much is the patience exercised! And this toil, this perseverance, this endurance of what is hard and what we naturally dislike, is the very discipline which we must meet all the way through life. Toil, patient toil, is our lot, and there is no place where the young can learn it so well as at school. . . ."[32]

The gradual acceptance of such a doctrine of discipline had a tendency to reduce attention to polite accomplishments and personal gratification as aims of education, and helped promote "solid studies" to a place of importance. Such outcomes were, of course, most completely realized in the early curricula of the full-fledged woman's colleges. Brackett, in *Woman and the Higher Education* (1892), expressed a fundamental belief in this formal discipline, averring that it should make the girl "level headed" and "able to meet any demands, no matter how unexpected. . . ."[33] McCabe, similarly, in the *American Girl at College* (1893), reflected the general attitude towards discipline when she declared that colleges did not aim to prepare women for professions, but gave them such training that they might meet all "developments."[34]

II. The Curriculum of the Female Seminary

The curriculum of female seminaries was a favorite object of criticism and ridicule, both for what it did and did not contain. An effort has been made to ascertain, as definitely as possible, what generally constituted it, both at the beginning of the seminary movement and during the period of its ascendency. The studies offered in a hundred and sixty-two institutions—a random selection, between 1742 and 1870, and from various states, as shown in catalogs, newspaper announcements, and other published accounts—have been examined and tabulated. The results, it is believed, are fairly representative of the seminary in Eastern, Southern and Western states. Approximately one hundred additional courses have been examined, between 1805 and

[32] Todd: *op. cit.*, 11–17.
[33] *Op. cit.*, 177–8.
[34] *Op. cit.*, 4–5, 14.

1870, the addition of which would naturally affect the volume but not the general character of the findings.[35]

In general, the data warrant the conclusion that none of the criticisms launched against the seminary curriculum were unjust or too harsh. Leaders of the seminary movement, such as Willard, Beecher, and Emerson, felt that female schools tried to teach too many subjects and failed to teach much in any one. A glance at the great variety of items, ranging from spelling and chirography to mythology, ouranography, mezzotint and calisthenics, of which many a seminary was not abashed at offering anywhere from twenty to forty or more, convinces one that the critics were, at least, not guilty of exaggeration. At the beginning, there was no such thing as a definite course; pupils took subjects as they or their parents desired. Emerson, by 1826, however, had pointed out the need of definite regulation of the number of studies pursued, the order in which pursued, and the fixing of stated times of entrance, leaving, and so on. At Wethersfield he established a three-year course, and accepted none under thirteen years of age. For this innovation he was warmly commended. The practice spread. Between 1825 and 1870, the specification of two, three, or four (or, in one instance, even five) year courses, on the completion of which some certificate was awarded, became common. Generally, the three year course was accepted as most satisfactory. Several factors, doubtless, entered into this definition and extension of the course: the need of more thorough study to equip young women for teaching; increase of wealth, permitting more attention to education; more general acceptance of the idea that women ought to be educated; the advancement of educational knowledge and its general diffusion; establishment of permanent schools under some sort of oversight; and also a gradual shifting of the marriage age. Youthful marriages, we have noted, were most common in Colonial days. As one said, if not married by twenty-one she was thought a "stale maid." Later, it appears the young lady had no cause for alarm until she reached the "antient age" of twenty-five:

[35] Statements in this section are based on tables, in possession of the author, derived from original catalogs of schools in Northern, Southern and Western states.

" . . . But lovers now have ceased to bow
"No way they can contrive
"To poison, hang or drown themselves
"Because I'm twenty-five."[36]

Not much uniformity is found as to the age of entrance.
Eight to twelve years was mentioned by Bethlehem Female
Seminary as appropriate; but the seminaries of the nineteenth
century ranged from twelve to sixteen years. It was common
practice to omit reference to the age required for entrance.

The preparatory studies were, at first, as uncertain as age requirements. Not until age requirements and established courses
appeared, indicating a school much more definitely secondary
and apart from the elementary, was there much emphasis laid on
entrance studies. From 1825 onward, emphasis on entrance
studies increased; but many schools still ignored them. Where
no definite course was outlined, a student entered with whatever
. . ppened to have "had" and "took" what she could. The
range of studies required for entering was great; but not many
were required by any one institution. Spelling, reading, writing, English grammar and arithmetic were often required; some
of the best institutions demanded an elementary knowledge of
literature, languages, some mathematics, science, and history.

Though, as has been said, the studies of the seminary seem
numerous,[37] they do not cover much space if reduced to their
general classifications: elementary English studies, advanced
English studies, mental science, Latin, Greek, German, French,
Spanish, Italian, mathematics—pure and applied—religion,
science, history and political science, ornamentals, business preparation—only a few taught bookkeeping and shorthand—and
calisthenics. By subdivision, a formidable appearance was given
the three or four year course; and parents were caused to see
how broad was the stream of learning at which their children
might drink!

The early seminaries had only a limited range of studies; up
to about 1800, English grammar, arithmetic, geography, some
history and a modern language generally marked the limits of
the highest schools for young ladies. Reading, writing, and some
ornamental studies rounded out the course.

[36] *St. Croix Courier*, Mch. 18, 1834.
[37] 180 items appear on the tables mentioned above; see Appendix II, 563.

Of the elementary English studies, spelling, reading and writing continued as constants throughout the period, to 1870. Sometimes they were relegated to the place of preparatory studies; this was increasingly true after 1840. English grammar and composition were the core of higher English studies to 1860; around these basic studies were grouped other kindred subjects, not so universally taught. Rhetoric, after 1800, became as constant as English grammar; while elocution, criticism, chirog-

CERTIFICATE OF PROFICIENCY IN PENMANSHIP

raphy, grammatical analysis and parsing, and the history of various literatures became increasingly popular. Logic and mental philosophy—or psychology, as one called it—were gradually injected into "female studies" after 1800; they appeared occasionally till about 1820, became much more common between 1820 and 1840, and were well-nigh universally taught between 1840 and 1870.

Throughout the history of the female seminary, modern languages, particularly French, less often German or Italian, were considered as desirable provisions of the female mind as were ribbons for external covering. In general, it may be said that both served the same purpose,—adornment. The language texts[38] indicate that a considerable range of literature was cov-

[38] Appendix I, 552.

ered, as well as the grammar.   Latin and Greek were apparently
not usually offered in regular academies,—though a few adventure
masters taught them to girls, if desired,—until the nineteenth
century.   Latin grammar, then, with a considerable

DIPLOMA ISSUED BY LAGRANGE FEMALE COLLEGE (1858)

number of Latin classics, became fairly constant, appearing in
more than half of the schools listed between 1810 and 1870.
Greek grammar was offered about half as frequently as the
Latin.

Of mathematical studies, the first favorite, arithmetic, continued with almost unabated approval till 1870; but, after 1840, it was frequently mentioned as a preparatory study, and the work done in the seminary course was probably, therefore, of more advanced character than before. Mental arithmetic was frequently specified after 1830. Algebra appeared about 1825, and became very common in the girls' seminaries, being specified by about three-fourths of the schools listed between 1825 and 1870. Plane geometry appears to have entered slightly earlier, a school listed having offered it in 1812; but its frequency was approximately the same as that of algebra. Other mathematical studies were introduced in the nineteenth century but to a much less extent than the foregoing. These were, in the order of their frequency, plane trigonometry, bookkeeping, surveying, mensuration, navigation, conic sections, solid geometry, and spherical trigonometry. The last three occurred so seldom as to be of little consequence; surveying and navigation were principally in schools for both sexes, a few of which are included in the list, and were probably seldom, or never, studied by girls.

In one respect it may appear that the foregoing does not give a true idea of the seminary. The institution was frequently the outgrowth of religious endeavor, or established on a sectarian basis. Catalogs, and other announcements, almost universally stressed the religious and moral atmosphere of the school: sometimes, doubtless, to reassure parents, who still saw learning as the first ally of the devil. Nevertheless religion and the Bible appear as regular subjects of instruction in but about thirty of the institutions listed. Second thought suggests what was taking place in the nineteenth century: the advance beyond Colonial Puritanism, which regarded the Bible as the first and only authority. The nineteenth century schools were beginning to rationalize religion; and, while they point to the religious and moral atmosphere, they are more inclined to develop such studies as moral philosophy, the Evidences of Christianity, natural theology, Butler's celebrated *Analogy of Natural and Revealed Religion*, and even certain sciences, than to rely on the Bible and direct religious teaching as the sole sources of ethical and moral instruction.

The advance of science, and its rapid extension into schools, was doubtless a great factor in promoting this tendency to

explain Christian religion rationally.   The first steps were, however, feeble.   Phelps, it is recalled, pointed to geological study
as desirable for young ladies because of the proof it gave to the
story of the creation.   Geography was the first science for girls,
and was almost universally offered until 1840; thereafter it was
not offered so regularly in seminaries, but did appear more and
more as a preparatory study.   Ancient and modern geography
were frequently named specifically after 1820, and correlated
with ancient and modern history, which appeared about the same
period and with about the same frequency.   Physical geography
occurred with fair regularity after 1855 or 1860; rarely before
that time.

Natural philosophy and astronomy were regular interests of
the seminary course after 1810; chemistry and botany were well
established in it after 1825.   Natural history and philosophy of
natural history occurred sporadically after 1815.   Physiology
became fairly constant after 1835, with occasional mention of
anatomy and hygiene.   Calisthenics, as a means to promote
health, appeared in girls' schools about 1825, but was not universally introduced at that time.   The best seminaries, however,
were leaders in this effort to promote health education.   After
the epoch-making work of Dio Lewis, about 1860, physical education became the general rule.   Popular scientific knowledge
found a place in instruction, as witness: familiar science, ouranography, object lessons and conchology.

In spite of considerable agitation on the question of domestic
economy as a proper subject of scientific study for ladies, from
the time of Emma Willard and Catherine Beecher, the seminary
continued to offer the fripperies of filigree, painting, music, and
drawing in far greater profusion.   For these they doubtless found
a better market.   Some schools came gradually to the point of
relinquishing the ornamentals as not ''solid'' or ''disciplinary''
enough, and below their dignity; for the same reason they were
reluctant to soil their hands with housework or domestic economy.
Considering all kinds of needlework, they clearly became less
popular after 1830; as for painting, music, and drawing, they
were fairly constant till the end of the period.

An important place was assigned the social sciences by realistic
educational philosophy.   Of these, history was the first important
one to appear.   It was mentioned in the earliest schools that

claimed to offer advanced education to girls, and retained a permanent place in the fully established and organized seminary or academy. Though subdivided in manifold and mysterious ways, it was a constant member of the family of studies, and doubtless a troublesome one for the young ladies, from 1800 onward; troublesome and a good discipline, no doubt, for, as one of its designations indicated, it was chronology or the "science of ascertaining the true historical order of past events and their exact dates."

Education, penmaking, and the "science of common school teaching" occupied a place in the studies of the seminary—probably a more important place than is at first suggested by the number designating it specifically as a subject. This is due to the fact that only by a few leaders was the science of teaching considered a separate study in itself. Joseph Emerson specified penmaking and education as special subjects, and Zilpah Grant also; but most teachers prepared future teachers by giving special attention to methods, subject matter, and school management, in connection with other academic subjects.

When these became well recognized subjects of instruction, and when a professional regard for special pedagogical instruction developed, the normal school was created, to which young women were drawn off from the seminaries and specifically prepared for the common schools. Nevertheless, as has been pointed out,[39] in numerous cases it was specified that the academies and seminaries should prepare, and many took especial interest in preparing, teachers. It has been said that, in 1867, in 86 academies of New York State, 363 male and 1,122 female pupils were being instructed in the science of common school teaching.[40]

Though housework played a part in the everyday life of some institutions, such as Bethlehem Seminary and that at South Hadley, and manual labor was introduced into some schools, it was for the purpose of economy and to enable poor students to get an education, and not because of their educational value. Mary Lyon insisted on this view of manual labor. In general, it is true that manual labor departments dropped out as the institutions became better established and the communities, from which students came, became more well-to-do. Oberlin's manual

39 See p. 403 ff.
40 Randall: *Hist. Com. Sch. System of N. Y.*, 383.

labor features declined as her prosperity increased.[41] Other factors, too, doubtless accounted for the decline.[42]

Taking into consideration the seminaries between 1749 and 1871, 162 in number, one may gain an impression as to (1) relative stress laid on the several fields of knowledge throughout the whole period; and (2) the fluctuation of emphasis on particular key studies. The number of cases is small, but it is believed that the trends and stresses suggested are fairly reliable. Table I shows the per cent of institutions which offered the thirty-six main studies, 1749–1829, 1749–1871, and between 1830 and 1871. All the branches of study named are given, with the number of institutions mentioning them, in Appendix II, at the end of this volume. Reading across the table, the rise or decline of a subject's importance may be estimated; reading down, one may see how each subject compared with another. The figures probably have less reliability in some subjects than others. Calisthenics, for example, may have had some place in an institution but may not have been considered and listed as a study in the catalog.

Besides regular studies, students appear to have interested themselves occasionally in outside activities, other than calisthenics, and the more sedate accomplishment of walking. The favorite outlet for superfluous energy was found in the establishment of societies, usually with a religious, missionary, or literary purpose. At Troy, New York, an association was formed to promote female education in Athens,[43] but this was due to the influence of Emma Willard rather than the initiative of the girls under her tutelage. At New Hampton Female Seminary, New Hampshire, and at the Ipswich Seminary, religious and literary associations were formed. The missionary and religious interest of the early academies is also to be seen in the religious meetings at Mount Holyoke, and in the establishment (1832) of the Female Association of West Bradford Academy for the Education of Heathen Youth. Forty-three members subscribed, at twenty-five cents each, and donations were also made. At each meeting "persons [were] chosen . . . to select and prepare to read some missionary intelligence for the next." The purpose of the Sister

[41] See also the *Record of Holliston Academy*, by Loomis.

[42] Cyril Pearl discussed them, in relation to boys' schools, in the *Yankee Farmer*, May 29, 1841, 4, cols. 2–3.

[43] *Am. Annals of Ed.*, III, 189.

TABLE I

PER CENT. OF INSTITUTIONS OFFERING CERTAIN SUBJECTS

Subjects	1749–1829 (55 schools)	1749–1871 (162 schools)	1830–1871 (107 schools)
Spelling	43	49	51
Reading	89	73	65
Writing	75	52	41
Composition	50	59	64
English Grammar	89	86	84
Logic	25	50	62
Mental Philosophy	22	62	82
Rhetoric	49	75	88
Latin Grammar	24	47	59
Greek Grammar	11	23	29
German	9	14	16
French	46	55	60
Arithmetic	86	81	79
Algebra	15	60	83
Plane Geometry	27	62	79
Plane Trigonometry	2	27	40
Evidences of Christianity	11	36	50
Moral Philosophy	36	65	80
Geography	82	70	63
Natural Philosophy	50	76	90
Chemistry	30	70	90
Geology	2	40	60
Botany	24	62	82
Astronomy	46	72	85
Physiology	2	37	55
Calisthenics	3	14	19
History	58	47	41
Ancient History	14	35	44
Modern History	14	32	41
U. S. History	16	35	45
Political Science	2	23	34
Plain Needlework	42	12	5
Ornamental Needlework	43	23	12
Painting	25	37	43
Drawing	49	49	50
Music	21	27	30

Circle of Bradford Academy, about 1818, was similar. Though few records of such organizations are to be found, considering the religious animus of the seminaries, it is probable that such organizations were the rule. At Maine Wesleyan Seminary, the Calliopean Society[44] was organized December 31, 1828, being com-

[44] Calliopean was a favorite name in female seminaries. Oxford Female College's Calliopean Society followed the practice of giving a "Never Despair" certificate to its members upon their graduation.

posed of both girls and boys.[45] Its object was "the encouragement of science and morality in this Institution." This society began (1841) to bind its literary contributions; and, in 1865, they experimented with publication of *The Calliopean*, which, however, did not prove a successful venture. Some of the topics

THE FAIR  EPHEMERAL.

Female Seminary, Washington, Pa., Friday, March 29, 1844.

Address of the Ephemeral.

Fair ladies and fair gentlemen, I make my humblest bow,
I come, a stranger, bearing my credentials on my brow;
I'm very young and diffident; to-night I have 'come out'
To mingle in your merriment, and see what you're about.
By the ladies I have been induced to grace this Hall to-night,
My reign is o'er, my life is done, when beams the morrow's light;
But to gratify my gentle friends who've made me fit for th' occasion,
I'll try to be agreeable, and talk without persuasion.
I hope I find you are well pleased with what you've heard and seen
At the Examination, which you all, of course, have been:
"The pupils all did well," you say; "the music, too, was good;
To hear such interesting care, I hope it long will stand,"
I'm glad to think it was so fine; for though I do not make
Pretensions to great scholarship, I certainly do take
Deep interest in the Institution called the Seminary,
Whose Teachers are so competent; the pupils all so merry:
Under Miss Foster's fostering care, I hope it long will stand,
To prove a useful ornament and blessing to our land.
And now, to wind the matter up, you see, the ladies have
Assembled here their choicest works, your patronage to crave:
Of fancy articles a rich profusion you will find,
And useful, pretty, tasteful things, to suit each different mind.
'Twere useless to attempt a list of the numerous fair creations
Of female skill collected here, of all denominations;
The magic "Bower of Fate" is here, where Fortune's stern decree
Presents before the startled gaze your future history;
Then, in the "Post office" you'll find a very charming letter,
Expressly written for your case; it could not hit you better;
And then, to tempt the Epicure—perhaps you'll like it best—
A table with rich viands spread, in choicest fashion dressed:
Hot coffee, oysters, chicken-salad, pickles, ham, and tongue;
Apples, oranges, and cakes and candies, are among
The number of enticing things with which they are supplied;
Then come and taste, and all enjoy; and when the whole you've tried,
Return to me, and well peruse my contents at your leisure,
That nature cannot fail to yield a vast amount of pleasure.
Below you'll find an Essay which must every person please,
A 'private conversation' styled, 'between the Pleiades;'
A burning genius glows along each classic word and line,
Which merits, and that richly, the appellative sublime:
To be in keeping with my name, so very transcendental,
I have some gems of poetry, to please the sentimental;
And then, to give variety, which is the spice of life,
I'll add a few nonsensicals, with wit and talent rife.
Now, gentlemen and ladies all, I'll close my introduction,
Hoping that on my character you'll put a fair construction:

And to the object of this fair give hearty approbation,
For 'tis of great importance to the interests of the nation;
A choice selection of rare books to purchase 'tis designed,
With which intent, to sell their goods the ladies have combined;
They labored unremittingly at home, and in society,
Taxing their inventive powers to have a rare variety;
Aware that every gentleman would feel a partiality
For 'home industry,' and to buy display some liberality:
With this broad hint, I feel assured, to offer and to sell,
And hoping that your heart is big, I bid you now farewell!

A PRIVATE CONVERSATION BETWEEN

THE PLEIADES,

BY MISS L. VIRGINIA SMITH.

Read at an Examination of the Pupils of the Washington Female Seminary, September, 1843.

Twilight had deepened into night around our little village, and the sunset banners which waved their "glory-pencilled folds" along the western sky, had faded to a sombre hue. The evening breeze, as it crept along the undulating bosom of our little stream, and sighed away its existence amid the foliage of the surrounding trees, brought to my ear the vesper hymn of the forest-bird, as he sank to his leafy dwelling. The shrill life of the catydid, and the roll of the beetle's drum, told of the joys of fairy-land; while the pure air around me seemed a rarer element, where the soul might soar away to the blue expanse, and revel in dreams "pure and bright as the morn of life." The palace of the forest-king on some ivy shore; or rich as the cloud-wrought drapery of a summer's sunset in a more genial clime." Methought that, as nature hung her white mists upon the bosom of the hills, and veiled the lustre of her charms with twilight's sober drapery, I could hear her still small voice whispering me to gaze afar, where countless worlds, surrounded by their attendant worlds, gradually appeared.

The beautiful Comet, then on a visit to this system, flashed like a brilliant gem upon the coronet of night; and the milky-way shone upon the sky, a river of light rolling in the land of stars. It was just such a night as the mind delights to dwell upon; when the world, and all its splendid nothings, recede from the eye of thought, and leave the soul to expand in the region of sublime contemplation. As evening melted into night, star after star lit its lamp at the altar of glory, and burned far up in the mid-heaven. My attention was arrested by that beautiful cluster denominated the Pleiades, which hung in gem-like brilliancy upon the verge of the horizon; and the words of the inspired writer came forcibly to my mind: "Canst thou bind the sweet influence of the Pleiades, or loose the bands of Orion?" "Canst thou bring forth Mazzaroth in his season, and guide Arcturus and his sons?"

Long and earnestly I gazed upon them, till "a change came o'er the spirit of my dream;" and I felt myself floating away with a wavy motion, through the sky, and knew that I was borne aloft upon Imagination's wing, to revel for a time amid the high and beautiful things of her own wild creation. Soon I arrived at the Pleiades, but never shall I be able to describe the delicious emotions I then experienced, when my ear caught the deep symphonies of Nature's voice, swelling her song of praise, like a thousand tiny harps, touched by those fairy shadows seen in the twilight dim. Before me were the seven sisters, reclining upon the rich folds of a

crimson cloud. Their robes were a tissue of sun-beams, gemmed with stars, and mingled with the shades of the rain-bow.—Above them streamed a burnished canopy of rosy light; while here and there, the beautiful spirits of air sported upon the bosom of the cloud, or fanned their shining wings in the flood of glory which encircled them.

A remarkable resemblance existed between six of the sisters. There were the same lofty brows; eyes whose glance was sunshine; and lips on which the fire of genius and of passion breathed.

First, I noticed Alcyone; called by many, the "light of the Pleiades;" and was struck with awe at the air of dignity and command which she possessed; for there was a rich flush upon her cheek, a light upon her sunny brow, and a fire in the flashing of her glittering eye, which altogether presented a picture bewildering to gaze upon. Around her, sat Electra, Sterope, Maia, Tayeta, and Celeno, over whom the spirit of youth seemed to shed its most touching grace. The glance of playful gaiety which revelled in their full dark eyes, was softened by the look of ineffable sweetness which awoke in them all a transparent veil, but heightened the beauties it would have fain concealed. Though they now appeared somewhat serious, yet love, lurking in the dimple which their arch smile created, seemed to claim the lovely creatures as his own; and the overwhelming expression which floated in their sun-like eyes, told they were not of earth.

In the centre of the group, and in perfect contrast to her queenly sisters, appeared the gentle Merope. Her blue-dissolving eye-beam was like the timid glance of the western star, when he sheds his pale light upon the summer sky, and rich curls clustered around her snowy brow, soft and bright as the sun's last fading blush, when it glows upon the purple mists of evening. The shadows of deep and holy memories rested upon her lovely countenance, while the consciousness of innocence shed its softness around her, grateful and pure, as the summer dew lingers upon the bosom of the rose. She was speaking, and the silvery tone of her voice came upon the ear like the "memories of days that are past—pleasant and mournful to the soul."

"It is because I have married a mortal," said she, "that our Father cast a shade upon my brow. So that I am alone in your midst; a stranger in mine own land; for I am not now as one of you. The light of my Father's smile has gone out upon my path. The joy of former years has passed away. Even the bright beam of my earthly love has departed, never—never to return!"

Her low voice appeared to die away, from very sweetness, they all gathered around to caress her—for she was the darling of that little band —and as their white arms wreathed lightly about her, the night-breeze lovingly mingled her golden curls with the raven tresses of the sisterhood.

"Sweet Merope!" said Alcyone, as she folded her sister to her bosom, "be comforted; and though recollection may delight to dwell on that era, when early love first shone upon the horizon of your existence, and tinged every feeling with its genial glow, apply now to us for that affection which the heart of Sisyphus would have lavished upon you in all its tenderness; and let Hope cheeringly teach us to muse upon the time when your affection shall bestow its best blessings upon us; and the finger of smiling felicity daily weave such hours of bliss in the web of our existence, as fancy's sweet idea gives to the joys of a better and a brighter world."

The warm tide of reviving tenderness rushed o'er the kindling soul of Merope.

"Thus blessed with a sister's love, O, how could I complain!" she exclaimed, as she returned the warm embrace of Alcyone; while a rich glow of pleasure quivered upon her cheek, sudden and beautiful as the summer lightning, when it plays upon the snowy bosom of a sustained cloud.

"Indeed, sisters," cried Celeno, while an arch smile frolicked upon her ruby lip, "I cannot see that any of you have reason to complain, except myself; for if you believe it, Arcturus has not

THE FAIR EPHEMERAL (1844)

written upon by the young ladies are suggestive of the atmosphere of the female seminary between 1830 and 1860; "Solitude," "Benevolence," "Twilight," "A Dream," "Soliloquy," "Ghosts of Fashion," and "The Lost Sister" are fairly typical;

45 *MS. Record Book*, at the school, Kents Hill, Maine.

they are choice essays, but not quite equal to those by young ladies of Nashville (Tennessee) Female Academy, who wrote upon "Morning's Gems are but Midnight's Tears," "I'll not Forget," "Triumphs of Genius," "Whence? Where? Whither?" "Earth's bright morn soon o'er cast with clouds," "Can Time teach Man Forgetfulness?" "The Eloquence of Decay," "Day and Night of the Soul," and similar themes.[46]

Other early attempts at journalism are found in *The Fair Ephemeral,* published at the Female Seminary, Washington, Pennsylvania, in 1844. The following polite address accompanied its debut:

"Fair ladies and fair gentlemen, I make my humblest bow,
"I come, a stranger, bearing my credentials on my brow;
"I'm very young and diffident; tonight I have 'come out'
"To mingle in your merriment, and see what you're about.
"By the ladies I have been induced to grace this Hall to-night,
"My reign is o'er, my life is done, when beams the morrow's light;
"But to gratify my gentle friends who've made me for th' occasion,
"I'll try to be agreeable, and talk without persuasion.
"I hope I find you are well pleased with what you've heard and seen
"At the Examination, where you all, of course, have been:
" 'The pupils all did well,' you say; 'the music, too, was good;
"To hear such interesting things, you could all night have stood.'
"I'm glad to think it was so fine; for though I do not make
"Pretensions to great scholarship, I certainly do take
"Deep interest in the Institution called the Seminary,
"Whose Teachers are so competent; the pupils all so merry:
"Under Miss Foster's fostering care, I hope it long will stand,
"To prove a useful ornament and blessing to our land.
"And now, to wind the matter up, you see, the ladies have
"Assembled here their choicest works, your patronage to crave:
"Of fancy articles a rich profusion you will find,
"And useful, pretty, tasteful things, to suit each different mind."

In the same year, "under the [editorial] supervision of the Board of Instruction" of Wesleyan Female Collegiate Institute, Wilmington, Delaware, there appeared *The Female Student and Young Ladies Chronicle.* It proposed issuing on the first of every month, and promised to contain "original communications

46 *Southwestern Monthly,* July, 1852, 63.

THE FEMALE STUDENT,

AND

YOUNG LADIES' CHRONICLE,

PUBLISHED AT THE WESLEYAN FEMALE COLLEGIATE INSTITUTE.

Vol. 1. WILMINGTON, (DEL.) AUGUST, 1844. No. 1.

THE FEMALE STUDENT (1844)

from the young ladies connected with the Institute, and those who have been so connected. . . ." It was to be "devoted exclusively to the advancement of female education"; for where, they ask, "in the long list of periodicals" of our country, "is there one devoted exclusively to . . . [this cause]?" "Is it presumptous in us to hope that by this means female talent will be elicited, and female energies awakened, and that many a flower—born to blush unseen—. . . will, through this medium, diffuse its fragrance around it?"

III. *Method of Instruction and Government in Seminaries*

In general, methods employed in the female seminaries were not novel; they followed, for the most part, the customary procedures of their period. Some divergence therefrom may, certainly, be noted in the use of the system of pupil-teachers, *dizainieres,* at the Ursuline Convent at its beginning (1727), and the early emphasis upon 'learning to do by doing' which was in vogue especially in the Moravian seminaries at Bethlehem and Salem, in connection with the practical arts of the household.[47] Books were not so plentiful in the eighteenth century and, consequently, great stress fell upon oral instruction. But this was true of boys' schools as well. Old manuscript arithmetics and geometries[48] bear witness to the fact that boys and girls made their books while they studied the subjects. Eliza Southgate wrote: I "expect now to begin my large manuscript arithmetic"; again, "I have finished my large manuscript arithmetic and want to get it bound." Later, she explained she had done a "small geometry book" and was going to begin "a large one."[49]

As long as the curriculum remained limited—for instance, before 1800, little was taught beyond reading, writing, arithmetic, religion, English grammar, rhetoric, domestic arts, accomplishments and geography—the method continued to be very formal, most emphasis being placed on memorizing the material taught. In the nineteenth century a movement began to rationalize the learning and teaching process. This is first evident in the sci-

[47] See Reichel: *Bethlehem Souvenir,* 34 and 35.

[48] See, for example, p. 157; also those of the *Norris Collection* in the library of the Historical Society of Pennsylvania, referred to in Woody: *Early Quaker Educ. in Pa.,* 196.

[49] Cook: *A Girl's Life Eighty Years Ago,* 11 and 15.

ences; but other studies, too, it was argued, could be taught so as to be understood as well as remembered. Pestalozzian method was eagerly acclaimed by enthusiastic writers on female education, because its adoption would transform the formal studies of the seminaries into agencies for producing "balanced minds," "observing capacities," "thinking beings," and so forth.

CERTIFICATES OF PROMOTION ISSUED BY HUNTSVILLE FEMALE SEMINARY (1836–1837)

In Emerson's Seminary at Wethersfield, it was proposed to "follow the indication of nature; to teach those things first, those branches and parts of branches, which may be understood by themselves, and gradually proceed to others, which more immediately and intimately depend upon these.''[50] As he says, it is manifestly absurd to ''teach multiplication to a person ignorant of addition, or to teach division to one unacquainted with subtraction and multiplication,'' but ''inconsistencies like these are probably to be found, in a greater or less degree, in almost every literary institution.'' He does not feel he will be able to avoid all inconsistencies, for such cannot be until ''intellectual philosophy is better understood,'' but he does propose to ''proceed gradually from the more easy to the more difficult'' and holds that a certain sequence of studies is necessary, which he explains: ''It is manifest that Arithmetic must be in some measure known, in order to understand Geography. In almost every page of Geography, numbers are brought to view; and these cannot be understood without some knowledge of Arithmetic, which is the science of numbers. To the study of Geography, some acquaintance with Geometry also is a prerequisite equally important. For the want of this, it is often the case, that those who have devoted much time to the study of Geography, know scarcely anything of latitude or longitude, of the comparative magnitudes of countries, &c. of the distances and bearings of places, and of some of the most important properties of maps.

''Geography and Chronology are the 'eyes' of history. How many, alas, have attempted to grope their way through the historic field, without these lights! How dark and bewildering has been their course! The study of History, then, should be preceded by that of Geography, and either preceded or accompanied by that of Chronology.

''A considerable acquaintance with Arithmetic and some knowledge of Geometry should also precede the study of Natural Philosophy.''

Studies pursued as above indicated will not only ''furnish that knowledge and that skill which are constantly needful for practical application in every walk of life,'' but will also be conducive to the discipline and improvement of the ''mental faculties.''[51]

In her annual report (1826), Mrs. Thayer, of the Elizabeth Female Academy, Washington, Mississippi, explained how she

[50] *Am. Jour. Ed.*, I, 531–44.
[51] *Ibid.*

had combined the method of Pestalozzi and the systematic instruction of Lancaster, *i.e.*, class instruction:

"*System of Instruction.* This, I have already said, is the inductive system, by which I mean that system which embraces the cultivation of the faculties of attention and judgment, rather than of memory. This system was invented by Pestalozzi, and is founded on the popular doctrine that our ideas are received through the medium of the senses. Pestalozzi wished to illustrate every thing to the senses, and reasoning only from facts, and carrying illustration by the side of theory, he wished a child to advance no faster than it understood. Our plan is formed by the union of these principles, with the systematic arrangements of Joseph Lancaster. Pestalozzi has developed the philosophy of mind, and shown us what we ought to teach. Lancaster has taught how to impart instruction with facility, to a much greater number than could possibly be instructed in the same time, on the old system. By the systematic movements of our plan, it fills up every moment, and thus avoids that ennui which always attends children when idle. It gives a succession of studies, and that prevents satiety and disgust. Its minute classification affords each scholar the chance of advancement, and if there be a superior intellect, it must develope itself and take its appropriate rank, unannoyed by envy and unshackled by pride. The common practice is to load the memory of pupils with a mass of undigested knowledge, and, provided they can recite a certain number of pages, they are supposed to be well taught. On our plan every lesson must be fully explained. The scholars are not urged on faster than they understand, and sensible objects are employed for the purposes of illustration. By the old system, a teacher had nothing to do but hear recitations; by this, the teacher's duty is laborious, and the pupil's comparatively light.

"To make this subject clear, I beg your indulgence while I delineate, as briefly as possible, my method of teaching two of the most important branches, grammar and arithmetic.

"Supposing a class prepared for grammar, who have had no previous instruction on the subject, I proceed in the following manner:—Placing the class before me, I call their attention to the subject of classification in general—ask what is meant by the term—explain it fully, and illustrate by a variety of examples, such as the genus tree for instance, which I teach them to divide into several classes, as forest trees, fruit trees, &c. and again into subdivisions, as oak, ash, maple, hickory, &c. The whole kingdom of nature is before me for illustrations; and if I find one is not clearly understood, I select another, and persevere until my meaning is clearly apprehended. I then proceed to explain the cause of classification, which must be likeness or fitness in the objects classed. Here I refer to our school for an apt illustration, and explain why the children, who listen to me, are classed together. Having thus established this first position taken, I proceed to a second, which is, that all the words which compose our language may be divided into a very few classes, and these classes have names, as articles, nouns, verbs, &c. The first is a very small class, and is soon learned; the second, nouns, is very numerous, including all names of things. Having explained and illustrated this, and fully understood that my pupils are able to name an article and a noun wherever they find them, I assign them, for a lesson, to learn from their grammar, the definitions of these parts of speech, and the exercise closes. At the next recitation, I review the ground gone over, and explain the verb. We now construct sentences, and parse the words etymologically. The next lesson introduces adjectives; the next, divisions of tense; the next, mode, and so on, advancing, step by step, explaining and parsing while we are going through the grammar.

"In arithmetic, I begin with very young children, because I have found from experience that some knowledge of numbers is pre-requisite to any considerable progress in geography. I make a few figures on the black board, which I teach the children to read according to the place they occupy, whether as units, tens, or hundreds. I begin with small numbers, and teach them to add, subtract, multiply and divide, mentally, while one stands by the board to put down the result as it is named. Making each add a column of figures, or subtract, or multiply a single number, and pronounce the result aloud, I engage the attention of all at the same time, errors are corrected, the idle are compelled to attention, and the whole are interested. As they advance, I explain every rule, and illustrate it by examples on the board before the class, and then require similar explanations and illustrations from them. Time will not permit me to be more explicit, I shall therefore only add on this head, that numerous as our studies are, and minutely as they are explained by a systematic appropriation of time and regular succession of studies, there is time for all. That no pupil may be idle is the grand principle upon which we proceed, and by the aid of an assistant governess and a few monitresses, a due proportion of attention is given to each class."[52]

From the above statement it is clear that while Pestalozzi suggested improvements in the method of presenting material to the mind, Lancaster opened a way to facilitate instruction for the many. The pupil-teacher system, as noted above, was not new, as the Ursulines had a similar scheme in their early existence; but, with the rapid spread of girls' seminaries, the necessity of training teachers became a more urgent problem, and the pupil-teacher system of Lancaster, being the most ready remedy, and, at the moment, the best advertised, was frequently adopted. Numerous high schools and academies were doubtless opened because this inexpensive system of teaching offered itself. Even where the Lancasterian system was not fully adopted, it suggested the possibility of training teachers quickly to take up a part of the head teacher's burden. Grant, Beecher, Lyon and Willard all recognized the need and trained their assistants. The latter declared her steps of teaching to be: first, to make the pupils by explanation and illustration *understand* their subject; second, to make each scholar recite "in order that she might *remember*"; and, third, to make her capable of *communicating* her knowledge. "Scholars thus instructed were soon capable of teaching; and here were now forming my future teachers; and some were soon capable of aiding me in arranging the new studies, which I was constantly engaged in introducing."[53] Her biographer, Fowler, makes clear that the school was not run to train teachers, but that the training of the pupil-teacher was to be a benefit to both Mrs. Willard and her protegé:

"Mrs. Willard, when she prepared her 'Plan,' did not at all contemplate the special training of teachers; and she never turned aside to accommodate the school to them, but rather the reverse. With a pupil-teacher of advancement and improved character, she would place in the same room, a petted, self-willed Miss of wealthy parents. This was an advantage to both parties

[52] *Ibid.*, II, 633–7.
[53] Barnard: *Am. Teachers*, 134–5.

—for while the teacher-scholar was aiding Mrs. Willard in a difficult and delicate duty, she was brought into more contact and conversation with her principal, by whom it was her special business to profit; and on the management of difficult pupils—the most critical portion of the business she was to learn."[54]

Another writer on "intellectual instruction" of females[55] sharply criticized the "prevailing practice of indiscriminate study" which "ranges over the surface of everything," and pointed out possible ways of improving the teaching of certain "things most essential in the intellectual department of female education." The studies named are not all-inclusive, and some may be omitted in particular cases; but when used, the method must be improved to get the greatest values.

Reading, he says, is a basic necessity, often supplanted by studies less useful, and made uninteresting by an unquestioning method of teaching. Questions in reading must be "close enough to reach the meaning of every word," and a part of every lesson should deal with "illustrations of the difference in the sense of words usually taken as synonymous." Poetry should be introduced for the "discipline of taste" and "moral improvement." Orthography, also, is not made "sufficiently practical." To be more so, teachers must use words from reading books rather than from spellers, thus laying stress upon the words in common use rather than those more difficult and freakish, yet seldom used; and spelling lessons should be written as well as oral. The tendency of teachers of English grammar to stress etymology, "theoretical acquaintance with the subject," "verbal knowledge" and "parsing" is lamented, and they are urged rather to "make the whole subject intelligible and familiar, by plain conversation and constant practical exercise" both in speaking and writing.[56]

In similar manner, other studies common in girls' schools are discussed briefly, emphasis being everywhere laid upon making the subject "practical" and "useful." Here, too, is to be found a profound faith in the discipline of certain subjects. In chirography, "to make . . . [it] a useful and improving exercise to the mind,"—any formal discipline obtainable is regarded as the most practical of results—"the teacher's first and chief care

54 *Ibid.*, 154.

55 *Am. Jour. Ed.*, II, 676–82.

56 *Ibid.*

should be accuracy of perception, and exactness of execution. Every other attainment should be subsequent to this, and . . . entirely subordinate. The habit of observing with close and persevering attention any succession of forms (and especially when the object is to imitate them), constitutes an excellent discipline of all the powers employed in expression. . . . There is a peculiar value in the cultivation of penmanship, from the very circumstance that it is an exercise so mechanical, and so well adapted therefore to the ability of the young mind. All the elementary efforts of children should be closely connected with the exercise of the senses. The eye and the hand should be made to minister to the improvement of the mind. . . ." But with "disciplinary values" a practical one is to be combined. Instead of endless repetitions of single words or letters and awkward or trite maxims, pupils should learn to write by making "bills and receipts and business accounts, . . . [by] letter writing," and by copying "from suitable books, the elements of useful science."[57]

Geography and history "are peculiarly appropriate to the circumstances of female life," but how seldom are they taught so as to be "interesting or practical?" This may be remedied by not "skimming over a general history from Creation downwards" but by giving attention to the United States or New England history, which would "favor a more natural progress of the mind in learning" and "tend to improve its habits of practical observation and direct application, by the influence of association with objects of proximity and of living interest." The study also needs to be made more than "a naked record of events" and may be strengthened by more strict attention to "chronology" and "antiquities," without which the "historical ideas . . . fall to pieces and gradually disappear from the memory."

In arithmetic little was formerly done, progress generally not going beyond the Rule of Three, so that "females . . . were permitted barely to discover what a puzzling thing arithmetic was." But now "the female mind . . . may be considered as privileged to all the benefits of thorough mathematical discipline, and to the free study of the various branches allied to it." Not only has its study been opened to them but the subject itself has become more a rational process, thanks to the works of Colburn. "The in-

[57] *Ibid.*, 734–42.

ductive method of teaching has happily put an end to much of this evil [memoriter learning of arithmetic] ; and the simple and intelligible works now compiled . . . enable teachers to impart to their scholars much excellent mental discipline along with their exercises in arithmetic.''[58]

Rhetoric is condemned because it is chiefly a formal study of Blair and Walker, and reading is a ''mechanical result of rules''; whereas it should be recognized that ''expression, whether read or written, cannot be naturally cultivated without direct reference to that which is expressed. . . .'' The ''piece'' to be read must ''be fully understood'' and ''thoroughly felt.'' ''A simple, unpretending, natural style of reading, is most effectually taught by early accustoming children to read pieces which they understand and like and by familiar directions for avoiding unmeaning and objectionable tones. The chief injury to the style of reading among children, is entailed on them by the attempt to read formal pieces which they do not understand, and in which the language is entirely different from that of common life. Here is the true origin of the difficulty which mothers often feel in endeavoring to instruct or entertain their children by reading to them, and of the rarity of that accomplishment so useful and so agreeable in young women—the power of reading in an easy, graceful, and interesting manner.''

The teaching of composition is condemned on similar grounds. Much attention is given to rules of composition and writing upon ''didactic themes,'' rather than expression of spontaneous thoughts; whereas the critic thinks ''a full mind is the only true source of fluent expression'' and narrative and descriptive themes are the only natural ones for young minds. Narration of simple things, which we have read from authors or which we ourselves have experienced, represents the best first step in composition.

Other studies, such as Latin, French, Italian, or ''any contemporaneous languages of Europe,'' are recommended, if they need not cost the neglect of something more directly useful. The critic has, however, no suggestion to make as to improved methods of instruction. A study of the human mind is urgently required, since the female sex is the natural guardian of the ''opening faculties of infancy'' and ''rational methods of government''

[58] *Ibid.*

can only spring from "a knowledge of the mind." All natural studies such as chemistry, botany, mineralogy, zoölogy, physical geography, and astronomy are to be taught by the method which relies least on books and "most on actual observation and experiment." Accomplishments are important when well taught and become real; but a smattering of drawing and playing upon an instrument are not accomplishments. Humble domestic arts properly occupy a place in female education if "an illiberal view of female character and influence" does not assign them too great an emphasis.

The South Carolina Female Institute, in a description of its proposed work, subscribed to principles of method similar to those above, stipulated that teacher and pupil must understand each other, and concluded:

"It will constitute a primary object of the institute to form such a subdivision, in the order of studies, that there will be a gradation from the simplest elementary branches to the higher departments of letters. In order to effect this, mere subordination is insufficient; a subordinate class must, as it respects the instruction imparted, be immediately preparatory to that in advance of it. The translation of a scholar into a higher class, must be but a single step in an ascending series."[59]

In the above criticism of methods employed, there is always evident a distinct stress upon the newly introduced Pestalozzian theory of teaching and learning. This, coupled with belief in method as a means to secure mental discipline, continued to prevail throughout the period when seminaries were the dominant institutions for higher education of girls. As yet the doctrine of interest was not understood to be in conflict with that of discipline.[60]

It must not be thought, however, that all practice was quickly modelled upon the Pestalozzian plan, as the criticism indicated should be the case. The account given below of the method employed at Hartford Female Seminary will suggest some applica-

[59] *Ibid.*, III, 583–94.

[60] An interesting development of the Pestalozzian influence is seen in the collection and exchange of cabinets of minerals, plants, etc., indulged in by the children of many schools. See the *Fortieth Report of the Public School Society*, 1846 (N. Y.). Some letters are quoted by Reigart: *Lancasterian System in N. Y. C.*, 60–2.

tion of the new theory, but it was still, on the whole, a very bookish system of instruction.

"A short account may be interesting of the mode adopted in several of the branches taught. In geography, the pupils are first required to learn all that can be obtained from the maps, and during the course they are required to draw maps from memory on the slate or black board, and then to give a minute account of the country thus portrayed. After thus completing the maps, Woodbridge's large Geography is used, from which selections are made according to the discretion of the teacher. These selections have reference to the previous knowledge acquired, and also the time which the pupil is able to devote to an education; as those who will pursue their studies a number of years, can enter more minutely into this study than those whose time and opportunities are more limited.

"For mental arithmetic, the classes use Colburn's work, and in doing each sum are required to state aloud the processes by which the answer is obtained, and the reason for it.

"In written arithmetic, by the aid of a little work prepared for the purpose, the pupils are taught to explain the principles upon which the most important rules are constructed. They are accustomed also to do sums upon the black board, and explain the principles of each process as they proceed. There is no study in which the immediately beneficial effects are discovered so much as in this. The command of the thoughts which this process requires, the precision of language demanded, and the accuracy of thinking and reasoning which it induces, are most desirable and important.

"In teaching history, the excellent set of charts just published by Mr. Henry Bostwick, of New York, are used. It is believed that all teachers, when they become practically acquainted with their peculiar excellencies, will consider them an invaluable acquisition. The method pursued is, first to give them a general outline of ancient geography as drawn out on the map at the head of the chart. This is done by dictation from the teacher, and notes are written by the scholars. Each pupil is provided with a chart which she examines as the teacher proceeds, and with the aid of the chart and the notes, learns the lesson for the next day.

"After the geography is acquired, the chart being divided into certain regular periods, one, two, or three lectures are given on each period, by the teacher, according to the number and importance of the events included in it. While the teacher is presenting a description of the most interesting characters and events, the pupils find the country, the date, the names of the characters, their genealogy, and the general history of the several nations, all presented to the eye on their charts, which thus greatly assists in fixing the lecture in their memory. Some notes are taken at the same time, and the next day the class is examined on the previous lecture. It is found necessary in order to make this branch interesting, that at least two terms should be devoted to it; and hereafter, ancient history will be pursued in the winter term, and modern history in the summer.

"In chemistry, a course of experimental lectures is delivered by a professional gentleman, each one of which is intended to illustrate the daily lesson given out and explained by the teacher. On account of the heat occasioned by performing the experiments, this branch will be pursued only during the winter term.

"In rhetoric and logic, the classes are required to analyze the ideas, arguments and arrangement of certain pieces pointed out by the teacher. They are also required to compose examples of the various figures of rhetoric, and of the various modes of argument, syllogisms, &c., pointed out in logic.

"In geometry, the pupils are accustomed to draw their own diagrams on the black board, while demonstrating, and to place different letters from those in the book. The black board is also used in algebra.

"In composition, the following method is pursued. A pupil is never required to write stories, descriptions, conversations and humorous pieces, that a suitable command of language may be acquired. When this is in some measure attained, a didactic subject is given out by the teacher to whom this branch is committed. The nature and method of the several parts required in a composition, are then pointed out, explained, and somewhat illustrated. The faults common in an introduction, in the arrangement, and in the style and language, are also pointed out. A regular plan is then given, and the mode of expanding and illustrating explained. The class when thus prepared, is then required to write on this subject. After the composition is written, the faults are pointed out, and the piece is to be re-written. An exercise either in composing or rewriting, is required every week. After some practice in this manner the pupils are ready to originate and prepare their own subjects.

"Wednesday mornings are devoted to exercises in reading and spelling. The work used for reading is Porter's *Analysis,* and the teachers first read over the pieces together themselves, before instructing their classes. One hour also on Wednesday afternoon is devoted to botany, or some other miscellaneous and interesting study.

"Saturday morning is devoted to grammar by those who are not well acquainted with its principles. The others read the best parts of Paradise Lost, when its beauties are pointed out, and its allusions explained by the teacher. In this exercise, Addison's critique on this work is read, the Classical Dictionary consulted, and every method sought to render interesting and intelligible this sublime poem.

"In addition to the general care of the regular studies and other business of the school, the principal teacher has the immediate charge of the moral and religious instruction of the pupils. It is the constant aim to induce the scholars to act from conscientious motives in discharging all their duties.

"In imparting religious instruction, one thing is ever borne in mind—that the susceptibilities of youth, and especially of young females, are not to be strongly called forth; nor is religious influence to depend chiefly upon these. The conscience and the understanding are addressed more than the passions, and the effects which follow are then to be more valued and trusted. Neither is it considered desirable to make any effects which may follow the faithful discharge of Christian duty a subject of notoriety and remarks."[61]

IV. Government of Students

In several of the seminaries there developed some practical phases of self-government, responsibility being placed on students by such leaders as Mrs. Willard, Miss Beecher and Mary Lyon. Many favored self-government theoretically for its effect on character formation; but self-government on the present-day

[61] *Am. Jour. Ed.,* III, 461–5; Miss Beecher's methods are also referred to at some length in her *Educational Reminiscences,* 34 *ff.*

scale was not attempted in practice. The intelligence of Mrs. Willard and the rest really guided the "officers of the day," the "circles," and so forth. The machinery necessary for functioning of the will of the student body was not created. The most complete approach seems to have been made by Miss Beecher, when, before her absence on account of illness, she arranged that the school "should be resolved into a sort of republic and attempt self-government at least for a short experiment." "Circles" were established with a teacher at the head of each, and to each was committed "one department of my responsibilities." The temporary experiment was a success, according to all reports, but Miss Beecher's severance of relations as head of the school necessarily brought it to a close. One teacher wrote: "I wish to say one word as to the prosperity of our Republic. . . . Since I have been in school I have never seen the young ladies so exactly what they should be as today."[62]

As a general rule, discipline, though mild, was centered in the hands of the principal or delegated to a first assistant. These officials usually took the shortest way to good order, as they understood it, by publishing rules. Few schools were without printed rules. In some they were numerous. Only a few codes, which are self explanatory, are given, as they are representative.[63] The regulations of the Moravian Seminary, Bethlehem, Pennsylvania, have already been mentioned.[64] Ann Smith, at Lexington, Virginia, wrote the names of offenders opposite the rules.[65] The rules established for the Litchfield Academy (1825) follow:

"You are expected to rise early, be dressed neatly and to exercise before breakfast. You are to retire to rest when the family in which you reside request you. You must consider it a breach of politeness to be requested a second time to rise in the morning or retire of an evening.

"It is expected that you attend public worship every Sabbath, except some unavoidable circumstance prevent which you will dare to present as a sufficient apology at the day of judgment.

---

[62] *Reminiscences*, 73.

[63] Rules of Elizabeth Female Academy, published in *Miss Hist. Soc. Pub.*, II, 172–4.

[64] See p. 331 *ff*.

[65] See p. 440.

"Your deportment must be grave and decent while in the house of God; all light conduct in a place of worship is not only offensive to God but an indication of ill breeding; and highly displeasing both to the good and the polite.

"Every hour during the week must be fully occupied either in useful employments, or necessary recreation. Two hours must be faithfully devoted to close study each day, while out of school: and every hour in school must be fully occupied. The ladies where you board must mention it if you do not study your two hours each day.

"You must suppress all emotions of anger, fretfulness and discontent.

"No young lady is allowed to attend any public ball, or sleigh party, till they are more than 16 years old.

"Speaking or moving once in school hours either with or without liberty will take off a part of the extra—unless they move to recite or practice, or write at the tables. Speaking more than once will take off the whole extra and often give you a quarter of a miss.[66]

"You must not walk for pleasure after nine o'clock in the evening. A reward will be given to those who do not waste money, books, clothes, paper, or quills, during the term. To those who have their studies performed at the proper time. To those who have not been peevish, homesick, or impolite. To those who always attend meeting or church. To those who never write carelessly."[67]

One is sometimes tempted to say the best school does not make much of rules. If true, Joseph Emerson's school was a worthy exception. It was recognized as one of the best, and had more rules than any other. In 1826, there were twenty-six:

"1. That they regularly and seasonably attend to the exercises of public worship on the Sabbath;

"2. That they do not spend any part of that sacred day in visiting, or unnecessarily walking or riding abroad;

"3. That they never treat religion with levity or disrespect;

"4. That they do not go more than two miles, from the Seminary Hall, without special permission;

[66] The code does not make quite clear the meaning of an "extra" and a "miss."

[67] White: *Hist. of Litchfield*, 115–16.

"5. That they do not walk in any field, pasture, or other enclosure without the consent of the occupant;

"6. That they regularly and seasonably attend the devotional and literary exercises of the Seminary;

"7. That when addressing a teacher in time of exercise, their posture be standing;

"8. That they do not attempt to communicate ideas privately to each other, in time of exercise, either by whispering, writing or circulating billets;

"9. That their studies in the Hall, be performed with most perfect silence;

"10. That they do not leave their seats in time of exercise;

"11. That they do not unnecessarily change their seats, either in the Hall or at public worship;

"12. That they keep their books closed during recitations;

"13. That in time of exercise, no one engage in any employment, which may divert attention from the subject of general pursuit;

"14. That they do not remove the inkstands from their places;

"15. That they do not make any letters, marks, or defacements upon any object whatsoever, without the owner's consent;

"16. That they do not open any box without the consent of the occupant or teacher;

"17. That they do not partake of any food, fruits, or refreshments in time of exercise;

"18. That they avoid scattering or leaving in the Hall, or near it, any object, that may offend the eye of taste, or injure their character for neatness.

"19. That at all times, they avoid unnecessarily interrupting or retarding the useful progress of others;

"20. That they never treat with reproach or unkindness those who when requested give information of faults;

"21. That they never indulge themselves in saying *can't* or in any way expressing their inability to perform any exercise required;

"22. That they never consider want of preparation to perform, as a reason of absence from any exercise required;

"23. That they never neglect any required exercise on account of company, except the company of friends not residing in the village;

"24. That they never neglect any exercise, for the sake of others, that are to be subsequent;

"25. That in cases of absence, tardiness, non-performance, or gross misdemeanor, they offer their apology, or confession in writing;

"26. That they endeavor at all times to conform themselves to the rules of propriety, according to the best of their judgment;

"And it is most earnestly recommended that the members of the Seminary continually exert themselves to promote each other's greatest improvement and highest welfare."[68]

Abbott Academy, in 1844, stated its purpose was "to secure self-government" and "due self-reliance." No one was to enter the institution "merely to be instructed and governed, but to learn to govern herself on the strictest rules of propriety." This was not brought about by any form of student government; but there was less emphasis on elaborate regulations.[69]

Lagrange Female College, Lagrange, Georgia, published the following rules in 1858:

"1st. Seven hours a day in the winter, and eight in summer, are appropriated to study in the Institution building, during which each pupil shall apply herself assiduously to study, and observe the ordinary rules of decorum.

"2d. Every young lady shall study at least two hours after supper, in her own room.

"3d. Punctual attendance at the tolling of the bell, and prompt discharge of duty, are imperative requisitions.

"4th. Attendance at the Church and Sabbath School of her parents' choice, at least once on Sabbath, is most strictly enjoined. (Parents, when they enter their daughters, must communicate to us their wishes in these regards.)

"5th. The young ladies, in intercourse with teachers or each other, are required to be kind and respectful, and to be governed by that high standard of moral right, which every lady (that deserves the name) will erect for her own moral conduct.

"6th. While extravagance to any extent will never be tolerated, young ladies are required at all times to be neat in person and dress, making a proper use of the hair, tooth and nail brush.

68 *Prospectus* of the school at Wethersfield, 1826, 23–4.
69 *Catalog*, 1844, 14.

"7th. Pupils from abroad, boarding in the village, must have a temporary guardian appointed for them, by their parent or guardian, to do their shopping, nor will any pupil in the absence of such guardian be allowed to make purchases for herself. (We call the attention of patrons especially to this rule, for we cannot hold ourselves responsible for the extravagant purchases of those who, by the neglect of their parents, are made their own guardians.)

"8th. No pupil of this Institution will be permitted to attend parties or places of amusement, receive or entertain, or correspond by letter or otherwise, with any one of the opposite sex, except it be near relations."

Holliston [Massachusetts] Academy, for both girls and boys, had the following rules about 1840:

"1. It is required that the Students at all times manifest a proper regard to their instructors.

"2. All the students are required to meet at the academy for prayers at a quarter before nine o'clock A. M.

"3. All are required to be in their rooms, attending to their respective duties, during the hours of study.

"4. All the students are required to attend the public exercises of Wednesday of each week.

"5. No student shall absent himself from any recitation or other exercise without permission previously obtained.

"6. All the students are required to attend public worship twice every sabbath—once in the forenoon, once in the afternoon.

"7. No member of the Institution shall at any time make use of wine or any other intoxicating drink as a beverage.

"8. No member of the Institution shall at any time make use of profane language—play at cards, checkers, chess, or any other similar game of skill and chance.

"9. The Gentlemen and Ladies are not permitted to walk in company without special permission from the principal."[70]

The Bourbon Academy, Paris, Kentucky, which admitted boys and girls, provided they had in their possession "Webster's *Spelling Book*, Baldwin's *Fables*, *New Testament*, the *American Preceptor*, Weem's *Life of Washington* and the *Columbian Orator*," established several interesting rules: Every student more than fourteen years old "shall, in the presence of his fellow

[70] Published Rules of Holliston Academy.

students bind himself by promise to obey all the laws of the institution.'' All must come at eight in summer and nine in winter and ''attend morning prayers with becoming decency and respect.'' They must avoid ''unnecessary talking, whispering, and laughing'' and treat their fellows with politeness and due respect. Moreover—for the boys, doubtless—they shall carefully avoid ''idle and vicious company; and shall abstain from drinking, gambling and every kind of vice and dissipation.''

RULES OF ANN SMITH ACADEMY (1815)

Breaking of rules was punishable by reproof, chastisement, or expulsion—the last at the discretion of the president and tutors, with the assistance of the trustees. One student only is recorded as having fallen into vicious behavior and threatened to stab the president; for this he was expelled.[71] Girls seldom had to be disciplined harshly, it appears; in one case, however, the master of Danville Academy, Virginia, knocked a large girl down for returning the compliment when he slapped her face.[72] Ann

[71] MS. Record of Bourbon Academy Trustees.
[72] Dame's MS. History of Danville.

Smith was reputed to be a mild disciplinarian, in spite of her list of rules and the practice of posting the offender's names on it; nevertheless, she had to expel a girl who was found guilty of the heinous crime of "breaking up a Bonnet."[73]

V. Criticism of the Seminaries

Educational institutions are generally open to many criticisms, and the female seminary was no exception. Though condemned at one time or another, by persons more or less qualified to judge, for nearly everything it did or did not do, or attempt to do, the criticisms were chiefly concerned with (1) organization; (2) superficiality of studies, attention to accomplishments, and need for specialization; (3) imperfect equipment, (4) incapacity of teachers; (5) lack of attention to moral, domestic (professional), and physical education; (6) appeal to emulation to secure results; (7) the choice of schools and the rapid changing of pupils.

Some most widely known institutions—such as Troy and Mount Holyoke, for example—were, in fact, living criticisms of the practices followed by others. The same might be said of Ipswich, Hartford, and a few others. Among the most unfaltering critics of the usual organization of the female seminaries was Catherine E. Beecher. She saw early, as had many others from Rush down to her day, that it was bad to have an educational institution controlled by one proprietor-principal. Rush had been glad to see Poor's academy under the control of a board of trustees, and Mrs. Willard had pointed out in her *Plan* the irresponsible character of private institutions. Miss Beecher's reforms in organization extended beyond control by trustees, however, and proposed that teachers be "co-equal," thus sharing responsibility with the principal for the management of the school.[74] In a number of respects her proposed reforms of organization suggested the college.

Miss Beecher likewise saw the need of specialization, and lamented the fact that in female schools one teacher must instruct in "reading, spelling, grammar, geography, arithmetic, composition, history, natural philosophy, chemistry . . ."—perhaps as many as twenty subjects—while "in our colleges, where our elder [male] youth are assembled, those whose minds have, to

[73] *MS. Minutes of Ann Smith Academy*, Lexington, Va.
[74] See pp. 320 and 324; and *Am. Jour. Ed.*, II, 219–23.

some degree, been made discriminating by discipline, and mature by age, . . . this principle [of division of labor] to a considerable extent has been introduced, so that ordinarily not more than one or two branches are committed to the care-of one person.''[75]   Not only was the teacher at a disadvantage who had to teach numerous subjects, but the wide range, coupled with the unsubstantial nature of studies, was in itself an evil to pupils.   These evils were commented on perhaps more than any other.[76]   The *American Lady's Preceptor* declared (1821) : ''The only cardinal defect in the education of our females . . . is, perhaps, an undue appropriation of time to the acquisition of those light accomplishments, which serve well to enliven and decorate . . . but are attended with no durable advantages.''   Margaret Fuller, herself fitted with an education of more substantial nature, gained from private schooling, declared (1839) that women were taught more than men but had no place or opportunity to use it:

''Women are now taught, at school, all that men are.   They run over, superficially, even *more* studies, without being really taught anything.   But with this difference: men are called on, from a very early period, to reproduce all that they learn.   Their college exercises, their political duties, their professional studies, the first actions of life in any direction, call on them to put to use what they have learned.''[77]

Much criticism of the lightness of woman's education appeared in the *American Annals* and the *American Journal of Education,* of which the following is typical:

''What an abandonment of useful knowledge,—what a trifling away of time,—what a skimming over the surface of literature,—what a strong desire to impress the fashionable follies of the day, does it unfold.   The whole circle of attainment bears upon one subject—the desire of display.   To display what? a knowledge of the beauties of nature,—the resources of science,—the treasures

---

[75] Extracts from Beecher's *Suggestions* in *Am. Jour. Ed.,* V, 63–6; also II, 219–23.

[76] See, for example, *Am. Annals Ed.,* V, 360–3 and 464–7; *Am. Jour. Ed.,* II, 219–23; Coxe: *Demands of the Country on Am. Females,* II, 140–8; Butler: *The Am. Lady,* 56–8; *American Lady's Preceptor* (1821), IV–V; Todd: *The Daughter at School,* 204–5; Howe: *Margaret Fuller,* 83; *The Nation* (1878), XXVII, 55; Brackett: *Woman and the Higher Education,* 158, and many others.

[77] Howe: *Margaret Fuller,* 83.

of art,—the intellectual pleasures which adorn while they enrich?
No.—These are objects beneath the attention of a young lady who
is to shine in society, and to receive the attentions of some newly
fledged graduate of a college, whose time has been as well occupied as her own, and whose attainments are as respectable.
They would take up too much of that time devoted to the reading
of novels, or of that occupied by the more important business of
discussing the merits of the recently imported foreign fashion.
The alpha and omega of fashionable education is, to unfit the
lovely pupil for the rational enjoyments of life,—to prepare her
to dance a sunny hour in the halls of flattery and deceit, to drink
the intoxicating draught of vanity to the dregs,—then to retire,
sated with unreal pleasures, to the gloomy recesses of an uncul-
tivated and perverted intellect.

"We have no desire to reject the fashionable accomplishments
of female education, or to detract from their merits. They add
a charm and variety to its social relations, and enhance the value
of higher and nobler acquirements. But when they are made to
usurp the place of those acquisitions which render their object a
moral, intelligent, and accountable being, they become an evil to
society, and should either be circumscribed or abandoned. It is
time that the female mind should be exalted to its proper grade,—
that the tinsel and trapping of exterior decoration should give
place to that interior cultivation, which, while it guides its pos-
sessor safely through the vale of time, enables her to look back,
at its close, with the confidence of one who has not, like the
servant of old, hid her talent in the earth, but is ready to return
it to the giver, increased in profit and interest. There is no
incapacity in the female mind for exertion in the highest departments of literature and science. If it has not shone forth as
frequently as in the higher sex, its coruscations have, at least,
been as brilliant and as pure; but while our young ladies are
taught that, to be admired they need only to be seen, . . . we
can expect to see the displays of talent proceeding only from
those whose independent energies have outstripped the instructive lessons of youth, and marked out for themselves a pathway
in the regions of intelligence and worth. . . .'"[78]

[78] *Am. Annals*, V, 464 *ff.*; for similar criticism see also *Hillsborough*
[N. C.] *Recorder*, Sept. 7, 1825, 4, col. 2; and *Ed. Jour. of Va.*, Aug. 1871,
368–9.

The above was answered by a sharp retort in the next issue, wherein an effort was made to show that female education was really improving and did not deserve such harsh condemnation. For the most part, however, no particular defense of the studies was offered; and private schools continued pretty generally to offer many, and with a tendency towards showy, subjects. So much so, in fact, that as late as 1892, Anna Brackett could say with little fear of contradiction that "the socalled education of many American girls has produced a mere hodge-podge of bits of information, of no use to themselves, and, what is of more consequence, of no use to any one else."[79]

To correct the practice of allowing girls to choose what they liked from assorted studies, efforts were made by the most conscientious teachers to establish regular courses involving (1) a definite period of time, generally from one to two or three years; (2) certain studies taken in the most beneficial sequence; and (3) the necessity of doing to complete satisfaction the work of one year, or one study, before advancing to the next. The *regular course* idea was stressed by such teachers as Joseph Emerson, Emma Willard, Catherine Beecher, and Mary Lyon, and was frequently advocated in those periodicals which were friendly to female education.

The *American Journal*[80] declared that "the greatest evils incident to female schools of the higher order . . . result from the fact that far too many and too varied duties are . . . demanded from one person. The amount of knowledge required to complete the education of a young lady . . . the number of studies considered as important, has nearly doubled within the last few years. Fifteen years ago [i.e., about 1810] a tolerable knowledge of Grammar, Geography, Arithmetic and History was considered as a good education for the generality of females . . . [but now] it is a fact that more different branches have been pursued in one year in the school under the care of the writer, than in their regular course engage the attention of young gentlemen during a four years' residence in college. By this is not intended, that any one individual pursued such a variety of studies or that they are pursued to the same extent as in colleges; but only that among them all, the teachers were obliged to

[79] Brackett: *op. cit.*
[80] II, 219 *ff.*

instruct in a greater variety of branches than are ever regularly pursued in any college. The following is a list of the branches pursued in the school mentioned, during one year: Reading, Spelling, Writing, Composition, Grammar, Geography, Arithmetic, Chemistry, Logic, Mental Philosophy, Chronology, Algebra, Geometry, Latin, and some work of a theological nature, beside Drawing, French, and Music, which have had separate teachers.

"In reviewing this list of studies, two inquiries will very naturally arise. The first is, can it be necessary or desirable that women should be made acquainted with such a variety of branches; and then, if it is important, why must they all be pursued in one school at the same time?"

The writer states that the above is no unusual example and urges the only proper remedy—the establishment of schools where students can take only what they are really prepared to study:

"To accomplish this, a regular course of study should be instituted, and so established that no scholar can enter the higher classes, till properly prepared by a thorough knowledge of the fundamental branches. Though the greater part of parents are willing to leave the direction of the studies to the teachers of a school, yet others are not; and at the present time so extensive is the mania for studying the higher branches that it often happens that chemistry, philosophy, or logic, are demanded before the pupil can properly parse, or even spell her own mother tongue. Both parents and pupil sometimes thus demand the superstructure and ornaments of an education before the indispensable foundations are laid. It is this fact, together with the difference in age, intellect, and acquirements, which produces the great variety of employments in female schools. There are always some, whose early education has been so imperfect as to need instruction in the branches which should be learned in primary schools. There are others, who are prepared for some of the higher branches and others still whose advanced education makes yet greater demands."[81]

Incapacity of teachers was a natural concomitant of the situation in which so many studies were required to be taught; also,

[81] *Ibid.*

it could not but be expected, since now, for the first time, girls were being offered the opportunity to prepare themselves to become teachers. But if a better situation could hardly have been expected, it is nevertheless true that the seminaries were criticized both because they had poor teachers, and also because they did not fully perform the function of preparing teachers for elementary schools. The female seminaries, either consciously or unconsciously, depending on circumstances, generally prepared teachers for lower as well as higher schools. But it was, to a considerable extent, a rather blind performance, and they were repeatedly taken to task for partial failure in this regard.[82] Finally the normal school arose, making teacher-preparation its sole function. Recognition of the incomplete success of the academy and seminary as teacher-training institutions assisted in furthering the normal school movement. Mann pointed out[83] that for fifty years the academies and seminaries had failed, and called upon the state to create an institution that would succeed. Spencer, in a report to the New York Senate (1826), pointed out failure in the same function in that state, but showed that it was due, in large part, at least, to the state's failure to support the seminary, and concluded that "they had found no reason" why "seminaries for the education of females . . . should not participate, equally with those for the instruction of males, in the public bounty."[84]

Being a newcomer among educational institutions, the female seminary was at first poorly supported, and therefore ill-equipped so far as buildings, furniture, and apparatus were concerned. Money first went for teachers, then buildings, books and apparatus. Many excellent schools existed long before a board of trustees could be found to manage and support the erection of a permanent building. These schools were excellent because of an individual teacher, but they declined because no permanent organization, endowment, or location existed to stabilize them and enable them to stand until successors could be secured to carry on the work. Leaders were agreed as to the necessity of securing those material aids. Emma Willard appealed to the

[82] Other reasons for few and untrained teachers were of course recognized. See, for example, *Am. Jour. Ed.*, III, 583-94.

[83] See p. 472.

[84] Randall: *Hist. Com. Sch. System of N. Y.*, 53-4.

legislature of New York to endow women's education; she went to Troy upon being promised a building. Mary Lyon raised the first funds by popular subscription to build a female seminary that would be permanent. Catherine Beecher succeeded in getting special buildings and laid the foundations for successful institutions; but, like the others, she failed to get the endowments desired at Hartford, Cincinnati, Dubuque, and Milwaukee. Excepting small gifts, woman's education received no endowments before the rapid development of colleges that came after the Civil War.

Buildings and equipment were more obvious needs than were endowments; consequently they were more often stressed. Every plan called attention to the need of them, and no critic of the situation of female education failed to point out the lack of these material aids usually supplied in men's institutions. The following is typical:

"To the difficulties already mentioned as embarrassing female education, may be added, the great disadvantages experienced from a want of suitable apparatus and facilities for instructing.

"It would naturally be inferred, that young minds, unaccustomed to thought, and unfurnished with the allied and collateral knowledge which maturer minds possess, would pre-eminently need the aid of tangible and visible objects, to enable them to comprehend those subjects, which with the best facilities require no little effort of mind to grasp.—The first principles of Natural Philosophy including Astronomy and Optics, are now generally taught in female schools. For the instruction of young men in these branches, a previous knowledge of mathematics—lectures—diagrams—and an expensive apparatus, are deemed indispensable.

"But it is expected that a teacher of females should communicate to young pupils, who have little or no preparatory knowledge to aid them, the first principles of mechanics, the balance of fluids, the complicated motion of the heavenly bodies, and the varied operations of nature as displayed both in Chemistry and Philosophy, without apparatus, without any thing to aid, but small compends of about 200 pages, and these so imperfectly constructed that sometimes it might puzzle even those who understand the science, to know what is meant.—No person can realize without experience, the difficulties a teacher finds, in explaining such subjects as Philosophy and Chemistry, to young and reflecting minds, without any facilities for doing it, or with only such as can be contrived by the genius of a teacher, who is driven to the utmost limits of invention to discover some remedy for so great a deficiency. During the past season an attempt was made by the writer to remedy some of these difficulties, by a course of lectures on Philosophy, more easy and intelligible than the work studied; but after a few were completed, the labor was found to be of little avail without apparatus, and the effort was relinquished as hopeless. In several other branches, also, a want of time and facilities are greatly felt. In history, for example, a far greater amount of knowledge might be communicated in the same time were proper facilities afforded. In schools it is very difficult for pupils to go through a long course of history— and there are no books fitted to be used in schools, for this purpose. History must therefore be chiefly studied by means of compends; which may be termed only the bone of history and without filling up, are as dry and as bare of interest and beauty, as was the gloomy collection in the valley of vision. But the following might afford some hints of a method which could be pursued, were a teacher afforded time and accommodations.

"Such a work as Worcester's Elements of History, might be used as the text book for the pupil to study. A certain portion of this might be given out as a lesson, such for instance as the short chapter including the history of Persia. The pupils then, (being provided with proper histories for consultation,) might receive from the instructor certain topics or subjects on which they are to search for more information in other books—such as the names of the most distinguished characters, events, &c. of that period and nation.

"The recitations might be performed in a room fitted up with suitable charts of history and chronology, and with maps of ancient countries, these so large, that the class might see with one glance, on the chart, the relative situation of each character and event, and on the map, the places where each incident occurred.

"When the class assembles before these charts and maps, the teacher may demand, from the class, the summary contained in the text book, and all the additional knowledge gained from other works—meanwhile pointing out on the chart and map, the spots to be noticed during recitation. When this exercise is finished, the teacher may add any other important information respecting that period, notice contemporary nations, and present the connection of history with science, civil institutions, and religion.

"It is believed that by such a method pupils might in one season, obtain a methodical and connected knowledge of History, Chronology, and Ancient Geography, while at the same time the study would be transformed, from one of the most tedious, to one of the most delightful of school avocations.

"Another particular in which female schools suffer great inconvenience is the want of suitable school rooms.

"In our public institutions, even where the number of pupils is small, it would be considered extreme folly to congregate professors, tutors, and scholars all in one room, and have all their different exercises and recitations performed in the same place. And in those other schools where a great number are brought together, it is a fact, that but comparatively few branches are pursued. In our primary schools the fundamental branches only are taught—our grammar schools are chiefly devoted to the dead languages. But a female school, where are summoned the various pursuits of the primary school, the grammar school, and the college; often must all be assembled in one room. Here are performed the various exercises in reading, writing, spelling, arithmetic, and grammar—the recitations in chemistry and philosophy, and the variety of other branches enumerated, while at the same time the school must if possible be kept still, and the pupils pursue their studies. This difficulty has been peculiarly felt by the writer during the past season, while from seventy to eighty pupils have been assembled in one room, so large as to increase every noise by its reverberation, while it requires a painful effort for the teacher to speak so as to be properly understood. The recitation of one class must necessarily interrupt the studies of another, and when it has been necessary to have two or three recitations performed at the same time, the confusion from this cause and the necessary noise of so large a number, has been enough to shake the strongest nerves, when under the additional pressure of that excitement which every good teacher must feel when communicating knowledge.

"This difficulty prevents an increased number of teachers, which the income of a large school might support.

"Another difficulty which the teachers of female schools must often feel, is the want of suitable books for consultation on the several branches taught. In our public seminaries, a library is open for the aid both of instructors and pupils, but when the resources of a teacher of females fail, the books which might aid are not at command. Then the libraries of friends must be searched, the book-stores laid under contribution, or some other method devised to remedy the difficulty. No teacher can attempt to instruct in any branch thoroughly, without feeling the need of books for consultation. Much more when endeavoring to teach nearly the whole round of sciences, as some unfortunately are doomed to attempt."[85]

To one looking back from the present, the female seminary seems to have been the very home of moral, religious, and domestic training. But to contemporary writers who had *their* mothers and grandmothers in mind, the seminary often appeared to encourage a lack of religious sentiment and the relinquishment of domestic arts as the true portion of woman, notwithstanding the fact that the most conspicuous leaders of the seminary movement were known for their moral and religious bias, as well as for their belief that domestic affairs, rather than public, should be the chief occupation of woman. In the *American Journal of Education*,[86] one writer asserted: "The great prevailing error in the education of females, especially is that moral culture is assumed rather than conferred: that while anxiety . . . is felt . . . that children should be highly accomplished . . . little pain is taken . . . to do anything . . . adequate [for] the formation of character. . . . It is not . . . the difficulty of the subject, but the want of exertion about it, that is the proper ground of complaint. Teachers usually leave this branch of education to the care of parents, or rest contented with occasionally reprehending a pupil who transgresses, or commending one who does well; and a few, perhaps, attempt a formal and systematic course of moral philosophy, or a doctrinal course of religious instruction." Such criticisms increased in proportion as the tendencies of the nineteenth century became more pronounced. An emphasis upon "accomplishments" was held to be incompatible with proper attention to morals and religion. One critic saw the

---

[85] *Am. Jour. Ed.*, II, 264–9; see also II, 339 *ff*.

[86] II, 604–9.

decline of society: "Fashion and accomplishments and amusements, and unnecessary display in literature and science absorbed the whole time of the females of this period. Domestic cares and virtues seem to have descended to the tomb with their Granddames; . . . domestic skill was lost, . . . domestic habits forgotten or despised. . . ."[87] *Harper's New Monthly Magazine* published a satirical thrust at the "Finishing School" education of the mid-century, in which morals were quite forgotten in the pursuit of fashion, as harmful to society in general as to Mary Degai. The school of Madame Cancan is represented as continuing its work, in spite of the wrecks it causes.

"No flirting of course was permitted. Oh dear!
"If Madame Cancan such a word were to hear
"She would look a whole beltful of dagger-blades at you,
"And faint in the style of some favorite statue.
"The men were invited alone to impart
"To her young protegées that most difficult art
"Of conversing in ease; and if ease was the aim
"That Madame had in view she was not much to blame,
"For I vow she succeeded so well with her she's
"That her school might take rank as a chapel of ease!

* * *

"Madame Cancan still lives, and still ogles and teaches,
"And still her lay sermons on Fashion she preaches;
"Still keeps of smooth phrases the choicest assortment;
"Still lectures on dress, easy carriage, deportment;
"And spends all her skill in thus moulding her pets
"Into very-genteely-got-up marionettes.
"Yes! Puppet's the word; for there's nothing inside
"But a clock-work of vanity, fashion, and pride!
"Puppets warranted sound, that without any falter
"When wound up will go—just as far as the altar;
"But when once the cap's donned with the matronly border,
"Lo! the quiet machine goes at once out of order."[88]

Similar (though more prosaic) criticisms of this socially useless education which did not concern itself with the home were common. One writer quoted, with great approval, Napoleon's opinion that to "stay at home and take care of her children" was woman's greatest glory, and declared: "The fact is that there is an abundance of folly in the modern fashionable system of

87 *Am. Annals of Ed.*, V, 360 *ff.*
88 *Op. cit.* (1858), XVII, 435 and 445.

female education; there is too much of learning and teaching.''[89]
Beecher, though she would not agree *in toto* with Napoleon, did,
in large measure, condemn the foolish accomplishments usually
stressed, when she declared: ''Woman is not trained for her
profession. . . . Women are not trained to be housekeepers, nor
to be wives, nor to be mothers, nor to be nurses of young children,
nor to be nurses of the sick, nor to be seamstresses, nor to be
domestics.''[90]

To be successful mothers and housekeepers women must retain
health. It was repeatedly urged that education at seminaries
was ruining, or would ruin, the health of young women; and,
though many leaders enthusiastically took up the promotion of
physical health, by means of calisthenics, chiefly,[91] vigorous
criticism of the lack of attention to health by the great majority
continued, and was to a great extent merited. About 1827, an
observer declared that ''of all the defects of the common plan
of education for females, few are more serious than the entire
neglect of the regular cultivation of health. . . .''[92] Another
asserted, in reply to his hypothetical question put to school girls,
concerning what they had been taught about health: ''No, we
have attended to almost everything more than to this. We have
been taught more concerning the structure of the earth, the laws
of the heavenly bodies, the habits and the formation of plants,
the philosophy of language and the art of cutting awkward capers
to music, than concerning the structure of the human frame and
laws of health and reason.''[93]

Allusion has been made to certain constructive developments
in methods of the seminary, influenced chiefly by a faith in
Pestalozzianism, the monitorial system of Lancaster, and the
theory of a formal discipline of the mind. The system of Lancaster laid great emphasis upon rewards, stimulated emulation;
and these in a rather short time came in for sharp criticism, as it
was believed such competition was especially bad for health, disposition, and character of young ladies. One citation will suffice to suggest the character of the objections raised.

[89] *Am. Annals*, V, 464–7.
[90] Quoted from *Harper's New Mo. Mag.* (1864), XXIX, 766.
[91] See ''Physical Education,'' ch. III, Vol. II.
[92] *Am. Jour. Ed.*, II, 339–43.
[93] *Conn. Com. Sch. Jour.*, IX, 284.

"We decline following into particulars all the evils entailed on character by excessive application, or by habits of undue devotion to intellectual pursuits, and would pass to the consideration of a class of motives which, from the prevalent use of them in schools, have a more extensive operation and a more lasting effect on the mind: we allude to all stimulants calculated to excite emulation. 'But what are we to do without emulation?' is the question with which objections to this principle of action are usually met—somewhat as the intemperate man asks, 'But what am I to do without stimulus?'—If it is the case—and we appeal not to teachers, but to parents for the truth on this point —if it is the case that even the fairest form of emulation deteriorates the character, by leading to the obtrusion of self; if it produces an avaricious desire for marks of personal distinction, and sinks very often into baser feeling; if it excites the mind so unduly as to produce wakeful nights, painful days, and tears of disappointment, it is a hindrance to happiness, and to the improvement of the character, the true end of education; and it ought to be banished at all hazards.

"Rank, places, medals, and badges, are very appropriate excitements to military virtues. But a school for girls should be a scene of peace and gentle self-forgetting happiness, such as forms the best resemblance to the aspect of family life. No young person, if we would cherish in her a disinterested disposition, should be so situated, for a moment, as to make another's loss her gain. But this is always the case where any mark of honor is lost and won. . . .'"[94]

The system proved hard to eradicate. Brackett, writing in the nineties, bore testimony to its continuance even to that date.[95] The gradually encroaching influence of the doctrine of interest has been at work for a century, and more particularly for the past generation; but still the system, under one name or another, plays a part in school life.

Other points often criticized had to do more intimately with the parents and daughters, and only partially reflect discredit on the seminary. This perennial difficulty was very early

---

[94] *Am. Jour. Ed.*, II, 549–55; for other criticism of the same practice see, for example, Butler: *The Am. Lady*, 49–51; *Com. Sch. Jour.*, I, 373–4; II, 76–7; and other educational periodicals.

[95] *Woman and the Higher Education*, 184.

recognized: that one could not, without great pains, make an intelligent choice of a school. For as Beecher said, "Most parents . . . are influenced in their choice of schools, either by what the teachers profess to accomplish in their advertisements, or by the recommendation of friends, or by the wishes or caprice of their children."[96] An English woman was convinced that, in America, choice of a school was "very frequently left entirely to children";[97] and this was borne out by many observers. That parents and daughters might be misled by advertisements, as hinted by Beecher, would be clear to anyone who rereads them now or is familiar with the difference between school catalogs and school courses. Fathers and mothers were well-nigh powerless to judge a school in advance. They were (and are), indeed, in much the same situation as the Irish nursemaid who remarked that if the baby came out red the water was too hot; if blue, too cold.

Partially as a result of this difficulty of selecting the right school, and the tendency to allow much freedom of choice to the girl, there arose a new evil: the rapid change of students from one school to another. "Nearly one third of the pupils who have attended the school," says one contributor to the *American Journal of Education*,[98] "entered after the regular classes were formed, and left before any study could be completed." Another pointed out this "error in female education" and submitted figures for two institutions,—one at Marietta, the other at Steubenville, Ohio. At the former, of about two hundred students attending during its five years' operation, two students remained three years; six two years; fifty to sixty, one; one hundred, six months; and between thirty and forty, "less than a year." Of the two hundred and twenty at the latter, five studied between four and five years; eight, three to four years; twenty, two to three; thirty, one to two; and one hundred and fifty-seven, one half year.[99]

The writer drew as conclusions, "not that these schools do not furnish good advantages, nor that higher advantages will not be

96 Extracts from her *Suggestions* in the *Am. Jour. Ed.*, V, 63–6.

97 Brackett: *op. cit.*, 185–6.

98 II, 264–9.

99 *American Annals of Education*, V, 492–4; at Steubenville the regular course was four years, "degrees" being granted upon completion.

DIPLOMA ISSUED BY PATAPSCO FEMALE INSTITUTE

furnished, when there are those who will accept them; but that there is a shameful apathy in the community on the subject of Female Education. In one of these schools, one-half of those who have entered, left at or before the expiration of six months; in the other, nearly three-fourths; and this too, in a town of 4000 or 5000 inhabitants, furnishing nearly one-third of the whole number of the school, in whose case no unusual expense of boarding is necessary!''

At the school of Zilpah Grant, operated for fifteen years, first at Derry, New Hampshire, and later at Ipswich, Massachusetts, only one hundred and fifty-six of the sixteen hundred pupils finished the three-year course and received the certificate.[100] The proportion of those completing the course at Troy, Milwaukee, and South Hadley was likewise small. One critic of this tendency thought it might be due, too, to a belief that education, like cream, might be skimmed off quickly, first at one institution and then another. In such a case, to remain long at one school

[100] See p. 352.

was a waste of time. Complaint against this rapid changing was quite common between 1825 and 1875. To combat it, the better schools began the practice of establishing regular courses leading to degrees or diplomas, and compelling entrants to remain a specified time, unless removal was necessitated by serious cause.

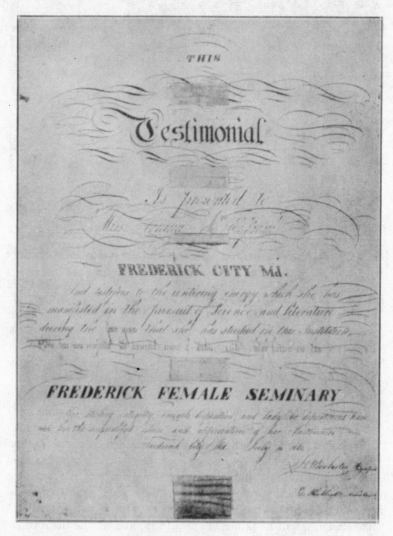

DIPLOMA ISSUED BY FREDERICK FEMALE SEMINARY (1843)

VI. *Influence of the Female Seminary*

The female seminary became a well defined institutional type after 1775 and continued to be most important for woman's education until about 1870. With respect to organization and curriculum, as advocated by its greatest exponents, and also the spread of the idea of the feasibility and usefulness of woman's higher education, the seminary clearly paved the way for women's colleges. But, coming before high schools and colleges, it was in its day "all things to all men"—both an intermediate and a higher school. In time many seminaries came to be *called* colleges, and some really were, except in name.

The second influence was in the field of elementary education. Particularly in the first half of the nineteenth century, when, with the rise of enthusiasm for universal education, there came an equally insistent call for teachers of common schools, the female seminaries and academies became the nurseries of teachers, until institutions could be established specially designed for that purpose. To go out—sometimes a great distance—to become a common school teacher required missionary zeal even more than pedagogical skill. Troy, Hartford, Mount Holyoke, Ipswich,[101] and numerous others, were recruiting centers for those who possessed it. The recruits were armed with instruction and inspired by a belief that on common school education depended the salvation of the country.

The extent of this service to common schools performed by one institution alone, between 1830 and 1835, was summarized in the *American Annals*:[102] "From September 1830 to September 1835, no less than fifty-three females who had been members of the Ipswich Female Seminary, had been employed as Teachers at the West and South; while during the same time only twenty-five young men went to the West and South either as teachers or ministers from the Andover Theological Seminary; and only about the same number from Princeton.

"Of these fifty-three female missionaries of education, three are now at home with their parents, several are married, and four are dead; but forty-two of them still continue to fill stations of high responsibility in the business of education. Five of these

[101] Miss Grant wrote on the difficulties of sending out these teachers in the *Am. Annals*, VII, 129–32.
[102] VI, 236.

are connected with female seminaries in New England, and thirty-seven are still at the West and South. Besides these, several have accompanied their parents or other friends to the West and South and have done what they could for the general object, on a smaller scale.

"The teachers above mentioned were distributed as follows: Twenty-two were employed in Ohio, five in Illinois, three in Kentucky, three in Tennessee, three in Michigan, three in Mississippi, one in Indiana, and one in Missouri; and twelve in the Southern States."

The influence of but a few seminaries in creating other institutions can be mentioned specifically. Georgia attempted a female seminary as a result of Mrs. Willard's *Plan*.[103] The missionary influence of Mount Holyoke, through teachers sent out and institutions created in her likeness, is conspicuous. The founder of Wellesley College, who was also a trustee of Mount Holyoke, sought to carry on in the new institution the best features of the school of Mary Lyon. As he put it, there was no danger of having "too many Mount Holyokes"; and if any students desired additional training, they might receive it at Wellesley or Smith after they had completed the course at Mount Holyoke Seminary or similar institutions. Very early the request was made that a Holyoke school be established in Persia. This was about 1843. Many other institutions of this type were established in missionary fields. In 1851 the Cherokee Seminary was established (at Park Hall, Arkansas), after the chief of this Indian tribe had decided that the Holyoke plan was best adapted to the promotion of Christianity among his people. Other seminaries upon the Holyoke plan that might be named were the Western Seminary at Oxford, Ohio (1855); Lake Erie Seminary, Painesville, Ohio, which succeeded Willoughby Seminary which had been established in 1847; the Michigan Seminary at Kalamazoo, which was modelled after the institution at Mount Holyoke, and opened in 1867; and also Mills Seminary and College, established in California for the purpose of doing "for the far West what Mount Holyoke Seminary does for the East."[104]

Save from an intellectual and professional point of view, the seminaries contributed but little to the emancipation of women.

[103] Barnard: *Am. Teachers*, footnote, 144.
[104] Stow: *op. cit.*, 159, 163, 239, and 327.

Generally, its leaders denied any desire for equality with men in any complete sense. But freedom and equality in intellectual pursuits, gradually offered by the seminary, and the entrance to the profession of teaching, constituted the natural first step towards complete emancipation in political and economic life, demanded by the next generation. With education, women became more competent to understand and remedy the evils of their position. A change of attitude towards subjection was the logical result. In 1818, Mrs. Willard appealed to "the enlightened politicans" and was then disillusioned; thirty years later, women were ceasing to pray to their "enlightened" leaders and were beginning to ask that they might be so.

CHAPTER X

WOMEN ENTER THE TEACHING PROFESSION

I. *Teaching the Most Natural Profession for Women*

Women were mistresses of the early dame schools of New England, appeared in 1727 as teachers in Louisiana, and, in Quaker communities, were prominent in the work of school committees as well as teachers of the rudiments, reading and writing, and often domestic arts.[1] Private adventure schools,[2] in the eighteenth century, were often taught by women, as well as for them; and here their instruction ranged from the simplest rudiments and arts to some subjects of secondary education. Mrs. Rodes, as early as 1722, offered to teach young ladies "to read and write French to perfection."[3] But, with few exceptions, men were regarded as the natural teachers and most desirable; women were cheaper, and, as they increased in the business of schoolkeeping, the discrepancy between their pay and that of men continued to prevail.

With the expansion of educational opportunities for women, by the establishment of seminaries and the rise of the movement for universal elementary education, women as teachers came to be regarded in a new light. The common schools created a new demand and the seminaries, for a time, offered the chief preparation for women teachers. The expense of common schools was the most objectionable feature to taxpayers; thus any cheap teacher supply was a great asset. Soon voluminous arguments appeared—chiefly the expression of the enthusiastic promoters of the common school movement and those interested in the progressive emancipation of women—to the effect that women were the natural teachers of youth, could do the job better, were therefore to be preferred, and, eventually, that they should receive equal pay for equal work.

[1] Woody: *Early Quaker Ed. in Pa.*, 22, 54, 72–3, and 204 *ff.*; and *Quaker Ed. in the Colony and State of N. J.*, 297.

[2] See Chaps. IV, V and VI; also Seybolt: *The Private School*, Bul. 28, Vol. XXIII, No. 4 (1925), published by the University of Illinois.

[3] *Am. Wkly. Mer.*, May 16–23, 1722.

WOMAN TEACHING A SUMMER SCHOOL

To support the statement that the need for female teachers was fully realized, it would be possible to point to the words of most friends of the common school movement. Among the most influential advocates were Hall, Carter, Mann, Grant, Russell, and Woodbridge. Another was Thomas H. Gallaudet, who alluded to the newly arisen need in the *Connecticut Common School Journal*[4] and asked:

"How shall we get good teachers for our district schools, and enough of them? While we should encourage our young men to enter upon this patriotic, and I had almost said, missionary, field of duty, and present much higher inducements to engage them to do so, I believe every one must admit, that there is but little hope of attaining the full supply, or anything like it, from that sex. This will always be difficult, so long as there are so many other avenues open in our country to the accumulation of property, and the attaining of distinction. We must, I am persuaded, look more to the other sex for aid in this emergency, and do all in our power to bring forward young women of the necessary qualifications to be engaged in the business of common school instruction."

The same note was struck by Beecher; and few, if any, commanded such an audience as did she: "But where are we to raise such an army of teachers as are required for this great work? Not from the sex which finds it so much more honorable, easy, and lucrative, to enter the many roads to wealth and honor open in this land. But few will turn from these to the humble, unhonored toils of the schoolroom and its penurious reward.

"It is WOMAN who is to come at this emergency, and meet the demand—woman, whom experience and testimony have shown to be the best, as well as the cheapest guardian and teacher of childhood, in the school as well as the nursery."[5]

Not only did the friends of education proclaim the necessity of filling vacant schools with women; they also claimed the schools would be better taught by them. Teaching, it was said, "is woman's natural profession." Beecher declared: ". . . It is ordained by infinite wisdom, that, as in the family, so in the social state, the interests of young children and of women are

4 I, 10.
5 Beecher: *True Remedy*, 240–2.

one and the same";[6] and her sister, Mrs. Stowe, held that "if men have more knowledge they have less talent at communicating it, nor have they the patience, the long-suffering, and gentleness necessary to superintend the formation of character."[7] Mann, in his *Seventh Report*,[8] mentioned expediency, and other reasons, for the entrance of women into the profession.

"In former reports, I have dwelt at length upon the expediency of employing female teachers, to a greater extent, in our schools. Some of the arguments in favor of this change have been, the greater intensity of the parental instinct in the female sex, their natural love of the society of children, and the superior gentleness and forbearance of their dispositions—all of which lead them to mildness rather than severity, to the use of hope rather than of fear as a motive of action, and to the various arts of encouragement rather than to annoyances and compulsion, in their management of the young. These views have been responded to and approved by almost all the school committeemen in the State; and, within the last few years, the practice of the different districts has been rapidly conforming to this theory."

A committee on the subject of employing female teachers in New York State, 1844, gave it as their judgment that it was not "gallantry," "complaisant homage," or "superior science" that had accorded to women an "unequivocal preference in teaching and controlling the young," but rather "superior skill in the use of that science; . . . it is the *manner* and the very weakness of the teacher that constitutes her strength, and assures her success. For that occupation she is endued with peculiar faculties. While man's nature is rough, stern, impatient, ambitious, hers is gentle, tender, enduring, unaspiring. One always wins; the other sometimes repels; the one is loved; the other sometimes feared." "The woman quickly possesses herself of the affections of the children, which is the key, and this explains the superior success of female teachers with small scholars."[9] Also the committee finds that "the habits of female teachers are better and their morals purer; they are much more apt to be content with, and continue in, the occupation of teaching."

[6] *Ibid.*, 97–9.

[7] Fields: *Life and Letters of Harriett B. Stowe*, 85–6.

[8] See the *Common School Journal*, VI, 154–5.

[9] Randall: *Hist. Com. Sch. System of N. Y.*, 185–6.

"It was asserted, in the *Connecticut Common School Journal*,[10] that "the common schools can be improved by the more extensive employment of female teachers during the winter season. The best interests of the children demand, during all their early school life, that the more kind, parental humanizing influence of woman should surround them like an atmosphere. Their opening and inquiring natures turn more readily to her gentle teachings and answering sympathies."

The Michigan superintendent's report of 1842 discloses a similar preference for female teachers:[11]

"An elementary school, where the rudiments of an English education only are taught, such as reading, spelling, writing, and the outlines barely of geography, arithmetic, and grammar, requires a female of practical common sense with amiable and winning manners, a patient spirit, and a tolerable knowledge of the springs of human action. A female thus qualified, carrying with her into the schoolroom the gentle influences of her sex, will do more to inculcate right morals and prepare the youthful intellect for the severer discipline of its after years, than the most accomplished and learned male teacher."

Dr. Humphrey, writing on "Female Teachers in Summer Schools,"[12] made it clear that "even if there were no difference between the wages of males and females, the latter would deserve the preference," for "they have a tact in the management and instruction of small children, which males have not." These points of excellence were repeated over and over again in educational periodicals by editors and contributors, who made the most flattering estimates of their success. A memorial to the Congress of the United States[13] likewise asserted most confidently "that young women are the best teachers"; it has been "proved and acknowledged by those men who have made trial of the gentle sex in schools of the most difficult description, because of the superior tact and moral power natural to the female character."

Some saw in woman's teaching a service to common school education, and thus to society and the nation at large. This social view was very generally expressed. Others saw, in addi-

10 II, 53–4.
11 *Ibid.*, IV, 140.
12 *Ibid.*, II, 119.
13 See *Godey's Lady's Book*, Jan. 1853, 176–7.

tion to this public service, the possibility of woman's independence, and believed it was a clever move whereby "a profession is to be created for women . . . a profession as honorable and as lucrative for her as the legal, medical, and theological professions are for men. This is the way in which thousands of intelligent and respectable women, who toil for a pittance scarcely sufficient to sustain life, are to be relieved and elevated." In another passage, Beecher made even clearer the connection, as she understood it, between educational service and the emancipation of women. She wrote, in 1851:

"Inasmuch, then, as popular education was the topic which was every day rising in interest and importance, it seemed to me that, to fall into this current, and organize our sex, as women, to secure the proper education of the destitute children of our land, was the better form of presenting the object, rather than to start it as an effort for the elevation of woman. By this method, many embarrassments would be escaped, and many advantages secured.

"With this end in view, I first endeavored, by personal discussion and by correspondence, to influence a number of the most sensible, practical, and benevolent ladies among my acquaintance in different parts of the country, chiefly at the West, to unite with me in attempting an organization of our sex, to carry out an enterprise, having for its object the education of more than two million children of our country whom the census had disclosed as entirely destitute of schools."[14] One result of Beecher's view was the formation, in Boston, of the Young Ladies' Society for Promoting Education at the West. Her sister Harriett wrote of this venture: "We mean to turn over the West by means of model schools in this, its capital. . . . We have come to the conclusion that the work of teaching will never be rightly done till it passes into female hands."[15] As noted above, after 1850 some urged the creation of normal schools in each state, subsidized by Congress, and thus "free for female teachers of common schools"; the arguments were chiefly that (1) 20,000 additional teachers were needed and (2) women were better teachers anyway.

[14] *True Remedy*, 23, 41, 97–9, and 240–2; see also *Godey's Lady's Book*, Nov. 1852, 484.

[15] Fields: *Life and Letters of Harriett B. Stowe*, 85–6.

II. Need of Pedagogical Training

At the same time that women were being proposed as the most natural teachers of youth, a movement arose, partially in response to Pestalozzian influence, favoring special training to direct and refine the native gift for teaching. It had too long been customary to buy a teacher "as is." Reformers pointed in derision to the schoolmaster of Waldbach, who, when asked what he taught, said: "Nothing, because I know nothing." And thus he explained his appointment as schoolmaster: "Why, sir, I had been taking care of the Waldbach pigs for a great number of years, and when I got too old and infirm for that employment, they sent me here to take care of the children."[16] Even the unwise could see the parallel. Gradually, it was realized that as in astronomy the trained observer is a most necessary adjunct to the telescope, so the teacher is the trained observer without which schools and books are of little use. As Bowditch put it, "Without good teachers, it is vain to look for good schools. And how can we have good teachers, unless they have encouragement properly to prepare themselves for their arduous and responsible tasks. . . . There is literally no such profession as that of a female teacher. The whole business is conducted by raw apprentices, in place of experienced workmen—young girls, just grown up, who adopt . . . it merely for some temporary purpose. . . . But what can be expected from inexperienced young girls . . . with views like these? Is it not rather surprising that they effect as much as they do?"[17] Thomas H. Gallaudet expressed the same view: "We need, exceedingly, a much larger supply of first rate teachers. In order to have first rate teachers, they must be trained for their employment; and for this purpose one or more seminaries devoted to the object are necessary."[18] The new faith in professional training was practically demonstrated by New York, which, in 1832, provided for the distribution of Hall's *Lectures on School Keeping* to every school district of the state.[19]

Such facts and statements would at first suggest that no training had as yet been available for female teachers. Rather, it is

[16] *Com. Sch. Assistant* (1837), II, 25–6.
[17] Quoted from the *Com. Sch. Jour.*, II, 284–6.
[18] *Conn. Com. Sch. Jour.*, I, 49.
[19] *Laws of N. Y.*, 1832, 513.

JAMES G. CARTER

evident from these and numerous other expressions of opinion
that certain things were recognized: first, that the present supply
of trained teachers was inadequate; second, that mere information on a subject and native ability did not constitute full
qualification for teaching. As one protagonist put it, "the
knowledge of Sir Isaac Newton could be of but trifling use to a
school while it was locked up safely in the head of a country
school master," unable to communicate it.[20] Teachers were
urged to take advantage of some of the several agencies for their
professional improvement. More than one pedagogical journal
challenged women in terms like the following:

"Are those females, who propose to be candidates for teaching
the Summer Schools, doing anything, by reading, conversation,
or study, to fit themselves for a proper discharge of the duties
they propose to undertake;—or do they think that the skill and
the spirit, to perform the most difficult and most important of
human labors, are to be miraculously given to them, when they
cross the threshold of the schoolhouse door?"[21]

To give this necessary professional training, various agencies,
some effective and others not, were tried from time to time.
Siljeström[22] mentioned the use of (1) periodical educational
literature, (2) the public press,[23] (3) further study in the elementary school, (4) private academies with special classes for teachers, (5) teachers' associations, (6) teachers' institutes, and (7)
normal schools. He quoted from Maine school reports, showing
that 1,280 women and 1,074 men had attended institutes in 1849,
and referred to like practice elsewhere. That 320 teachers of a
New York county had attended institutes at an expense of $10
each, he considered one of many proofs of their interest in their
improvement.[24] Besides the above agencies, others might be
mentioned: (1) organizations, such as the American Lyceum,
1831, which were to arouse interest in the education of women
and girls;[25] (2) special lectures and courses of lectures;[26] (3)

[20] Carter's *Outline of an Institution for the Education of Teachers.*

[21] *Com. Sch. Jour.,* II, 82.

[22] Translation, by Frederica Rowan, of his *Education in the United States*
(1853), 200 *ff.*

[23] Especially *New York Tribune.*

[24] *Op. cit.,* 205.

[25] In 1835, Catherine Beecher wrote and presented, at the Lyceum's request, "An Essay on the Education of Female Teachers," published later
in the same year at New York.

voluminous and monotonous letters to teachers which often found
their way into magazines;[27] (4) gratuitous instruction in seminaries and academies for a few proposing to teach;[28] and (5) an
increase of pay.   This last argument,-voiced by many, was sustained by Gallaudet; for, as he pointed out, "If our young men
and young women are to be induced to spend their time and
money in qualifying themselves to be first-rate teachers, they
must see a fair prospect of being remunerated for this expenditure. . . . Raise the wages of good female teachers, and you
will give an impulse to the whole movement that will be seen
and felt at once.''[29]

But of all the agencies enumerated, it was generally agreed
that normal schools—or teacher's seminaries, as they were first
called—would prove the most reliable means for preparing
teachers. Obviously, occasional lectures, courses of lectures,
institutes, articles in periodicals, and so forth, would only produce irregular results, never to be entirely relied upon. But
academies and seminaries had already been tried and had prepared many teachers, in an academic way at least. Troy,[30]
Ipswich,[31] and Hartford had wide reputations as sources of good
teachers. Ipswich, in 1831, had "120 pupils, about half of
whom . . . [had] been . . . employed as teachers."[32] Beecher,
in her *Essay on the Education of Female Teachers for the United
States*[33] made it clear that the institutions which she would have

---

[26] See, for instance, *Conn. Com. Sch. Jour.*, I, 43; and *Com. Sch. Jour.*,
II, 42.

[27] See, for example, *Com. Sch. Jour.*, III, for a series of 19 letters from
a teacher to her young female friend who was just about to commence keeping school.

[28] Thus the principal of Winsted Academy would receive, free of charge,
a few young ladies who would qualify to become teachers; and Hartford
Female Seminary gave a course of gratuitous instruction to a "class of
females" who had "engaged" to teach in common schools; Gallaudet, Barnard, Stowe, and other friends of education were to assist in giving this
course.—*Conn. Com. Sch. Jour.*, II, 52 and 116.

[29] *Ibid.*, I, 49.

[30] For some phases of teacher preparation at Troy see Barnard: *Am.
Teachers*, 154.

[31] The organization, content, and methods of the work of the Teachers
Seminary at Ipswich were fully set forth in the *Am. Annals*, III, 69–80.

[32] *Ibid.*, I, 83.

[33] See footnote, p. 467, and *Am. Annals*, V, 275–8.

Thomas H. Gallaudet

opened and endowed at public expense would only "repeat and extend, and render permanent, those efforts for preparing female teachers, which have been so successfully made at the seminaries in Ipswich, Hartford and Troy, and about to be attempted at Northampton." These permanent, endowed schools, free from the caprice of parents and students, would be under proper superintendence; would have a uniform course of instruction; would stress, in addition to the academic preparation, the care of health, domestic duties, and the formation of character by means of "moral discipline and religious instruction." She did not approve, however, of granting "titular degrees to females," as it would be bad taste, would cause "needless ridicule" and "painful notoriety," and would appear, many thought, as "an attempt to unsex them."[34]

The idea of special teacher training institutions did not of course originate with Beecher; rather, she adopted the idea so that women might be prepared for their profession. In 1823, Samuel Reed Hall had established his Model School at Concord, Vermont; in 1829 he published *Lectures on School Keeping* and, later, *Lectures to Female Teachers*. In 1837, he became principal of Holmes Plymouth Academy, which had abandoned the original purpose of theological preparation, upon his advice, and had become a teachers' seminary for men and women. The male department offered a four years' course and the female, three.[35] Gallaudet also published, in the *Connecticut Observer*, his "Letters of a Father," which were issued, in 1825, as a pamphlet entitled *Plan of a Seminary for the Education of Instructors of Youth*. Twenty-five years later, its author had the privilege of witnessing the opening of a State Normal School at New Britain for the preparation of men and women teachers. Another significant work was that of Walter Johnson, of Pennsylvania, who published (1825) *Observations on the Improvement of Seminaries of Learning in the United States: with Suggestions for its Accomplishment*. While Gallaudet's "Letters" and Johnson's *Observations* were appearing in Connecticut and Pennsylvania, James G. Carter, under the signature of "Franklin," published a series of "Essays on Popular Education" in the *Boston Patriot*, one of which was "An Outline of an Institu-

---

[34] *Ibid.*

[35] Barnard: *Am. Teachers*, 169–81.

tion for the Education of Teachers.'' Two years later he presented the following memorial to the legislature:

''. . . The undersigned begs leave most respectfully to represent: ''That he is about to open a seminary in a central part of the state, for the general instruction of children and youth of both sexes, and also for the particular instruction of those who may resort to him for that purpose, in the science of education; or in the best means of developing the physical, moral, and intellectual powers of the young by judicious and wholesome exercise of those powers, and, at a subsequent period, of conveying to their minds the greatest amount of useful knowledge.''[36]

The memorial was favorably received, and a bill drawn providing an appropriation, but it failed by one vote in the senate. Carter, then, at his own expense, planned a teacher training academy at Lancaster, which terminated in failure due to local opposition.[37]

Other significant private efforts were made by Bache, who (1840) offered a ''Plan'' for a seminary for female teachers and high school for girls at Philadelphia; and William Russell who (1849) opened a private training school on the Pestalozzian principles at Lancaster, Massachusetts, assisted by Whittaker, Krüsi, Tenny and Dana Colburn. The ''Plan,'' of the former, proposed a two years' course for pupils entering at sixteen, after they had completed high school. Each entrant was to agree, if elected, to teach two years in the First School District, at the minimum compensation. The first year was to be devoted to a review of studies of the elementary and the high school, the principles of education and occasional practice teaching; the second continued some review, but more attention was to be given to ''lectures on the science and art of teaching, with practice in the different departments of the Model School and in the lower classes of the High School.'' The officers were to be: a principal, in charge of the High School as well as the Teachers' Seminary, who was also professor of theory and practice of teaching; a professor of English language and literature, with two female assistants; one of mathematics, with an assistant; and a professor of natural philosophy. ''Occasional lessons'' were to be given by professors of moral and mental science,

[36] *Ibid.,* 192.
[37] Barnard: *Normal Schools,* 75–84.

natural history, drawing and writing, and vocal and instrumental music. The professor of moral science might also have charge of rhetoric, logic, and the Latin in the Seminary. One of the women assistants was to instruct in "female work," another in housewifery (unless it proved desirable to have special teachers of these subjects), and another have charge of the playground.[38]

A significant step in teacher training, and one of the earliest, was the development of city training schools out of the Lancasterian model classes. These were conspicuous in such cities as Philadelphia and New York, but not limited to the larger places, as the model class was an essential part of the monitorial system. In Philadelphia, 1848, the monitorial training was merged in the Girls' Normal School (later the Girls' High School); while Boston, Oswego (N. Y.), and New York City created similar institutions in 1852, 1861, and 1867, respectively.

III. Establishment of State Normal Schools

In the thirties, the movement for training teachers took more definite form, with emphasis on founding an institution entirely for that purpose; though great dependence was, in practice, still put upon the academies and seminaries, experienced school men and women urged the inadequacy of these agencies. A committee report of the New York Senate, 1826, stated: "Our academies, also, have failed, to supply the want of teachers to the extent which was within their power . . . the committee admits that the establishment of a separate institution for the sole purpose of preparing teachers would be a most valuable auxiliary";[39] and, about 1839–40, commenting upon the continued failure of their academy and seminary system, it was declared that the Massachusetts Board of Education had been wise in setting aside the first normal school, 1839, to the exclusive use of training female teachers.[40] But, in spite of the fact that many in New York were of this same opinion, the policy of establishing departments for the instruction of teachers in existing institutions and of subsidizing academies and seminaries, according to the number of pupils to whom they had taught "the science of common school

[38] Seminary for Female Teachers, Phila., 1840. From Bache's "Plan"—
Conn. Com. Sch. Jour., III, 164.

[39] Randall: *Hist. Com. Sch. System of N. Y.*, 53–4.

[40] *Com. Sch. Jour.*, I, 84–6.

teaching," was continued.[41] Mann expressed his belief that seminaries had really failed for fifty years to provide enough teachers,[42] and that the special training school was an imperative need. Gallaudet showed that women had been successful even in schools with scholars[43] from eighteen to twenty and asked:

"How are teachers to be thus qualified? Shall this important matter be left to accidental and fluctuating circumstances to control, or shall some united and systematic effort be made with regard to it? Shall we not make provision, on a well-digested plan, for training up, for the performance of their duties, the instructors of our common schools? Shall this be done in connection with academies already in existence, as has been attempted in the State of New York, or by the establishment of a distinct institution, or institutions, for the purpose?"[44] "What city, or town, in the State of Connecticut, will begin the enterprise of establishing a Seminary for Female Teachers . . ." as they are doing now in Massachusetts?[45] Barnard's first report to the Connecticut Board of Education took a definite stand on the same point, though successful action was to be delayed for several years. He said:

"To give the additional qualification, one or more seminaries, for female teachers, with model schools attached, should be provided, free, as far as tuition is concerned, and so located as to admit of their finding profitable employment for a small portion of the time to meet the incidental expenses of their residence there, without retarding their improvement.

"Thus prepared with the requisite general information, and the specific training for the work, female teachers could enter our schools with far better chances of success than now. But to get the full benefit of their peculiar talents, they should be employed where it is practicable, in the same school, so as to bring it under the combined influence of a male and female teacher; or, if this cannot be, in the appropriate work of unfolding the youthful intellect."[46]

[41] *Laws of N. Y.*, 1838, Ch. 237, Sect. 7, 222; 1852, 333; and 1853, 800.
[42] See page 403.
[43] *Conn. Com. Sch. Jour.*, I, 34.
[44] *Ibid.*, 17–18.
[45] *Ibid.*, 105.
[46] *Ibid.*, 168.

To these views might be added numerous others, but let it suffice to mention Calvin E. Stowe and Thomas Burrowes. The former argued that if Prussia, with 14,000,000 people, two-thirds of them poor, could maintain forty-two teachers' seminaries, surely Ohio, and other states, with populations of over a million, and none of them very poor, could support one.[47] Burrowes declared that Pennsylvania had "nearly thrown away" $5,000,-000 and ten years of effort, because not one dollar had "been spent to secure this great prerequisite, good teachers," and for that reason "the system has become unacceptable to the people, and will be more and more so. . . . If my gifts and domestic relations permitted, I should devote myself to a mission in this and other states, for the purpose of impressing on legislatures, philanthropists, and teachers, the necessity of Teachers' Seminaries."[48]

The first successful effort for a state-supported normal training school was made by Massachusetts. An appropriation was lost by but one vote in 1827 and another ten years' agitation was necessary to bring the legislature to favorable action. In 1838, Edmund Dwight promised a sum of $10,000,[49] provided the state would give a like amount "for qualifying teachers for our common schools." This was done on April 19th, 1838, and the schools were established at Lexington, July 3, 1839; at Barre, September 4, 1839; and at Bridgewater, September 9, 1840.[50] The one at Lexington was later transferred to West Newton, 1844, and that at Barre to Westfield.[51]

The first normal school was appropriated exclusively to women, while the others were open to both sexes.[52] For this reason, and the fact that one could not enter for less than a year, the number was at first small, there being but twenty-one in the second term.[53] Entrants were to be sixteen or over, in good health, had to prove themselves of good intellectual capacity and high moral character, and agree to teach after finishing the course. All must pass an

[47] *Ibid.*, II, 104.
[48] Quoted in Beecher's *True Remedy*, 84–7.
[49] *Com. Sch. Jour.*, VIII, 283.
[50] Boyden: *State Normal School*, Bridgewater, 9–10.
[51] *Com. Sch. Jour.*, VI, 265–6.
[52] *Ibid.*, I, 86.
[53] *Ibid.*, II, 98–9.

FIRST STATE NORMAL SCHOOL, LEXINGTON, MASSACHUSETTS

examination in the common branches and be "well versed in orthography." None were to be admitted for less than a year, and the complete course was to last three years. Tuition was free, but pupils had to pay for board, books, and all incidentals.[54] The institution was placed in the hands of Cyrus Peirce,[55] who had been conspicuously successful in a public school at Nantucket. Of the school he wrote (1841) that the principal was the only teacher of the Normal School and that its pupils taught the Model School. To that date, forty-one had been in attendance at the former and thirty, the usual number in the latter. The studies actually pursued were: "all the common branches, particularly and fully; together with Composition, Geometry, Algebra, Physiology; Natural, Intellectual, and Moral Philosophy; Natural History, Botany, Political Economy, Book-Keeping, Vocal Music, and the art of Teaching. The books used in the school are Worcester's Dictionary, and Worcester's Fourth Book, Abbot's Teacher, Russell's First Lessons, Testament, Grund's Geometry, Colburn's Sequel and Algebra, Wayland's Moral Philosophy, Newman's Political Economy, Hitchcock's Book-Keeping, Combe's Constitution of Man, Combe's Physiology, Brigham's Mental Excitement, Smellie's Natural History, Comstock's Botany, Abercrombie's Mental Philosophy, Combe's Moral Philosophy, Story's Constitution of the United States, Newman's Rhetoric, Hayward's Physiology, Day's Algebra; Scientific Class-Book, by Johnson, for the various branches of natural philosophy."[56]

Of the method of conducting the Model School he wrote: "This school consists of thirty pupils, of both sexes, from the age of six to ten, inclusive, taken promiscuously from families in the various districts of the town. The children pay nothing for tuition; find their own books, and bear the incidental expenses. This school is under the general superintendence and inspection of the Principal of the Normal School. After it was arranged,

[54] *Ibid.*, I, 96.

[55] A valuable volume on *The First State Normal School in America: The Journals of Cyrus Peirce and Mary Swift*, with an introduction by Professor A. O. Norton, published by the Harvard University Press, 1926. A cut of the Normal School is reproduced, p. 474, by permission of the author and the Alumnae Association of the Framingham State Normal School; Barnard: *Am. Teachers*, 405 *ff.*; and *Com. Sch. Jour.*, III, 164–7.

[56] *Com. Sch. Jour.*, III, 164–7.

the general course of instruction and discipline being settled, it was committed to the immediate care of the pupils of the Normal School, one acting as superintendent, and two as assistants, for one month in rotation, for all who are thought prepared to take a part in its instruction.   In this experimental school, the teachers are expected to apply the principles and methods which they have been taught in the Normal School, with liberty to suggest any improvements, which may occur to them.   Twice every day the Principal of the Normal School goes into the model school for general observation and direction, spending from one half hour to one hour each visit.   In these visits, I either sit and watch the general operations of the school, or listen attentively to a particular teacher and her class, or take a class myself, and let the teacher be a listener and observer.   After the exercises have closed, I comment upon what I have seen and heard before the teachers, telling them what I deem good, and what faulty, either in their doctrine or their practice, their theory or their manner. Once or twice each term, I take the whole Normal School with me into the model schoolroom, and teach the model school myself, in the presence of the pupils of the Normal School, they being listeners and observers.   In these several ways, I attempt to combine, as well as I can, theory and practice, precept and example.   In regard to the materials of which it is composed, and the studies attended to, the model school is as nearly a facsimile of a common district school, as one district school is of another.   In regard to the discipline and management, I am aware there may be more dissimilarity.   The superintendent is not situated precisely as she will be, when placed alone in a proper district school.   This could not be effected without having several model schools.   But, limited as is the field of operation for the superintendent it is wide enough, as the teachers find, for the development of considerable tact and talent.   From the model school we exclude all appeals to fear, premiums, or emulation; and yet we have had good order, and a fair amount of study.''[57]

Generally speaking, the success of the first woman's normal school was incontestable.   George B. Emerson, the enthusiastic principal of a girls' private school, in Boston, declared that what he saw there, on his visit, far surpassed his expectations.

[57] *Ibid.*

CYRUS PEIRCE

The instruction, the mode of government, and the earnestness in study which the embryo teachers had imbibed, led him to believe that the only drawback could be that ''from the entire devotion of the teacher, and the intense interest excited in the pupils, the health of both should suffer.''[58] Emerson's fear for the health of young ladies at normal schools was shared by Beecher, who felt that to lose her health struggling after logarithms, algebra and astronomy was too great a price to pay for a chance to teach school.[59]

Samuel G. Howe asserted it was the ''best school I ever saw, in this or any other country''; of this he was convinced, although he had held some ''theoretical objections to normal schools.''[60] In part, his remarks dwelt upon discipline and the method of teaching: ''The discipline of the school is perfect; the pupils regard their teacher with profound respect, yet tender affection; their interest in their studies is deep and constant; their attainments are of a high order; and they thoroughly understand every subject as far as they go.

''But not for these things do I give this School the preference; for others in this country and in Europe may equal it, in these respects; but I prefer it, because the system of instruction is truly philosophical; because it is based upon the principle that the young mind hungers and thirsts for knowledge, as the body does for food; because it makes the pupils not merely recipients of knowledge, but calls all their faculties into operation to attain it themselves; and finally, because, relying upon the higher and nobler parts of the pupils nature, it rejects all addresses to bodily fears, and all appeals to selfish feelings.

''I have said, sir, that the pupils were thoroughly acquainted with the various branches of an English education, as far as they advanced in them, and that they bore well a very severe examination. But this is faint praise; for a teacher may cause a class to make very great intellectual attainments by pursuing a system which, nevertheless, is ruinous to the moral nature of his pupils. But, at the Lexington School, the moral nature is as much cultivated as the intellectual, and the training of each goes on at the same time.

[58] *Ibid.*, II, 236–7.
[59] *Educ. Reminiscences*, 180–2.
[60] *Ibid.*, 238–9.

"There is one point of view, however, in which this School particularly interested me, and in which it presented a beautiful moral spectacle, the memory of which will dwell long in my mind; it was the fact, that every pupil seemed impressed with a deep sense of the importance of the calling which she was to follow; they seemed to feel that at least the temporal weal or woe of hundreds of human beings might be dependent upon the fidelity with which they should perform their duty as teachers. Consequently, every one was desirous of becoming acquainted with the philosophy of mind; and they received such excellent instruction, that they seemed to understand the various springs and incentives to action, which exist in a child's bosom."[61]

Voluminous favorable comments were made from time to time, some on the part of the Board of Visitors, by those who had been enthusiastic proponents of the institution before its creation, as well as those who had been skeptical, and others from school committees that had employed normal school pupils in their schools.[62] Siljeström, about the middle of the century, confirmed the favorable reports, and commented upon the clientele of the school, as well as the excellent quality of women teachers in America. There were then two classes, junior and senior, under the care of a principal and three female teachers. Pupils were drawn from various groups as follows: 23 "daughters of laborers, 16 of farmers, 14 of tradesmen, 4 of captains of merchant vessels, 3 of clerks, 2 of newspaper editors, 2 of railway inspectors; 7 were daughters of men following as many different callings, 3 were orphans, and 29 widows.

"It was truly delightful to behold the sober and pleasing manners of these pupils, who all gave promise of exercising a most beneficial influence on the schools which should in future be entrusted to them; and I may say the same of all other female pupils of normal schools and all female teachers I saw in the United States. Although I have, on the whole, no reason to have other than a favorable opinion of the male teachers also, I nevertheless give the preference to the females. It is incontestable that woman, otherwise in point of education on a level with the other sex, far surpasses the latter in refinement of feeling and nicety of perception, and these qualities give her a decided

61 *Ibid.*

62 *Ibid.*, VII, 66–7 and 260–2; see also IV, 33–4, 85, 316; II, 98–9.

superiority as a teacher of childhood. With these the American
female teachers combine another no less important quality,
namely, a firmness of character which is less frequently found
among women in Europe. The spirit of freedom which reigns
in America gives even to woman there a superior degree of
independence and decision, and a greater power of action; and
the respect, bordering upon submissiveness, with which she is
treated by the other sex, imparts to her character a loftiness, I
might almost say pride, which cannot but strike every stranger,
and which renders it easy for her, in her capacity of schoolmistress, to command the necessary deference. In a word, I have
been highly gratified at the combination of manly earnestness and
womanly gentleness which, in most cases, I have met with among
the female teachers of America, in addition to all the other
qualities of mind which one loves best to see in a woman.''[63]

It must be understood, however, that all did not consider the
work of normal schools so nearly perfect. Bowditch[64] asserted
that ''seminaries for teachers have been established in various
parts of the country, sometimes as independent schools, at others,
as branches of academies or colleges; but as yet the beneficial
results have been trifling. . . . The plan has commonly been
to extend the knowledge of the students to the higher branches
of learning, rather than to instruct them in the art of teaching. . . . The practical part, also, is wanted in these seminaries.
Theory alone is not sufficient. . . . This is a subject well worthy
the attention of visitors and superintendents of teachers seminaries.'' There was also criticism by those who opposed the creation of the normal schools. The minority report of the Committee on Education attacked the position of those in the majority, who proposed discontinuance of the experiment, March 11,
1840:

''The Committee speak of our Normal Schools as possessing no
advantages for qualifying teachers, above what are possessed by
our academies and high schools. We cannot suppose that they
have formed this opinion from having visited them. The two letters . . . contain the opinions of men who speak that which they
know. With their testimony before the public, it is not necessary
for us to enlarge on this subject.''[65]

[63] Siljeström: *Education in the United States*, 194–7.
[64] In his Memoirs, quoted in the *Com. Sch. Jour.*, II, 284–6.
[65] *Com. Sch. Jour.*, II, 233–4.

This opposition was, of course, unsuccessful. The other two schools were established, one at Barre under Professor S. P. Newman of Bowdoin College, which, in December, 1841, had "about seventy male and female pupils";[66] the other at Bridgewater, under Mr. Tillinghast, which, by 1844, had admitted 137 female and 136 male pupils.[67] At Westfield, whither the school at Barre had been transferred, in 1847, 81 per cent., or 83, of the pupils were the children of farmers and mechanics. Sixty-one female and forty-one male pupils were in attendance.[68]

As success attended these first normal schools, and the need for teachers became more, rather than less, acute, similar institutions were created elsewhere. By the middle of the century, one had been established at Albany (1844), at Philadelphia (1848), New Britain, Connecticut (1849), and at Ypsilanti, Michigan (1849).[69] The great need for a normal school to prepare women teachers is seen in the figures for the first school district of Pennsylvania, in 1850, which indicate to what an extent the work of the lower schools had come into the hands of women. There were 256 public schools, 23,706 male and 21,677 female scholars, and 81 male and 646 female teachers.[70] The census of 1850 showed 80,978 public schools, 91,966 teachers and 3,354,- 011 pupils in the schools of the United States.[71] It was at the same time evident that though many schools and teachers were serving the children of the country, there were "more than two million," according to some, "destitute or nearly so" of means of education. The enthusiasm of school reformers and of the promoters of women's professional interests, at this time, culminated in a memorial being sent to Congress for "Free Normal Schools for Female Teachers of the Common Schools":

"Whereas there are now, within these United States and Territories, more than *two millions of children and youth* destitute, or nearly so, of proper means of education, requiring, at this moment, 20,000 additional teachers, if we give to each instructor the care of one hundred pupils, quite too many for any common school with only one teacher—therefore we beg to call your attention to the following propositions:—

[66] *Ibid.*, IV, 317.
[67] *Ibid.*, VII, 62.
[68] *Ibid.*, X, 88–9.
[69] Barnard: *Normal Schools*, 8, 201, and 223.
[70] *Ibid.*, 218.
[71] DeBow: *Compendium of the Seventh Census*, 142.

"1. That to find 20,000 young men, who would enter on the office of pedagogue, would be utterly impossible, while the great West, the mines of California, and the open ocean, laving China and the East, are inviting them to adventure and activity.

"2. That, therefore, young Women must become the teachers of Common Schools, or these must be given up.

"3. That young women are the best teachers has been proved and acknowledged by those men who have made trial of the gentle sex in schools of the most difficult description (see Reports of the 'Board of Popular Education,' 'Reports of Common Schools in Massachusetts,' &c.), because of the superior tact and moral power natural to the female character.

"4. That female teachers are now largely employed, on an average of five of these to one male teacher, in New England, New York, Pennsylvania, Ohio, and wherever the common school system is in a prosperous condition; and everywhere these teachers are found faithful and useful.

"5. That, to make education universal, it must be moderate in expense, and women can afford to teach for one-half, or even less, the salary which men would ask, because the female teacher has only to sustain herself; she does not look forward to the duty of supporting a family, should she marry; nor has she the ambition to amass a fortune; nor is she obliged to give from her earnings support to the State or Government.

"6. That the young women of our land, who would willingly enter on the office of teacher, are generally in that class which must earn their livelihood; therefore these should have special and gratuitous opportunities of preparing them for school duties; thus the Normal Schools, in educating these teachers of Common Schools, are rendering a great national service.

"7. That, though the nation gives them opportunity of education gratuitously, yet these teachers, in their turn, will do the work of educating the children of the nation better than men could do, and at a far less expense; therefore the whole country is vastly the gainer by this system.

"8. That it is not designed to make a class of celibates, but that these maiden school-teachers will be better prepared to enter the marriage state, after the term of three or four years in their office of instructors, than by any other mode of passing their youth from seventeen or eighteen to twenty-one.[72]   That earlier marriages are productive of much of the unhappiness of married women, of many sorrows, sickness, and premature decay and death, there can be no doubt.

"From the foregoing facts and statements, showing the importance of woman's agency in the instruction of the young, and the pressing need of female teachers in the Common Schools throughout the land, we venture to request that your honorable body would make some provision for the suitable education of those young ladies who are willing to become teachers, if the way is opened before them.

"We respectfully ask the attention of Congress to this subject. While the public domain is parcelled out and granted for internal improvements and plans of national aggrandizement, we would humbly suggest that a small portion be set apart and allotted for the benefit of the Daughters of the Republic.   Three or four millions of acres of land would be sufficient to found and endow one Free Normal School for the education of Female Teachers in every State of the Union.   These institutions could be modelled and managed in each State to suit the wishes of its inhabitants, and young ladies of every section would be trained as instructors for children in their own vicinity.   This would be found of immense advantage in the States where schools have hitherto been neglected.   In short, the value of all the physical improvements in our country will be immeasurably enhanced by this provision for Female Education; because in the influence of intelligent and pure-minded women lies the moral power which gives safety and permanence to our institutions, and true glory to our nation."[73]

The enthusiastic plea for national subsidy of female normal schools was doomed to disappointment; but, by 1872, there were 101 normal schools in the United States, 48 aided by states, 2 by counties, 7 by cities, and 44 operated in connection with other institutions.   Ten states, six of them Southern, reported no state normal school, though normal training was offered in departments of other schools.   The total of students reported was 11,778.[74]   In 1892, there were 135 public and 43 private normal

[72] This view was commonly held.—Stow: *Hist. of Mount Holyoke Seminary*, 127.

[73] Quoted from *Godey's Lady's Book*, January, 1853, 176–7.

[74] *R. C. E.*, 1872, XXVII–XXIX.

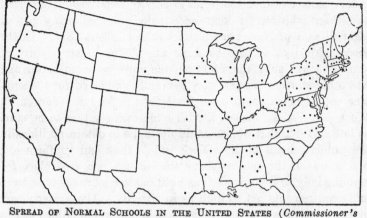

SPREAD OF NORMAL SCHOOLS IN THE UNITED STATES (*Commissioner's Report, 1890*)

schools, with about 35,000 pupils.[75] By 1917–1918, 172 state, 57 private, 34 city and 45 county normal schools had been established and were attended by 21,287 men and 116,887 women.[76]

IV. *The Woman Teacher and Her Position*

While women were thus beginning preparation to enter the teaching profession, it was often pointed out that they would use the position merely as a waiting station until the train came to bear them to their wedding. To this, the first reply was that it was no worse than to use teaching as a stepping-stone to the ministry or the bar. Another justification offered was that teaching was, in fact, the best preparation for the office of mother. Such was the view of Catherine Beecher; and it appeared frequently elsewhere. A letter to Horace Mann declared (1843): ". . . The great purpose of a woman's life—the happy superintendence of a family—is accomplished all the better and easier by preliminary teaching in school. All the power she may develop here will come in use there.'"[77] But the need for teachers was so great that the possible or probable brevity of women's service was an ineffectual argument against their employment, regardless of what use they could make of their experience afterward.

[75] *Ibid.*, 1892, I, 544.
[76] *Biennial Survey of Education*, 1916–1918, IV, 10 and 20.
[77] *Com. Sch. Jour.*, V, 353–5.

As a matter of fact, the terms of service were frequently short, and those who taught long, as a rule, occupied many places. Randall said of New York district schools about 1871, "In the great majority . . . the teachers are changed every year";[78] and, without doubt, the situation was nowhere much better and was often worse. Women were generally employed for the summer only, if men could be secured for the winter. Manson, in *Work for Women*, declared, with some exaggeration to be sure, as late as 1882, that women could not hope to obtain positions in the public schools of New York unless they had "influence"; but he was of the opinion that "the country is a good place for a young lady to begin work," as positions are more easily secured and requirements not so high as in the city. The western part of the country was rated "a good field for well-qualified teachers" but they must "be endowed with some courage."[79]

The schools for which young women, and men too, with little preparation and experience, were employed were far from attractive, and generally lacked equipment. Lack of books is often commented upon.[80] Fairly reliable pictures are called to mind by the school of Ichabod Crane, Eggleston's *Hoosier Schoolmaster*, and Burton's *District School As It Was*. The latter says the school of District No. 5 was in the exact center of the district because of the obstinate insistence of all residents that is should be no more advantageous to one than another. It stood on a high hill which became "literally the hill of science to generation after generation." The exterior, whether square, octagonal or hexagonal, was often dilapidated and doubtless bore a marked resemblance to the cartoons published by the American Common School Society; the crude, limited equipment of the interior, the "birchen rod, the strap, the raw hide," and so on, has been described by Barnard.[81]

Burton leads us inside. "First, there is an entry, which the district were sometimes provident enough to store with dry pine wood, as an antagonist to the greenness and wetness of the other fuel. A door on the left admits us to the schoolroom. Here is a space about twenty feet long and ten wide, the reading and

78 *Op. cit.*, 438.
79 *Op. cit.*, 117–18.
80 *Com. Sch. Jour.*, III, 67–8.
81 *Am. Jour. Ed.*, XXXII, 970 *ff*.

spelling parade.   At the south end of it, at the left as you enter, was one seat and writing bench, making a right angle with the rest of the seats.   This was occupied in the winter by two of the oldest males in the school.   At the opposite end was the magisterial desk, raised upon a platform a foot from the floor, the fireplace was on the right, half way between the door of entrance and

A DISTRICT SCHOOL OF 1852

another door leading into a dark closet, where the girls put their outside garments and their dinner baskets.''[82]

The schools of the West were even more unattractive, offered more difficulties than those in the East, and quite truly demanded "some courage" on the part of a woman who would go out to teach in them.   Many letters to Beecher and others who assisted

[82] Quoted in the *Com. Sch. Jour.*, I, 125.

in providing female teachers for Western schools, give a vivid picture of the social and educational situation. One woman opened school in a small log house, with forty-five pupils, one-half of them boys, and some of them grown up; but she had no trouble with discipline. The parents were farmers, had come from North Carolina, Tennessee and Germany, and were chiefly interested in making money. She described her surroundings at some length, as follows:

". . . They seem desirous to have their children educated, but they differed so much about almost every thing, that they could not build a schoolhouse. I was told, when I came, that they would not pay a teacher for more than three months in a year. At first, they were very suspicious, and watched me narrowly; but, through the blessing of my heavenly Father, I have gained their good will and confidence, so that they have provided me a good frame schoolhouse, with writing-desks and a blackboard, and they promise to support me all the year around.

"I commence school every day with reading the Bible, and prayer: this was new to them, but they made no objections. The people here spend Sunday in hunting, fishing, and visiting. I have commenced a Sabbath-school, and invited the parents to come with their children. They seem much pleased, and many come three and four miles. They never heard of a Sunday-school before. Last Sunday there were fifty present, and I proposed that we should have a Bible-class for the men, and that Mr. ————, a professor of religion near this place, should take charge of it, while I attended to the women and children. There being no church nearer than seven miles, the people think it too much trouble to go to it. I have persuaded them to invite the nearest clergyman to preach in my schoolhouse next Sunday.

"My greatest trials here are the want of religious privileges, the difficulty of sending to the distant postoffice, the entire want of social sympathy, and the manner in which I am obliged to live. I board where there are eight children, and the parents, and only two rooms in the house. I must do as the family do about washing, as there is but one basin, and no place to go to wash but out the door. I have not enjoyed the luxury of either lamp or candle, their only light being a cup of grease with a rag for a wick. Evening is my only time to write, but this kind of light makes such a disagreeable smoke and smell, I cannot bear it, and do without light, except the fire. I occupy a room with three of the children, and niece who boards here. The other room serves as a kitchen, parlor, and bedroom, for the rest of the family. . . .

"The people here are very ignorant; very few of them can either read or write, but they wish to have their children taught. They spend Sunday in visiting and idleness, and the fact that I kept Sunday-school for them without pay convinced them that my real object was to do good. The people in the settlements around are anxious to have more of the teachers come out. They have sent for Miss H————, who came out with me, but she was engaged. I was sorry, as it would have been a comfort to have had one friend in reaching distance.

"When I came here, I intended to stay only one term; but the people urged me so much to remain, and have done so much in building me a schoolhouse, that I concluded to stay longer. I did not leave my home to seek pleasure, wealth, or fame, and I do believe my heavenly Father will bless my labors here, even if I never see the fruit. The people seem to like me, say their children never behaved so well before, visit the school, were present at my examination, and like the Eastern way of keeping school."[83]

Another teacher, located in the county seat of a newly organized county, was even more distressed by her surroundings: "The only church built here is a Catholic. Presbyterians, Campbellites, Baptists, and Methodists, are the chief denominations. The last are trying to build a church, and have preaching once a fortnight. The sabbath is little regarded, and is more a day for diversion than devotion.

"I board with a physician, and the house has only two rooms. One serves as kitchen, eating and sitting room; the other, where I lodge, serves also as the doctor's office, and there is no time, night or day, when I am not liable to interruption.

"My school embraces both sexes, and all ages from five to seventeen, and not one can read intelligibly. They have no idea of the proprieties of the schoolroom, or of study, and I am often at a loss to know what to do for them. Could you see them, your

[83] Beecher: *True Remedy*, 163–7.

sympathies would be awakened, for there are few but what are ragged and dirty in the extreme. Though it is winter, some are without stockings, and one delicate little girl came with stockings, and no shoes. The first day, I felt like having a thorough ablution of both the room and the occupants, they were so filthy.

"I had to wait two weeks before I could get broken panes mended, and a few poor benches brought in. My furniture consists now of these benches, a single board put up against the side of the room for a writing-desk, a few bricks for andirons, and a stick of wood for shovel and tongs. I have been promised a blackboard, but I find that promises are little to be relied on. The first week I took a severe cold by being obliged to keep both doors open to let out the smoke. The weather is much colder than I expected, and the houses are so poor we feel the cold much more.

"I am told they are abundantly able to support a minister, and pay a teacher; but could you see them grouped together on Sunday, you would think they could do neither. I learn that the place is considered not a healthy one; still I do not wish to leave on this account, if it is judged best for me to remain. I came, expecting to make sacrifices, and suffer privations. When Sunday evening comes, I feel more than ever the want of some place for retirement, where I can join in concert with those who at this hour unite in prayer for this noble cause. Those seasons of social communion and prayer at Hartford I shall never forget; they come like balm to the spirit when oppressed with care. There is so much to do, and, where all are so ignorant, so much instruction to give, one can not but feel anxious to know what will be most profitable. I long, and hope, to see things wear a more cheerful aspect, and for this would labor untiringly. 'Hope on, and hope ever,' I would take as my motto.''[84]

Other teachers, doubtless, were more happily situated; but, as a rule, teachers were, and continued to be, forced to pursue a lonely existence. On the frontier, the teacher shared the crude living arrangements; in the more populous centers of the East her physical comfort was more easily secured. But, for the most part, in neither place did she find much intellectual and social diversion. She served society for a miserable sum, but outside

[84] *Ibid.*, 169–72.

the school little account was taken of her. Caroline Dall, in *College, Market and the Court*, found this to be true; and, in many instances, the social position of the woman teacher is not much better at present, though better financial reward has tended to put her in a more independent and desirable position. Of the woman teacher, Dall asserted, in 1861: "Society offered her no welcome. . . . Their meager salaries prevent them from dressing as ladies must be dressed for a large company. For the same reason, their boarding-places are obscure and lonely. The middle class of artisans, &c., who send their children to the public schools, seek no intercourse with those whose refinement seems to isolate them; the upper class look down upon them very kindly, but never think of inviting them to meet distinguished people, of showing them rare books or pictures, of stimulating their worn-out faculties in any way. Why do we not make these teachers our first care? Should we not be more than repaid—if pay we must have—by the cheer and comfort added to the school-room in which our children are to be taught? I have tried the experiment of bringing these tired souls into contact with those who ought to refresh them. It does marvellously well, until the crucial question is asked 'Who is she.' If I answer, 'The teacher of a primary school,' what a change of countenance, what a fading of the cordial smile, what passive indifference! and this, in cases where, in refinement and delicacy of manner, the young lady might pass unchallenged anywhere. But let the subject of my experiment be a girl of genius; with such cultivation only as a Normal School could add to the education of a country home; deficient still in the minor graces of deportment; too energetic and adventurous, perhaps, to be elegant; and *who* will take a motherly interest in her, draw her within the charmed circle where she shall learn to carry herself with reserve and dignity, and to veil her flashing powers, that they may warm where they have hitherto consumed?"[85]

Though much had been said, and done, to exalt the profession of teaching, it nevertheless remained true that it was one of the most lowly, lonely, and unattractive means to a living. Probably only those who were filled with a missionary and philanthropic zeal for service came to love it. Certain it is that many entered teaching because it was the nearest thing at hand, and relin-

[85] *Op. cit.*, 13–14.

quished it as soon as a more interesting career opened before them; this is proved by the rapid turnover. Some have frankly related the story of their reluctant apprenticeship as teachers. Lucy Larcom said:

"I liked the thought of self-support, but I would have chosen some artistic or beautiful work if I could. I had no especial aptitude for teaching, and no absorbing wish to be a teacher, but it seemed to me that I might succeed if I tried. What I did like about it was that one must know something first. I must acquire knowledge before I could impart it, and that was just what I wanted. I could be a student, wherever I was and whatever else I had to be or do, and I would! . . .

"This was the plan that indefinitely shaped itself in my mind as I returned to my work in the spinning-room, and which I followed out, not without many breaks and hindrances and neglects, during the next six or seven years,—to learn all I could, so that I should be fit to teach or to write, as the way opened. And it turned out that fifteen or twenty of my best years were given to teaching."[86]

Gail Hamilton, after being duly educated in all things necessary for women, at Cambridgeport and Ipswich, gave up teaching because she was "tired of learning lessons [and] . . . teaching them, tired of going to school at nine o'clock every day, tired of never visiting anybody . . . I mean to come. I won't stay another minute after this term. As for wearing out my life, and soul, and brain, and lungs, in teaching and getting just enough to keep body and soul together, I won't do it any longer. If I stay at home I shall be some company for you, and I can try for one year on Mr. Cowles' plan and see whether my pen may not do something for me. I can at least be no worse off than I am now. I have had it on my mind to write to you about this for some days, as I did not know but that you supposed I was getting rich with rapidity. I am glad, however, that you are not deceiving yourself in this respect. I have tried teaching some four years, and I think it is quite time to see whether something else will not be as profitable and less wearisome and wearing."[87]

Much dissatisfaction arose concerning the inadequate and unequal salaries paid to women, and a movement soon appeared for

[86] Larcom: *A New England Girlhood*, 161.
[87] Gail Hamilton's *Life in Letters*, I, 79–80 and 112–13.

equal salaries for men and women where the same services were performed. They were, of course, pitiably small for the former as well as the latter. Mary Lyon began teaching at seventy-five cents a week; Polly Hovey, a teacher in Maine, 1792, was paid $1.50 a week; two women in Iowa are said to have received at one time but $4.29 per month;[88] while fifty cents and "board round" was a common fee. In the thirties and forties it was not uncommon for women to be paid one-half, two-thirds, or three-fourths less than men.

Some superintendents, and others responsible for common schools, were greatly in favor of capitalizing the low wages of women and thus cutting down the expenditures necessary to support the system. The state superintendent of Ohio presented this argument:

"The number of male teachers in the aggregate, exceeds that of females. In the northern counties, the schools to say the least, are as good as in any counties in the state, and their practice is to employ females for teaching the small children. These counties are not surpassed in educational enterprise by any counties in the state, and by availing themselves of the help of female teachers, they are able to do twice as much with the same money as is done in those counties where female teachers are almost excluded. As the business of teaching is made more respectable, more females engage in it, and the wages are reduced. Females do not in the northern counties, expect to accumulate much property by this occupation; if it affords them a respectable support and a situation where they can be useful, it is as much as they demand. I, therefore, most earnestly commend this subject to the attention of those counties who are in the habit of paying men for instructing little children, when females would do it for less than half the sum, and generally much better than men can. Those counties that have large school funds could by a judicious expenditure keep their free schools open, at least eight months in the year."[89]

Discussing summer schools, a writer, about 1840, said the teacher should expect to receive "a dollar a week and her board; not more, it is admitted, than half as much as she can earn . . .

[88] *Harper's New Mo. Mag.* (1878, LVII, 608–9.)

[89] *Conn. Com. Sch. Jour.*, II, 155, from the *3d Annual Report* of the Ohio Superintendent of Schools.

[but] she has a higher object in view in teaching, than merely to gain a livelihood. She is moved to be useful. She has compassion on the ignorant and vicious. . . ."[90] Nathaniel Bowditch declared, about the same period, that "in this profession alone, except in the cities and large villages, no one can gain even a scanty subsistence."[91] Barnard declared in his *Report* for 1841 that, in Connecticut, "the wages of this class of common school teachers are far below the real worth of their services; are not equal to the compensation realized in private schools, or in the factory and the work-shop; and are altogether disproportionate to the average compensation of male teachers. [Besides, the position of women teachers is made more undesirable by] the practice of 'boarding round,' [which] still prevails very generally in the country districts. It may not be objectionable to young men, to be thus deprived of a regular and quiet home, but to young ladies of education and refinement, it is attended with so many inconveniences, that many are driven from this their appropriate field of labor and usefulness rather than encounter them."[92]

In Pennsylvania, 1840, men received an average salary per month of $19.39½ and women, $12.03. Only in the large cities were wages more comparable with the service. Boston, 1839–40, paid primary school teachers $250 annually,[93] but throughout Massachusetts as a whole women teachers were little better off than elsewhere. Mann's *Eleventh Report* to the Board of Education[94] emphasized the inadequate pay for all teachers and the inequality of wages paid men and women:

"Look at the average rate of wages paid to teachers in some of the pattern States of the Union. In Maine, it is $15.40 per month to males, and $4.80 to females. In New Hampshire, it is $13.50 per month to males, and $5.65 to females. In Vermont, it is $12 per month to males, and $4.75 to females. In Connecticut, it is $16 per month to males, and $6.50 to females. In New York, it is $14.96 per month to males, and $6.69 to females. In Pennsylvania, it is $17.02 per month to males, and $10.09 to

90 *Com. Sch. Jour.*, II, 166–8; also I, 161–2.
91 *Ibid.*, 284–6.
92 Quoted in the *Conn. Com. Sch. Jour.*, I, 168.
93 *Ibid.*, III, 155–6.
94 96–7.

females. In Ohio, it is $15.42 per month to males, and $8.73 to females. In Indiana, it is $12 per month to males, and $6 to females. In Michigan, it is $12.71 per month for males, and $5.36 for females. Even in Massachusetts, it is only $24.51 per month to males, and $8.07 to females. All this is exclusive of board. . . .''

A survey of the entire territory of the United States would probably have revealed little, if anything, more favorable to women than in the states named. As late as 1869, Utah reported women's wages a little less than half of men's.[95] Randall said, 1871, that women were employed ''at a low rate.''[96] Dall, in *College, Market and the Court,* declared: ''These wages are not yet in fair proportion to what are paid to men for the same work; and the shameful argument is still used that we employ women, chiefly, because men will not work for the same price.''[97] Dearborn, in his recent study, gave statistics for twenty-three states, in 1875–1876 and 1876–1877, showing that in the former year men's salaries averaged $389.88 and women's, $262.64; in the latter, $437.98 and $290.69, respectively.[98] The study shows a great rise of the salary level for those who had graduated at Oswego, the average of their salaries being more than twice that of women teachers generally in the twenty-three states.

While salaries were so meagre, there was well-nigh universal agreement that remuneration should be increased. Barnard declared that every friend of common schools ought to protest against the inadequate and disproportionate compensation given to female teachers.[99] Gallaudet believed an increase of wages would stimulate the schools at once, and recommended that towns ''advance the money necessary to procure for them a year, or certainly six months' instruction . . . and let it be refunded in whole or in part. . . .''[100] Such action was taken by Salem, it being agreed that two young ladies should be sent to Lexington at the expense of the city for a year. These were to agree to become assistant teachers (according to the law passed by Massa-

[95] *R. C. E.* (1870), 328.
[96] *Hist. of Com. Sch. System of N. Y.,* 438.
[97] *Op. cit.,* 16–17.
[98] Dearborn: *The Oswego Movement* (1925), 30.
[99] *Conn. Com. Sch. Jour.,* I, 167–8.
[100] *Ibid.,* I, 49.

chusetts March 18, 1839) in Salem and a part of their salary was to be deducted each year.[101]

A letter to Horace Mann, 1843, published in the *Journal*,[102] asserted: "We could obtain vastly more talent, skill and wisdom for the purpose of teaching in women, than . . . in men, at the same price. And if we will pay female talent, and power of accomplishing purposes, as well as we do the male, we should have, in many instances, better schools than we now have. Let our committees offer twenty dollars a month for the greatest quantum of capacity for government and teaching, male or female, and they will make much the best bargains in purchasing this of the women. Unhappily, we graduate the prices of the respective services of the male and female teachers, not by the worth of their services, but by other and extraneous notions. In the district before alluded to, they gave cheerfully eighteen or twenty dollars a month to men, that were good for nothing, and hesitated at giving eight or ten dollars a month to a woman who accomplished all their purposes.

"If districts would offer fifteen or twenty dollars to women qualified for the winter schools, we should soon see a generation of female teachers, such as we have not seen, and they would have a power and influence over the whole schools, such as the male teachers cannot now possess."

Caroline Dall, a generation later, insisted it was woman's duty to secure equal pay for equal service rendered. But there has been much opposition to this idea, even if, in some cases, steps have been taken to provide more nearly equal pay. The Commissioner's Report for 1874 stated that, in California, "females employed as teachers in the public schools of the state shall in all cases receive the same compensation as is allowed male teachers for like services when holding certificates of the same grade."[103] In 1918, Will C. Wood commented on California's case as follows: "The law on the subject is plain and clear. The time has passed for discriminating in the matter of salary on account of the sex of the worker. The cave man's dominance over women finds a modern counterpart in the policy of paying women less than men, although they may render equal service. Such a

101 *Com. Sch. Jour.*, I, 111–12, 345–7; and II, 204–5.
102 V, 353–5.
103 *R. C. E.* (1874), 18.

policy must go the way of the sabre-toothed tiger and the cave man's club. The modern world must accord to woman position and pay commensurate with her service and her ability.'"[104]

Harper's New Monthly Magazine, in 1878,[105] in discussing the success of women in filling places in common schools, alluded to the progress made up to date in the payment of equal salaries: "In the city of St. Louis no distinction is made between the sexes in fixing the teachers' salaries; and the California Legislature of 1873 enacted that the female teachers in the public schools should in all cases receive the same compensation as men for like services. A few of the Southern States, which employ more men than women, pay the same salary for the same work to both sexes; and Idaho, Nevada, and Arizona report the same custom. Nevada, which supports but few schools, pays her teachers $100.56 per month; and in Arizona where the schools are all of a primary grade, and the larger portion of the children of Mexican birth, teachers are paid from $100 to $125 per month. . . ."

On October 30, 1911, the New York State Legislature passed an equal pay bill, due to the persistent agitation of the Interborough Association of Women Teachers which had been organized in 1906.[106] Previous to the enactment, the maximum for men teachers of elementary schools was $2400; for women, $1500. The maximum for male elementary school principals was $3500; for women, $2500. Male teachers of the high schools might rise to $3000, but women only to $2400. Naturally, there was vigorous objection to this radical change. Perry saw in the change a great economic wrong, though he congratulated the women for their adroitness in securing the state's recognition of their position. He wrote:

"No business man, no business corporation, would think for a moment of making to any employee a gift of $750 a year in the form of a salary $750 above the market rates. No employer would say to an employee: I can get any number of other women to do the work that you are doing on the salary I am paying you; nevertheless, I will pay you a bonus of $750 because, if I needed a man, I should have to pay him that extra amount. But the

104 *N. E. A. Jour.* (1918), LXXXVIII, 239.

105 608–9.

106 *Laws of N. Y.* (1911), III, 2749–50; and *Educational Review* (1912), XLIII, 344–5.

city of New York is forced to do just this—to follow this uneconomic, unbusinesslike policy—by the order of the government of the state of New York. Keep in mind, then, as the crux of the whole matter, that the city is now compelled by legislative fiat to employ its teachers in violation of economic law. With this clearly before us, we may proceed to the real, the vital issue at stake. . . .[107]

"Whatever the causes, society faces the fact that a considerable proportion of its women are without the normal family life. They are without the position in the family prescribed for them by nature and they are without the economic support which comes to the normal woman who is the wife of a family-supporting man. Fortunately for society, these women are in a minority, are exceptional. Nevertheless, in all justice, society must meet this condition by granting to these women a position in the economic world and an opportunity to recover that economic reward for their labor which they would have received in leading the normal biologic and social life. And what is that reward? Clearly it is economic support for herself. Most assuredly it is *not* economic support for a family which does not exist. In other words, the right of the woman to a position of self-support is indubitable; her claim to a position yielding family support is unwarranted. Having herself to support, she must be paid by society a wage that will make her self-supporting; having no family to support, society can not in any justice to itself pay her a wage that will give her alone the support that should go to a family."[108] A somewhat similar view was taken by Elizabeth Hodgson, who opposed the position endorsed by the National Education Association for equal pay for equal service, her chief reason apparently being that woman's profession should be marriage.[109]

V. Increase of Women Teachers

When common schools were first established, it was generally felt that women were able to handle summer sessions but not those in winter when big boys attended. Due to the difficulty of getting men for the low salaries offered, however, the number of women in school positions began to increase rapidly. Foreign

107 *Ibid.*, 348–9.
108 *Ibid.*, 351–2.
109 *Education*, XXXV, 371 *ff.*

travellers were especially struck by the number of schools taught by women. Siljeström, at the middle of the century, gave particular attention to the fact and remarked that "this custom is becoming more common every year."[110] But there was, of course, a great variation in the practice of the several states.

When Barnard made his report for Rhode Island (1845) he said that outside of Providence and the primary departments of a few central districts, he found only six female teachers; but his successor, fifteen years later (1861) found more than two hundred employed in the whole state.[111] The figures of Massachusetts from 1837 to 1850 tell the same story of rapid substitution of women for men:

	Men	Women
1837	2370	3591[112]
1842	2414	4301[113]
1850	2437	5238[114]

In the report of Lowell, Massachusetts, the statement was made that their primary schools (twenty-two in number) were taught entirely by women.[115] Barnard, in his *Journal*,[116] said there were 996 male and 296 female teachers in Connecticut, but that these figures would be reversed for the summer schools. "The great ambition in many districts seems to be to have a 'man's school' in the winter, and a 'woman's school' in summer." In Pennsylvania, 1840, the returns showed 4,488 male and 2,050 female teachers;[117] while Ohio had 4,569 men and 2,946 women teachers.[118] Ten years later, Ohio had 9,130 men and 7,742 women teachers. In general it is found to be true that in the West the decline in the proportion of men to women was not so rapid as in Eastern states, such as Massachusetts and Pennsylvania. The cities of the West, however, tended to the employment of women more than rural places, though not to the same degree as in the East. Cincinnati (1839–40) had 21 men

---

110 *Op. cit.*, 185–7.

111 *Harper's New Mo. Mag.* (1878), LVII, 608–9.

112 *Com. Sch. Jour.*, VIII, 117–19.

113 *Ibid.*

114 Quoted from Siljeström: *op. cit.*, 183–4.

115 *Conn. Com. Sch. Jour.*, III, 156.

116 1838, I, 167.

117 *Ibid.*, II, 193.

118 *Ibid.*, I, 118–19.

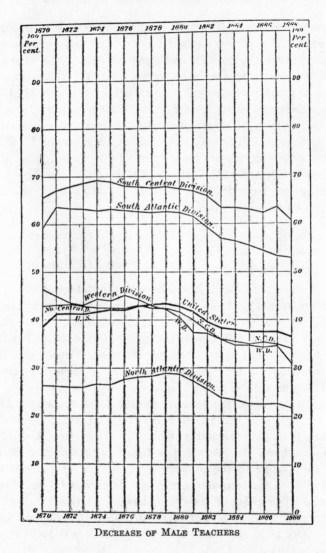

DECREASE OF MALE TEACHERS

and 42 women teachers;[119] Brooklyn's women teachers (1851) numbered 103 and men, 17; while in Philadelphia, there were 82 men and 699 women.[120] By 1888, in the United States at large, women furnished 63% and men 37% of the teachers. In

[119] *Conn. Com. Sch. Jour.*, III, 167–8.

[120] From figures for various places quoted in *Godey's Lady's Book*, May, 1852, 405.

the cities of the United States at the same date, 90.4% of the teachers were women and 9.6% men.[121]

Since 1880 the statistics of teachers in the United States are more complete. They show a rapid, steady decline in the proportion of men, a continuation on a broad scale of the same tendency seen in Massachusetts between 1837 and 1850. In 1880, 57.2% of the teachers in the United States were women, and 42.8% men; in 1890, 65.5% women and 34.5% men; in 1900, 70.1% women and 29.9% men; in 1910, 78.9 women and 21.1% men; and in 1918, women constituted 83.9% and men 16.1% of

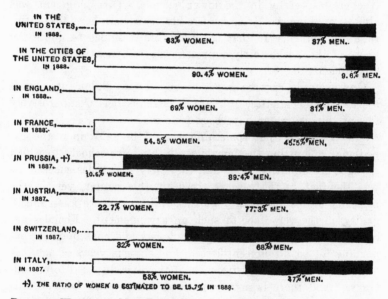

RATIO OF WOMEN TO MEN TEACHERS IN THE UNITED STATES AND ABROAD
(*Courtesy, D. Appleton and Company, New York*)

teachers.[122] In 1921–22,[123] 87% of the public elementary school teachers, 64% of public high school teachers, 86%[124] of private elementary schools, 61% of private secondary schools, 60% of teachers of teacher training schools, 52% of commercial and business schools, 100% of kindergarten, and 71% of teachers of

[121] Klemm's translation of Lange's *Higher Education of Women in Europe* (D. Appleton and Co., New York, 1890), p. XIII.

[122] *Biennial Survey of Education*, 1916–1918, III, 89 *f*.

[123] See *Statistical Survey of Education*, 1921–1922, pub. by the Bur. Ed. [Bul. 1924, No. 38], Govt. Printing Office, 1925.

[124] Estimated.

"other schools" were women. Only universities and colleges, and the professional schools of theology, law, medicine, dentistry and pharmacy, had withstood the movement of women into teaching. In the former (colleges and universities) women constituted not quite 26%, and in the latter (professional schools) they formed but .028 of the teaching force.

VI. Success of Women Teachers

Few years of service were required to convince public school officials of the ability, and even the superiority, of women as teachers, especially in the lower schools. This judgment was almost unanimous. It is impossible to review here the entire range of evidence to that effect. It must suffice to quote the views of those who fairly represent the judgment of competent school men.

One example may be given of an adverse judgment, passed by the school committee of Ware, Massachusetts. Comparatively few of this character have been found.

"It is proper that something should be said upon the expediency of putting the female sex into winter schools, to which all ages are admitted. Though they may sometimes succeed, as was the fact in the case referred to, this winter, yet, in the majority of instances, they make a failure. There is an incongruity on the very face of such an arrangement. Females are of too delicate a texture for the rudeness and consequential importance of boys fourteen, fifteen, and sixteen, years of age. A woman can do nothing with such, if they are disposed to be contrary. And there is a very natural feeling with boys of this age, that it is pusillanimous to obey a woman. The committee honor the sex, and would not abridge their influence, in the least, in its proper sphere. Their fitness to instruct girls of any age, and boys under ten, they do not question. They regard them as perhaps superior here to the sterner sex. But they would not recommend them as the best fitted for our winter district schools. Sometimes, it may be expedient to employ them."[125]

Favorable sentiments would naturally be expected from Mann, one of the earliest and most progressive advocates of women in the schools. His *Reports* and *Journal* are a mine of favorable

[125] *Com. Sch. Jour.*, II, 278.

judgments on women teachers.[126] It is significant, however, that his judgment was not reversed after he had had much actual experience with their service. In the *Fourth Annual Report,* he stated: "That females are incomparably better teachers for young children than males, cannot admit of a doubt . . .";[127] and four years later he recorded his approval and the consensus of opinions gathered from reports of school committees throughout the state:

"Reason and experience have long since demonstrated that children, under ten or twelve years of age, can be more genially taught and more successfully governed by a female than by a male teacher. Six or eight years ago, when the employment of female teachers was recommended to school committees, not a little was said against adopting the suggestion. But one committee after another was induced to try the experiment, and the success has been so great that the voice of opposition is now silenced. So far as can be learned from the committees' reports, I believe there is now an unbroken unanimity among them on this subject. It is found that females will teach young children better than males, will govern them with less resort to physical appliances, and will exert a more genial and kindly, a more humanizing and refining influence upon their dispositions and manners."[128]

Reports such as the following, relative to summer schools, were received from time to time from school committees. Brimfield (Massachusetts) asserted: "Females, other things being equal, are in nine cases out of ten better adapted to promote the improvement of our children in learning than teachers of the other sex; Randolph was "decidedly of the opinion that female teachers are far the most preferable to be employed in such schools"; and Rutland stated, "There has been less failure on the part of female teachers, indeed they have generally excelled. . . . Three-fourths of the pupils could be better taught by them than by our most able male teachers. . . ."[129]

[126] See, besides those mentioned below, the *Com. Sch. Jour.*, II, 386; and V, 353–5, etc.

[127] *Com. Sch. Jour.*, III, 303–4.

[128] *Ibid.*, VIII, 117–19.

[129] Quoted by the *Conn. Com. Sch. Jour.* from the Massachusetts school returns of 1838–9.

Thomas Gallaudet, in reply to the question whether women could handle winter schools, made it a particular point that women handled older and younger scholars with great success, whenever given the opportunity. "Not a few instances, both in our own and other States, have come to the writer's knowledge, where district schools of the usual size in point of numbers, and embracing scholars of both sexes, the older ones eighteen and twenty years of age, have been kept by young women, and as thoroughly taught and successfully conducted as they had ever been by male teachers. Particular inquiry was made with regard to their government, and in this respect there was no failure. The young men, it was said, had a sense of propriety, and a polite deference for the female teacher, that led them to yield to her gentler authority quite as readily as they had been accustomed to do to that which is made of masculine and sterner stuff."[130]

Siljeström, after his investigation of the schools of the United States, asserted that "in America the thesis is received as an axiom" and "experience has shown that, as regards the education of youth, women are not only equal to men, but that in many respects they are much more qualified for the task. . . ."[131]

Governor Seward, of New York, expressed a firm belief in woman's better qualifications for teaching the young, rather than a judgment of her success which he, himself had witnessed.[132] The superintendent of schools of New York (1842), however, gave this summary of the experience of the state and those nearby:

"The result of a careful investigation of the reports of the visitors of common schools in our own State, as well as of the reports of the several committees and boards of education in Massachusetts and Connecticut, concur in demonstrating the superior efficacy and utility, especially in the elementary branches, of schools taught by competent and well qualified female instructors. From the greater confidence which children naturally repose in them—the familiar acquaintance with the habits, dispositions and character of the young, which their situation and pursuits necessarily involve—and the peculiar adaptation of

130 *Conn. Com. Sch. Jour.*, I, 34.
131 Siljeström: *op. cit.*, 185–7.
132 *Com. Sch. Jour.*, I, 224.

their minds to the business of instruction, it cannot be doubted that the more general employment of female teachers would essentially promote the interests of education, and conduce to the welfare and prosperity of the common schools."[133]

Randall gave his personal experience and observation to the effect that there was a "decided superiority of female over male teachers" and advised Mr. Sands, who had written him, and "the trustees of the several school districts under your jurisdiction, . . . by all means, to secure the services of competent and well qualified female teachers, for the winter as well as summer school, in preference to male teachers of equal or even superior attainments and scholarship. . . ."[134] Superintendent Rice, likewise, strongly maintained that women's services were superior to men's.[135]

Willard, President of the Board of Education, Wilmington, Delaware, asserted, 1869: "They commenced by employing male teachers, but, although successful in procuring teachers of superior ability, they learned by experience that female teachers were better, and they have, therefore, employed them exclusively for years, as principals and assistants, and both the government and instruction of the schools are reported better for the change."[136]

In Pennsylvania, Schaeffer stated that the German communities continued for years to "put the schools in charge of men" and they supposed women had not enough strength and muscle to control mischievous boys.   But during the Civil War, when men were away, the schools passed into the hands of women teachers.   In bad schools women "invariably . . . brought order out of chaos.   Experience has shown that some women are born teachers, and they succeed where men have failed."[137]   In his *Women and Men*, Thomas Wentworth Higginson merely summarized what was generally expressed by school officials throughout the United States—views that had become common since Horace Mann urged the trial of women because it was more eco-

[133] Quoted by the *Conn. Com. Sch. Jour.*, IV, 135.
[134] *The New York Teacher*, April, 1859, 299–300.
[135] Randall: *Hist. of the Com. Sch. System of New York*, 366.
[136] *R. C. E.* (1870), 104; also 95.
[137] *Pa. Sch. Jour.* (1903), LI, 360–1.

nomical, and because "he regarded women as the natural teachers of all children."[138]

The tendency, in the United States, to employ so many women teachers had long been wondered at by foreigners. Germany, France, and England were inclined to regard the influence of a man necessary for discipline and the development of manly character. And, with the gradual exclusion of men from the public schools, there were reverberations of the same sentiments in the United States. Notwithstanding their success in actually imparting instruction and meeting the problems of discipline, it was urged by many that too much feminine influence on boys and girls was bad.[139]

In the work of Butler,[140] the report of Mr. Fraser[141] was quoted to the effect that "there is a strong preference in the United States for the employment of females as teachers, chiefly on the score of superior cheapness, but also, in the estimation of many, on the ground of superior efficiency." Interest in the reputed success of women as teachers continued, and about 1890 the Joint Education committee of Wales and Monmouthshire made a systematic effort to collect information concerning it. Their questionnaire was distributed by the *Educational Review* to the Commissioner of Education and others. The following answers to some of the questions were made by the Commissioner, who summarized "his impressions and conclusions regarding the United States as a whole." At this time, 65.5% of the entire teaching force of the United States were women.

To the question, "Are women employed as teachers of classes either (a) of boys only, or (b) boys and girls together?" he replied: " . . . Women are employed as teachers of classes in many schools exclusively for boys, but the employment of women as teachers of classes of boys and girls together is much more frequent. To another, "Does their work . . . require supplementing by that of men?" he stated: "The work of women in any of the grades from the primary up to the college does not need supplementing for any reasons of scholarship, but it is generally believed that the young should have the personal influence

[138] *Op. cit.*, 243-7.
[139] See pages 505 *ff.*
[140] *Woman's Work and Woman's Culture*, 56.
[141] Schools Enquiry Commission, 67.

of both men and women. . . . '' As to their success in (a) giving intellectual training and (b) maintaining discipline and order, he asserted: ''Women, I think, as a rule succeed better than men in getting work out of pupils of all kinds. . . . They also maintain better discipline and order than men, and with less corporal punishment. But there is a drawback to the intellectual training and discipline of the women in the fact that their training is more like that of the family and less like that of the State. It is evident that the child needs both of these kinds of training, and therefore he should have instruction from male as well as female teachers.'' As to the question of salaries, he said 'women receive only about 60% of that of men.' Regarding the number of married women teaching and their success in teaching, the Commissioner found that ''in those cities where married women act as teachers, I think it is often found that they have an advantage as compared with those who are unmarried; but the tendency in cities is to discriminate against married women. Some have gone so far as to exclude them by rule from the corps of teachers.''[142]

VII. The ''Woman Peril'' in Schools

Among the above statements, two, especially, suggest that the good effect of the predominant influence of women in the public schools was asserted by some and denied by others. The Commissioner but reflected current views in his statements that ''. . . the young should have the personal influence of both men and women . . . '' and '' . . . the child needs both these kinds of training and . . . should have instruction from male as well as female teachers.'' For throughout American schools were to be found those who believed in and feared the menace of our feminized schools. This fear of the ''woman peril'' became more and more acute in the last twenty years of the past century, and is felt by some today.

We shall not presume here to present all the views relating to this question, as limited space forbids it, but only so much as is necessary to gain an appreciation of the growth of this new attitude towards the dominating influence of women in public schools. In 1886, in the discussion of a committee report, Mr. Sheldon declared: ''Horace Mann said that ninety per cent of all

[142] *Educational Review* (1891), II, 358–61.

elementary instruction should be conducted by women. I believe
that the opinion was one of his greatest mistakes. A certain per
cent of the schools of Massachusetts would be benefitted by more
male teachers, especially girls' schools. . . . There is something
in man's instruction that is especially helpful to a class of girls.
If I had a few bad boys, I would seek to place them in the care
of a woman teacher. I should like to see more men in schools.
So many women are teaching not because they are better, but
they can be hired cheaper, than can men. The lamented Dr.
Philbrick was of the same opinion, and so expressed himself to
me a few months before his death. Twenty-five per cent. of the
women teachers ought to be removed, and men substituted.''[143]
Mr. Hinsdale asked what per cent of Massachusetts teachers were
males and Sheldon answered, ''five.'' Mr. Hagar was of the
opinion this was too low.

Attention was given to this tendency in the Commissioner's
Report for 1891. It was found that the number of male teachers
had increased but 4.39 per cent in the last year, while female had
advanced 5.27 per cent. Fifty years ago most teachers were
men; now ''it is the exception to find more than one man in any
one building. . . . '' 'In places women have not only become
teachers but principals as well. Wilmington, Delaware, has 193
teachers, only five of them men, and they are all in the high
school. In other cities it is much the same.' The historical
reasons for this state of affairs were cited:

''The change which resulted in this condition of affairs was
brought about in consequence of the conviction that women are
naturally better fitted than men to be teachers of young children,
and also by the lower price at which women may be employed.

''The latter was at first the principal reason for the initiation
of this change, for it was begun at the instance of Horace Mann,
Henry Barnard, and their contemporaries, when the public-
school system was in its infancy. Money was scarce and every
device that could be thought of was utilized to increase the number of schools and the number of people reached by them. But
the change has gone much further than was ever intended or
dreamed of by the original advocates of the employment of
women, and further than the general sentiment of school men

[143] *N. E. A. Proceedings* (1886), 302.

now approves. It has had many consequences that were not foreseen and which are difficult to overcome. The business of school
teaching is coming to be considered a woman's business, and
therefore, offers less attraction to young men than formerly,
especially in the subordinate positions, where the low salaries also
operate to repel them.''[144] In fact, the author continued, ''there
is danger that the increasing femininity of the schools . . . may
be productive of serious results. The already noticeable decrease in the proportion of boys in the higher grades is ascribed
by many to this cause. . . . ''

That many school officials became alarmed at the increase of
women is shown in their statements concerning needed reforms.
Aaron Gove, of Denver, said, 1891–2:

''One of the most desirable reforms in the administration of
the American common school at the present day is that whereby
more men may be employed as teachers. Not that a man is a
better teacher than a woman. This is not true. But there are
elements in the teaching profession which belong to sex, and the
elements proper to both sexes are needed in training and character making, the main work of the school. A complete course
of twelve years can be established only by an equal allotment of
teachers from each sex. I would year by year alternately place
the pupil under the companionship of, first, a man; second, a
woman, and so on, from the first to the twelfth grade. In the
present condition of society and of the financial world, this is
impossible. But the change will come, and improvement will
follow in the increase of the number of men teachers.''[145]

Philadelphia, to check the rising tide, established the School
of Pedagogy for men and agreed that, in future, men should be
named for positions in the two highest grades of boys' grammar
schools. Isaac A. Sheppard, of the Board of Education, 1892,
explained more fully the facts which justified this step:

''In this city the number of women teachers on the roll is 2,745,
and the number of men teachers is 126. For many years past the
pupils of both sexes, of the eleventh and twelfth grades, have
been taught by women. And in multitudes of instances it has
been found that in matters that pertain to the common every day

[144] R. C. E. (1891–1892), II, 668–71.
[145] Ibid.

business of life the boys remain untaught in much that they ought to know. . . .

"As a tree is known by its fruit, so is the worth of a teacher disclosed by the development of the pupil. The fact is that a woman teacher can not in the nature of things gain the confidence of a class of boys to the same extent that a man will do; and the preceptor who establishes a feeling of confidence between himself and his pupils, gains an influence of unmeasurable value in the pupils' advancement.

"In 1881, the Committee on Central High School called attention to the fact that 'a more careful and thorough training of the candidates for admission into the school should be exacted from the lower schools.' In 1883, President Richie, of the Central High School, in his report to the Board, said: 'Many boys in the lower classes of the school seem incapable of intellectual effort either from lack of natural ability, or from not having been trained to habits of study. These boys not only derive but a minimum of benefit from the instruction given them, but what is worse, they retard the work of the teachers in almost all of the departments; and the testimony of the teachers in the higher schools entirely accords with these statements.' In 1887, President Steel, in his report to the Board of Education, said: 'The greatest weakness of the school department is the small number of men in it; and the need of the department in this respect is so apparent that it is beyond discussion'; and he earnestly asked the attention of the Board to the subject. In 1888, Superintendent MacAlister, in his report said: 'It is my conviction that the Board has now before it no more important question than the best means of bringing into service a sufficient number of young men, possessing the education, character, and ambition to make successful teachers.' . . . After mature deliberation, this Board, by a unanimous vote, wisely adopted rules which designate the places where men teachers are needed; namely, for the boys in the eleventh and twelfth grades.''[146]

In 1890–91, the Chicago Board of Education took a strong stand "for the restoration of the element of masculinity," though no new regulation was made as in Philadelphia. Mr. Nettelhorst's chief reason for the adoption of the new policy was that ". . . after the children have grown to reach a certain age,

[146] *Ibid.*

say 10 to 12 years, I do not think it wise to intrust their education to women only. In my opinion it is necessary that the more
sturdy character of men should be allowed to have an influence
upon our growing generation, and while it may be necessary that
the gentle hand of woman should guide and lead our little ones,
I believe that the more firm hand of man should be employed in
teaching the older ones [and take] part in molding and shaping
their character. . . . A man (if he is the right kind of a person,
and, if not, he has no place there) will inspire the children with
more respect, after they have advanced to a certain age, than a
woman, and they therefore will be more ready to listen to the
teachings of the man and pursue their studies more diligently
than if they are in the hands of a woman.''[147]

The rising wave of opinion adverse to women as teachers had
an effect upon the New York Board of Education, which adopted
a by-law especially directed at married women, apparently judging that marriage in itself was a disqualification for teaching, or
that a married woman ought to be supported by her husband and
leave school positions to the unmarried. The by-law stated:

''No woman principal, woman head of department, or woman
member of the teaching or supervising staff shall marry while in
the service. It shall be the duty of a District Superintendent to
bring to the notice of the Board of Superintendents the marriage
of any such person in his district, and such fact shall be reported
to the Board of Education, which may direct charges to be preferred against such teacher by reason of such marriage.''[148]
Again, ''No married woman shall be appointed to any teaching
or supervising position in the New York Public Schools unless
her husband is mentally or physically incapacitated to earn a living or has deserted her for a period of not less than one year.''
The position of the Board was at once attacked and ridiculed.[149]

[147] *Ibid.*

[148] Quoted by the *Educational Review* (1903), XXV, 213–14.

[149] From *Are Women People?* by Alice Duer Miller, Copyright (1915)
by George H. Doran Company. Pp. 89–91. The Board interviews three
women candidates, as follows:

  Chorus by Board:
      Now please don't waste
      Your time and ours
      By pleas all based
      On mental powers.

The by-law was modified in 1913 and 1915; and on May 26, 1920, it was "stricken out in its entirety."[150]

Another reaction against women teachers, possibly stimulated by the action of the Board of Education, developed among their male colleagues. In 1904 an interesting report of the Male Teachers Association of New York was reviewed in the *Educational Review*[151] under the heading "Are there too many women teachers?" After pointing out the fact of their increase in cities and the country at large, not only in elementary but in high schools, and also the fact of gradual feminization of the student body as well, the report asks whether this tendency is good, viewed from the sociological, the educational, and administrative angles. Sociologically, the practice is found to be bad because (1) it may diminish the "extent, power and influence of the home"; (2) the continuance of such a work may be too great a

---

She seems to us
The proper stuff
Who has a hus-
Band bad enough.
All other pleas appear to us
Excessively superfluous.

1st Teacher:
My husband is not really bad—
Board:
How very sad, how very sad!
1st Teacher:
He's good, but hear my one excuse—
Board:
Oh, what's the use, oh, what's the use?
1st Teacher:
Last winter in a railroad wreck
He lost an arm and broke his neck.
He's doomed, but lingers day by day.
Board:
Her husband's doomed! Hurray! hurray!
2nd Teacher:
My husband's kind and healthy, too—
Board:
Why, then, of course, you will not do.
2nd Teacher:
Just hear me out. You'll find you're wrong.
It's true his body's good and strong;
But, ah, his wits are all astray.
Board:
Her husband's mad. Hip, hip hurray!

strain upon the physical well-being of women—"are there not signs that their greatest and best physical powers are being broken?"—and (3) differentiation of the sexes indicates a differentiation of vocation, and by employing women as teachers, and taking them away from homes, society is running counter to nature. Educationally, women are bad for boys above ten years of age because (1) men are necessary as ideals for boys; (2) a boy needs forceful, manly control, and he should learn it of a man; (3) men are less mechanical in instruction than women; (4) women feminize the course of study; and (5) they feminize the method of teaching. The sixth reason given really suggests that women teachers have the best "immediate intellectual" results in teaching, but that these are not the true tests. "The true test of educational efficiency is what the boy is and does as a man."

From the administrative point of view, there were many evils: (1) the rapid changing of women teachers has made an excessive amount of supervision necessary; (2) marriage has been a constant deterrent to efficiency because teaching "must cease with

---

3rd Teacher:
　　My husband's wise and well—the creature!
Board:
　　Then you can never be a teacher.
3rd Teacher:
　　Wait. For I led him such a life
　　He.could not stand me as a wife;
　　Last Michaelmas, he ran away.
Board:
　　Her husband hates her, Hip, hurray!
Chorus by Board:
　　Now we have found,
　　Without a doubt,
　　By process sound
　　And well thought out,
　　Each candidate
　　Is fit in truth
　　To educate
　　The mind of youth.
　　No teacher need apply to us
　　Whose married life's harmonious."

[150] Letter and copy of the by-laws from Joseph Miller, Secretary of the N. Y. C. Board of Education, Jan. 26, 1926.

[151] (1904) XXVIII, 98–105.

her marriage''; (3) teaching has been used as a temporary employment, as women leave it to get married (Men left the profession, too, but not to marry; other reasons were more legitimate); (4) teaching has been made a cheap profession because women were able and willing to teach for little pay; (5) education of all classes has been put in the hands of a single class; and (6) there has resulted an unwise expenditure of public funds to support normal schools to train these imperfect and temporary educational agents—women. All the objections were fortified by quoting Mosely's statement that ''one of the greatest faults in the American school system was its dearth of male teachers.''[152]

Having thus annihilated all possible excuses for woman's being in the schools, the Association desired to pay ''tribute to the most praiseworthy effort and faithfulness of our admirable associates, . . . women teachers,'' who have done ''all that they could . . . as women. . . .'' They then passed this final judgment and made recommendations to govern employment of teachers: ''They may be employed as teachers of girls and young boys. Our contention is, however, that it is far better for women, for boys and for the schools as a whole, that fewer women be employed as teachers.'' In the future, they proposed:

''1. That all normal boys, upon entering their tenth year of life, should be, during their attendance at school, under the direct control of a man teacher.

''2. That the administrative authorities of the schools of our country, and especially of the great cities, be urged to adopt a policy to employ only male teachers for boys above the age of ten years.

''3. That fair, graded salaries, tenure of office, and pensions be put in force to the end that able men may be attracted to the work of teaching as a life profession.

''4. And especially do we urge that in New York City steps be taken to extend the policy of employing men teachers until all boys in the last four years of the elementary schools are taught by male teachers.''[153]

[152] Dr. Gray, of the Commission, said: ''There is a tendency for women teachers, when dealing with boys of such advanced age, to instill (unconsciously, no doubt) sentimental views of facts, rather than to derive principles of conduct from them.''—*R. C. E.*, 1905, I, 9.

[153] *Ibid.*

Along with the attack of school boards and organizations went that of individuals. Charles W. Eliot argued that there were too many women in the schools.[154] His article met with vigorous opposition by teachers for months afterward. Chadwick[155] revived the discussion of "The Woman Peril" in 1914, and many other writers came forth either to uphold or controvert his views. He declared, dogmatically, that for generations the American boy had been under woman's tutelage and that "the effect of such procedure has had so evil an effect upon the manhood of the country, on the qualities that go for making the masculine character, that it is more than full time to consider most seriously this great and vital question." As a result of female teachers we have "a feminized manhood, emotional, illogical, non-combative against public evils. . . . We have in this result the cause in greatest degree, of our supineness in municipal affairs. . . . I lay down the broad statement that no woman, whatever her ability, is able to bring up properly a man child. . . . Men think in terms of steamships, railways, battleships, war, finance, in a word, the greatest energies of the world, which the woman mind never, in a practical way, really concerns itself with, nor can it do so." Woman's influence does violence to the "masculine nature." Prussia, "the most advanced and highly civilized state in the world," has kept boys under the tutelage of men. He quoted the percentage of women in several states and cities and concluded: "That such a state of things should continue is unbelievable. It cannot be that we shall be willing to continue this down-hill process of character; that we shall continue to warp the psychics of our boys and young men into femininity." It will cost more to put men in the place of women, he pointed out, "but, if we are to take education seriously, whatever the cost, the change should be made. We may economize safely in many things but not in this which touches the great fundamental of education—character."[156]

It was urged by some, however, that "available men" were not only more expensive but below the "ideal masculinity" which

154 *N. E. Jour. Education*, I, 254.

155 See *Educational Review* (Feb. 1914), XLVII, 109, 115–16, 117, and 118.

156 *Ibid.*; also recent views expressed, in an interview, by Dr. C. W. Burr. —[Philadelphia] *Public Ledger*, Dec. 12, 1926; and Sept. 4, 1927.

Chadwick hoped to reintroduce into boy's education. Passano attacked this view in 1915, and declared that ideal men or women could not be obtained and that "of the non-ideal teachers available, men are more suited than women to teach boys."[157]

But if the foregoing references, selected from a great array of articles during the past forty years, indicate a reversal of the sentiments of those who first promoted the introduction of women into the schools, it is also true that numerous equally competent judges deny the evil influence that has been attributed to women. The *American Educational Review*[158] stated:

"Professor John Dewey, of Columbia University, is recently quoted as saying there is no more efficient body of workers in America than the great army of its woman teachers. They 'feminize' boys? Nonsense! Or where are our effeminate boys, if you please? The notion that our splendid women teachers are making mollycoddles of their boy students is utterly absurd. Why, women themselves are anything but mollycoddles in these days of basket-ball and athletic 'stunts' without number! They'd be the first to despise the 'feminine' boy—instead of petting him into being."

Thus the wisdom of employing women teachers continues to be a matter of opinion, where scientific proof is so difficult. Opinion abroad[159] has generally been in favor of men teachers; whereas, in America, many arguments have been found to justify the employment of women, but none so irrefutable as the historic ones of economic expediency and the successful performance of women teachers. Many would, no doubt, take the position of Flora Cooke, of the Francis Parker School of Chicago, that "the ideal arrangement is to have both."[160]

VIII. *Women as Educational Leaders and School Officers*

On this subject, as well as their position as teachers, there has been much difference of opinion. Henry Barnard, in the middle

157 *Educational Review* (1915), XLIX, 407.

158 XXXI, 690.

159 In England, but recently, the National Association of Schoolmasters, at Nottingham, declared in favor of men teachers for all boys over seven years—because "women emotionally are unable to understand or control boys." See an article on the divergent views of American and English teachers in the [Philadelphia] Sunday *Public Ledger*, May 24, 1925.

160 *Ibid.*; see also Noble and Roy: *The Personnel, Preparation and Progress of the High School Teaching Staff of Louisiana*—Foreword by T. H. Harris, who favored the half-and-half idea.

of the century, was convinced of the capacity of women to serve as school supervisors, and one, at his suggestion, took charge of schools in a rural district of Rhode Island and "accomplished wonderful results"; but Henry Raab, of Illinois, felt it unwise even for directors "to employ and for women to accept places in ungraded country schools."[161]   We have seen that Mrs. Willard became a supervisor at Kensington and was instrumental in the work of the Female Association for the Improvement of Common Schools after 1839,[162] but the advancement of women in these positions of importance and leadership was slow.   It was not until 1903 that Celeste Bush, of Niantic, Connecticut, invited some sixty women, representing the Women's Christian Temperance Union, Collegiate Alumnae, Daughters of the American Revolution, State Federation of Women's Clubs, Motherhood Club, Wellesley Club, Mount Holyoke Club and women teachers of the state, to a gathering at Hartford, where the first Woman's Council of Education in the United States was inaugurated.[163] Even as late as 1904, Chancellor[164] declared that women as a class "seldom furnish valuable school board members";[165] and that women were "out of place in a teaching principalship" (high school) and only slightly preferable in elementary principalships "while they are comparatively young and still have the maternal instinct toward children."   He concluded that higher salaries should be secured "as far as possible" so as to obtain men, for ". . . the feminization of schools has gone altogether too far."[166] Dutton and Snedden took a more moderate view.[167]

But while there were bitter opponents who insisted that women could not teach schools attended by large boys, could not serve on school committees or act as principals and superintendents, the way did gradually open and they took charge of these posts. The legislature of New Hampshire, 1872, approved the election of women to the prudential committees of school districts, or

[161] R. C. E., 1890–1891, II, 1057–8.

[162] Conn. Com. Sch. Jour., IV, 187, and 193–4.

[163] Article by M. I. Jenkins in Educational Foundations (1909–10), XXI, 579.

[164] Our Schools, Their Administration and Supervision (1906), 13–15.

[165] His views on women as school board members were criticized by Pauline Steinem, to name no others, in the Ohio Educational Monthly, LV, 230.

[166] Chancellor: op. cit., 181–3.

[167] Administration of Public Ed. in U. S., 138.

school committees of cities and towns of the state. The state reports of Connecticut and Rhode Island for 1873 advocated women as school visitors. Boston, in 1872, elected four women to the school committee; and women were also chosen in several cities. Massachusetts passed an act, in 1874, declaring women eligible for membership on school committees.[168] In Philadelphia, 1882, Mary E. Mumford, who was serving as chairman of the Education Committee of the Century Club, was asked by the "Committee of One Hundred" to stand as a candidate for the Sectional School Board in the 29th ward. She was elected, served six years, and, in 1889, was appointed to the Central Board of Education.[169] The first woman on the Central Board was Anne Hallowell, appointed in 1886.[170]

In the West the change of view was reflected in the law of Illinois,[171] which made women, married or single, eligible to school offices, if over 21, and possessing the same qualifications prescribed for men. Eleven women county superintendents were elected under this law in 1873. In Iowa and Kansas, women,[172] under similar provisions, had become superintendents. Michigan, Ohio, and Pennsylvania moved in the same direction. In the far West, an act approved by California[173] declared: "Women over the age of 21 years, who are citizens of the United States and of this State, shall be eligible to all educational offices within the State, except those from which they are excluded by the constitution. . . ."

The admission of women as officers was as hesitatingly and grudgingly permitted, and apparently for much the same reasons, as was their first service as teachers. A statement attributed to a committee of Massachusetts, and witnessed by Colonel T. W. Higginson, to a considerable extent describes the attitude of many as they speculated on this innovation: "As there is neither honor nor profit connected with this position, we see no reason why it should not be filled by a woman." But, if there was "neither honor nor profit" for women, they are

168 *Laws of Mass.*, 1874, 443; and *E. C. E.* (1873), CXXXIII–CXXXIV.
169 *Jour. Board of Educ.*, Phila., 1889, 30.
170 Letter July 8, 1927, Secretary, Phila. Board of Education.
171 *Laws of Illinois*, 1873, Hurd's *Rev. Stat. of Ill.*, 1874, 982.
172 See article in the *Pa. Sch. Journal*, XXXV, 407.
173 *Statutes of California*, Mar. 12, 1874, 356.

ELLA FLAGG YOUNG

reported to have filled the new positions honorably and profitably for society. Rhode Island[174] took the view that as women had proved better teachers, so they could with "equal propriety and efficiency" act as school officers, because of their natural fitness and special experience as teachers; and the *State Report* of Kansas declared (1873) that they had already proved themselves:

"As county superintendents, the verdict is that those elected in this State 'have done their work faithfully and well, as well as the best and far better than many of the men.' The superintendent hopes that this new field, as well as professional chairs in high schools and colleges, will remain open to all, male and female, in fair and honorable competition."[175]

Notwithstanding the favorable reports on women as officers, wherever tried out,[176] the increase of their numbers was slow until after 1900. In 1896 only two women held state superintendencies,[177] twelve held city superintendencies, and 228 were at the head of county systems. In eleven states they could hold "any school office," and in others they could hold certain offices.[178] The Commissioner's *Report* of 1899–1900[179] showed a gain of 56 county superintendencies, while, by 1903, there were 324 women county superintendents.[180] The entrance of women to these positions increased rapidly in the next ten years. A review of the statistics, given in the *American Educational Review*,[181] stated: "Four States—Colorado, Idaho, Washington, and Wyoming—have women at the head of their State school systems, and there are now 495 women county superintendents in the United States, nearly double the number of ten years ago. In some States women appear to have almost a monopoly of the higher positions in the public-school system. Wyoming has a woman State superintendent; the deputy State superintendent is a woman; and of the fourteen counties in the State, all but one are directed educationally by women. In Montana, where there

174 In the *State School Report* for 1873, 90–3.
175 *Report* for 1873, 23–5; see the *R. C. E.*, 1874, 124–5 and 379.
176 *R. C. E.*, 1873, CXXXIII–CXXXIV.
177 In Colorado and Idaho.
178 *R. C. E.*, 1896–7, II, 1528.
179 II, 2589.
180 *Ibid.*, 1903, II, 2457.
181 (1913) XXXIV, 289–90.

are thirty counties, only one man is reported as holding the position of county superintendent.

"The increase in the number of women county superintendents is most conspicuous in the West, but is not confined to that section. New York reports 42 women 'district superintendents,' as against 12 'school commissioners' in 1900. Other States showing marked increases are—Iowa, from 13 in 1900 to 44 in 1912; Kansas, from 26 in 1900 to 49 in 1912; Nebraska, from 10 to 42 in the same period; North Dakota, from 10 to 24; Oklahoma, 7 to 14. In only two states is a decrease reported—Tennessee had 9 in 1900 and only 5 in 1912, and Utah had one less than a decade before."[182]

[182] Figures for the present date are not available.—Letter, W. S. Deffenbaugh, Jan. 22, 1926.

CHAPTER XI

NEW OPPORTUNITIES FOR GIRLS' SECONDARY
EDUCATION

I. Early Girls' High Schools

In the early twenties of the nineteenth century, there arose an effort to create for youth a public institution which would do without cost that which the academy had done for a fee. This new institution, first called the English Classical School, in Boston, became generally known as the high school. The movement to establish such a public institution was common in the circles of female as well as male education.

The Boston English Classical School, for boys, was opened in 1821, and became the High School in 1824. Thus far, it appears the first high school for girls was established at Worcester, Massachusetts, in 1824. On August 22, 1823, a special committee reported certain recommendations, among which was one to the effect that a girls' school, "of a higher order," and "to be composed of the scholars most advanced from all the other female schools," should be established. This school for girls was opened not later than June, 1824. One plan, proposed March 17, 1824, would have opened the Latin Grammar School to girls; but this met with opposition on the part of the Select Men who controlled the Latin School, and was defeated. It is perfectly clear that, having failed to open the Latin Grammar School to girls, the "First Female School" was meant to fill the same place for them that the Latin School did for boys. Lincoln's *History of Worcester*[1] stated that the Female High School[2] was the "highest in rank," corresponded to the Latin Grammar School, and that promotions were made to it from the primary schools. Grizzell, after a careful study of the early records, stated: "So far as is known, the girls' high school had its origin here, and, throughout the period from 1824 to 1845,

[1] P. 304.

[2] This name does not appear earlier than April 13, 1827.

this institution provided a superior type of secondary education for girls.''[3]

The next year (1825) the Boston school committee considered ''the expediency and practicability of establishing a public school for the instruction of girls in the higher departments of science and literature. . . . ''   A month later (June) it was agreed to establish ''such a school . . . on the monitorial system, and the city council was requested to appropriate two thousand dollars for this purpose.''   Such an appropriation was approved by the Common Council, September 26, 1825.[4]   Throughout the summer the plans for the new institution went forward and, in November, public notice was given[5] that the school committee would select a master, ''prepared to teach'' on the ''monitorial or mutual instruction'' system.   Ebenezer Bailey opened the school, February 27, 1826, with one hundred and thirty pupils,[6] one-half of whom came from private and the others from public schools.[7]

The school proved immensely popular; indeed, as Quincy said, it was ''an alarming success,'' and was therefore abolished in 1828.   It was said that ''not one voluntarily quitted it, and there was no reason to suppose that anyone admitted to the school would voluntarily quit for the whole three years, except in the case of marriage.''[8]   In commenting on its discontinuance, the *American Annals,*[9] several years later, said it was ''because it was found that a single school of this description would not accommodate more than one fourth part of those who ought to attend such an institution.''   Though efforts were made from time to time to improve the condition of girls' education, nothing was accomplished for more than a score of years.   Siljeström,

[3] For accounts of the beginning of this school at Worcester see Grizzell: *Origin of the High School in New England,* 48–53; Jones: Early Schools in Worcester [*Educational Administration and Supervision,* IV, No. 8, Oct. 1918]; Lincoln: *History of Worcester,* 304.

[4] Barnard: *Am. Jour. of Ed.,* XIII, 243; see also the *Am. Jour. of Education,* 1826, I, 96–105.

[5] *Columbian Centinel,* Nov. 5, 1825, 3.

[6] Some authorities give 135 as the number; see *Am. Jour. of Ed.,* I, 380–1.

[7] Barnard: *Am. Jour. Ed.,* XIII, 243 f.

[8] Higginson: *Common Sense About Women,* 200–1; Barnard: *Am. Jour. Ed.,* XIII, 247.

[9] VI, 137.

(*Courtesy of the Boston Athenaeum*)

EBENEZER BAILEY

writing of the education of girls in Boston, at the middle of the century, pointed out that the girls remained in the lower schools until sixteen or seventeen years of age, for there were "no schools of a higher grade for them."[10]   The number of girls in the lower schools at that time was 4,487 and that of boys, 4,315.[11]

The first girls' high school in New York City was opened shortly before that of Boston.   The New York High School Society, influenced by the experiences of John Griscom abroad, established its first school for boys on March 1, 1825.   About a year later, February 1, 1826, the Female High School was opened, its establishment being due, it appears, to the fact that the one for boys had been entirely satisfactory.   D. H. Barnes was associated with Griscom as principal.[12]   The school experienced rapid growth.   The new three-story building, erected on the lot purchased in Crosby Street, was completed and occupied in 1826.   In 1827, three hundred and seventy-four students were reported in attendance, and the Society felt assured that the combined effect of their male and female institutions "must be most powerfully felt in this community." and were, therefore, "fully sensible of the high importance of the charge committed to them."[13]

The germ of the high school movement made its appearance in Connecticut, at Bridgeport, in 1826, with the establishment of a school with departments for both sexes.   The *American Journal of Education*,[14] in commenting upon it, made clear the fact that it was an imitation of the "New York High School."   The studies pursued were to include the branches of an English education necessary "to prepare youth for the active pursuits of future life."   The pupils numbered from 200 to 240 at this time. It appears that the High School did not continue permanently.[15] Other institutions, designated as high schools, were established at North Glastenbury (1828), East Hartford (about 1828), and

[10] Siljeström: *Education in the United States,* 113–14.

[11] *Ibid.,* 111–12.

[12] See *Reports of the New York High School Society,* pamphlets bound in three small volumes; *Am. Jour. Ed.,* I, 59–60; Randall: *Hist. of the N. Y. School System,* 48; Gifford: *Hist. Development of the New York State High School System,* 22–3; also Brown: *Making of Our Middle Schools,* Ch. XIV.

[13] *Am. Jour. Ed.,* II, 59–60.

[14] III, 489.

[15] Consult Steiner: *Hist. of Educ. in Conn.,* 56; and Grizzell: *op. cit.,* 223.

Guilford (1838) ; but neither they nor that at Bridgeport appear to have fully merited the name.[16]

The interest evinced by Worcester, Boston, and New York in girls' high schools was quickly noted, and private high schools, controlled by trustees or individuals, began to spring up to meet the new demand.   At Greenfield, Massachusetts, about 1828, "the proprietors . . . observed with interest the progress of public sentiment on the subject of female education," and were convinced that "any expense in assembling facilities for the formation of the minds and characters of young ladies" would meet with "ample and generous patronage."   This was to be a boarding high school.   The plan was described at some length:

"The house, of which a sketch will soon be given to the public, is spacious and built in a style of superior elegance, affording accommodations for boarding and lodging the principal and his assistants with from 40 to 50 scholars.   A contemplated addition will accommodate 30 more.   Ample conveniences for the school are likewise included.   The situation is airy and delightful, commanding a beautiful view of surrounding scenery. . . .

"Col. Root, the former proprietor, and still sharing in the capital, has consented to become the steward of the establishment, and the utmost confidence is reposed in the kind and maternal treatment which every pupil will experience in his family.   It is expected that every scholar from abroad, will board at the institution, and be always under the parental oversight of the instructors.

"The department of instruction will be filled by a principal with one or more assistants in the regular branches of English education, a native teacher of the French, also qualified to instruct in the Italian or Spanish language, a teacher in Music, another in Drawing, Painting, and Ornamental Needle-work, and another in Penmanship.   The proprietors conceive themselves particularly fortunate in having secured for their principal the Rev. Henry Jones, a graduate of Yale College, of whose character and talents they have received full satisfaction.   Teachers in Music and in Penmanship are likewise engaged.

"A word respecting the general course of education to be pursued.   In the various branches of natural science, the most ap-

16 Griffin: *Evolution of the Connecticut State School System,* 58 and 157 *ff.*

John Griscom

proved authors will be studied, and illustrated at successive recitations, as the subjects may require, in the way of experimental lectures and demonstrations. The more abstract sciences will be pursued so far as they promise a happy influence in forming the female mind, and preparing it for the various duties of life. Individuals designed to qualify themselves for the business of instruction will be conducted as far in these branches as they may desire. But we are willing to say that the character of the institution will be rather literary than scientific. In our judgment the most important of all acquisitions for a young lady, is a correct, unaffected and graceful use of her own language, both in conversation and composition. To this end the attention of our pupils will not be limited to grammatical and rhetorical rules. The accurate and precise use of words will be constantly inculcated; the standard authors in English literature will be critically read and analyzed; a library embracing the best models of style shall be always accessible, and frequent exercises in composition will be required.

"A due regard will be paid to the religious and social habits, the manners and general deportment of the pupils."[17]

Though the success of the movement for a public high school at Providence, Rhode Island, was long delayed (until 1838), there was an institution at least ten years earlier which was the result of private initiative. In 1828, John Kingsbury and G. A. Dewitt published their proposals for the Providence Young Ladies' High School.[18] The charges were $12 per quarter, or $20 for two from the same family. When the ordinance providing a public high school was passed (1838), it was specified that not more than one hundred, or half, of the pupils "shall be females, except when the number of males shall be less than one hundred: in which case, an additional number of females may be admitted, until the school shall be filled. . . . "[19]

At Middletown, Connecticut, a permanent high school, with departments for girls and boys, was established in 1840. This

[17] *Greenfield Gazette*, May 19, 1828, quoted in the *Am. Jour. Ed.*, III, 488-9.

[18] *American Journal of Education*, III, 427-9; also, in the *Cyclopedia of Education* [Ed. by Paul Monroe], consult article on Kingsbury.

[19] *Records of the Providence School Committee*, quoted by Grizzell: *op. cit.*, 257.

school was under the control of the City School Society of Middletown, which had been incorporated the previous year.   In 1838, a high school movement, sponsored by such men as Henry Barnard, Horace Bushnell, James A. Bunce, Amos Collins, and others, was begun at Hartford, and resulted finally in the opening of a high school in 1847.   It was established as "a free high school for instruction in the higher branches of an English, and the elementary branches of a classical education, for all the male and female children of a suitable age and acquirements in this Society who may wish to avail themselves of its advantages."[20] In the first year there were one hundred and thirty-seven female and one hundred and twenty-two male students.

On October 5, 1840, Alexander Dallas Bache submitted, to the Controllers of the Public Schools of Philadelphia, a plan for a *High School for Girls and of a Seminary for Female Teachers.*[21] Students were to be admitted at twelve years of age, after having passed a satisfactory examination.   They should remain in the high school four years, and at sixteen be ready for the teachers' seminary.   The Girls' High and Normal School, however, was not actually established until 1848.   It appears not to have been considered a high school but rather a normal school for girls. Siljeström, on his visit, described it as "a normal school for the training of female teachers. . . . "   Speaking of its importance, he exclaimed: "Yes, the High School for Girls!—that is what Philadelphia lacks, and must have before the city attains her highest eminence.   Educate the girls properly, and the world will soon see a better and nobler race of men."[22]

II. Purpose and Character of Girls' High Schools

From the very outset, it is evident that the high school was proposed as a public institution to extend the limits of girls' education.   It has been seen that the seminaries and other private schools paid great attention to accomplishments, and that there was a great deal of dissatisfaction with such a superficial education.[23]   Attempts were being made by leaders to reform

---

[20] *Quinquennial Catalogue*, 1910, quoted by Grizzell: *op. cit.*, 203.

[21] *Reports on Public Schools*, Philadelphia, Vol. II, 1831–1841, 38 pages; also *Conn. Com. School Jour.*, IV, 163–4.

[22] *Op. cit.*, 124–5; *Godey's Lady's Book*, July, 1853, 84–5.

[23] See pp. 441–56.

seminary education; and to lay more stress on 'solid' studies. Naturally the high school, newly created in this atmosphere of reform, fell in with this current of thought. It was easier to accomplish the reform in a new institution. In some cases seminaries and academies became high schools. That the reform movement was successful may be seen from a glance at the courses of the new high schools and the changing character of the curricula of the seminaries.

Worcester aimed to "provide an education for girls comparable to that provided for boys in the Latin Grammar School and the English School."[24] Boston lamented the fact that girls had "no provisions for their instruction in the higher departments of literature and science"; and the committee therefore voted, on May 10, 1825, that "a public school" be established to make such provision.[25] More specifically, the new school was to be created for the purpose of satisfying certain social needs. First, the general argument was put forth, though the committee was aware such an argument was unnecessary before "this board," that on account of the "weight of female influence in society, in every stage of moral and intellectual advancement," and the "abiding influence of mothers upon every successive generation of men . . . " the general expediency of giving women "such an education as shall make them fit wives for well educated men . . . " could not be doubted. In the second place, a higher institution would make more profitable the city institutions already created "for the public education of its daughters," by providing an outlet for those who excel in their studies but are forced to remain in lower schools " . . . two and sometimes three years, very inadequately and unprofitably employed." The "more sprightly girls . . . are in constant danger of falling into habits of inattention, and mental dissipation . . . [during the last] two or three . . . years . . . in the public schools." Third, the school would furnish teachers for the lower schools. Fourth, a valuable experiment could be made " . . . of the practicability and usefulness of monitorial or mutual instruction. . . . " Finally, in answer to any opposition that could be raised on account of expense, the committee urged it would not

24 Jones: *op. cit.*, 419.
25 *Am. Jour. of Education*, I, 96–105.

cost much (1) because of the "mutual instruction" plan and (2) because no new building would be needed the first year. But, whatever expense might be entailed, the social utility would outweigh the cost. For " . . . in regard to the expense at which the contemplated school is to be instituted and sustained, your committee think the same remark may be made of this, as of all our other public schools. When liberally supported they more than support themselves. They are a source not of honor only, but of pecuniary profit, to the city; for, taking into view—as an enlightened policy does take into view—the whole period during which these institutions exert their influence upon the community, they more than indemnify the city for the expense of their maintenance, in that the knowledge they diffuse through the great mass of the population, throws open new and wider fields to enterprise, gives higher aims to ingenuity, and supplies more profitable objects to industry."[26]

In an address delivered by John T. Irving, at the opening of the New York High School for Females, emphasis was placed on ". . . the great individual and public advantages, which will be derived from an attention to female education." Specifically, "how shall the girls struggle with the hardships and meet the vicissitudes of life, without an education? Every father is concerned by such a question, but . . . little attention has been hitherto paid to female education." Women must be educated for ". . . their domestic happiness and . . . usefulness . . ." and to be fit companions for their husbands, to "enliven" their prosperity, to be a solace in misfortune and advisers in their difficulties. Finally, women must be educated because of their great influence on society through their children and the home circle:

"These children who now repose on the bosom of maternal affection, are to be the future arbiters of the state. These are to form our magistrates, our legislators, our rulers. To their keeping are to be intrusted all the immunities we possess. If they are intelligent and virtuous, in their hands these immunities will be safe: if they are ignorant and base, by their instrumentality may those great blessings be jeopardized or lost. Let their minds therefore be taken hold of early and powerfully, let them be trained from childhood to the exercise of manly thought, and be imbued with the principles of a strict and unyielding integrity.

26 *Ibid.*

"In every point of light therefore, in which it can engage our attention, how important is the female character, how great its influence upon the well-being and the operations of man! Wherever an opportunity has been afforded to it of developing its capacities, it has shown itself worthy of all the culture it has received, and equal to what it has undertaken to perform; respectable in all those departments of literature in which it has been employed, unrivalled in those of taste, of fancy, and of feeling.

"Thus calculated both to adorn and to instruct, if we but improve the natural talents of our female children; if we but give to them a good education, we prepare them to become the ornaments of their families, a blessing to their children, and to rank deservedly among the useful and meritorious members of the community."[27]

More at length the speaker delineated what he believed should be the scope of girls' education:

"I would not wish to be understood as advocating their attention to any abstruse branches of science. Such knowledge is not necessary for them, nor would it be useful, and the prejudices against female learning may have arisen from its being in some cases improperly directed; but I do advocate their being made thoroughly acquainted with those branches of knowledge which will be particularly useful in all the various concerns of life. They should be made critically acquainted with their own language; and it would be well that they also receive instruction in other modern languages, and especially in the French, the use of which at present so generally prevails. They should be made acquainted with the world in which they live; its form, countries, beings, and properties. Their studies should be directed to practical arithmetic, to geography thoroughly, and to the principles of astronomy. All these branches of education are comprehended in the course of instruction which is prescribed for this Seminary; and it will be found upon examining this course, that those subjects of knowledge which are necessary for females in domestic economy, have not been sacrificed to those which are ornamental. Such a judicious selection has been made both of study and employment for the pupils as is suited to their sex, and will prepare them for presiding with skill and prudence in those domestic stations, for which Providence has designed them. This

[27] *Ibid.*, 271-8.

course of education will, as far as it is practicable, be pursued upon the monitorial system of instruction. The advantages of this system, in regard to elementary instruction, we have had sufficient time and opportunity to test fully during the last year, in our school for male children; and as some have expressed apprehensions, lest in so great a collection of female children, it might be difficult to preserve that order and neatness which their sex peculiarly requires, I would answer those apprehensions by referring those who entertain them to the public schools established for the education of poor female children in various parts of this city. I have never witnessed more discipline—neatness—propriety of conduct, and greater proficiency among pupils, than I have witnessed in those public schools. In fact, I would invite those who doubt, to visit those schools—it is the most powerful argument I can use; for I venture to say, that no one can visit them without feelings of the deepest emotion, and without being fully convinced of their great utility in all those elementary principles of education to which those schools are devoted.''[28]

That the purposes considered most important were those recognized by the school society may be seen by comparing the following statement with those preceding:

''. . . It would be a great mistake if we were to consider female education as calculated merely to render ladies useful and agreeable as companions in domestic life. That is undoubtedly one important object. But it has a higher and nobler purpose: the best and most durable lessons, and the most happy direction which the youthful mind receives, is from the mother. It is her task to inspire her sons with the earliest love of knowledge, to teach them the precepts of religion, the charities of life, the miseries of vice, and to lead them into the paths of a just and honourable ambition. Lessons flowing from such a source, enforced by the most pathetic exhortations and the highest example, are most likely to be tenaciously retained, and to survive if they do not entirely control the tumults of the passions and the conflicts of the world. In this view, therefore, as well as in many others, this female school is entitled to the most active and zealous patronage, by all well wishers to the honour and prosperity of our country.''[29]

[28] *Ibid.*
[29] *Ibid.*, III, 121–2.

Similar purposes were alluded to in other cities. The Providence High School's proprietors declared no attempt would be made to gain the approval of those who preferred "showy and superficial accomplishments"; rather they sought the support of those who "wish their daughters to acquire a thorough education."[30] At Bridgeport, in 1827, "the studies pursued [were] intended to embrace the various branches of English education necessary to prepare youth for the active pursuits of future life."[31] The Lowell High School prepared young men for college and carried forward ". . . the education of both sexes in the studies previously pursued in the grammar schools as well as in astronomy, practical mathematics, natural history, moral philosophy, bookkeeping, composition, and the evidences of Christianity."[32] Hartford's committee believed the English course embraced a ". . . sufficient variety of subjects to qualify the graduated student to occupy any place in society or business, with credit and success."[33] Bache's plan for a Girls' High School at Philadelphia, 1840, clearly aimed to prepare pupils for their pursuits in "after life," and also to furnish a basic training to which the special training of the seminary for teachers was to be added.[34]

This second purpose, mentioned by Bache, was generally recognized elsewhere. Herein is evident the close relationship of the seminary and the high school. Their purposes were substantially the same. The common schools needed teachers badly; therefore, seminaries did what they could as private agencies. To eke out their contribution, however, normal schools had eventually to be established. In the meantime, as high schools arose, it was urged they, too, would help increase the teacher supply. The Girls' High and Normal School of Philadelphia (1848) and the revival of the Boston Girls' High School in the Normal School (1852), which was in turn converted into a Girls' High School two years later, with a normal class provided in it, are cases which forcefully suggest the intimate connection of the girls'

[30] *Ibid.*, 427-9.
[31] *Ibid.*, 489.
[32] *Conn. Com. Sch. Jour.*, III, 156.
[33] *Outline of Studies* (1848?) at Hartford, quoted by Grizzell: *op. cit.*, 207.
[34] *Phila. School Reports*, 1831-1841, Vol. II.

high schools with teacher training. As the Boston committee argued at the time of its first experiment, "these schools are daily gaining the confidence of the community, and consequently are daily furnishing a greater and greater proportion of the children to our grammar schools. Of course, it is of continually increasing importance that these first schools should be taught by those who are themselves well educated. They are, and probably will be, taught exclusively by women; and it is doing no injustice to the city, or to the gentlemen who so faithfully superintend these schools, to say, that they are not always able to find women qualified as they ought to be, to take charge of these very interesting public institutions. A school like that now in contemplation, would certainly and permanently furnish teachers for the primary schools, competent in every respect to render the city efficient service; and especially in this respect; that they will have gained by their own experience a thorough knowledge of our whole system of public instruction, and the relations of its several parts to each other. Thus, the city will insure to itself a greater excellence and uniformity in the primary schools than is possible at present, and be always able to recur to its own resources, to meet its own wants;—exhibiting thus, in morals —what has been so long a desideratum in mechanics—a piece of machinery that, by its own operation, produces the power by which itself is driven."[35]

A similar purpose was explicitly stated in Salem. As early as 1827 schools for girls had been called "high schools,"[36] and again in 1836; but it was not until 1845 that the creation of a genuine girls' high school was undertaken. Early in that year, Mr. Oliver "gave notice" he would soon recommend the same. In general, the plan was to put the newly proposed school under a male principal and "connect with it a primary school under a female teacher, in which the scholars of the higher class in the new school should, by turns, be employed as assistants,—thus enabling them to become somewhat versed in the art of teaching,—it being intended that the assistant teachers of the grammar school, and the teachers of the primary schools should be taken from this quasi-city Normal School."[37] Shortly there-

35 *Am. Jour. Ed.*, I, 96–105.

36 Felt: *Annals of Salem;* also Grizzell: *op. cit.,* 69 *f.*

37 *Com. Sch. Journal*, VII, 267–8.

after, Mr. Oliver committed the project to the standing committee for consideration, and on June 30, 1845, it was voted "expedient to establish a High School for Girls. . . ."[38]

From the foregoing, it appears that the high school's aims were: first, an extension of the range of girls' education, supported by the public; second, increased social usefulness on the part of women; third, specific preparation for teaching in the lower schools. Eventually, preparation for college, which had been long an objective in boys' high schools, became legitimate for the girls' institutions also. But for some time they remained, like the academies and seminaries, the "finishing schools" for girls.

One of the greatest obstacles in the way of a new institution, supported by the public, was the expense which would have to be borne by taxpayers. Consequently the monitorial system was often adopted as the best means to an end. Some masters, to be sure, became so enthusiastic about "mutual instruction" that it was declared, in the case of the Boston school, that, regardless of economy, the system was to be preferred.

"Upon the whole, if the monitorial system possesses some defects,—and what system is perfect in every respect?—they are more than counter-balanced by its commanding and salutary influence upon character, in a moral and intellectual point of view,—by its tendency to inspire decision and energy and thought, and to promote habits of industry, a cheerful spirit, and a correct deportment. Here its advantages are great and peculiar. In bearing this testimony in favor of monitorial instruction,—against which I formerly felt some prejudices, in spite of myself, although I theoretically understood, as I thought, its various advantages and defects,—I make no account of the common argument of economy. The system of education is to be preferred which is best, not that which is cheapest. Neither am I influenced by motives of personal ease; for my cares, confinement, and labors, are vastly greater than they have ever been in any other school. Independently of all such considerations, I estimate the new method with reference to its merits alone,— its practical influence upon mind, manners and character. If it did not enable a master to teach a single additional scholar,

[38] *Ibid.*

I should still regard it as a great and invaluable improvement in conducting the business of education."[39]

It was proposed, at this time, not only to introduce mutual instruction into the high school but into the whole Boston system. The committee, however, were of the opinion, highly as they valued the system, that "so important a change" should not be made so suddenly and "to the extent proposed." The new system "ought, perhaps, to be more thoroughly tested before being universally adopted."[40]

The generous praise given the system, its adoption in so many schools of the United States,[41] and the fact that it was one of the chief agencies that made possible the establishment of high schools,—all these warrant a complete view of its operation in practice. The following description concerns the monitorial plan as it was employed in the Girls' High School of Boston.

"The government of the school is vested in a set of books, in which is recorded an accurate and minute account of every scholar's performances, deportment, absence, and tardiness; and at the end of each quarter, she is advanced to a higher, or degraded to a lower, section or seat, as this record shall appear in her favor or against her. The whole business is regulated by fixed principles, that are well understood; and every individual is, literally speaking, the artificer of her own rank, which is affected by every exercise she performs, and by every error she commits, either in recitation or conduct. Everything depends upon numerical calculation; and, were it expedient, the school might be classed by the scholars themselves.

"A Credit is given to every member of the school, for each regular recitation which is performed in a correct and satisfactory manner.

"A Check is given to such as fail in their lessons. Thus, in every recitation, each pupil receives either a check or a credit.

[39] *Am. Journal of Education*, II, 185–7.

[40] *Ibid.*, I, 96–105.

[41] New York and Indiana are perhaps as good examples of the wide-spread use of the monitorial system as can be named. It became a dominant factor in elementary schools, academies, and high schools until about 1840; and, though it began to lose caste, and many objected to its mechanical character, it continued in many places for more than a generation thereafter. Many elements of school management today may be traced back to this system.

"Merits are awarded for correct and orderly deportment, for excellence in the usual exercises of school, and for voluntary labors.

"The marks which indicate violations of order and improper conduct, for the want of a better name, are called Misdemeanors. For the more common instances of misconduct, only one is given; but for higher offences, such as disrespect to a teacher or monitor, the number would be graduated by the circumstances of the case.

"Forfeits are incurred by neglecting to attend to required exercises, at the proper time, and in a proper manner, by making appeals without sufficient grounds, and by slight irregularities of conduct.

"In making the quarterly records of the school, by which the rank of the scholars is determined, every check cancels one credit, or two merits, and every misdemeanor, five merits. These principles were discussed and settled by a large committee of the scholars themselves. The forfeits are not entered upon the records, but kept on the bills until they are redeemed by an equal number of merits.

"Various classes of agents are employed in the government, instruction, and general administration of the affairs of the school, to each of which are assigned specific duties.

"The Head Monitor holds the highest and most responsible situation. She has the general superintendence of the school, and in the absence of the Principal, she supplies his place. The Monitor of Attendance, and the Monitor of Dictation, in addition to their own proper duties, act as assistants to the head monitor. Their authority extends over the whole school, and they are selected to fill their respective places, as marks of distinguished and general merit. They occupy an elevated desk, which commands a view of the other scholars.

"The Monitors of Sections, as such, are not employed in the instruction of the school; but their duties are nevertheless important. Each one has the superintendence of the section next below her; in which if she observe any disorder, it is her duty to report it to the head monitor without delay. I would here remark, that spies and informers, receive no encouragement in the school. All complaints to be regarded, must be made in official form, and by those whose duty it is to make them. These monitors also keep class bills of their respective sections, in which they record the results of their recitations, and report them to the head monitor weekly, to be entered in her Journal. In selecting the monitors of sections and their Assistants, who perform the duties of the monitors, in their absence, I pay no regard to scholarship, unless it is connected with ingenuousness, and observance of order, and an amiable and lady-like deportment; as a reward for which high qualifications, if I should not rather say cardinal virtues, these appointments are exclusively reserved.

"The Examiners pass through their respective sections, every morning to attend to such voluntary exercises as may be offered; and, under certain limitations, to award the merits they deserve. They keep the bills of merits and forfeits, as do the monitors, those of credits and checks; and, like them, they make weekly reports to the head monitor.

"In selecting the Teachers, particular attention is paid to their attainments in the several branches, in which they are to give instruction, and their aptness for the business. In those studies, however, which require little more in the teacher, than to hear a recitation, the reverse of this rule is sometimes adopted, by a selection of such as will be the most benefited by reviewing what they have already learned. No teacher, ordinarily, hears the same section in two branches; and no one is required to hear another class while her own is reciting. The scholars are encouraged to detect the errors of their teachers and of each other; this secures their undivided attention to the exercise before them, makes the teacher careful in the discharge of her duty, and brings to her assistance all the knowledge of her pupils. An account of the recitation is entered on a slate provided for the purpose, and read to the class, that the errors, if any, may be corrected at the time. It is then transferred to the bill of the proper monitor. The teachers are held responsible for the order of their respective classes, from the time they leave their seats till they return to them again.

"The Messengers are the highest scholars in their several sections. Through them are made all communications to and from the Principal, while their classes are reciting; and by their agency much disorder and delay are prevented. To illustrate the nature of their duties, suppose a scholar does not give a prompt and satisfactory answer to a question proposed; her teacher says 'check!' Should she think the question not an important one, or that her answer was sufficiently accurate,—as they are encouraged in the use of their own words, instead of those of their books,—her reply is 'appeal!' The messenger then brings the case before the instructor for his consideration, stating all the circumstances, except the name of the individual. This is done in writing, when it can be with convenience. The check is continued or removed, according to the decision given.

"As there is but one instructor, it seemed necessary that provision should be made for the school to go on without his being present. So far as order is concerned, this has been effectually done, by vesting the government in books of record; and the past head monitors, are constituted a Board of Appeal, whenever the master is detained from school, by sickness or any other casualty.

"The only penalty for absence, is, that scholars obtain neither credit nor merit marks; and for the plain reason, that they do nothing to earn them. Excuses for absence are not now required; and yet the attendance is highly gratifying, even in the most inclement weather.

"From this account,—too brief I fear to be distinct, although much longer than was contemplated,—the operations of the school may appear complicated and confused. But nothing could be farther from the truth. All understand their duties, because they are precisely defined; and the parts are so adjusted, that there is no jarring, or crossing each other.

"It may be supposed, too, that the business of the records must be cumbrous and unwieldy, and occupy a large share of the time both of the master and many of the scholars; and yet a stranger might spend days in the room and know nothing of the matter, unless it were pointed out to him. The work is so distributed and arranged, that no one has much to do, in this department, except the head monitor, who requires an hour, perhaps, on Saturday to make up her journal for the week. The system is so compact, that a single quire of paper will serve as a waste-book for the whole school, in which all the facts are entered in detail, for almost three years; and in the permanent record, which is kept by the master, four lines give the whole history of a scholar's progress, even to the minutest facts, for a year.

"It may be asked, what security we have that these various agents perform their respective duties, with fidelity and impartiality? It might be sufficient to answer, the same security which we have that any person will perform his duty, in any situation; for I am yet to learn that the young, with their glowing and generous feelings, are less ingenuous, less liable to be governed by sentiments of justice and principles of integrity, and less tenderly alive to all the sweet influences of truth and honor and honesty, than they whose judgments may be more mature, but who have been longer hackneyed in the crooked ways of the world. Let the moral sense be properly cultivated,—let scholars learn to respect themselves, by seeing that they are respected by others,—let a prudent and generous confidence reposed in their integrity, prompt them to an exact and faithful discharge of their duties, and there is little to be apprehended on the side of injustice, or from the abuse of power.

"But all the means, which circumstances allow, are used to prevent even 'the appearance of evil.' Every award, either of merit or censure, must be made openly, and in the presence of all interested, that if any error is committed, or injustice done, it may be at once corrected. An appeal from the decision of a monitor or teacher, may at all times be made to the Principal, for which a uniform and easy course is prescribed. Indeed, appeals have been made to the desk, and not infrequently with success, against decisions of the master himself when acting in the capacity of a monitor or teacher. In a word, such is the system of checks established, to detect all violations of the rules of the school and to secure equity and good order, that no individual can suffer injustice to be done to herself, or partiality to be shown to another, but through her own negligence or fault.

"To be sure that the teachers do their duty faithfully, I regularly review the scholars in all their studies. The books of the school are divided into proper and convenient stages; and a section cannot go forward to a new stage, before they have passed a thorough and critical examination in the last. In this way, I eventually attend to all the studies of the school in person. The salutary influence of these reviews, both upon the teachers and their pupils, will be readily conceived. The pupils, on their part, are anxious to go on fast, that the slower sections may not pass by them; and the teachers are as anxious that they should go on well, that they may not incur the mortification which must result from an unsatisfactory review."

The opposite page gives a "Plan of the Record Book."

PLAN OF THE RECORD BOOK

Names.	Quarters.	Absent	Tardy	Misdemeanors	Checks	Credits	Merits	Sections	Seats	Remarks
A. B.	January. April. July. October.									
C. D.	January. April. July. October.									
E. F.[42]	January. April.									

[42] The names are arranged in alphabetical order. The matter for the Record is furnished by the Journals of the head monitor and the monitor of attendance.—*Am. Jour. Ed.*, II, 206–10.

In New York the monitorial system was already well known by reason of its successful employment in the schools of the New York Free School Society, and it had great vogue throughout the state by reason of the enthusiastic praise of DeWitt Clinton. Griscom had visited the High School under Dr. Pillans at Edinburgh, and was greatly impressed by the fact that the monitorial plan could be used in higher as well as lower schools. Accordingly, the monitorial system was cautiously tried out in New York, both in the boys' and girls' schools. A year after the opening of the girls' school, it was stated that "the monitorial system, with all the improvements which its trial in the boys' school has suggested, is carried into practice in this new institution, with a success commensurate with the highest expectations of the trustees."[43]

It was openly recognized in some places, and quietly, no doubt, in the rest, that high schools for girls—the earliest ones, at least—were experimental. Of Boston it was said: ". . . This institution is an experiment, and it cannot be fairly tested without patient and laborious exertions. A free school for the instruction of females, founded on principles so liberal, is in itself a novelty; but such a novelty argues well for the spirit and improvement of the age, and of the community wherein it is fostered."[44] Moreover, it was an experiment to test the utility of the monitorial plan, which "might be introduced into all our public schools, to the benefit of the schools, and to the pecuniary advantage of the city. . .".[45] As in many first experiments, there were numerous failures. But failure itself was sometimes, as in Boston, an evidence of the success and popularity of the school. The New York institution, likewise, was popular and well filled. Its discontinuance, in 1831, was doubtless due in part to some organized opposition and administrative problems, partially connected with the application of the Lancasterian system to the work of the High School.[46]

In admitting girls to the High School, the Boston committee specified they should be between eleven and fifteen, but that some

[43] *Ibid.*, II, 59–60.

[44] *Ibid.*, I, 380–1.

[45] *Ibid.*, 96 *ff.*

[46] Griscom: *Memoirs of John Griscom*, 209 *ff.*; see also Gifford: *Hist. Development of the New York State High School System*, 23.

"allowance . . . be made [in particular cases] according to the discretion of the school committee. . .".[47] Among those actually admitted, however, it was found there were 37 between 11 and 12 years of age, 69 between 12 and 13, 72 between 13 and 14, 94 between 14 and 15, and 14 who had recently passed the fifteenth birthday.[48] Bache specified in his plan that candidates for entrance should be twelve years of age,[49] and this appears to have been generally the minimum age. Naturally ages of pupils covered a wide range, for the irregular and sometimes ineffective lower schools could not carry the youngster far (Bache would require the entrant to have had "at least six months in regular attendance upon one of the public schools."), and the fact that normal training was often connected with the high school naturally drew more mature students.[50]

Besides the variable, and sometimes non-existent, age requirements, admission depended in some places on examinations. Standards in examinations varied. Boston directed that they be based on the work of the "public grammar schools of the city and . . . be strict or otherwise, as the number of candidates shall hold relation to the accommodations provided for them. . . ."[51] After the examination, it was stated that it covered "reading, English Grammar, geography, arithmetic, and writing; and in all these . . . was critical and thorough." Only 135 (some authorities say 130) were admitted, though 286 had applied.[52] At New York, 374 were in the introductory, junior and senior departments combined, at the end of the first year. Bache's plan also included the examination of the twelve-year old applicants in reading, writing, spelling, arithmetic—to the rule of three, inclusive—grammar, and geography. An examination was to be given each half year.[53] Other schools might be mentioned where examinations were the rule.[54]

An interesting estimate of the significance of the American girls' high schools is found in the work of Siljeström, who visited the United States during the middle of the past century:

[47] *American Journal of Education*, I, 96 ff.
[48] *Ibid.*, 380–1.
[49] *Conn. Com. Sch. Jour.*, III, 163 f.
[50] Compare Grizzell: *op. cit.*, 355.
[51] *American Journal of Education*, I, 96 ff.
[52] *Ibid.*, 380–1.
[53] *Conn. Com. Sch. Jour.*, III, 163–4.
[54] Grizzell: *op. cit.*, 190, 80 f., etc.

"I will here, however, seize the opporunity of drawing the attention of the reader to the great importance and significance of such high schools for girls as are daily becoming more numerous in America. The objections which were at first raised, by class-prejudice in particular, against the establishment of public schools for girls, have been confuted by actual experience in the schools established, and it is, therefore, to be expected that the number of these establishments will rapidly increase. The course of instruction imparted in these schools, as well as in a great many of the academies which will be mentioned hereafter is, in every respect, the same as the course in the boys' schools. In addition to a very extensive knowledge, practical as well as theoretical, of the English language, and of the subjects included under the name of humanities, an acquaintance with elementary geometry, one or two degrees of algebra, the natural sciences, the Latin, and sometimes the Greek, language constitute the more substantial accomplishments which form part of the higher education of women in America.

"The comparatively high degree of culture which women of all classes in America possess, as also the influence which, in consequence, they exercise in their families and in society, cannot but strike European travellers. The more developed the life of a community is, the greater is the influence and significance of woman; and the position which woman holds in America is at one and the same time a standard by which to measure the high degree of culture attained by the American nation, and one of the best guarantees of its stability and of its future development."[55]

While he attached great significance to the schools for girls, he found that provisions were much more liberal for boys. It is noted that although Boston had two high schools for boys, there was but one for girls; and the same was true of New York. Hartford, however, had placed girls' education upon an equal footing with boys'. As he says, "The school in Hartford, which is in common for both sexes, forms an exception to this rule. This last-mentioned school presents the strange spectacle (strange, as regards our habits and ideas) of girls and boys of the ages of 15 and 16, assembled in a common school-room under the guidance of female as well as male teachers. Girls and boys enter by

[55] Siljeström: *Education in the United States,* 308-9.

separate doors from the street, have separate entrance rooms, &c., and are placed on separate sides of the large school-room; otherwise they are upon quite an equal footing, and in the recitation rooms you may see classes composed of both sexes. There can be no doubt but that this system of allowing boys and girls to receive their education in common, must tend to refine the manners and morals of the school, while at the same time it must exercise a great influence on the position of women, not only as regards education, but also afterwards in society.''[56]

From one of the teachers we get another view of the Hartford institution in 1854. She makes it clear that there were some classes of boys. Her experience with them and her feelings regarding the "Fathers of the School" may doubtless stand as typical of those of many a "school ma'am."

". . . Don't wonder if my similes smack of battle, for I have a class of loyal boys who wax enthusiastic every day over Yankee prowess and British pusillanimity, as displayed in our impartial American histories. I have studied about wars and rumors of wars, till I have become quite pugilistic myself. Did you ever teach boys? I cannot tell you how strange it seemed to me at first. Great burly fellows; they poured into the recitation room the first day, coming down upon me like a seventy-four gun ship till I almost gasped for breath. They frightened me out of my senses. I walked about in a dream the first week. They seemed so like men. Every time one of them rose to answer me, it seemed to me as if he was going to make a speech. For a little while I thought I had mistaken my calling and looked forward to Thanksgiving with inexpressible longings, but I am now fain to say that these boys have diminished very perceptibly in size and numbers and, taken together, are really a very gentlemanly set, though I find them in their classes much more restless than girls, or perhaps it is because when they do move they make more noise about it than girls. The high school house is a fine large three-story brick building, classical department on the first floor, general assembly room on the second, gymnasium on the third, laboratory, dressing-rooms, etc., in the basement. Everything is entirely different from any private school I was ever in, though I cannot tell the reason why. There seems to be much more machinery. There are five teachers, three gentlemen, one lady,

[56] *Ibid.*, 302 *f.*

and Abby Dodge, all excellent in their way. Did you know that
the teachers have to be examined? What an idea! They thought
they were going to examine me, but they didn't. I told Mr.
Curtis in Boston that I would not be examined. I repeated it in
Hartford with an emphasis. He called with the other teacher
at my boarding-house, was to take us both to the 'Fathers of the
School' to be tested, analyzed, twenty-five per cent., Arithmetic,
fifteen ditto Geography, etc., bottled up, labelled and prepared
for use. I protested. He spent half an hour in reasoning and
entreating. I was convinced by his argument and moved by his
eloquence, but at the end of all remained in *statu quo ante bellum*
and parried all his shafts with the clear simple forcible English
declaration, 'I won't go.' So I didn't go, so he went without
me, so the committee did not have the pleasure of dissecting me,
so it is laid down as a law for all future teachers, that if they
prefer to be examined by their classes, or in their classes, they
can. How grateful ought all my successors to be to me! Do
you think I did wrong? I did not parry or evade anything. I
told him I was willing to suffer the penalty of the law, to go
home the first morning, or I could be hung if indispensable, but
that one solitary thing I could not, should not, and would not do.
I was quite willing they should come in and hear my recitations
every hour in the day, for every day in the week. Anyway, I
have not yet repented, and would do just so again.'[57]

III. *Organization and Studies of Girls' High Schools*

We have already noted[58] that an effort was being made, from
the twenties onward, to organize and grade the work of the seminaries. The tendency was to recognize a four, three, or at least
a two years' course. In the high schools of the same period,
the length of the English course was frequently three years; the
classical, four; and a normal training course connected with high
schools generally occupied one or two years. In the first school
at Worcester there was no grading, though by 1831 three classes
were recognized.[59] At Boston, in 1826, the course was three
years; and Worcester's "English Department," in 1845, gave a
three-year course. Hartford's English course, in 1848, required

---

[57] Hamilton: Letters, I, 73–5.
[58] Chapter VIII, 343; and IX, 444 *f.* and 455 *f.*
[59] Grizzell: *op. cit.*, 296.

four years and, ten years later, five years.[60] At New York, in 1826–27, there were three departments,—introductory, junior and senior;[61] while Bache's plan for the school at Philadelphia (1840) contemplated four years in the high school (12–16 years of age) preparatory to entering the normal school.[62] Later, courses were usually four years in length.

Just as there was a range in organization from none at Worcester, 1824, to the strictly outlined three, four and five-year courses at Boston, Philadelphia, Hartford and elsewhere, so there was a considerable variation in the studies at different schools, especially between those of the earlier and those of the later institutions. The similarity, however, between high school and seminary courses may be readily seen. Siljeström was apparently impressed by the Hartford provision that girls might omit "etymology, the geography and history of the United States, natural philosophy, chemistry, and philosophy" and substitute for them the study of Latin. He felt the tendency of American girls' education was away from the practical, and that this was a great defect. It was, indeed, contrary to one of the original purposes of the high school. He urged that education of girls, as well as boys, be of "serious and substantial character," preferring the sciences, geometry, and geometrical drawing to the great emphasis on algebra and arithmetic. He was, certainly, unable to know the work of all the high schools intimately, but he did sense a growing tendency in favor of formal studies.[63]

As the public high school developed, there was a definite tendency to favor the four-year course. Sometimes, studies were designated as belonging to scientific, classical, and the "girls' department." In the West, however, the tendency was to favor coeducation and the same course for both sexes. Such studies as reading, writing, spelling, mental arithmetic, written arithmetic, English grammar, geography, and history of the United States were often mentioned as requirements for admission; but a review of them frequently came in the high school work. A detailed comparison of the studies has shown the similarity between high school studies and those of the female

60 *Ibid.*, 302–13.

61 *American Journal of Education*, II, 59–60.

62 *Philadelphia School Reports*, 1831–1841, Vol. II.

63 Siljeström: *op. cit.*, 308–9.

seminaries at the same dates.[64]   It is to be noted that elementary English studies tended to drop out, whereas in the seminaries they had been important.   This shifting was doubtless largely due to better and more general preparation in elementary schools. So also with arithmetic and geography, which had been favorites of the female seminary.

Sciences, being on the increase in popularity, naturally bulked prominently in this new school of the people, as they had in the earlier pioneer institution, the seminary.   Much less emphasis was laid on religion, ethics and philosophy.   History, civics or political economy were always represented under one name or another.

Languages do not appear to have taken as prominent a place in the high schools as they occupied in the seminaries, though Latin was almost always offered, even if not required.   Sometimes French, German, and Greek were offered, even in the general course, which made the high school course look like that of the female seminary.

Perhaps the greatest contrast between high school and seminary courses was in their range of subjects.   The former narrowed down gradually, as a general rule, to rhetoric, composition, a language or two, algebra, geometry, ancient and modern history, physics, chemistry, botany, and zoölogy, and perhaps a little drawing or music for aesthetic culture.   In the seminary, however, a young lady could study almost any subject she elected and for which she was willing to pay.   The high schools, as a rule, used the same textbooks as the seminaries, to about 1870.

IV.   Progress of High Schools for Girls

The development of the public high school in the United States was slow before the Civil War.   To 1850, the states were chiefly concerned with establishing state-supported elementary schools. H. H. Barney, in his *Report on the American System of Graded Free Schools,* a report made and printed by order of the school board of Cincinnati, 1851, declared that only eighty cities had such schools.   Harris said, ten years later (1860), that there were but forty high schools in the whole country.[65]   Many more

[64] From tables prepared by, and in possession of, the author; studies of a few high schools are indicated in Appendix III, 566 *ff.*

[65] Recent Growth of Public High Schools [*Proceedings of the N. E. A.,* 1901, 174–80].

were reported, certainly; but these were only called high schools, while in reality they were elementary in character. Many states counted more high schools within their borders than there were genuine institutions of that grade in the whole country. In early reports of the Commissioner of Education, a great many high schools reported the dates of organization of their forerunners as the date of their own beginning. Certainly, numerous institutions in the South, indicated as high schools in 1880, were academies, seminaries or institutes at the dates given for their organization. Such faulty tables, used uncritically, led to assertions which were far from true, concerning the number of high schools in early decades of the high school movement.

Between 1850 and 1860, and especially after 1865, the number of high schools increased, so that at the end of the decade (1870) there were at least 160. In 1880 there were nearly 800; in 1890 there were 2,526; and, in 1900, 6,005.[66] By 1910, there were 10,213, and in 1920, 14,326 public high schools.[67] Since 1890 the population of the United States has nearly doubled. In that time attendance of girls and boys at high school has been multiplied approximately by ten.

While the public secondary school has thus been gaining in popularity, the private agencies have been decreasing in proportion. In 1880, of the 1264 secondary institutions which reported to the Commissioner's office only 82 were called high schools.[68] These figures were most incomplete both for high schools and academies, but undoubtedly the public high school was still far short of the numerical level reached by the private institutions. The relation of private to public secondary institutions is shown in the table following:[69]

TABLE I

	1890	1900	1910	1920
Private High Schools and Academies	1,632	1,978	1,781	2,093
Public High Schools	2,526	6,005	10,213	14,326

The rôle played by the secondary school in girls' education may be seen by comparing the enrollment and graduation of

66 *Ibid.*
67 *Biennial Survey of Education,* 1918–1920, Bulletin 1923, No. 29, 497.
68 *R. C. E.,* 1880, Table VI, 523–68.
69 *Biennial Survey,* 1918–1920, 497 and 537.

girls and boys during the most recent period for which figures
are available.

TABLE II

Private High Schools and Academies:	1890	1900	1910	1920
Boys	47,534	55,734	55,474	84,222
Girls	47,397	55,063	61,926	99,931
Boys Graduating		6,226	6,876	10,590
Girls Graduating		5,990	7,533	13,576
Public High Schools:				
Boys	85,451	216,207	398,525	822,967
Girls	116,351	303,044	516,536	1,034,188
Boys Graduating	7,692	22,575	43,657	90,516
Girls Graduating	14,190	39,162	67,706	140,386

Since 1900, the number of girls in private schools has been
rising above that of boys, while in public high schools girls have
been the predominant factor throughout the period. Thus the
past century has witnessed the transition from the private seminary (the first institution to attempt more than elementary
education for girls), and the first public high schools for girls
(which were of very short duration, due in one case at least to
great popularity), to the modern public high school, attended
more often by girls than boys. Public high schools are mainly
coeducational. The *Biennial Survey*[70] indicated (1918–20) but
39 public high schools for boys only, and the same number for
girls. Of the private secondary schools in 1920, 980 were coeducational, 728 for girls and 385 for boys.

V. Problems of the Girls' High School

With the remarkable growth in the number of high schools,
and the increasing proportion of girls attending them, there
have developed many special problems. Back of these problems
of the schools there were, of course, the changing factors in
social and economic life, which have thrown many burdens on
a public institution which were previously borne by the family.
A detailed discussion of these problems of the present day is,
manifestly, inappropriate here. A satisfactory treatment of
any one of them would require a volume of considerable extent.

The attention of those engaged in secondary school teaching
and management has, during the past thirty years, increasingly

[70] *Ibid.*

been turned upon special problems attendant on the presence of girls in high schools. Within the past fifteen years there has resulted a definite realization that a special officer should be designated to handle such problems. When high schools were small, and the home performed religious, moral, social and economic functions which to-day it fails to do, the high school principal and teachers gave all the advice—moral, vocational, and so on—that was needed. Personal contact with teachers was the rule rather than the exception. Now, with numbers mounting to hundreds, and tens of hundreds, and the tendency to emphasize departmentalization and specialization, the principal is, generally, no longer the personal adviser to those who may wish to come; and teachers, likewise, with a heavy burden of instructional duty, are incapable and sometimes unfitted for the task. Consequently, new shoulders are sought on which to place these responsibilities. "Advisers" and "deans" are the result.

Literature on the "dean of girls," "adviser," "vice-principal," or other officers designated for assisting girl students,[71] is largely a product of the past fifteen years. J. W. Raymer reported (1912) on "advisory systems" in 198 schools throughout the country.[72] Susan M. Dorsey's address on the work of advisers was published the next year;[73] and in 1916, G. W. Gaylor wrote regarding the dean of girls at Canton, Illinois.[74] Since then, the subject has taken up a great many pages in various periodicals and has received more extended attention in books as well.[75] The appearance of the dean of girls may, from one point of view, no doubt, be regarded as an extension downward of the practice of colleges; but it was a genuine need, not a mere desire for imitation, that led to such a development. Mathews' *The Dean of Women* was doubtless suggestive to such officers, regardless of their location in colleges or high schools. A national organization of deans of women was effected and a first meeting was held in 1914, but not until 1918 was much attention given to high school questions. The growth of the

[71] "Dean of girls" seems to be generally preferred.—See the studies of Miss Stevens and Miss Barker, and the *Report of the Committee of Fifteen* of the California High School Teachers' Association.

[72] *Educational Review*, 1912, 466.

[73] *N. E. A. Proc.*, 1913, LI, 495.

[74] *Educational Administration and Supervision*, III, 1917, 496.

[75] Belting: *The Community and Its High School*, Ch. IV.

importance of deans of girls in high schools is indicated by the
fact that, in 1923, a section devoted to their problems was
recognized in the national organization.[76]   No one knows how
many high schools to-day have deans, advisers, or similar officers,
to look out for girls' welfare; but the number has doubtless
increased manifold since Stevens (1917) found 365, out of 3,658
returns to a questionnaire, which reported such an official.[77]

Since this position of dean has become of such importance as
to occupy a considerable place in educational literature, it is
worth while to note the causes assigned for its creation, and the
benefits the occupant is supposed to confer.   Among the causes
assigned are: first, the large high school; second, the increasing
complexity of the high school, socially and intellectually; third,
the feeling on the part of some, at least, that the high school
should develop social manners; fourth, the conviction that girls
should have someone to whom they can look for physical, intellectual, moral and vocational guidance;[78] and fifth, a vague sense,
doubtless definite enough on the part of some, that the whole of
secondary education needs focusing, reorganization, adjustment,
and so forth—like a camera, which is useless unless properly
adjusted and expertly operated.   The adviser of girls is only one
of the means proposed to make the institution more effective.

Interestingly enough, the new position and its occupant have
added new questions and problems to the list they were to solve.
There is great variety of opinion as to what a dean should be,
do, or attempt to do.   Should she be a college graduate, a Master,
a Doctor?   What qualities must she possess?   How old should
she be?   What should she be called; and how much paid?
Should she teach regular classes; and how many?

Taking the last question first, we find almost no agreement.
California's Committee of Fifteen found advisers' teaching a
variable quantity: 15.4 per cent. taught from one to ten hours
a week; 37.2 per cent., eleven to twenty-five; and 29.5 per cent.
were teaching the same hours as other teachers.[79]   Fretwell was

[76] See *Proc. of the N. E. A.*, 1923, 623.

[77] *T. C. Record*, September, 1919, 301–23.

[78] See, for example, the *N. E. A. Proc.*, 1913, 495; *Educational Administration and Supervision* (1917), III, 496 *f.*; and *Journal of Education*, April
17, 1913, 436.

[79] *Report of Committee of Fifteen*, California High School Teachers Association, 1923, 200.

of the opinion that ". . . at the present advisers of girls are devoting the major part of their time to the work for which such a position exists."[80] Stevens found the variation to be from three to thirty hours per week, and Barker's questionnaire showed that 73 per cent. were teaching one or more classes per day.[81]

Investigations made thus far indicate that the majority of deans have a Bachelor's degree, some the Master's, a few the Doctorate, and some no degree at all. Stevens found the median age to be 41 years and the range from 25 to 70. In California, 41.4 per cent. were between 31 and 40. The title of "dean" is apparently most favored. The salaries of deans vary greatly. Barker found them ranging from $1,200 to $4,500, the median being $2,241. In California the range was between $1,500 and $3,600, with a median of approximately $2,400. The tendency has been to employ women who have had many years of experience as teachers.

That most deans possess some academic degree has been noted. But their job being highly specialized, it has been thought that a bag of academic units, sufficient to get a degree of one denomination or another, is not enough. Consequently, some special courses for deans and advisers of women and girls have been offered by leading institutions for several years past. In 1926, Teachers College offered twelve courses specially designed for advisers, leading to the diploma of "Adviser of Women and Girls." The chief elements in the work outlined were educational guidance of women, psychology, history of the family, and the education of women.[82]

In addition to teaching, the California Report states that advisers are concerned with girls' activities, conduct, attendance, health, program-making, scholarship, student council, registration, vocational guidance, and related subjects. Their work is concerned with innumerable detailed problems relating to the physical, social, mental, moral, religious, and economic welfare of the individual student.

A unique individual is undeniably needed to perform such wonders. California high school principals voted the following

[80] *Ed. Administration & Supervision*, X, 72.
[81] *Op. cit.*
[82] Teachers College *Catalog*, 1926–27, 102–4.

attributes necessary for a dean: sympathy and understanding, 90.7 per cent. (i.e., 90.7 per cent. of the principals indicated this as a determiner in selecting advisers); tact, 85.6 per cent.; fine womanhood, 83.5 per cent.; attractive personality, 79.4 per cent.; appearance, 67.0 per cent.; social experience, 65.0 per cent.; age, 55.6 per cent.; and special training, 12.4 per cent. The adviser must be philosopher, guide and friend. Again we are told, "In spirit she is expected to be as bright and buoyant as the sunshine, but in substance as old and stable as the hills."[83] Solomon, without a doubt, expressed the virtues of this rare person more succinctly than the high school principals, though their judgments correlate well with his:

> "Strength and dignity are her clothing;
> "And she laugheth at the time to come.
> "She openeth her mouth with wisdom;
> "And the law of kindness is on her tongue."

In the summer of 1924, a conference of deans of girls at New York University passed the following resolution:

"Since the modern high school is not a school for any selected class of students but enrolls in constantly increasing numbers girls and boys of all social and economic classes and of widely differing degrees of mentality; and,

"Since the high schools of America should be so socialized as to prepare students for citizenship in a democracy and for useful and happy lives as individuals; and,

"Since many high schools of the country have, with benefit to the students and to the community, officially recognized the position of the dean of girls,

"We, therefore, record it as our conviction:

"1. That every high school in which there are girls should establish the position of dean of girls, and should give this dean sufficient time-allowance for her responsibility as dean so that she may have a chance to make her work effective; and,

"2. That the aim of a dean of girls in a secondary school should be threefold:

"a. To be a friend to every girl. To be so thoroughly genuine, sincere and human that every girl will feel free to confide in her.

[83] *Educational Review* (1924), LXVII, 42—an editorial.

"b. To supervise the social life. As a group leader she may develop among the girls a social life which considers the happiness of others rather than mere personal pleasure.

"c. To develop character. To develop through responsibility in school affairs the character of every girl and the qualities of initiative and leadership in many which will make their lives of value to the community."[84]

It is, of course, impossible to judge how fully a mere human being can perform the manifold and high duties mapped out for these foster mothers of the high school girl.   It is, however, worth while to record that most of the principals in California schools voted that advisers were either excellent, essential, good, helpful or satisfactory.   Only 6.3 per cent. felt their service was doubtful, and 3.1 per cent. judged it valueless.

[84] *Sch. and Soc.*, August 23, 1924, 241-2.

APPENDICES

I

TEXTBOOKS MENTIONED IN ACADEMY AND SEMINARY CATALOGS
(1780–1870)

Algebra

Bailey: Algebra
Colburn: Algebra
Colburn and Smyth: Algebra
Davies: Algebra
Davies' Bourdon: Algebra
Davies: University Algebra
Davy: Algebra
Day: Algebra
Greenleaf: Algebra
Loomis: Algebra
Perkin: Algebra
Robinson: Algebra
Robinson: New University Algebra
Smyth: Algebra
Thompson's Day: Algebra
Totten: Algebra

Analysis

Bullion: Analysis and Parsing
Fowler on the English Language
Goldsmith: Analysis of Prose and
    Poetry
Green: Analysis of the English
    Language
Porter: Analysis
Richard and Orcutt: Parsing
    Book
Student's Companion (for par-
    sing)
Town: Analysis
Welch: Grammatical Analysis

Archeology

Jahn: Archeology

Arithmetic

Adams: Arithmetic
Adams: Mental Arithmetic
Adams: New Arithmetic
Colburn: Arithmetic
Colburn: First Lessons and Sequel
Colburn: Mental Arithmetic
Colburn and Davies: Arithmetic
Daboll: Arithmetic
Davies: Arithmetic
Davies: Mental Arithmetic
Davis: Arithmetic
Eaton: Arithmetic
Eclectic Arithmetic
Emerson: Arithmetic
Greenleaf: National Arithmetic
Greenleaf and Davies: University
    Arithmetic
Mt. Vernon: Arithmetic
Ostrander: Arithmetic
Parley: Arithmetic
Ray: Arithmetic
Ray: Little Arithmetic
Robinson: Arithmetic
Smith: Arithmetic
Stoddard: Intellectual Arithmetic
Thompson: Arithmetical Analysis
Thompson: Larger Arithmetic
Tracy: Child's Arithmetic
Tracy: Written Arithmetic

Astronomy

Blake: Astronomy
Bouvier: Familiar Astronomy
Burritt: Astronomy

Astronomy (cont'd)
  Burritt: Geography of the Heavens
  Guy: Astronomy
  Kendall: Ouranography
  Kiddle: Astronomy
  Mattison: Astronomy
  Mattison and Burritt: Astronomy
  Norton: Astronomy
  Olmstead: Astronomy
  Comstock: Chemistry
  Parley: Sun, Moon and Stars
  Robinson: Astronomy
  Ryan: Astronomy
  Smith: Astronomy
  Snell's Olmstead: Astronomy
  Vose: Astronomy
  Vose's Burritt: Geography of the
    Heavens
  Wilkins: Astronomy
  Willard: Astronography

Bookkeeping
  Bennett: Bookkeeping
  Foster: Bookkeeping
  Fulton and Eastman: Bookkeeping
  Harris: Bookkeeping
  Hitchcock: Bookkeeping
  Lowell: Bookkeeping
  Marsh: Bookkeeping
  Marsh and Harris: Bookkeeping
  Preston: Bookkeeping

Botany
  Beck: Chemistry
  Bigelow: Botany
  Bigelow: Florula Bostoniensis
  Botany of Linnaeus
  Child's Botany, The
  Comstock: Botany
  Eaton: Botany
  Gray: Botany
  Lincoln: Botany
  Lincoln and Eaton: Botany
  Olmstead: Botany
  Phelps: Botany
  Thinker: Child's Botany
  Woods: Botany

Chemistry
  Beck: Botany
  Blake: Chemistry
  Cotting: Chemistry
  Eaton: Chemistry
  Gray: Chemistry
  Johnston: Chemistry
  Jones: Chemistry
  Jones: Conversations on Chemistry
  Park: Chemistry
  Phelps: Chemistry
  Porter: Chemistry
  Quackenbos: Chemistry
  Renwick: Chemistry
  Silliman: Chemistry
  Stockhardt: Chemistry
  Turner: Chemistry
  Webster: Manual on Chemistry
  Wells: Chemistry
  Youmans: Chemistry

Chirography
  Emerson: Chirography
  Foster: Writing Books
  Marshall: System of Writing
  Pomeroy: Writing Exercises
  Quackenbos: Penmanship
  Schuster: Cards

Conic Sections
  Bridge: Conic Sections

Criticism
  Kames: Elements of Criticism

Dictionaries
  Oswald: Dictionary
  Union Bible Dictionary
  Walker: Dictionary
  Webster: Dictionary
  Worcester: Dictionary

Domestic Economy
  Beecher: Domestic Economy
  Youmans: Household Science

Drawing
Thenot: Practical Perspective
Whitlock: Drawing

Electricity
Wells: Philosophy of Electricity
and Galvanism

Elocution
Bronson: Elocution
Porter: Elocution
Russell: Enunciation
Sanders: Series

English Classics
Addison: Spectator
Cowper: Poems
Cowper: Task
Homer: Translations of Poems
Milton: Paradise Lost
Pollock: Course of Time
Pope: Works
Scott: Marmion
Thompson: Seasons
Wordsworth: Works
Young: Night Thoughts

English Composition
Arnold: Prose Composition
Barton: English Composition
Brookfield: Lessons in Composition
Green: Scholar's Composition
Greenleaf: Punctuation
Parker: Aids to English Composition
Parker: Exercises in English Composition
Quackenbos: Composition
Smith: Lessons in Composition Writing
Wilson: Punctuation

English Grammar
Barton: English, Grammar
Brown: English Grammar
Bullion: English Grammar
Butler: Primary Grammar
Clark: English Grammar
Fisk's Murray: English Grammar

English Grammar (cont'd)
Fowle: Grammar
Graham: English Synonyms
Greenleaf: English Grammar
Greenleaf and Murray: Universal Grammar and Exercises
Ingersoll: English Grammar
Kirkham: Grammar
Latham: Handbook of the English Language
Murray: English Grammar
Murray: Exercises in Syntax
Pinneo: Grammar
Pond's Murray: Grammar
Quackenbos: English Grammar
Smith: English Grammar
Smith: Intellectual and Practical Grammar
Smith and Bullion: English Grammar
Smith and Fisk: English Grammar
Tower: English Grammar
Webster: English Grammar
Weld: English Grammar
Wells: English Grammar

English Literature
Brown: Classical Literature
Chambers: English Literature
Chambers and Cleveland: English Literature
Cleveland: Compendium of English Literature
Schlegel: History of Literature
Spalding: English Literature

Etymology
Crabb: Synonyms
Lynde: Etymology
Roget: Thesaurus
Trench: Study of Words

Familiar Science
Abbot: About Common Things
Wells: Science of Common Things

French
Aventures de Gil Blas
Boileau

French (cont'd)

Bolmar: Dictionary
Bolmar: Fables
Bolmar: Grammar
Bolmar: Grammar of Levizac
Bolmar: Phrases
Bolmar: Verbs
Boyer: Dictionary
Bruyère
Bugard: Practical Translator and French Teacher
Callot: French Reader
Callot: Levizac's French Grammar
Chapsal and Wanostrocht: Grammar
Charles XII
Chouquet: First Lessons
Colloquial Phrases
Corbett: Grammar
Corinne
Cours de Litterature par Théry
de Fiva's Reader (advanced)
De L'Allemagne par Madame de Stäel
Dramatic French Reader
Études Géographique par D'Levi
Exiles of Siberia, The
Fasquelle: Colloquial Reader
Fasquelle: Course
Fasquelle: Dumas and Napoleon
Fasquelle: Large Grammar
Fasquelle: Racine
Fasquelle: Reader
Flemming and Tibbins: Dictionary
Fontaine: Fables
French First Classbook
French Phrase Book
Girard: Précepts de Rhétorique
Histoire de Napoléon
Histoire Grecque
Histoire Romaine
History of the U. S. (French)
Keetel: Progressive French
L'Arithmétique de E. Arnold
L'Arithmétique de la Croix
Le Grand Père
Le Livre des Petites Enfants
Le Répertoire

French (cont'd)

Levizac: Grammar
L'Histoire de France
Longfellow: Grammar
Madame de Peyrac: Reader
Manesca: Grammar
Meadow: Dictionary
Modèles de Litterature
Noel and Chapsal: Grammar
Nugent: Dictionary
Numas Pompilius
Ollendorf: French Grammar
Peter the Great
Petit Carime de Misillon
Picciola Laintine
Piccioli and Chapsal: Litterature Francaise
Picot and Bolmar: Series
Pinney: French Series
Proverbes Dramatiques
Racine: Works
Rhétorique Française
Spiers and Surrenne: Dictionary
Siège de Rochelle
Surault: Grammar and Exercises
Surault: Questions on Sir Walter Scott's Tales of a Grandfather
Talbot: Pronunciation
Télémaque
Traducteur Francais
Vie de Washington
Voltaire: Henriade

Geography

Butler: Ancient Geography
Carter: Modern Geography
Cartier: Physical Geography
Colton and Fitch: Geography
Cornell: Geography
Cornell: Primary Geography
Cumming: Geography
Guyot: Earth and Man
Hughes: Scriptural Geography and History
Huntington: Geography
Keith on Globes
Lothrop: Use of Globes
Lyell: Geography
Malte-Brun: Geography and Atlas

Geography (cont'd)

Mitchell: Ancient Geography
Mitchell: School Geography
Monteith: Child's Geography
Morse: Geography
Olney: Geography
Olney: Geography and Atlas
Olney, Woodbridge, and Malte-Brun: Modern Geography
Parley: Geography
Pelton: Key to the Outline Maps
Smith: Geography
Somerville: Physical Geography
Warren: Elementary Geography
Warren: Modern Geography
Warren: Physical Geography
Willard: Ancient Geography
Woodbridge: Geography
Woodbridge: Large Geography
Woodbridge: School Geography and Atlas
Woodbridge: Universal Geography
Woodbridge and Willard: Geography
Woodbridge and Willard: Modern Geography
Woodbridge and Willard: Universal Geography
Worcester: Ancient Geography
Worcester: Atlas
Worcester: Geography
Worcester: Modern Geography
Worcester: Scriptural Geography

Geology

Bakewell: Geology
Comstock: Geology
Dana: Geology
Gray and Adams: Geology
Hitchcock: Geology
Loomis: Geology
Lyell: Geology
Mather: Geology
Phelps: Geology
Ruschenberger: Geology
St. John: Geology

Geometry

Brewster's Legendre: Geometry
Davies: Analytical Geometry

Geometry (cont'd)

Davies: Geometry
Davies: Legendre
Emerson: Geometry
Greenleaf: Geometry
Holbrook: Geometry
Legendre: Geometry
Loomis: Solid Geometry
Playfair: Geometry of Euclid
Robinson: Geometry
Simpson: Geometry
Thompson: Legendre
Walker: Geometry

German

Adler: Dictionary
Adler: Progressive German Reader
Ahn: Grammar
Bokum: Introduction
Buckhardt: Dictionary
De Wette: German Bible
Dramas of Schiller and Goethe
Eclectic Reader
Elwell: Dictionary
Faust
Follen: German Reader
Follen: Grammar
Kallschmidt: Dictionary
Nöliden: Dictionary
Nöliden: Grammar
Ollendorff: Grammar
Ollendorff: New Method
Schiller: William Tell
Undine
Weber: Dictionary
Woodbury: Grammar

Greek

Anthon: Lessons
Anthon: Reader
Bullion: First Lessons in Greek
Bullion: Grammar
Buttman: Grammar
Champlin: Greek Grammar
Cleaveland: Epitome of Grecian Antiquities
Donnegan: Lexicon
Felton: Homer's Iliad
Fisk: Grammar
Fisk: Greek Exercises

Greek (cont'd)

Goodrich: Grammar
Goodrich: Greek Exercises
Goodrich: Greek Lessons
Graeca Majora
Greek Testament
Grove: Lexicon
Hadley: Grammar
Harkness: First Book
Jacobs: Reader
Leusden: Greek Testament
Liddell and Scott: Lexicon
Porter: Greek Antiquities
Sophocles
Wilson: Testament
Xenophon: Anabasis
Xenophon: History of Greece

History

Abbot: Illustrated History
Baker and Hall: History of the
  United States
Bancroft: United States
Berard: United States History
Blair: Outline of Chronology
Bloss: Ancient History
Bloss: History
Bostwick: Historical Charts
Campbell: History of Virginia
Dickens: History of England
Frost: History of America
Frost: United States
Goldsmith: France
Goldsmith: Greece
Goldsmith: Rome
Goldsmith: History of England
Goodrich: Ancient and Modern
  History
Goodrich: History of the United
  States
Grimshaw: France
Grimshaw: History of the United
  States
Guizot: History of Civilization
Hale: United States
Irving: Washington
Keightly: History of Greece
Keightly: Roman History
Liddell: Rome

History (cont'd)

Macaulay: History
Magnall: Historical Questions
Magnall: The Reason Why
Marsh: Ecclesiastical History
Marshall, Chief Justice: Life of
  Washington
Morse and Parrish: History of
  New England
Parley: Common School History
Parley: First Book of History
Parley: General History
Parley: History of the United
  States
Picot: First Reader
Quackenbos: History of the
  United States
Robbins: Ancient and Modern
  History
Robbins: Compend of General
  History
Robertson: History
Robertson: Hume
Rollin: Ancient History
Russell: History of the United
  States
Russell: Modern Europe
Schmitz: History of Rome
Smith: History of Greece
Student's Hume
Titler and Worcester: General
  History
Tuttle: Compend of History
Tytler: Universal History (2 vols.)
Weber: Universal History
Webster: History of the United
  States
Whelpley: Ancient History
Whelpley: Compend of History
Whelpley: Modern History
Willard: American History
Willard: Ancient and Modern
  History
Willard: Chronographer
Willard: Historic Guide
Willard: History of the United
  States
Willard: Republic of America

History (cont'd)

Willard: Universal History and Chronographer

Wilson: American History

Wilson: History of the Middle Ages

Wilson: Outlines of History

Wilson: Outlines of Modern History

Worcester: Elements

Worcester: Outlines of Ancient History

Worcester: Outlines of History

Italian

Bachi: Fables

Bachi: Grammar

Bachi: Phrases and Dialogues

Bossut: Phrase Book

Chrestomazia Italiana

Conversazione Italiana

Gerusalemme Liborata

Graglia: Dictionary

Il Picolo Pietro

Il Tesoretto Dello Scholare Italiano

Le Notti Romane

Meadow: Italian Dictionary

Nuove Testamento

Ollendorff: Grammar

Scella di Prose Italiane

Silvio Pellico: Le Mie Prigione

Soave: Novelli Moralli

Surault: Tesoretto

Tasso

Vergani: Grammar

Latin

Adam: Grammar

Adam: Roman Antiquities

Ainsworth: Dictionary

Andrews: Latin Grammar

Andrews: Latin Lessons

Andrews: Latin Reader

Andrews: Lexicon

Andrews and Stoddard: First Lessons

Andrews and Stoddard: Latin Grammar

Latin (cont'd)

Andrews and Stoddard: Reader

Anthon: Caesar's Commentaries

Anthon's Carey: Latin Versification

Anthon: Cicero

Anthon: Classical Dictionary

Anthon: Horace

Anthon: Lessons

Anthon: Roman Antiquities

Anthon: Sallust

Anthon: Virgil

Anthon and Andrews: Sallust

Arnold: Exercises and Reader

Arnold: Latin Prose and Composition

Arnold: Nepos

Ars Poetica

Baird: Classical Manual

Bojesen: Grecian and Roman Antiquities

Bowen: Virgil

Bullion: Caesar

Caesar: Commentaries

Cicero: De Amicitia

Cicero: De Officiis

Cicero: De Senectute

Cicero: Oration for the Poet Archias

Cicero: Orations against Cataline

Cicero: Select Orations

Cooper: Virgil

Dillaway: Roman Antiquities

Frieze: Virgil

Fulsom: Livy

Goodrich: Latin Lessons

Gould: Excerpta ex Ovidio

Gould: Latin Grammar

Gould: Ovid's Metamorphosis

Gould: Virgil

Hanson: Caesar's Commentaries

Hanson: Cicero

Hanson: Prose Book

Harkness' Arnold: First Latin Book

Harkness: Grammar and Reader

Historiae Sacrae

Horace

Latin (cont'd)
Jacobs: Latin Reader
Kingsley: Tacitus
Kirliner: Grammar and Reader
Kirliner: Latin Exercises
Leverett: Dictionary
Leverett: Latin Tutor
Liber Primus
Livy
Mair: Introduction to Latin Syntax
McClintock: Introduction to Latin
Oration for the Manilian Law
Phaedrus: Fables
Pliny: Letters
Richard: Latin Lessons
Salkeld's Fish: Classical Antiquities
Sallust: Orations
Selectae ex Profanis Scriptoribus
Spencer: Latin Lessons
Smith: Antiquities
Tacitus
Virgil
Virgil: Aeneid
Viri Romae
Vita Washingtona
Weld: Latin Lessons

Logic
Gerhart: Philosophy and Logic
Hedge: Logic
Mahan: Logic
Tappan: Logic
Thompson: Laws of Thought
Whateley: Logic

Mechanics
Olmstead: Mechanics
Wells: Philosophy of Mechanics

Mensuration
Davy: Mensuration
Day: Mensuration

Mental Philosophy
Abbot: Learning to Think
Abercrombie: Intellectual and Moral Powers
Abercrombie: Intellectual Philosophy

Mental Philosophy (cont'd)
Brown: Intellectual Philosophy
Champlin: Intellectual Philosophy
Comstock's Watts: Improvement of the Mind
Haven: Mental Philosophy
Hedge: Abstract of Brown
Hickok: Mental Philosophy
Mason on Self Knowledge
Stewart: Philosophy of the Mind
Upham: Mental Philosophy
Upham on the Will
Watts on the Mind

Meteorology
Brocklesby: Meteorology

Mineralogy
Comstock: Mineralogy
Dana: Mineralogy

Moral Philosophy
Abbot: About Right and Wrong
Abbott: Little Philosopher
Beattie: Moral Science
Hickok: Moral Science
Paley: Moral Philosophy
Parkhurst: Moral Philosophy
Stewart: Philosophy
Upham and Wayland: Moral Philosophy
Wayland: Moral Science
Whateley: Lessons on Morals

Music
American Glee Book
Bertini, Hunten and Czerney: Instruction for Piano
Carmina Sacra
Carhart: Instructor
Carulli and Carcasi: Instruction for Guitar
Hunten: Instruction Book for Piano
Kingsley: Juvenile Choir for Classes
La Blache
Mason: Cottage Glee Book
Mason: Manual
Mason: Vocal Classbook

Music (cont'd)
Peters' Burrowes: Primer
The Jubilee
The Juvenile Singing School
The Young Choir
The Young Choir's Companion

Mythology
Dillaway: Mythology
Dwight: Mythology
Kreighton: Mythology

Natural History
Agassiz: Natural History
Goodrich: Animated Nature
Guyot: Earth and Man
Ruschenberger: Natural History
Smellie: Philosophy of Natural
History

Natural Philosophy
Arnot: Physics
Blake: Natural Philosophy
Bryan: Natural Philosophy
Comstock: Natural Philosophy
Conversations on Common Things
Gale: Natural Philosophy
Ganot: Physics (Peck's edition)
Grund: Natural Philosophy
Johnston: Natural Philosophy
Jones: Conversations on Natural
Philosophy
Olmstead: Natural Philosophy
Parker: Natural Philosophy
Phelps: Larger Natural Philoso-
phy
Phelps: Natural Philosophy
Snell's Olmstead: Natural Philos-
ophy
Wells: Natural Philosophy

Natural Theology
Chadbourne: Natural Theology
Gallentz: Natural Theology
Paley: Natural Theology
Paxton: Plates

Navigation
Bowditch: Navigator
Davy: Navigation

Philosophy
Hamilton: Metaphysics
Johnston: Philosophy
Parker: Little Philosophy
Quackenbos: Philosophy
Swift: Philosophy

Physiology
Comstock: Physiology
Cummings: Physiology
Cutter: Anatomy and Physiology
Fowler's Combe: Physiology
Griscom: Physiology
Hayward: Physiology
Hitchcock: Physiology
Hooker: Physiology
Jarvis: Physiology
Lambert: Anatomy and Physiol-
ogy
Lee: Physiology
Loomis: Physiology
Taylor: Child's Physiology
Willard: Circulation of the Blood

Political Economy
Bayard: Constitution
Conversations on Political Econ-
omy
Goodrich: Political Science
Governmental Instructor
Mansfield: Political Grammar
Newman: Political Economy
Phelps: Legal Classic
Shephard: Constitution of the
United States
Shephard: Constitutional Text-
book
Shurtleff: United States Govern-
ment
Stansbury: Catechism on the
Constitution
Sullivan: Political Classbook
Wayland: Political Economy

Readers
Abbot: Franconia Series
Abbot: Learning to Read
Blake: Historical Reader

Readers (cont'd)
Emerson. Poetic Reader
Goodrich: Readers
Heman: Reader
McGuffey: Eclectic Readers I–IV
Mitchell: Geographical Reader
Murray: Reader
Murray: Sequel
Parker: Rhetorical Reader
Phelps: Fireside Friend
Porter: Reader
Russell: Reader
Russell and Goldbury: Reader
Sanders: Readers
Sargent: Readers
Scholar's Companion
Stone: Introduction
Town: Series of Readers
Webb: Series
Young Ladies' Class Book

Religion
Alexander: Evidences of Christianity
Althans: Natural History of the Bible
Bible
Butler: Analogy
Dobie: Key to the Bible
McCosh on Divine Government
McIlvain: Evidences of Christianity
Nevin: Biblical Antiquities
Nicholl: Help in Reading the Bible
Nicholl: Introduction to the Study of the Bible
Paley: Evidences of Christianity
Porter: Evidences of Christianity

Rhetoric
Alison on Taste
Blair: Rhetoric
Blair: Rhetoric (University Edition)
Boyd: Rhetoric
Campbell: Philosophy of Rhetoric
Day: Rhetoric
Jamieson: Rhetoric
Newman: Rhetoric
Parker: Rhetoric

Rhetoric (cont'd)
Porter: Rhetorical Reader
Quackenbos: Higher Rhetoric
Quackenbos: Rhetoric
Schlegel: Dramatic Art and Literature
Village Rhetorical Reader
Whateley: Rhetoric
Worcester: Abridgment of Blair's Rhetoric

Spanish
Costas Marruccas
Cubi: Grammar
El Traductor Español
La Historia de Los Estados Unidos
Newman: Dictionary
Newman and Barrett: Dictionary
Novelas Españolas
Ollendorff: Grammar
Ollendorff: Reader
Pizzaro: Phrases
Poesias de Melendez Voldes
Quijote
Rabbaden: Grammar
Sale: Grammar
Sloane's Newman: Dictionary
Solis: Conquista de Mejico
Velasque: Reader

Spellers
Comly: Speller
Denman: Students' Spelling Book
Hazen: Speller and Definer
Hodges: Speller and Definer
Hooker and Gallaudet: Speller
McGuffey: Speller
Parker and Watson: Spelling and Reading
Sanders: Spelling Book
Sargent: Standard Speller
Swan: Scientific Speller
Town: Speller
Webster: Spelling Book
Wright: Speller

Surveying
Davies: Surveying and Levelling
Flint: Surveying
Gummere: Surveying

II

STUDIES OFFERED IN FEMALE SEMINARIES[1]
(1742–1871)

79 Spelling
2 Pronunciation
119 Reading
85 Writing
30 Chirography
4 Punctuation
4 Dictation
6 Letter Writing
96 Composition
139 English Grammar
19 Defining
5 Etymology
9 Syntax
33 Grammatical Analysis and Parsing
3 Prosody
10 Mythology
8 Belles Lettres
13 History of Literature
2 American Literature
16 English Literature
23 English Authors
43 Criticism
14 Analysis, English Authors and Poets
81 Logic
100 Mental Philosophy
1 Psychology
121 Rhetoric
32 Elocution
76 Latin Grammar
24 Latin Reader
15 Latin Composition
13 Caesar
28 Virgil
9 Cornelius Nepos

16 Sallust
5 Livy
19 Cicero
4 Ovid
8 Horace
6 Tacitus
12 Roman Antiquities
37 Greek Grammar
12 Greek Reader
8 Greek Composition
7 Greek Testament
2 Iliad
8 Grecian Antiquities
22 German
89 French Grammar and Literature
17 Italian
23 Spanish
1 Portuguese
1 Indian
132 Arithmetic
23 Mental Arithmetic
97 Algebra
100 Plane Geometry
4 Solid Geometry
44 Plane Trigonometry
4 Spherical Trigonometry
5 Conic Sections
14 Surveying
7 Navigation
10 Mensuration
30 Bookkeeping
6 Religion
23 Bible
1 Exegesis
4 New Testament

[1] The figure preceding each subject indicates the frequency with which it was offered by the 162 institutions.

5 Jewish and Biblical Antiquities
41 Analogy of Natural and Revealed Religion
43 Natural Theology
59 Evidences of Christianity
106 Moral Philosophy
2 Ethics
113 Geography
2 Universal Geography
15 Physical Geography
54 Ancient Geography
8 Sacred Geography
31 Modern Geography
18 Maps
36 Globes
15 Map Drawing
2 Familiar Science
123 Natural Philosophy
2 Electricity
1 Physics
1 Hydrostatics
1 Optics
4 Mechanics
1 Technology
112 Chemistry
65 Geology
27 Mineralogy
101 Botany
1 Gardening
116 Astronomy
3 Meteorology
3 Ouranography
60 Physiology
2 Hygiene
11 Anatomy
8 Zoölogy
22 Natural History
25 Philosophy of Natural History
1 Object Lessons
2 Conchology
7 Domestic Economy
2 Housework
11 Chronology
76 History
13 Sacred History
57 Ancient History
12 Greek History
16 Roman History

3 Mediaeval History
21 Ecclesiastical History
52 Modern History
1 History of New England
9 French History
20 English History
57 U. S. History
16 Universal History
38 Political Science
1 International and Constitutional
   Law
7 Civil Government
13 Government of United States
2 Constitution and History of
   Kentucky
1 History of Virginia
2 Marking
29 Plain Needle
2 Knitting
1 Darning
1 Spinning
37 Ornamental Needle
1 Millinery
20 Embroidery
3 Filigree
2 Tambour
7 Waxwork
1 Grotto work
2 Rug work
2 Shell work
1 Bead work
1 Lace work
1 Silk Drawing
1 Tapestry
4 Artificial Flowers
1 Basket making
60 Painting
10 Water Color
8 Oil Painting
7 Painting Velvet, Silk, etc.
1 Gilding
3 Mezzotint
2 Miniatures
2 Psalmody
39 Music
48 Vocal Music
46 Instrumental
1 Melodeon

30 Piano
 5 Organ
 3 Harp
16 Guitar
 1 Spinet
10 Dancing
 1 Soirée
 2 Conversation

 4 Politeness
80 Drawing
 2 Architecture
 2 Sculpture
 2 Education
 2 Penmaking
 3 Shorthand
22 Calisthenics

Spelling	Writing	Reading	Length of course	Name / Date	Reference
				Name / Date	Reference
×		×	3	Boston Girls' H. S. / 1826	*Barnard's Jour. Ed.*, XIII, 246
×	×[15]	×	11	New York Girls' H. S. / 1827	*Am. Jour. Ed.*, 1828, III, 121
×		×	4	Philadelphia Girls' H. S. / Planned by Bache, 1840	*Bache's Report on a High School for Girls*, 1840, 4 *ff.*
			4	Cincinnati H. S. / 1847	Data collected by Eleanor O'Connell
			4	Louisville Girls' H. S. / 1856	Board of Ed. *Report*, 1856
			4	Dubuque H. S. / 1857	Data from Mr. O. P. Flower, Superintendent of Schools
			3	San Francisco H. S. / 1858	Data from Mr. A. W. Scott, Girls' High School
			4	St. Paul H. S. / 1865	Data from Mr. J. W. Smith, Public Schools
×		×	4	Savannah Girls' H. S. / 1866	Data furnished by Albert S. Otto, School Statistician
			4[14]	St. Louis H. S. / 1867	*Barnard's Jour. Ed.*, XIX, 535 *f.*
		×	4[14]	Chicago H. S. / 1867	*Ibid.*, XIX, 572 *f.*
			9	Portland H. S. / 1869	From Annual Report, Collected by Eva M. Brandburg
		×[6]	3	Richmond H. S. / 1872	An historical leaflet, pub. by Richmond Board of Ed.
		×	4	Denver H. S. / 1873	Data from Denver Public School Records, furnished by Wm. H. Smiley
			4	Trenton H. S. / 1874	Data furnished by Superintendent of Schools
			4	Salt Lake City H. S. / 1890	Data furnished by Superintendent of Schools

- Defining
- Dictation
- Penmanship
- English Grammar
- Analysis and Parsing
- Composition
- Etymology
- Literature
- Rhetoric
- Elocution
- Criticism
- Logic
- Mental Arithmetic
- Written Arithmetic
- Bookkeeping
- Stenography
- Typewriting
- Business Letters
- Commercial Arithmetic
- Commercial Law
- Geometry
- Analytical Geometry
- Demonstrative Geometry
- Algebra
- Mensuration
- Surveying
- Navigation
- Civil Engineering
- Plane Trigonometry
- Spherical Trigonometry
- Calculus
- Modern Geography
- Ancient Geography
- Physical Geography

III—Continued

Name	Date	Reference	Commercial Geography	Projection of Maps	Globes	Natural Philosophy or Physics	Chemistry
Boston Girls' H. S.	1826	Barnard's Jour. Ed., XIII, 246		x[1]	x	x	
New York Girls' H. S.	1827	Am. Jour. Ed., 1828, III, 121				x	x
Philadelphia Girls' H. S.	1840	Planned by Bache, 1840 Bache's Report on a High School for Girls, 1840, 4 ff.		x	x	x	x
Cincinnati H. S.	1847	Data collected by Eleanor O'Connell				x	x
Louisville Girls' H. S.	1856	Board of Ed. Report, 1856				x	x
Dubuque H. S.	1857	Data from Mr. O. P. Flower, Superintendent of Schools				x	x
San Francisco H. S.	1858	Data from Mr. A. W. Scott, Girls' High School				x	x
St. Paul H. S.	1865	Data from Mr. J. W. Smith, Public Schools				x	x
Savannah Girls' H. S.	1866	Data furnished by Albert S. Otto, School Statistician				x	x
St. Louis H. S.	1867	Barnard's Jour. Ed., XIX, 535 f.				x	x
Chicago H. S.	1867	Ibid, XIX, 572 f.				x	x
Portland H. S.	1869	From Annual Report, Collected by Eva M. Brandburg				x	x
Richmond H. S.	1872	An historical leaflet, pub. by Richmond Board of Ed.				x[5]	
Denver H. S.	1873	Data from Denver Public School Records, furnished by Wm. H. Smiley				x	x
Trenton H. S.	1874	Data furnished by Superintendent of Schools				x	x
Salt Lake City H. S.	1890	Data furnished by Superintendent of Schools	x			x	x

Botany

Zoölogy

Astronomy

Geology

Object Lessons

Physiology

Calisthenics

Hygiene

Natural Theology

Evidences of Christianity

Moral Philosophy

Ethics

Mental Philosophy

History of the United States

Civics

Political Economy

General History

History of Greece

History of Rome

Ancient History

History of England

Modern History

Latin Grammar[12]

Latin Reader

Latin Exercises

Prose Composition

Caesar

Cicero

Virgil

Ovid

French[12]

Télémaque

Racine

German[12]

Greek	Mechanical Drawing	Drawing	Vocal Music	Art	Name / Date	Reference
				x[1]	Boston Girls' H. S. 1826	*Barnard's Jour. Ed.*, XIII, 246
				x	New York Girls' H. S. 1827	*Am. Jour. Ed.*, 1828, III, 121
		x	x	x	Philadelphia Girls' H. S. Planned by Bache, 1840	*Bache's Report on a High School for Girls*, 1840, 4 *ff*.
			x	x	Cincinnati H. S. 1847	Data collected by Eleanor O'Connell
				x	Louisville Girls' H. S. 1856	Board of Ed. *Report*, 1856
					Dubuque H. S. 1857	Data from Mr. O. P. Flower, Superintendent of Schools
					San Francisco H. S. 1858	Data from Mr. A. W. Scott, Girls' High School
					St. Paul H. S. 1865	Data from Mr. J. W. Smith, Public Schools
					Savannah Girls' H. S. 1866	Data furnished by Albert S. Otto, School Statistician
x			x	x	St. Louis H. S. 1867	*Barnard's Jour. Ed.*, XIX, 535 *f*.
			x		Chicago H. S. 1867	*Ibid*, XIX, 572 *f*.
					Portland H. S. 1869	From Annual Report, Collected by Eva M. Brandburg
					Richmond H. S. 1872	An historical leaflet, pub. by Richmond Board of Ed.
	x[r]	x	x	x	Denver H. S. 1873	Data from Denver Public School Records, furnished by Wm. H. Smiley
			x	x	Trenton H. S. 1874	Data furnished by Superintendent of Schools
	x[10]	x	x	x	Salt Lake City H. S. 1890	Data furnished by Superintendent of Schools

Marking on Linen	x
Sewing	x x[19]
Housewifery	x

[1] Offered but not required.

[2] This included ancient, mediaeval and modern history.

[3] No doubt, not all the languages mentioned were required.

[4] Algebra and geometry, at least, were probably included under "mathematics."

[5] "Science" probably included physics, chemistry and botany.

[6] "Review of the work of the grammar grades" probably included reading, spelling, writing, grammar and arithmetic.

[7] "May be substituted for English branches except mathematics."

[8] Ancient and modern history.

[9] "Oral expression."

[10] Doubtless not all required.

[11] Three departments mentioned probably indicate a course which required three years for completion.

[12] Where German, French or Latin are checked, other studies beyond the grammar were probably pursued in most cases, though the books read and the exact nature of the exercises are not indicated.

[13] Also mediaeval.

[14] General course is checked. Classical and normal courses were also outlined.

[15] "Writing on slates and on paper."

[16] Bache makes special note that he does not "at present recommend the introduction of any foreign language. . . ."

[17] And Pennsylvania history especially.

[18] Including comparative anatomy and the study of natural history.

[19] Probably included under "female work."

INDEX TO VOLUME I*

* Index to Volumes I and II, page 591, Volume II.

Needlework, 51, 73, 80, 150 *f.*, 153, 194, 198, 271 *f.*, 274, 277, 280 *ff.*, 290, 292 *f.*, 295, 297, 299, 339, 342, 415, 418, 522

Negative confession, 3

Negro, girl, gifted student, 132; school, 229; slaves, 267

Nesbitt, F., in Aimwell School Account Book, 206

Neshaminy, 213

Nettelhorst, Mr., 508

Nettement, M. Alfred, 61, 70

Nevada, teachers' salaries, 495

New Britain (Conn.) Normal School, 480

New England and the South, contrasted, 238 *f.*

New England, changing society of, 172, 174 *f.*; education of girls in, 124 *ff.*; Quakers in, 94; town schools generally closed to girls, 142 *f.*

New England Girlhood, 373

New England School of Design for Women (Mass.), 364

New England Seminary for Teachers, Plan of, 358

New Glasgow Female Academy (Va.), 392

New Hagerstown Female Seminary (O.), 367

New Hampshire, advanced education of women in, 396; teachers' salaries, 492; women on school committees, 515 *f.*

New Hampton Female Seminary (N. H.), 417

New Haven, private schools at, 154; school dame of, 141 *f.*

New Jersey, advanced education of women in, 396; Quakers in, 94

New London, town school, 145

New Netherlands, position and character of women in, 93 *f.*

New Orleans Female Collegiate Institute, 386

New Providence, 211

New Testament, required as school book, 439

New York, academies for girls, 365, 396; estimate of women teachers, 502 *f.*; girls' high schools, 521, 538 *f.*, 543; private schools in, 230; Quakers in, 94; salaries of teachers in, City, 495–6; teachers' salaries, 492 *ff.*; women teachers in, City, 509 *ff.*

New York Yearly Meeting, 207

Newbern Academy (N. C.), 381

Newburyport, private school at, 154; town school, 145

Newman, S. P., 480

Newman's Political Economy, 475

Newman's Rhetoric, 475

Newnham College, 55

Newport News Female Seminary, 393

Newport (R. I.), private schools, 152

Newspapers, among the Germans of Pennsylvania, 94; schools advertised in the Colonial, 149–53, 217–30; supported in Northern and Southern colonies, 238

Newton County Female Seminary (Ga.), 387

Newtonian Philosophy, 233

Nichols', Miss, Detroit Seminary, 370

Nickolls, Salina, 391

Nineteenth century, conservatism of, 43

Nixon, William, schoolmaster, 295

Noble, Mary Ann, ferry-keeper, 260

Noble, Stuart G., 514

Nodden, Charles, 258

Noel, Garrot, publisher, 226, 233

Nohle, on German education, 83

Normal schools, 109, 301, 305, 310, 324, 403 *ff.*, 466–83, 512; in France, 60; men and women teachers in, 499; statistics of, 482 *f.*

Norman, Sarah, schoolmistress, 282 *f.*

North Carolina, education in 19th century, 380 *f.*, 383, 393, 396; position and education of women in, 243, 245 *f.*, 248, 251

North Carolina Yearly Meeting, 207

North Glastenbury (Conn.), high school, 521

Northampton Female Academy (N. C.), 381

Northampton, town school, 143

Northwest Territory, girls' education in, 363

Norwalk Female Seminary (O.), 367

Novels, popularity of, criticized, 274 *f.*, 304, 312

Nugent, Mr., schoolmaster, 149

Nunneries, destroyed, 26

Nursing, 192, 258, 452

Nuthead, Dinah, publisher, 241, 261

Nutmaker, Mrs., merchant, 163

Oakland Female Seminary (Mich.), 370

Oakland Female Seminary (O.), 367

LC1752 .W6 1966   010101 000
Woody, Thomas, 1891-1960.
A history of women's education

0 2002 0067298 4
YORK COLLEGE OF PENNSYLVANIA 17403

LC
1752   WOODY
.W6   A HISTORY OF WOMEN'S
1966   EDUCATION IN THE
V.1   UNITED STATES

55996

DISCARDED

YORK COLLEGE PENNSYLVANIA LIBRARY

4